PUBLICATIONS OF THE RICHARD RAWLINSON CENTER

AEDIFICIA NOVA

PUBLICATIONS OF THE RICHARD RAWLINSON CENTER

Publications of the Richard Rawlinson Center is a scholarly series covering the general field of Anglo-Saxon culture, with particular emphasis on the study of manuscripts. The series is published by the Richard Rawlinson Center for Anglo-Saxon Studies and Manuscript Research in association with Medieval Institute Publications, Western Michigan University.

A list of books in the series appears at the end of this book.

Medieval Institute Publications is a program of
The Medieval Institute, College of Arts and Sciences

 WESTERN MICHIGAN UNIVERSITY

AEDIFICIA NOVA

Studies in Honor of Rosemary Cramp

EDITED BY

Catherine E. Karkov

AND

Helen Damico

Publications of the Richard Rawlinson Center

MEDIEVAL INSTITUTE PUBLICATIONS

Western Michigan University

Kalamazoo

Library of Congress Cataloging-in-Publication Data

Aedificia nova : studies in honor of Rosemary Cramp / edited by
Catherine E. Karkov and Helen Damico.
    p. cm. -- (Publications of the Richard Rawlinson Center)
  Includes bibliographical references and index.
  ISBN 978-1-58044-110-0 (casebound : alk. paper)
 1. Art, Anglo-Saxon. 2. English literature--Old English, ca. 450-1100.
3. Archaeology, Medieval--Great Britain. 4. Anglo-Saxons--Material
culture. I. Cramp, Rosemary. II. Karkov, Catherine E., 1956- III.
Damico, Helen.
NX543.A43 2008
941.01--dc22

                                                        2008003389

ISBN 978-1-58044-110-0

Printed in the United States of America
C   5   4   3   2   1

CONTENTS

ABBREVIATIONS

A. Clon.	Denis Murphy, ed., *The Annals of Clonmacnoise*
AFM	John O'Donovan, ed. and trans., *Annals of the Kingdom of Ireland by the Four Masters*
AI	Seán Mac Airt, ed. and trans., *The Annals of Inisfallen*
ALC	W. M. Hennessy, ed. and trans., *The Annals of Loch Cé*
ASE	*Anglo-Saxon England*
ASSAH	*Anglo-Saxon Studies in Archaeology and History*
A. Tig.	Whitley Stokes, ed. and trans., "The Annals of Tigernach"
AU	W. M. Hennessy and B. MacCarthy, eds. and trans., *Annals of Ulster*
Bede,	*Bede's Ecclesiastical History of the English People,*
Hist. eccles.	ed. B. Colgrave and R. A. B. Mynors
CBA Res. Rep.	Council for British Archaeology Research Report
CCSL	Corpus Christianorum Series Latina
CS	W. M. Hennessy, ed. and trans., *Chronicum Scotorum*
EETS	Early English Texts Society
Excavations	Annual summary accounts of excavations in Ireland (Bray: Wordwell)
HMSO	Her Majesty's Stationary Office
Jnl.	Journal
JRSAI	*Journal of the Royal Society of Antiquaries of Ireland*
JWCI	*Journal of the Warburg and Courtauld Institutes*
MA	*Medieval Archaeology*
Misc. Irish A.	Séamus Ó hInnse, ed. and trans., *Miscellaneous Irish Annals (A.D. 1114–1437)*
NM	*Neuphilologische Mitteilungen*
PL	J.-P. Migne, ed., *Patrologiae cursus completus, Series Latina* (Paris, 1844–82)
PRIA	*Proceedings of the Royal Irish Academy*
PSAS	*Proceedings of the Society of Antiquaries of Scotland*
RCAHMS	Royal Commission on the Ancient and Historic Monuments of Scotland

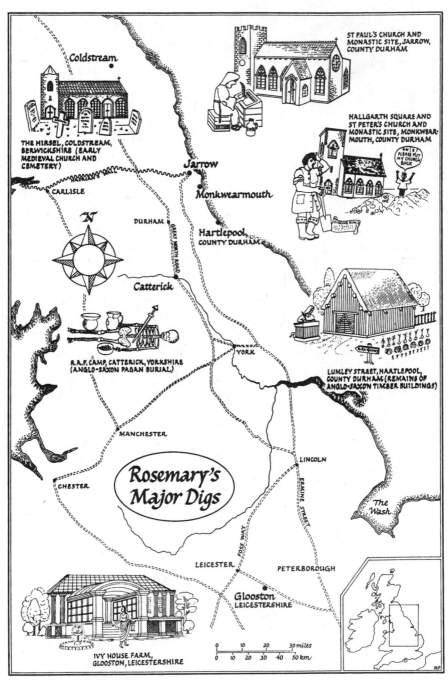

St Paul's Church and Monastic Site, Jarrow, County Durham

The Hirsel, Coldstream, Berwickshire (Early Medieval Church and Cemetery)

Hallgarth Square and St Peter's Church and Monastic Site, Monkwearmouth, County Durham

BUT PLEASE MAY I HAVE MY CHURCH BACK

DIGGING KIT

R.A.F. Camp, Catterick, Yorkshire (Anglo-Saxon Pagan Burial)

Lumley Street, Hartlepool, County Durham (Remains of Anglo-Saxon Timber Buildings)

Coldstream

Jarrow

Monkwearmouth

Hartlepool, County Durham

HADRIAN'S WALL

CARLISLE

DURHAM

GREAT NORTH ROAD

Catterick

YORK

MANCHESTER

LINCOLN

CHESTER

ERMINE STREET

The Wash

Rosemary's Major Digs

FOSS WAY

LEICESTER

PETERBOROUGH

Glooston, Leicestershire

Ivy House Farm, Glooston, Leicestershire

| 0 | 10 | 20 | 30 miles |
| 0 | 10 | 20 | 30 | 40 | 50 km |

RP

Courtesy of Reginald Piggott

CATHERINE E. KARKOV AND HELEN DAMICO

"For any archaeologist, the problem of assessing the date of the context created by the *Beowulf*-poet for his hero is the same as that of assessing the date and meaning of an archaeological 'layer.'"[1]

In this statement made some thirty-six years after her groundbreaking article "*Beowulf* and Archaeology," Rosemary J. Cramp makes explicit her complex perception that materiality, whether found in literature or in the earth, takes place in time. That temporality, however, is plural and variable, for it takes into consideration the variance between the particular time and environment of a work's production or creation and the relational time and environment in which it is received by later generations. Imbued with symbolic and metaphoric significance, these tangible objects function as nonverbal communicators of a societal norm. No material object is transparent or neutral; rather in its particular framework and social context, it makes an ideological statement about the realities of the past.

Rosemary Cramp's reflections upon and dynamic involvement with past reality began at the age of sixteen when she unearthed a coin while walking near her family farm in Leicestershire. Presaging the importance of later and more significant discoveries, the results of this first "excavation" were reported in the *Journal of Roman Studies*.[2] The essays in this volume are meant to mark and celebrate a career that spans over a third of a century, and whose action has been to meditate upon and hold dialogue with tangible objects in order to uncover the meaning of a past that existed as a physical reality rather than as a literary or historical supposition. Our title is taken from Asser's *Life of King Alfred*, where it is used to refer to new treasures, wonderfully made, that surpassed those of earlier times.[3] Rosemary Cramp has given us the treasures of her discoveries and her scholarship, always beautifully crafted, and as diverse and plentiful as the precious objects about which Asser wrote.

1. Cramp, "The Hall in *Beowulf* and Archaeology," p. 334.
2. *Journal of Roman Studies*, 36 (1946), 142; 38 (1948), 81–104.
3. Keynes and Lapidge, *Alfred the Great*, pp. 91, 101. See also Webster, "*Ædificia nova*."

The essays we offer to Professor Cramp in this volume were all delivered at the Kalamazoo Medieval Congress in 2000. While varied in subject, discipline, and methodological approach, they center on interpretations of the material world, whether that materiality appears in literature, in stone, or in the artifacts removed from an archaeological dig. They deal mainly with the Germanic and Celtic worlds, but incorporate motifs and themes from eastern Christian and Roman cultures. They address themes of time in history; societal and ideological change and continuity; iconic style and polysemous textuality; symbolic and representational interpretation; gender-specific economic production; definitions of social and political structures; and social processes of eclecticism and adaptation. Hence, the approaches are interdisciplinary, contextual, comparative, and fluid in their integration of texts and images, where the text represented is as crucial to the meaning as is the image or object; they, therefore, represent the study of the material culture of the Anglo-Saxon period at its best.

The prime example of a multilayered and fluid reading of material objects is provided by Rosemary Cramp herself who, in her lead essay "The Changing Image, Divine and Human, in Anglo-Saxon Art," explores three main aspects of figural representation in Anglo-Saxon Art: mask, icon, and dramatic actor. Incorporating myths and symbols common to native Celtic and Germanic cultures and integrating Eastern and Roman Christian figural motifs, she demonstrates the varied treatment and evolution of divine figures over a six-hundred-year period; these changes in figural representation, she argues, significantly illuminate our understanding of a cultural phenomenon, the tendency toward individual rather than collective piety in late Anglo-Saxon England.

The essays that make up the rest of the volume are organized loosely by discipline. George Brown, Éamonn Ó Carragáin, Roberta Frank, and John Hines focus largely on texts, albeit in Ó Carragáin's paper on a text inscribed on a sculpted stone monument. In each case, however, these texts are situated within the larger religious, historical, or material culture of the Anglo-Saxons: the monastery, reading practices, warrior culture, the grave. The essays offered by Gale Owen-Crocker, Elizabeth Coatsworth, Susan Youngs, Carol Neuman de Vegvar, Jane Hawkes, and Leslie Webster concentrate on the art historical sources. Together the essays in this section of the book cover an impressive range of material, from textiles and sculpture to metal- and enamel-working. The final section of the book is devoted to archaeology. It opens with Colleen Batey's essay on the excavation of the St. Ninian's Isle beads. This is an excavation report and, as such, an example of the type of hands-on work and primary data on which interpretation of the history and material culture of the Anglo-Saxons rests. The essays by Catherine Hills, Elizabeth O'Brien, Kelley

Wickham-Crowley, and John Bradley that follow then provide examples of the multifaceted ways in which raw archaeological data can be synthesized with the documentary record to provide insight into burial practice, gender roles, material production, societal and spatial organization.

Within and beyond the disciplinary arrangement of the essays, variable perspectives and themes repeatedly reverberate throughout the volume. Roberta Frank focuses on one type of material object (the boar-helmet) and the ways in which it helps to define the cultural milieu of a text. After examining the image of the boar-helmet in *Beowulf* in the context of medieval Latin and Continental literature, she explores the ways in which the material world of *Beowulf* may have its roots in North Sea culture and concludes that the references to the boar-helmets in *Beowulf* are closely aligned to references in tenth- and eleventh-century skaldic verse. John Hines shifts the perspective from object as text to literary text as object and argues against the "overtextual approach" of contemporary Beowulfian criticism. As is evident from its title, Hines's essay revisits Rosemary Cramp's 1957 thesis and expands upon it in light of new archaeological discoveries and theories. The materiality of *Beowulf*, he posits, with its archaeological counterpart in the "real" world argues against its being imaginary, but rather evinces a reality of the Anglo-Saxon world the poem represents.

While Frank's and Hines's essays focus on shifting critical perspectives of the material and literary records, the essays of Leslie Webster, Éamonn Ó Carragáin, and Jane Hawkes make pivotal the interrelationship between literary and material texts. Their essays integrate texts and material artifacts to reveal underlying cultural significations. Webster interrelates apocalyptic images, particularly those found in ivory carvings, with sermons and poems of the late tenth and eleventh centuries and argues that these objects function as private meditations or reflections upon a disordered world—an interpretation that gains support from the use of similar imagery in the proems of contemporary charters. Meditation as a viable vehicle for interpretation of a material object is at the heart of Éamonn Ó Carragáin's paper on the Ruthwell Cross. Ó Carragáin argues for the integrity of design and liturgical purpose of the cross, for Roman influence on the designer of the Ruthwell Cross, and for the intentional and contemporaneous carving of the runic passages on the cross for use in both prayer and worship—in opposition to critics who argue for a later less clearly defined purpose for the carving of the runic inscription. Like Ó Carragáin, Jane Hawkes fuses image and figural decoration in her examination of the Iona crosses, especially that of St. Martin, on which both figural and nonfigural motifs are employed to represent the Crucifixion and Resurrection of Christ, and the mysteries of the church.

Two essays deal with change within the continuum of time. The concept that distinctions of the nature of time and the resultant temporal systems are human constructs that reflect ideological and social practices underlies George Brown's essay on "Bede and Change." Brown presents Bede as an adapter and modifier of patristic thought and a creator of a new construct of temporal development and historical change. Brown's essay is particularly pertinent as the world of Bede and the cultural context created in the writings of Bede are at the heart of several of the essays in this volume, as well as so many of Rosemary Cramp's own projects. Later in the volume, Catherine Hills explores the ways in which some of these same ideas and processes are manifested in the material remains of the early Anglo-Saxon period in her interpretation of the archaeological evidence provided by two excavation sites—Spong Hill and Icklingham. Hills understands time as a continuum; she regards earlier archaeological interpretations, based on temporal periodization of the artifacts (e.g., Iron Age, Roman, Saxon), as having resulted in a bundling up of complex social activity into isolated episodes, entirely disconnected from the material reality of land use and the production and consumption of material culture over time and changing sociopolitical structures. In her interpretation of the material records of Spong Hill and Icklingham, Hills proposes a more fruitful way to discuss the transition between Roman and Saxon communities in East Anglia as being one of both continuity and change. She further argues for breaking down the barriers between ethnicity and cultural materiality; instead she would substitute a heterogeneous cultural dynamism in which variation and overlapping between indigenous and Continental social practices would more closely reflect the reality of the regions.

Kelley Wickham-Crowley, Elizabeth Coatsworth, and Gale R. Owen-Crocker examine what Wickham-Crowley calls "soft artifacts," woven materials generally produced by women. The appearance of cloth, embroidery, and woven textiles solidify women's presence in the economic structure of Anglo-Saxon society. Wickham-Crowley argues that women's productivity was critical to the Anglo-Saxon economy, especially to the economy of sainthood, where the shroud and the shroud maker heightened the reputation of the dead. Coatsworth points to professional embroiderers and designers who produced exquisite objects. In particular, she focuses on the ingenuity of artists who appropriated a design in its entirety from one medium to another (what archaeologists call a skeuomorph), as, for example, the image of a reliquary in the form of a bag or pouch that is prominently reproduced in metalwork and adapted to textile work. In textile decoration, in all its forms, but especially trimmings and edgings, Coatsworth examines the adaptation of the oppositional ideas of binding and separation as they are refashioned from other pre-Conquest English art forms such as metalwork and sculpture. In textiles, for instance, Coatsworth's decorative "edges" emphasize the idea of difference as they mark boundaries between different types of material surfaces, enclosed and open spaces, or types of design (p. 142); in metalwork, on the other hand, edgings often disguise separateness by covering the joints of the material surface (p. 145).

In the context of material culture, cloth has a transformational symbolic potency in appearance and production. The technique of weaving symbolizes a mental construct of time and space; the product of that activity—cloth—protects, binds, and restores; the materiality of the cloth itself changes in execution and in the type of design imposed upon it. For Wickham-Crowley, cloth changes meaning in the construction process: in the secular sphere, cloth signifies wealth and opulence; when constructed as shrouds for saints it is imbued with a sacral meaning. For the shroud, once having enclosed and enveloped the holy body, is imbued by and becomes a material manifestation of the saint's holiness; the material fabrication of threads into cloth has thus been transformed into a secondary relic.

Transformation and polysemy of decorative design is also at the heart of Owen-Crocker's essay. The thirty-nine zoomorphic-headed terminals in the Bayeux Tapestry—apart from their transparently obvious decorative function—perform as structural and thematic signifiers in the graphic representation of the Bayeux narrative. In addition to creating a repetitive chain-like pattern, each terminal speaks to the craft of individual embroiderers; moreover, in their contextual relationship and appropriation of space the terminals become iconic and polysemous, in their assigning connotative value to the main narrative and in their self-referentiality as hybrids, "embroidered picture[s]" (skeuomorphs) of wooden ornaments (p. 114).

The production of a culture's materiality is to be understood as articulating a dynamism in early English society. Susan Youngs's essay, for example, discusses the far-ranging early uses of enamel for dress ornament (ca. early sixth century) and its later uses in hanging bowls as signifying the nature of regional economic production (especially that of East Anglia) and a readiness to embrace foreign elements be they British or Continental. The development of complex enameling reflects the merging and overlapping of contemporary Continental uses and design and their importation and appropriation in native art. As Youngs shows, "the new Anglo-Saxon styles of artifact and their decoration were badges of success"; however, enamel would have to "wait for another three centuries before it made a significant contribution to Anglo-Saxon art and ornament" (p. 175). Colleen E. Batey's essay likewise argues for the interpretation of the material record as a reflection of a multilayered complex social structure. Batey reads the beads of St. Ninian's Isle, unexamined since Andrew C. O'Dell's excavations forty years ago, not as isolated remnants, but bundled with beads from other Pictish sites. Perhaps most important in a collection of this nature where so many of the essays rely in one way or another on textual evidence, Batey provides us with an example of a study in which texts fail completely. There are no Pictish texts; Anglo-Saxon texts deal with the Picts only in passing; and there exist very few contemporary parallels for the beads, making an understanding of the exact cultural context in which they were produced difficult. In order to confirm their Pictish origins, further scientific analysis of other types of "culturally diagnostic material" will be necessary (p. 259).

The intersections of Celtic and Germanic elements in the creation of Anglo-Saxon material culture surface in the essays by Carol Neuman de Vegvar and Elizabeth O'Brien. Neuman de Vegvar argues that the hell-mouth motif believed to have had its origins in Anglo-Saxon art in all probability had its immediate source in Irish metalwork of the eighth and early ninth centuries. Elizabeth O'Brien surveys burial practices in liter-ary sources to determine their social, religious, or political significance and sees them as providing insights to the cultural practices revealed by archaeological excavations in seventh- and eighth-century Ireland and Anglo-Saxon England (p. 299), cultural practices that negotiate the space between the temporal and material here and now and the passage of the dead to the gates of heaven or the mouth of hell.

Finally, in light of Rosemary Cramp's important excavations at Wear-mouth and Jarrow and at Hartlepool, the collection would be incomplete without a discussion of monastic sites, and this collection thus closes with John Bradley's essay on Celtic monasteries and monastic towns. Bradley sets himself the task of determining the difference between a monastery and a monastic town, outlining the development and central characteris-tics of the latter and offering seven prime examples of Irish monastic cen-ters, among which are the well-known sites of Armagh, Kells, Kildare, and Glendalough. Bradley demonstrates that while the Irish monastic town was "an entity in its own right, a fully fledged phenomenon with specific settlement characteristics, which was part and parcel of the functioning fabric of society," it was also symptomatic of a much more widespread "European experience" (p. 360).

In this introduction we have outlined some of the most obvious con-nections between the essays that make up this volume, but they are by no means the only connections to be made. Readers interested in specific topics will find that the subjects dealt with resonate with each other in interesting and complex ways. Éamonn Ó Carragáin, for example, opens the possibility of female designers or sculptors having had a hand in the design and carving of the Ruthwell Cross, a possibility that is particularly interesting in light of Kelley Wickham-Crowley's discussion of the cultural production of women and their role in the preservation of memory and the care of the dead. Susan Youngs and Colleen Batey both draw our attention to the important advances offered by the scientific analysis of enamel and glass; while Roberta Frank, John Hines, and Gale Owen-Crocker all raise questions about the levels of reality that underlie works of literature and art like *Beowulf* or the Bayeux Tapestry. The variety of disciplines represented in the essays that follow and the range of topics covered by the individual scholars give some indication of the enormous scope of Rosemary Cramp's impact on the study of Anglo-Saxon Culture.

Professor Cramp has worked tirelessly to raise the profile of the material culture of Anglo-Saxon England as a field archaeologist, an art historian, and an administrator. Her excavations at Wearmouth and Jarrow changed our notions of what an Anglo-Saxon monastery looked like, how its spaces and buildings were organized, and how its economy functioned. Her fieldwork became the inspiration for Bede's World, a project that has helped to teach so many about what everyday life was like in early Anglo-Saxon Northumbria through restoration and reconstruction of its material culture. Professor Cramp is the director and guiding spirit behind the *Corpus of Anglo-Saxon Stone Sculpture*, an indispensable reference tool for art historians and archaeologists alike. In the *Corpus* project, as well as in her many articles on Anglo-Saxon art and archaeology, and in her article "*Beowulf* and Archaeology," to which so many of the essays in this volume refer, she has provided a model of interdisciplinary scholarship; perhaps most importantly, she has been a friend and mentor to students and scholars in a variety of fields and from numerous countries.

The editors wish to thank Tom Seiler and Patricia Hollahan of Medieval Institute Publications, Paul E. Szarmach, former director of the Richard Rawlinson Center for Anglo-Saxon Studies and now executive director of the Medieval Academy of America, Randy Morehead and the Interlibrary Loan staff at Zimmerman Library, University of New Mexico, our contributors, and most of all Rosemary Cramp herself.

AEDIFICIA NOVA

The Changing Image, Divine and Human, in Anglo-Saxon Art

Rosemary Cramp

This essay has grown out of a long-standing preoccupation with the problem of what constitutes the distinctive nature of Anglo-Saxon art, indeed how valid it may be to group together the art styles of six hundred years under one heading—Anglo-Saxon—when to the most untutored eye the results are so disparate.[1] Nearly thirty years ago, at another conference in America, I delivered a paper called "The Viking Image," which gave a first airing to several of the themes I wish to explore further in this essay, and I make no apology for restating some of the conclusions since I happen to believe them still. Much exciting scholarly work has been published in the intervening period, however, providing new insights into the meaning of Anglo-Saxon images, and I think in particular of the work of C. R. Dodwell[2] and Barbara Raw,[3] as well as that of many of those contributing to this publication. Their works, together with recent studies of Byzantine images, have provided new directions for inquiry, and new stimuli.[4]

The study of Anglo-Saxon art and architecture is a comparatively recent phenomenon when considered alongside classical art and architecture, which was studied as a basic part of education from the sixteenth century. The study of the Anglo-Saxon language and its texts had begun seriously in the eighteenth century, but consideration of the physical remains of the post-Roman/pre-Norman period was a much later development, and the physical remains (unlike the language) proved difficult

---

1. It was a great honor to give the Rawlinson Lecture for the year 2000, and I would like to thank the Richard Rawlinson Center for its generous sponsorship. My thanks also for the great privilege I enjoyed at a conference in which so many of my friends from both sides of the Atlantic gathered together. I am grateful to them for giving up their time to come and to create this program, but my deepest gratitude must go to those who organized the event, Paul Szarmach, Catherine Karkov, and Helen Damico, with George Brown and Kelley Wickham-Crowley, who so meticulously prepared all the arrangements, and thus made this such a happy and stimulating occasion.

2. Dodwell, *Anglo-Saxon Art*.

3. Raw, *Anglo-Saxon Crucifixion Iconography*, and Raw, *Trinity and Incarnation*.

4. See especially Gameson, *Role of Art in the Late Anglo-Saxon Church;* Ó Carragáin, "Ruthwell Crucifixion Poem"; Belting, *Likeness and Presence*.

to identify and to characterize,[5] and to some extent this is still the case. The primacy of the study of the language and literature of Anglo-Saxon England has almost inevitably molded attitudes in the study of the visual arts, but it is possible for Anglo-Saxon art to provide some counterreflection for the student of literature.

By the 1920s the distinctiveness of Anglo-Saxon art was recognized, especially by foreign scholars: "Whether I turn to the remains of Anglo-Saxon churches, to the crosses, or to the MSS. of the time of Bede, I feel in the presence of an art which differs from every other art in the world":[6] so wrote Josef Strzykowski in 1923. He continued with a theme that will be referred to several times here: the affinity of Anglo-Saxon Christian art with that of the Christian world of the Near East. The precise elements that constituted the distinctiveness of Anglo-Saxon art, however, proved difficult to define. In 1926 Peers characterized its Englishness as "adaptive to outside influences, backsliding" (presumably toward barbarism), but with "a constant element of good judgment, of reasonableness, a dislike of the fantastic and exaggerated."[7] (That probably is how he defined "English" in general rather than being specifically applicable to Anglo-Saxon art!) The monumental series of volumes by Baldwin Brown addressed more cogently, however, the problems of how variation in context and period molded Anglo-Saxon art and also, in considering its adaptiveness, compared the aesthetic of the Celtic and Germanic worlds, seeing that "where the Celtic artist shows his superiority is in his feeling for line, and in his use of the contrast between plain and enriched passages on an ornamental surface," while the Germanic artist's conventional beast ornament may be regarded "only as the enrichment of the surface by a sort of uncertain dappling."[8] (This feature of surface enrichment is observable not only in the animal ornament, but in other elements of later Anglo-Saxon art.) The adaptive nature of Anglo-Saxon art continued to be stressed by later writers, as a generalized comment for the whole period; for example David Wilson in 1984 said, "English Art is and always has been eclectic, drawing for inspiration on its own traditions (often far back) and on such foreign influences as are immediate to English taste."[9] What, however, is "English taste"? Jane Hawkes in a thought-provoking article entitled "Symbolic

5. At one stage Stonehenge was given to the Saxons; Anglo-Saxon interlace can sometimes, even today, be characterized as "Celtic." Defining Anglo-Saxon architecture was a long and painful process, and perhaps as a reaction to the paucity of previously accepted examples, the three great volumes by Taylor and Taylor, *Anglo-Saxon Architecture,* can be found too inclusive.

6. Strzykowski, *Origin of Christian Church Art,* p. 233.

7. Peers, "English Ornament," p. 54.

8. G. Brown, *Arts in Early England,* 1:17.

9. Wilson, *Anglo-Saxon Art,* p. 9.

Lives"[10] has provided one answer in suggesting as a constant element the taste for "ambiguity," and this is indeed an aspect of Anglo-Saxon art that can be traced from the Migration Period to the Norman Conquest. The most wide-ranging and innovative study of Anglo-Saxon taste was, however, provided by C. R. Dodwell who supported his views by extensive reference to contemporary comment.[11]

Today, we not only have a constantly increasing body of evidence for the art from the Anglo-Saxon period—whether discovered by excavation and fieldwork[12] or reidentified in the light of new research—but also contemporary scholars have extended interpretation beyond identification and the establishment of chronologies and have provided multilayered interpretation of images. Nevertheless, although we no longer see the social customs of half a millennium, between the establishment of the Anglo-Saxon ascendancy and the Norman Conquest, as monolithic and unchanging, there is still a tendency to see temporal, regional, even individual differences in the visual arts and in literature in terms of large political groupings: Northumbrian, Mercian, West Saxon, or Northumbrian and Southumbrian. I would cite here the excellent recent study of the St. Andrews sarcophagus[13] in which it was felt necessary to search for influences on this important monument from each of the major territories in Britain and Ireland, only to find that they were not there.

The adoption of Christianity throughout the whole island, with exposure to Christian exegesis and Christian art, could have been expected to provide some common interpretations of images that would transcend Insular boundaries, but a distinctive Anglo-Saxon treatment of these was apparent even in the earliest works. By the time Christian images were adopted by the Anglo-Saxons, the artistic traditions and exegetical preoccupations in the various territories through which Christianity had spread had modified and developed images so that there was a wide choice of models. But, whatever might be available, and attractive, to the newly converted Anglo-Saxons, it was the importation of this art that introduced a range of human figural illustrations to them. I have chosen to concentrate on figural representation because this does at least provide a limited field of inquiry, and also because figures have the potential for the greatest depth of interpretation. There are three main aspects of figural representation in the Anglo-Saxon period that I would like to explore in this essay,

10. J. Hawkes, "Symbolic Lives," pp. 333–34. See also the collected essays in Karkov and G. H. Brown, *Anglo-Saxon Styles*.

11. See note 2 above.

12. Best known of the recent finds is, of course, the discovery of the princely burial at Prittlewell: Museum of London, *Prittlewell Prince*.

13. S. Foster, *St. Andrews Sarcophagus*.

each of which can be present in any phase but which tend to be dominant
in chronological sequence. I give them the shorthand titles of mask, icon,
and dramatic actor.

The art (in all media save metalwork) that has come down to us from
Anglo-Saxon England is so overwhelmingly Christian, and so well supported by Christian exegesis, that it is sometimes discussed as though
pre-Christian symbolism is utterly irrelevant for its understanding. But in
the art of all Christian cultures—even the most theocratic such as the Byzantine—the continuing presence of popular subcults has been noted. In
Britain such pre-Christian manifestations should involve the native Celtic
as well as transferred Germanic elements, which anyway from La Tène
times onward have involved common myths and symbols such as shape
changers, masks, and head cults. Relicts of one such cult can be seen in
the impressive stone heads that occur in some numbers in the pre-Roman
through post-Roman periods in Britain and Ireland (fig. 1).[14] These possess a remote malignancy that is truly haunting, and as in a mask, the
features and expression are strongly but simply conveyed. The idea that
the whole of a being can be encapsulated in the head does seem to be
at the center of decapitation rites and head cults, but could be reflected
also in the early representations of Christ and his evangelists in Hiberno-
Saxon art, where the heads are abnormally large and the bodies abstractly
conveyed.[15]

Van der Leeuw, in a penetrating study of the holy in art, says "Primi-
tive and classic man represent primarily, in fact almost exclusively, those
beings with whose power they are impressed, gods, spirits, kings, animals.
In them man recognizes a power which he does not possess at all or only
partially."[16] Despite the fact that we know very little about the religion,
and images of power, of the North Germanic peoples in the Migration
Period, or indeed how the images and their meaning survived or changed
when transported to a new setting, it is not unreasonable to suppose that
they were not obliterated, but rather transformed and given new meanings in the way that pre-Christian legends whether Hebraic or Germanic
were reinterpreted in literature. Certainly animal forms (which are not the

14. Hickey, *Images of Stone*, pp. 23–30. Similar detached, malignant, faces are found
in later artifacts that seem to be symbols of power, for example, the whetstone from Sutton
Hoo and its smaller affinities: Evans, *Sutton Hoo Ship Burial*, fig. 72.

15. As, for example, in Irish metalwork such as the Athlone Plaque, or a contemporary
shrine mount, Youngs, *"The Work of Angels,"* pp. 141–42, and for masklike heads used as
metal weights from England, see p. 143. Examples from manuscripts are the well-known
depictions of the symbol of St. Matthew from the Book of Durrow, Dublin, Trinity College
Library, MS 57, fol. 21v, or the Crucifixion page from the Durham Gospels, Durham,
Cathedral Library, MS A.II.17, fol. 38v.

16. Van der Leeuw, *Sacred and Profane Beauty*, pp. 161–62.

main concern of this essay) are a constant theme in Anglo-Saxon art and have been used as one of the main chronological indicators, but they may also have been, throughout the period, significant images of power.[17]

In human terms, the images of imperial power that seem to have been transmitted from the Roman to the barbarian world included the victorious mounted warrior, the victorious huntsman and slayer of beasts, the emperor or consul as controller of men and animals presiding over the contests at the circus, and the seated figure of the ruler in judgment. The commonest superhuman image for the North Germanic peoples is of the armed man whose power is in his weapons, who, like the heavily armed Roman, prevails over other lightly armed humans or the natural strength of beasts. Some beasts are of greater significance than is naturally apparent because they are the alter egos of the gods, and such beasts need to be appropriated through their representation, for with every representation an attempt is made to approach what is represented and to hold it fast.

The much discussed Torslunda dies, for making the plates on helmets such as those from Vendel and Sutton Hoo, are an obvious example of this interpenetration of the supernatural and natural, animal and human worlds and include beasts and men in combat, men with beast masks, masked men dancing with spears.[18] I would point out that although the helmets on which they are placed were themselves a disguise, the depictions that surround the Vendel or Sutton Hoo helmets show processions of men so heavily armed that their human characteristics dwindle beneath the weight of their armor and their bird and boar images, although the mounted figures are less disguised. All of these, like the mounted figures on the much earlier Gundestrup Cauldron or later in Pictish art,[19] are shown in profile, whereas other figures differently dressed with elaborate

17. Boar images such as those found on seventh-/eighth-century helmets (see Roberta Frank this volume) occur also as late as the Alfred Jewel, where the gold boar's head terminal with its garnet eyes could well be a deliberate reminiscence of earlier symbols of royalty. There is also a resurgence of animal ornament on stone crosses not only in the north in the Viking Age, but also in one group in the West Saxon kingdom. No doubt these creatures were seen to embody new Christian meanings when they are prominently placed on public Christian monuments, as indeed were birds, both in the initial conversion period for the Anglo-Saxons and again in Northumbria during the Viking Age. For the earlier period, see Bailey, "Sutton Hoo and Seventh-Century Art," pp. 33–36, and Wickham-Crowley, "Birds on the Sutton Hoo Instrument." The ambivalence of such images in suggesting old and new meanings was no doubt an important factor in their promotion.

18. For a discussion of these pieces in which some of the scenes are seen as myths, which are ultimately Persian, but have been translated through Sassanian and Alemannic art to the North Germanic peoples, see Stiegemann and Wemhoff, 799 *Kunst und Kultur der Karolingerzeit*, pp. 436–38 and fig. VII.4.

19. For the Gundestrup Cauldron with its profile processions of armed warriors and forward-looking masks, see Green, *Celtic Myths*, p. 13. Profile mounted figures or processions

headdresses and often dancing with spears are shown frontally. If the profile figures represent the idealized contemporary warrior, do the frontal figures represent priestly figures performing ritual dances to the gods or even the gods themselves among men? There is no conclusive answer to such a speculation, but the difference between profile and frontal figures is significant in many cultures and is significant also in later Anglo-Saxon Christian art, although it could have been transmitted from other Christian sources rather than by direct descent from Migration-Period art.

In his discussion of "Frontal and Profile as Symbolic Forms" Meyer Schapiro says, "The profile face is detached from the viewer and belongs with the body in action . . . in a space shared with other profiles on the surface of the image. It is, broadly speaking, like the grammatical form of the third person, the impersonal 'he' or 'she,' while the face turned outwards is credited with intentness, a latent or potential glance directed to the observer, and corresponds to the role of 'I' in speech with its complementary 'you.'"[20] Later he says "profile and frontal are often coupled in the same work as carriers of opposed qualities. . . . The duality of the frontal and profile can signify then the distinction between good and evil, the sacred and the less sacred or profane, the heavenly and the earthly, the ruler and the ruled, . . . the living and the dead, the real person and the image."[21] He also states that sometimes the message of the relative importance of images is conveyed by the figures being shown as frontal, three quarter, or profile, with the schematized three-quarter face being the commonest, since Late Antiquity, in Western European art. I shall return to this language of positioning on several occasions below.

Masks of course depend for their greatest impact on the frontal view. In the mask, man powerfully creates a second countenance that can convey a clear message: a mask from the cult center of Aqua Sulis in Bath is probably the image of the god/goddess, while, at another level, the face mask on Roman parade helmets can produce a second countenance of idealized youth and beauty above the face of even a grizzled old veteran.[22]

---

are of very frequent occurrence on Pictish stone monuments; see, for example, Fowlis Wester, in Allen and Anderson, *Early Christian Monuments of Scotland,* fig. 306B, and in contrast St. Vigeans no. 11, ibid., fig. 282B, with, on the cross face, two frontal ecclesiastics and, on the back, also two frontal ecclesiastics holding books and scepters or crosiers, with below two hooded profile figures holding round-topped staffs, which in their form are like Roman consular staves. Although Allen interpreted these last as "? ecclesiastics," surely these are authoritative secular figures. See now also the discussion of the same monuments in G. Henderson and I. Henderson, *Art of the Picts.*

20. Schapiro, *Words and Pictures,* pp. 38–39.

21. Schapiro, *Words and Pictures,* p. 43.

22. For the mask, see Cunliffe and Davenport, *Temple of Sulis Minerva at Bath,* plate 4; and Roman parade helmet, Bruce-Mitford, *Sutton Hoo Ship Burial,* 2:222–25, fig. 169.

For the person commemorated in Mound One at Sutton Hoo the second countenance that the helmet mask provides is supernatural; it has the ambiguity of the masks on brooches that intimidate by their mixture of animal and human characteristics, because in a mask separate types of being can be fused into a new whole.[23] The flying dragon, the serpent, and the boar images on the helmet create the features of the ruler/priest in a very controlled way. In contrast, in a recent interpretation of such images on a sixth-century brooch from Ekeby in Uppland, the composition of demonic animal masks devouring human heads and the maze of struggling beasts and humans has been interpreted as the chaos of the final day of Ragnarok, when the mythical beasts will overwhelm both men and gods.[24] The ambiguity between the images of men and beasts that David Leigh described as a characteristic of Style 1 animal ornament[25] perhaps predisposed Anglo-Saxon artists to search out similar ambiguity in Christian art.

The fascination with creatures that link two worlds, whether griffins, dragons, angels, or evangelist symbols, remains throughout the period, and in Christian terms they can be interpreted either as benign or terrifying, even as representing the dual nature of Christ himself, while grotesque masks continue to appear tucked away in less prominent places, for example on the Canon Tables of manuscripts. It is not until late in the period, however, that there is a thoroughgoing orgy of representation of monstrous creatures in the Marvels of the East (e.g., London, British Library, MS Cotton Tiberius B. v), and in these overt representations something of the horror of the half-described, undepicted, or ambivalent image is lost. Strange creatures have ceased to be the dominant symbol of power and become mere titillation.

The separation of human and animal in God's chain of being was an essential part of Christian acceptance for the Anglo-Saxons. The important first message for the missionaries was to place the natural world, with all its strange manifestations, within a controlled hierarchy of creation, and to demystify it. That was demonstrated in Gregory's admonition to Augustine to allow his Anglo-Saxon converts, who were accustomed to ritual feasts of animals, to eat their animals in a convivial nonreligious feast outside the church,[26] and Paulinus's clear-cut order to his young acolyte, "shoot the bird down swiftly with an arrow," when a crow had terrified the catechumens of King Edwin's retinue by croaking "from an unpropitious

---

23. Evans, *Sutton Hoo Ship Burial*, pp. 46–48 and plate III.
24. For the brooch from Ekeby, Uppland, see Magnus, "Firebed of the Serpent," pp. 201–02, fig. 91.
25. Leigh, "Ambiguity in Anglo-Saxon Style 1 Art."
26. Bede, *Hist. eccles.* 1.30, pp. 108–09.

quarter of the sky." Paulinus waited until after his Christian instruction to
the group was finished and then presented the dead crow as a sign that
idolatry was "in all respects useless; 'for,' he said 'if that senseless bird was
unable to avoid death, still less could it foretell the future to men who have
been reborn and baptized in the image of God who have dominion over
the fish of the sea and over the fowl of the air and over every living thing
upon earth.'"[27] This was then the new concept: a powerfully controlled creation with man remade in the image of God, a god not this time masked
or weaponed but facing each individual soul in a direct communion.

How could there be an image of this Christian God? The Bible supplied images such as fire for God the Father or a dove for the Holy Spirit,
but the most frequent image was of God in his incarnation in human form
in the person of Jesus Christ, an icon. By the time the Anglo-Saxons were
Christianized, disputes concerning God's image were long standing and
of some complexity, and the first flowering of Anglo-Saxon Christian art
coincided with the time when the dispute concerning images was reaching
a climax in the Eastern church. The Western church was closely in touch
with East Christian ideas, linked no doubt to the many Greek-speaking
exiles such as Theodore, archbishop of Canterbury, and the Syrian popes
who ascended the papal throne in the eighth century. According to Bede,
the first public display of Christian art to which the Anglo-Saxons were
introduced was the silver cross and "the image of our Lord and Savior"
painted on a panel, which Augustine and his monks carried before them
as they began the conversion of Kent in 597.[28] There is no reason why the
Anglo-Saxon converts would not have been introduced to the most up-to-
date images. The surviving remnants of both seventh-century Byzantine
art and contemporary wall paintings in Rome suggest that there was in
this period an increasing emphasis on the isolated figure or the dominant
figure presented frontally.[29] I stress this point since, although Augustine
traditionally also brought books, notably the St. Augustine Gospels that
was painted with narrative miniatures of the life and miracles of Christ, in the
surviving public art of sculpture it is the individual figure devoid of context (the icon) that seems most common in the seventh and eighth centuries.

If only we had a fraction of the literary evidence from Anglo-Saxon England that we have from Byzantium from which Gervase Mathew claimed it
is possible "to gain a uniquely complete knowledge of the tastes, beliefs and

27. Colgrave, *Earliest Life of Gregory the Great*, chap. 15, pp. 97–99.
28. Bede, *Hist. eccles.* 1.25, pp. 74–75.
29. Mathew, *Byzantine Aesthetics*, p. 99, and see for example the sixth-century icons of
Abraham of Bawit, St. Mark, and the archangel Michael, or the early seventh-century icon
of the Madonna and Child from the Pantheon at Rome: Belting, *Likeness and Presence*, figs.
45–47 and fig. facing p. 264.

aesthetic standards of sixth-century Constantinopolitan bureaucracy."[30] We may not have a record of the taste and aesthetic standards, but we do know something of the beliefs and they seem not far from those of Procopius: "Even human nature cannot be precisely understood by man, still less can the things that appertain to the nature of God. . . . For I personally will say nothing whatever about God except he is altogether good and holds all things in his power."[31]

"For he is altogether good and holds all things in his power" might have been said by Bede, and it is because of Bede's much-discussed testimony that we have any account of the attitude toward images in early Anglo-Saxon England, and one moreover that has been traditionally linked with Gregory the Great's famous letters to Bishop Serenus of Marseilles in 599 and 600. These have been very fully discussed by a series of scholars, but what I would like to comment on is Bede's interesting variations on Gregory's texts, one of which said, "For a picture is displayed in churches on this account, in order that those who do not know letters, may at least read by seeing on the walls what they are unable to read in books," and in a letter the following year, "For it is one thing to adore a picture, another through a picture's story to learn what must be adored, for what writing offers to those who read it, a picture offers to the ignorant/illiterate who look at it, since in it the ignorant/illiterate see what they ought to follow. Thus especially for the gentiles (*gentibus*) a picture takes the place of reading."[32] Gregory makes it clear that pictures have to be interpreted so that when recollected they bear the correct interpretation and keep in mind the memory of Christ, and the support for images as a reminder of

---

30. Mathew, *Byzantine Aesthetics*, p. 70; cf. Gameson, *Role of Art in the Late Anglo-Saxon Church*, p. 3: "aside from the grievous losses of works of art themselves, undoubtedly the greatest handicap for one trying to study the role of the visual arts is the dearth of contemporary written comment on that subject itself."

31. Mathew, *Byzantine Aesthetics*, p. 70.

32. Translation taken from Chazelle, "Pictures, Books, and the Illiterate," p. 139. A view from the East Christian world, a fifth-century letter of Nilus of Sinai, interestingly supports the use of human images and the simple sign of the cross, as against decoration of churches with hunting scenes and "representations of flying, walking, and creeping beasts and every kind of plant," saying "no-one but a babe or a suckling would wish to pervert the eyes of the faithful with such trivialities." At the east end of the house of God, there should be "nothing but the cross alone; for by the single sign of salvation mankind is saved and hope universally proclaimed to the hopeless, but it is not unfitting to decorate both sides of the holy temple by the hand of the finest painters with scenes from the Old and New Testaments, that the man who is ignorant of writing and unable to read the holy scriptures may gaze upon the painting and gain knowledge of the fathers of all virtue, who served the true God; and that he may thus be roused to emulate them in the great and celebrated deeds of heroism, through which they won heaven in exchange for earth." Quoted by Strzykowski, *Origins of Christian Church Art*, pp. 144 and 163–64.

the reality of the Incarnation and as a focus for prayer was maintained in Bede's lifetime by Popes Gregory II and Gregory III.[33]

Bede had been brought up with the sequence of panel paintings that Benedict Biscop and Ceolfrid had imported from the Continent and hung in the churches of Wearmouth and Jarrow. These illustrated, across the east wall at Wearmouth, Mary, the Virgin mother of God, and the twelve apostles, on the south wall depictions of the Gospel story, on the north visions of St. John's Apocalypse. Later, scenes from the life of Christ were added to the Wearmouth churches while at St. Paul's Jarrow was displayed a visual concordance of the Old and New Testaments. The texts in which Bede described these pictures, and also, with reference to Gregory, defended the use of representational art, have been fully explored by Paul Meyvaert, C. R. Dodwell, and others,[34] and here I only wish to make two points. Bede supported his case by the traditional argument of Gregory and his successors, but his own experience of the spiritual benefit of Benedict's icons is apparent in his description of how they were placed, "in order that all men who entered the church, even if they might not read, should either look whichever way they turned upon the gracious (lovable) faces of Christ and His saints, though it were but in a picture; or might call to mind a more lively sense of the blessing of the Lord's incarnation, or having as it were, before their eyes the peril of the Last Judgment might remember more closely to examine themselves."[35] In this he has described all the sequences of paintings in Wearmouth as a source of meditation, and in his treatise *On the Temple* he recalled those in St. Paul's by comparing the serpent lifted up by Moses and a painting of Christ lifted up on the cross, adding that if it is permissible for Moses to display the brazen serpent,

> why is it not permissible that the exaltation of the Lord our Saviour on the cross, whereby he conquered death, be recalled to the minds of the faithful pictorially, or even his other miracles and cures whereby he wonderfully triumphed over the same author of death, since the sight of these things often tends to produce a feeling of great compunction in the beholders, and also to make available to those who are illiterate a living narrative of the story of the Lord? For in Greek too a painting is called . . . "living writing."[36]

33. Raw, *Trinity and Incarnation*, pp. 54–64, in an extended discussion of the icon, examines the papal and Bedan statements in depth.

34. Other significant comments on Bede's contribution to the debate on religious depictions can be found in Dodwell, *Anglo-Saxon Art*, pp. 84–85; Meyvaert, "Bede and the Church Paintings at Wearmouth/Jarrow"; and G. Henderson, *Bede and the Visual Arts*.

35. Bede, *Historia abbatum* 6, pp. 369–70. Trans. in *Bede the Venerable Homilies on the Gospels*, p. 143.

36. Bede, *On the Temple* II, 19.10, p. 91.

Bede constantly in his homilies shares his fascination with the meaning of words, and here is equally personal in his emphasis on the amiable face of Christ and his saints (in contrast to the inhuman malignant images that must have been still around at that time), but also conveys that the awe-inspiring Last Judgment scenes in the church must have made a very deep impression, as is also articulated in his Death Song.[37]

Bede's views were, as noted above, at one with those of contemporary popes, but his own towering reputation more locally may have overcome, in many Northumbrian centers at least, any tendency to iconoclasm in public Anglo-Saxon art in the period when its arguments prevailed in Byzantium and apparently were largely accepted on the Continent. Moreover some of the subjects represented on the Wearmouth and Jarrow icons seem to be repeated in Northumbrian art throughout the late seventh and early eighth centuries.

The Cuthbert coffin (AD 698) is one of the few closely dated pieces of early Christian art in Northumbria, and its well-known carvings comprise the twelve apostles, the Virgin and Child, the archangels, and Christ surrounded by the beasts of the Apocalypse. Kitzinger considered the possibility of a link between the images brought by Benedict to Wearmouth and Jarrow and the twelve apostles, but explicitly denied a relationship between them, saying that the coffin apostles were all taken from the angel model.[38] That does not, however, invalidate a proposition that the carvers of the coffin knew about, or had seen, the Wearmouth icons and, as with the relationship of the Lindisfarne Gospel portrait of St. Mathew (London, British Library, MS Cotton Nero D. iv, fol. 25v) and the scribe portrait in the Codex Amiatinus (Florence, Biblioteca Medicea-Laurenziana, MS Amiatinus 1, fol. 5), could have adapted what they saw.[39] These apparently artless figure carvings reflect something of the native tradition in their large heads and prominent eyes, but this could be a reflection of the styles of their models, and there is a language in the imagery of the coffin that implies wider knowledge. Christ in apocalyptic mode is strictly frontal (fig. 2) as is the *imago hominis*, whilst the other symbols are shown in profile, and although as a child he is seated across the Virgin's knee, his face and upper body are frontal. The Virgin, like Gabriel and Michael, faces the viewer directly, but the angels' noses, unlike hers, are shown in half profile. The other angels and apostles are also depicted in half profile but, as befits his importance above the rest, Peter's features are shown frontally, and both he and Paul are provided with their common attri-

---

37. Bede's Death Song, in Sweet, *Oldest English Texts*, p. 149.
38. Kitzinger, "Coffin-Reliquary," pp. 265–68.
39. On the Lindisfarne Gospels, see M. Brown, *Lindisfarne Gospels*.

butes, the tonsure and key for one and the bald head and ragged beard for the other (fig. 3), while John is distinguished by the gesture (as also in the Lindisfarne Gospels) in which his hands are held to his breast to show his divine inspiration. Whether the large heads and staring eyes come from the Insular tradition or from imported icons,[40] it is possible that both the type of faces and the stance of the Christian models appeared particularly apt to the Anglo-Saxons.

In the ordering of the apostles after the litany of the Mass, as Kitzinger pointed out, the Lindisfarne artist showed the ability to adapt and to interrelate word and image in an individual way, but the stance of the figures confirms their hierarchy. Whether frontality and semiprofile or profile can be used to distinguish hierarchies that involve only secular figures is more debatable. In the much discussed scenes of the Franks Casket,[41] the Virgin and Child are shown frontally and the three Magi in profile, but this is the normal positioning for this scene and could have been slavishly copied from a model; on the other hand in the Weland scene the smith and the bird catcher are in profile, the female figure on the left in semiprofile, but the female figure holding a bottle is a passive frontal figure. This might just be compositional variation, but on the top, the back, and the left side all figures are in profile, while on the mysterious right side only the central figure of a woman gripped between two hooded females is frontal. Whatever the myth depicted on the front and the right side of the casket, I would maintain that the frontal facing figures gain attention as the most important, or possibly of another more sacred order of being; the other figures are engaged in actions played out within their own narrative rather than engaging with the viewer.

Positioning is obviously not the only means of elucidating an image, as was clear from the Cuthbert coffin, and attributes, such as books for evangelists and apostles, vestments and crosses or staffs for bishops, were adopted from a common heritage in earlier Christian art. The pictures that are discussed in Continental sources are paintings whether on boards or on walls, and wall paintings could have existed in the seventh and eighth centuries in England, although it is not until two centuries later that we have any physical evidence for figures, as opposed to abstract patterns, on Anglo-Saxon wall paintings.[42] But the Insular peoples developed their own devotional monuments in low-relief sculptures whether inset in

40. Large heads and prominent staring eyes are also found in Byzantine icons at this period, for example the images cited in note 29 above.

41. Webster and Backhouse, *Making of England*, pp. 101–02.

42. The relevant information has been gathered together in Cather, Park, and Williamson, *Early Medieval Wall Painting and Painted Sculpture in England*.

church walls or on the faces of cross-shafts, and these combined the functions of an iconostasis and classical triumphal columns. It is perhaps no accident that some of the most impressive of these are on the margins of the Anglo-Saxon kingdoms and sometimes in places, such as Bewcastle, that had a pagan holy site. At such sites there was the greatest need to establish a presence for the new faith. As Bede says, "He took upon himself a body immune from all stains of iniquity, and entered the world in it, so that he might destroy the cult of idolatry, and make clear the true light of divinity to the shadowy and dark hearts of the gentiles."[43] Painted relief sculpture on crosses was a robust response to any surviving images from Roman and sub-Roman Britain.

Among the earliest surviving depictions of Christ and his apostles and saints in Anglo-Saxon England, the images are serious but kindly, set against an empty background sometimes with an identifying inscription. They are clothed in classical costume and have beardless, young, and rounded faces, like many on late Roman ivories.[44] The sequence of early "icons" on the crosses at Ruthwell and Bewcastle could have played a part in the enactment of an elaborate liturgy as Ó Carragáin has suggested,[45] but also, even if there were only one image, this could serve as a focus for personal or group devotions. From the beginning kings and aristocrats were patrons of the Anglo-Saxon church, and a list of personal names, probably of laymen, occurs prominently on the Bewcastle shaft, but did the images of such patrons earn a place alongside religious images in the early eighth century, and how possible is it to make such identifications? Of the three images on the Bewcastle Cross,[46] Christ the Judge might have been identified by the combination of his halo, the scroll that he holds, and his central frontal position, even without the inscription with his name. The identity of the topmost figure has been more disputed, but it is haloed, points to the Lamb that it is holding, and is most convincingly interpreted as John the Baptist with the Lamb of God. The lowest figure with a bird has been identified, from the nineteenth century onward, as a layman, sometimes just as a falconer, and at other times has been compared with depictions on coinage that are seen as lay, aristocratic or royal, images rather than as St. John with his eagle attribute.[47] I have in the past

43. Bede, *Homeliae* 2.15, in *Bede the Venerable Homilies on the Gospels*, p. 143.

44. Morey, *Early Christian Art*, figs. 141–45.

45. Ó Carragáin, *City of Rome*, pp. 30–38.

46. Bailey and Cramp, *Cumberland, Westmorland and Lancashire-North-of-the-Sands*, ills. 99, 94–96.

47. G. Brown, *Arts in Early England*, 5:125. Karkov, "Bewcastle Cross," pp. 16–19. It seems probable that the ambiguity in this image is intentional, just as the inscription above the

vacillated between the religious symbolism that provides a neat antithesis of the two St. Johns at the top and bottom of the shaft and a lay depiction, accepting that the different dress of this figure separates it from the figures of Christ and John the Baptist above. I would now add further support to this—the distinctive stance in which, in contrast to the frontal figures above, the body is half turned away but the head is looking back at the spectator. This sets him somewhat below the frontal figures above but engages him with the spectator in the manner seen much later in the New Minster Charter portrait of King Edgar.[48]

How would an image of an Anglo-Saxon ruler be identified ca. 700? This is not an easy task before the early tenth century, when Anglo-Saxon kings started to be depicted wearing crowns. Before then, on coinage, they were depicted wearing a variety of diadems and sometimes, as Baldwin Brown and Catherine Karkov have noted, with a bird. I have discussed this problem recently in relation to the Glastonbury monuments.[49] However, I missed an important image in previous discussion, namely the heads at the end of the Breedon friezes. These heads were originally considered to be recut into the friezes in the thirteenth century, but Richard Jewell's reinstatement of them as contemporary with the rest of the friezes is very convincing.[50] He compares them with the coinage of Offa, but I would compare them also with Byzantine ruler portraits that have the same elaborately dressed hair, neatly trimmed beards, and caplike diadems.[51] They reflect then the influence of East Christian art as do some other motifs from Breedon, but they could well represent the lay patrons of these distinctive, elegant friezes. Perhaps the fact that lay rulers can be represented by heads alone is influenced by the heads on coinage.[52] It is interesting to note as an aside, however, that secular and clerical rulers are distinguished by their positioning: in the early ninth century, innovative frontal images occur on the coinage of the archbishops of Canterbury

---

image of Christ as Judge at Bewcastle has been seen as reminding the reader of the words that Bede ascribes to King Oswiu in attempting to convert the pagan king of the East Saxons, and so relating human and divine sovereignty. For this parallel, see Schapiro, "Religious Meaning of the Ruthwell Cross," p. 171. See also Gannon, *Iconography of Early Anglo-Saxon Coinage*, pp. 96–98.

48. London, British Library, MS Cotton Vespasian A. viii, fol. 2v; see Backhouse, Turner, and Webster, *Golden Age of Anglo-Saxon Art*, plate 4.26; Karkov, *Ruler Portraits of Anglo-Saxon England*, pp. 85–93.

49. Cramp, "Pre-Conquest Sculptures of Glastonbury Monastery," pp. 154, 161.

50. Jewell, "Anglo-Saxon Friezes at Breedon-on-the-Hill," p. 109.

51. See, for example, the portrait of Constantine in a mosaic in the Katholikon of the monastery of Hosios Loukas in Greece: Maguire, *Icons of Their Bodies*, fig. 29.

52. Gannon, *Iconography of Early Anglo-Saxon Coinage*, pp. 25–41.

and York, in a form that copies Byzantine models, while the contemporary images of the kings remain in profile.[53]

The lively miniature figures on the Breedon friezes coexist with more static and larger-scale figures, framed in panels, and these and related individual figures at Peterborough and Fletton nearby include the same repertoire of Christ, Our Lady and the apostles, and angels as was found on the Cuthbert coffin.[54] This repertoire continues throughout the eighth into the ninth century in the north on crosses, although during that period the style of their representation changed. Contemporary with the more sympathetic understanding of the varied styles of Late Antique art that was being developed on the Continent in manuscripts and ivories, Christ himself and the apostles were depicted under architectural frames in more varied and relaxed attitudes, and with a greater understanding of perspective. This is the beginning of a movement away from the awed contemplation of Christ and his surrounding saints and angels as distanced if benign, to the more personalized devotion to different human aspects of Christ and in which the worshiper is named as an individual, as in the Cynewulfian poetry. In a recently published article, the late Jim Lang identifies the Christ figure on the Easby Cross as the Risen Christ holding up his right hand to show his wounds, flanked by St. Peter and St. Paul in a scene which he identifies as the *Traditio Legis*.[55] This type of gesture with open palm is found elsewhere, for example on a Continental ivory in which the Virgin is flanked by two similar figures, and the standing figure of Christ from the Metz chancel screen displays the same gesture and, like the Easby Christ, holds up a circular feature that could be the host.[56] This gesture with an open palm could be a "peace be with you" statement of the risen Christ who is eternally present in the Eucharist, or it could be an early example of emphasizing the humanity of Christ and his suffering, so common in later Anglo-Saxon art. Both Bede and Ælfric developed the idea that on the great Day of Judgment the wicked will see Christ as he was when he died, as Ælfric said "in the form of a man so that his killers can recognize him."[57] The Easby Cross is not only

---

53. Conveniently illustrated for both York and Canterbury in Webster and Backhouse, *Making of England*, no. 120, pp. 155–56, and no. 226, pp. 252–53.

54. Cramp, "Schools of Mercian Sculpture," figs. 56–58.

55. Lang, "Apostles in Anglo-Saxon Sculpture," p. 273.

56. Hubert, Porcher, and Volbach, *Europe in the Dark Ages*, fig. 288 for the Saulieu ivory of the Virgin, and fig. 291 for the Metz closure slab.

57. These passages from Bede's homily on the Vigil of the Ascension and Aelfric's Catholic Homilies, 1 xxi, are quoted by Barbara Raw in a discussion of the linking of Christ's death with the Second Coming in eighth-century manuscripts: Raw, *Anglo-Saxon Crucifixion Iconography*, pp. 108–09.

a complex monument iconographically, but carved by a master who could indicate realistically in the seated figure the body beneath the fine drapery, in the manner of an early Carolingian manuscript, and indeed parallels with Carolingian art have been adduced from its first full publication by Margaret Longhurst onward.[58] The apostles exhibit the variation in facial type, and posture of the head, that is found in Early Christian art, and some have the rather wistful expressions, as with a figure on a cross from Otley, which many years ago I compared with the evangelist figures in the St. Medard de Soissons Gospels (Paris, Bibliothèque nationale de France, MS lat. 8850).[59] Nevertheless despite some variation the Easby figures are fairly static and remain confined within their frames, very much like the Evangelist portraits in contemporary manuscripts such as the Stockholm Codex Aureus (Stockholm, Royal Library, MS A.135). The individual image continued as the representational norm into the ninth century and was indeed transmitted to the Viking settlers who also raised crosses that depicted figures of ecclesiastics, although they introduced in addition secular armed figures, often in profile, so combining secular and religious images of power.[60]

By the end of the eighth century and beginning of the ninth there are indications of change—a widening of context and grouping of figures even within the most confining of media, sculpture. Most of the scenes are taken from the life and miracles of Christ, and some individual scenes are clearly extracted from larger cycles. One example is the little group, perhaps from a Passion cycle, on the Cundall/Aldborough Cross (fig. 4) that could be Christ before Pilate, in which Pilate is seated with a scribe at his feet and Christ stands in front of a building. Also on that cross is a panel showing Samson bearing off the gates of Gaza, which would have been part of an Old Testament cycle such as is found on the Masham column (fig. 5). Both monuments have been assigned to the same sculptor,[61] and indeed the isolated images on Cundall/Aldborough probably were enough to remind a viewer of the larger cycles on the Masham column. That monument records an evolving understanding of God's relationship with the created world, from the parade of fantastic animals at the base through the witness of the Old Testament precursive heroes such as Sam-

58. Longhurst, "Easby Cross."

59. Cramp, "Position of the Otley Crosses in English Sculpture," pp. 60–61.

60. The intrusion of the lay "portrait" into the composition of the Nunburnholme shaft is a noteworthy example, and has been fully discussed in Lang, *York and Eastern Yorkshire*, pp. 189–93, illustrations 721–24.

61. Lang, "Apostles in Anglo-Saxon Sculpture," pp. 271–82; Lang, "Monuments from Yorkshire in the Age of Alcuin."

son or David to the events of Christ's own life, as witnessed and recorded by the apostolic *comitatus*.

Despite new fashions for miniature series and groups, individual figures of saints and apostles remained popular during the ninth century. By this time England had produced some notable indigenous saints, and it has been proposed that some of the images on cross-shafts could have been of contemporary Anglo-Saxon ecclesiastics.[62] I have suggested before in relation to a small group of crosses at Collingham, Crofton, and Halton that the figures who carry a cross and wear a skull cap were bishops, and this generic image could have been used to represent local bishops without any necessity to reflect a likeness.[63]

So far we have looked at indicators of types for ecclesiastics and possibly rulers, but was there any attempt to produce likenesses of individuals? There has been considerable discussion of the reality and likeness that contemporary witnesses perceived in Byzantine images, which to our eyes today appear very formalized. A similar situation is to be found in later Anglo-Saxon art in the third, more dramatic phase that I am considering, when contemporary human beings penetrate the world of Christ and his saints and are present in the unfolding dramas of the Gospel narratives. In literary sources near-contemporary figures are recorded as possessing their own attributes, so William of Malmesbury notes of Siward, an abbot of the late ninth or early tenth century: "Paintings testify that his habits did not conflict with his name, for each time he appears in them he is shown with a scourge or a birch." However, the claim of likeness is also made, as Dodwell noted, in the case of an eleventh-century observation by Osbearn that a local priest resembled St. Dunstan as he was known from his representations.[64] Can we really see much resemblance between the figures of Dunstan kneeling at Christ's feet in "St. Dunstan's Classbook" (Oxford, Bodleian Library, MS Auct. F.432, fol. 1), and Dunstan seated with Æthelwold and King Edgar in London, British Library, MS Cotton Tiberius A. iii, folio 2v? And yet the two images of the ecclesiastics are individual and distinctive, and moreover the same two figures are rep-

62. For example, G. Henderson in his *Vision and Image in Early Christian England*, pp. 172–73, speculated as to whether St. Wilfrid might have been represented on the Dewsbury, Otley, and Halton Crosses.

63. Cramp, "Position of the Otley Crosses in English Sculpture," pp. 61–62, but here Crofton was not mentioned, and it might be added that the flock of sheep depicted on the Halton Cross (Collingwood, *Northumbrian Crosses of the Pre-Norman Age*, fig. 87, Collingham; fig. 92c, Halton) could well be conceived of as an attribute of a bishop who, like Peter, would feed Christ's lambs. The image could have an additional resonance for any depiction of St. Cuthbert who was called to the monastic life while tending his master's sheep.

64. Dodwell, *Anglo-Saxon Art*, pp. 93–94 and 275.

licated in a Durham manuscript where two ecclesiastics are seated alone (fig. 6).[65] Whether these are seen, however, as Æthelwold and Dunstan or as generic images of clerics is difficult to say, but they are distinctive among the many depictions of clerics in late Anglo-Saxon manuscripts. Perhaps after an image had been first promoted it established a norm for subsequent representation, so people then recognized what they had been led to expect. Henry Maguire summed up this situation perceptively and with humor in using, to discuss likeness in Byzantine icons, the *New Yorker* cartoon of a teacher receiving a visit from a mother with the caption "Mrs. Hammond I would know you anywhere from little Billy's portrait of you."[66]

In this dramatic phase the formal and distanced images of the icon type can coexist together with chattering group expressionism, and the contrast adds meaning to the image. In the depiction of St. Benedict being presented with his Rule from the Arundel Psalter, Benedict makes a distant gesture of acceptance (fig. 7) but does not turn to look at the book as in some representations of the same incident. He is frontal, distanced in his richly colored shrine, almost oblivious to the flippant group of monks who have invaded his space. There are clear identifiers of importance and role in posture and attributes, but it is the exaggerated movements and gestures that command the attention and may semaphore the messages. Some of the gestures may indeed have developed, as Dodwell suggested, from a knowledge of the plays of Terence;[67] others perhaps mirror the increasingly dramatic liturgy of the time. The breaking out of the frames and even the pillaging of frames for the action, the intrusion of contemporary props into the biblical landscapes in which Old and New Testament scenes were enacted, even a movement of the contemporary human into divine space, all created an exciting participation in events rather than tranquil recollection, which the icon induced.

The informality of some of the images contrasts very markedly with contemporary work on the Continent, and none more so than in the ruler

65. For "Dunstan" in the "Classbook," see Temple, *Anglo-Saxon Manuscripts*, fig. 41; for King Edgar with St. Dunstan and St. Æthelwold, see ibid., fig. 313. For a discussion of the proposition that the kneeling monk in the "Classbook" is not Dunstan, see Gameson, *Role of Art in the Late Anglo-Saxon Church*, pp. 79–81.

66. Maguire, *Icons of Their Bodies*, pp. 15–16, fig. 7.

67. This gesture of acceptance in which the thumb and forefinger are curled together Dodwell has seen as one of the gestures derived from the Roman stage, claiming that by the eleventh century knowledge of the illustrated plays of Terence could have introduced a new language of gesture into Anglo-Saxon art: Dodwell, *Anglo-Saxon Gestures and the Roman Stage*, pp. 122–23. Richard Gameson has also noted that in later art, "particularly in manuscripts gesture is all important," but facial expression and interaction with the viewer is not so: Gameson, *Role of Art in the Late Anglo-Saxon Church*, p. 261.

portraits. In the earliest surviving manuscript portrait, Æthelstan's presentation of a book to St. Cuthbert,[68] there is still a formality and division between the king and the bishop: the king, in contemporary dress and crowned, is facing sideways and bent with an exaggeratedly humble gesture; Cuthbert, by contrast, facing outward from his vestigial church and gazing into the distance, is a still solemn figure. The architectural backdrops for each figure serve to distinguish further their lay and religious roles. In the equally well-known scene in which Edgar presents a charter to the New Minster at Winchester,[69] the king, in recognition of the new sacral nature of kingship, is transported to a higher realm in which he shares the same space as St. Peter and the Virgin, and can even touch the heavenly host, but his lesser state than Christ above is emphasized by the amount of space his zone occupies and also by the manner in which he swivels between his roles to engage with the spectator. The main space on the page, however, is given to Christ and his angels. In the presentation scene of a gold cross to the New Minster by Cnut and Emma,[70] the king and queen with their splendid presentation cross occupy the main space on the page. They are actively occupied in their presentation, and even the angels are distracted from their heavenly zone to attend them. Barbara Raw, however, has suggested that this scene has a more than localized significance in noting that the drawing prefaces a representation of the Last Judgment, which could confirm the suggestion that the figures of the Virgin and St. Peter (now moved to a position on either side of Christ) are interceding for the king and queen, and asserting the belief that the cross would bring one safely to heaven.[71] Nothing illustrates better than these royal images the lack of pomposity in Anglo-Saxon figural painting, which is one of its defining characteristics.

In sculpture, the single awe-inspiring image of Christ or his angels and saints remained popular throughout the Anglo-Saxon period, only increasing in scale and with a specific emphasis on large-scale crucifixes or images of judgment. This late style is exemplified by figures such as the Bristol Christ or those on a newly discovered stele from Somerset, possibly Congresbury.[72] On this last the figure of Christ is holding a cross in his left

68. Cambridge, Corpus Christi College, MS 183, fol. 1v (Temple, *Anglo-Saxon Manuscripts*, fig. 29); Karkov, *Ruler Portraits of Anglo-Saxon England*, pp. 55–68.

69. BL, Cotton Vespasian A. viii, fol. 2v (Temple, *Anglo-Saxon Manuscripts*, fig. 84); note 48, above.

70. London, British Library, MS Stowe 944, fol. 6 (Temple, *Anglo-Saxon Manuscripts*, fig. 244); Karkov, *Ruler Portraits of Anglo-Saxon England*, pp. 21–45.

71. Raw, *Anglo-Saxon Crucifixion Iconography*, pp. 26 and 144–45.

72. For the Bristol Christ, see Kendrick, *Late Saxon and Viking Art*, plate 37. The Congresbury stele is discussed in Cramp, *South-West England*, pp. 149–51, ill. 204–20.

hand and blessing with his right, in the stance of the Second Coming or
the Harrowing of Hell. The tonsured ecclesiastic could represent St. Peter
or a local saint (see figs. 8 and 9). The architectural details of the frames
can be paralleled in late tenth-/early eleventh-century manuscripts, and
the distinctive folds across the belly and knee are reminiscent of the drapery on an ivory figure of John the Baptist, dated to ca. AD 1000.[73] The
discovery of new and unweathered figures such as these demonstrates how
much has been lost in late Anglo-Saxon sculpture, yet their period style is
evident and despite their gravitas these figures could hardly be mistaken
for any on seventh- to ninth-century monuments.

Dodwell in his perceptive exploration of Anglo-Saxon taste does seem
to consider that there was little difference throughout the period. Certainly
there is a continuum in the use of certain words in Anglo-Saxon texts that
evoke a characteristic that is distinctive in the art throughout, namely the
play of light and shade flickering on a surface. This is expressed in terms
like *fah, brun,* or *fealu,* which convey nuances of brightness. But, though
the words may be the same, the effects to which they refer are very different. The bright reflections of gold and the deep shadows of the garnets, in
the seventh and eighth centuries, produce this effect, as do in a different
way the flowing and swirling backgrounds that support the gesticulating
figures in late Saxon manuscripts. The strong primary colors of the earlier palette differ greatly, however, from the range of hues in soft pinks,
milky blues, and greens and the gold of the later.

There is indeed a great change from the generality of the kindly but
severely remote divine figures of the early icons to the animated, even
histrionic, figures of the later period. Their relationship to the viewer
becomes more intimate, and depictions of the physical differences between
human and divine are less sharp. Despite the changes to contemporary
costumes there is no real portraiture, but the impression is that the simple
cues to figural identification no longer surface, and the viewer is expected
to extract more from the context. The divine beings, and those filled
with divine power, are, however, still marked out by their traditional Late
Antique dress and, unless actively occupied, by their frontality.

In the later Anglo-Saxon period, growth in lay learning and in the
importance of the individual rather than the group voice, as well as wider
patronage, resulted in a changed environment for figural representation.
In such a world men and women could imagine the events of the Passion
so vividly that they themselves became part of the event and could be
demonstrably present in a depiction.[74] Traditional iconography could then

73. Wilson, *Anglo-Saxon Art,* fig. 266.
74. See further O'Reilly, "Rough Hewn Cross in Anglo-Saxon Art," pp. 155–57; Schapiro, "Image of the Disappearing Christ."

Figure 1. Romano-British head from the fort at Appleby, Cumbria. By permission of English Heritage. Copyright author.

Figure 2. Lid of the Cuthbert Coffin showing Christ surrounded by the beasts of the Apocalypse. By kind permission of the Dean and Chapter of Durham Cathedral. Copyright Durham Cathedral.

Figure 3. "Apostle Side" of the Cuthbert Coffin showing Peter and Paul with their attributes. By kind permission of the Dean and Chapter of Durham Cathedral. Copyright Durham Cathedral.

Figure 4. Part of the Cundall/Aldborough shaft at Aldborough. Copyright author.

Figure 5. The Masham column. Copyright author.

Figure 6. Durham, Cathedral Library, MS B.III.32, folio 56v, showing two ecclesiastics. By kind permission of the Dean and Chapter of Durham Cathedral. Copyright Durham Cathedral.

Figure 7. London, British Library, MS Arundel 155, folio 133. St. Benedict being presented with his Rule. By permission of the British Library.

Figure 8. Head of Christ and a saint from shaft from Congresbury (Somerset). Photo John Crook. Copyright *Corpus of Anglo-Saxon Stone Sculpture*.

Figure 9. Drapery from a figure from Congresbury (Somerset). Photo John Crook. Copyright *Corpus of Anglo-Saxon Stone Sculpture*.

be manipulated in an individual way; so Goscelin described the scenes of Christ's Passion as painted on the walls of Edith's chapel at Wilton "as she had pictured them in her heart."[75] The greatest gap in our understanding of popular and individual piety in the pre-Conquest period is the loss of wall paintings and other forms of interior decoration such as wall hangings, since it may be true, as William of Malmesbury said, that the Anglo-Saxons were committed not to the largeness of buildings but to the sumptuous nature of their contents.[76] The Anglo-Saxons throughout the pre-Conquest period do not seem particularly concerned with grand public display, and the expression of their piety on the eve of the Conquest had become informal and individual.

I have tried to demonstrate some of the very definite changes in the treatment of the human and divine figure in the art of the Anglo-Saxon period, and indeed changes in the relationships between them. The same verbal imagery can be seen to cloak very different manifestations, yet there are distinctive characteristics that emerge, like carefully bred strains, through the repeated choice in limited directions from a wide range of available models. A fancifulness and ambiguity that manifests itself most characteristically in late Saxon colored ink drawings (but is apparent even in the eighth-century stone sculptures), surface texturing, a lack of "volume," and above all, even at its most serious, a lack of pomposity and grandiose settings, all distinguish the language of this figural art.

75. Raw, *Anglo-Saxon Crucifixion Iconography*, p. 60; Goscelin, "La Légende de Ste Edith en prose et vers," pp. 86–87.

76. William of Malmesbury, *Willelmi Malmesbiriensis Monachi De Gestis Regum Anglorum Libri Quinque* 2, p. 205.

BEDE AND CHANGE

GEORGE H. BROWN

When we consider Bede's sublime composure, calm career, monastic stability, conservatism, and strong dedication to order and orthodoxy, my title "Bede and Change" may seem incongruous. In substance and style he advocates a changeless, divinely ordered cosmos. Because he emphasizes the allegorical meaning of Old Testament texts and in his commentaries on Old Testament books pursues typological relationships so relentlessly, the impression is given of historical stasis and inert abstraction. Moreover, Bede is tradition bound; everyone who reads him is aware of his deference to the bedrock of patristic authority in the Roman church. In his exegetical writings he often avers that he is but following the footsteps of the Fathers (*sequens vestigia patrum*).[1] He is so careful to establish his credentials as a traditional mediator of patristic teaching that during four post-Renaissance centuries his exegesis was dismissed as derivative. This attitude continued into the modern period; for example, even in celebrating the twelfth centenary of Bede's death in 1935, Dom Bernard

An essay on Bede seems an appropriate tribute to Rosemary Cramp, whose scholarship and fieldwork mark her as the greatest contributor to our archaeological knowledge of Bede's sister monasteries at Wearmouth and Jarrow. Her energy and drive were the leading force in the construction of the great educational complex Bede's World. Her work as an author and general editor of the *Corpus of Anglo-Saxon Stone Sculpture* and her numerous studies of Northumbrian art, architecture, and ornament have provided those of us working primarily in literature with complementary cultural enrichment and the ability to unite the literary with the material record. She has inspired and supported my work on Bede since I was first introduced to her and her work in the 1960s. She has frequently guided me to the Bedan sites and landscapes of Northumbria and welcomed me to her home to meet eminent friends and scholars, especially during my tenure as fellow of University College, Durham. She is a dear friend to me, to my wife, and to my sons. I am honored to be among the colleagues who contribute their essays to this book; I offer this study to Professor Cramp in gratitude and admiration.

1. Of Bede's frequent use of this expression to assert his exegetical debts, see, for example, *In primam partem Samuhelis libri iv*, Prologus, p. 10, lines 53–54; *In Regum librum xxx quaestiones*, Prologus, p. 293, line 23; *De templo*, Libri II, I, p. 191, lines 1754–55; *In Cantica Canticorum*, Prologus, p. 180, line 504; *Homeliarum Euangelii libri ii* II.11, p. 258, lines 191–92; *De temporum ratione*, chap. 5, p. 287, lines 86–87.

Capelle considered Bede as an exegete "périmé" (out-of-date) because of his allegorical penchant and patristic dependence.[2] Beryl Smalley, in her influential *The Study of the Bible in the Middle Ages,* concludes her tepid and brief treatment of Bede with the words, "His importance lies in his faithful presentation of the tradition in its many aspects."[3] Henri de Lubac, while linking Bede to the conservative patristic tradition, does give him credit for being the most scientific spirit of the early Middle Ages, the first to formulate the four modes of biblical interpretation (literal, allegorical, tropological, and anagogical), and the first to list as the canonical four doctors of the Latin church Ambrose, Augustine, Jerome, and Gregory.[4] However, only recently has it become clear why the ninth-century acclamation of Bede as himself a Father and Doctor of the Latin church is truly merited. With the emergence of critical editions of Bede's works in the Corpus Christianorum Series Latina and a dozen translations of his individual exegetical works, along with newer and more perceptive evaluations and interpretations of his exegesis by theologians such as Arthur Holder and Bertrand de Margerie, Bede's contribution to the exegetical tradition is becoming manifest. De Margerie points out that Bede himself intended to "note and add to" *(adnotare, superadicere)* the commentaries of the Fathers on Holy Scripture, by which "Bède nous communiquait, en cet aveu, un projet d'originalité dans la continuité" (Bede communicated to us, in that avowal, a project of originality in the continuity).[5] De Margerie then gives examples and analyses of some of Bede's sensitive and nuanced original additions to patristic expositions of the New Testament. Bede is astutely editorial in his selection and expansion of his sources. Historians such as Paul Meyvaert, Faith Wallis, and the many scholars who have given the annual Jarrow Lecture have demonstrated how Bede made genuine and extensive contributions in every monastic discipline, not only in exegesis, but also in pedagogy, computus, poetry, homiletics, and history.

2. "En tant qu'exégète, il faut reconnaître que Bède est, dans l'ensemble, périmé. Il l'est pour s'être trop tenu à l'exégèse allégorique; il l'est pour avoir trop emprunté aux anciens." (As an exegete, it must be recognized that Bede is on the whole out-of-date; that is for his being too devoted to allegorical exegesis, for his having borrowed too heavily from the ancients.) Capelle, "Le rôle théologique de Bède le vénérable," p. 25.

3. Smalley, *Study of the Bible in the Middle Ages,* p. 36.

4. De Lubac, *Exégèse médiévale,* I, p. 26, 664. For an English translation (first reference only), see de Lubac, *Medieval Exegesis,* trans. Sebanc, I, p. 4. Bernice M. Kaczynski provides a more detailed account of the formation of the canon in her essay "Bede's Commentaries on Luke and Mark," pp. 18–20.

5. De Margerie, *Introduction à l'histoire de l'exégèse,* p. 188. Bede's statement is found in *Hist. eccles.* 5.24, p. 566: "haec in Scripturam sanctam meae meorumque necessitati ex opusculis uenerabilium patrum breuiter adnotare, siue etiam ad formam sensus et interpretationis eorum superadicere curaui."

Besides Bede's talents in all these fields as an original contributor who augments and modifies the texts of his sources, he possesses another, related attribute: that of recorder of change. Bede recognizes and deals with this constant change in human history; he espouses and even promotes change in his own time and society. While recognizing this complex topic to extend beyond the scope of this essay, I propose now to look at two major areas of Bede's scholarship: his treatises on time, especially the *De temporum ratione* (or, as Faith Wallis gives as the title to her fine translation and commentary, *The Reckoning of Time*), and his historical works, the *Historia ecclesiastica* and *The Letter to Bishop Egbert*.[6]

In his strong affirmation of activism and zeal for change even while standing for stability and discretion, Bede is following patristic precedents, especially the enormously influential shaper of Christian orthodoxy in the West, St. Augustine. He shares Augustine's sense of linear history that proceeds from Creation and the Fall to Christ's Incarnation and redemptive act, active in the ever-changing present while moving inexorably to the final end. In the chronicles that he attaches to his two works on time reckoning, he has as his model *Chronikoi Kanones* of Eusebius of Caesarea as translated and edited by Jerome (who continues it to AD 378) and augmented by Prosper (to 445) and Marcellinus Comes (to 534).[7] Among ecclesiastical historians who shaped the history of their ages, Bede's models are, again, Eusebius of Caesarea, Augustine, and also Gregory of Tours, who provide Bede with methods of creative historiography, some of which he finds useful to emulate and modify and some of which he rejects as unsuitable to his purpose and the reality of the very different conditions of his land and society. Therefore, while seeking to steer clear of sheer panegyric and hagiography on the one hand and cynical criticism on the other, I want to navigate a few of the major ways in which Bede adapts, modifies, and extends the thought of his patristic forebears and formulates a new construct of temporal development and historical change. In his approach to his textual sources, Bede may be usefully compared with the Anglo-Saxon artists and viewers discussed by Rosemary Cramp in the preceding essay, who adapted traditional images and iconographies to suit individual goals and changing times.

Bede's two treatises on time were among his educational treatises. Although he did not advocate any wholesale educational reform, he augmented the curriculum in every subject. He followed the prescriptions of Augustine's *De doctrina Christiana* concerning the role of learning in the

---

6. Bede, *Reckoning of Time*, pp. xlvii–xlviii. For a convenient English translation with notes of both the *Historia ecclesiastica* and the *Letter to Egbert*, see Bede, *Ecclesiastical History of the English People*, ed. McClure and Collins.

7. Bede, *Reckoning of Time*, pp. 354–58.

Christian, and for him in the specifically monastic, community. *"Doctrina Christiana* sees Christian erudition as a means to an end; the training of exegetes and preachers—men who could understand the Word of God and convey its message accurately and persuasively."[8] That pragmatic purpose provided the basis of Christian education. Since the monk was to learn only what was useful for salvation, and shun what was useless or harmful, Bede's model of learning was not based on the trivium and quadrivium of late pagan antiquity but on a curriculum of useful sciences contributing to a deeper knowledge of the Bible. During the Carolingian Renaissance, when the educational curriculum was constituted for clergy and court, Alcuin, though he considered himself a disciple of Bede, restructured monastic educational training by reinstituting the late classical trivium and quadrivium. But Bede remained faithful to the ideal of Augustine's *De doctrina,* in which all learning was related to an understanding of the central text of the Christian religion. Bede really was consistent in following that ideal, which to later secular ages would seem restrictively narrow. Thus, even his extirpation of pagan classical examples in favor of Christian citations in his educational works shows how dedicated he was to that Augustinian ideal, more consistently indeed than Augustine himself. For Augustine, like Jerome, frequently quotes or echoes pagan classical authors, while Bede eschews all of them except Virgil.

By rejecting the pedagogical structure of the quadrivium and the ancient format of science, as Brigitte Englisch convincingly argues, Bede and the monastic *magistri* actually liberated science from the speculative and circumscribed subject of classical mathematics, which left little room for experimentation, and moved it to the pragmatic, problem-oriented, empirical, and rational methods of temporal reckoning according to both lunar and solar cycles, that is, computus.[9] In his treatises on time and computus, *De tempore* and especially *De temporum ratione,* Bede "was obliged not only to harmonize scientific data with theological implications, but to transform the calendar into a reproducible system, logically consistent and hence capable of resolving doubts and refuting criticism."[10]

The Reckoning of Time is a treatise on measuring time and establishing a Christian calendar. It represents the earliest comprehensive treatment of this subject, as Wallis points out, for although much calendrical work was done before Bede's time, it was both fragmented and biased in character.

---

8. Wallis in Bede, *Reckoning of Time,* p. xxi.
9. Englisch, *Die Artes liberales im frühen Mittelalter,* section 2.1; and "Realitätsorientierte Wissenschaft oder praxisferne Traditionswissen?" pp. 19–21. Summarized by Wallis in Bede, *Reckoning of Time,* pp. xxvi–xxvii.
10. Wallis in Bede, *Reckoning of Time,* p. xxxvii.

> Bede's book is very different in form and content. Although he is also the partisan of one form of Paschal table—the Alexandrian 19-year cycle, as elaborated by Dionysius Exiguus—he sought to establish its credibility by making it the basis of a comprehensive manual of time reckoning. It was a gamble that paid off. So lucid, thorough and well-organized was Bede's exposition, so easy was it to teach from and learn from, that it can be said to have not only guaranteed the ultimate success of Dionysius' system, but to have made computus into a science, with a coherent body of precept and a technical literature of its own.[11]

Bede's work was thus truly revolutionary and established a deep channel from the many rivulets and errant streams that preceded his work. The many manuscript copies of both treatises (but especially the amplified one) right up to the sixteenth century, along with derivative works such as Byrhtferth's *Computus* (988–96) and *Manual* or *Enchiridion* (1011), attest to the potent transformation he wrought. As the editors of the *Enchiridion* affirm, "Bede wrote *De Temporum Ratione* (*DTR*) in the year 725. To say that *DTR* is the most important work on chronology produced in the Middle Ages is inadequate. Bede was, as much as Dionysius Exiguus, responsible for the shape of the calendar before the Gregorian reform, and even our modern calendar might look rather different were it not for his influence."[12]

It is common knowledge that, taking up the suggestion of the sixth-century computist Dionysius Exiguus (already brought to the attention of the English by Wilfrid at the Synod of Whitby), Bede in the *Historia ecclesiastica* is the first medieval historian to use the dating system of *anno Domini*. Why, though, does he use the AD dating in the *Historia*, but in the great chapter 66, called the Greater Chronicle, of *The Reckoning of Time* he uses instead the age of the world, *annus mundi*, as the basis of temporal reckoning? Faith Wallis tells us succinctly:

> Bede uses *annus mundi* throughout the chronicle because it underscores this continuity; he uses *annus Domini* reckoning in the *Ecclesiastical History* because all its action takes place within the sixth age of the world, and because the Dionysian computus associated with *annus Domini* era plays such an important role in his overall story. Like his choice of genre, Bede's choice of era was deliberate and strategic: what is irrelevant to the *Ecclesiastical History*, is all-important to *The Reckoning of Time*, and vice versa.[13]

11. Wallis in Bede, *Reckoning of Time*, pp. xvi–xvii.
12. Baker and Lapidge in Byrhtferth, *Enchiridion*, p. lxxxvi. See also Lapidge's entry on Byrhtferth in Lapidge et al., *Blackwell Encyclopaedia of Anglo-Saxon England*, pp. 78–79.
13. Wallis in Bede, *Reckoning of Time*, pp. lxx–lxxi.

Bede's realignment of time reckoning in these two complementary works indicates his genius and originality. Such a flexible and rational adjustment also reveals his methods of structuring history and recording change.

Why does Bede add to the sixty-five chapters of computistical reckoning of *The Reckoning of Time* the last six chapters, which constitute the comparatively long and seemingly separate world-chronicle, followed by five chapters on future time and the end of time? As von den Brincken and Tristram noted in their separate studies of the *Sex aetates mundi*, it is Bede who forges an essential link between computus and chronology.[14] The initial inspiration for this came from Isidore and the Irish, but Bede's treatment is quite special. In pressing the Augustinian analogy of the six ages with the six days of Creation and also with the six ages of man (infancy, childhood, adolescence, manhood, middle age, and old age), he introduced a major modification in the tradition. He replaced the Eusebian chronology of the first two world-ages, reckoned from the dates given in the Septuagint version of the Old Testament, with the chronology based on Jerome's translation of the Hebrew text, the *veritas hebraica*, of the Old Testament. "Where the Septuagint assigns 2,242 years to the First Age and 942 to the Second, Bede, following the Vulgate, gives 1,656 years to the First Age and 942 to the Second Age. The upshot is that the birth of Christ, which Isidore, following Eusebius, dated to AM 5197, is dated by Bede to AM 3952."[15] The revised chronology occasioned the greatest possible insult to the supremely orthodox Bede, that of heresy. There was a common belief that each of the six ages was a thousand years, seemingly supported by the text "One day is with the Lord as a thousand years, and a thousand years as one day" (2 Peter 3:8; cf. Psalm 90:5 [89:4]).

As a result of the redating of the age of the world (following Jerome), Bede was accused in the court of his diocesan superior, Bishop Wilfrid, of putting the birth of Christ in the fifth age and not in the sixth, as it should be. Bede ferociously defends his position in his Letter to Plegwin, which angrily includes even an argument ad hominem, so uncharacteristic of Bede.[16] In chapter sixty-six of *The Reckoning of Time*, however, he more moderately and extensively sets forth his position. He makes the central point of his argument that not all the world-ages are of equal length, so that the duration of the sixth age is humanly unknowable. By this Augustinian insistence Bede avoids the critical danger of inexorably linking computus, history, chronology, and the end of time. As Richard Landes

14. Von den Brincken, *Studien zur lateinischen Weltchronistik*, pp. 38–49; Tristram, *Sex aetates mundi*, pp. 12–15.

15. Wallis in Bede, *Reckoning of Time*, p. 358.

16. Bede, *Epistola ad Pleguinam*, pp. 617–26.

has explained, the fusion of computus and chronology can easily lead to chiliasm and millenarianism, because by literal reckoning of units of one thousand years, the world should end in *annus mundi* 6000, ushering in a seventh age, a cosmic sabbath period equivalent to the Lord's day of rest in the Creation.[17] "Chronology then becomes unwittingly the accomplice of both a heretical chiliasm and an explosive millenarianism."[18] In the last chapters of *The Reckoning of Time* Bede firmly argues against chiliasm, that is, that the world will end in the thousandth year of the sixth age, and also against millenarianism, that is, the belief that there will be a post-Judgment seventh historical age, in which the saints will reign with Christ on earth. The seven days of Creation, Bede says,

> signify, not six thousand years of labor and a seventh of the reign of the blessed on earth with Christ, but rather six Ages of this fleeting [*labentis*] world in which the saints labor in this life with Christ, and the Seventh Age of rest in another life which the holy souls, released from their bodies, will possess in Christ. The sabbath of souls is rightly believed to have begun when Christ's first martyr [i.e., Abel], slain in the flesh by his brother, was translated in spirit into eternal rest. But it will come to an end when the souls shall have received incorrupt bodies on the day of resurrection. And because each of the five Ages in the past is found to have run its course in a thousand years, but some in more, some in less, and none had the same total of years as another, it follows that this [Age] likewise, which is now running its course, will have a duration uncertain to mortal men, but known to Him alone who commanded His servants to keep watch with loins girded and lamps alight "like men waiting for the lord, when he shall return from the marriage feast" [Luke 12:35–36].[19]

Here Bede adopts with enthusiasm Augustine's interpretation that the seventh age is the duration of the church expectant, the totality of all the elect from the time of Abel to the end of the world, concomitant with our time but outside our time sphere, waiting in peace for the eighth age of eternal completion. The antichiliasm and antimillenarianism present only seminally in Bede's early *Commentary on the Apocalypse* and featured here and there throughout his exegetical tracts and homilies is here explicitly expressed. Both diversity and change are the historical reality, not neatly fixed limits and humanly predictable segments.

17. Landes, "Lest the Millennium Be Fulfilled," pp. 142–49.
18. Wallis in Bede, *Reckoning of Time*, p. 360.
19. Bede, *Reckoning of Time*, p. 240.

Just as Bede insists in *The Reckoning of Time* on leaving his Chronicle open-ended, so in his *Historia ecclesiastica* he ends with the account open to the future and to change. In contrast to the *Letter to Bishop Egbert,* the *Historia ecclesiastica,* intended for general public consumption, finishes on an upbeat: "In these favorable times of peace and prosperity, many of the Northumbrian race, both noble and simple, have laid aside their weapons and taken the tonsure, preferring that they and their children should take monastic vows rather than train themselves in the art of war. What the result will be, a later generation will discover (*posterior aetas videbit*). This is the state of the whole of Britain at the present time (*inpraesentiarum universae status Britanniae*)."[20]

But it is not just the end of the *Historia ecclesiastica* that is firmly set in continuing time. Every reader of the *Historia ecclesiastica* must realize how frequently and intensely Bede inserts dating, temporal reckoning, and especially the correct method of calculating the date of Easter, and the detail with which it is discussed. Roger Collins and Judith McClure, in their edition and translation of the *Historia ecclesiastica,* deem his concern about the correct dating of Easter obsessive: "By the time that Bede was writing the *EH* in 731 the issue was hardly a living one, yet he gives it an extraordinary prominence, which is also matched in his Chronicle by references to the subject and to those who wrote about it. Whereas his interest in the miraculous was common, his interest in Easter-dating must appear somewhat idiosyncratic."[21] Even though by contemporary secular historical standards Bede's fixation on the topic may seem excessive, now that we have discussed Bede's ardent involvement with the subject in the two works on time, we can better understand why he gives it this high profile in the *Historia ecclesiastica.* If space permitted, we could show the same purpose in his exegetical works, such as the *Commentary on the Acts of the Apostles,* where Christianity that was born in Jerusalem expands over the centuries to the ends of the earth, to the territory of the Angli. With proper adjustment for the different forum of the *Historia ecclesiastica,* Bede is maintaining the same thesis. He had engaged himself in a long and complex investigation on the nature of time, its reckoning, and the necessity of keeping the correct dating of Easter, the temporal fix of the supreme feast of the Christian Church within constantly changing time on the celestial matrix. It clearly has a major role in an *ecclesiastical* history. Bede is a theological historian, imbued with Augustinian understanding of the critical importance of marking the cosmic mileposts along the line of Christian history. And Bede insists on keeping the relationship between actual time and annual liturgical commemoration right.

20. Bede., *Hist. eccles.* 5.23, p. 561.
21. In Bede, *Ecclesiastical History of the English People,* ed. McClure and Collins, pp. xix–xxi.

Of course, the *Historia ecclesiastica* manifests the creative shaping of much other data within its complex order. Bede arranges (sometimes suppresses) and edits the materials and sources acknowledged in the Preface. As Richard Fletcher puts it, "Bede was an exceptionally careful and honest historian, though in using him we have to bear in mind that his aims and methods in writing history widely differed from those of today."[22] Clever scholars such as Walter Goffart bring to the surface some of the likely motives and stratagems buried in the subtext of the marvelously smooth surface of the *Historia*. One of Bede's most potent ploys is the consigning to oblivion or to carefully limited treatment those elements that do not conduce to his ends. A notable example of this, as Goffart and others have noted,[23] is Bede's diplomatically selective portrayal of Bishop Wilfrid, in contrast to the enthusiastic apotheosis in the *Vita Sancti Wilfrithi* by Stephen of Ripon.[24] Conversely, other events and personages he spotlights prominently. As D. P. Kirby has recently called to our attention, Bede enhanced Cuthbert as monk, bishop, and Northumbrian patron.[25] Cuthbert served only the briefest time as bishop of a lesser diocese, unwillingly dragooned into the post and relinquishing it for a return to eremetical seclusion on the isolated isle of Farne. Other saints, such as Aidan, rivaled his good works and sanctity. But Aidan was Irish and, though eminently holy, followed the Irish dating of Easter and shape of tonsure.[26] Bede saw in Cuthbert, as Simon Coates has shown, the ideal mix of the monastic contemplative and the active pastor of souls.[27] Cuthbert was a pastoral monk-bishop like Aidan but English and united with the universal catholic church in Easter reckoning and tonsure. Bede was right in his choice. From the eighth century on to the present Cuthbert stands as an emblem and symbol of Northumbrian piety. To this day St. Cuthbert is a presence, a living force, a revered patron. It was Bede's three versions (prose life, poetic life, and epitome in the *Historia ecclesiastica*) that textually reinforced the cult and insured the future patronal eminence of Cuthbert. So, just as Bede created a text that forever fixed the events and personalities of early Anglo-Saxon England, he also fixed the hagiography and hieratic ranking of the Northumbrian saints.

We have noted that the *Historia ecclesiastica* ends on a positive note. But his Letter to Bishop Egbert, also written toward the end of his life, is

22. Fletcher, *Conversion of Europe,* p. 4.
23. Goffart, *Narrators of Barbarian History,* pp. 235–328.
24. Eddius Stephanus, *Life of Bishop Wilfrid.*
25. Kirby, "Genesis of a Cult," esp. p. 383.
26. See Bede's description of Aidan's virtues in *Hist. eccles.* 3.5 and his detesting his lack of the proper observance of the Easter dating in 3.17.
27. Coates, "Bishop as Pastor and Solitary."

a more personal and troubled document (surviving in only three manuscripts, two quite late). It is labeled by Roger Collins and Judith McClure "a free-standing moral treatise,"[28] but I consider it rather an early predecessor of the "Sermo ad clerum" type, an admonition to a prelate by an upright clerical critic, notably developed during the early modern period by Colet and Latimer. Bede's letter calls for a reform of the Northumbrian ecclesiastical system by doing away with the numerous small private familial *Eigenkloster* and inaugurating twelve episcopal sees, as envisaged originally by Pope Gregory, to assist the metropolitan in his vast territory. Bede will have the sees based on monastic sites. That way there would be no need for new and expensive foundations, and the bishops would be of the type of Aidan and Cuthbert, humble missionary-bishops (unlike the grasping prelate Wilfrid) working among the people in the distant villages of the vast Northumbrian hill country. Here Bede calls for radical change, and in so doing presents a grim picture of present pastoral care or rather the lack of it. But this letter, like the Chronicle and the *Historia ecclesiastica,* is open-ended toward the future, nonapocalyptic, looking to a reform within the continuation in linear time against the unforeseeable eternal endpoint.

In all his works of exegesis, history, and chronology, Bede is engaged with time, and with change. Bede monitors change in the church and in society, and by his writings attempts to channel and direct it. He is historian of the labent, eliding sixth age, the end of which he refuses to predict, since it is given to no one to know (Matt. 24:36; Mark 13:32).

28. In Bede, *Ecclesiastical History of the English People,* ed. McClure and Collins, p. xxx.

WHO THEN READ THE RUTHWELL POEM
IN THE EIGHTH CENTURY?

ÉAMONN Ó CARRAGÁIN

In a paper given at University College Cork in late 1975, Rosemary Cramp reexamined the relationships between Old English literature and Anglo-Saxon archaeology, a subject on which she had years before written a highly influential paper.[1] She was cautious about the possibilities of making direct links and stressed the different methodologies and problems of the two disciplines. But she ended her lecture by making an important exception. There was one site where the archaeologist had to take an interest in literature, while the literary scholar had to take an interest in archaeology and iconography: the Ruthwell Cross, on which poetry and iconography formed a unity. The present essay is a footnote in memory of that inspiring lecture, the occasion on which the present writer first met Rosemary Cramp. She has always seen the Ruthwell poem as a primary feature of the monument:

> Even if one supposes the runic poem was inscribed to fill in the ugly wide margins (which would have to be left for reasons of symmetry on the narrow sides) there seems no convincing reason why they should have been carved in later. . . . There is nothing in the cutting of the runes, as Baldwin Brown and Blyth Webster first pointed out, to suggest that the inscription was a later addition to the cross, quite apart from the common-sense improbability of leaving the broad margins blank.[2]

To appreciate the force of Rosemary Cramp's remark about the "the commonsense improbability of leaving the broad margins blank," one need only look at the related Bewcastle Cross (fig. 1). There is a major difference in design between it and the Ruthwell Cross. The Bewcastle shaft has rounded corners. Two long thin vertical incisions on each face, parallel with and close to the corners, mark out at each corner a slender scroll (a roll molding), partially detached from the shaft. Thus while all the panels have wide vertical borders, these borders are all curved and unsuitable for

1. Cramp, "*Beowulf* and Archaeology."
2. Cramp, "Anglian Sculptured Crosses of Dumfriesshire," p. 12.

inscription. All the inscriptions are on the flat spaces *between* panels, not on the vertical borders with their roll moldings.[3] But the Ruthwell cross-shaft has squared corners (fig. 2). Its panels have flat vertical borders suitable for inscription.[4] The vertical borders of every surviving large panel are inscribed, except for those of the Crucifixion on the base, and that was certainly a later addition to the cross. There are many Anglo-Saxon monuments with inscriptions, but the Ruthwell Cross is unique among them in being designed to have inscriptions on the vertical borders of all of its four sides. If all scholars admit that the Latin inscriptions on the broad sides are original features of the cross, there is no logical reason to deny that the runic poem on the narrow sides is similarly an original feature of the cross. That the Ruthwell designer should have provided *tituli* for all the large panels on the broad sides, but none for his largest panels, the vine scrolls on the narrow sides of the lower stone, was clearly, to use Cramp's expression, a "commonsense improbability."

Rosemary Cramp's position on Ruthwell was implicitly challenged, in 1973, by Professor Ray Page, who gave a highly censorious account of the layout of the *tituli* to the two vine scrolls on the lower stone:

> The runes of the top stone were cut sensibly so as to run in fairly long text lengths along the borders they filled. Not so those of the lower stone, for where these occupy the vertical borders of the east and west faces they are set, not along the length of the border, but in a succession of short horizontal lines of two, three or four letters each. Thus that section of the text which fills the top and then the right-hand vertical border of the east face is divided up "[.]gere / da / hi / næ / go / da / lm / eg / tti / gþ / ah / ew / al / de / on / ga / lg / ug / ist / iga / *mod* / igf / [.] [.] / men / [.]." This looks absurd and is maddeningly hard to read. So odd does it appear that I incline to think it may not be part of the original design for the cross, and to wonder if these runes were added by a later carver who had less command over the space he had to fill. But this is a heretical view and not shared by art historians.[5]

Page's vivid and highly judgmental phrases, "looks absurd," "maddeningly hard to read," and "odd," were clearly based on his own experience as an epigrapher and runologist, and on a personal sense of what was fitting. He saw it as sensible to lay out inscriptions in a continuous

3. See the description by Rosemary Cramp in Bailey and Cramp, *Cumberland, Westmorland and Lancashire-North-of-the-Sands*, pp. 61–72.

4. See the plates in Cassidy, *Ruthwell Cross*.

5. Page, *Introduction to English Runes*, p. 150 (2nd ed., p. 147).

line from left to right, or from top to bottom, even when such inscriptions ran along a vertical border at right angles to the reader's vision. Conversely, he considered it absurd to lay out inscriptions in vertical columns without word divisions, even when such a layout ensured that the letters were the right way up when the reader looked at them. Page also implied that Anglo-Saxon runes did not provide any directly comparable material, because nothing survives that is quite like Ruthwell. With some 260 surviving runes (and perhaps as many as 480 runes originally), the Ruthwell poem is by far the longest continuous runic inscription from England to survive. The second longest group of runes to survive from England is that of the Franks Casket, which has over 260 runes in all; but these are divided between the four sides and the top of the casket, so that there are "five sculptured panels, each with one or more runic legends, making up eleven discrete inscriptions on the casket."[6] Otherwise, the corpus of English runic inscriptions comprises "perhaps forty significant texts, and several of these consist only of personal names in the nominative case,"[7] and no other surviving runic inscription from England compares in length to the Ruthwell poem. As we shall see, a major difficulty in understanding what the Ruthwell designer was about has stemmed from the fact that his design is unique among surviving runic inscriptions. As far as we know, no other English designer of runic inscriptions was remotely as ambitious. The designer of the Franks casket set out his inscriptions (a mixture of runic and Roman scripts) in a variety of ways: some inscriptions are upside down as the casket stands; one group of runes is retrograde, so that each rune is back to front, and the inscription reads from right to left; one inscription is encrypted, using unique forms for all the vowels.[8] It hardly seems likely that the designer of the Franks Casket shared Page's criteria of what was "sensible" and what "absurd." But it was the Ruthwell inscription, not that on the Franks Casket, that Page described as "absurd," and in doing so he failed to cite any comparative material from nonrunic scripts.

In 1978, Professor Ute Schwab provided the comparative and historical material that previous discussions had lacked. She pointed convincingly to the rich Roman and Byzantine tradition of inscribing the uprights of crosses, or vertical borders of reliquaries, in short groups of letters reading left to right without word division, so that the inscription forms a solid vertical column of letters, as at Ruthwell.[9] Schwab's contribu-

6. Page, *Introduction to English Runes*, p. 175 (2nd ed., p. 173).

7. Page, *Introduction to English Runes*, 2nd ed., p. 14, modifying his first edition, p. 15, which referred to "under thirty significant texts."

8. See Page, *Introduction to English Runes*, pp. 174–82 (2nd ed., pp. 172–79); and the plates and excellent survey in Webster, "Iconographic Programme of the Franks Casket."

9. Schwab, "Das Traumgesicht vom Kreuzesbaum."

tion was of the greatest importance: it provided new evidence to support the arguments of earlier scholars, such as Fritz Saxl and Rudolf Wittkower, that Mediterranean contexts are important for understanding the Ruthwell and Bewcastle Crosses.[10] As we shall see in the present essay, this tradition was to be seen on at least two of the relics most revered in seventh- and eighth-century Rome: the Cross of Justin II and the miraculous icon of Santa Maria in Trastevere.[11] One might have expected that Schwab's study would have settled the scholarly debate: she demonstrated conclusively that the layout of the *tituli* to the Ruthwell vine scrolls had close analogues in a major tradition of Early Christian epigraphy and, in particular, of epigraphic verse. This tradition was exemplified in highly prestigious objects to be seen in Rome, the city that in the eighth century was for Anglo-Saxons, kings and clerics alike, the most sought-out pilgrimage center in Europe.[12]

In 1987, the present author built on Schwab's work in order to argue that there were particular reasons why the Ruthwell designer should have followed this tradition for the verse *tituli* of the vine scrolls on the lower stone.[13] To understand the designer's procedure, we need to make a distinction between, on the one hand, his layout for the *tituli* of the panels on the broad sides and the vine scrolls of the upper stone and, on the other, his layout for the runic verse *tituli* of the vine scrolls on the lower stone. All the *tituli* on the upper stone, and those for the panels on the broad sides of the lower stone, were relatively short, because all of those panels are relatively small. In general (with some exceptions, such as the Man Blind from Birth on the first broad side) the incipit of each *titulus* ran across the top of a panel; it then continued down the right side. The *titulus* usually ended on the left vertical border (reading downward), and where the inscription was particularly long, it could end on the lower margin of the panel (this happened in two cases: the panels depicting Mary Magdalen at the feet of Christ on the first side of the lower stone, and John the Baptist pointing to the Agnus Dei on the second side of the upper stone). The parts of the *tituli* on the vertical borders usually run downward; those on the horizontal borders invariably run from left to right. To this there is a major exception on one large panel: the now fragmentary runic *titulus* for the Visitation panel on the first side of the upper stone seems to have run upward along the left vertical border (on this border the inscription,

10. Saxl, "Ruthwell Cross"; Schapiro, "Religious Meaning of the Ruthwell Cross"; Saxl and Wittkower, *British Art and the Mediterranean*, §§ 15–18.

11. Schwab, "Das Traumgesicht vom Kreuzesbaum," pp. 156–62.

12. See Levison, *England and the Continent in the Eighth Century*, pp. 15–44; Stancliffe, "Kings Who Opted Out"; Ó Carragáin, *City of Rome*.

13. Ó Carragáin, "Ruthwell Crucifixion Poem."

largely lost, ended with the surviving word "[-] m(a)rþ(a)"), then across the upper border (perhaps "mar [-] m r", though this inscription is doubtful in the extreme: in most lights nothing can be made out on the upper border), and then downward on the right border (where the inscription began with the word "dominnæ [-]": its continuation is lost). In an ingenious but ultimately unsatisfying reconstruction of this inscription, Page failed to consider what is likely to have been lost in the damaged borders before "marþa" and after "dominnæ", and thus reconstructed a single complete sentence out of these few fragments; this imaginative procedure was followed by David Howlett who, within the narrow limitations of that procedure, gave a better account of the surviving fragments.[14]

On the vertical borders of all these panels, the *tituli* are set out at right angles to the reader's vision. As Page has put it, such relatively short *tituli* are "cut sensibly, so as to run in fairly long text lengths along the borders they filled."[15] The layout is indeed sensible, but only because these *tituli* are all relatively short. Thus, as a rule, they have a reasonable balance between text that runs from left to right (along the top and in two surviving instances the bottom margin of a panel) and text that runs in a single continuous line along the right or left margin. Readers could usually read, or recall, one of these *tituli* by looking at a line of horizontal script. Then they could read or recall the rest of the *titulus* simply by making a single quick sideways tilt of the head. To take in the sideways inscription on any one of these short vertical borders, a reader would have had to make two, or at most three, eye movements.[16] Such a balance between horizontal and vertical layout was not available to the designer in the *tituli* for the vine scrolls on the lower stone. If, as originally designed, the two Ruthwell verse *tituli* may together have comprised over 480 runes, each *titulus* may have originally comprised some 240 runes. Allowing about ten runes for each horizontal incipit, each of the two vertical columns in each *titulus* may have had, say, 115 to 120 runes. In 1987, the present writer concluded that:

> The designer may have felt that to inscribe each margin, practically the whole length of the lower stone, with a continuous row of runes laid at right angles to the onlooker's vision, might have had the Ruthwell community murmuring of cricks in their necks, or else of runes running up and down before their eyes.

14. For discussion of this difficult inscription, see Ó Carragáin, *City of Rome*, p. 34 and nn. 144–46.

15. Page, *Introduction to English Runes*, p. 150, quoted above (2nd ed., pp. 146–47).

16. See the discussion of how the eyes move in reading, in Saenger, *Space between Words*, pp. 1–9.

By adopting the solution he did, the designer at least ensured
that all the runes of the poem were the right way up when the
cross was erected, even if he sacrificed logical word-division
in the process. As the margins around the foliage scrolls grow
broader towards the bottom of the stone, the designer was free
to choose when to change from two to three, or from three to
four, runes per line. In this way he could use the space available to him in the most economical way, and at the same time
keep the runes to a consistent size throughout the design of
the border. By using short lines, therefore, it was easier for the
designer to ensure that the area covered in runic script was
aesthetically coherent.[17]

Ute Schwab had already called attention to close contemporary analogues; now, in addition, a close examination of the problems facing the
Ruthwell designer indicated that his layout was the most realistic way of
coping with these problems.

Schwab's important paper had far less impact than it should have
done. Four years after her study appeared, but without any reference to
it, Paul Meyvaert published the first of two studies of the Ruthwell Cross,
both of which accepted as original all the *tituli* to the panels on the broad
sides. However, he too viewed the runic *tituli* to the vine scrolls on the
lower stone as secondary and added later. Instead of referring to Schwab's
examination of contemporary analogues, Meyvaert provided a series of
schematic diagrams of how inscriptions might ideally be laid out, in order
to show that the layout of the *tituli* to the vine scrolls on the lower stone are
"a total anomaly" and "a complete anomaly."[18] "Anomalous" is, of course,
simply the negative for "unique." Again, the argument was weakened by
a lack of knowledge of the relevant comparative material. In 1992, in his
second paper, Meyvaert still based his rejection of the *tituli* as integral
to the vine scrolls on the lower stone simply on his study of runic monuments:

> As regards the runic verses—linked to the Old English *Dream
> of the Rood*—that are incised around the borders enclosing the
> inhabited vine-scroll, and that loom so large in the literature
> on the Ruthwell cross, nothing has been said in the preceding
> pages. This is only because I consider these verses to be a later

17. Ó Carragáin, "Ruthwell Crucifixion Poem," p. 9. I wish to acknowledge the assistance of Professor Jane Roberts, who first pointed out to me that the designer probably
chose his layout for the runic *tituli* on the lower stone to cope with the fact that its vertical borders gradually grew broader from top to bottom. See now Roberts, "Some Relationships."

18. Meyvaert, "Apocalypse Panel on the Ruthwell Cross"; Meyvaert, "New Perspective on
the Ruthwell Cross," pp. 164–65 ("a total anomaly"), and n. 266 ("a complete anomaly").

addition, which did not influence the original design and iconography of the cross. I have encountered no new evidence, or
serious criticism of the argument I presented in 1982, to prompt
me to change my opinion on this point. On the contrary, an
even broader survey of the manner in which runic inscriptions
were displayed through the centuries, always with a view to legibility, has kept me convinced that the lay-out at Ruthwell is a
total anomaly demanding a very different kind of explanation.
The explanation put forward in 1982—which has since been
accepted by others—still seems to me the most logical and reasonable one, namely, that the cross was no longer lying flat, in
sections, in the stonemason's workyard, but was standing erect
in the church, when the runes came to be incised upon it.[19]

While Meyvaert once more rejected the *tituli* to the vine scroll on the
lower stone as later, he now explicitly stated that the fragmentary *tituli* to
the vine scrolls on the upper stone were original. For him, all depended
on the notion of what was a "sensible" layout: "The runic inscription which
once occupied the upper stone of the cross, of which now only a few runes
remain . . . , was laid out in exactly the same manner as the Latin inscriptions, thus indicating that it belongs to the original carving, done before
the cross was erected. The problem is to explain how the shaft came to be
incised so differently."[20] The footnote to that passage continues with an
explicit rejection of the present author's defense of the layout of the runes
on the lower stone as practical:

> Ó Carragáin . . . has recently suggested that the new procedure
> was intended to facilitate reading and prevent the Ruthwell
> community from getting the crick in the neck that would have
> resulted, had the runes been incised in the same way as the
> Latin letters. But anyone who peruses the numerous illustra-
> tions of runic monuments—some with very long inscriptions—
> shown in E. Moltke, *Runes and their Origin, Denmark and Else-
> where,* Copenhagen (1985) will have to conclude that the runes
> on the Ruthwell shaft represent a complete anomaly, demand-
> ing some explanation unrelated to legibility or twisted necks.
> My own explanation is to suggest that the tall cross was already
> standing when the decision was made to add the runic verses.[21]

19. Meyvaert, "New Perspective on the Ruthwell Cross," pp. 164–65.
20. Meyvaert, "New Perspective on the Ruthwell Cross," p. 164.
21. Meyvaert, "New Perspective on the Ruthwell Cross," n. 266. Elisabeth Okasha is
more circumspect than Page and Meyvaert on the question: "the runic texts, whether or not
they were always intended to be part of the design of the cross, are certainly highly decorative and enhance its appearance": "Literacy in Anglo-Saxon England," p. 88.

Meyvaert here refers to the very passage in which the present writer had pointed out the importance of Schwab's work, and on that very page he had listed some of the most important analogues adduced by Schwab and paraphrased (with due acknowledgement) some of her discussions of these objects.[22] The central weakness of Meyvaert's argument thus becomes his refusal even to consider Schwab's evidence. He wrote as if for him runes existed in a self-enclosed Germanic cultural world so that, in considering their layout, only runic tradition need be considered. Apparently, the practices of Northumbrian Christian rune-masters of the eighth century were to be assessed solely in the light of the achievements of other Germanic rune-masters, including those of the Scandinavians, even though eighth-century Christian Northumbrians, fortunately for them, had not yet seriously encountered Scandinavians in large social groups. On the other hand, it was evidently felt that the Roman or Greek epigraphic traditions set forth by Schwab could be ignored, even though Northumbrian ecclesiastics (such as, say, Bishop Acca of Hexham) had certainly been to Rome and clearly valued the ecclesiastical traditions they found there.[23] Meyvaert not only ignored Schwab's evidence and conclusions, his dismissal of Schwab also implied a rejection of the demonstrations by Saxl, Schapiro, and Wittkower that Mediterranean traditions were central to the Ruthwell monument. The assumption that runes occupied an autarchic German epigraphic tradition recalls the assumptions of nationalist German scholars such as Helmut Arntz.[24] David Parsons has recently made it seem even less likely that runes can be understood in isolation from other contemporary scripts, with his convincing suggestion that it was the monastic communities that propagated the seventh-century Anglo-Saxon reform of the *futhorc:*

> Roman script appears at much the same time in much the same areas, and it is used for much the same purposes, as Christian-period runic script, and its spread is surely due to the Church.

22. Ó Carragáin, "Ruthwell Crucifixion Poem," p. 9. In addition, Schwab's article is listed in the bibliography to the volume in which Meyvaert's remarks appear: Cassidy, *Ruthwell Cross*, p. 194.

23. See Ó Carragáin, *City of Rome*, passim.

24. Arntz, *Handbuch der Runenkunde*, see pp. 124 and 210, where the Ruthwell runes are discussed without any reference to their iconographic or Christian contexts. Arntz's National Socialist assumptions are amply set forth in his "Vorwort," pp. vii–x. John M. Kemble had already delivered a magisterial rebuke to such romantic epigraphic nationalisms in 1840: "as nearly every inscription we have must be referred to Northumberland, we find this the more intelligible, when we bear in mind, that before the close of the eighth century Northumberland was more advanced in civilization than any other part of Teutonic Europe" ("On Anglo-Saxon Runes," p. 338).

It is tempting, therefore, to wonder whether the dissemination of the standard *futhorc* might also have been due to the Church. This hypothesis . . . not only accords with the distribution of inscriptions, it also links what appears to be a swift and—on present evidence—complete change in runic practice to the institution which was effecting profound cultural changes across Anglo-Saxon society. What other authority, around the turn of the eighth century, is likely to have exerted an influence away from heterogeneous local practice and towards a standard that was observed from East Anglia to Northumbria?[25]

If Parsons is right, then runic inscriptions demand to be seen in the context of all other evidence of Anglo-Saxon ecclesiastical interest in varieties of script and alphabets, ancient and modern.

The arguments of Page and Meyvaert were adopted with enthusiasm by Eric Stanley.[26] His article attempted to document the philological consequences of their theories about layout. Understandably, Stanley also ignored Schwab's evidence. His philological arguments are inconclusive: the impression left by his paper is that runes simply cannot be accurately dated on philological grounds alone. Although Stanley could find no evidence definitively to exclude an eighth-century date, he nevertheless suggested that the poem might have been added as late as the tenth century.[27] He did not discuss the question why, if the runes were added in the tenth century (i.e., long after the Viking invasions and settlement), no one had yet suggested Scandinavian influence on the form of the runes or the language. In his fundamental article, published in 1840, John Mitchell Kemble had pointed out that the Ruthwell runes were Northumbrian, pre-Viking in form.[28] Stanley's arguments did not find acceptance among other specialist philologists.[29] While Page was characteristically polite to Stanley's methodology, he implicitly rejected his tenth-century dating.[30]

---

25. Parsons, *Recasting the Runes*, pp. 97–98. See also two important earlier studies, each of which independently argues that runes, which are regularly associated with Roman script on ecclesiastical sites, were widely used in Anglo-Saxon monasteries in the eighth and ninth centuries: Parsons, "Anglo-Saxon Runes in Continental Manuscripts"; and Fadda, "Aspetti e significati della compresenza delle scritture romana e runica nelle iscrizioni anglosassoni."

26. Stanley, "Ruthwell Cross Inscription."

27. Stanley, "Ruthwell Cross Inscription," p. 396. Stanley's iterations of Meyvaert's conclusions are listed by Ó Carragáin, "Ruthwell Crucifixion Poem," p. 7 and n. 9 (on p. 55).

28. Kemble, "On Anglo-Saxon Runes," p. 352.

29. His dating is rejected explicitly by Fulk, *History of Old English Meter*, p. 342.

30. Page, *Runes and Runic Inscriptions*, pp. 43–46, 336.

By the end of the last century, the mutually reinforcing opinions of Page, Meyvaert, and Stanley had become widely influential among English-speaking Anglo-Saxonists. Weak though their arguments were, they set a new fashion. By the early 1990s opinions based on their studies were so widely iterated on the Ansaxnet discussion list as to become canonical.[31] As the present writer put it in 1987, "a new centrifugal orthodoxy, . . . a new consensus" had been created in which the Ruthwell poem was seen as having nothing to do with the cross.[32] By the 1990s Rosemary Cramp's interdisciplinary approach to the cross and her ideas about the relevance of the poem to the cross had become distinctly unfashionable. Not Page but Cramp now held to heretical opinions. The orthodox scholarly consensus, following Page, held that the layout of the runic *tituli* on the lower stone showed them to be an afterthought to the cross, and hence irrelevant to its iconographic program, although not all scholars did, or do, subscribe to this view.[33]

As we have seen, the arguments about the layout of the *tituli* on the lower stone summarized above can only be upheld by dismissing the comparative evidence put forward by Schwab. In addition to their reluctance to consider nonrunic analogues, the work of Page, Meyvaert, and Stanley shared another methodological weakness: a failure to consider how the act of reading was conceived in eighth-century monasteries. For the rest of this essay I shall concentrate on some early medieval attitudes to reading, particularly of *tituli*. The question is best approached by considering a later contribution by Ray Page. Good jokes are rare in Anglo-Saxon scholarship, and the following is one of Page's best. In 1984, he provided a learned and helpful discussion of how to transliterate English runes. He said that one way of presenting runes was to reproduce in the transcription their original layout. In such a procedure a transcript of the Ruthwell poem would roughly correspond to the shape of the borders of the lower stone. Page gave an example of how this would look, and then commented: "This is certainly useful in showing how inefficiently the runes are set out on the cross and how hard it must always have been to understand the texts."[34] Page then continued in a footnote that showed that his negative opinion of the Ruthwell runic *tituli* had not mellowed over the years: "This lay-out helps to justify my suspicion that these runes, so clum-

---

31. See, for example, the remarkable discussion of the Ruthwell Cross on Ansaxnet in October 1992 and following months. Search Ansaxdat under the keyword Ruthwell at www.mun.ca/Ansaxdat.

32. Ó Carragáin, "Ruthwell Crucifixion Poem," p. 7.

33. See, for example, Karkov, "Naming and Renaming."

34. Page, "On the Transliteration of English Runes"; repr. Page, *Runes and Runic Inscriptions*, p. 261.

sily arranged, are a later addition to the cross, not part of its original plan. However, U. Schwab has pointed to foreign models for this lay-out."[35] Yet Page gave no consideration to the significance of Schwab's "foreign models"; instead, immediately after the reference to Schwab, he prints nine short columns of letters, which readers will find amusing to decipher:

Pro	amp	hed	his	out	ien	ein	eei	sag
fes	tel	oes	way	tex	t,b	ter	fot	ree
sor	lsm	not	ofs	tsi	uti	est	her	wit
R.J	eth	thi	ett	nef	twi	ing	rea	hhe
.Cr	ats	nkt	ing	fic	llb	tos	der	r.

When the original version of the present essay was read in the presence of Rosemary Cramp at Kalamazoo in May 2000, the audience deciphered the nine columns in unison and aloud. At the end of their *praelectio* they all burst out laughing, and none laughed more heartily than Rosemary herself. The joke is marvelous fun, and the audience agreed that it had an added and perhaps unintended charm. The joke shows clearly how far, when he laboriously composed it, its author was from appreciating why the Ruthwell designer laid out the runic *tituli* on the lower stone in the way he did, and how he or she intended those *tituli* to be read. Let us examine why this is so.

1. Page's satires on the Ruthwell *scriptura continua* imply that a more "sensible" norm had prevailed by the eighth century. They would have some force if regular word-division was normally to be found in the Early Christian inscriptions valued by Northumbrian ecclesiastics. But this was not the case. In the ancient world, lack of word division had been the rule in all kinds of writing.[36] A text, before it could be read out, had to be got by heart in the process of *präelectio*, preliminary reading.[37] Readers first assimilated the text, mentally providing their personal word-division and punctuation, as it were. Once they had performed the arduous process of *praelectio*, they could subsequently refer back to the written text as a mnemonic aid to recitation. *Scriptio continua* or *scriptura continua* was the norm

---

35. Page, "On the Transliteration of English Runes," repr. p. 261, n. 47.

36. See Parkes, *Pause and Effect*, pp. 1–15; Saenger, *Space between Words*, pp. 6–13.

37. On *praelectio*, see Parkes, *Pause and Effect*, pp. 11 and 14; Saenger, *Space between Words*, pp. 6–9.

in the ancient and Early Christian world. In the eighth century it had all the prestige of being ancient, like the oldest Christian manuscripts known to the Anglo-Saxons and the verse inscriptions they saw, for example, in the Roman basilicas. The verse dedication-inscription over the entrance door at Santa Sabina (dated to the reign of Leo I, 440–61) provides an example. Here I print a transcript with word divisions and an interlinear translation; these aids to *praelectio* are intended to help the reader to read the original verse inscription, given in figure 3, with enjoyment:[38]

CVLMEN APOSTOLICVM CVM CAELESTINVS HABERET
  When Caelestinus used to hold the apostolic height (= AD 422–32),
PRIMVS ET IN TOTO FVLGERET EPISCOPVS ORBE
  And when he, first among bishops, was shining throughout the whole world,
HAEC QVAE MIRARIS FVNDAVIT PERSBYTER VRBIS
  A priest of the city founded this which you are now admiring
ILLYRICA DE GENTE PETRVS VIR NOMINE TANTO
  A man called Peter of Illyria, of such a great name
DIGNVS AB EXORTV CHRISTI NVTRITVS IN AVLA
  Worthy (i.e., to be called Peter); from birth brought up in Christ's hall:
PAVPERIBVS LOCVPLES SIBI PAVPER QVI BONA VITAE
  Rich to the poor, making a poor man of himself: fleeing the good things
PRAESENTIS FVGIENS MERVIT SPERARE FVTVRAM
  Of the present life, he was justified in hoping for the future (life).

The verse *titulus* demands to be interpreted in the context of the two flanking figures who represent the Church chosen both out of the Jews ("Ecclesia ex circumcisione," "the Church of the circumcision") and out of the gentiles ("Ecclesia ex gentibus," "the Church taken out of nations"). Here, as on the Ruthwell Cross, visual and verbal icons complement each other. The dedication *titulus* was not simply designed to impart information, but also to be enjoyed as design: it forms a pleasing visual unity. From this coherent block of script, careful *praelectio* yields a meditation on membership of the Church. Verbal meaning emerges from visual spacing: in the course of *praelectio* the reader comes to see that at the center of the unified block of script is PETRVS, the fourth word of the fourth line in the seven-line titulus. PETRVS refers at once to Peter the apostle, the rock on whom Christ founded his Church, and to Peter's namesake, the priest Peter from Illyria, who built this local church on the Aventine during the reign of Pope Celestine (422–32), St. Peter's late successor in the "culmen apostolicum."[39]

38. Text from Duchesne, *Le Liber Pontificalis*, 1:235, Life of Sixtus III, AD 432–40; interlinear translation by the present author. See also Krautheimer et al., *Corpus Basilicarum Christianarum Romae*, 4:75 and 91.

39. The centrality of "Petrvs" to the inscription has been examined by Higgitt, "Design and Meaning in Early Medieval Inscriptions"; Higgitt, "Emphasis and Visual Rhetoric."

Malcolm Parkes has demonstrated that it was Irish and Anglo-Saxon monks, working from the sixth to the eighth centuries, who gradually introduced word division and the features of layout that make a text easy to read at the first try, such as the use of majuscule and minuscule scripts on the same page.[40] When the Ruthwell Cross was erected, word division was a modern innovation, still in the process of development. If one wanted to tell in verse an ancient story, it still made sense to require of your reader the additional effort of *praelectio*. Page himself has argued that runes seem to have been valued, not as magical, but rather as a script of historical interest, suitable for inscription on Christian monuments.[41] If so, it made sense to lay out the long runic *tituli* on the lower stone in *scriptura continua*, long venerated in Christian tradition.

2. The joke is funny precisely because the message hidden in the columns of letters is so banal. We are persuaded to spend some time and effort making out a prosaic message that, if it were laid out "sensibly," we could have read in seconds. In this joke bathos triumphs: we laugh because we have been intrigued into wasting our time. The puzzling layout is intended to provide an amusing contrast to what is implied to be the only "sensible" way of laying out texts: so as to enable the reader to assimilate the maximum amount of new information in the minimum amount of time. But we do not read verse *tituli* like that. Poems yield pleasure when ruminated on and, if the poem is good, the longer the better. It was by contemplating the Ruthwell poem at leisure, "memorizing it and ruminating over it, like some clean animal chewing the cud," that monastic readers gradually came to see the quality of the verse, how intelligently it was edited for the cross, and its centrality to the whole iconographic program of the cross.[42] The patient effort of *praelectio* needed to assimilate the Ruthwell verse *tituli* and get them by heart was and is, for any reader sensitive to poetry, its own reward.

3. The joke exposes a third flaw in Ray Page's understanding of the Ruthwell runes. All of the lines in his nine columns, except the final line, consist of three elements: either three letters or two letters and a punctuation mark. But we have seen that the Ruthwell Cross poem is not laid out like that. Page evidently failed to realize the significance, for a sophis-

---

40. Parkes, "Contribution of Insular Scribes"; see also Saenger, *Space between Words,* pp. 14–44.

41. Page, "Anglo-Saxon Runes and Magic"; Page, *Introduction to English Runes,* pp. 116–17 (2nd ed., pp. 96–116).

42. For the phrase, "rememorando secum et quasi mundum animal ruminando," see Bede's account of the poet Cædmon, in his *Hist. eccles.* 4.24.22, pp. 418–19. See the classic account of the centrality of leisure (*otium*) in monastic culture, as a normal precondition for contemplation, in Leclercq, *Love of Learning,* pp. 73–75, 250–65.

ticáted rune-master, of the fact that the available space on the tapering lower stone of the Ruthwell Cross widens gradually: that is, that it is
broader at its base than at its apex. The margins around the foliage scrolls
grow broader toward the bottom of the stone. Only by laying out the runes
as he did could the designer keep his runes to a consistent size throughout each *titulus*. If the designer had been compelled to lay out his runes
"sensibly" in a single line running downward at right angles to the reader's
vision, not only would the audience have been complaining of sore necks,
they are likely also to have complained that the runic *tituli* on the lower
stone were very ugly. The runes at the bottom of each vertical border of
that stone would have been much bigger than the runes at the top of that
border. The Ruthwell designer was, in the matter of inscriptions, at once
more sophisticated and more practical than any of his modern critics.
We may permit ourselves to rejoice that, as the Ruthwell designer clearly
was an expert in the layout of inscriptions, he had freedom to make the
choices he did.

The rationale behind Page's layout is best appreciated by looking at
one of the most precious reliquaries of the treasury of St. Peter's basilica
on the Vatican in Rome: the sort of reliquary of the True Cross that early
Anglo-Saxon pilgrims to Rome are likely to have admired and venerated.[43] The reliquary Cross of Justin II (fig. 4) contained one of the major
relics of the Holy Cross in St. Peters. (Pope Sergius was to find another
one, forgotten by the monks who ran the basilica, in the *sacrarium* of St.
Peter's about 700.) The Cross of Justin II is likely to have been displayed
in the *porticus* or chapel of the Holy Cross, near the baptistery area of the
north transept (the transept to the right as one faced the principal altar).[44]
The feast of the Exaltation of the Cross developed at Rome from the second quarter of the seventh century, precisely in this *porticus*-chapel at St.
Peter's, and perhaps around this very reliquary.[45] The Cross of Justin II
enables us to see how natural it was to inscribe the upright of a cross in
such a way that the inscription could be read without tilting the cross or
bending one's neck. Like the vertical borders around the vine scroll on
the lower stone at Ruthwell, the upright of this reliquary becomes narrower as the inscription descends. It then becomes broader again toward
the base. Thus we move from groups of three letters to single letters, and
then back to three-letter groups again.

43. On the reliquary Cross of Justin II, see Schwab "Das Traumgesicht vom Kreuzesbaum," p. 156 and n. 134; Belting-Ihm, "Das Justinuskreuz in der Schatzkammer der Peterskirche zu Rom"; Cameron, "Artistic Patronage of Justin II."
    44. On the "porticus ubi vivificae crucis vexillum servatur" in Old St. Peters, see
Ó Carragáin, "The Term *Porticus* and *Imitatio Romae*," p. 25.
    45. See Van Tongeren, "Vom Kreuzritus zur Kreuzestheologie."

Let us try to imagine the stages in which literate early medieval pilgrims might have instructed themselves by *praelectio* of the inscription on this Roman cross. During the first stage of their *praelectio,* they would have made out the individual letters. There must have been false starts, initial mistakes about word order. The result of this preliminary study might perhaps be represented by the following transcript:

[SHAFT]:
+LI/GNO/QUO/CH/RI/ST/US/HU/MA/NV/M/S/VB/DI/DI/TH/OS/TE/M/DA/TRO/MAE
[CROSS BEAM]: JUSTINVSOPEM / ETSOCIADECOREM

The second stage would be to decide how the letters made sense: deciding where the word divisions came; realizing that the end of the inscription on the upright ran on to the beginning of the inscription on the crosspiece; beginning to see that the inscription was in verse; and starting to get some sense of its meter. How the inscription might have been understood by readers after this second stage might perhaps be represented as follows:

[SHAFT]:
+ LIGNO QUO CHRISTUS HUMANVM SVBDIDIT HOSTEM DAT ROMAE
[CROSS BEAM]: JUSTINVS OPEM ET SOCIA DECOREM

The third and final stage of *praelectio* would have involved realizing that the verse formed a unified distych. To come to such a decision, the best way would have been to murmur the Latin text out loud, or at least under the breath. In the act of making out that it existed, a literate reader would have more or less learned the distych by heart. Monastic readers would have recited the verse *titulus* "like a clean beast ruminating" in order to produce a personal "edition" of the verse in their memories, and so appreciate it as poetry. The way the text was understood after this final stage might be represented as follows:

+ LIGNO QUO CHRISTUS HUMANVM SVBDIDIT HOSTEM
  DAT ROMAE JUSTINVS OPEM ET SOCIA DECOREM
(With the wood by which Christ overcame the enemy of humanity:
to Rome Justin gives the work, and his consort the decoration.)

By the third and final stage, the Latin distych would have come free from the cross, as it were. The readers now hold it in their memory, but have not forgotten how it was originally laid out. They can appreciate how the second line of the distych, which begins on the upright, is completed on the crosspiece. They also no doubt appreciate how, reciting the poem

by heart but with occasional reference to particular letters on the cross
itself, their eyes perform a "sign of the cross." The act of reading becomes
a symbolic recognition that the Cross of Justin II is itself a symbol of the
relic contained within it. Memory of how the distych was laid out reinforces
the memory of the whole reliquary. By making the effort of *praelectio,* the
readers of the Cross of Justin II find that they have discovered a poem;
and the poem preserves the memory of the cross and of its donors. The
effort needed to get the poem by heart is its own reward: it is pleasing and
instructive. The Latin poem, while competent, is hardly outstanding. How
much greater was the contemplative pleasure and instruction provided by
praelectio of the crucifixion poem on the Ruthwell Cross.

Now let us look at a second Roman relic, the icon of Santa Maria in
Trastevere (fig. 5). From the seventh century, the icon of the Madonna in
that basilica was venerated as an *acheiropita,* a relic not made by human
hands. A seventh-century pilgrim-guide describes the icon of the church
as "the icon which was made by itself" ("quae per se facta est").[46] It is difficult to imagine any Anglo-Saxon pilgrim not visiting Santa Maria in order
to venerate such a miraculous icon. The icon we have at present has been
variously dated: as early as the reign of the Emperor Justin II (565–78)
or as late as the reign of Pope John VII (705–07).[47] In any case we can be
sure that the present icon was the icon of Santa Maria in Trastevere from
707, perhaps a generation before the Ruthwell Cross was erected. Here
again we have a poem, and this time the poem runs across the top of the
icon, down its right side, and then down the left side. This corresponds to
the design of the *tituli* for the vine scrolls on the lower stone at Ruthwell.
On the icon the verse *titulus* is sensibly laid out: in *scriptura continua* and
upright, so that onlookers do not have to tilt their heads to read it. This
ancient procedure is followed even though the designer of the icon did
not have the additional motivation that the Ruthwell designer had, that
each vertical border grew broader as its runic *titulus* descended. Like the
two Ruthwell verse *tituli,* this verse *titulus* is not a mere label; instead,
it is a concise meditation on the theological significance of the icon it
frames. Although the inscription is badly damaged, enough remains for
us to see that the effort to puzzle out the *titulus* would have been worth-
while: the poem leaves in readers' memories a verbal icon, a souvenir that
recalls the significance of the object that they once saw with their eyes.
The transcript below, based on Bertelli's work, provides word divisions

46. Bertelli, *La Madonna di Santa Maria in Trastevere;* Belting, *Likeness and Presence,* pp.
126–27 and color plate II.

47. Bertelli, *La Madonna di Santa Maria in Trastevere,* argues for the late dating; this is
accepted by Belting, *Likeness and Presence,* p. 126; the early dating was proposed by Andaloro, "La datazione della tavola di S. Maria in Trastevere."

but still divides the verse according to its layout around the icon. It thus corresponds to the second stage of the process of *praelectio* as we reenacted it for the reliquary Cross of Justin II. The reader can follow the original layout from figure 5:

TOP BORDER: + ASTANT STYPENTES ANGELORYM PR
RIGHT BORDER: INCIPES GESTARE NATYM . . . A . . .
LEFT BORDER: DS QYOD IPSE FACTYS EST Y. . . ER . . .

To complete the act of *praelectio,* educated pilgrims would have had to divide the text into three verses. That is, they would have had to use their aural imaginations to free the *titulus* from its layout. Holding the *titulus* in their memory, but referring where necessary to the written text on the icon, they would have "edited" it into three lines of poetry. The end result might have looked something like the following (the second half of the second line is so badly damaged that Bertelli did not try to restore it):

+ ASTANT STYPENTES ANGELORYM PRINCIPES
GESTARE NATYM . . . A . . . DS
QYOD IPSE FACTYS EST (y)T(t)ER(o tvo).

(+ The princes of the angels [ANGELORYM PRINCIPES] stand wondering; [they see you] bearing Him who was Born [GESTARE NATYM]; because [QYOD] God [DS] has made himself in/of your womb.)

Modern epigraphers, in order to advance our knowledge, have had to develop a technique of reading that is silent, solitary, and skeptical. Silent, because they need to get every last letter, every last rune, faithfully copied and carefully drawn into their notebooks: one can hardly imagine scientific epigraphers chanting the verse as they transcribe it. Solitary, because they must not be distracted by suggestions from others of what might be there. Above all skeptical, because the whole point of publishing a new epigraphic study of a monument is to improve on earlier studies: in effect, modern epigraphers must always hope to prove their predecessors wrong, if only in minutiae.

Those necessary scholarly requirements have resulted in a quite different form of reading from anything we may imagine taking place in the eighth century. The eighth-century readers were hardly solitary when (as in the case of Ruthwell) the inscription was on an ecclesiastical site.[48] There was no reason for them to cultivate the skeptical attitude of the modern epigrapher: they can have had no inhibitions in getting advice from mem-

---

48. For the archaeological evidence that there was an ecclesiastical site at Ruthwell in the early Middle Ages, see Crowe, "Excavations at Ruthwell."

bers of the community or friends.[49] Unlike modern epigraphers, they did not have to copy every last rune accurately into a notebook. Once monastic readers had become reasonably familiar with the text, it is likely that their eyes no longer needed to swivel from left to right along each short line of the runic columns, as a modern epigrapher's must do in order to make a minutely accurate written transcript. Because of the relative narrowness of the short lines (from two to four runes per group), the eyes of eighth-century readers could move smoothly downward along the familiar text of the vernacular song, while they recalled the text by chanting it.[50] In order to transcribe the Ruthwell runic verse *tituli*, modern epigraphers have to perform an exquisitely frustrating task: they have to interrupt the act of reading continually in order to draw individual runes, and then find their place once more in a *titulus* designed to be seamless. Influenced by his frustrating experience of transcribing the Ruthwell verse *tituli* rune-by-rune, perhaps on more than one occasion, Page naturally saw this seamlessness as a frustrating problem. He failed to realize that for the Ruthwell editor-designer it had been an opportunity to show the unity and coherence of his two runic verse *tituli*. The designer gave each *titulus* an easy-to-read incipit, which ran in a continuous line from left to right. He or she placed the incipits, not on the upper stone, but at the top of the lower stone: this ensured that they would be well within the visual range of any reader with reasonable eyesight. Each *titulus* has two *sententiae*, and each of these is completed in a single long and seamless column. Their layout recalls the *per cola et commata* system: it displays each sentence as a separate unity. This is an epigraphic analogue for the way St. Jerome had recommended that sentences of scripture should be separately displayed.[51] In contrast, Page divided his cryptic prose message into nine neat short columns, none of which makes sense on its own. The resulting joke shows no appreciation of the subtlety with which the four *sententiae* of the Ruthwell poem were edited and thematically balanced against each other.[52]

Because modern epigraphy is deservedly prestigious, the epigrapher's specialized "scientific" form of reading has been projected onto the very different cultural conditions of an early medieval ecclesiastical commu-

---

49. John Higgitt has written two important studies of how monuments may have been actively explained in the Middle Ages: "Words and Crosses" and "Early Medieval Inscriptions in Britain and Ireland."

50. The discussion of the reader's eye movements while reading texts in *scriptura continua*, in Saenger, *Space between Words*, pp. 1–13, is relevant to this process.

51. See Parkes, *Pause and Effect*, pp. 14–15; Saenger, *Space between Words*, p. 16 and fig. 2.

52. On the ways in which the themes of the first *titulus* are recalled and sometimes reversed by the second, see Ó Carragáin, "Ruthwell Crucifixion Poem," pp. 15–29, 36–38.

nity. This projection has led to the unconscious assumption that because freer forms of reading are unscholarly by modern "scientific" standards they are without value in understanding eighth-century monasticism. As a result, a curious idea has grown up that no one could have read the Ruthwell poem in the early Middle Ages.[53] But early medieval monks saw epigraphy, not as a specialized antiquarian discipline, but as a living poetic form, taught as such in monastic schools like Wearmouth and Jarrow. Michael Lapidge has demonstrated that Bede was an accomplished and original epigraphic poet.[54] We owe the earliest and most influential syllogae of Roman inscriptions to Insular monks, who made their compilations toward the middle of the seventh century, the period when Benedict Biscop and Wilfrid first reached Rome. Irish monks, who had got to Rome at least a generation earlier, may already have initiated such collections.[55] Monks had three good reasons for compiling these syllogae. First of all, they wanted to teach, in their monastic schools, the ancient and living genre of epigraphic verse; such a skill might enable poets to compose new *tituli* for northern churches and ecclesiastical objects such as reliquaries.[56] Second, proper performance of and participation in the Roman liturgy encouraged an informed interest in the religious topography of the *caput urbium;* to memorize verse inscriptions from particular basilicas was a practical way to deepen this interest. The third reason followed from this: to commit to memory some of the most important Roman Christian inscriptions was to anticipate Rome pilgrimage. By imagining the basilicas of Rome through their inscriptions, a monk or nun could make an imaginary pilgrimage to Rome, as preparation for an actual pilgrimage there.

It is unlikely that eighth-century readers were silent while making out the Ruthwell verse *tituli*. All the surviving accounts of how Anglo-Saxon poetry was performed refer to it as sung: from Bede's account of the poet Cædmon, to *Beowulf* and *Widsith*, and even to Cynewulf, certainly a literate poet.[57] Surviving accounts of early medieval reading imply that people normally used their voices and articulated the letters and syllables when

---

53. An idea explicitly developed by Okasha, "Literacy in Anglo-Saxon England."

54. On the genre, see Bernt, *Das lateinische Epigramm in Übergang von der Spätantike zum frühen Mittelalter,* pp. 42–149. On Bede as an epigraphic poet, see Lapidge, *Bede the Poet,* pp. 1–5. On Bede's sense of the continuity between past and present, see George H. Brown's essay in this volume.

55. See Silvagni, "Nuovo ordinamento delle sillogi epigraphiche di Roma anteriori al secolo XI"; Silvagni, "La silloge epigrafica di Cambridge." St. Columbanus had founded Bobbio in 612; on early Irish pilgrims to Rome, see Ó Carragáin, *City of Rome,* pp. 1–5.

56. See Bede's *titulus* for the apse of the basilica built by Bishop Cyneberht of Lindsey (d. 731), collected in the sylloge of Bishop Milred of Worcester (745–75); it is quoted and discussed by Lapidge, *Bede the Poet,* p. 2.

57. See O'Brien O'Keeffe, *Visible Song.*

making them out. But it is in the nature of music and chant that, once singers have recalled the beginning or an important phrase in the chant, they can recall the whole chant. Anyone with an elementary interest in music knows that the incipit of a song or chant helps to recall a lot more of the song: examples, from the Latin Mass, are "Kyrie," "Gloria," "Credo," "Benedictus," and "Agnus Dei." The same is true for secular music: for example, "Rule Britannia," or "Oh say can you see." It is significant, therefore, that the incipit of each *titulus* runs from left to right transversely through the vine scroll, along the top border of the lower stone. This arrangement ensured that, when the cross was erected, each runic incipit would be easily legible, as well as being within easy visual range. Further, it ensured that text and image were perceived as one. The incipit of each *titulus* is by no means maddeningly difficult to read, and the present writer finds no reason to abandon his conclusions of 1987:

> The kind of reader who might not have found the text maddeningly difficult, in short, is precisely the kind of reader for whom the text is likely to have been intended: a permanent member of a community at Ruthwell who knew the monument from years of use, and who probably knew the poem off by heart from hearing it from other members of the community, from hearing it sung, or from reading some version of the poem in a manuscript. The primary function of the runes would therefore have been mnemonic. A cleric at Ruthwell might, at one period in his or her monastic life, have given time to puzzle them out, or have got one of the community to explain them. Ever after, the whole text, or a whole *sententia* from the text, could have been called to mind by nine or ten runes read in sequence.[58]

The Ruthwell Cross demands to be seen in the context of the diocese of Hexham, or of the diocese of Whithorn that had been recently founded (731), with the cooperation of Bishop Acca of Hexham. Hexham had a special devotion to the cult of the cross and that of the Virgin Mary. The Hexham devotion to the cross was based on the Hexham monks' yearly commemoration of King Oswald at the site of his victory, in the sign of the cross, at Heavenfield. In his *Historia ecclesiastica*, Bede records that this cult had been in existence for a long time (*multo iam tempore*), but that as part of its recent development, a chapel had recently (*nuper*) been built at the site.[59] Acca himself probably commissioned that new chapel, perhaps in the late 720s. We know how the particular Hexham devotion to the Virgin Mary began. Returning from Rome in early 705, the seriously

---

58. Ó Carragáin, "Ruthwell Crucifixion Poem," p. 10.
59. Bede, *Hist. eccles.* 3.2, pp. 214–18.

ill Wilfrid had a vision of St. Michael the archangel at Meaux in Francia. In the vision, St. Michael told Wilfrid that the Virgin Mary had successfully interceded with God to grant Wilfrid some extra years of life, so that Wilfrid would have time to build a church in her honor. After the vision, Wilfrid's first act was to call out for Acca, his companion and chaplain, to tell him what he had seen and heard.[60] Wilfrid's angelic vision is best understood in the context of the election of Pope John VII on 1 March 705 (that is, either shortly before Wilfrid received his visionary message or shortly after it). John VII proclaimed himself, in Latin and Greek inscriptions, to be *servus Mariae*, "the slave of Mary"; evidence of his devotion to the Virgin survives in his frescoes in Santa Maria Antiqua in the Roman Forum (where he placed the bilingual inscriptions just mentioned) and in the surviving fragments of his funerary chapel in honor of Mary at St. Peter's basilica. These commissions were recorded in his official biography, known to and used by Bede.[61] In effect, St. Michael the archangel inspired St. Wilfrid to reproduce at Hexham the very latest Roman devotion. In this, Hexham may have been more up-to-date than the rest of Northumbria, with the possible exceptions of Wearmouth and Jarrow and Whithorn. The Hexham cults of the cross and the Virgin Mary, as developed by Bishop Acca after Wilfrid's death, provide a relevant intellectual background for the Ruthwell Cross: it combines devotion to the cross with a uniquely rich sequence of scenes celebrating Mary. The *titulus* for the Annunciation panel, on the first side of the lower stone, proclaims that Mary is "blessed among women."[62] The now fragmentary runic *titulus* for the Visitation panel, on the first side of the upper stone, develops the theme that Mary is "blessed among women" by relating her to other "ladies" including "marþa" of Bethany.[63] Mary is represented a third time on the Return from Egypt panel, on the second side of the lower stone.[64]

60. Eddius Stephanus, *Life of Bishop Wilfrid*, pp. 122–23.

61. Nordhagen, "Mosaics of John VII"; Nordhagen, "John VII's Adoration of the Cross in S. Maria Antiqua"; Nordhagen, *Frescoes of John VII*. On the possible influence of John VII's artistic commissions on contemporary Northumbrian art, see Nordhagen, "Carved Marble Pilaster in the Vatican Grottoes"; Nordhagen, "Italo-Byzantine Painter at the Scriptorium of Ceolfrith"; Nordhagen, *Codex Amiatinus and the Byzantine Element*.

62. To the left of the figure of Gabriel the letters "T[E] . . . B[E]" can be read. Thus, with reference to Luke 1:28, the *titulus* for the Annunciation panel can be reconstructed as: "[top margin]: [+] INGRESSUS ANG[EL]us / [right margin:] ad eam dixit ave gratia plena dominus / [Left Margin:] T[E]cum B[E]nedicta tu in mulieribus."

63. The inspiration for this link between the Virgin and Martha and Mary of Bethany is clearly the Mass for the Dormition of the Virgin on 15 August, where Luke 10:38–42, the episode of Martha and Mary, was read to celebrate Mary's entry into heaven: "Mary has chosen the better part, and it shall not be taken from her" (Luke 10:42): see Ó Carragáin, *City of Rome*, p. 35.

64. See Ó Carragáin, "Necessary Distance," pp. 196–97.

Such close association between devotion to the Virgin and devotion to the cross is consistent with what we know of Hexham in the time of Bishop Acca (709–31). Even if the Ruthwell Cross were to be assigned to a slightly later date, important local cults inspired by St. Wilfrid and developed by Bishop Acca are unlikely to have ceased abruptly when Acca was deposed in or about 731. One is tempted to ask where Acca may have gone between his expulsion from Hexham and his death (and burial at Hexham) about 740. Perhaps to the shrine of St. Ninian, whose cult was recently developed at Whithorn by Bishop Pehthelm, another member of Bede's scholarly circle?[65] Or to the large monastery at Hoddom with its many standing crosses?[66] Or to a smaller monastery such as Ruthwell, near Hoddom and perhaps dependent on it, with its single great cross?[67]

It is likely that at Ruthwell the liturgical *cantatores* (cantors), at least, were in touch with Hexham. Bishop Acca was described by Bede as "a most expert cantor, very learned in sacred writings" ("cantator peritissimus, in litteris sanctis doctissimus"); he was assisted by Maban, whom Bede described as "a really outstanding cantor" ("cantatorem . . . egregium").[68] Bede tells us that Maban had been instructed in methods of singing by the successors of the disciples of St. Gregory in Kent, and that Acca brought him to Hexham to teach him and his people. Acca kept Maban at Hexham for twelve years (perhaps 719–31?) teaching them such music as they did not know, while the music that they once knew and that had begun to deteriorate by long use or by neglect was restored to its original form.[69] This description reminds us that liturgical chant was in this period an oral tradition, like the separate vernacular oral tradition that gave us the Ruthwell runic poem: there was as yet no way of writing down music. Acca and Maban were familiar with Roman traditions and considered them important. To understand the Ruthwell Cross we must try to appreciate the ways in which the text of a song would have been read by a cantor like Maban, a man to whom song and chant were natural everyday forms of expression. The ideal eighth-century reader of the Ruthwell poem, and indeed the ideal editor for all the *tituli* of the monument, is perhaps the *cantator* of whatever small ecclesiastical community then inhabited the Ruthwell settlement: some mute inglorious Maban there may rest.

65. On the cult of St. Ninian, see P. Hill, *Whithorn and St Ninian*.

66. Pending the publication of the definitive report on Hoddom some ten miles from Ruthwell, see Lowe, "New Light on the Anglian 'Minster' at Hoddom"; Lowe, *Angels, Fools and Tyrants*.

67. The life of Acca is conveniently summarized in Bede, *Venerabilis Baedae opera historica*, 2:329–30.

68. Bede, *Hist. eccles.* 5.20, pp. 530–33.

69. Bede, *Hist. eccles.* 5.20, pp. 530–33.

In monastic culture reading was often seen as serving a deeper process by which texts, and even more so chants and songs, were assimilated. We can find visual evidence of this in the gradual elaboration of important texts in the Gospels, from the Book of Durrow to the Book of Kells. In the Insular tradition Gospel texts were progressively elaborated, not in the direction of legibility, but rather in the direction of symbolism and mystery. The Gospel incipits in Durrow are all easy to read, but those of Kells assume that a monastic reader already knows the text and wishes, not to read it for information, but to be reminded of the immense implications of each Gospel. Similarly, the "XPI autem generatio" text (Matthew 1:18) was elaborated from the modest clarity of Durrow to the cosmic mystery of Kells.[70] Monastic artists could rely on educated members of their community having the major scriptural and liturgical texts by heart.[71]

The eighth-century Sacramentary of Gellone provides a good example of such reliance. In the Roman liturgy, the preface to the Canon of the Mass was (and is) the classical expression of the idea that, as the liturgy is a sharing in Christ's own prayer to the Father, each liturgical celebration on earth participates in the liturgy of heaven.[72] The Gellone scribe wrote the opening sentences of the second part of the preface in normal Latin script, using the word divisions propagated by Insular monks. The last sentence in Latin script is the request that our voices should be joined with the songs of the angels in the heavenly liturgy. But when that song begins, when he comes to the Hebrew word "Sabaoth," the scribe begins to write his Latin text in Greek characters. The reason is decidedly not that he expects his text to be read only by a celestial or "divine audience."[73] The reverse is true. By this stage of the Mass, the celebrant using the sacramentary is singing a solemn and invariable chant. As he knows the chant by heart, Greek letters would provide the celebrant with ample cues. Confident that this would be so, the scribe felt free to symbolize the antiq-

70. See G. Henderson, *From Durrow to Kells*, pp. 70–71, 104–05, 124, 159–61.

71. The classic account of monastic memory is Leclercq, *Love of Learning*, pp. 76–93.

72. The standard discussions include Peterson, *Angels and the Liturgy;* Emery, *Communion of Saints*, pp. 14–31, 65–75, 184–227; Markus, *End of Ancient Christianity*, pp. 21–26.

73. Elisabeth Okasha suggested that Ruthwell was intended to be read not by men but by "a divine audience": "Literacy in Anglo-Saxon England," p. 88 (repr., pp. 73–74). But liturgical celebration was based on precisely the opposite idea: that since the Incarnation (and precisely since the "Gloria in excelsis" was sung on Christmas Night, Luke 2:8–14) men and angels had praised God together. The idea that the Ruthwell Cross inscriptions were intended, not for an audience of living human beings, but for a divine audience was first suggested by P. Wormald, "Uses of Literacy in Anglo-Saxon England," p. 96. Wormald argues that the Ruthwell poem "might just as well have been addressed to the Redeemer himself," a suggestion trenchantly and convincingly dismissed by Ray Page: "In no way is it addressed to the Deity: it implies a human readership" (*Runes and Runic Inscriptions*, p. 297).

uity and solemnity of the Latin chant by writing it out in the ancient and
graceful Greek alphabet, while the artist adorned the sung text with two
angels: the cherubim or seraphim to whom the chant refers. Their figures
link the "Sanctus" chant to the figure of Christ on the cross. Christ dying
on the cross performed the fundamental act of prayer in which Christians
participated by means of the liturgy. To symbolize this, representations of
the Crucifixion always showed Christ's hands outstretched in prayer, in
the *orans* posture. At this point of the Mass, the celebrant's hands would
also be outstretched in the *orans* gesture, as he chanted:

> Caeli caelorumque virtutis ac beata seraphyn socia exultatione
> concaelebrant, cum quibus et nostras uoces ut admitti iubeas
> deprecamur, supplici confessione dicentes:
> Sanctus sanctus sanctus, dominus deus SABAOTH PLENI SUNT
> KELI ET TERRA KLORIA TVA. HOSANNA IN EXKELSIS.
> BENEDIKTUS QUI UENIT IN NOM DNI. HOSANNA IN
> EXKELSIS.[74]

> (The heavens and the Virtues of the heavens and the blessed
> Seraphim cocelebrate with a joy united to our own: we beg that
> you would allow our voices to be joined to theirs, saying in pray-
> erful confession:
> Holy holy holy, Lord God SABAOTH; HEAVEN AND EARTH
> ARE FILLED WITH YOUR GLORY. HOSANNA IN THE
> HIGHEST. BLESSED IS HE THAT COMES IN THE NAME
> OF THE LORD. HOSANNA IN THE HIGHEST.)

The Ruthwell verse *tituli* are similarly symbolic. They surround the
vine scrolls, the most important symbol on the cross, with a song that
brings out what the vine scroll implies: that Christ long ago poured forth
his blood on the tree of the cross in a uniquely heroic action that restored
Paradise for humankind. This restored happiness is symbolized by the
birds and animals feasting on the vine scrolls. The designer knew that any
small group of runes read in sequence would act as a musical cue, reminding literate monks or nuns of oral versions of the song they knew. Once
they identified where, in the song, a particular word or phrase came, it
would have been easy for them to make out the rest of the inscription
by chanting their version of the song and seeing where it was reflected
in the newly edited runic *tituli*. Monastic readers are likely to have been
particularly intrigued by any phrases in the edited runes that did not correspond to the oral versions of the song they were used to singing. Any

74. Paris, Bibliothèque nationale de France, MS lat. 12048, fol. 143v, ed. Dumas, *Liber
Sacramentorum Gellonensis*, 1:253 (where the Greek letters are transcribed in Greek capitals); see also vol. 2, fig. 99.

such phrases would have required, and perhaps received, a particularly attentive *praelectio*.

Monastic reliance on liturgical reminiscence can be seen, not only in elaborate texts like Gellone, but in the simplest and briefest inscriptions. In the pillar with an inscribed cross at Reask (Co. Kerry) the cross is provided with a laconic *titulus,* "dne": an invocation to Christ (fig. 6).[75] With perfect economy, the *titulus* identifies the cross as the symbol of Christ, the sign that will appear in the heavens before the Last Day to announce his Second Coming. As the vocative "Domine" provided the *incipit* of many liturgical prayers, the three inscribed letters would have reminded educated monastic readers of whatever sacramentary they used at Reask. The reminder encouraged them to pray, either in Latin or in the Irish vernacular. The word "dne," which also encouraged them to identify the eschatological symbol of the cross with Christ himself, suggested the mode of their prayer: to Christ through his symbol the cross.

When they discussed the *tituli* to the vine scrolls at Ruthwell, those scholars who found their layout absurd mistook the nature of what they had before them. As philologists and epigraphers, they were trained to look at, and decipher, inscriptions, but the Ruthwell poem is not primarily an inscription, to be read in isolation. Instead, it is primarily a *titulus,* a caption designed to complement, indeed, perhaps even to be a part of, the two great inhabited vine scrolls or trees of life that cover the narrow faces of the lower stone. Page, Stanley, and Meyvaert never asked why the uniquely original crucifixion narrative of the *tituli* should have been inscribed around vine scrolls and wrote as if the vine scrolls were merely decorative: if not quite invisible, at least an irrelevance to "the runic verses" that happen to surround them. But this was to misunderstand fundamentally the design of the narrow sides of the Ruthwell Cross, and to fail to understand the significance of the pioneering study by Franz Dietrich, who already in 1865 had written eloquently on the symbolism of the vine scrolls and saw their relevance to the poem inscribed around them.[76] There is a meaningful contrast between the layout of the poem and the vine scrolls for which it provides *tituli:* while the poem reads downward and describes a heroic death, each image of the tree of life, inhabited by feeding animals and birds, attracts the eyes of the audience upward. In this way the heroic narrative of each *titulus* is balanced, immediately and consistently, by images of sustenance and life. The two runic *tituli* of the foliage scrolls fulfill the normal function of early medieval verse *tituli.*

---

75. See Okasha and Forsyth, *Early Christian Inscriptions of Munster,* pp. 23–24, where various uses of the word "dominus" in Munster inscriptions are listed.

76. Dietrich, *De Cruce Ruthwellensi,* pp. 5–7.

They do not act simply as identifying labels: their narrative expands the significance of the iconographic image of which they form an essential element. The narrative provides supplementary considerations that the onlooker, having memorized the *tituli* or reminded himself of them, can carry away in his memory as part of the image itself.[77] They supplement the central visual icon of the vine scrolls with a verbal icon (itself visually pleasing), a prosopopoeia that makes the whole Ruthwell monument, upper and lower stones, identify itself with what it was always designed to represent, the Holy Cross. In short, the narrow sides of the Ruthwell Cross provide a unified symbol, at once verbal and visual, of the unity of the Easter triduum (from Good Friday to Easter Sunday): the Passover in which Christ died, was buried, defeated the powers of darkness, and rose again from the dead to bring life to the world. For the Ruthwell community of the eighth century, this life was mediated through the *sacramenta* of baptism, penance, and Eucharist: and these communal rituals provide the key to the iconographic programs of the broad sides.[78] The Ruthwell Cross primarily represents a life-giving tree, at once world tree and *lignum Domini*.[79] If so, the vine scrolls and their runic *tituli* were designed to be its heart, and without them the cross cannot be understood in its entirety. They symbolize the progression from death to life, the *Paschale sacramentum* at the heart of the symbolic variety of the broad sides that, in their turn, represent the sacramental means of entering into the paschal mystery.[80]

To conclude: arguments that separate the poem from its iconographic context or that view its layout as absurd provide no evidence whatever that at Ruthwell the runic *tituli* to the vine scrolls were added later, nor that the lower stone was already erected when the *tituli* were inscribed. They may with confidence be consigned to the lumber room of superseded Ruthwell scholarship. Two scholars, Rosemary Cramp and Ute Schwab, each a *mulier fortis*, provide far more reliable guides to the intentions and achievement of the Ruthwell designer. To lay out the *tituli* in columns of

77. This function of ancient and early medieval verse *tituli* is amply demonstrated by Arnulf, *Versus ad Picturas*. He has a good discussion of the theoretical issues raised by this verse genre, pp. 9–29. As Arnulf puts it, the relation of verse *tituli* to the images they accompany can be not merely explanatory, but also expository and allusive ("der erklärend, auslegend oder hinweisend sein mag," p. 20).

78. See Ó Carragáin, "Necessary Distance."

79. See the excellent discussion of the non-Christian religious significance of trees in ancient Northumbria by North, *Heathen Gods in Old English Literature*, pp. 273–96.

80. For the phrase "paschale sacramentum," see the Easter Vigil prayers in the Old Gelasian sacramentary, ed. Mohlberg, *Liber Sacramentorum Romanae Aeclesiae Ordinis Anni Circuli*, par. 434, p. 70: "[per] paschale sacramentum Abraham puerum tuum uniuersarum, sicut iurasti, gencium efficis patrem."

Figure 1. The Bewcastle Cross, detail. University of Durham, Department of Archaeology. Photograph: Tom Middlemass.

Figure 2. The Ruthwell Cross, detail. University of Durham, Department
of Archaeology. Photograph: Tom Middlemass.

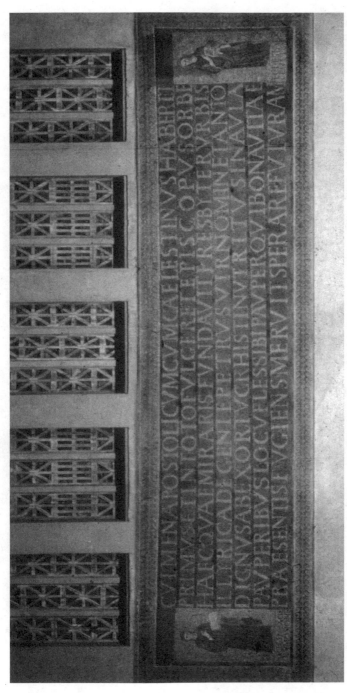

Figure 3. Rome, Santa Sabina, Dedicatory Inscription. Photograph: Santa Sabina, Dominican Community.

Figure 4. St. Peter's, Vatican. Reliquary Cross of Justin II, reverse with inscription. Photograph: Fabbrica di San Pietro, Rome.

Figure 5. Rome, Santa Maria in Trastevere, Madonna della Clemenza.
Photograph: Soprintendenza archeologica di Roma.

Figure 6. Reask (Co. Kerry) inscribed cross-slab. Photograph: Archaeology Department, National University of Ireland Cork.

runes in *scriptura continua* made sense within the Byzantine and Roman traditions identified by Ute Schwab. The layout was consonant with the many other reminiscences of the liturgy on the cross. The layout was also eminently practical. It ensured that later, when the lower stone was erected, the runes would be the right way up. It coped excellently with the problem that the borders of the lower stone grew broader from top to bottom. It made sense within an early medieval monastic context, in which texts were regularly chanted, and interpreted with reference to communal liturgical actions regularly performed, and thus familiar to all members of the community. The Ruthwell designer provided all the major panels with *tituli* that recalled intoned lections and well-known chants, in Latin and in English. Scholars may proceed with confidence on the sensible hypothesis to which Rosemary Cramp has always held: that the vine scrolls and their runic verse *tituli* formed from the beginning the central element in the design of the Ruthwell Cross, the symbolic heart of the monument.

The Boar on the Helmet

Roberta Frank

> Without at least an intuitive grasp of the life of the detail in the
> structure, all love of beauty is no more than empty dreaming.
> Walter Benjamin, 1928[1]

Our image of the boar-helmet is blurred and vague, a visual equivalent to the indeterminate schwa, a portrait produced by combining features from photographs taken at different times and places. Gundestrup,
Hounslow, Liechtenstein, Issendorf, Monceau-le-Neuf, Brumath-Stefansfeld, Vendel, Valsgärde, Torslunda, Guilden Morden, Benty Grange, Sutton Hoo, Wollaston, Leningrad: a sonorous roll-call not of great battles
but of notable boars. Authors of twentieth-century historical romance
have placed this headgear on a smorgasbord of legendary Danish kings.[2]
But where the *Beowulf* poem dwells lovingly on the construction and special features of these helmets, as if its audience might never have seen
one, more recent fiction averts its gaze, keeping both helmet and reader
in the dark. In 1838 Henry Wadsworth Longfellow described the teen-
aged Beowulf as "a famous Viking . . . who had slain sea-monsters, and
wore a wild-boar for his crest."[3] Modern illustrations of the poem present
this boar in a variety of positions, shapes and sizes, colors and materials.
The creature is legless and bodiless in Rockwell Kent's 1931 drawing, a
terminal grunt.[4] Severin's 1954 design—a dashing boar's-head beret—sits
rather fetchingly on Beowulf; or so Grendel's mother seems to think.[5]

1. Benjamin, *Ursprung des deutschen Trauerspiels (Origin of German Tragic Drama*, trans.
Osborne, p. 182).
2. See Mjöberg, *Drömmen om sagatiden*, 2:200, 281–84, 368.
3. Longfellow, "Anglo-Saxon Literature," p. 103. All five appearances of boar-helmets
in *Beowulf* are recorded in John Mitchell Kemble's edition (*Anglo-Saxon Poems of Beowulf*)
and translation (*Translation of the Anglo-Saxon Poem of Beowulf*). The Icelander Grímur Jónsson Thorkelin, first editor of the poem (*De Danorum rebus gestis secul. III & IV. poëma danicum dialecto anglo-saxonica*), had recognized OE *swin* (ON *svín*) but not OE *eofor* ("boar,"
cognate with ON *jofurr* "prince"), thereby halving the number of boar crests in the poem.
The first English sighting of a boar on Beowulf's head is in Conybeare, *Illustrations of Anglo-
Saxon Poetry*.
4. Tharaud, *Beowulf*, p. 148; illustrations from Jones, *Prints of Rockwell Kent*.
5. Serrailler, *Beowulf the Warrior*, p. 27.

Sheila Mackie's 1987 helmet supports the complete boar, exuding down-home porcine charm from upturned snout to friendly corkscrew tail.[6] The crest remains in the mind's eye not as a menacing abstraction, cloaked Grendel-like in mist, but as the little tusker next door.

This essay—a footnote to Rosemary Cramp's classic article on "*Beowulf* and Archaeology"—looks with wary eyes at the boar-helmets of archaeologist and poet, hunting for evidence that they might have different cultural affiliations, be old-fashioned and non-Christian in different ways. The boar image, whether forged by metalworker or wordsmith, is malleable, adaptable, promiscuous in its attachments, like any symbol worth its keep.[7] In the late 1890s, Kipling adopted the swastika as his personal seal, plastering this "auspicious Indian sign" (his description) on his works and on much else; he even persuaded Edward Bok, editor of the *Ladies' Home Journal,* to name his new house Swastika.[8] Thirty-five years later, the Nazi party officially took the emblem as its own—an appropriation that sent Kipling's good luck charm packing. The powerful and articulate boar-helmets of *Beowulf,* drenched in northern paganism and rooted in northern legend, may have similarly affected responses to the three English boar-helmets so far found in seventh-century burial deposits. Both the poem and the finds are Anglo-Saxon messengers, speaking an archaic diction that we must strain to hear. Rosemary herself has never stopped seeking "the life of the detail" in the dispersed and fragmentary traces of the Anglo-Saxon past, and it is to her and her love of beauty that this piece is dedicated.

A century and a half of archaeological and literary scholarship on Anglo-Saxon boar-helmets has emphasized moments of harmony and consonance, resemblance and reconciliation. In 1849, shortly after a boar-helmet was dug up in Benty Grange, Derbyshire, William J. Thoms

---

6. Glover, *Beowulf, an Adaptation,* p. 62.

7. On the various symbolic connotations of the boar in early Continental literature, see Schwab, "Eber, aper und porcus in Notkers des Deutschen Rhetorik"; on the boar image in Anglo-Saxon England, see Speake, *Anglo-Saxon Animal Art,* pp. 78–81; Hicks, *Animals in Early Medieval Art;* J. Hawkes, "Symbolic Lives," esp. pp. 326–27. For illustrations, see also Schouwink, *Der wilde Eber in Gottes Weinberg.* Recent studies of boar symbolism from France include Fabre-Vassas, *La Bête singulière* (trans. as *Singular Beast*), and Walter, *Mythologies du porc.*

8. See Lycett, *Rudyard Kipling,* pp. 314–15. The town of Swastika (Ontario) was named in 1906; in 1940 residents defied government pressure to change the name to Winston. See Rayburn, *Naming Canada,* p. 65. My gratitude to Ian and David McDougall for this reference and much more. In the early years of the last century, the American Girls' Club issued a monthly magazine named *The Swastika* and "good luck" cards sported the symbol: see Heller, *The Swastika: Symbol beyond Redemption?* On the boar in Pictish art, see now G. Henderson and I. Henderson, *Art of the Picts.* See also Rosemary Cramp, this volume, p. 9.

matter-of-factly confirmed that the figure most often found perched on
Germanic helmets was the boar, "and it is to this custom that reference
is made in *Beowulf* where the poet speaks of the boar of gold, the boar
hard as iron."[9] In 1852 Charles Roach Smith was struck by the similarity:
"Nothing can be more satisfactory than the explanation of the hog upon
the Saxon helmet found in Derbyshire presented by citations from . . .
Beowulf."[10] The next boar-helmet to emerge, that of Sutton Hoo, Mound
One, has served the poem loyally for more than a half century now. As
Rosemary Cramp first pointed out, the gilt-bronze boar heads that form
the eyebrow-terminals of the Sutton Hoo helmet are located, like the
golden boar images on Beowulf's helmet, "over cheek [or face]-guards"
(*Beowulf*, line 303): each monument sheds light on the other.[11] The Anglo-
Saxon boar-helmet found in 1997 alongside a Roman road at Wollaston,
Northamptonshire (fig. 1), has not yet had time to bond with the poem,
but it will.[12] Derbyshire, Suffolk, and Northamptonshire together occupy
a sizeable chunk of England, suggesting that the boar-helmet was a widespread habit in the early seventh century, not the quirk of a nostalgic
fringe group.

The helmets found at Benty Grange, Sutton Hoo, and Wollaston are
latecomers in a procession led by La Tène prototypes in the fourth century
BC, joined by Gaulish models in the first century BC, and reinforced by
late Roman parade armor in the fourth century AD. Boar-helmeted warriors are famously depicted on a cauldron from Gundestrup, Denmark,
Celtic or Dacian work of the first century BC.[13] A free-standing Celtic
bronze boar from Liechtenstein, along with three from Hounslow, Middlesex, are probably unmounted helmet crests from the same BC period.[14]
The boar served as emblem for the Twentieth Legion, long stationed in
Roman Britain; wherever the garrisons went, a sounder of bronze and iron
hogs followed.[15] A fourth-century grave in northern France has produced
two large, conjoined boar tusks, probable attachments to a leather hel-

9. Thoms, *Primeval Antiquities of Denmark*, cited in Bateman, *Ten Years' Diggings*, pp.
32–33. Cramp, "*Beowulf* and Archaeology," plate 10a.

10. Smith, *Collectanea antiqua*, 2:241. See Bruce-Mitford and Luscombe, "Benty Grange
Helmet"; also Bruce-Mitford, *Sutton Hoo Ship Burial*, 2:205–07.

11. Cramp, "*Beowulf* and Archaeology," pp. 60–63; Bruce-Mitford, *Aspects of Anglo-
Saxon Archaeology*, pp. 198–209; Bruce-Mitford, *Sutton Hoo Ship Burial*, 2:138–231.

12. Meadows, "Wollaston"; also Meadows, "Pioneer Helmet," with cover photograph.
See Webster, "Archaeology and *Beowulf*," pp. 188–90.

13. See Olmsted, *Gundestrup Cauldron;* Larsen, *Historien om det store sølvfund fra Gundestrup.*

14. Megaw, *Art of the European Iron Age*, cat. no. 224; J. Foster, *Bronze Boar Figurines*.

15. The Roman military site at Usk has turned up a medallion with the boar-insignia
of Legion XX: Branigan and Fowler, *Roman West Country*, pp. 37–38.

met, like the tusks from the late Roman cemetery at Brumath-Stefansfeld (Alsace).[16] Similarly mounted boar tusks have been found in late Roman contexts in Wiltshire and Kent.[17] An Anglo-Saxon boar-figurine from Guilden Morden, Cambridgeshire, is now described as the detached crest of a boar-helmet.[18] In seventh-century Sweden, warriors in such headgear are portrayed on helmet plates from Valsgärde, graves 7 and 8, and from Vendel, grave I, depictions apparently inspired by the late Roman imperial guard helmet, vintage AD 400.[19] A die or matrix for making these stamped plates was found at a seventh-century site in Torslunda, Öland.[20] Hundreds of identical decorative foils embossed with the same boar-helmeted figures may once have glittered, like beads on a string, along the shipping lanes of the North Sea and the Baltic.

Tacitus had nothing to say about boar-helmets, observing that Germans went bareheaded: "vix uni alterive cassis aut galea" (scarcely one or two have metal helmets or leather headgear) (chap. 6). When the *Germania* was rediscovered, however, its first printing included excerpts from Diodorus Siculus describing the headgear of the Gauls as follows: "They wear bronze helmets with high extensions, which give them an appearance of great size. On many helmets, one sees horns, attached in the expected places; on others, frontal images of birds or four-footed beasts" (5.30.2).[21] Plutarch placed similar helmets on the proto-Danish Cimbri (*Marius* 25), confirming what the humanists already knew. For Heinrich Bebel had established by 1500 that when ancient writers mentioned Gauls or Celts, they meant Germans as well.[22] Beatus Rhenanus, editor of the *Germania*, enthusiastically agreed: "Who will deny that those ancient Celts were similar to the Germans and in fact were Germans?"[23] By 1937, Rudolf Much

16. Werner, "Die Eberzier von Monceau-le-Neuf."

17. S. Hawkes and Dunning, "Soldiers and Settlers in Britain."

18. J. Foster, "Boar-Figurine from Guilden Morden."

19. For an overview, see Almgren, "Hjälmar, kronor och stridsrockar"; Almgren, "Helmets, Crowns and Warriors' Dress." See, in the same volume, Arwidsson, "Valsgärde," p. 77, and the full report, Arwidsson, *Valsgärde 7* and *Valsgärde 8;* for Vendel, see Stolpe and Arne, *Graffältet vid Vendel.* On the early adaptation in the north of Roman motifs, see Vierck, "*Imitatio imperii* und *interpretatio Germanica* vor der Wikingerzeit." For more boars, see Hauck, "Die bildliche Wiedergabe von Götter- und Heldenwaffen im Norden seit der Völkerwanderungszeit."

20. See Bruce-Mitford, *Aspects of Anglo-Saxon Archaeology,* pp. 214–22.

21. For editions of classical texts, see the bibliography in Glare, *Oxford Latin Dictionary.* See also the Perseus Digital Library at www.perseus.tufts.edu.

22. Bebel, *Schardius Redivivus,* 1:128–29; see Borchardt, *German Antiquity in Renaissance Myth.*

23. Beatus Rhenanus, *Castigationes in Libellum de Germania,* p. 422; see Hirstein, *Tacitus' Germania and Beatus Rhenanus,* pp. 212–13.

in his commentary to the *Germania* was confident that Tacitus, despite his silence, knew of Germanic boar-helmets: "Hier handelt es sich also um eine lange Tradition, und der Zeit des Tac., die zwischen diesen späteren Funden und Zeugnissen und dem Kessel von Gundestrup mitten inne liegt, können sie nicht fremd sein."[24] The tendency to insist on the Germanness of motifs that have a wider currency is still embedded in our scholarship. Tacitus's remark in the *Germania* (chap. 45) that the Baltic tribe of the Aestii worshipped a goddess whose emblem was "the device of a wild boar" regularly appears in commentaries on *Beowulf*, beginning with John Mitchell Kemble's edition of 1833; the latter also connects the boar to Freyja. As for the four Roman Legions that displayed the boar as emblem, no one ever mentions them.[25] So, too, in the Old English *Elene*, it has been cheerfully assumed, from Jacob Grimm on, that the boar-standards hovering above the (still pagan) Emperor Constantine and his troops are Germanic, even though such standards are common in Gaulish and Roman military contexts, as the triumphal arch of Orange and numerous Gaulish coins attest.[26]

The latest Anglo-Saxon material witness for the boar-helmet is a biblical illustration now in St. Petersburg, a solitary escapee from Bede's world.[27] The sketch, on the opening flyleaf of an eighth-century English manuscript, depicts David decapitating Goliath with the latter's sword, using the boar crest of the giant's helmet as a handhold. Goliath's bronze headdress is mentioned in the biblical account (1 Samuel 17:5); the boar-crest is not.

In the exegesis of the church fathers, from Origen and Augustine to Cassiodorus, Hrabanus Maurus, and beyond, the one boar lurking in the Bible (Psalm 79:14) is identified as Rome, destroyer of the vineyard of

---

24. Much, *Die Germania des Tacitus,* p. 94. Much's statement is repeated in the 2nd edition of his commentary, ed. Kienast, p. 94, and in the 3rd edition, rev. Jankuhn, ed. Lange, p. 145.

25. See, s.v. *signa militaria,* Daremberg and Saglio, *Dictionnaire des antiquités grecques et romaines,* 4.2:1310–11.

26. Grimm, *Deutsche Mythologie,* pp. 176–78; Grimm, *Andreas und Elene,* p. xxviii. On Gaulish coins depicting boar-standards, see Olmsted, *Gundestrup Cauldron,* p. 70. The entry s.v. *aper* (boar) in Glare, *Oxford Latin Dictionary,* includes "a figure of a boar used as a standard" (Plin. *Hist. nat.* 10.16). For OE *eoforcumbol* ("boar-standard," not "boar-helmet") in *El* 76 and 259, see Healey et al., *Dictionary of Old English: "E,"* s.v., and Cramp, *"Beowulf* and Archaeology," n. 13. Unless otherwise noted, editions and abbreviations are those used by the Toronto Dictionary of Old English project: see *DOE: Preface and List of Texts and Index of Editions* and *Abbreviations for Latin Sources and Bibliography of Editions.*

27. Swanton, "Manuscript Illustration of a Helmet of Benty Grange Type." Lapidge, *"Life of Saint Oswald,"* pp. 52, 57 n. 8, observes that the "bronze helmets" worn by Byrhtferth of Ramsey's "accursed Danes" associate them with Goliath and his *cassis aerea.*

Jerusalem.[28] In his commentary to Isaiah 27:10, Jerome matter-of-factly observes that the Psalmist, David, refers to the Roman army under the name "boar."[29] Historically, this "boar from the woods," "the singular beast,"[30] represents Emperor Vespasian or his son Titus; spiritually, it stands for the devil. David's victory over the Philistine giant not only foreshadowed Christ's over Satan; it proved that pagan matter (i.e., Goliath's sword) could be converted, like Egyptian gold and Canaanite women, to Christian use.[31]

In the late eleventh century, when the Holy, or Romano-Germanic, Empire was forging links with a Roman past, the boar suddenly emerges in German nonepic vernacular poetry as a positive emblem, symbol of Rome's all-powerful Caesars.[32] The boar images that attached themselves to helmets in the far north and west of seventh-century Europe may have conveyed a more ambiguous message. New excavations at Sutton Hoo reveal that the burial eminences would have had a fine view of Roman barrows across the river. The boar-helmet of Mound One, a vernacular version of the Late Antique parade helmet, resembles the type that a high-ranking legionary guard stationed on the Wall might have worn three centuries earlier. The deceased—or his armorer—must have suffered boars gladly. Four pairs are depicted on his two shoulder-clasps, splendid gold, garnet, and blue-glass millefiori ornaments that resemble but outdo the ornate hinged shoulder-clasps on the parade regalia of late Roman officers.[33] Such objects, like Edwin of Northumbria's standard (Bede, *Hist. eccles.* 2.16, p. 192) or Oswald of Northumbria's banner "made of gold and purple" (Bede, *Hist.eccles.* 3.11, p. 246), would have reflected the grandeur

28. For references, see Speckenbach, "Der Eber in der deutschen Literatur des Mittelalters," pp. 426–32. The electronic age offers shortcuts to hunters of this boar: e.g., the Chadwyck-Healey *Patrologia Latina* database (pld.chadwyck.com/), and the CETEDOC Library of Christian Latin texts (Turnhout: Brepols), and the electronic *Monumenta Germaniae Historica* (www.mgh.de/gesamtverzeichnis/).

29. Jerome, *Commentariorum in Esaiam* 8.27, par. 10, line 15.

30. French *sanglier* (boar), like Italian *cinghiale*, derives from Latin *singularis* (solitary one) of the Psalm verse: Gamillscheg, *Etymologisches Wörterbuch der französischen Sprache*, p. 792.

31. See, e.g., Augustine, *Enarrationes in Psalmos* 143.4; Gregory the Great, *Moralia in Job* 18.24.

32. Speckenbach, "Der Eber in der deutschen Literatur des Mittelalters." This is different from the "epic" warrior/boar comparison, which had an unbroken run from Homer to Asser: e.g., *Iliad* 13.470; *Aeneid* 1.324, 4.158, 10.708; *Metamorphoses* 8.280, 10.539. Cf. early Welsh *twrch* (boar) and Old Irish *torc* (boar), both used for a brave warrior. On Asser's praise of Alfred for acting courageously, *aprino more* (like a wild boar, *Vit. Ælf.* 38), see "Asser's *Life of King Alfred*," in Keynes and Lapidge, *Alfred the Great*, pp. 79, 242 n. 70. See Rosemary Cramp, this volume, p. 7 n. 17, for the possible boar's head on the Alfred Jewel.

33. Bruce-Mitford, *Sutton Hoo Ship Burial*, 2:533–34.

of Rome, advertising their owner as heir to Roman authority and Roman land. The boar on early seventh-century helmets, with its vaguely barbaric and Romano-Celtic flavor, probably announced continuity with the fused ancient traditions of Europe and the Mediterranean as well.

The heads in *Beowulf* seem blonder, their boar-helmets pointing not to Rome but toward the magnetic North. Worn by contemporary Geats and Danes, such hats accessorize nicely with the pagan sacrifices, cremations, drinking rituals, and auguries of these beefy breakers-of-rings.[34] As Beowulf and his men approach the Danish hall, a helmet glints: "boar images adorned with gold flashed above cheek-guards; gleaming and fire-hardened, it held guard over life" (303b–305).[35] Just before Danish "heads melt" on the pyre at Finnsburh, so do the boar-helmets that guarded them: "It was easy to see upon that pyre the bloodstained battle-shirt, the gilded swine, the iron-hard boar" (1110–12a). (One hungry commentator detected a sacrificial roast boar in these lines.)[36] A boar-helmet is mentioned in each of the three sections or fitts leading up to Beowulf's killing of Grendel's mother. The terror she inspires is said to be less than that of a man, "when the ornamented sword, a bloodstained blade, hammer-forged, its edges strong, slices the hostile boar from a helmet" (1285–87). The morning after her late-night house call, the Danish king, lamenting the death of his favorite companion, recalls the times the two of them "defended their heads when footsoldiers clashed, battered the boars" (1327–28a). Before Beowulf sets out for her place, he dons a helmet "hooped by splendid bands, as the weapon-smith had wrought it in ancient days, crafted it wondrously, set it round with boar shapes, so that afterwards no blade or battle-sword could ever bite it" (1451–54). The emphasis on boar power in the first part of the poem is deliberate, as is the setting in *fyrndagum*, in old heathen times.[37] The boar-helmets of *Beowulf* are not fossils, the casual imprints of a "merely inherited . . . verbal convention."[38] These hats map the temporal and cultural distance between the pagan Scandinavian past, the late fifth- and early sixth-century world of the chief actors, and the England of the poet's day.

34. Studies touching on boars in *Beowulf* include Stjerna, "Hjälmar och svärd i *Beowulf*"; Falk, *Altnordische Waffenkunde*, esp. pp. 157–60; Hatto, "Snake-swords and Boar-helms in *Beowulf*," pp. 155–60; Beck, *Das Ebersignum im Germanischen*, pp. 4–33; Beck, "Eber"; Glosecki, *Shamanism and Old English Poetry*, pp. 54–59, 192–97.

35. My punctuation and reading follow B. Mitchell and Robinson, *Beowulf.*

36. Leo, *Bëówulf,* p. 18: "The boar-insignia of the Geats, like the boar-sacrifice which accompanies the cremation of Finn's son, stand out as clear memories of the cult of Frouwo" (my translation).

37. On a possible sense "heathen" for OE *fyrn* (ancient, of old), see Robinson, "Sub-Sense of Old English *Fyrn*(-)."

38. Irving, "Christian and Pagan Elements," pp. 178–79.

It is frequently acknowledged that "the weaponry described in *Beowulf* only fits with the material culture from the sixth and seventh century";[39] "that there is a close link between objects . . . described in *Beowulf* and archaeological evidence from the sixth and seventh century A.D.";[40] that "in an English context, the archaeological horizon of *Beowulf* reflects the later sixth and seventh centuries with a striking consistency";[41] "that, in an Anglo-Saxon context, the archaeological horizon of *Beowulf* can be seen to extend no later than around the end of the seventh century";[42] and "that the most detailed and concrete descriptions—those of swords and helmets especially—probably reached their present form no later than the eighth century."[43] I am not so sure. The evidence of Viking Age skaldic verse suggests that northern poets were still summoning up boar-helmets at the turn of the millennium.

Literary horizons can seem boundless. The Mycenaean boar-helmet described in detail in the *Iliad* (10.261–70) would have been extinct for a half millennium or more when "Homer" sang.[44] This legendary Bronze Age headdress came with a pedigree of former owners: originally Amyntor's, it was stolen from him by the famous thief Autolykos, who gave it to Amphidamus, who gave it to the Cretan Molos, father of Meriones, who lent it to Odysseus. In just a few verses, the boar-helmet travels from Greece north of the Isthmus to the southern coast of the Peloponnese and then to Crete. Scandinavian prose texts from the late twelfth and early thirteenth centuries also know of a peripatetic boar-helmet, associated in turn with at least three characters in *Beowulf:* the much-praised Swedish king Onela, his nephew Eadgils, and—in events that take place after the poem ends—the Danish king Hrothulf.[45] Everyone, it seems, wants a piece of Onela's hat.

39. Nielsen, "Style II and the Anglo-Saxon Elite," p. 200.
40. Davidson, "Archaeology and *Beowulf*," p. 359.
41. Hines, *Scandinavian Character of Anglian England,* p. 296.
42. Newton, *Origins of Beowulf and the Pre-Viking Kingdom of East Anglia,* p. 37.
43. Webster, "Archaeology and *Beowulf*," p. 184 n. 4.
44. See Borchhardt, *Homerische Helme,* esp. pp. 18–37, 47–53, 77–83. Heinrich Schliemann was the first to link the boar-tusk plates of Mycenae with Homer's poetry: *Mykenae,* p. 312. See Lorimer, *Homer and the Monuments,* pp. 211–45; and Dickinson, "Homer, the Poet of the Dark Age," pp. 21 and 26–27.
45. For the legend, see Boer, "Studier over Skjoldungedigtningen"; Jakob Benediktsson, "Icelandic Traditions of the Scyldings"; Bjarni Guðnason, *Um Skjöldungasögu.* For the texts, see Bjarni Guðnason, *Sǫgur Danakonunga.* Snorri Sturluson relied on the saga in *Ynglingasaga,* chap. 29, in *Heimskringla,* ed. Bjarni Aðalbjarnarson, pp. 56–59, and in *Skáldskaparmál* (ca. 1220); in the latter treatise, he calls Onela's helmet both Hildisvín and Hildigǫltr (Battle-Boar), turning a skaldic kenning into a proper name: *Snorri Sturluson, Edda: Skáldskaparmál,* chap. 44, p. 58, lines 34, 37; st. 473, line 1. ON poetic lists include sev-

One incident in the poem, twice recounted, seems to explore through eponymy the *enfance* of this helmet. Toward the end of his life, Beowulf, recalling events from his childhood, tells of a Geat named Eofor (boar) fatally attacking the Swedish king Ongentheow, Onela's father, causing his *guðhelm* (battle-helm) to slip off (2487). Then, just before Beowulf's funeral, a messenger relating the origin of the feud between the Swedes and Geats again portrays Eofor shattering Ongentheow's *entisc helm* (gigantic helm, 2979). Eofor presents this helmet to Hygelac. If, after Hygelac's death, his son Heardred inherited the helmet, and if, after Heardred's death, his slayer, Onela, retrieved it, and if, after killing Onela, Eadgils (as Norse legend relates) took that king's famous headgear, then the poem ends with Eadgils sitting on the Swedish throne, waiting for Hrothulf and his troops to arrive and demand that same boar-helmet as prize. Perhaps the twin allusions in *Beowulf* to Ongentheow's looted helmet, like the preceding one to Heoroweard's missing mailcoat (2158–62), were intended to evoke the final act of the Scylding drama: the attack on Hrothulf at Lejre, when, according to Saxo's Latin rendition of *Bjarkamál*, Geats *cristatis galeis* (with crested helms) surprise and overwhelm the sleeping Danes.[46] Given the pileup here of unknowable unknowns, almost anything is possible. The one precious anchor in this sea of guesswork is that boar-helmets appear in a few Viking Age skaldic stanzas with English associations.

In the half century before *Beowulf* was written down in London, British Library, MS Cotton Vitellius A. xv, three or four Norwegian and Icelandic court poets speak of these helmets, the first in connection with Onela. In a stanza composed around 961 for Hákon the Good, ruler of Norway, Eyvindr Finnsson skaldaspillir designates "helmet" by the phrase "boar of Áli [i.e., Onela]":[47]

---

eral more helmet names based on "boar": e.g., Valhrímnir, Valglitnir, Balbassi, Hallhrímnir; Kock, *Notationes Norroenae*, § 2544, also takes *seimfarri* (gold boar) to be a boar-helmet. Snorri uses *hildigǫltr* (battle-boar=helmet) in his own verse: *Edda: Háttatal*, st. 2.

46. Saxo's poem in 298 hexameter lines comes at the end of Book 2 of the *Gesta Danorum;* for "crested helms" see verse 75 in the consecutive line-numbering of the text in Heusler and Ranisch, *Eddica Minora*.

47. Quotations from skaldic verse are based on the transcriptions and apparatus in Finnur Jónsson, *Den norsk-islandske skjaldedigtning* (hereafter *Skjd.*), vols. 1A, 2A, together with the corresponding B volumes (emended texts) and all other modern commentary available to me. For this stanza (*Skjd.* 1A, 72; 1B, 63), see also *Hákonar saga góða*, chap. 31, in Snorri Sturluson, *Heimskringla*, ed. Bjarni Aðalbjarnarson, p. 190, and Bjarni Einarsson, *Fagrskinna*, chap. 13, p. 91. Snorri may have interpreted *Ála él* as "battle," whose "boar" is the helmet named Battle-boar; the kenning *Ála él* occurs approximately six times in late tenth- and early eleventh-century skaldic verse. See Finnur Jónsson, *Lexicon Poeticum Antiquae Linguae Septentrionalis*, s.v. *él*.

> Ófælinn klauf Ála
> éldraugr skarar hauga
> gullhjǫltuðum galtar,
> grandaðr Dana, brandi.

Ála galtar éldraugr, grandaðr Dana, klauf ófælinn skarar hauga
gullhjǫltuðum brandi.

(The tree/perpetrator [warrior] of the storm [battle] of Onela's
boar [helmet], harmer of the Danes, unafraid clove mounds of
the hair [heads] with goldhilted sword.)

Eyvindr, the first skald to mention a boar-helmet, is also the first to
allude to the Scylding legend, in a kenning based on the gold-sowing
escape of Hroðulf from Eadgils.[48] The prince defined by this battle-boar,
Hákon the Good, had been fostered in England by King Æthelstan; he
returned to Norway ca. 935, driving out his half brother, Eric Bloodaxe,
who moved over to York, OE *Eoforwic* (Hog-town).[49] Egill Skallagrímsson
is said to have recited a stanza before King Æthelstan shortly afterwards,
reporting how he escaped with his life from Eric:[50]

> Arfstóli kná ek Ála
> Áttgǫfguðum hattar
> . . .
> ráða nú sem áðan.

Kná ek ráða nú sem áðan áttgǫfguðum arfstóli Ála hattar.

(I can now as before keep my noble inheritance-seat [head] of
Onela's hood [helmet].)

Egill here seems to be playing upon an English idiom (OE *yrfestole
wealdan*) and possibly also upon his English audience's knowledge of
Onela's headgear.[51]

Two Viking Age skalds after Eyvindr call a helmet "battle-boar."
Glúmr Geirason composed around 970 a stanza for Harald Greycloak,

---

48. *Fýrisvalla fræ* ("seed of Fýri-plains" near Uppsala): *Skjd.* 1A, 73; 1B, 64. Eyvindr's
stanza is preserved in a number of sagas (e.g, *Haralds saga gráfeldar* chap. 1, in Snorri
Sturluson, *Heimskringla*, ed. Bjarni Aðalbjarnarson, p. 201) and in Snorri's *Skáldskaparmál*,
chap. 44 (st. 185, p. 59).

49. The popular etymology that by the ninth century at the latest produced OE Eoforwic out of Colonia Eburacensis may already be reflected in Alcuin's spelling of the place-
name: Eubora(i)ca, Euboricensis (as opposed to Bede's classical Eboracensis/Eburacensis).
See Godman, *Alcuin*, pp. cxii–cxiii.

50. *Skjd* 1A, 55; 1B, 48; Nordal, *Egils saga*, chap. 61, p. 194.

51. See Hofmann, *Nordisch-Englische Lehnbeziehungen der Wikingerzeit*, p. 33.

one of the sons of his former patron, Eric Bloodaxe, praising this chip off
the old block for killing men of high rank, those wearing boar-helmets:[52]

> valgaltar lét velta
> vargfœðandi marga,
> ofvæginn réð jǫfra,
> jafnborna sér þorna.

Vargfœðandi lét marga valgaltar þorna, jafnborna sér, velta;
ofvæginn réð jǫfra.

(The wolf-feeder [warrior] caused many trees [warriors] of the
battle-boar [helmet], born equal to himself, to tip over; the over-
powering one put princes to death.)

Glúmr's word for "prince," *jǫfurr,* cognate with Old English *eofor* (boar)
complements, in typical skaldic fashion, the reference to "boar-helmet" in
the main sentence. For although ON *jǫfurr* always designates the human
animal, Viking Age skalds, unlike later ones, seem sometimes to play on
an underlying zoological sense.[53]

Finally, an association of boar-helmets with the god Freyr is hinted at
in a stanza composed around 1012 by Þormóðr Trefilsson, commemorat-
ing a slaying in Iceland:[54]

> Felldi folksvaldi
> fyrst ens gollbyrsta
> velti valgaltar
> Vígfús þann hétu.

Folksvaldi felldi fyrst velti ens gollbyrsta valgaltar; hétu þann
Vígfúss.

(The leader of the army first slew the tipper-over [warrior] of
the gold-bristled battle-boar [helmet]; they called him Vígfús.)

The second line of Þormóðr's half-stanza, *fyrst ens gollbyrsta,* is almost
identical to one in Úlfr Uggason's late tenth-century *Húsdrápa,* st. 7, telling how Freyr rode on a boar with gold bristles to Baldr's funeral pyre
(*Skjd.* 1A, 137; 1B, 129). Snorri, perhaps on the basis of this verse, names
the boar Gullinbyrsti (the gold-bristled), making it kin to the golden boars
of *Beowulf.*

---

52. *Skjd.* 1A, 76, 1B, 67; Bjarni Einarsson, *Fagrskinna,* chap. 14, p. 102.
53. E.g., Sighvatr's *Knútsdrápa,* st. 9 (*Skjd.* 1A, 250; 1B, 234).
54. *Skjd.* 1A, 206; 1B, 196; Einar Ól Sveinsson and Matthías Þórðarson, *Eyrbyggja saga,*
chap. 26, p. 67.

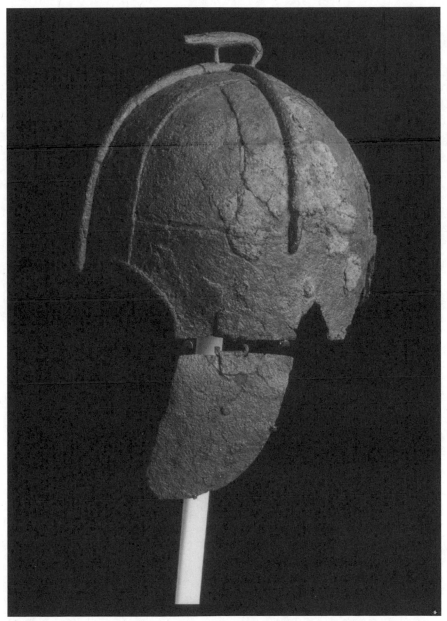

Figure 1. The Wollaston helmet. Photograph courtesy of Ian Meadows and Northamptonshire County Council.

The metonymy through which the compound "battle-boar" gets to mean "helmet" in skaldic poetry, the crest standing for the whole, recalls the description in *Beowulf,* lines 1327–28, of noble warriors battering the "boars" (i.e., helmets). Just as the material world portrayed in the Old English poem has been illuminated by sixth- and seventh-century grave goods, so, too, its lovingly described boar-helmets gain depth by being reunited with their cousins in tenth- and early eleventh-century skaldic verse.

The two poetries bear at moments an uncanny resemblance to each other, revealing the same allusiveness and habits of expression, and, sometimes, the same inventory of "things." The boar-helmets of *Beowulf* are rooted, like the heads they cap, in a North Sea culture whose poetic language had at some point gone its separate way. "Singularity," Sir Arthur Conan Doyle advised (not necessarily thinking of late Latin *singularis,* "wild boar"), "is almost invariably a clue."[55] The boar on the helmet is a little thing, but no object is so small that it cannot be seen to overshadow mountains if, as Rosemary Cramp has taught us, we pay attention to it for a long time and close up.

---

55. A. Doyle, "Boscombe Valley Mystery," p. 70. I am much indebted to Oren Falk, University of Toronto, for his thoughtful reading of this piece.

Beowulf and Archaeology—Revisited

John Hines

Archaeology and Literary Criticism

It is difficult to imagine an Old English scholar who is not utterly familiar with *Beowulf*. There will, however, be few such scholars with even a similarly thorough understanding and knowledge of Anglo-Saxon archaeology. It is consequently all the more daunting a task to try to make the case to the Anglo-Saxonist establishment that there is something to be gained from revisiting the pairing of *Beowulf* and archaeology yet again. This is not least so because we already have two recent studies, by Leslie Webster and Catherine Hills,[1] that are as thorough as the space available to them allows for in providing an archaeological elucidation of the various categories of artifact referred to in the poem. These commentaries, however, represent only one of the ways in which Anglo-Saxon archaeology and the study of Old English literature can be integrated, and they do not attempt to involve archaeology in the criticism of the poem. By the latter I mean the analysis, interpretation, and evaluation of it as a unitary work of literary art, and it is the purpose of this essay to show how substantial a role an archaeological perspective may play in such an enterprise.

In this respect, the polemical edge of the claim that *Beowulf* and archaeology should be revisited is directed against an overtextual approach to past cultural products that is characteristic of modern literary and especially Old English studies, rather than being a querulous criticism of archaeologists who have written about *Beowulf* for not having done enough. Nonetheless, even the latter have seemed to find it hard to escape a reductive position as they (literally) get down to details. Archaeological evidence would indeed seem to be of limited importance in critical terms if, in the end, all it can do, to quote Rosemary Cramp's conclusion to her 1957 article

I wish to thank Professor John D. Niles and Dr. Elizabeth Ashman Rowe for commenting on an earlier draft of this paper, and in particular for helping me to recognize points that could be made clearer for a readership with a background primarily in literary studies. Responsibility for the shortcomings that remain is still, of course, entirely my own.

1. Webster, "Archaeology and *Beowulf*"; Hills, "*Beowulf* and Archaeology."

on *Beowulf* and archaeology, is "to enrich the study of the poem" by being able to "supply relevant illustrations so that simple words such as 'hall' or 'sword' conjure up a precise picture."[2] This is somewhat less than the fundamental exploration of insights into Anglo-Saxon "society" and "life," in respect of which it was initially suggested archaeology and the poem could complement one another.[3] The problem may seem to be simple and irredeemable. Nearly all Old English poetry—with the possible exception of some of the riddles—is concerned to portray an ideal, not the real world. Meanwhile the splendid weapons and armor that are referred to, the horse trappings and ships, and the finest hall imaginable with its mead benches and ale cups, are meant to be rare and esoteric things, not the items and settings of mundane and daily Anglo-Saxon life. This is not to say that the elevated culture envisaged in the poem did not have its counterparts in the real world. But with such a limited interface between literature and life as it really was, what can archaeology do for the literature other than provide us with a rather limited series of illustrations? And what can the literature add to archaeology other than a set of names for things that we can already tell, on purely archaeological grounds, were special?

There is more than one solution to this basic problem. For one thing, it is possible to approach a work of literary art as an artifact capable of analysis in essentially the same terms as the diverse forms of material artifact that constitute archaeology's primary domain, so that the literature can consequently be fitted into a general cultural history. Such is an approach that has long been prominently championed by so well-known a figure as Jacques Le Goff,[4] although in fact textual sources remain dominant in his studies of the Middle Ages. Crucially for the present essay, however, this is a particularly awkward approach to take to *Beowulf,* where we have a single Anglo-Saxon manuscript copy of the poem of reasonably well-defined date but then a distinctly contentious debate over the origins, accretion, and transmission of the material that makes up this one version of the poem through something like the previous four centuries. I do not in fact regard the controversy over the date of *Beowulf* as an insuperable problem for such an approach, as is implicit in some of what follows, but nevertheless judge it simply unnecessary (for the purposes of the present discussion) to become entangled in this whole complex of problems.

The alternative approach that I shall seek to demonstrate through selected examples in this short essay takes its starting point in an understanding of archaeology as not simply a specialist knowledge of ancient

2. Cramp, "*Beowulf* and Archaeology," p. 77.
3. Cramp, "*Beowulf* and Archaeology," p. 57.
4. E.g., in his essays first published from 1956 to 1985 collected in Le Goff, *Pour un autre Moyen Âge* and *L'imaginaire médiévale.*

artifacts but rather a study of a more abstract phenomenon called "past culture"—culture being something that is implicit in and common to even such apparently different material products as, say, a type of grave, a pot, a ship, or a garment that can somehow be associated with a common source.[5] Archaeology is thus not concerned just to identify, classify, and date the artifactual inventory of past contexts but is far more profoundly concerned to understand what was done with those artifacts and how the many particularities of past behavior reflected by individual finds may relate to one another as part of some more coherent whole. I do not intend to attempt to give some all-embracing explanation and justification of such a concept of cultural coherency at this point. We can, I believe, amply justify assuming it to be a valid starting point in the present context by exploring *Beowulf* and looking for some system or systems of material culture there. This will be to read the text as the archaeologist reads material culture, and therefore to do much more than to approach the text as a catalogue of artifacts, of which we may or may not happen to have found examples.[6]

A different form of reading of the poem, not only informed by archaeology but really dependent upon it, is that of Gale Owen-Crocker,[7] who effectively suggests that a familiarity with particular material-cultural features is crucial to the full semantic recognition and interpretation of a key part of the poem. Drawing on parallels in a set of Migration Period to Viking Age furnished burials in central Sweden (the territory of the poem's *Sweoðeod*), she identifies allusions to funerary practices in the "lay of the last survivor" (2247–66),[8] which she then locates within the elaborate thematic structure she postulates for *Beowulf*, based upon this as one of four funerals. The poem is still, in her view, a late Anglo-Saxon Chris-

---

5. For a particularly clear definition and concise explanation of the archaeological concept of culture, see Childe, *Short Introduction to Archaeology*, pp. 16–19.

6. It would be improper not at least to acknowledge the need to discuss the relationship between the approach(es) advocated in this essay and Allen J. Frantzen's thoughtful and thought-provoking case for interdisciplinary—or rather comparative disciplinary—studies in his "Prologue: Documents and Monuments." It is not, however, purely an evasive rhetorical ploy to invoke *occupatio* here, on the grounds that this essay is not the place for an adequate or useful evaluation of Frantzen's more theoretical paper, the empirical contents of which are essentially retrospective, reviewing (inter alia) the limits and biases of mono-disciplinary traditions, and in particular the emphasis on the rich and the aristocratic in the links drawn between *Beowulf* and the Sutton Hoo ship burial excavated in 1939. I believe there is a fundamental congruency of purpose between what I seek to advocate here and the prospects optimistically outlined by Frantzen (ibid., esp. pp. 22–33); however, this essay seeks to yoke theory to practice from the start.

7. Owen-Crocker, *Four Funerals in Beowulf*.

8. All line references to and quotations from *Beowulf* are taken from B. Mitchell and Robinson, *Beowulf*. All translations are my own.

tian reflection upon a pagan past. It is undoubtedly important to be aware that any literature may use contextual allusions in a crucial way, which only a knowledge of the relevant archaeology will make accessible to a modern reader. Among my concerns about Owen-Crocker's argument, however,[9] is the fact that in this case it again limits the contribution of archaeology to a highly particularized and indeed esoteric association: one has both to know the material-cultural reference and then to make (and indeed believe in) the connection. Toward the end of the present discussion I offer an alternative interpretation of the dragon's hoard as unused treasure—unusable, as it appeared to the last survivor, who buried it as there was nobody else left to bury it with him as grave goods. The funerary associations of this vignette in *Beowulf* also appear to me to be much more significantly drawn out by its close association with two further cases of grievously inchoate mortuary rituals: the death of Herebeald (2435–71), slain by his brother, whose father cannot remedy the hostile blow (*fæghðe gebetan*, 2465), and the young man's body hanging on the gallows, pecked by ravens and bringing agony to his father (2444–59). Here indeed, I would rather argue, the explicit absence of proper obsequies acts as a powerful reminder of the pagandom in which *Beowulf* is set, a paganism that lurks just below the surface of the mythical, literary, and material allusions of the poem.[10]

We all ought to be familiar enough with the principal categories of material artifact referred to in *Beowulf*. Pride of place is taken by a special type of building that served as an elite gathering and meeting place, the hall, and various requisites for group entertainment and hospitality that go with it—the ale cup, the mead bench, and the harp, for instance. This is effectively the only element within the human settlement hierarchy and landscape that is evoked in the poem; apart from (even here only possibly) brief references to *londbuend* and *bufolc* (1345, 2220), no notice is taken of any substructure of farms and villages, or a farmed landscape like that which is regularly and formulaically recorded in Anglo-Saxon charters. The next most prominent category is military equipment, weapons and armor, and means of transport in the form of riding gear and ships. Jewelry is not exclusively female, but this category nonetheless serves as the equivalent, for the *goldhroden* woman, of the man's body armor of helmet and mailshirt.[11]

9. See Hines, review of Owen-Crocker, *Four Funerals in Beowulf.*

10. Consider, for instance, the propositions that Herebeald, Hathcyn, and the old man are euhemerizations of Baldr, Hǫð, and Óðinn in situations recorded for us in Old Norse mythology, and the then-conspicuous absence of the story of the attempts to retrieve Baldr from Hel after his violent death in those sources.

11. Cf. Fee, *"Beag & Beaghroden."*

Very importantly, in view of archaeology's concern with what was done with the artifacts of the past as well as with the fact of their existence, a further major category of material construct portrayed in *Beowulf* is a range of contexts for the deliberate deposition of objects. The type encountered most frequently, and conspicuously at the beginning and end of the poem, is the furnished funerary deposit, as in Scyld's burial at sea and Beowulf's grave in his barrow. There is also nonfunerary hoarding—obviously in the case of the dragon's lair; more arguably so in the case of the collection of weaponry and treasures in Grendel's underwater den. With this category we can see especially clearly how the artifact may serve not solely as a purely utilitarian, function-serving, and thus passive item—something that is simply used—but can also be used creatively in the negotiation of human relations, both social and circumstantial, and thus become invested with growing and changeable value, power, and significance. Therefore let us not jump to, or fail to pass beyond, those common, simplistic explanations of the provision of grave goods: that they mark the deceased's status or are for use in an afterlife. Why, then, bury artifacts like dead people in nonfunerary votive hoards? Should we perhaps look at things the other way round, and see the dead human body as treated as, in effect, an inconvenient or even dangerous encumbrance, to be disposed of like inanimate artifacts?[12] On the basis of such observations and questions, I propose to take a fresh look at instances of the use of material culture where I believe it forms a vital interpretative crux in each of the three main sections of the poem.

WEAPONS AND ARMOR—BEOWULF'S JOURNEY TO FIGHT GRENDEL

For all the familiarity of the importance of weaponry and armor to the heroic military elite portrayed in *Beowulf,* I am not aware that there has ever been any very detailed analysis of precisely how these items are used.[13] When Beowulf himself finally makes his entrance into the poem, in lines 189–98, after the building of Heorot and Grendel's depredations have been recounted, the main visual picture put before us is that of his

12. For careful discussions of the possible range of explanations of the early Anglo-Saxon furnished burial rite and the pitfalls associated with that, and at the same time striking examples of the almost automatic association between (non-Christian) burial practices and (pagan) religion, see Owen, *Rites and Religions of the Anglo-Saxons,* pp. 67–125, and Wilson, *Anglo-Saxon Paganism,* pp. 67–180. See also Elizabeth O'Brien's essay in this volume.

13. The discussion that follows here may be compared with van Meter, "Ritualized Presentation of Weapons," especially in respect of the lack of distinction amongst categories of weaponry and armor, and the maintenance of the conventional value attributed to the sword, in that study.

ship crossing to Denmark—evoked in considerable detail, and thus also echoing Scyld's arrival and departure across the sea. But there is a very marked change as soon as the troop of fifteen disembarks onto land, which is typically referred to with the simple word *wang* (225), a word that implies nothing more than a bare, open stage upon which the heroes can act. As the men move around rather than being carried, almost magically, in the boat, there is a completely new focus on their armor and weapons, which even chime in with the sound of the poem: *syrcan hrysedon, / guðgewædo* (mailcoats shook [or were clinking], war-garments, 226–27).

Such are certainly the terms in which we perceive the Geatish troop through the Danish coastguard's eyes: he sees them carrying their bright shields, their ready war-gear (*fyrdsearo fuslicu*, 232—it is very difficult to translate this halfline without personifying the armor); and in his challenge to them, he seems to identify their armor as a sort of uniform, and as being the particular point that he needs to ask them about: "Hwæt syndon ge searohæbbendra / byrnum werede?" (What armored men are you, troop in mailcoats?, 237–38). Now there is, of course, nothing very remarkable in a situation in which a group of men turning up fully armed should be perceived as a potential threat for precisely that reason and challenged to explain themselves. But the guard's words go beyond this. He says he has seen no shieldbearers (*lindhæbbende*) arrive *cuðlicor* (more conspicuously), and that one of them is the greatest warrior he has seen: "nis þæt seldguma / wæpnum geweorðad" (that is no hall-man adorned with weapons, 249–50). Thus both the appearance and behavior of the armed troop in these circumstances appear noble, and their war-gear plays a substantial part in this. The coastguard is, however, astute enough to know that appearances and material symbols alone are not enough to prove true identity and character, and thus they have to be questioned.

On its own, this episode would not give the material culture of the poem any more than a banal and self-evident significance, but these are terms of reference that not only remain at the forefront of attention from here on but play an increasingly powerful dramatic role. After Beowulf's speech declaring their purpose (260–85), in which he pointedly refers to Grendel as *sceaðona ic nat hwylc* (a ravager, I know not what, 274), they are told to proceed, in and with their war-gear: "Gewitaþ forð beran / wæpen ond gewædu" (Go and carry forth weapons and garments, 291–92), shortly after which we have the first reference to the famous boar-helmets, on which the *eoforlic scionon* (boar-shapes shone, 303–05). One can really note only in passing here that this image links the armor with a vitally important theme of light within the poem—immediately followed at this juncture, in fact, by a reference to the light of Heorot shining over many lands (307–11).

As the troop enters the hall, we again are told that their armor shines and sings: *guðbyrne scan* (the war-corslet shone, 321), *hringiren scir / song in searwum* (the bright ring-iron sang in the armor, 322–23), *byrnan hringdon* (the mailshirts rang, 327). Here, in fact, we also can begin to see the division of the war-gear into significantly different categories of body-armor and arms, as the shields and spears are put down, stowed into their proper place and almost, one might conceive, added to the structure of Heorot like the shields along the sides of the Gokstad ship (325–30).[14] The troop is truly identified with its armor as an *irenþreat* (iron-force, 330), and of course the first question of the spokesman, Wulfgar, is the same as the coastguard's:

> "Hwanon ferigeað ge   fætte scyldas
> græge syrcan   ond grimhelmas,
> heresceafta heap?" (333–35)

> ("Whence do you bring [these] plated shields, grey mail-shirts and visored helmets, [the] mass of troop-shafts?")

Beowulf replies:

> *heard under helme.*   "We synt Higelaces
> beodgeneatas.   Beowulf is min nama." (342–43; my emphasis)

> (*hard under helmet.* "We are Hygelac's table-companions. Beowulf is my name.")

Accordingly, in recommending them to Hrothgar, Wulfgar associates their equipment with their status, "Hy on wiggetawum wyrðe þinceaþ / eorla geæhtlan" (In their war-gear they appear worthy of the status of distinguished men, 368–69), and they are explicitly directed finally to approach Hrothgar in their armor but without their weapons:

> "Nu ge moton gangan   in eowrum guðgeatawum
> under heregriman   Hroðgar geseon.
> lætað hildebord   her onbidan,
> wudu wælsceaftas,   worda geþinges." (395–98)

> ("Now you may advance in your war-gear, beneath the visored helmets, to see Hrothgar. Let the slaughter-shafts of wood await here what words will decide.")

14. Nicolaysen, *Langskibet fra Gokstad ved Sandefjord;* Sjøvold, *Viking Ships in Oslo*, pp. 53–68.

At this point again, Beowulf's speech is introduced with emphasis on the fact that he speaks in his helmet and mailcoat (405–06). What is very clear in all this, then, is that the body-armor of helmet and mailcoat is understood and treated as being particularly personal in the sense of expressing the identity and status of its wearer in a way and to a degree beyond what any weapon does. From an archaeological perspective, we ought not to be in the least bit surprised by such an instance of culturally variable ways of clothing, grooming, or presenting the human body being used to express identity like this.[15]

All of this could, however, still be regarded as merely familiar and even predictable. The most startlingly dramatic use that is made of it in *Beowulf* is the turn that is announced in Beowulf's first speech to Hrothgar, when he forswears the use of weaponry (specifically sword and shield, at this point) in his anticipated battle with Grendel (433–40). Subsequently, indeed, we are told that he (finally) takes off his helmet and corslet when the Geats are left alone in Heorot that night awaiting Grendel (669–74). If this armor is so integral a part of his identity and status as we have been directed to believe, what are the implications of his divesting himself of it to fight Grendel? It is, of course, an ostentatious display of both courage and physical strength on Beowulf's part for him to do this, but I do not find that, on its own, a sufficient explanation. Beowulf does not seem abashed to have taken to the waters in a mailshirt and carrying a sword during his contest with Breca (530–606). We also learn retrospectively that a sword would be no use against Grendel anyway (798–805), but this appears to me more significant as one instance among a remarkably large number in which swords fail those who wield them at the point of need in *Beowulf* than as an explanation of Beowulf's conspicuous decision.[16]

15. See Hines, "Culture Groups and Ethnic Groups in Northern Germany," esp. pp. 225–29.

16. The most salient examples are the failure of the sword Hrunting, which Beowulf has accepted as a loan from Unferth to aid him in his battle with Grendel's mother (1455–64, 1522–28: see below), and the failure of the sword Nægling, which Beowulf has relied on in his final battle with the dragon (2516–24, 2575–80), a point to which particular attention appears to be drawn by being twice recalled subsequently (2680–82, 2904–06). Wiglaf's sword is admittedly more effective against the dragon, although it is Beowulf's *weallseax* that finishes the monster off (2697–705). A parallel to lines 794–805 occurs with the ineffective swords drawn by the men in Heorot, against Grendel's mother (1288–95). Of course, the sword does not have exclusively negative connotations, as Hrothgar's gift of a *mære maþþumsweord* (a famous treasure sword) as a reward to Beowulf (1023) and Beowulf's exchange of swords as gifts with Hygelac on his return to Geatland (2144–99) show. But these again can be balanced against the ominously central role played by swords in the tragedies of the rekindled feuds in the Finnsburgh and Heatho-Beard stories, closely juxtaposed in the text with the accounts of these gifts (1142–45, 2041–62).

A further consideration, whose significance we cannot easily set so low, is Beowulf's faithful and fatalistic trust in God:

> "ond siþþan witig god
> on swa hwæþere hond   halig dryhten
> mærðo deme   swa him gemet þince." (685–87)

(and then may wise God, the holy Lord, grant the glory on whichever side seems fitting to Him.)[17]

Potentially of substantial relevance to this, too, is Beowulf's further motivation, again revealed only later, of desiring to capture Grendel as a living prize (960–70). The frustration of this wish makes its own critical point: Grendel's body "failed" (*his lic swice*, 966) and broke apart, while at the same time even Beowulf's great bodily strength had failed to achieve what he desired—*wæs to foremihtig / feond on feþe* (the foe was too greatly powerful in his movement, 969–70). Altogether, then, the drama of signs has moved on through the fight with Grendel from a familiar type of functional material culture in which artifacts have a symbolic value in human terms to one in which they dramatically represent elemental forces and values. In the approach to and presentation of the fight with Grendel, material culture thus plays a substantial discursive role in expressing the deeper meanings of the poem.

THE OBJECT AS TOKEN—BEOWULF'S RETURN FROM THE MERE

The dynamic role played by objects as signs is nowhere more evident in the narrative of *Beowulf* than in the passage of just over six hundred lines in the middle of the poem dealing with the fight with Grendel's mother. The preceding four hundred plus lines have served to establish a familiarity with the major signs involved here: primarily, of course, Grendel's severed arm as a trophy and token of Beowulf's victory over him (832–36, 918–29, 970–90), but also the bloody tracks across the landscape and the bloodstained mere (840–41, 847–49), the gifts with which Hrothgar rewards Beowulf (1020–49), and even the sword Hunlafing placed in Hengest's lap in the Finnsburgh interpolation (1142–45). Grendel's arm is retrieved by his mother, and as its counterpart she leaves Æschere's head on the path to the mere for her pursuers to find (1417–21). Correspondingly, Beowulf decapitates Grendel, and brings his head back as his second trophy, along with the surviving hilt of the superlative sword with which he had achieved the feat. Reminding us that signs can be misread,

17. See also 312–19, 381–84, 441–42, and 478–79.

Beowulf's Geatish and Danish companions had assumed that this infusion of blood into the waters meant Beowulf's death (1591–95).

Beowulf goes to fight Grendel's mother in her lair, which is explicitly an antitype of the hall in which he met Grendel: *in niðsele nathwylcum* (in a hostile hall of unknown kind, 1513)—note again the unknown, indefinable element. The contrast in context is signified in other ways too. In the deployment of weaponry, it is implicit when Beowulf takes a bow and arrow (not a noble weapon) gratuitously to kill one of the lake beasts (1425–41): in case one should doubt the point, the only others to use the bow and arrow within the poem are the diabolical spirit who metaphorically strikes *oferhygd* into the unwary hero in Hrothgar's sermon (1740–47) and Hæthcyn killing his brother Herebeald (2435–40). As in his sea battle with the *niceras* during his swimming match with Breca, Beowulf equips himself and behaves appropriately as a man hunting down and defending himself against the beasts in their own element. Immediately after the beast is dragged to shore, "Gyrede hine Beowulf / eorlgewædum" (Beowulf equipped himself in warrior's clothing, 1441–42), and indeed the two items then described in detail are his mailcoat and helmet, followed by Unferth's sword Hrunting. Ironically, we hear of the sword that "næfre hit æt hilde ne swac / manna ængum" (in battle it never failed any man, 1460–61), because this indeed is what it is just about to do. It is interesting then to note that Grendel's mother is armed with a *seax:* presumably the one-edged knife/sword that proves a consistently reliable weapon, as Beowulf himself discovers, using his own *seax* to finish off the dragon (1545–56, 2702–05, 2900–06).[18]

When Beowulf emerges from the mere, it is striking how quickly he is greeted and disarmed. The surprise, pleasure, and celebrations of his remaining Geatish companions are dealt with in three rather prosaic lines:

> Eodon him þa togeanes,   gode þancodon,
> ðryðlic þegna heap   þeodnes gefegon
> þæs þe hi hyne gesundne   geseon moston. (1626–28)

> (They went toward him, and thanked God, the valiant troop of retainers; they rejoiced for their lord, that they were able to see him unharmed.)

He is similarly swiftly disarmed: "Ða wæs of þæm hroran helm ond byrne / lungre alysed" (Then the helmet and mailshirt were swiftly removed from

---

18. On *seaxes*, see Gale, "The Seax"; Siegmund, *Merowingerzeit am Niederrhein*, pp. 87–94; Jørgensen, *Waffen und Gräber*, pp. 44–67 and 120–75.

the mighty fellow, 1629–30). The emphasis at this point shifts, in the following nineteen-line passage, to the trophies, particularly Grendel's head,
that are being carried back to the hall. There is a parenthesis to underline
the labor of bearing Grendel's head back:

> —feower scoldon
> on þæm wælstenge   weorcum geferian
> to þæm goldsele   Grendles heafod— (1637–39)

> (—four of them were obliged laboriously to carry, on the slaughter-
> shaft, to the gold hall, Grendel's head—)

And this fitt remains focused on the spectacle, the "wliteseon wrætlice;
weras on sawon" (marvelous spectacle; the men gazed upon it, 1650).
Beowulf's account of the battle, which follows immediately afterward,
appropriately begins with direct reference to the *sælac* (sea-booty) that
they have brought Hrothgar, *tires to tacne* (as a token of glory, 1652–54).

Grendel's head is both a token of Beowulf's victory and a reminder
to the Danes of the terror they had faced; it is also compensation for
Æschere's head. The other item Beowulf presents Hrothgar with is the hilt
from the similarly truncated sword, *wundorsmiþa geweorc* (the work of wonder-smiths, 1681). It is noteworthy how often the term *wundor* is used in
Beowulf in a way that implies significance, often Christian. These wonders
are things to be pondered. *Wundor sceawian* (to scrutinize a wonder/mar-
vel) occurs twice as a formulaic halfline (840, 3032), and after Beowulf's
victory over Grendel Hrothgar avers, "a mæg god wyrcan / wundor æfter
wundre" (God can always perform wonder after wonder, 930–31).

At the end of the poem, *wundur* refers to the unknown end of the
story of human life, just as at the beginning no one knows who received
the load of Scyld's funeral ship:

> Wundur hwar þonne
> eorl ellenrof   ende gefere
> lifgesceafta. (3062–64)

> (It is a [matter of] wonder where, then, a distinguished man
> famed for his courage should meet the end of his allotted life.)

Just over forty lines after the hilt is attributed to "wonder-smiths," Hrothgar marks the beginning of the moralizing application of his synopsis of
Heremod's life to Beowulf in his *gidd* (song, utterance) inspired by the hilt
with the words:

> "Wundor is to secganne
> hu mihtig god   manna cynne
> þurh sidne sefan   snyttru bryttað
> eard ond eorlscipe." (1724–27)

("It is a wonder to be told how mighty God with his expansive heart apportions wisdom to humankind, land and nobility.")

It is true that in a number of other cases, *wundor* is associated with nouns apparently with a basic sense of "extraordinary," "magnificent."[19] But this semantic range from magnificent to significant seems only to underline the elastic but inseparable relationship between object and burgeoning significance in the material culture of *Beowulf.*

Even within this context, however, the hilt is an extraordinarily eloquent artifact. "Written" in some way on it, it has the beginning (*or*) of the struggle between God and the giants, the descendants of Cain; in looking toward God's *endelean* (final blow) in his battle with this kindred it had in some way foreseen what has now, narratively, just happened (1687–93). Also written on it, probably in runic letters (*runstafas*), is "for whom," "by whom," or possibly even "for what" (*hwam*) the sword was primarily made (1694–98). Immediately after this, the same combination of narrative and anticipation as is embodied in the hilt and its markings occurs in the sermon of Hrothgar inspired by his scrutiny of it: he summarizes Beowulf's achievement to date, tells the warning tale of Heremod, and gives Beowulf explicit moral advice for the future.

Here, therefore, at what we can properly see as a pivotal point within the poem, is an artifact that functions as the material, pictorial, and inscribed equivalent of a literary artifact, while the interpreter of that artifact is thus necessarily like a poet. Artifacts are literally described as singing, or as fundamentally involved in the generation of a *gidd*, surprisingly frequently in the poem.[20] They occupy a commemorative and instructive place alongside and very close to the lays of the *scop* in the culture of the heroic world portrayed in *Beowulf.* Critical theory has, in the relatively recent past, been tempted to overemphasize the significance of autoreferentiality in a work of literature.[21] We ought, however, to be careful still to attach sufficient weight to the engagement with material signs in this poem and the reading of the tales they tell, especially in comparison with the critical significance widely attributed to *literary* allusions and echoes in the conventional study of *Beowulf.*

19. I.e., *wundorbebod* (mysterious prompting), *wundordeað* (wondrous death), *wundorsion* (wondrous sight), *wundurmaððum* (marvelous treasure), B. Mitchell and Robinson, *Beowulf,* Glossary, p. 306.

20. See also lines 321–23, 628–30, 1423–24, 1520–22, 2152–54, and 2444–59.

21. See, for instance, T. Hawkes, *Structuralism and Semiotics,* esp. pp. 59–73.

THE DRAGON'S HOARD

Oferhygd is indisputably a, if not the, key moral theme linking Hroth-gar's sermon with the final section of *Beowulf*. As we have seen, Hrothgar's comments on *oferhygd* are inspired by an artifact, and the theme is worked out in Beowulf's later life in relation to an assemblage of artifacts, the dragon's hoard. In many respects, the use of material culture in this section is fully consistent with what has gone before—for instance in Wiglaf's choice of imagery to crown his assertion of loyalty to Beowulf:

> "urum sceal sweord ond helm
> byrne ond beaduscrud   bam gemæne." (2659–60)

> (to both of us shall the sword and helmet, the corslet and battle-coat, be in common.)

Just like the Grendels' den, the dragon's lair is an antitype of the noble hall: a *beorh* (hill, barrow) rather than a *burh* (stronghold), where *niðða nathwylc* (an unknown person: note the unknown element, yet again), ironically looking for a home (*ærnes þearfa:* in need of a house, 2225), steals the cup that in the hall serves to create social unity—the *fæted wæge* (gold-plated cup), the *frioðowær(-)* (peace-agreement, 2282).

One respect in which there is a very perceptible difference between this section and the previous ones, however, is the ever more pragmatic terms in which the contest with the fire-breathing dragon—otherwise no less imaginary and symbolic a creature than Grendel—is viewed. Hence the description of Beowulf's commissioning and carrying of an iron shield into the fight (2337–39). Particularly persistent is the emphasis on the practical economics of a well-armed kingdom: the need for treasure and land with which to reward one's troops and lieutenants. Beowulf recalls how he repaid the *maðmas* (treasure) and *lond* (land) that Hrethel gave him (2490–93), and Wiglaf remembers what he owes Beowulf likewise, for being allowed to inherit the dwelling place and "folkrights" his father had possessed and for gifts of weaponry and treasure (2606–08, 2633–42). The treasure hoard pried from the dragon's keeping should therefore be of practical value to the Geats, all the more so if bought with their ageing king's life (2747–51, 2794–801, 3011–14).

The final, challenging enigma of *Beowulf* therefore resides essentially in a set of material-cultural phenomena: objects and what is done with them. Why is the treasure hoard reburied with Beowulf? The morally ambivalent portrayal of Beowulf at the end of the poem should long have been familiar enough to all serious readers of the poem not to need recapitulation here[22]—the pertinent question to be articulated is rather in what ways the reburial of the treasure might affect our reading of that portrayal. Is the action to be understood as judgmental, with Beowulf's soul consigned to face his Maker by way of a pagan funeral in which his body has been burned and interred with heathen treasures that he proudly, covetously, and fatally sought? Or is it tonal, with the extravagant waste of the treasure, like the melancholy reflections and predictions of Wiglaf, the messenger, and the female mourner (2862–91, 2897–3027, 3150–55), to be taken as essentially rhetorical ways of marking the loss of such a great king? If one adopts the latter alternative, one might have to concede that at this point the archaeological perspective and the more purely literary or artistic reading part company, for, from the realistic standpoint, the ending of *Beowulf* is almost remorselessly bleak. The most substantial element creating this atmosphere is the (pseudo)historical realism of the wars between the Geats, the Swedes, and the Frisians, the renewal of which can now be anticipated. This goes hand in hand with the economically pragmatic view of military loyalty already noted in this section. The *hearpan sweg* (voice of the harp) is proleptically stilled (3023), and where the poetic tone has been persistently elegiac throughout the section the final occurrences of the word *gidd* refer to a dirge:

> woldon care cwiðan   ond cyning mænan
> wordgyd wrecan   ond ymb wer sprecan (3171–72; cf. 3150–55)
>
> (they wished to lament their care and keen for the king, utter a
> word-*gidd* and speak about the man.)

Even the *wundor* at the end of this story is explicitly an ignorance of where the warrior goes after death (quoted above, 3062–65).

Nevertheless, God's final judgment remains deferred, and the final, human, verbal *dom* is in a series of superlatives, three out of four of which are morally unambiguous:

> manna mildust   ond monðwærust,
> leodum liðost   ond lofgeornost. (3181–82)
>
> (mildest of men and kindest among them, most gentle to his
> people and most eager for renown.)

And heaven receives the smoke of the pyre (3155). The introductory emphasis on the heathenism of the gold is interesting (2216, 2276). It would be quite justifiable to take these deliberate references as invitations

---

22. Cf. Greenfield, *Interpretation of Old English Poems*, pp. 1–29 and 115–17.

to an exegetical reading, equating the *hæðen gold* with the treasures of the Egyptians, which were rightly appropriated by the Israelites and converted to the service of God.[23] Morally, then, the reburial of the treasure represents a failure on the part of the pagans of the poem to use such treasure properly in a Christian sense. In this context, it is impossible to ignore one particularly prominent feature of the hoard as it is seen by Wiglaf:

> Swylc he siomian geseah   segn eallgylden
> heah ofer horde,   hondwundra mæst
> gelocen leoðocræftum;   of ðæm leoma stod. (2767–69)

> (He also saw a standard covered in gold standing high over the hoard, the greatest of works of skill, dexterously crafted; from it came a light.)

The standard towering over the hoard strongly recalls the *segen gylden(ne)* that stands high over Scyld's head in his funeral ship (47–48). The sign or standard (*cumbol, hildecumbor, segen*) is frequently referred to in the poem and, archaeologically, is probably represented for us by the Sutton Hoo standard.[24] The most significant testimony to a sign in a relevant historical context is Oswald's Constantinian use of the cross at the battle of Heavenfield.[25] What is more, it was to a significant degree in the form of ecclesiastical treasures such as crosses that gold was taken out of social circulation and thesaurized by the Anglo-Saxon church.[26] In their effective rejection of the pre-Christian treasures, therefore, the pagan Geats could be seen as performing their own catharsis, rejecting the pagan system in readiness for the Christian one.

It is of crucial importance to note here that, in archaeological terms as well as to some degree in historical terms, *Beowulf* is demonstrably dealing with a *real* past, not an imagined one created out of references that are no more than a cluster of emblems. Within the text of the poem there is a knowledge, a recognition, and a demonstration of the fact that the honorific practices of the pagan past are no longer practiced, in the Anglo-Saxon community at least, and that there is a Christian alternative to them. I am not sure whether or not *Beowulf* as a poem has a definite concept of the Heroic Age, but it certainly had at its heart a consistent sense of the pagan past. That past was an era that had ended, but some

---

23. Augustine, *De doctrina Christiana* 2.40, pp. 124–27.

24. See now also the possible standard from the Prittlewell burial, a tall iron stand with a bowl for a lamp on top. Museum of London, *Prittlewell Prince*, pp. 29–30.

25. Bede, *Hist. eccles.* 3.2, pp. 214–19.

26. See Webster and Backhouse, *Making of England*, passim.

of its key principles and glories—its military heroism—were still effective, and still needed. It appears, then, to be especially through the use of the material culture of the past that the poem can express an appropriately ambivalent attitude to the pagan period, selecting and endorsing some elements while rejecting others.

CONCLUSION

What I have sought to provide examples of in the discussion above represents just one way in which archaeology and literary criticism can productively be integrated. This approach has involved reading the poem in the same way as an archaeologist would (or at least should) approach the totality of Anglo-Saxon archaeology, seeing the archaeology of *Beowulf* not just as a collection of exotic and valuable artifacts but as a highly meaningful system of material culture. As an attempt to contribute to the development of Anglo-Saxon studies, this does not consciously seek to change the way literary scholars view *Beowulf* by compelling them to take due account of the insights of archaeology so much as to affect the way literary scholars perceive Anglo-Saxon archaeology and the way archaeologists may view *Beowulf*. It may indeed be claimed that literary critics need no lessons or encouragement in the use of semiotics for the interpretation of poetry.[27] Good; and so there ought to be all the greater appreciation there of the potential contribution of archaeology, both as a sister discipline in Anglo-Saxon studies and as a methodologically neglected area in Old English studies.

In this particular case, the archaeological perspective not only encourages an awareness but provides examples that have not, so far as I know, been articulated before of the richness and sophistication with which *Beowulf* dramatizes the tensions of a human society's struggles to know and control its circumstances, and to come to terms with its dependency upon events of the past as it seeks to make the best of conditions for the present and future—and doing so using material culture as a key expressive medium, albeit vicariously, if not additionally, in a translated form, through the medium of literary discourse. In this case, too, the archaeological approach advocated depends upon an understanding of the character of archaeology as a generalized view of material culture, rather than a specific knowledge of Anglo-Saxon archaeology in the sense

27. See, inter alia, Niles, "Sign and Psyche in Old English Poetry"; Frantzen, "Writing the Unreadable *Beowulf*"; Schrader, "Language of the Giant's Sword Hilt"; Cronan, "Wiglaf's Sword"; Fee, "*Beag* & *Beaghroden*"; and van Meter, "Ritualized Presentation of Weapons."

of being able to identify and picture the objects alluded to. Whoever (singular or plural) wrote *Beowulf* likewise did not rely on an audience or readership's ability to classify and contextualize the objects referred to in an academic way; to this extent, yes, the work of literature is autonomous in that sufficient context is provided by the text of the poem itself. Yet it is inconceivable that the material artifacts are purely imaginary and symbolic creations, and that their well-attested, diverse, and detailed counterparts in the real world exist by sheer coincidence; while at the same time a key implication of the foregoing discussion is that the archaeology of the poem is not merely incidental realism—the product of a blind and unconscious frame of reference that thus encodes and can reveal the character (and date) of an original context for the poem.[28] Archaeology, as an intellectual and scientific appreciation of the systemic role played by material culture in human life in both the past and the present, is truly fundamental to the conception and achievement of *Beowulf.* For the richest possible reading of *Beowulf,* then, archaeology is neither an illustrative curiosity nor a pedantic factual burden. The archaeology is truly a vital part of the poetic composition.

28. As noted above, I wish to avoid being sidetracked into the controversy over archaeology and the possible date(s) of the poem in this essay. As Leslie Webster writes, however ("Archaeology and *Beowulf*," p. 184, n. 4), it is simply undeniable that, both in respect of specific details and as a whole inventory of material-cultural phenomena, the real counterparts to what is portrayed in the poem belong predominantly in seventh- and eighth-century England and Scandinavia rather than anywhere else (*pace* Hills, "*Beowulf* and Archaeology," esp. pp. 309–10; see also Owen-Crocker, *Four Funerals in Beowulf,* pp. 114–23). In view of the poem's incorporation of a Christian perspective on pre-Christian circumstances discussed in this essay, it is far from insignificant that this date embraces both the late pagan/Early Christian transition in England and a period when England had become Christian while Scandinavia, and much of the Germanic Continent, remained pagan, although within the sights of English missionary ambitions.

What this constitutes, however, is part of the background of *Beowulf,* not its date. The realism of the material imagery may have come into the poem by way of the accumulation of conventional imagery in poetic, perhaps specifically heroic, tradition, or from a knowledge of real archaeology as artifacts survived or were exhumed in the Anglo-Saxon period. Both of these sources nonetheless involve a form of direct diachronic contact with the material-cultural phase concerned.

EMBROIDERED WOOD:
ANIMAL-HEADED POSTS IN THE BAYEUX "TAPESTRY"

GALE R. OWEN-CROCKER

The Bayeux "Tapestry,"[1] which has been kept at Bayeux, in Normandy, since at least the fifteenth century, is now generally accepted as being of English design and, probably, English workmanship, since it borrows images from manuscripts known to have been in the libraries of St. Augustine's monastery, Canterbury, and the nearby Christ Church Cathedral.[2] Its patron is likely to have been Odo, bishop of Bayeux and earl of Kent, and the embroidery was probably completed by the 1080s. The Tapestry is our largest surviving nonarchitectural medieval artifact and has generated an enormous range of studies, both academic and popular.[3] Regret-

It is impossible to grow up in the northeast of England unaware of the region's heritage. The brooding presence of Hadrian's Wall and the towering domination of Durham Cathedral testify to the great civilizations of the past. The Anglo-Saxon and Viking presence is more subtly indicated yet more warmly remembered than the Roman and Norman. Every schoolchild of my own era came home with an essay to write "about the Venerable Bede," and many spoke with the same easy familiarity of "Saint Cuddie" as they did of the local folksongs, *The Waters of Tyne* and *Bobbie Shaftoe*. It is no longer fashionable to teach children through local culture; yet the Northeast remains proudly conscious of its place in English history. Rosemary Cramp has made an outstanding contribution to raising this awareness of our heritage, just as she has to the rediscovery of it, and I think of her with several different faces: as Professor at Durham University, elegant and authoritative, lecturing and chairing other distinguished speakers; as "archaeological expert" on local television, warmly wrapped up against the biting Northeast wind, bringing alive the medieval world she knows so well; and, my favorite personal memory, as the inspired and inspiring excavation director who could wield a pickaxe with far more dexterity than any of her volunteer diggers, to reveal, yes, the foundations of Bede's monastery wall exactly where she had predicted they would be! I am privileged to contribute to this volume in her honor.

1. The work is technically an embroidery, not a tapestry, since the decoration is stitched, rather than woven. As Tapestry has become the established English name for the work, and since it has become conventional to refer to any wall hanging of cloth as a tapestry, I use this term here, but flag it at the beginning of the essay with quotation marks.
2. The Canterbury association is accepted by most recent scholars with the exception of Wolfgang Grape, *Bayeux Tapestry;* George Beech, *Was the Bayeux Tapestry Made in France?* For my own suggestion that the borrowings were not merely convenient but thematically significant, see Owen-Crocker, "Reading the Bayeux Tapestry through Canterbury Eyes."
3. Major interdisciplinary books include Stenton, *Bayeux Tapestry*, and Bouet, Levy, and Neveux, *Bayeux Tapestry*. See also Owen-Crocker, *King Harold II and the Bayeux Tapestry*.

tably its importance as a textile has not yet been fully exploited due to its confinement in a protective case.[4] However, it has long been recognized as a major historical source for the end of the Anglo-Saxon period and the beginning of the Norman, and it has been regularly mined for socio-historical information on late Anglo-Saxon culture. The Tapestry is also of unique significance as an artwork. It is a visual analysis of a specific graphic motif that is presented in the following essay.

Since David Bernstein's publication of *The Mystery of the Bayeux Tapestry* we have been increasingly aware of the important suggestive power of detail. Bernstein demonstrated that the anecdotal scenes and the poses and actions of the animals depicted in the borders of the Tapestry are likely to have been intended as comments, often ironic, on the actions depicted in the central narrative. More recently, scholars have explored the ways in which weapons or horses contained within the main narrative panel might also be understood as commentary on the events depicted.[5] My own work has investigated the relationship of design, draftsmanship, and needlework and has convinced me that many small objects were included among the embroidered images not simply because they were facts of life, but because they had functional roles in the design of the Tapestry and acted as pointers to themes in the narrative.[6]

A recurrent feature of the first half of the Tapestry[7] is the addition of a zoomorphic or grotesque human head to a wooden post. There are thirty-eight such terminals: eighteen as parts of ships,[8] sixteen associated with furniture,[9] and four architectural details.[10] In the following study I will discuss the animal-headed terminals in each of these categories, estab-

---

Some "classic" articles are reprinted in Gameson, *Study of the Bayeux Tapestry*. For a full bibliography, see S. Brown, *Bayeux Tapestry* and "Bibliography of Bayeux Tapestry Studies 1985–1999." For a digital facsimile see Foys, *Bayeux Tapestry: Digital Edition*.

4. The most recent and authoritative studies are the six articles in the section "The Artefact as Textile," in Bouet, Levy, and Neveux, *Bayeux Tapestry*, pp. 65–123, though analyses that form the basis of the papers date back to 1982–83. New information on dimensions, number of pieces, fibers, and stitches is contained in Bédat and Girault-Kurtzeman, "Technical Study of the Bayeux Tapestry," and on colorants in Oger, "Bayeux Tapestry."

5. See, for example, Lewis, *Rhetoric of Power in the Bayeux Tapestry;* Keefer, "Body Language."

6. I have previously discussed horns, walking sticks, swords, and shafts. See Owen-Crocker, "Telling a Tale"; Owen-Crocker, "Bayeux Tapestry.'"

7. See note 85 below.

8. References are to plate numbers in the color facsimile, Wilson, *Bayeux Tapestry*. Ships' figureheads appear at 5–6, five; 26–27, one; 33–34, two; 37, two; 40–43, eight.

9. Wilson, *Bayeux Tapestry*, 1, one; 10, two; 13, two; 16, one; 19 (upper border), one; 25, one; 28, two; 30, one; 32–33, two; 34–35, three.

10. Wilson, *Bayeux Tapestry*, 17, two; 25, one; 27, one.

lishing the authenticity of each usage. I will suggest that the beast heads
can be used by modern analysts as stylistic indicators, reflecting different
hands at work within a single section of linen, and so, presumably, within
the same workshop, and between the different sections, which may have
had different draftsmen as well as different embroiderers. The discussion
will demonstrate that, apart from its obvious decorative value, the animal-
headed terminal may operate functionally at the graphic level, connecting
scenes and filling spaces. More controversially I will argue that a wooden
animal head sometimes reflects the situation or emotion of a human protagonist and thus functions as a subtle accessory to interpretation.

SHIPS

The existence of zoomorphic figureheads on ships is well attested
from archaeological and textual sources as well as from representations
in art. However, many of the animal terminals on the Bayeux ships are
quite large in proportion to the vessels they decorate. They look top-
heavy, lacking the aerodynamic efficiency of the ninth-century Oseberg
(Norway) ship's sinuous prow[11] or the compact neatness of the figurehead
found in the River Scheldt near Appels, Belgium,[12] leading one to question their realism. Many of them are elaborately decorated with the curling tendrils characteristic of the Anglo-Scandinavian Ringerike style and
its mainly Scandinavian relative, the Mammen style. One, as I will argue
below, may be Urnes style. We might question whether these ships' figureheads, together with the trees and the buildings of the Tapestry, are almost
totally stylized, while the human beings and their immediate trappings
are more realistic. The Bayeux Tapestry is traditionally believed to have
been produced near Canterbury because of its stylistic and iconographic
similarities with Canterbury manuscripts, and a glance at some Anglo-
Saxon drawings from Canterbury manuscripts will show that the stylistic
disparity seen in the Tapestry is indeed normal in eleventh-century art.[13]
We should note, however, that the apparent naturalism of the human figures is deceptive; they are also very stylized, and it is their medieval cloth-

---

11. Wilson, *Vikings and Their Origins*, p. 86, fig. 57.

12. Owen, *Rites and Religions of the Anglo-Saxons*, p. 111, fig. 20.

13. In the illustrated calendar in London, British Library, MS Cotton Tiberius B. v
(see McGurk, Dumville, Godden, and Knock, *Eleventh-Century Anglo-Saxon Illustrated Miscellany*, fol. 6v), for example, trees interlace like the Tapestry trees, and in the Old English
Hexateuch (London, British Library, MS Cotton Claudius B. iv; see Dodwell and Clemoes,
Old English Illustrated Hexateuch), though individual details of architecture may be authentic, the overall picture of any building is not because of the stylized ornamentation and lack
of perspective.

ing and their animation that make them convincing.[14] On the other hand, though I know of no survival of such massive figureheads, spiral curls of ironwork found with Viking ship burials at Ladby, Denmark, and at Île de Groix, Brittany, France, may derive from Ringerike style tendrils.[15] The "great beast" of Ringerike art was certainly considered appropriate decoration for eleventh-century ships since it ornamented metal vanes, once carried on ships, of which we have examples from Heggen, Norway, and Söderala, Sweden,[16] that have survived because they were reused on churches. The greatest flowering of the Ringerike style in English and Scandinavian art was in the first part of the eleventh century, but it persisted beyond that. The Urnes style in Scandinavia lasted from about 1040 well into the twelfth century. Both decorative styles might well have appeared on ships of the 1060s, the years depicted in the Tapestry, or of the 1080s, when it was probably made.

Animal-headed ships are particularly associated with the Vikings.[17] Snorri Sturluson describes the ship that was built for Harald Hardrada, the eleventh-century king of Norway: "On the stem was a dragon-head and on the stern a dragon-tail, and the sides of the bows of the ship were gilt. The vessel had thirty-five rowers' benches and was large for that size."[18] Snorri later describes the vessel as "a great ship," and the dragon-stem is poetically called "serpent-head with golden mane." He compares it in size with another vessel, called *Ormr*, "Serpent" or "Dragon."

This is the popular image of animal-headed ships that has survived to our own day. There is an assumption that the beast head always represented a dragon and that it was at the prow of a warship, which had a tail at the stern, effectively turning the vessel into a visual image of a ruthless, terrifying killer, which is the enduring impression of Viking fleets. Anglo-Saxon art, though, suggests that the head-and-tail arrangement was variable, and we find zoomorphic ships variously depicted with a head and tail, or with two heads, and we may find the heads facing outward or inward. Both the Tapestry and the Old English illustrated Hexateuch (London, British Library, MS Cotton Claudius B. iv) show what is meant to

14. That is, they wear medieval secular clothing rather than the classical garments in which Christ, angels, and saints are depicted. The clothing might, of course, have appeared stylized to contemporaries, since manuscripts were based on older Continental models.

15. Roesdahl, *Vikings*, p. 87.

16. Graham-Campbell and Kidd, *Vikings*, p. 168. The Heggen vane is illustrated at plates 9 and 99.

17. The Normans of the Tapestry were, of course, of Scandinavian descent, and England was an Anglo-Scandinavian kingdom by the eleventh century.

18. *Harald Hardradas Saga*, chaps. 59, 60; quoted from S. Laing, *Snorri Sturluson Heimskringla, Part Two*, "Harold the Stern," p. 203. The Old Norse text can be found in Snorri Sturluson, *Heimskringla*, ed. Finnur Jónsson, 3:155–56.

be the same ship consecutively with different arrangements of figureheads, in a discontinuity that is typical of the Anglo-Saxon artist in general and especially of the Bayeux designer. It is possible that heads might be turned round for convenience (they were certainly not integral to the construction of the vessel—Snorri's account of Harald's dragon-head prow includes the information that it was attached once the ship was in the river), but it seems improbable that they were moved or changed in the course of a journey. It seems, too, that animal heads on ships were not confined to dragons, St. Olaf, for instance, having a famous ship named "The Bison" (ON *Visund*) with a gilded head and tail.[19] Nor, it would seem from representations in art, were zoomorphic terminals reserved for warships. In both the Junius Manuscript (Oxford, Bodleian Library, MS Junius 11, pp. 67–68)[20] and the Old English Hexateuch (London, BL, Cotton Claudius B. iv, fols. 14r–15v), Noah's ark is represented as a grotesque beast, though it can do battle with no one and nothing but the surging water; and other seagoing vessels of no intrinsic significance are occasionally depicted with animal heads, for example in the Harley Psalter (London, British Library, MS Harley 603), folio 27v[21] and folio 51v (fig. 1).[22]

We should not, then, be surprised to find in the Bayeux Tapestry the ealdorman Harold, setting off on an apparently peaceable journey,[23] in a zooanthropomorphic ship (fig. 2). He has evidently embarked by means of a smaller boat, which lacks the distinctive terminals. His cross-channel transport, though, has a beast at one end and a man, identifiable by the human ear and eyebrow, at the other. The beast looks backward, connecting visually with the embarkation scene. The creature is, like all the Bayeux beast heads, stylized, but its interlaced execution is unique in the Tapestry, and if we observe that the color is filled in with lines of stem stitch rather than the laid and couched work that is mostly used as a filler for even the smallest shapes, such as shoes, we have reason to question whether this beast is part of the original work. There is no obvious evi-

19. *Magnus the Good* 19; S. Laing, *Snorri Sturluson Heimskringla, Part Two*, p. 142.

20. Ohlgren, *Anglo-Saxon Textual Illustration*, pp. 563–64. The ark appears twice on p. 67 of the manuscript with slight differences to the animal head.

21. Ohlgren, *Anglo-Saxon Textual Illustration*, p. 193.

22. There is another example in the Bury Psalter (Vatican City, Biblioteca Apostolica Vaticana, MS reg. lat. 12, fol. 108r), which like the Harley Psalter (London, British Library, MS Harley 603, fol. 51v) illustrates Psalm 103 (104):25–26, describing the sea and its contents as part of Creation; Ohlgren, *Anglo-Saxon Textual Illustration*, p. 290.

23. There are shields along the ship's sides and Harold carries a spear as the vessel approaches land, but there is no stowing of weapons and armor such as we find before William's invasion, or as described by the poet of the Old English *Beowulf* (Klaeber, *Beowulf and the Fight at Finnsburg*, lines 213–15). Since hounds and hawks are loaded on board, Harold's journey might be either a hunting trip or a diplomatic mission, in which case the animals could have been intended as gifts.

dence of modern reconstruction, however,[24] and all the colors are found elsewhere in the scene. This beast head is the first in the Tapestry and perhaps was executed before draftsman or embroiderer had settled down to the style that was to predominate. There is interlace elsewhere in the Tapestry, in the stylized depiction of tree branches, but not in the grotesque terminals. Perhaps the embroiderer misunderstood the outline of the cartoon, and with different coloring and technique this beast might have had Ringerike curls. Whether the artist intended it or not, what the embroiderer has produced might be seen as a manifestation of the later eleventh-century Urnes style, perhaps coincidentally, or possibly because this embroiderer was familiar with that style. It is found only rarely in England or Ireland, having probably evolved in Sweden;[25] some of its best-known manifestations today are in Norway, for example the ornament on a bone pin from Trondheim, which combines interlace with Ringerike-type curls, demonstrating the close relationship of these two styles.[26]

The second depiction of Harold's ship (fig. 3, left) has several differences that suggest another hand at work: the second version has no prominent keel plank; the steering oar is fixed differently; and the shields are depicted more economically, with the plain linen acting as a color contrast for alternate shields. The ship still has a man and a beast as finials, but their positions are reversed, and both gaze forward toward the approaching land, like the sailors themselves, especially the lookout on the mast and the man about to cast anchor at the bow, all taking our eyes on to the next event. The stern post curves inward here, both protecting and inflating the importance of the man at the steering oar, presumably Harold. The embroiderer has taken more trouble over the human head than was evident on the first version of the ship, adding a drooping mustache and protruding tongue, making the beard more prominent, and outlining the Ringerike tendrils in different colors. The beast at the prow appears to have horns, or ears, but this could be unfinished work. It is openmouthed with, again, what I take to be a protruding tongue, but it looks surprised rather than terrifying.

Perhaps it *is* surprised, for the next thing to happen will be that Harold is arrested as he steps on shore. The Latin commentary makes the

24. The eighteenth- and nineteenth-century copies published respectively by de Montfaucon and Stothard are very similar to the present appearance of the Tapestry at this point. I am grateful to David Hill for access to the early reproductions in his forthcoming publication: D. Hill and McSween, *Bayeux Tapestry*. The Tapestry and its copies may be compared in Foys, *Bayeux Tapestry: Digital Edition*.

25. Graham-Campbell and Kidd, *Vikings*, pp. 173–75. The best-known English examples are in metalwork, a brooch from Pitney, Somerset, and a mount from Lincoln (ibid., p. 177, fig. 106). There is an example in wood from Dublin, DW 49 (a knife-handle); see Lang, *Viking-Age Decorated Wood*, p. 27, fig. 57 and p. 67.

26. Graham-Campbell and Kidd, *Vikings*, plate 78.

circumstances clear: "Hic apprehendit VVido Haroldum et duxit eum ad Belrem" (Here Guy arrests Harold and took him to Beaurain). Harold is obviously angry and resentful. He brandishes a spear as he comes ashore and is restrained from using a knife by one of his own men.[27] He is defiant but impotent. The creature at the prow of his landing craft (fig. 3, right) may reflect this. It is certainly no dragon: it has a doglike muzzle and its ears droop. Yet its tongue sticks out defiantly.

Protruding tongues are recurrent in the Tapestry. Dragons, of course, spew flames, and if the animal-headed posts represent dragons then these tongues might be intended as fire. However, there are plenty of dragons in the borders of the Tapestry that can be usefully compared with the wooden animals. Several of those in the bottom register clearly breathe flames, but the depiction of fire there is dissimilar to these tongues. The border dragons exhale flames like rays (fig. 4) or as long, forked (fig. 5) or tripled (fig. 6) projections colored red or yellow. Although one might account for the difference in depiction by the fact that the border dragons are "alive" whereas the animal terminals are meant to be wooden and solid enough to withstand the elements, it is undeniable that the projections of the figureheads, which resemble the characteristic Ringerike style lobed tendrils, are short and fleshy, resembling tongues rather than flames. Their color offers no guidance: some are red, some yellow, and some, like Harold's landing craft beast (fig. 3), an unnatural green.

Projecting tongues have often been used on grotesques in art, going back to ancient Greek pottery on which Gorgons and grotesque masks were depicted thus.[28] Linguiform projections certainly feature in Anglo-Saxon and Scandinavian zoomorphic art, for example in a confusion of tongue and tendril on a grotesque from an eighth-century pin suite found in the River Witham at Fiskerton, Lincolnshire (fig. 7), and in the "great beasts" of the Ringerike style, as manifested on a slab from St. Paul's churchyard, London (fig. 8). The Witham animal is probably meant to be a dragon, but other creatures may not be, and I think it is clear that tongues in Anglo-Saxon art do not necessarily signify flame; but we might question if the stuck-out tongues of the Bayeux Tapestry are purely stylistic characteristics, or whether they have any deeper significance. We will return to this issue more than once.

The figureheads considered so far, which are all fairly elaborate, fall in the first of the nine strips of linen that make up the Tapestry.[29]

27. Wilson, *Bayeux Tapestry,* 6–7. The man's short tunic proclaims that he is English, not, as is generally assumed, one of Guy's men. In the first section of the Tapestry Normans mostly wear culottes.

28. See, for example Bérnard, Vernant, et al., *Die Bilderwelt der Griechen,* p. 229, Abb. 219.

29. Wilson, *Bayeux Tapestry,* 1–15.

In the second section, which was probably the production of a different workshop, we find the ship on which Harold returns to England depicted more simply (fig. 9). It has a small animal head with a single long lappet attached to its muzzle. The beast-headed post curves sharply inward, away from the climactic and humiliating scene where Harold swears an oath of allegiance to Duke William at Bayeux. The animal's mouth is open as if it is crying out, in keeping with the frenzied activity of Harold's sailors. It is perhaps significant that this ship comes home tail first,[30] as Harold returns to face a reproving king with his shoulders hunched abjectly and his physical distance from the monarch very noticeable (fig. 10). From the arrival at Bayeux through to Harold's reception by Edward and beyond, there are animals, which are not dragons, in the bottom border with extended tongues. The borders also feature birds and dragons biting their own wings, animals biting their tails, and birds hiding their heads. If there is anything to be read in this, it is shame and anguish for Harold; his homebound ship seems to represent the same emotions.

In the third strip of linen the animal heads are all fairly simple, and similar to one another. Each has a small pair of ears, but they lack Ringerike curls or lappets. Possibly this restraint reflects the house style of one particular workshop, but it may correspond to the fact that these ships do not carry any of the principal figures or feature in a major event. The vessel of the messenger who takes to Normandy the information that Harold is crowned king of England, and has thus betrayed his oath to William, has two forward-facing animals, both with long tongues, suggesting the eagerness of the messenger to tell his news (fig. 11). The ships of the invasion fleet under construction have no animal heads, but two vessels being launched have uncomplicated beast terminals, one openmouthed, the other with a protruding tongue.[31] The faces of the animals are uplifted, positive.

The fourth strip of linen begins with the embarkation of the Norman army, and the ships of the invasion fleet are clearly and elaborately delineated. There are heads on six of the ships that broadly resemble those found in the first strip of linen, but there are no exact parallels since the size, detail, and direction of curling tendrils provide variety. All are different: the first creature, with a bird's beak, mammalian ears, and a mane of Ringerike curls, is perhaps a griffin.[32] There is a simpler

30. Perhaps the ship was depicted backward because the inscription above says "reversus est," possibly as a witticism. The full inscription for the scene reads "hic harold dux reversus est ad anglicam terram," but it is very disjointed because it has to fit round the yard of the ship and the harbor building, so the phrase could easily have been taken out of context.

31. Wilson, *Bayeux Tapestry*, 37.

32. Wilson, *Bayeux Tapestry*, 40.

beaked creature,[33] several grotesques with Ringerike tendrils and protruding tongues,[34] a bearded man at the prow of a ship that ends in an
animal's tail,[35] and, on the Ducal ship, a near-full-length figure of a male
with a horn and flag.[36] This is surely meant to be a carving, not a Norman
sailor dangerously perched, because of the Ringerike tendrils round tunic
and head, the hair of "real" human beings in the Tapestry never being
depicted in this way. The horses are disembarked from a boat that has
been poled in stern first—perhaps this was the correct way to approach
land after all—and the animal figurehead at the prow is turned to face
them and the new land to be conquered (fig. 4). With its open mouth and
widely spread tendrils, it exudes enthusiasm and animation, suggestive
body language in a creature that is an image of an image, an embroidered
picture of a wooden ornament.

The animal heads on the ships are—usually—larger than the heads
of the men who man them and in most cases they stand out, tall against
the linen backcloth, giving personality to the ships. Their anthropomor-
phism conveys the emotions of their passengers: expectation, surprise,
embarrassment, eagerness to impart news, and finally, enthusiasm for the
imminent conquest.

FURNITURE

We have good evidence for the existence of animal-headed seats in
both Anglo-Saxon and Viking contexts. They can be found in manuscript
illuminations, often very stylized, from the eighth century (fig. 12), reap-
pearing with variations in the Old English Hexateuch (BL, Cotton Claudius B. iv, fol. 27v) and Tiberius calendar (London, British Library, MS

33. Wilson, *Bayeux Tapestry*, 42.
34. Wilson, *Bayeux Tapestry*, 41, 42, 43.
35. Wilson, *Bayeux Tapestry*, 41.
36. Wilson, *Bayeux Tapestry*, 42. Simone Bertrand identifies the figure as that of a
child, adding "une charmante tradition affirme qu'il fut sculpté à l'image du jeune fils du
duc, Guillaume le Roux" (*La Tapisserie de Bayeux*, p. 299). She does not indicate the source
of the tradition. The image corresponds in some respects to a description of the figurehead of a child blowing a horn on the *Mora*, the ship given to Duke William by his wife
Matilda, as described in a twelfth-century manuscript (Van Houts, "Ship List of William
the Conqueror," p. 166, and "Echo of the Conquest in the Latin Sources," esp. pp. 149–53).
However, without this external evidence the figure would probably not be identified as a
child. Recognition of children in medieval art works is problematic, since the distinctive
proportions of head to body had not yet been recognized. Children are only identifiable by
their relative size and even this is not always self-evident. Compare the small figures carrying bells who are depicted beneath the bier at Edward's funeral (Wilson, *Bayeux Tapestry*,
29), who could represent children or acolytes, or alternatively might represent adult figures
of lesser importance, fitted into the design where there is a space.

Cotton Tiberius B. v, fol. 4v). On an Anglo-Viking sculpture from Old Malton, near York (fig. 13), beast heads on either side of a human head indicate a chair; traces of color remain on the collar of one of the creatures, showing that it was originally painted. The remains of gilding on a wooden zoomorphic finial from Viking Dublin (fig. 14) likewise testify to the splendor of the chair it once decorated. Five wooden posts with animal-head terminals, which may derive from furniture survived from the ninth-century Oseberg ship burial,[37] and others have been recovered from later Scandinavian context.[38] There are stone examples from Monkwearmouth, County Durham, and Lastingham, North Yorkshire.[39]

The opening scene of the Tapestry (fig. 15) shows King Edward the Confessor on a lion-headed bench. The lion, with its upturned face, mane, and foot, is readable as an image of kingly authority and grandeur, a message conveyed also by the crown and scepter, the elaborate building, and the border animals, which include several more lions and preening birds. In contrast, the seat from which King Edward receives Harold on his return two years later has no lions (fig. 10). It is lower and its animal heads, level with the seat and horizontal instead of inclined, look like angry wolves. The change in the king's bench may result from the stylistic difference of the second embroidery workshop. However, when we note that the king himself has here deteriorated into old age, his scepter replaced by a walking stick and his beard and mustache lacking the elaborate grooming of the earlier depiction, it is tempting to see the transformation of his seat as a reflection of his decline.

The first bench we encounter during Harold's adventures on the Continent is that of Guy of Pontieu, who, as I have argued elsewhere,[40] is a little man who wants to be big. The Tapestry indicates that though he captures Harold, he is himself intimidated by Duke William, eventually being given a classic put-down on a horse with the mane and ears of a donkey. When Guy sits on a chair it has small, mute canine heads.[41] He has no canopy over him and no cushion, though he is two steps high and is accompanied by border lions and preening birds. While the latter reflect Guy's pretensions to grandeur, the animal heads suggest he has no voice and little power.

Duke William sits on a very similar bench as he primes his messengers to take Guy's prisoner Harold away from him,[42] but the animals' mouths

37. Graham-Campbell and Kidd, *Vikings*, p. 29. One of the posts is illustrated in Wilson, *Vikings and Their Origins*, p. 118, fig. 88.

38. Wilson, *Bayeux Tapestry*, p. 229 n. 65, cites Brøgger, Falk, Gustavson, and Schetelig, *Osebergfundet*, vol. 2, figs. 26–28 (Oseberg) and 56–63 (later examples).

39. Both are illustrated and discussed in Webster and Backhouse, *Making of England*, pp. 151–52, figs. 111, 112.

40. See Owen-Crocker, "Telling a Tale," pp. 54–55.

41. Wilson, *Bayeux Tapestry*, 10.

42. Wilson, *Bayeux Tapestry*, 13.

are open here, probably reflecting William's urgent spoken instructions. It may be no coincidence that the creatures are of similar size and proportion to the hunting dogs that are enjoying the chase in the lower border, as William is, of course, sending his messengers to flush out Harold. Border and bench thus work together to reinforce the meaning of the scene, that the duke is hunting his rival.

These animal-headed benches, variously depicting lions, wolves, and dogs, occur in the first strip of linen, and the type reoccurs in the third strip (below, p. 117). The second section of cloth, uniquely, depicts a different kind of seat, which has a single upstanding post with an animal-head terminal. There is a chair with a similar post in the Hexateuch that may have inspired the Bayeux examples.[43] A tiny figure in the upper border of the Tapestry, gesturing toward the Abbey of Mont-Saint-Michel, sits on a bench of this type,[44] and it is on a similar chair that William sits as he holds discussions with Harold in his palace at Rouen (fig. 6). A small animal head, strikingly executed in navy blue and yellow—quite unusual at this point in the Tapestry—perches like a glove puppet on the high post (fig. 16). This comes near the beginning of the section of linen where the embroiderers went to considerable length to elaborate items such as the cushions, garters, and brickwork, and this deliberate complexity may account for the detail on the animal head. The contrasting lines of stem stitch embroidery make the creature appear bridled, like the nearby horses, but it has a canine appearance and a clawed foot. With its open mouth and pricked ear it shares the animation of the human debaters; but it is the one head in this scene that does not turn in to the discussion. Perhaps the creature is more interested in the dogs outside, looking out to them as the gatekeeper looks out to the approaching riders. If it represents a fox, it may have a particular interest in hounds. If this suggestion is correct, the interaction between fox and hounds is a subordinate discourse in counterpoint to both the linear time-scheme of the narrative and the Tapestry's well-established principle of unity of place (here marked by the entrance tower): the hounds accompany Harold and William to the palace as the Latin caption makes clear; the conference takes place later, inside the palace. Interaction between animate and inanimate beasts is not unique to the Tapestry: the animal-headed ship in MS Harley 603, folio 51v (fig. 1) confronts a waterfowl.[45]

43. BL, Cotton Claudius B. iv, fol. 27v. The similarity is noted in Dodwell and Clemoes, *Old English Illustrated Hexateuch*, p. 72. The Hexateuch seat, however, is of the folding type, not a solid bench.

44. Wilson, *Bayeux Tapestry*, 19.

45. This may have been Anglo-Saxon wit. The Utrecht Psalter (Utrecht, Universiteitsbibliotheek, MS 32, fol. 59v) which is the source for BL, Harley 603, fol. 51v, depicts the same actors, but there is no interaction between them. The two illustrations are conveniently printed *en face* in Bernstein, *Mystery of the Bayeux Tapestry*, pp. 64–65.

The human faces in the Tapestry are almost expressionless—emotions are conveyed by posture and gesture. It is worth saying that it is difficult to achieve a satisfactory expression on a face in needlework. Though the embroidery wool is intrinsically flexible, the fact that every stitch is necessarily straight, however tiny, makes for rigidity in the image depicted. The choice of whether the needle is plunged in on one side or the other of a thread in the linen cloth may make considerable difference to the effect. We might bear this in mind as we consider Duke William's seat at Harold's oath taking (fig. 17). This is a triumphant moment for William. His bench on this occasion is awkwardly drawn, and largely concealed, but hints at grandeur. It has two areas of decoration—more than Edward's—as well as a cushion, and it is four steps high. There are two clawed feet. The animal head, slightly elevated and viewed at three-quarter angle instead of the usual profile, is outlined in stem stitch but not filled in with couched color.[46] Despite its minimalism, it has a complacent look that could be coincidental but would be appropriate as an indicator of William's feelings at this moment.

The throne on which Harold is crowned king of England has knobs rather than animal finials,[47] but in the twin scene that follows, where the sight of Halley's comet in the upper border provokes terror of an invasion fleet (seen in outline in the bottom border), the emotion is expressed in squawking birds' heads on the back of the king's chair (fig. 18). The birds and the chair itself are skewed, like the body of Harold, as, with spear replacing scepter and orb, he faces the possibility of losing the throne so recently gained. The impact of the birds on the throne is reinforced by the presence of birds on the roof of the building, again with open beaks; perhaps they prophecy doom for Harold.

The benches on which William and Odo sit to plan the invasion have beast terminals with the same kind of alert foxy faces as William's navy and yellow beast.[48] They are more naturalistic than any of the other furniture animals because the curved ends of the seats convey a sense of the animals' chests, leading to the legs and feet (a simple version of the kind of zoomorphic bench in the calendar in BL, Cotton Tiberius B. v, fol. 4v).

There is one other item of animal-headed furniture: King Edward's bed (fig. 19). There is what may be an animal-headed bed in the Hexateuch,[49]

46. The animal head on the adjacent building is treated the same way (see p. 119). Both may be unfinished or the linear technique may be deliberate; human faces are of course depicted this way.

47. Wilson, *Bayeux Tapestry*, 31.

48. Wilson, *Bayeux Tapestry*, 34–35.

49. BL, Cotton Claudius B. iv, fol. 55r. Dodwell identifies the piece of furniture as a bed and demonstrates the resemblance of the animal head and draped curtain to King Edward's bed in the Tapestry (Dodwell and Clemoes, *Old English Illustrated Hexateuch*, p.

which might have been the model for this one, but as there were beast finials on a bed found in the Oseberg ship[50] this must have been an authentic
type of furniture, not just artistic convention. The beast on Edward's bedpost, with its upward-turned, open mouth and long tongue, might be wail-
ing, like the adjacent figure of the soon-to-be-widowed queen, but it also
has spatial function. The artist at this point adopted the unusual device of
dividing the main register into upper and lower zones, probably adapting
both the deathbed scene above and the shrouding scene beneath it from
(independent) conventional illustrations of biblical or apocryphal scenes.[51]
The lower zone needed extra width for attendants at the head and foot
of the corpse, and the building that contains both scenes is designed to
accommodate it. The deathbed features a tight group of people facing
inward, leaving an empty space to the left. The animal on the bedpost
helps to fill this space, and like William's foxy animal earlier, it looks out
of the scene, in this case to Edward's funeral procession.[52]

---

72 and plate XI). The Hexateuch scene shows Judah with Shuah and their three sons. However, this would be an unusual way of indicating procreation. The couple are upright, as if
behind the piece of furniture, and wear clothes. Elsewhere in the Hexateuch, sexual activity
is indicated by a couple lying side by side, wrapped up, in bed, and birth by the presence
of a swaddled baby.

50. Wilson, *Bayeux Tapestry*, p. 218, fig. 12. The animal heads have projecting tongues.

51. The deathbed scene may have been reversed. The head of the dying person is
usually to the left. The death of the Virgin in the Benedictional of St. Æthelwold (London,
British Library, MS Additional 49598, fol. 102v, which is itself an echo of the Nativity in
the same manuscript; see Deshman, *Benedictional of St Æthelwold*, p. 134) provides general
parallels to Edward's deathbed scene in the position of the propped up figure, the pillow,
the weeping woman at the foot of the bed, the position of other figures (excluding Harold),
and the prominence of hands, though the exact gestures are not duplicated. Wilson (*Bayeux
Tapestry*, p. 219) claims the wrapping of a corpse is "formulaic in manuscripts." The shrouding of Mahalalel in the Hexateuch (BL, Cotton Claudius B. iv, fol. 11r; Genesis 5:17), with a
pillow and the suggestion of rich textile (on the bed?) is the closest parallel among several
conventional shrouding scenes in this manuscript, particularly at fols. 10v–12v, which chart
the lives and deaths of Adam and Eve's descendants. The Bayeux artist's choice of Mahalalel as a model for the saintly King Edward might have been motivated by knowledge of a
(false) etymology whereby "Mahalalel" was interpreted as "praiser of God." The etymologi-
cally suggested significance of the name is offered by Gollancz in his introduction to the
facsimile edition of Oxford, Bodleian Library, MS Junius 11, in which Mahalalel appears (at
p. 58) in *orans* position before an altar, an iconography not suggested by the surrounding
text (the Old English poem *Genesis A*); see Gollancz, *Cædmon Manuscript of Anglo-Saxon Biblical Poetry*, pp. xliii, 58. See also Kelley Wickham-Crowley's discussion of Edward's deathbed scene, and of shrouding in general, in this volume.

52. The funeral processes from right to left, from the deathbed/shrouding scene to
Westminster Abbey.

ARCHITECTURE

There are only four architectural beast heads in the Tapestry, which is perhaps surprising since it depicts many buildings and there is considerable corroboration that architectural decoration of this kind existed. There is evidence of decorated woodwork on Insular and Viking buildings,[53] and animal heads are depicted, for example, on an eighth- or ninth-century, house-shaped reliquary casket from Scotland,[54] on a painting of the temple in the Book of Kells (Dublin, Trinity College Library, MS 58, fol. 202v),[55] and on the gable ends of hogback tombstones.[56] The Anglo-Saxon church of St. Mary at Deerhurst, Gloucestershire, has stone beast heads at the ends of hood moldings over both exterior doorways and the original chancel arch as well as *prokrossoi* (projecting animal heads) over three doorways.[57] There are similar *prokrossoi* over windows at Barnack, Northamptonshire, and Alkborough, Lincolnshire.[58] Wooden, animal-headed gables can be found on stave churches at Borgund and Lom, Norway, both twelfth-century buildings but perhaps preserving an older architectural tradition.[59]

An unobtrusive animal gapes down at the party arriving at Bayeux,[60] and there is another on the building at the unidentified English port to which Harold returns from Normandy (fig. 9). The building seems to be actually in the water.[61] There are a lookout on the balcony and four faces at the windows. The beast, which is neither a hood molding nor a gable end, but more like a *prokrossos,* also looks out to sea, and like King Edward's bedpost adds a little fill to the empty space. With its beak-shaped mouth it looks severe, which would be in keeping with the general interpretation that Harold has done badly in his encounters abroad. The beast has horns, like a snail, and perhaps there is the implication that Harold has

53. Karkov, "Decoration of Early Wooden Architecture."

54. Graham-Campbell and Kidd, *Vikings*, p. 34 and plate 12. The casket was preserved in Norway and is now in Copenhagen, Denmark.

55. P. Brown, *Book of Kells*, plate 36.

56. Lang, "The Hogback."

57. Taylor and Taylor, *Anglo-Saxon Architecture*, 1:193–209. The chancel arch beasts still bear traces of color (ibid., p. 199).

58. The comparison is made by Taylor and Taylor, *Anglo-Saxon Architecture*, 1:194. Barnack is described at pp. 43–47 and Alkborough at pp. 23–24.

59. Blindheim, *Norwegian Romanesque Decorative Sculpture*, p. 32, figs. 95–96 (Borgund; a late medieval copy), 97–98 (Lom).

60. Wilson, *Bayeux Tapestry*, 25. See note 46.

61. Bertrand relates the animal head to the function of the structure it ornaments: "un embarcadère orné comme un navire, d'une curieuse figure de proue" (*La Tapisserie de Bayeux*, p. 273).

been very slow to return (he had been away for over a year);[62] but possibly the artist intended a simple version of the lobed Ringerike tendrils we have seen elsewhere and failed to delineate this clearly in the cartoon, which was accordingly mutilated by the embroiderer.

The other two architectural beast terminals appear together in the famous and controversial scene cryptically labeled "ubi unus clericus et Ælfgyva" (fig. 6). The animal heads are again used for spatial effect here: it is unusual in the Tapestry to find two adjacent architectural structures as we have at this point, and, like King Edward's bedpost, the beasts add interest to an awkward empty area; but it is necessary to consider whether they have any other significance.

In order to investigate this question it is desirable to consider the beasts in relation to the whole of the Ælfgyva scene, and its context as a subscene to the debate in the palace. I do not have a definitive answer to the problem of Ælfgyva's identity, but I have noted a number of parallels in manuscripts, of the kind that Francis Wormald called "quotations,"[63] that enable us to "read" something of the scene's significance.

I do not think the beasts in the Ælfgyva scene are dragons breathing flame, though the fact that there are two dragons doing just that in the bottom border may be a signifier;[64] but the frequency of lobed tongues in Ringerike style animal ornament seems to me sufficient to claim these as stylistic. The tongues are very prominent here, and one function of them may be to direct us to the humans who are engaged in animated conversation. The Anglo-Saxons recognized that the tongue was the instrument of slander: cutting off of the tongue was a legal punishment for this crime.[65] It seems very likely that William and Harold are slandering Ælfgyva, if we take up the sexual hints in the lower border.[66] The two men may well be quarreling: the upper border shows two beasts apparently having a tug of war or punching one another with heads averted, as well as birds with raised wings back-to-back. There are also two peacocks, remarkable for

62. That the snail was already a byword for slowness in Anglo-Saxon times is clear from its use in Exeter Book Riddle 40 ("Creation"): "me is snægl swiftra, snelra regnwyrm / ond fenyce fore hreþre"; Dobbie, *Exeter Book,* p. 202, lines 70–71 (the snail is swifter, the earthworm quicker, and the fen-frog more rapid in its going than me).

63. F. Wormald identified specific instances in Canterbury manuscripts: "Style and Design," pp. 30–33. "Quotation" is discussed by Bernstein (*Mystery of the Bayeux Tapestry,* pp. 39–50) and by Dodwell in his introduction to Dodwell and Clemoes, *Old English Illustrated Hexateuch.* (See also below, note 79.) I have identified other possible examples (see notes 2, 76 and Lasko, "Bayeux Tapestry and the Representation of Space," p. 38 n. 5).

64. It may signal, for example, that emotions were heated over the matter depicted above.

65. Alfred 32; Liebermann, *Die Gesetze der Angelsachsen,* 1:66.

66. McNulty, *Narrative Art of the Bayeux Tapestry Master,* pp. 52–58.

being the only instance of these creatures in the upper border.[67] Instead of being placed in the mirror-image relationship that is usual for paired border creatures, the peacocks faintly mimic the positions of the men beneath them, also duplicating the colors of their costumes.[68] If the modern connotation of "proud as a peacock" was already attached to these birds, their presence may imply arrogance in the human protagonists. The tongue pulling of the beast heads above Ælfgyva could be a reaction to that arrogance or, since the animals are back-to-back, a comment on the men's intransigent attitude to one another.

The beast heads are at the corners of a frame. Wilson compared this structure to the frames of the illuminations in Winchester School manuscripts and the placing of Ælfgyva specifically to the representation of St. Æthelthryth in the Benedictional of St. Æthelwold (London, British Library, MS Additional 49598, fol. 90v),[69] but this is a misleading generalization because the Bayeux structure is neither arched like the characteristic architectural frames of illuminations nor covered in acanthus like the rectangular ones. Inhabited frames are relatively uncommon in surviving late Anglo-Saxon manuscripts, and I have found no close parallels.[70] Ælfgyva's structure is not a true frame; there are stepped pillars at the sides, and there is no base. The architecture suggests, rather, the posts and lintel of a doorframe. Doorframes are common in late Anglo-Saxon art, though they are usually associated with buildings.[71] They often have figures framed in them, usually seated. Beast heads, however, are not a regular feature of doorframes, and the animals above Ælfgyva are probably the least authentic wooden zoomorphs in the Tapestry. They are perhaps inspired by the beast heads that decorated illuminated initials in late Anglo-Saxon manuscripts. The closest parallel I have found is in the beasts whose tongues spew the letter B in the opening words (*Beatus vir*) of the Harley Psalter, folio 2r (fig. 20).

67. There is a less colorful pair in the lower border as the Normans advance, on horseback, "viriliter et sapienter," to battle (Wilson, *Bayeux Tapestry,* 58). Border birds are discussed in detail in Owen-Crocker, "Squawk Talk."

68. William and the left-hand bird are in navy blue, yellow, and pink; Harold and the right-hand bird in green, pink, and yellow. I am grateful to Richard Crocker for this observation.

69. Wilson, *Bayeux Tapestry,* pp. 178–79.

70. There are inhabited frames in the Galba Psalter (London, British Library, MS Cotton Galba A. xviii), but they are dissimilar: at fol. 2v a beast bites at each of the four corners; at fol. 10v beasts project from the bottom corners; at fol. 11v two beasts spring from the center top toward the corners (Ohlgren, *Anglo-Saxon Textual Illustration,* pp. 129, 137–38). In Bodl. Lib. Junius 11, p. 51, there are beast heads at the upper corners of the frame but they are full face and do not project (ibid., p. 551).

71. The doors themselves are sometimes included, but often omitted. Frequently there are curtains, which drape round the pillars. A simple lintel of the Bayeux kind is unusual, and there is usually a triangular architrave or an arch.

The Bayeux doorframe may simply be an indicator that the woman
is either in another room in William's palace (that is, a different location
from the scene of William's discussion with Harold) or in another building
altogether, but the dislocation of Ælfgyva's frame from any other architecture, its unusual zoomorphic decoration, and the fact that she stands
(rather than sits) within, or behind, it may be significant. Both the Anglo-
Saxons and the Vikings seem to have used a freestanding framework of
this kind as a symbolic portal into another dimension. The Arab observer
Ibn Fadlan recorded that a construction "like a door-frame" was used in
the sacrificial ritual associated with the funeral of a Viking chief. The
slave girl about to be sacrificed first looked over the frame three times and
claimed to see her parents and kinsmen and her dead master in Paradise,
before being killed to join her master.[72] There is a graphic use of such a
frame, this time with a stout door attached, in Bodl. Lib. Junius 11, p. 46,
as an angel ushers Adam and Eve out of the Garden of Eden. The angel
stands in the doorway; Adam and Eve are exiled and outside it (fig. 21).

Perhaps Ælfgyva is depicted in a doorframe because at the time of the
discussion she was in a different dimension in that she was no longer living; and if the lady under discussion was either Ælfgyva of Northampton,
Cnut's mistress, or Ælfgyva-Emma, Cnut's queen, she was certainly dead
by this time.[73] The cupping gesture that the *clericus* makes toward her
face[74] may be seen as a metaphorical "raising up" of Ælfgyva: it resembles
the gesture of a man (not Christ) who draws the risen Lazarus from his
sepulcher in the St. Augustine Gospels (Cambridge, Corpus Christi College, MS 286, fol. 125r; fig. 22) and the cupping of God's hand round
the face of a man in the Paris Psalter (Paris, Bibliothèque nationale de
France, MS lat. 8824, fol. 2v), where the Old English text reads "Drihten
me awehte, and me upp arærde" (the Lord awoke me and raised me up:
Psalm 3:4).[75] The unusual tower to the right of the Ælfgyva scene[76] may
contribute to this interpretation since it bears some resemblance to the

72. Quoted in translation in Owen, *Rites and Religions of the Anglo-Saxons*, pp. 99–100.
73. Either woman might have been mentioned in a dynastic discussion. Both were the
mothers of Cnut's sons. Emma was also mother of Æthelred's son, now King Edward the
Confessor, as well as Duke William's aunt.
74. Sometimes interpreted as a sexual gesture relating the role of the *clericus* to the
naked male figure in the bottom border (Bernstein, *Mystery of the Bayeux Tapestry*, p. 19). For
a contrasting view, that Ælfgyva is not only alive but the embodiment of virtue and that the
clericus gestures toward a bridal veil, see D. Hill, "Bayeux Tapestry and Its Commentators."
75. Ohlgren, *Anglo-Saxon Textual Illustration*, pp. 50, 299.
76. The structure graphically balances the tower on which a watchman stands as the
party of riders approaches William's palace. The watchman's building is clearly intended
as part of the architecture of Rouen: windows, brickwork, staircase towers, and a door are

aedicula of Lazarus[77] in the St. Augustine Gospels (fig. 22) and to the sepulcher of Christ in the Harley Psalter (BL, Harley 603, fol. 8r; fig. 23).[78] Both of these were Canterbury manuscripts the Tapestry designer almost certainly knew.[79] There is, then, very probably some reference to resurrection iconography here, though Ælfgyva is dressed in clothes, as if alive, and not in a winding sheet. Developing David Hill's suggestion that the figure of Ælfgyva herself derives from one of the personified Virtues in a Canterbury manuscript of Prudentius's *Psychomachia* (London, British Library, MS Cotton Cleopatra C. viii),[80] we can find a close parallel in the depiction of *Spes* (Hope), on folio 17r (fig. 24).[81] As the Virtue *Humilitas* (Humility) shows the severed head of the defeated Vice *Superbia* (Pride) to *Spes*, *Spes* denounces pride,[82] making with her right hand what C. R. Dodwell has identified as a well-established variety of a traditional gesture of approval.[83] The embroidered right hand of Ælfgyva, unusually clumsy-looking among the hands in the Tapestry, may be the result of an attempt to copy in needlework this gesture, in which the middle finger makes an incomplete circle with the thumb, leaving the index finger extended. The

delineated. The building beside the Ælfgyva scene is of similar, but not identical, shape, and it could, conceivably, also represent the entrance tower, perhaps a back view of it; but the subdivisions of the structure have been differently interpreted by the embroiderer and it seems to have a different kind of entrance, rectangular double doors like Lazarus's tomb in the St. Augustine Gospels (see fig. 22).

77. This small Roman sepulcher had been the conventional realization of Lazarus's tomb since the earliest-known (fourth-century) depictions of the scene, though the biblical account (John 11:38) specifies a cave. See Schiller, *Iconography of Christian Art,* 1:182.

78. The sepulcher of Christ is elsewhere shown as a single-story apse attached to a building or buildings with pitched roofs, as in BL, Harley 603, fol. 71v (Ohlgren, *Anglo-Saxon Textual Illustration,* p. 243) and the Sacramentary of Robert of Jumièges (Rouen, Bibliothèque Municipale, MS Y 6 [274], fol. 72v); J. Alexander, "Some Aesthetic Principles," plate VIII.

79. See note 63. The scene of William's feast at Hastings is copied from a depiction of The Last Supper, which is on the same folio as the Lazarus scene in the St. Augustine Gospels, a sixth-century, Late Antique manuscript believed to have come to Canterbury with the Roman mission at the end of the sixth century. A figure bringing in provisions for the feast at Hastings is copied from a personification of *Labor* in a Canterbury copy of Prudentius's allegorical poem *Psychomachia,* now London, British Library, MS Cotton Cleopatra C. viii. BL Harley 603 is a copy made about 1000, probably in Canterbury, of the ninth-century, Carolingian Utrecht Psalter (Utrecht, Universiteitsbibliotheek, MS 32).

80. D. Hill, "Bayeux Tapestry and Its Commentators," p. 26.

81. The positions of the hands and feet are closer to Ælfgyva's than those in Hill's drawing, which is taken from *Patientia* (Patience) on fol. 12r, reversed (pers. comm., David Hill).

82. "Desine grande loqui; frangit Deus omne superbum" (An end to thy big talk. God breaks down all arrogance); Prudentius, *Prudentius,* 1:298–99; see Ohlgren, *Anglo-Saxon Textual Illustrations,* p. 81.

83. Dodwell, *Anglo-Saxon Gestures and the Roman Stage,* pp. 61–65, 122–29, plates XLIIa–XLVb.

Figure 1. London, British Library, MS Harley 603, folio 51v, detail. Animal-headed ships confront a sea-bird. Drawn by the author.

Figure 2. Detail from the Bayeux Tapestry, eleventh century. Harold sets off in a ship with an interlaced beast head and a human head. By special permission of the City of Bayeux.

Figure 3. Detail from the Bayeux Tapestry, eleventh century. Left, the second depiction of Harold's ship; right, Harold's landing craft, headed by a droop-eared animal with protruding tongue. By special permission of the City of Bayeux.

Figure 4. Detail from the Bayeux Tapestry, eleventh century. William's invasion fleet arrives. Eager horses disembark from a ship with an eager animal head. Lower border: dragons breathe flames like rays. By special permission of the City of Bayeux.

Figure 5. The Bayeux Tapestry. A border dragon breathes forked flames. Drawn by the author after Wilson.

Figure 6. Detail from the Bayeux Tapestry, eleventh century. Arrival at Rouen, with hounds; discussion between William and Harold; Ælfgyva. Upper border: peacocks and quarreling beasts; lower border: sexual innuendo and (right) dragons breathing triple flames. By special permission of the City of Bayeux.

Figure 7. Beast on one of a set of eighth-century pins found in the River Witham. Drawn by the author.

Figure 8. Ringerike style beast on an eleventh-century stone carving from St. Paul's, London. Drawn by the author.

Figure 9. Detail from the Bayeux Tapestry, eleventh century. Harold's ship returns to England, tail first; a severe-looking animal gazes out from the port. Lower border: beasts bite their tails, birds bite their wings. By special permission of the City of Bayeux.

Figure 10. Detail from the Bayeux Tapestry, eleventh century. Harold returns, abject, to an aged King Edward on a wolf-headed seat. Lower border: birds bite their wings; animals stick out their tongues. By special permission of the City of Bayeux.

Figure 11. The Bayeux Tapestry. Eager beast heads on the messenger's ship. Drawn by the author after Wilson.

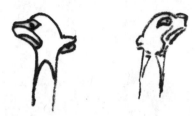

Figure 12. Lichfield Cathedral, MS *sine numero,* p. 218. Animal finials from St. Luke's chair. Drawn by the author.

Figure 13. Fragment of stone carving from Old Malton, near York. Man's head and finials of a chair. Drawn by the author.

Figure 14. Two sides of a wooden chair finial from Dublin. Drawn by the author.

Figure 15. Detail from the Bayeux Tapestry, eleventh century. King Edward on a lion-headed bench. Borders: lions and preening birds. By special permission of the City of Bayeux.

Figure 16. Detail of Figure 6. The beast head on William's seat at Rouen.

Figure 17. The Bayeux Tapestry. The beast head on William's seat at Bayeux. Drawn by the author after Wilson.

Figure 18. Detail from the Bayeux Tapestry, eleventh century. Disaster anticipated for King Harold, on a bird-headed throne. Upper border: Halley's comet and birds on the roof; lower border: the outlines of ships. By special permission of the City of Bayeux.

Figure 19. Detail from the Bayeux Tapestry, eleventh century. King Edward's deathbed. By special permission of the City of Bayeux.

Figure 20. London, British Library, MS Harley 603, folio 2r. Illuminated initial. Drawn by the author.

Figure 21. Oxford, Bodleian Library, MS Junius 11, p. 46. Adam and Eve leave the Garden of Eden by a doorway. Drawn by the author.

Figure 22. Cambridge, Corpus Christi College, MS 286, folio 125r, detail. Lazarus is drawn from his sepulcher. Drawn by the author.

Figure 23. London, British Library, MS Harley 603, folio 8r, detail. The sepulcher of Christ. Drawing by the author.

Figure 24. London, British Library, MS Cotton Cleopatra C. viii, folio 17r, detail. *Spes* (Hope) from Prudentius's *Psychomachia*. Drawn by the author.

gesture, which is not used elsewhere in the Tapestry, may have been distorted in transmission. The interesting question is whether the designer took over anything of the significance of this scene as he may have done when he copied the figure personifying *Labor* on folio 30r of the same manuscript.[84] The context is that *Spes* and *Humilitas* have triumphed in a long struggle against *Superbia,* depicted in a series of eleven illustrations including the decapitation of the Vice by *Humilitas* wielding a sword of vengeance and culminating in the ascension of *Spes* to Heaven. If we add the context of the borrowed figure-drawing to Bayeux's border peacocks we can deduce that there has been a situation (in the debate between William and Harold) where pride was exhibited, but this has been defeated. Possibly the deceased Ælfgyva has been vindicated. The situation is hopeful. In the immediate context of the Tapestry the sequel is indeed positive—William and Harold ride off to campaign as allies.

My interpretation of the scene is that Ælfgyva is being metaphorically resurrected in the conversation about her. The *clericus* is probably not a real actor in the drama, just a graphic convenience to draw Ælfgyva forward. The writer of the caption was perhaps unable to describe this action (either because he did not understand the nonliteral nature of it, or because it was too complex for brevity) and resorted to merely naming the protagonist and *unus clericus* without a defining verb. The animals on Ælfgyva's doorframe are not realistic architectural features, and the dislocated structure they decorate is symbolic not naturalistic. It is the function of the beast-heads, in conjunction with the border figures and animals, to indicate to us that the adjacent conversation was slanderous and quarrelsome and, possibly, that the humans were being slightly absurd.

CONCLUSION: THE PLACE AND FUNCTION OF THE BEAST-HEAD TERMINALS

The animal-headed posts all occur in the first half of the Tapestry, up to the disembarkation of the Norman troops.[85] After this, there are no more depictions of ships. When William and his brothers appear seated later in the narrative they are at temporary encampments on their cam-

84. See note 63. *Labor* (Suffering) is ostensibly transformed into labor (hard work). However, the artist's derivation of the Bayeux figure from *Labor,* an associate of the Vice *Avaritia* (Avarice) expelled along with *Metus* (Fear), *Vis* (Violence), *Scelus* (Crime), and *placitae fidei Fraus infitatrix* (Fraud that denies accepted faith), and the fact that in the *Psychomachia* this follows a sermon by *Operatio* (Good Works) on Christ's theme of "Think not of the body" and injunctions against begging (Matthew 6:24–36; 10:9–10, 29; see Thomson, *Prudentius,* 1:320–23) reflects a perception of the Norman pillagers as greedy and sinful looters, an irony only apparent to those who knew the manuscript.

85. According to my analysis of the design of the "Tapestry," the original halfway point

paign of conquest, and it may have been thought inappropriate to decorate their benches with zoomorphic terminals. There are occasional buildings, but the artist does not choose to ornament them this way. This may
mark a change of artist and/or changes in approach to the subject matter.
Many of the animal finials in the first part of the Tapestry, as I have
demonstrated, offer, it seems to me, an ironic commentary on the human
protagonists. They suggest underlying emotions and secret thoughts, and
sometimes undercut the pomposity of the major actors. The wooden creatures, therefore, like certain of the border animals, provide a witty and
potentially subversive subtext to the Tapestry's narrative. The second half
of the embroidery is not without humor: border irony is still occasionally present, and the main register exhibits both esoteric wit[86] and a new,
somewhat clownish, comedy.[87] There are of course many more horses in
the second part of the Tapestry than the first, and these to some extent
occupy the functional, ornamental, and spatial roles of the wooden animals, but the artist does not choose to anthropomorphize the horses in the
same way. Although they walk, trot, gallop, suffer injury, and fall horribly,
they appear to be obedient beasts with expressionless faces, which do not
rear, roll their eyes, or show their teeth in fear.[88] The Tapestry is designed
to suggest that, once the Norman army is mounted at Hastings, it sweeps
to victory,[89] massed and largely anonymous; and though the horses support their riders to inexorable success they do not comment on the action
in the way their wooden counterparts do. The animal-headed posts take
part in the story at earlier points where the desires and expectations of
individual men are pitted against one another; though events could have
turned out very differently, both Harold of England and Guy of Pontieu
find themselves outmaneuvered, and William of Normandy constantly
takes the initiative. The wooden animals provide a commentary on the
characters, aspirations, and disappointments of these individual protagonists. The "real" horses of the victorious battle are surprisingly "wooden"
in contrast.

---

was the Norman disembarkation; see Owen-Crocker, "Brothers, Rivals and the Geometry
of the Bayeux Tapestry."

86. See note 84.

87. The blowing of the horn in a man's ear (Wilson, *Bayeux Tapestry*, 47); two men
fighting with spades (ibid., 49).

88. This contrasts with the earlier depiction of the horses being transported across
the Channel and splashing through the shallows where their open mouths, without bits,
give them (perhaps entirely coincidental) expressions of pleasure (see, especially, Wilson,
Bayeux Tapestry, 41 and 43–44).

89. See Owen-Crocker, "Brothers, Rivals and the Geometry of the Bayeux Tapestry,"
p. 121. Although the Normans did not have the battle entirely their own way (Wilson,
Bayeux Tapestry, 65–68), obviously the outcome was known to the artist and the intended
audience of the Tapestry; the Normans are depicted as confident.

Design in the Past:
Metalwork and Textile Influences on Pre-Conquest Sculpture in England

Elizabeth Coatsworth

It would be true to say that, without the *Corpus of Anglo-Saxon Stone Sculpture,* for which I was Research Assistant from 1969 to 1979, the Manchester Medieval Textiles Project would never have gotten off the ground.[1] The former project, under Rosemary Cramp's guidance, was an unparalleled training ground in handling large bodies of material and for acquiring knowledge both of Anglo-Saxon sculpture from all areas and of comparative material, especially in ivories, manuscripts, and metalwork.[2] The latter, which essentially began in 1994 in collaboration with Gale Owen-Crocker, has revealed that the textile arts comprise a body of material hitherto largely neglected by the mainstream, as important in many respects as metalwork in its own right, and also as comparative material in relation to the other arts. It was the revelation of these close links that inspired the current essay.[3]

Anglo-Saxon Decorated Textiles: The Evidence

The Textiles Project takes the form of a catalogue of all surviving medieval textiles in the British Isles and Ireland 450–1500, with an annotated bibliography to guide the interested scholar or student through the great range of published material.[4] For the purposes of the present discussion I have drawn on the impressively large body of material from Anglo-Saxon England only. It will be obvious that the relevant material is

---

1. *Corpus of Anglo-Saxon Stone Sculpture,* vols. 1–8 are as follows: Cramp, *Durham and Northumberland;* Bailey and Cramp, *Cumberland, Westmorland and Lancashire-North-of-the-Sands;* Lang, *York and Eastern Yorkshire;* Tweddle, Biddle, and Kjølbye-Biddle, *South-East England;* Everson and Stocker, *Lincolnshire;* Lang, *Northern Yorkshire;* Cramp, *South-West England;* Coatsworth, *Western Yorkshire.*
2. Coatsworth and Pinder, *Art of the Anglo-Saxon Goldsmith.*
3. Coatsworth and Owen-Crocker, *Medieval Textiles.* The substance of this essay was given at the 35th International Congress on Medieval Studies at Western Michigan University, Kalamazoo, Michigan, May 2000, but it included some material from a companion paper given at ISAS (International Society of Anglo-Saxonists), Notre Dame, Indiana, 1999.
4. It is intended to begin publication of the material as an online catalogue.

all from decorated textiles, both embroideries and those with other forms of applied decoration; perhaps less obvious will be that it is the structures and techniques used in that decoration that are as relevant in the comparison with other arts as the depiction of patterns or iconography.

Having established this body of evidence, we can begin to examine how relevant these remains are to our understanding of the wider material culture of the Anglo-Saxons. We have a few complete textile objects or large remnants: for example, the ninth-century embroidered strips and the equally early silks and linens from Maaseik;[5] fragments of what are probably Anglo-Saxon embroidery comparable in style and date to those from Oseberg;[6] and the early tenth-century stole, maniple, and the bands called maniple 2 (which I believe are part of a secular royal dress) from the tomb of St. Cuthbert in Durham.[7] From the same tomb there is a fragment of what may be an eighth-century dalmatic, with its hem and braided edge (see below, p. 150). From the early tenth century are the charred fragments of a fine embroidered linen garment from Llangors in Powys, Wales;[8] and from a later period, and judging from its context a lower social stratum, a pouch with its roughly embroidered cross, possibly a reliquary pouch from Viking Age York.[9] From the very end of the period there is of course the largest single early medieval textile object from anywhere, the Bayeux Tapestry (or rather embroidery), in part the subject of Gale Owen-Crocker's essay in this volume.[10]

On the other hand, several thousand archaeological textiles from the British Isles survive, usually either as tiny fragments or in the rust on the back of metal objects such as those from the site of Cleatham, Humberside.[11] Among these are pieces that preserve part of their original structure, such as the piece from Sutton Hoo (below, p. 150), or the fragments from the cuff of a very early Anglo-Saxon lady's dress from Mitchell's Hill, Icklingham, Suffolk, which were found still attached to their metal wristclasps.[12] In comparing textile details with other media, fragments pre-

---

5. Budny and Tweddle, "Maaseik Embroideries"; Budny and Tweddle, "Early Medieval Textiles at Maaseik."

6. Ingstad, "Functional Textiles from the Oseberg Ship."

7. Battiscombe, *Relics of St Cuthbert*, esp. pp. 375–432; for the redesignation of the bands, sometimes described as another maniple or a girdle in the previous literature, see Coatsworth, "Embroideries from the Tomb of St. Cuthbert."

8. Granger-Taylor and Pritchard, "Fine Quality Insular Embroidery."

9. Tweddle, "Silk Reliquary Pouch in Compound Twill," plate XXVII and pp. 377–81.

10. See also S. Brown, *Bayeux Tapestry;* Grape, *Bayeux Tapestry;* Stenton, *Bayeux Tapestry;* Wilson, *Bayeux Tapestry;* Foys, *Bayeux Tapestry: Digital Edition.*

11. Coatsworth, FitzGerald, Leahy, and Owen-Crocker, "Anglo-Saxon Textiles from Cleatham."

12. G. Crowfoot, "Anglo-Saxon Tablet Weaving."

serving stitches or structure can be even more revelatory than the famous larger pieces. We know from the frequent mentions of embroideries in the documentary evidence that richly decorated textiles were valuable and highly regarded, an important part of portable wealth (as indeed they continued to be throughout the medieval period), and we would expect that importance to be reflected in various ways in those other arts and in contemporary commentary on them.[13]

The relationship between commissioner, designer, and craftsperson is as difficult to determine for the textile arts as it is for every other art of the period. There is evidence for an apparently professional embroideress recorded in Domesday Book, Leofgyth of Knook, Wiltshire, who worked for both an Anglo-Saxon king and queen and William the Conqueror's queen, Matilda.[14] As Dodwell pointed out, Matilda's will appears to point to the existence of two further professional embroiderers, one in Winchester.[15] These professionals may be distinguished from famous noblewomen and queens noted for their embroidery, such as Æthelswyth, a noblewoman who gave rich embroideries to Ely,[16] or Queen Edith, whose husband Edward the Confessor according to William of Malmesbury wore garments woven with gold which the queen had further richly embellished,[17] or Ælfflæd, second wife of Edward the Elder, whose name appears on the stole and maniple from the tomb of St. Cuthbert (see above, note 7). In the last case it is quite clear that Ælfflæd was commissioner rather than maker, and in noble and royal households it is more than likely that most of the work was executed by servants or slaves, even if these great ladies were expert needlewomen themselves. In asserting this the surviving embroideries and the descriptions of vast quantities of gold-encrusted embroidery provide their own testimony, for those that survive provide evidence for many more hours of work than could ever be accomplished by one woman, even working full time.[18]

It is interesting as well as relevant that the only evidence for a designer in Anglo-Saxon England concerns an embroidery. This is the story of St. Dunstan who was asked by a noblewoman called Æthelwynn "to design for her a stole for the divine service with various figured patterns, which she

13. Dodwell, *Anglo-Saxon Art*, esp. chap. 5.
14. Domesday Book I, 74r. See Thorn and Thorn, *Domesday Book 6*, 67:86.
15. Dodwell, *Anglo-Saxon Art*, pp. 75, 78, 227, and n. 227 on p. 268 and n. 100 on p. 327.
16. Blake, *Liber Eliensis* 2.88, p. 158.
17. William of Malmesbury, *Willelmi Malmesbiriensis Monachi De Gestis Regum Anglorum Libri Quinque*, 1:271.
18. Helen Stevens demonstrated the professional standards of execution and the commitment of time required for the Maaseik embroideries. See Stevens, "Maaseik Reconstructed."

could afterwards embellish and diversify with gold and precious stones."[19] Unfortunately this brief mention leaves unresolved the process by which the design was transmitted. In later medieval practice, artists were often designers for a whole host of crafts, from flags and bed-hangings to saddles and stage scenery, and perhaps we have to assume, though there is no direct evidence for it, that either Dunstan drew directly onto a prepared silk or linen strip, as happened later in the medieval period, or that he provided a fully worked-out design or series of motifs in some other medium that the embroiderer could transfer by tracing or pouncing onto the fabric as needed.[20] Certainly later in the Middle Ages it was quite common to find artists supplying designs for embroiderers, although the documentary evidence for this is better for Italy than England.[21]

Edges and Trimmings and the Interrelationship of the Arts

It is possible to pursue the links between textiles and other contemporary media such as metalwork and sculpture quite a long way within the pre-Conquest period, using internal evidence from the artifacts themselves. This is particularly the case when looking at the edges, borders, and trimmings of textiles. These are important both decoratively and functionally among textiles: if it can be shown that they appear as copies of textile forms in other media they can be very informative indeed both about contemporary textiles when relatively few pieces of this fragile medium actually survive and about the design relationship between the various arts.

The edges and borders of Anglo-Saxon art works have received little attention save in some very specialized instances, such as the architectural frames for canon tables in major manuscripts from the Lindisfarne Gospels (London, British Library, MS Cotton Nero D. iv) onward. They are, however, an important though underrated feature in every medium of Anglo-Saxon art: paintings, sculpture, ivories, wood, metalwork, and textiles. It is often the edges that tell us the most about the structure of an object, and when edge details are copied in other media in which they are no longer structurally necessary, they become informative as to what the Anglo-Saxons valued in art, and therefore about the relative status of the

19. *Vita S. Dunstani auct. B,* in Stubbs, *Memorials of St. Dunstan,* pp. 20–21.

20. See J. Alexander, *Medieval Illuminators and Their Methods of Work,* pp. 50–51; Cennini, *Craftsman's Handbook,* pp. 3–4, 84–85. See also Coatsworth and Pinder, *Art of the Anglo-Saxon Goldsmith,* chap. 6 in which early medieval evidence for the design process is discussed. The indications of metalwork designs in Oxford, Bodleian Library, MS Junius 11, pp. 225 and 230 (ibid., plates 29 and 30) are also relevant to this discussion.

21. Staniland, *Medieval Craftsmen: Embroiderers,* pp. 19–26.

arts. Edges are also important to artists and craftsmen: they are transitions between the object and its surroundings, between different patterns and motifs, between separately made parts, or between different materials or surfaces. In the special case of skeuomorphs (that is, representations of complete objects originally in one medium by means of another), they may show something of their makers' deeper beliefs about what was spiritually or socially important. It is instructive in this connection to contrast the Anglo-Saxon period with a different era of art, that of the Gothic, in which one medium, architecture, was preeminent. Its forms were used to embellish and inform every medium, including textiles such as the early fourteenth-century Bologna Cope,[22] or to articulate a structure in another medium such as a bench or chair,[23] or as a more subtle expression of underlying structural form and geometry, as in an octagonal French royal cup.[24]

In the early medieval period neither aesthetics nor symbolism in art were discussed directly, but as Dodwell and others have shown in studies of early medieval taste, aesthetics, or artistic practice, they can sometimes be deduced from the objects themselves, and sometimes from the qualities that contemporaries praised in art. It is perhaps in the edges and borders of objects, and the way their parts are fitted together, that both aesthetic values and artistic cross-fertilization is most easily discovered. For example, Rosemary Cramp has identified a series of early, rather plain crosses from Northumbrian monastic sites and has seen some of these as representations in stone of an earlier tradition of carving crosses in wood, such as a cross with a simple incised outline from Whitby that may have enclosed a painted inscription.[25] The new stone architecture of early Northumbria also shows traces of a preexisting vernacular building tradition in wood, as Catherine Karkov has shown.[26] There is, for example, evidence of wood paneling with edge moldings from Iona. The influence of this tradition can be seen in the paneled layout of many Northumbrian crosses, with their relatively broad edge and finer inner moldings. The relationship between cycles of paintings, such as those recorded for Wearmouth and Jarrow,[27] and paneled crosses has been suggested before, but the way the panels are treated supports this hypothesis, from flat edge moldings with inscriptions on the Ruthwell Cross to the arched panels and fine inner moldings of the Bewcastle Cross.[28] A panel from Monk-

22. Staniland, *Medieval Craftsmen: Embroiderers*, plate 9.
23. See for example Mercer, *Furniture 700–1700*, plates 94–96.
24. Lightbown, *Secular Goldsmiths' Work in Medieval France*, p. 45.
25. Cramp, "Reconsideration of the Monastic Site of Whitby," esp. pp. 68–70.
26. Karkov, "Decoration of Early Wooden Architecture," esp. pp. 32–34 and fig. 2.
27. Bede, *Historia abbatum*, pp. 369–70.
28. Cassidy, *Ruthwell Cross*, plates 11–32 (Ruthwell) and 49–52 (Bewcastle).

wearmouth, which is related to the manuscript style of the Book of Durrow (Dublin, Trinity College Library, MS 57), is possibly a closure slab
from the sanctuary or an altar panel. It has multiple fine moldings that
look indicative of a fine woodworking style.[29] The fact that these edges go
on into the vocabulary of stone sculpture does not detract from the argument about their origins.

Stone architecture itself came to Anglo-Saxon England along with
Roman Christianity, and its high status in Northumbria is attested in
numerous descriptions of the building campaigns of major figures such
as St. Wilfrid,[30] in poetic accounts of buildings real and visionary, like
those in Æthelwulf's poem *De Abbatibus,* and in the importance attached
to exegesis of Solomon's Temple, especially in Bede's *De templo.* The earliest Anglo-Saxon stone architecture from sites such as Hexham or Wearmouth and Jarrow includes sculptural decoration. Yet it is not easy to show
that the new architecture itself directly influenced even the apparently
closely related art of stone sculpture, for as a source of artistic inspiration architectural motifs are unique neither to Anglo-Saxon England nor
even to the early medieval period, and in many cases it is clear that the
Anglo-Saxons were merely copying from models in which architecture
was part of the iconography. Thus paneled scenes set within the frame of
architectural colonnades, such as the panel from a possible altar frontal
from Hovingham, Yorkshire, owe a great deal to an iconographic model
that originated outside Anglo-Saxon England.[31] In this example, and in
numerous others throughout the period, the architectural setting signifies, according to context, a church or palace and is used as a shorthand
to convey either spiritual importance or rank or both. It is not necessarily
related to the influence of local or contemporary architectural styles.

In fact the influence of stone architecture on the design structure
of early Northumbrian cross-shafts of the period in which the new stone
buildings were going up seems to me to be singularly lacking. A rare
example of such influence from the south of England is the eighth- to
ninth-century cross-shaft from Codford St. Peter, Wiltshire, which is
explicitly architectural[32] and on which the edge molding takes the form
of segmented columns with stepped capitals. These in turn support
plain square-sectioned corner moldings with a truncated frieze of plant
ornament between them. Above this is an abbreviated stringcourse with
another frieze of fret above that, and there is a baluster frieze like a rail at

29. Cramp, *Durham and Northumberland,* plate 656.
30. E.g. in Eddius Stephanus, *Life of Bishop Wilfrid.*
31. See J. Hawkes, "Mary and the Cycle of Resurrection"; Lang, *York and Eastern Yorkshire,* pp. 144–48, esp. p. 148.
32. Cramp, *Studies in Anglo-Saxon Sculpture,* pp. 80–83, 89.

the foot of the panel. The friezes are familiar from surviving examples in seventh- to eighth-century churches such as Hexham, and also from the ninth-century church at Breedon in Leicestershire. The Codford St. Peter shaft is a convincing but rare example of the influence of contemporary architectural style as a high-status art, used structurally to articulate a monument in another medium.

The case for prototypes of fine metalwork for stone sculpture, on the other hand, has long been accepted. As I noted in an earlier study of the pectoral cross of St. Cuthbert, the effect of metalwork design on early Northumbrian sculpture was profound, becoming a major element of the period style.[33] There would also have been large-scale examples of jeweled metalwork crosses, as we know from a picture and a small fragment of a great standing garnet and gold altar cross reputedly made by the great seventh-century Frankish goldsmith Eligius.[34] The eighth-century Anglo-Saxon cross from Bischofshofen, a wooden cross covered on three sides with chased gilt-bronze sheets, stands 1.58 meters high.[35] The inspiration for these larger crosses survives in stone skeuomorphs such as Acca's cross at Hexham.[36] Acca's cross had a head of the same type as the Cuthbert Cross, of which only the lower arm survives, apparently attached to the shaft by a collar with alternate pelleted and square-cut moldings, imitating metalwork forms. Sculptures at Hexham, Jarrow, and Northallerton also represent jeweled cross-heads with central settings and dogtooth borders and, on the sides, details that have sometimes been said to be sculpturally inspired friezes of balusters, but that are more likely to be representations of joining strips and concealed rivets, as on the side of the Cuthbert Cross.[37]

In metalwork many of the edging details were originally functional elements, either essential to construction, as on strips that joined the back and front of a brooch, or a disguise for what would otherwise have been an ugly join. For example, a feature that occurs only in seventh- to eighth-century Anglo-Saxon art and in some related Frisian jewelry is the reeded strip covering the join between the back and the front of composite brooches.[38] This detail is found transferred directly to sculpture on, for example, part of an eighth-century pillar or church furnishing from Escomb, County Durham, of which the front is a simple wirelike twist (figs. 1 and 2).[39]

33. Coatsworth, "Pectoral Cross and Portable Altar."
34. See Hubert, Porcher, and Volbach, *Europe in the Dark Ages,* plates 266–67.
35. Webster and Backhouse, *Making of England,* pp. 170–73.
36. Cramp, *Durham and Northumberland,* plates 167–71.
37. See Coatsworth, "Pectoral Cross and Portable Altar," esp. pp. 289–96.
38. Pinder, "Aspect of Seventh-Century Anglo-Saxon Goldsmithing."
39. Cramp, *Durham and Northumberland,* plate 55, ills. 266–69.

Some borders of cross-shafts have edges like cable twisted wire, such as on the eighth-century cross from St. Andrew Auckland.[40] Others have various forms of beading identical to those known from brooches. The edges of some keystone garnet disc brooches, for example, can be compared to those on the edge of a ninth-century or later grave marker from Gainford (fig. 3).[41] In the sculpture, the cabling or beading, or the collar effect, or the reeded strip were always unnecessary, but they were not only used to convey the overall impression of a gigantic metal cross or piece of precious goldsmith work. The whole object is a skeuomorph, but the edge detail, though not functionally necessary, is also used structurally to articulate the monument, to manage and make coherent transitions between different parts of the cross—between faces, for example—or the join between shaft and head. It therefore functioned at an aesthetic level. These features go on into later Northumbrian sculpture as part of the vocabulary of a sculptural style for crosses that are no longer skeuomorphs of real metalwork objects at all.

Some metalwork borders and interlace panels, however, were already cast or carved skeuomorphs of patterns that could also be carried out in wire or thread, and these are very widespread. Obvious examples of these are forms of knitted work in wire, such as the scourge from the ninth-century Trewhiddle hoard, or in Irish art the panels from the underside of the ca. 700 Ardagh chalice. In Anglo-Saxon metalwork there are panels of filigree ornament that are true interlace, as on the eighth- to ninth-century Windsor sword pommel.[42] On the other hand, the beaded filigree on the early seventh-century buckle from Taplow only appears to be interlaced as there is no real under- and overplaiting.[43] Where the wires appear to go under, the ends in fact just butt up against the apparently overlying strand, and the three-dimensional effect is enhanced by placing the wire on top of a foil formed with the same pattern. As Gwenda Adcock has pointed out, early illusionistic interlace in paint, stone, or cast metal originates from real interlace, and the earliest examples in sculpture and metalwork are always representations of interlace that could be made using wire or thread.[44] The metalwork and sculpture therefore possibly provide evidence for missing or fragmentary textile detail.

40. Cramp, *Durham and Northumberland*, plates 1–5.

41. Compare disc brooches from Faversham and Gilton in Avent, *Anglo-Saxon Disc and Composite Brooches*, plates 1–3, with Gainford in Cramp, *Durham and Northumberland*, plate 69, ills. 347–48.

42. Webster and Backhouse, *Making of England,* cat. nos. 180, 225–26.

43. J. Campbell et al., *The Anglo-Saxons,* plate 39.

44. Adcock, "Study of the Types of Interlace," pp. 35–42.

EVIDENCE FROM SCANDINAVIA

Clear evidence for the influence of textiles on other forms of art survives from Scandinavia, where there is an interesting use of knots, plaits, and embroidery using wire, found particularly in ninth- to tenth-century contexts in Birka, Sweden. There they are more common than the thread wound around with gold or other metal, which is what we usually think of as a textile or embroidery medium.[45] There were two types of wire employed: plain round wire produced by drawing and used on its own, and spiral wire, essentially even more finely drawn wire, tightly twisted around a textile core. The objects made in these three materials—wire, spiral wire, and gold thread—were all found as garment trimmings, either of the caftanlike garments identified at Birka or of various forms of headgear. There seems to be great uncertainty as to the origin, even the place of origin, of these trimmings, which have no direct parallel outside Scandinavia and few parallels within it. Agnes Geijer, in her 1938 study of the Birka textiles, was in fact rather ambivalent about whether these costume trimmings were actually imports. Although she implied an ultimately "eastern" origin for the technique, and also connected one particular metalwork technique with the Saamis, with whom the traders of Birka were in contact, she also pointed out, though very briefly, some points of comparison with native Viking art. In a later brief update of her views on the Birka textiles she appeared to have recanted the identification of most of the fine textiles as native or even western European products.[46] In the case of the works in gold and silver wire, the argument seems to be that there is some embroidery of the "western" type at Birka, but by this she seems to mean particularly stem stitch embroidery done with spun gold thread. She was also clearly influenced by the fact that the Anglo-Saxon embroideries from Maaseik and Durham (of the ninth and tenth centuries respectively and therefore of the same date as Birka) used spun gold thread, not wire, in both the edge braids and the embroideries, with the thread laid singly, not paired as in the Birka braids. In the case of the trimmings, rather than the embroideries or the braids, she still referred to the likelihood that the technique of spiral wire was acquired from the Saamis, who used pewter wire in a similar way.

Inga Hägg in a study of the dress at Birka was most concerned to demonstrate that it was not representative of ordinary Scandinavian dress and that the style and decoration were evidence of the costume of an elite, whose origins were "oriental."[47] The most detailed study of Viking Age

45. Geijer, *Birka*, vol. 3, chaps. 8 and 9, pp. 99–127.
46. Geijer, "Textile Finds from Birka."
47. Hägg, "Die Tracht."

oriental imports into Scandinavia, of which there were many, commented however that the use of the term "oriental" in connection with the textiles and their decoration was often vague, and usually included Byzantine as well as truly oriental influences and imports.[48] Jansson found evidence of the same dress and ornamentation in Scandinavian settlements in Russia at least in the tenth century, but pointed out that the evidence for the origin of the characteristic caftanlike costume was difficult to assess, since many of the features of dress, though ultimately Iranian, could be found in both the Byzantine sphere and within the Muslim world of the Caliphate by the period in which Birka flourished. Evidence for the decorative details coming from there or from other eastern areas such as the Steppes could not be proved for lack of research on the material from those areas. The evidence for comparable wire decoration comes only from those parts of Russia that had Scandinavian trading settlements, and in association with other Scandinavian finds. The only slight evidence from the Muslim sphere comes from a few wall paintings that seem to show costume with borders and hanging trimmings that might be comparable to those of the Scandinavian material, though it has to be said that neither of the examples illustrated indicates any richness of patterning of any type in the trimmings. There appear to be no examples of the trimmings from any of the areas of putative influence.

In one sense it may be that the source, or even whether the objects were imported into Scandinavia at all, is unimportant. The fact is that these extraordinary trimmings, which combine the goldsmith's and the embroiderer's art, existed in Birka from the ninth into the tenth century and that they parallel closely most of the features of the Borre style that flourished at the same time in metalwork and sculpture. The Borre style is characterized by the ribbon plait commonly known as the ring chain, a ribbon animal, a quadruped with a masklike head, and an animal seen in profile, usually with a backward-turned head and a lappet. In his book on Viking art, David Wilson observed that the Borre style grew out of the preceding Scandinavian styles, such as that found at Oseberg, but he also saw a connection in the cast or carved versions of the style with another metalwork technique, that of filigree work.[49] He came to this conclusion because of the way that the interlace was structured, with a double strand of which each ribbon was decorated with a series of transverse nicks. It is true that this feature could be copying beaded filigree, but it could also be copying the effect of spiral wire thread, as in an example from Birka grave 944 (fig. 4). In this example the pattern of the wire seems to be a

48. Jansson, "Wikingerzeitlicher orientalischer Import in Skandinavien," esp. pp. 592–614.

49. "The Borre Style," in Wilson and Klindt-Jensen, *Viking Art,* pp. 87–94.

true interlace, not a ring chain, which as its name suggests is a simple plait into which is inserted a series of loose rings; however, some of the trimmings follow exactly that form (fig. 5). These Birka ornaments have survived because they are made of wire not textile, but there is some evidence from Birka of similar knots and plaits in purely textile form, and as various writers have shown, there are objects in church treasuries throughout Europe that show the importance of knots and plaits as a major decorative form (see below, p. 152). To my mind, the link with the chain patterns on Viking Age crosses and other artifacts in England is obvious. It can be seen, for example, on the Gosforth Cross, where the ring chain on all sides, including the curious winged version, can be paralleled among the wire ornaments from Birka (see figs. 6, 7, and 8). The influence on the development of the Borre style then may come from textiles and textile-related arts, as well as from other prestigious metalwork techniques, such as work in fine gold filigree. Might not then the influence on sculpture have come not only from metalwork, but also directly from the textile arts: needlework, weaving, plaiting, and embroidery?

The Evidence from Anglo-Saxon England

Luckily, examples of textile details that might have influenced metalwork and sculpture do survive, often as edgings or borders that in fact turn out to be important in early north European dress, and possibly in other forms of textiles. Elaborate stitching, narrow woven braids, and plaited threads or strips were functional as well as decorative. They were used to disguise seams or hems, and this makes them similar to the original function of beaded and filigree wires in metalwork. Examples of plaits occur in the textiles from St. Cuthbert's tomb, Durham, and also from other graves, both Anglo-Saxon and Scandinavian. From the kind of rich furnished graves in which they tend to be discovered they were obviously also functional in a sociological sense, as expressions of wealth and social status. In addition, decorations made of expensive imported materials or worked in labor-intensive techniques were often confined to narrow strips displayed on edges and borders. Moralistic complaints about these edges testify to their widespread use and importance. For example, St. Boniface, writing to Cuthbert, archbishop of Canterbury, about 745 condemns "those ornaments of dress with embroidered margins (or margins of worms) on the borders; they announce Antichrist and are sent by his guile and through his ministers into the monasteries to induce fornication and extravagance."[50] This long-lasting fashion can be seen on the chasu-

50. Boniface, *Briefe des Bonifatius,* pp. 252–54, letter 78. In this edition the letter is dated to 747.

bles for clerics and rich cloaks for the laity depicted in later manuscripts, though the borders might have been either braids woven with gold thread or embroidered. Examples can be seen on the dress of St. Æthelwold on folio 118v of his Benedictional[51] and on the cloak of King Edgar in the frontispiece to the Charter of the New Minster.[52] Among surviving braids used to edge expensive embroidered objects or garments is a rather splendid example on the sleeve of a tunic ascribed to a seventh-century abbess, St. Bertille, from Chelles, France, but incomplete fragments of such braids are found in rich Anglo-Saxon graves, too. The fragment is especially important, however, because of Bertille's well-known close connection to Anglo-Saxon England.[53]

I have already mentioned embroidery actually made in the form of strips in the ninth-century Maaseik embroideries, which also have their own stitched and braided edgings. The strips, and the monograms from the same group (which were painted as well as embroidered), were appliqués, possibly from an altar frontal, but they could equally have adorned some form of ecclesiastical dress.

Other surviving examples throw up connections with other media. For example a braid from St. Cuthbert's coffin in Durham is an edging from a garment thought to be a dalmatic of the seventh or eighth century.[54] The braid is on one edge of the object, and the central area of the braid is woven. At both outside edges there are sewn-on plaits, defining a border in which the ground is completely covered by closely spaced blanket stitching in bars of red, yellow, green, and blue. This embroidered edging has been compared to the barred effect of the cloisonné edging of the Sutton Hoo purse lid. The chevron border edging of the Maaseik arcade strips can also be paralleled in metalwork. On the Durham braid, the stitching and plaits are of course decorative, but they also cover and neaten hems and cut edges.

From Sutton Hoo there is a fine woolen fabric with a seam decorated with a plaitlike stitch (reconstruction, fig. 9). First, two cut edges were joined by a running stitch, then the seam was opened out flat and turned under. The fabric was in two shades of blue, and the plait stitch covering

51. The Benedictional of St. Æthelwold, London, British Library, MS Additional 49598; Deshman, Benedictional of St. Æthelwold, plate 35.

52. The New Minster Charter, London, British Library, MS Cotton Vespasian A. viii, fol. 2b; Keynes, Liber Vitae of the New Minster and Hyde Abbey, plate 1.

53. Bertille was the first abbess of Chelles, one of the most important links between the Frankish and Anglo-Saxon churches, and a refuge for Anglo-Saxon noblewomen wishing to take up the religious life. Hild, for example, was on her way to join her sister Hereswith at Chelles when she was called back to Northumbria by Bishop Aidan. Bede, Hist. eccles. 4.23, p. 406.

54. Granger-Taylor, "Weft-patterned Silks and Their Braid," plates 54–55.

the seam picked out one of the shades. Elisabeth Crowfoot compared this to a seam reinforced and decorated with herringbone stitch on a woolen pillow cover from the famous burial at Mammen, Denmark.[55] The Sutton Hoo stitch is not a self-standing plait, but it is more interlace than stitch, as can be seen in the reconstruction. It is also exactly comparable to the trimmings and wire "embroidery" from Birka, being the stitch first defined by Geijer as "Ösenstich," which she later translated into English as "reversed chain stitch."

Sculptures that might have been inspired by textile constructional forms include a shaft from Coppergate, York, with its plaits and twists.[56] James Lang dated this piece to the tenth century but related it closely to the fragment with a reeded edge reminiscent of an early and characteristically Anglo-Saxon metalwork technique from Escomb, which has been dated two centuries earlier (above, p. 145).

At Lastingham, East Yorkshire, there is a sculptured chair arm that has, on its upper edge, a linear heart-shaped leaf pattern.[57] This same pattern is found in manuscript art, but it is also like the rosebud/petal design on tablet-woven bands such as a fragment from the abbey of St. Peter, Salzburg, now in the Los Angeles County Museum of Art, thought to be Insular but copying an oriental design.[58] The braid has plaits on the edges, decorated with hemispherical silver bosses, of which five remain. The use of metal attachments in textiles is another area of crossover between the two arts.

At Bewcastle, the checkerboard pattern might not seem obviously textile related but it does represent a type of woven pattern—as in a braid with an inscription of an Insular style from San Apollinare in Classe, Ravenna, that has a woven or brocaded checkered pattern on the front.[59] In fact the side of the Bewcastle Cross on which this pattern occurs appears to be a strip with woven and embroidered patterns.

It has been noted before that there are skeuomorphs of complete textile objects in both metalwork and sculpture. An obvious example is the grave cover from Kirkdale in Yorkshire, with its embroidered surface and its fringed and tasseled edge.[60] To this I would add a cross-base from Lindisfarne, which seems to have a cover with girdlelike ties.[61] There are

55. E. Crowfoot, "The Textiles," p. 422; for Mammen: see Hald, *Ancient Danish Textiles from Bogs and Burials*, p. 282 and fig. 295.

56. Lang, *York and Eastern Yorkshire*, p. 103 and plates 333–36.

57. Lang, *York and Eastern Yorkshire*, pp. 172–73 and plates 614–17 and 623–66.

58. Museum No. 55.57.1. Webster and Backhouse, *Making of England*, pp. 83–84.

59. For Bewcastle, see Cassidy, *Ruthwell Cross*, plates 49–52; and see Granger-Taylor, "Weft-patterned Silks and Their Braid," plate 56.

60. Lang, *York and Eastern Yorkshire*, pp. 162–63 and plates 563–67.

61. Cramp, *Durham and Northumberland*, p. 201 and plates 196–97.

also literary descriptions of vestments spread on tombs, in *De Abbatibus,* for example. Textiles from inside tombs also survive, as fragments, in Anglo-Saxon bed-burials,[62] but also sometimes in splendid condition, as in a pillow and sudarium embroidered in the ninth century for the tomb of Bishop Hincmar of Rheims.[63] The sculptors at Kirkdale and Lindisfarne therefore seem to be representing actual early medieval practices.

The reliquary in the form of a bag or purse is another type of textile skeuomorph that has previously been identified in metalwork. Surviving textile examples include the York silk pouch with a crudely embroidered cross, which has been dated both ca. 975 and the early to mid-eleventh century due to its archaeological context.[64] This has been identified as a reliquary pouch because of its decoration and because it seems to have been completely enclosed. There are other textile examples, some small and insignificant like the York piece, but a more impressive example of the genre survives from outside Anglo-Saxon England in the form of a purse from Nürnberg, Germany, of ninth- to eleventh-century date that has plait-covered seams and plaited or knitted tassels.[65] Skeuomorphs of these reliquaries in metalwork include the Winchester reliquary of the late ninth century, but there are numerous Continental examples of the type, including examples of small reliquaries imitating textile purses from Tongres in Belgium and the ninth-century Enger reliquary in Berlin.[66]

There is considerable evidence from the Anglo-Saxon pagan and transitional periods that objects of status or value (sometimes of personal or religious value), which could include weapons or tools as well as jewelry or plate, were placed in rich furnished graves, often wrapped in fine textiles or enclosed in purses and satchels of textile or sometimes leather. These are usually reconstructed from their metal or ivory fittings. In rich female graves, for example, an ivory closing ring for a pouchlike bag is often noted. The Sutton Hoo purse has already been mentioned, and there are examples from the Allemannic site of Krefeld Gellep, as well as others from Germany.[67] A leather satchel or bag for scales was found in a late seventh-century Anglo-Saxon grave from Watchfield, Oxfordshire;[68] another leather bag has been reconstructed from the finds in a rich bed-burial from Swallowcliffe Down, Kent, also from the seventh century.[69]

---

62. Swallowcliffe Down, for example: Speake, *Saxon Bed Burial on Swallowcliffe Down.*

63. Volbach, *Early Decorative Textiles,* pp. 106, 111, and plate 68; Starensier, "Art Historical Study of the Byzantine Silk Industry," 2:606–08.

64. Tweddle, "Silk Reliquary Pouch in Compound Twill."

65. Von Wilckens, *Die Textile Künste von der Spätantike,* p. 174, fig. 194.

66. Tweddle, "Silk Reliquary Pouch in Compound Twill."

67. Bruce-Mitford, *Sutton Hoo Ship Burial,* 2:520, fig. 383.

68. Scull, "Excavations and Survey at Watchfield," esp. p. 181.

69. Speake, *Saxon Bed Burial on Swallowcliffe Down,* pp. 72–80.

Figure 1. Escomb 4, Side D, County Durham. Photo copyright Department of Archaeology, Durham University.

Figure 2. Escomb 4, Side A, County Durham. Photo copyright Department of Archaeology, Durham University.

Figure 3. Gainford 21, Side B, County Durham. Photo copyright Department of Archaeology, Durham University.

Figure 4. Birka, Grave 944, interlacing wire trimming. By kind permission of the Museum of National Antiquities, Sweden.

Figure 5. Birka, Grave 944(?), wire trimming in the form of a ring chain. By kind permission of the Museum of National Antiquities, Sweden.

Figure 6. Gosforth 1, Cumbria, face A, detail of ring chain. Photo copyright Department of Archaeology, Durham University.

Figure 7. Gosforth 1, Cumbria, face D, detail of "winged" chain. Photo copyright Department of Archaeology, Durham University.

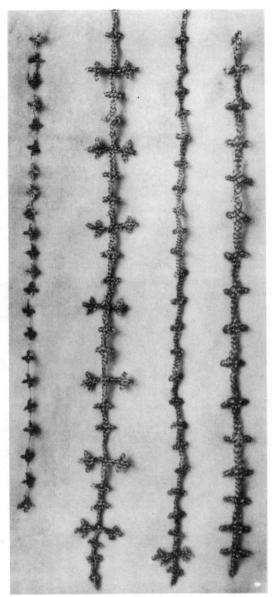

Figure 8. Birka, Grave 736, wire trimming in the form of a "winged" chain. By kind permission of the Museum of Antiquities, Sweden.

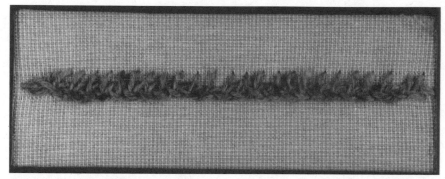

Figure 9. Reconstruction of embroidery on Sutton Hoo (SH9), showing the interlace stitch used to join and conceal the seam. The original is wool on wool. Copyright Alexandra Lester, photographer Stephen Yates.

Figure 10. Falstone 2, Northumberland, face A. Photo copyright Department of Archaeology, Durham University.

This practice seems to lie behind the development of the textile reliquary and its metalwork skeuomorph.

Is it possible that this form too was carried over into sculpture? A grave marker from Falstone, Northumberland, has been described as an incomplete house-shaped tomb and as a skeuomorph of a metalwork reliquary with its locks and hasps.[70] I would like to suggest instead that it is in fact the sculptured version of the textile or leather bag. It is very small, only 12¾ inches long by 7 inches high and 6 inches deep (fig. 10). It has two inscriptions, one in runic and one in Insular majuscules, recording that this *becun* was set up by a man for his uncle. If the object is reinterpreted as a bag or satchel, the twist on the top and on the left edge falls into place as a plait edging covering a seam, the handlelike appearance of the upper molding also makes sense, and so does the vertical feature, which does not come quite to the lower edge, as a strap and buckle fastener, in which the rounded termination of the strap above the bottom edge is quite clear.

CONCLUSION

The early medieval evidence assembled in this essay demonstrates that edges and trimmings may be diagnostic of stylistic trends and betray the primacy in time and in taste for certain arts over others. This has particularly important ramifications for our understanding of the development of Anglo-Saxon stone sculpture. In England, edges and trimmings may, as in the case of woodworking, textiles, and metalwork, show that the Anglo-Saxons, at least in pre-Viking Northumbria, used the techniques and structures of their native arts to decorate but also to articulate and make sense of the new art of stone sculpture. Where this occurs, some of these features go on to influence developing sculptural styles more widely. Full skeuomorphs also function on the level of metaphor, for expressing what is spiritually or socially valued. They may develop into a class, like the *crux gemmata* in stone, or they may be one-offs, like the embroidered cover from Kirkdale or the purse from Falstone. The edges and sides of Anglo-Saxon sculpture demonstrate that none of these arts developed in isolation or was uninfluenced by the others, and that the classicizing trends that arrived with Christianity did not, even in the arts most associated with Christianity, completely displace the taste for the native arts, in either style or medium.

70. Cramp, *Durham and Northumberland*, pp. 172–73 and plate 166.

MISSING MATERIAL:
EARLY ANGLO-SAXON ENAMELING

SUSAN YOUNGS

Since 1923 when Sir Cyril Fox published his observations on early Anglo-Saxon enamels, it has been recognized that in the sixth century smiths
producing dress fasteners in Anglo-Saxon style occasionally used enamel
inlay and that finds of this enameled work were concentrated in parts of
East Anglia, on the fen edge of eastern Cambridgeshire and Suffolk in the
Lark valley.[1] Following his publication several scholars have added items
to the corpus, but while new finds have broadened the distribution with
some distant outliers and also the range of artifacts carrying enamel, they
have made no significant difference to the marked concentration in south
Cambridgeshire and Suffolk.[2] Further interpretations have been based on
this phenomenon. It has been accepted that enameling was unknown in
the Continental homelands and was not imported with the Germanic settlers; that it therefore represents the adoption of a technique that survived
from the Roman period in Britain; and that this occurred locally in East
Anglia as the result of direct contact with indigenous peoples who had
retained this skill. Further it has been argued that these eastern aborigi-
nal craftsmen were, in turn, subsequently influenced by Germanic styles
and techniques in the production of more complex enamel work in their
own idiom, when making decorative fittings for hanging bowls. Increasingly large claims are being made for cultural survival, exchange, and
interaction in this relatively confined area of eastern Britain in the sixth
century.[3] Most recently, a case has been made that the transmission of

My first debt is to the dedicatee of this volume, under whose vigilant eye I first made physical contact with Bede's world while digging at Wearmouth and Jarrow. Her support over a
very long period, as well as her scholarship, have been and continue to be a source of strength
and a stimulus. My thanks are also owed to Leslie Webster, John Hines, and Barry Ager for
information, comment, and advice. Jim Farrant went beyond the call of duty to provide the
artwork for this essay.

1. Fox, *Archaeology of the Cambridge Region*, p. 260.
2. Evison, "Enamelled Disc from Great Saxham"; D. Brown, "Swastika Patterns"; Scull,
"Further Evidence from East Anglia for Enamelling"; Hines, *New Corpus of Anglo-Saxon Great
Square-Headed Brooches*, pp. 220–21.
3. D. Brown, "Swastika Patterns," pp. 230–31; Scull, "Further Evidence from East
Anglia for Enamelling," pp. 120–21.

enameling skills from imperial Britain included polychrome glass work, primarily in the form of millefiori inlays, allowing very early dates for key native pieces of complex enameling.[4] In the light of recent finds and improved knowledge of old ones these views deserve to be reconsidered, and that is the purpose of this essay.

If all the arguments advanced above are correct, it is surprising that when used in Anglo-Saxon mode, where enamel was used almost exclusively on dress items, it was employed in a very restricted way as a substitute for cold inlaid translucent garnet or glass and set in small precast fields. These basic champlevé cells are simple circles or rectangles, a few having a "bull's eye" outer line imitating composite inlaid glass (fig. 1). The new material is opaque red enamel used in ways determined by the insets for which it was substituted. On many pieces enamel was combined with gilding. This is unknown in sixth-century native metalwork and very rare in the first half of the seventh century, a development inhibited by the use of leaded bronzes for fine casting, alloys that are unsuitable for mercury gilding. Given the relative temperatures involved for enameling and gilding, this establishes that the enamel was part of the original decoration, fired in its cells before the mercury gilding process, and not added later to make good the loss of an original inlay. This primary use is confirmed by the use of enamel on two cruciform brooches from Ixworth, Suffolk (fig. 1), and the observation that gold overlays the enamel on some pieces.[5]

Only opaque red enamel was used with one noteworthy exception discussed below.[6] All of these Anglo-Saxon pieces are of sixth-century date, with some from the first half of the century. A bronze sword pommel from Hemingby, Lincolnshire, may date from before 500 and is at present a unique example of enamel on a weapon fitting (fig. 2). The pommel is of Brighthampton type, which makes it the oldest example of Anglo-Saxon enameling.[7] It carries a variation on the "bull's eye" pattern in which the central field is triangular, is not gilded, and appears to have no exact equivalent in garnet inlay.

4. L. Laing, "Bradwell Mount and the Use of Millefiori."

5. London, British Museum, PE 1927,12-12,21 and (fig. 1) 1971, 1-1,1; West, *Corpus of Anglo-Saxon Material from Suffolk*, p. 70.

6. The use of blue enamel on a brooch from grave 40 Little Wilbraham cemetery, Cambridgeshire, was reported by E. T. Leeds, repeated by Günther Haseloff (*Email im frühen Mittelalter*, p. 150), and reported and then discounted by John Hines (*New Corpus of Anglo-Saxon Square-Headed Brooches*, pp. 220, 333).

7. Evison, *Fifth-Century Invasions*, pp. 42, 105, fig. 11; Menghin, *Das Schwert im frühen Mittelalter*, pp. 309–10; Vera I. Evison, pers. comm.; Professor Dr. Wilfried Menghin in correspondence. An unassociated unpublished metal-detected find, London, British Museum, PE 1997,1-1,1.

An apparent exception to the above is a damaged five-spiral saucer brooch from Bury St. Edmunds, Suffolk. It has been suggested that the spirals were reserved against a field of red enamel and that this brooch forms a link with enameled "Durrowesque" spirals, the spiral and trumpet pattern found on some native hanging bowls.[8] This incomplete and damaged brooch has areas of shiny, pale green laminated surface left in the depressions between the spirals whose original upper surface is otherwise missing. Such a surface is not characteristic of degraded enamel and is probably the result of cremation. It lacks any beds prepared for enamel. On many early enameled pieces the incomplete bonding achieved with the red cuprite glass has led to the preferential loss of enamel, so that its survival on a brooch with almost totally degraded surface would be exceptional, but not unprecedented. Optical examination has convinced this writer that the Bury St. Edmunds brooch was not enameled and that this piece cannot, therefore, support arguments based on it having "spirals" reserved against enamel.

The use of the Vitruvian wave on this brooch is certainly a common design link with some hanging bowl ornament, but this motif is also well known on Germanic metalwork from Britain and on the Continent and is not expressed with any Insular characteristics on this brooch. It is also the case that the archaeological parallels for this brooch date it to the late fifth and earlier sixth centuries, so that it comes from a period earlier than we are able to establish for the hanging bowl mounts. For these bowls we are largely dependent on a *terminus ante quem* based on their deposition dates, most of which lie in the seventh century.[9] The hair spirals and trumpet patterns drawn in the Book of Durrow (Dublin, Trinity College Library, MS 57) were drawn a hundred years after the brooch was made.[10]

Because enamel is used on Anglo-Saxon metalwork in the heartland of East Anglia, while the historically attested "free" British communities supporting smiths who used enamels in native styles lay to the west and north of the Anglo-Saxon territories, it has been customary to posit a local British enclave where the technique of inlaying glass by heating was imparted to the incomers, or was adapted to embellish new metalwork in their preferred styles. This must have happened around, if not before, 500 to judge by the products. A hot inlaying technique was something already familiar to some Anglo-Saxon smiths who worked with niello, although

8. Scull, "Further Evidence from East Anglia for Enamelling," pp. 117–20.

9. Scull, "Further Evidence from East Anglia for Enamelling," pp. 119–21, for the date of the brooch; for a discussion of deposition dates, see Geake, "When Were Hanging Bowls Deposited," where the case for *all* deposits being made in the seventh century is overstated.

10. G. Henderson, *From Durrow to Kells*, pp. 54–55, with further references.

it is more common in Kent and Merovingian France. There is, however, some tantalizing, fugitive evidence to suggest that enameling was known in early Scandinavia,[11] and the influence of Migration-Period Scandinavia on East Anglian metalwork is well attested. While the two enameled items so far noted from Norway are of second-century date, enamel reappears in Swedish Vendel period metalwork of the seventh century. Two similar enameled disc brooches, one from a Merovingian grave, the other a metal-detected piece from Kent, have been dismissed as Roman by a leading scholar in the Merovingian field, but are not accepted by romanists.[12] Enamel is an often fugitive material that needs to be recognized in a degraded state and often needs to be looked for.

Accepting, however, that it remains an Anglo-Saxon regional phenomenon in the late fifth and sixth centuries, enamel in England achieved no great status and was not, for example, employed to render the complex patterns of the composite garnet brooches and pendants. Anglo-Saxon is a term used here as a convenient label for those people in eastern England who had adopted the new material cultural and funerary practices and are therefore highly visible in the archaeological record. With one exception, there is no evidence that the heirs of the earliest East Anglian enamelers went on to develop or adopt the styles and colors and polychrome millefiori inlays that transformed British and Irish enameling around 600.[13] Once acquired, say from an enslaved British smith, the skill of working with ground or softened red glass at relatively low temperature could readily have been handed down through a local family of craftsmen who, even if British speaking in 500, were probably assimilated Old English speakers by 550. This is not to challenge any of the evidence for the continued existence of British-speaking elements in the population of East Anglia into the seventh century, but to argue that early Anglo-Saxon enameling does not necessarily depend on or relate to the survival of a culturally distinct element in the population.

More importantly it does not support or prove the existence of British craftsmen continuing to work *within* the Anglo-Saxon kingdom of East Anglia into the seventh century in their own techniques and styles, with independent cultural development expressed in fine metalwork. An enameled hanging bowl found near Ipswich (detail, fig. 3a) has rightly been recognized as being a unique hybrid of medieval Celtic and Anglo-Saxon

11. Hines, *Scandinavian Character of Anglian England;* Hines, "Scandinavian Character of Anglian England: An Update."

12. The brooch said to come from Kent is in private hands and the parallel is published in Salin, *Le Haut Moyen Age de Lorraine,* plate xvii. I owe this reference to the encyclopedic knowledge of Cathy Haith.

13. Carroll, "Millefiori in the Development of Early Irish Enamelling."

decorative and technical traditions but, in my view, wrongly interpreted as a local product produced by an isolated community working in archaic style.[14] The styles of ornament have been used to pull the piece back from the mid-seventh century, a date argued on constructional grounds, to "hardly earlier than the middle of the 6th century."[15] It is argued below that both style and construction place it at the end of the British-made series.

There is a basic conundrum. Several richly and elaborately enameled hanging bowls have been found in the region, with the finest examples from the Sutton Hoo barrow cemetery in Suffolk. This evidence has been used to support the argument for "native craftsmen" working directly for Anglo-Saxon patrons, but perceptions have been distorted by proximity. The evidence of grave furnishings from the late sixth and seventh centuries indicates that bronze vessels from any source were deemed appropriate and desirable additions to a burial assemblage. Bowls decorated with enamels were highly prized, or were at least desiderata that were ranked alongside imported Byzantine and Frankish bronze vessels. The possibility that the presence of enamels and polychrome glass inlays on some bowls may have been of little or no importance, as compared with the value of the metal bowl itself as a container, is not supported by the presence of the most elaborate and technically ambitious enameled bowl in the richest surviving burial of the period, the ship burial in Mound One at Sutton Hoo, Suffolk. This bowl was so esteemed by its last owner that the bronze of the bowl had been repaired in precious metal, patched with silver plates decorated in typical Anglo-Saxon style.[16] There are other examples of the bowls from graves being patched and repaired, rebottomed and bodged by smiths incapable of matching the original fittings. There was no local technology available to mend or to make these lathe-turned bowls in the late sixth and early seventh centuries.

If, as has been argued for the complex and interesting bowl found near Ipswich, there were craftsmen working in polychrome enamels and making fine wheel polished bowls locally, why was the Sutton Hoo bowl treated like an exotic heirloom? It is now increasingly clear from repairs and replacements that the bowls deposited in Anglo-Saxon graves were

---

14. Scull, "Further Evidence from East Anglia for Enamelling," pp. 120–22; a clear illustration of the complete bowl and its decorated mounts is published in West, *Corpus of Anglo-Saxon Material from Suffolk*, p. 187; Bruce-Mitford with Raven, *Corpus of Late Celtic Hanging Bowls*, no. 86.

15. Scull, "Further Evidence from East Anglia for Enamelling," pp. 120–22.

16. Full publication in Bruce-Mitford, *Sutton Hoo Ship Burial*, 3:202–43; further references, illustration, and discussion in Brenan, *Hanging Bowls and Their Contexts*, cat. no. 54; Bruce-Mitford with Raven, *Corpus of Late Celtic Hanging Bowls*, no. 88.

also exotic imports in terms of current boundaries and not local commissions. The Anglo-Saxon feature of the Ipswich bowl is its gilded band of two-strand three-ply interlace (fig. 3a). Simple interlace of this type was not restricted to East Anglia. We know from the evidence of a disc found at Dunadd, Argyll, and from molds excavated at the Mote of Mark in Dumfries in contexts dated to the seventh century that Germanic interlace was both imported and imitated in very distant workshops in Britain at this period.[17] Derivative interlace patterns were used, for example, on an elaborately mounted bowl found at Lullingstone in Kent.[18]

The Ipswich bowl is one of a restricted group that carries slices of millefiori glass set in its enamel, a group that includes two from Mound One, Sutton Hoo, and three bowls found in Lincolnshire.[19] The basal disc with millefiori was made in two parts (fig. 3a) and it shares this composite construction with a set of millefiori inlaid mounts found in Northumberland. This feature, married with the use of external rivet holes on the hook mounts, is strong evidence of development and change and indicates a late date in the British-found series.

It has been argued, however, that the use of millefiori glass indicates a very early date for all these pieces.[20] There is certainly no archaeological evidence to support the idea of a direct flow of polychrome enamel work from its common and widespread use in Britain in the second century through to the fourth let alone the fifth century. These inlays were long out of vogue and out of production before the fourth century. The use of small fields of opaque red enamel in a local, in the sense of native, archaizing style provides the only link between the metalworkers of the fourth century and those using enamel in the following centuries in Britain and Ireland. A very small number of brooches and dress pins in this Romano-British idiom, as exemplified by a dress pin in a coin hoard from Oldcroft in Gloucestershire that is dated to the fourth century, are the carriers or transmitters of the enameling tradition. Indigenous British and Irish enameling from the fifth and sixth centuries is similarly restricted,

17. Lane and E. Campbell, *Dunadd*, pp. 245–46, illustration 7.10; for the Mote of Mark, see L. Laing, "Mote of Mark and the Origins of Celtic Interlace." For the latest evidence for the early date of this material, see Longley, "Mote of Mark."

18. Brenan, *Hanging Bowls and Their Contexts*, cat. no. 40; G. Henderson, *From Durrow to Kells*, pp. 52, 68, fig. 65; Bruce-Mitford with Raven, *Corpus of Late Celtic Hanging Bowls*, no. 43.

19. The different phases of millefiori type and use are discussed in Carroll, "Millefiori in the Development of Early Irish Enamelling." For finds up to 1990, see Brenan, *Hanging Bowls and Their Contexts*, and for Lincolnshire finds, see Bruce-Mitford, "Late Celtic Hanging-Bowls"; Bruce-Mitford with Raven, *Corpus of Late Celtic Hanging Bowls*, pp. 18–19, List 11, pp. 185–215. To these should be added an unpublished find with millefiori from the Horncastle area.

20. L. Laing, "Bradwell Mount and the Use of Millefiori," pp. 145 and 150.

insofar as we can identify pieces from this period, to fine lines and small fields of red enamel. The implications of this are not lack of skill but limited access to other glasses.

Anglo-Saxon goldsmiths certainly cold set reused slices of Roman millefiori glass, sometimes using large sheets with a monocolored layer wrapped outside the bundles of rods, a technique characteristic of Roman millefiori work. Such glass must have been highly prized and was probably traded alongside Roman glass tesserae used for bead making. Again, the archaeological contexts and artifacts indicate a revival of interest in and access to traded millefiori glass in the second half of the sixth century.

Outside the Anglo-Saxon trading nexus the millefiori glasses are not identical, although sometimes made from highly complex rods, and were not prefused into large sheets. Circular "sun burst" rods were available. Slices of millefiori glass were individually set into a matrix of red enamel by heating, with evidence for the attendant risks of the inlays moving about before the enamel matrix solidified. On sixth- to seventh-century enameled Irish brooches we can see experimentation using precast recesses and collars to fix these bright inlays in position. Angular cells (of the type mentioned below) were conveniently filled by pieces of millefiori glass, and increased availability of millefiori through local production may have provided the impetus toward this design change, one that is fully established in the eighth century, with several good examples from the Shanmullagh, County Tyrone hoard.[21] But this is also a *reinvention* of the treatment of extensive areas of contrasting millefiori glass seen on second-century Roman plate-brooches, enameled boxes, and similar objects. It does not suggest that there was a surviving tradition of millefiori working in post-Roman Britain that was passed on to the medieval world.

This summary introduces a fascinating enameled disc from Great Barton in Suffolk. In his analysis of this piece David Brown rightly emphasized its many distinctive features: the use of angular interlocking cells, the use of millefiori glass, the four outer elements of the design (fig. 4).[22] It is a key piece that marks a transition from variations on compass-based curvilinear, archaic, La Tène–derived ornament to a style characterized by interlocking angular cells that lend themselves, as here, to rectangular fields. In Irish enameling this style was established by the end of the seventh century and came to dominate in the eighth century. While such ornament appears to mimic earlier Germanic cloisonné work in gold and garnet, this assumed derivation from sixth- or early seventh-century Germanic metalwork does not stand up to close analysis. The cell shapes are

---

21. Illustrated in Bourke, *Patrick, the Archaeology of a Saint*, pp. 26, 27, 34.
22. D. Brown, "Swastika Patterns," pp. 227–37.

very restricted, mainly L-, T-, or S-shaped, when compared with the proposed models; they are also much bolder and much larger, unlike the
false cloisonné glass studs that do compare in size and cell shapes with the
sword beads they imitated. There were other models available for these
enameled designs and these were Late Antique or in the Late Antique
tradition, now best represented in durable materials by the third- and
fourth-century mosaics of Roman Britain, and in other materials that continued in use in churches across the western and eastern Roman world, as
many commentators have observed. The contemporary Christian milieu
also has plentiful examples of swastikas and other angular crosses derived
from Greek-key patterns. To cite one public example, a sixth-century
stone choir screen in San Apollinare Nuovo, Ravenna, carries openwork
swastikas combined with examples of that much-discussed and typically
Irish motif, the ringed cross (fig. 5).

If it is accepted, as is argued in summary form above, that hanging
bowls are British, that is, non-Anglo-Saxon products, then they were made
originally for patrons who were predominantly Christians, a view supported by the overtly Christian decoration on some of the bowls. These
thin, often ornately decorated bowls were impractical luxury items, and
the Christian elite for whom most bowls and their mounts were made
will have been familiar with and interested in what was perceived to be
Roman, as indeed the idea of hanging bowls themselves was in origin.
Late Antique Christian Rome was their acquired cultural heritage, filtered
and distorted by time, distance, relative isolation, and through language
barriers. This makes contemporary models and styles in the Romanocen-
tric Christian culture of real significance when looking for sources of the
new angular art style. As Christopher Scull pointed out in his analysis of
the motifs on the Ipswich bowl, the scrolls on its hook mounts recall the
Tree of Life motif (fig. 3b), but this does not, as he argues, necessarily
hark back to the Early Christian tradition; rather it reflects the traditions
of the Romani available in the seventh century, the century into which the
Ipswich bowl with its millefiori fits most convincingly.[23]

It is the isolation of the swastika pattern formed from interlocking L-shaped cells on the Great Barton disc that makes the arguments
developed from this piece unconvincing. By concentrating on this element because it forms a swastika, the central pattern is divorced from
its frame and supporting elements (fig. 4). The whole central device is
a lozenge with a circular finial at each corner emphasized by the use of
yellow glass. It resembles in outline a well-known, second-century Roman
enameled plate-brooch or seal box form. The four independent support-

---

23. Scull, "Further Evidence from East Anglia for Enamelling," p. 121.

ing elements, though crudely executed, are simple swags between volutes. Such a swag between volutes, as on a simple Ionic capital, can be seen in combination with classical key-pattern on a mount from a hanging bowl from Capheaton in Northumberland.[24] In a much nativized form "swags" frame openwork spirals on one of the mounts on a hanging bowl found at Garton Station, Humberside. It is a motif that was used on Irish brooches in the eighth century, enriched with spirals in the volutes and trumpet pattern in the swags in contemporary Irish style. On the Great Barton disc the whole composition, including the swags, is classicizing. The design was not necessarily dependent on swastikas seen on sixth-century potters' stamps in East Anglia. From its use of yellow glass and millefiori insets and its relation to the angular style of Irish enameling of the late seventh and eighth centuries, this piece should be no earlier than the first half of the seventh century. It does not look like the work of an innovating craftsman but is a relatively crude version of the elements it carries.

It is also unlikely that the Great Barton disc was made anywhere near where it was found. Local enameling in Anglo-Saxon style does not continue through the seventh century. The piece is probably a mount from the base of a hanging bowl. Its angular cell work, like that of a basal disc on a bowl from Manton Common, Lincolnshire, links it to the later Irish-made series found in Viking graves in Scandinavia, a shift in production and patronage that probably marks the reduction and conquest of British kingdoms of central, western, and northern Britain in the course of the seventh century.[25]

Polychrome enameling was reintroduced to Britain by the late sixth or early seventh century with yellow, blue, and green glasses in addition to the brilliant sealing-wax red. This suggests new access to different colored glasses with melting temperatures compatible with the prevailing red. Yellow glass appears early and uses the same type of glass as was used for beads found in Anglo-Saxon graves. There is, however, an Anglo-Saxon bucket from a grave at Great Chesterford, Cambridgeshire, that has both red and yellow enamel in four unique decorative plates at the rim (fig. 6).[26] The bucket is a distinctive type that has been dated to the first half of the sixth century. Each plate carries two panels with a quatrefoil in low relief, one set against red enamel and one against yellow. In size and

24. For the examples cited, see Brenan, *Hanging Bowls and Their Contexts*, cat. no. 13; J. Hawkes, *Golden Age of Northumbria*, p. 33, fig. 28.

25. For the Scandinavian finds, see Petersen, *Viking Antiquities in Great Britain and Ireland*, pp. 83–111, and list 3 in Wamers, *Insularer Metallschmuck in wikingerzeitlichen Gräbern Nordeuropas*, pp. 113–16.

26. J. Cook, "Bronze-bound Buckets."

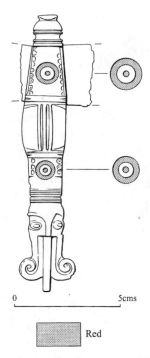

0   5cms

Red

Figure 1. Enamel inlays on an Anglo-Saxon cruciform brooch made from the same model as a brooch from Ixworth, Suffolk. Drawing by James Farrant, British Museum.

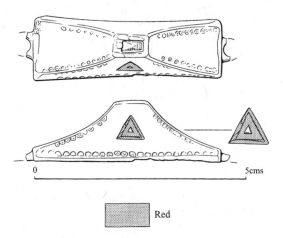

0   5cms

Red

Figure 2. Bronze sword pommel with red enamel inlay on one side only, from Hemingby, Lincolnshire. Drawing by James Farrant, British Museum.

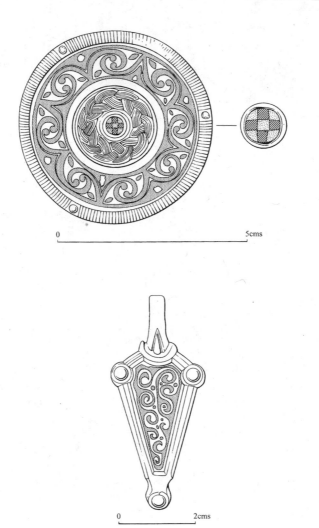

Figure 3. Basal (a) and hook (b) mounts from a bronze hanging bowl from Hadleigh Road, Ipswich, Suffolk. The interlace on the disc is gilded, the other areas are inlaid with red enamel and a central piece of millefiori glass in blue and pale yellow. Drawing by James Farrant, British Museum.

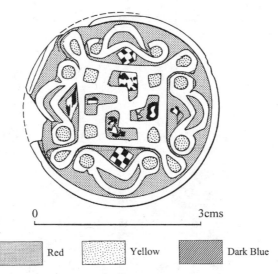

0 ———————————————— 3cms

Red   Yellow   Dark Blue

Figure 4. Bronze disc inlaid with fields of yellow enamel against a red background and inset with millefiori glass, from Great Barton, Suffolk. Drawing by James Farrant, British Museum.

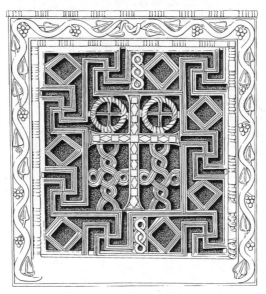

Figure 5. Ornament on a sixth-century pierced stone panel from San Apollinare Nuovo, Ravenna. Reduced. Drawing by James Farrant, British Museum.

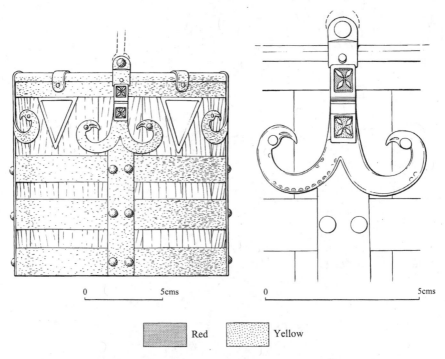

Figure 6 and detail. The enameled plates on a bronze-bound wooden bucket from Great Chesterford, Cambridgeshire. Drawing by James Farrant, British Museum, after Evison, "Anglo-Saxon Glass from Cremations."

decoration the fittings resemble a type of wrist-clasp, but the use of these mounts with their two-colored enamel inlay remains without parallel.[27] Yellow glass has not been identified on native-style British or Irish enamel of this date. Was this pioneering work, or an experimental piece imitating Roman vessels that carry enameled versions of this same quatrefoil motif? The Roman fort at Great Chesterford is still rich in enameled metalwork. Other examples of the same bucket type with elaborate birds-head terminals do not carry enamels or equivalent mounts, and this bucket could have been made and embellished locally. Is this evidence for sub-Roman craftsmen working in the area, indulgently allowed by a local patron to experiment with new colors? Perhaps it was a local smith trying a new line that did not become widely popular. Perhaps this is best accepted as a reminder that we have partial and incomplete evidence of the past.

The earliest enameled Anglo-Saxon piece was found at Hemingby, Lincolnshire. The old kingdom of Lindsey in north Lincolnshire has a unique concentration of hanging bowls in graves, with more than seventeen complete examples, in contrast to a total of five from Suffolk, and also a contemporary enameled buckle, against a background of earlier native British enameled brooches.[28] Here, too, crudely repaired and incomplete bowls argue against local manufacture. By the late sixth century it may have been an entrepot or gateway for such items into Anglo-Saxon territories.[29] In the sixth century we are not looking at the native tradition informing those of the incomers. In a period of rapid cultural dominance that saw the end of the British language, influences are going from the patron to the supplier, from the dominant forces to the subservient or unsuccessful polities. The new Anglo-Saxon styles of artifact and their decoration were badges of success. Enamel had to wait for another three centuries before it made a significant contribution to Anglo-Saxon art and ornament.

27. My thanks to John Hines for pointing out the relation to wrist-clasps. Hines, *Scandinavian Character of Anglian England*, form B 12, pp. 77–79, 106–07, fig 2.45; a good parallel for these decorative panels in the form of a wrist clasp comes from a multiperiod site at Coddenham, Suffolk (West, *Corpus of Anglo-Saxon Material from Suffolk*, p. 23, fig. 25.3).

28. Vince, *Pre-Viking Lindsey*. The enameled buckle with millefiori from Keelby, Lincolnshire, must be a local British product, as Lloyd Laing suggests in "Bradwell Mount" (p. 149), *contra* Youngs, "Recent Finds of Insular Enameled Buckles," pp. 192–94 (where this buckle is given the incorrect provenance of West Ravendale throughout). An Irish origin for the two buckles of this type is unlikely. Enameled brooches have been recorded by Kevin Leahy at the North Lincolnshire Museum and await publication by the author.

29. Bruce-Mitford, "Ireland and the Hanging-bowls," p. 38.

THE DOORS OF HIS FACE:
EARLY HELL-MOUTH ICONOGRAPHY IN IRELAND

CAROL NEUMAN DE VEGVAR

Among her many contributions to the study of Insular art and archae-ology, Rosemary Cramp has demonstrated through her work the necessity of deriving possible meanings of sites and objects from their literary and historical contexts. Her work has cleared a path for many of us who have ventured after her into the thorny thickets of the Insular world, show-ing by example the obligation incumbent upon scholars of early medieval material and visual culture to form as clear an idea of cultural setting as the evidence will support, as the primary prerequisite to interpretation. In an era where some have called for the isolation of archaeology from the history of art and the separation of the study of material culture from textual sources of any kind, Professor Cramp has been a steady voice for an understanding of culture and its artifacts as an integrated whole. For this, as for so much else, an entire generation of scholars owes her a pro-found debt of gratitude, for which this volume may serve as a sign. The unified approach exemplified in Professor Cramp's work has direct bear-ing for the study of the development of new iconographic types for which the wellsprings of inspiration may not have been entirely visual. A case in point is the development of a particular early visualization of the mouth of hell, where exegesis, popular cult, and liturgical innovation as well as earlier visual formulations may all have played a critical role in stimulat-ing artistic imagination.

The image of the mouth of hell, jaws agape, swallowing demons and sinners alike with appalling gourmandise, is one of the deliberately ter-rifying images developed in medieval art as an admonition to transgres-

My thanks are owed to several colleagues without whom this project would not have reached fruition: to Michael Ryan for the initial idea for the project; to Richard Schneider and Bill Clark for encouraging me to present a very preliminary version of this inquiry at the Eigh-teenth Annual Canadian Conference of Medieval Art Historians (York University, Toronto, 19–21 March 1998), the discussion of which led to the development of the project to its present form; to Catherine Karkov for inviting me to participate in the sessions in honor of Rosemary Cramp at the International Congress on Medieval Studies at Kalamazoo in May 2000; and above all to Professor Cramp herself for the inspiring excellence of her work, for her many kindnesses, and for her enthusiasm for the field and all who labor in it. Any remaining errors are the responsibility of the author.

sors. One variant of this type is the lionhead doorpull with a human head in its teeth. Such doorpulls proliferate in the Romanesque period; this essay will propose a far earlier origin for this type, in eighth- or early ninth-century Irish metalwork, and examine both the visual and the textual elements available in that context that may have contributed to the articulation of this new pictorial type.

Current art historical understanding places the origin and evolution of hell-mouth iconography in Anglo-Saxon England; however, this assertion may be challenged as the early Anglo-Saxon examples, both textual and visual, are problematic. In his *vita* of Guthlac, written around the middle of the eighth century and frequently adduced as the earliest evidence of hell-mouth imagery in Anglo-Saxon England, Felix describes Guthlac as carried by demons "ad nefandas tartari fauces." Bertram Colgrave translated this as "to the accursed jaws of Hell," but *fauces* may also be translated "chasm."[1] None of the following text explores a metaphor of ingestion; instead the text refers to *atras cavernas*, which suggests that the gate of hell is an abyss, not a gullet. On the Repton Stone, dated to the eighth or ninth century and now in the Derby Museum, face B (fig. 1) shows a scene of a human-headed serpent swallowing the heads of two embracing or grappling male figures. This has been identified as a hell-mouth scene by Martin Biddle and Birthe Kjølbye-Biddle;[2] however, the scene has no absolute iconographic parallels. If it is indeed a hell-mouth scene it is not the start or an example of an extant iconographic tradition. On an ivory of the Last Judgment now in the Victoria and Albert Museum (fig. 2), the lower right corner displays a large quasi-leonine quasi-human head in profile, swallowing the damned one at a time while the rest queue to wait their turn. John Beckwith identified this ivory as Anglo-Saxon and late eighth or early ninth century in date, but others have considered it Continental work: Adolph Goldschmidt saw it as a ca. 800 product of Tours, and most recently Jonathan Alexander has referred to arguments for a later ninth-century Carolingian origin.[3] The hell mouth on this ivory

1. Felix, *Life of St. Guthlac*, chap. 31, pp. 104–05.
2. Biddle and Kjølbye-Biddle, "The Repton Stone," pp. 246–50, 273–79.
3. Beckwith, *Ivory Carvings in Early Medieval England*, cat. no. 4, pp. 118–19 and illustration 1; Goldschmidt with Hübner and Homburger, *Die Elfenbeinskulpturen aus der Zeit der karolingischen und sächsischen Kaiser*, 1:85; J. Alexander, "Last Things," pp. 48, 61 n. 17 for bibliography; Jonathan Alexander, conversation with author, Kalamazoo, Mich., 7 May 2000. This ivory (London, Victoria and Albert Museum, inv. no. 253.67) is now paired with an ornamental panel (London, Victoria and Albert Museum, inv. no. 254.67); in the late Carolingian period, both were cut down to form the doors of a shrine. However, the ivories are of different thicknesses and were not originally a pair; parallels for the motifs on the ornamental panel do not address the issue of the origin of the Last Judgment panel; see D. Wright, "Byzantine Model of a Provincial Carolingian Ivory."

seems to share a common ancestry with similar images in the Utrecht
Psalter (Utrecht, Universiteitsbibliotheek, MS 32), which depict partial
ingestion of evildoers by a gigantic but human head or figure, identified by Ernest DeWald as a personification interchangeably of Hades or
Death, which inhabits but is not identical with hell.[4] In the Utrecht Psalter,
according to DeWald, the image for Psalm 1 (fol. 1v) shows Hades with the
arm of a sinner in his mouth; in Psalm 17 (fol. 9r) a figure stands up to
his hips in the mouth of Death; and in Psalm 138 (fol. 78r), Hades is about
to devour a sinner head first, pulling him eagerly toward his mouth. The
illustration to Psalm 102 (fol. 59r) shows Death with a head in his mouth;
here as elsewhere in the Utrecht Psalter, Death is anthropomorphic and
seen in profile as on the Victoria and Albert ivory, not frontal and leonine
as on the doorpulls.[5]

A more consistent application of hell-mouth imagery develops in later
Anglo-Saxon manuscript illumination, as in the Harrowing of Hell in the
Tiberius Psalter (London, British Library, MS Cotton Tiberius C. vi, fol.
14; fig. 3) where the mouth of hell is shown as a vast yawning leonine jaw
in which an entire crowd of sinners can stand, a sort of infernal Jacuzzi.
The late Anglo-Saxon illuminators' repeated use of this image has been
linked to the monastic reform movement.[6] However, the lionhead doorpulls with human heads in the lion's jaws seem to have evolved separately
from textual sources, as compositionally they have nothing in common
with the gaping hell mouths of the Anglo-Saxon manuscript tradition.

The leonine ring handle had a long and distinguished history before
its arrival in medieval art. In classical architectural ornament and the decorative arts, the type is found in sacral, imperial, and funerary contexts.[7]
Textual sources reveal that lionhead doorpulls opened the door from the
pronaos into the *cella* of the Parthenon, and similar ring handles decorate
the arms of chairs on consulary diptychs.[8] The lionhead ring handle also
had funerary associations in Greek art already from the fourth century

4. DeWald, *Illustrations of the Utrecht Psalter,* pp. 4, 11, 47, 60.

5. A similar profile view of an open toothy jaw was sketched in the lower border of a
manuscript of Bede's *Ecclesiastical History* (London, British Library, MS Cotton Tiberius C.
ii, fol. 5r); however, the artist has not shown the mouth as an entrance to a place of damnation; see Schmidt, *Iconography of the Mouth of Hell,* p. 38. The date of this sketch is debated;
Schmidt considers it ninth century, contemporary with the manuscript's gloss; however, J.
Alexander dates it possibly as late as the twelfth century (*Insular Manuscripts,* p. 60).

6. Schmidt, *Iconography of the Mouth of Hell,* p. 38; Galpern, "Shape of Hell in Anglo-
Saxon England," p. 154; Ohlgren, *Insular and Anglo-Saxon Illuminated Manuscripts,* p. 357
and passim.

7. Mende, *Die Türzieher des Mittelalters,* pp. 128–36; Michael Ryan, "Zoomorphic Handle Assembly; Donore, Co. Meath," in Youngs, *"The Work of Angels,"* cat. no. 64, p. 69.

8. Mende, *Die Türzieher des Mittelalters,* p. 130, plate 350.

BC onward; in late antiquity it is consistently found on sarcophagi and cineraria and on tomb doors and their images in art.[9] Ursula Mende sees the classical lionhead motif as apotropaic, deriving its force from its visual similarity to the *gorgoneion* or gorgon head and from the identity of the lion as the premier predator in the Near East and Egypt.[10]

The classical lionhead doorpull is commonly considered to have been revived in the Carolingian period with the doors of the Capella Palatina at Aachen, ca. 800 (fig. 4), and to have spread from there to the rest of Europe and the British Isles, appearing at Durham Cathedral ca. 1133. In Germany, this type is thought to have fused with hell-mouth imagery to produce a number of doorpulls with a human head in the jaws of the lion. Of these the earlier series of examples were made in twelfth-century Magdeburg and are today found at the cathedral of St. Sophia, Novgorod, and at the monastic church of the Premonstratensian community at Czerwinsk.[11] A series of later examples, dated to about 1400 and probably influenced by the Magdeburg type, include the doorpull of the Raising of the Cross Church at Luborzyca, near Cracow, and three examples in England: on the sacristy door of St. Gregory, Norwich; on the south portal of the Church of St. John the Baptist at Adel in Yorkshire (fig. 5); and on the north portal of the Church of All Saints, York.[12]

The responsibility of the Carolingian Capella Palatina at Aachen for the revival of the classical leonine ring handle and for its introduction to the northern European medieval artistic repertory must be shared with Irish smiths and the clergy for whom they produced fine metalwork. At least one pre-Carolingian western medieval lionhead handle has been found in Ireland; part of the assemblage of eighth-century door fittings from Donore near Moynalty, Co. Meath (Dublin, National Museum of Ireland; fig. 6).[13] This doorpull may predate the Aachen doorpulls and demonstrates that the concept of the leonine handle was not introduced to early medieval northern Europe exclusively by the Carolingians but was also available in Ireland. Nor is the Donore ring handle unique in Irish metalwork. A second simpler version of the same design was also found at Donore.[14] Another Irish ring handle similar to the more complex

9. Mende, *Die Türzieher des Mittelalters*, pp. 128–30.

10. Mende, *Die Türzieher des Mittelalters*, pp. 133–34.

11. Mende, *Die Türzieher des Mittelalters*, cat. no. 78A/B, plates 145–46, 150–53.

12. Mende, *Die Türzieher des Mittelalters*, cat. nos. 153–56; plates 254–57. E. Meyer, "Deutschordenskunst im mittelalterlichen England," compared the central European examples with the lion heads on a baptismal font at Elbing, dated 1387 and associated with the Bernhuser workshop active ca. 1400 probably in Königsberg.

13. M. Ryan, "Zoomorphic Handle Assembly," p. 69; M. Ryan, "Donore Hoard."

14. Michael Ryan, "Enamelled Handle; Donore, Co. Meath," in Youngs, *"The Work of Angels,"* cat. no. 66, p. 70.

Donore example was at one time preserved at Killua Castle; here the animal head is somewhat more generic, although Armstrong claimed to be able to identify it as a horse.[15] Similar handles of Irish origin were found in Norwegian eighth- to ninth-century Viking graves at Vik and Tornes.[16]

An iconographically more interesting eighth- or ninth-century example was found in 1848 in the excavation of a railway cutting at Navan, Co. Meath (Dublin, National Museum of Ireland; fig. 7).[17] It was discovered in dark soil along with an assemblage of horse trappings and human and animal bones and has been published consistently as a harness mount.[18] However, the identification of the assemblage by James Graham-Campbell in 1976 as a Scandinavian burial, potentially containing a mixture of metalwork looted by Viking raiders, and the resemblance of the handle to the Donore doorpull have led to the reidentification of the Navan handle as a doorpull or shrine handle, possibly from a coffin-reliquary.[19] However, the Donore and Navan handles are mutually distinct in one significant detail; the Donore lion bares its teeth at the viewer gripping the handle, but the Navan mount shows the additional feature of a bearded human head in the jaws of the lion.

The Navan handle is not a unique example of the human head in the jaws of a beast in early Irish art. This motif is found in metalwork in three other examples: first, an eighth-century terminal, probably from a crosier, from Helgö in Sweden, now in the Statens Historiska Museum in Stockholm (fig. 8); second, a pair of late eighth- to early ninth-century mounts in the Musée des Antiquités nationales, Saint-Germain-en-Laye, probably from the gable-end finials of a massive house-shaped shrine (fig. 9); and third, two similar but badly damaged fragments from a woman's grave at Gausel, Norway, which Egil Bakka has suggested come from the corresponding finials at the other end of the gable of the same shrine.[20] In 1938, Françoise Henry catalogued several examples of the same motif

15. Armstrong, "Some Irish Antiquities," pp. 6–7; Raghnall Ó Floinn, "Animal-headed Mount; Ireland," in Youngs, "The Work of Angels," cat. no. 68, pp. 70–71.

16. Wamers, Insularer Metallschmuck in wikingerzeitlichen Gräbern Nordeuropas, cat. nos. 34, 75; pp. 93, 98; plates 6.6, 31.7; Leslie Webster, "Door-ring; Vik, Stamnes, Bruvik, Hordaland, Norway," in Youngs, "The Work of Angels," cat. no. 67, p. 70.

17. Armstrong, "Some Irish Antiquities," p. 6.

18. Armstrong, "Some Irish Antiquities," p. 12; Wilde, Descriptive Catalogue of the Antiquities, p. 611; Raghnall Ó Floinn, "Harness Mounts; Near Navan, Co. Meath," in Youngs, "The Work of Angels," cat. no. 113, pp. 117–18.

19. Graham-Campbell, "Viking-Age Silver Hoards," p. 60; and Michael Ryan, conversation with author, Dublin, 15 July 1996.

20. Leslie Webster, "Pair of Mounts; Unprovenanced," in Youngs, "The Work of Angels," cat. nos. 138a, b, p. 145; and "Terminal, probably from a Crozier; Helgö, Ekerö, Uppland, Sweden," in ibid., cat. no. 147, p. 152; F. Henry, "Deux Objets de bronze irlandais"; Bakka, "Some Decorated Anglo-Saxon and Irish Metalwork."

in stonework: on a capital from the Romanesque Church of the Saints at Inchagoyle (Co. Galway), on the Ferbane Cross (Co. Offaly), and on a small stone capital at Maughold on the Isle of Man, probably an import from Ireland.[21] The Book of Kells (Dublin, Trinity College Library, MS 58) also includes a number of hostile encounters between human figures and lions.[22] Of these, one shows human heads in lions' mouths; at the bottom of folio 188r, in the reserved area for the letters NIAM of *Quoniam* at the opening of Luke, two of the descenders of the M terminate in lions' heads that bite the heads of recumbent figures (fig. 10). George Henderson agreed with Henry that the scene must refer generically to the torments of hell.[23] These examples demonstrate that the motif of the human head in the jaws of a lion was not uncommon in the preeminent media of early Irish art. The human face on the Navan handle may most probably be understood as an adaptation of a locally popular motif to the format of the leonine handle or doorpull, which was also available in the same milieu.

Lions figure in the Bible as both positive and negative signifiers, but explicit references to a devouring lion as the embodiment of damnation after death are predominantly exegetical rather than scriptural. In the Bible, the enemies of this world are sometimes identified with a consuming lion, and elsewhere lions identified with the Devil seize or devour their victims, but no biblical text explicitly situates these assailants in the afterlife. The Psalms refer to lions as the embodiment of malice suffered in the course of earthly life. Psalm 7:2–3 asks for deliverance, "Save me from all them that persecute me, and deliver me. Lest at any time he seize upon my soul like a lion, while there is no one to redeem me," but the identity of the soul seizer is not declared. Elsewhere the Psalms are even more openly worldly in their concerns: in Psalm 9:30 the sinner lies in wait for the poor man like a lion in his den; and in Psalm 16:12, the psalmist's enemies plan like lions to attack him. Psalm 21:14 refers to enemies who "have opened their mouths against me, as a lion ravening and roar-

21. F. Henry, "Deux Objets de bronze irlandais," pp. 206–07.

22. J. Alexander, "The Illumination," pp. 276–77; F. Henry, *Book of Kells*, pp. 200–04, 206–07; M. Ryan, "Book of Kells and Metalwork," pp. 276–77. At the opening of the Gospel of Mark (fol. 130r), a nude male figure is seized around the torso and upper arms by a lion; the victim resists by seizing the lion's tongue. At the opening of Luke (fol. 188r), in addition to the example cited in the text, the head of a lion, projecting from the top frame of the initial, is juxtaposed with several nude or partially clad figures in a framed space directly below. At the opening of John (top of fol. 292r), a seated figure holding a cup confronts a huge lion head; see also G. Henderson, *From Durrow to Kells*, p. 178.

23. G. Henderson, *From Durrow to Kells*, pp. 165–68; F. Henry, *Book of Kells*, pp. 200–04 and n. 98. Henderson read this scene as possibly depicting the two witnesses killed by the beast from the abyss (Rev. 11:7).

ing"; and verse 22 of the same psalm petitions for salvation but again from earthly malice: "For many dogs have encompassed me; the council of the malignant hath besieged me . . . But thou, O Lord, remove not thy help to a distance from me; look toward my defense. Save me from the lion's mouth; and my lowness from the horns of the unicorn. I will declare thy name to my brethren: in the midst of the church will I praise thee."[24] The last line suggests the speaker is understood to be very much alive at the conclusion of his metaphoric animal encounters.

The Petrine and Pauline Epistles echo and expand upon the psalmist's leonine motifs. In 2 Timothy 4:17, Paul refers to delivery from persecution as salvation "from the mouth of the lion" but, like the psalmist, in the present world. Only in 1 Peter 5:8 do the lion and the devil explicitly cross paths: the faithful are admonished, "Be sober and watch: because your adversary the devil, as a roaring lion, goeth about seeking whom he may devour"; but here the need for vigilance in the present suggests that the danger of ingestion applies to the living, not the dead. Neither Bede nor the Irish exegetes who wrote on the Petrine epistles consider the eschatological potential of this passage.[25] Other scriptural texts concerning the swallowing of sinners, whether by hell or Sheol or by the ground, tend to visualize the opening as a mouth, but without specific reference to natural or supernatural creatures.[26] It was left to exegetes and visionaries to identify the lion with the all-consuming mouth of hell awaiting sinners in the hereafter.

Most early western commentators on the mouth of hell, notably Caesarius of Arles and Peter Chrysologus, both writing in the fifth century, refer to the size and depth of the mouth of hell without association with a particular species of beast. However, later writers may have taken inspiration from the *Visio Sancti Pauli,* one of the earliest eschatological visionary texts in the Christian tradition, where a dragon consumes sinners. The *Visio* was initially written in Greek possibly as early as the third but certainly no later than the fifth century.[27] It reached Ireland before the end of the ninth century, where it was widely used in the subsequent development of Irish eschatological texts.[28] The so-called Long Latin redactions of the *Visio Sancti Pauli* describe the swallowing of evil princes and their ministers by a dragon in hell. Redaction VII, preserved in an eleventh-cen-

24. See also Psalm 90:13.

25. Bede, "Expositio super Epistolas Catholicas"; McNally, *Scriptores Hiberniae minores,* pp. 35 and 97; J. Kelly, "The Devil in Hiberno-Latin Exegesis," p. 140.

26. Schmidt, *Iconography of the Mouth of Hell,* p. 33.

27. Silverstein, *Visio Sancti Pauli,* pp. 3–5; Sozomen, *Ecclesiastica Historia,* p. 331; Duensing, "Apocalypse of St. Paul," p. 755.

28. Silverstein, *Visio Sancti Pauli,* p. 12; C. Wright, *Irish Tradition in Old English Literature,* pp. 109–13; Borsje, *From Chaos to Enemy,* pp. 271–75 and passim.

tury manuscript in Paris (Bibliothèque nationale de France, MS lat. 2851), extends the swallowing to generic sinners; but it is uncertain whether this particular recension was known and widely circulated in Ireland.[29]

A text certainly well read in Ireland was Gregory's *Moralia in Job*, with its multiple references to the devouring of sinners by Behemoth and Leviathan. Eschatology was a central component of Gregory's cosmology, notably in the *Moralia* and in Book IV of the *Dialogues*.[30] In the *Moralia* as elsewhere Gregory himself may have been influenced by the *Visio Sancti Pauli*.[31] In Gregory's text, Behemoth can take on the identity of several different animals, including a lion; he consumes the life of sinners; he lies in ambush for the faithful; and "even after the knowledge of the Redeemer, he seizes many with his open mouth."[32] Gregory's vivid image of the ingestion of sinners by a leonine monster stoked the imaginations of northern European visionary writers and artists for centuries to come.[33]

The *Moralia* was available in many parts of northern Europe by the seventh century and used widely as a source within a few centuries of its composition.[34] It was in Ireland already by the seventh century, where it was republished in condensed form as the *Eclogues* of Laidcenn of Clonfert-Molua.[35] In the incipits of two early manuscripts of the *Eclogues*, St. Petersburg Public Library, MS F.v.I, no. 7 (fols. 41r–104v), dated to the late eighth century, and Karlsruhe, Badische Landesbibliothek, MS Augiensis CXXXIV, of the ninth century, and in the ninth-century catalogue of the library at Murbach, Laidcenn is identified as "son of Baith."[36] This in turn serves to identify the author of the *Eclogues* with the *Laidhggen sapiens*

---

29. Silverstein, *Visio Sancti Pauli*, p. 205.

30. Manselli, "L'escatologia di S. Gregorio Magno"; McNally, "Gregory the Great."

31. Cracco, "Gregorio e l'Oltretomba," p. 256.

32. Gregory, *Moralia in Job* 32.13.18, 32.15.25, 33.6.12, pp. 1642–43, 1648, 1681; Gregory, *Morals on the Book of Job*, pp. 524–25, 530, 566.

33. Galpern, "Shape of Hell in Anglo-Saxon England," pp. 142–54. In addition to 1 Peter 5:8, Gregory may have been inspired by references in Marcus Manilius's first-century *Astronomica* to the dreadful hunger and horrifying jaws of the monstrous lion in the constellation Leo (4.176, 4.464–65, 4.535–41, 5.206, pp. 236–37, 258–59, 264–65, 316–17).

34. Manitius, *Geschichte der lateinischen Literatur des Mittelalters*, pp. 97–100; de Lubac, *Exégèse médiévale* 1:2, pp. 537–48; Wasselynck, "L'influence de l'exégèse de S. Grégoire le Grand"; Wasselynck, "Présence de Saint Grégoire le Grand"; Milde, "Paläographische Bemerkungen zu den Breslauer Unzialfragmenten der Dialoge Gregors des Großen"; Meyvaert, *Bede and Gregory the Great;* Bonner, *Saint Bede in the Tradition of Western Apocalyptic Commentary.*

35. Gougaud, "Le Témoignage des manuscrits"; Kenney, *Sources for the Early History of Ireland*, pp. 278–79; Bischoff, "Turning Points in the History of Latin Exegesis," p. 105; J. Kelly, "Catalogue of Early Medieval Hiberno-Latin Commentaries," p. 561; cf. Wasselynck, "Les Compilations des 'Moralia in Job,'" pp. 11–14.

36. Manitius, *Geschichte der lateinischen Literatur des Mittelalters*, p. 100; Laidcenn, *Ecloga de Moralibus Iob*, pp. vi–vii.

mac Baith Bannaigh (Laidcenn the wise, son of Baith the Victorious) whose death is recorded in the Irish Annals for 661.[37] The *Eclogues* demonstrate a decided taste for the more visual aspects of Gregory's allegoristic text, consistently selecting the vividly descriptive over the moralizing passages and perhaps assisting in setting the stage for the emergence of hell-mouth iconography in Ireland.[38]

This process was no doubt assisted by the enormous popularity of Gregory in Ireland, as demonstrated by the evidence of the Irish cult of Gregory compiled by François Kerlouégan.[39] The *Moralia* and the *Dialogues* were both quoted extensively by hagiographers, exegetes, and composers of penitentials, and the accomplishments of the sainted pope were a regular subject for Irish authors, by whom he is also reputed to have taught and ordained Irish saints and to have been the recipient of their monastic *regulae,* the subject of their visions, and the recipient of visions concerning them; indeed Kenney noted that Gregory is the standard name for the pope in Irish saints' legends.[40] Kerlouégan also compiled legends concerning Gregory's Irish connections; in both the *Aru na naemh* (Aran of the saints) and the possibly eleventh-century *Betha Grighora* (Life of Gregory) Gregory was of Irish descent and was interred on Aran Island.[41] Given both Gregory's personal popularity and the wide circulation of his texts in Ireland, it is no surprise to find echoes of his writing in Irish ecclesiastical writing and art.

In the period in which the Navan handle was produced, Gregorian eschatology was influential in the increasing popularity of the Mass for the dead throughout western Europe. Gregory's eschatology introduced the notion of individual judgment at the time of death, rather than a period of waiting in anticipation of the collective Last Judgment at the end of time; those in purgatory could be released from torment to beatitude by means of private masses said for their benefit.[42] One offertory of the Mass for the dead, *Domine Iesu Christe,* calling for the delivery of the deceased from various torments, eventually became part of the stan-

---

37. Laidcenn's death is recorded in parallel entries in the Annals of Ulster (*AU*), Inisfallen (*AI*), and Tigernach (*A. Tig.*); he is also commemorated on January 12 in the martyrologies of Tallaght and Drummond and the *Félire* of Oengus (Grosjean, "Sur quelques exégètes irlandais," pp. 93–94). On the title *sapiens,* see Ó Cróinín, *Early Medieval Ireland,* pp. 194–95; Ireland, "Aldfrith of Northumbria"; Mac Lean, "Scribe = Artist (but Not Monk)," pp. 57–71.

38. Laidcenn, *Ecloga de Moralibus Iob,* passim; Wasselynck, "Les compilations des 'Moralia in Job,'" pp. 12–13; Braga, "*Moralia in Iob*," pp. 562–63.

39. Kerlouégan, "Grégoire le Grand et les Pays Celtiques."

40. Kenney, *Sources for the Early History of Ireland,* p. 219 n. 176.

41. Kerlouégan, "Grégoire le Grand et les Pays Celtiques," p. 594.

42. Vogel, "Deux conséquences de l'eschatologie Grégorienne," pp. 268–69.

dardized requiem Mass in the Roman missal. The *Domine* includes the line "Libera eas de ore leonis" (Free them from the mouth of the lion).[43] Debate concerning the date and origins of this offertory is extensive. The oldest extant manuscript sources for the text as offertory date to the tenth century, suggesting that its appearance in this liturgical role dates from that time.[44] However, the text's many archaisms suggest that it had an earlier history as a prayer before being adapted as an offertory chant.[45] Raynerius Podevijn suggested that its responsorial structure places it with similar prayers of the eighth to the tenth century.[46]

The offertory is clearly not Roman in origin; it is unlike any other offertory preserved in the Roman liturgy and does not appear in Roman sacramentaries until the beginning of the twelfth century.[47] The offertory exhibits some similarities with the Gallican liturgy, notably the invocation, following eastern models, of the Son rather than the Father, as opposed to the dictates of the third Council of Carthage.[48] But Irish texts offer by far the most consistent parallels. Bonifacio Serpelli first suggested an Irish author or school if not a provenance in Ireland for the *Domine;* he noted the offertory's tendencies to the rich phraseology, vivid imagery, and incantatory repetition typical of early Hiberno-Latin texts, and the emphasis on St. Michael, the focus of an extensive cult in Ireland but a

43. The offertory in full reads: "Domine Iesu Christe, rex gloriae, libera animas omnium fidelium defunctorum de poenis inferni et de profundo lacu. Libera eas de ore leonis; ne absorbeat eas tartarus; ne cadant in obscurum. Sed signifer sanctus Michaël repraesentet eas in lucem sanctam. Quam olim Abrahae promisisti, et semini eius. Hostis et preces tibi, Domine, laudis offerimus: tu suscipe pro animabus illis, quarum hodie memoriam facimus; fac eis, Domine, de morte transire ad vitam. Quam olim Abrahae promisisti, et semini eius."

44. The earliest manuscript sources are the Amiens Sacramentary, Paris, Bibliothèque nationale de France, MS lat. 9432 (Sicard, *La Liturgie de la mort dans l'église latine,* p. 188); St. Gall, Stiftsbibliothek, MS 339, fol. 114r; and a probably early tenth-century transcription in an Insular hand in Vatican City, Biblioteca Apostolica Vaticana, MS Palatinus lat. 14, fol. 178v (Serpelli, *L'Offertorio della messe dei defunti,* pp. 24, 27).

45. Cabrol, "L'Offertoire de la messe des morts," p. 167.

46. Podevijn, "Het Offertorium der Doodenmis," pp. 341, 345; Podevijn, "Addendum to Het Offertorium der Doodenmis," pp. 250–52; see also Maertens and Heuschen, *Doctrine et Pastorale de la liturgie de la mort,* p. 86.

47. Cabrol, "L'Offertoire de la messe des morts," p. 165; Serpelli, *L'Offertorio della messe dei defunti,* p. 25; cf. Beran, "L'Offertorio 'Domine Iesu Christe.'" The contention of the seventeenth-century Spanish Jesuit theologian Juan Azor, revived in the 1930s by Franciscus X. Hecht ("De offertorio missae defunctorum") and Johannes Obernhumer ("Nochmals: Das Offertorium der Totenmesse"), that the "mouth of the lion" is a direct reference to the entrance to the lowest level of a Roman prison has largely been put to rest since the 1940s: see Soressi, "L'Offertorio della messa dei defunti," p. 8.

48. Cabrol, "L'Offertoire de la messe des morts," p. 168; Serpelli, *L'Offertorio della messe dei defunti,* p. 17.

latecomer to Rome through Gallican liturgical influences.[49] Serpelli suggested that the offertory originated at ninth- or tenth-century St. Gall, on the basis of the early appearance of the offertory in St. Gall, Stiftsbibliothek, MS 339, folio 114r. If so, it was written in a period when the abbey was a flourishing center of liturgical music. However, for Serpelli the *Domine* was produced under strong Irish influence, and a provenance in Ireland remained a second possibility.[50] Brian Grogan has suggested additional parallels between the *Domine* and texts with Irish connections: notably the *Priscillian Fragments* and the apocalyptic *Vision of Adomnán*.[51] If he and Serpelli are correct in their assertions, the leonine imagery of the *Domine* may well have been in circulation in eighth- or ninth-century Ireland, at the time of the production of the Navan handle.

It is evident that a critical mass of textual iconographic source material was available in Ireland by the eighth or ninth century to permit the evolution of leonine hell-mouth imagery. But is it also possible that Irish doorpulls or shrine handles ultimately served as models for the examples from twelfth-century Magdeburg and, through the latter, for the late medieval examples from Königsberg and England? Irish missions to the Continent continued into the eleventh and twelfth centuries. Although the concentration of Irish foundations in central Europe tended to cluster in what is today southern Germany and Austria, missionary activity extended considerably further north and east. In his eleventh-century *Gesta Hammaburgensis ecclesiae pontificum*, Adam of Bremen records the work of a Bishop John from Ireland who undertook missionary work in northern Germany, probably in Mecklenburg, where he was martyred about 1066.[52] The anonymous *vita* written in 1184/85 of Marianus, abbot of St. Peter at Ratisbon, describes the foundation of the *Schottenklöster*, a congregation of monastic communities that developed in the late eleventh and early twelfth centuries in southern Germany. These communities were supported by gifts from Ireland; by the thirteenth century the congregation also included one or more houses in Ireland itself.[53] The

---

49. Serpelli, *L'Offertorio della messe dei defunti*, pp. 25–26, 92.

50. Serpelli, *L'Offertorio della messe dei defunti*, p. 28; see also Soressi, "L'Offertorio della messa dei defunti," p. 7.

51. Grogan, "Eschatological Teaching," pp. 52–55. Grogan's third example, a prayer in the ninth-century Book of Cerne (Cambridge, University Library, MS Ll. i. 10, fol. 57r), "Ut non apponat leo et draco qui consuetus est animas/miserorum rapere et ad aeterna tormenta perducere" (Kuypers, *Prayerbook of Æduald the Bishop*, pp. 113–14), is probably not, as Grogan claims, a prototype for the *Domine*, but is closely linked to the *Contestatio* in the Gallican liturgy for the dead: "Non se ei opponat leo rugiens, et draco devorans, miserorum animas rapere consuetus" (Mabillon and Germain, *Museum Italicum*, 1:385).

52. Kenney, *Sources for the Early History of Ireland*, p. 614.

53. Kenney, *Sources for the Early History of Ireland*, pp. 605–06, 616–18.

Figure 1. Repton Stone (eighth or ninth century), face B: possible hell-mouth scene. Derby, Derby Museum and Art Gallery. Photo: author/Derby Museum and Art Gallery.

Figure 2. Last Judgment, ninth century. London, Victoria and Albert Museum. Photo: V&A Picture Gallery.

Figure 3. Tiberius Psalter (London, British Library, MS Cotton Tiberius C. vi), folio 14r. The Harrowing of Hell (mid-eleventh century). By permission of the British Library.

Figure 4. Aachen, Capella Palatina, lionhead doorpull mount (ca. 800).
Photo: Bildarchiv Foto Marburg/Art Resource.

Figure 5. Adel, Yorkshire, Church of St. John the Baptist, south portal doorpull (ca. 1400). Photo: author.

Figure 6. Door fittings from Donore, near Moynalty, Co. Meath (eighth century). Dublin, National Museum of Ireland. Photo: National Museum of Ireland.

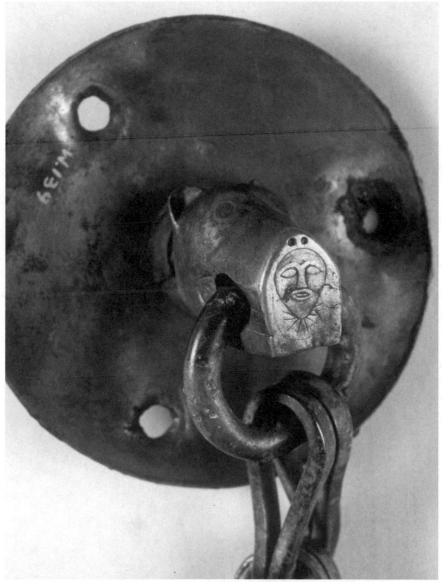

Figure 7. Doorpull or shrine handle from Navan, Co. Meath (eighth or ninth century). Dublin, National Museum of Ireland. Photo: National Museum of Ireland.

Figure 8. Terminal, probably from a crosier, from Helgö (Ekerö parish), Uppland (eighth century). Stockholm, Statens Historiska Museum. Photo: Antikvarisk-topografiska arkivet, National Heritage Board, Stockholm.

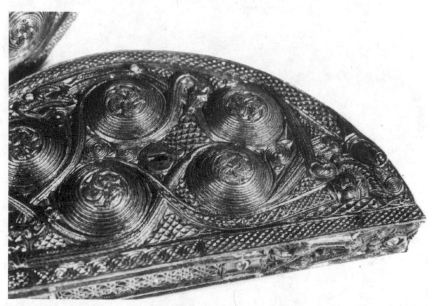

Figure 9. One of a pair of mounts, probably from a shrine (late eighth to early ninth century). Saint-Germain-en-Laye. Musée des Antiquités nationales. Photo: © Photo RMN.

Figure 10. Book of Kells (Dublin, Trinity College Library, MS 58), folio 188, opening of Luke (ca. 800). Photo: The Board of Trinity College Dublin.

monks of the *Schottenklöster* traveled as missionaries outside southern Germany: the *vita* of Marianus also describes the missionary journey of a monk named Mauricius to Kiev in Russia, where he not only succeeded in establishing a mission but also obtained a consignment of furs that funded the completion of the *Schottenklöster* of St. James at Ratisbon in 1090. A letter to Wratislaw, king of Bohemia, also mentions this mission, confirming the report in the *vita*.[54] Certainly among the gifts to the *Schottenklöster* from Ireland in this period would have been portable reliquaries and book shrines that could have traveled with the missionaries going north and east or served as gifts in exchanges with indigenous ecclesiastical communities elsewhere in Germany. Although specific records of such objects are lacking, one may speculate that the handles on these objects could have served as vectors of the hell-mouth handle type from Ireland to the later Romanesque doorpulls from Magdeburg and their Gothic successors from Königsberg. It may be only by an ironic historical accident that three doorpulls of the Königsberg type ended up in the islands at the northwest corner of Europe, at Norwich, Adel, and York, so close to the source of the idea that gave rise to their form.

This study of the origins of the leonine hell mouth with human head draws together several strands of inquiry: exegesis, cult, liturgy, and the history of Irish missions on the European mainland. The resultant cloth is no doubt somewhat tattered even in the weaving by the concealments and distortions of historical distance, but on the whole, the fragments suggest an Irish provenance of the type, parallel to but separate from Anglo-Saxon and Continental hell-mouth imagery, and at least one possible path for its dissemination to the continent. The variety of the evidence adduced here reflects the continuing legacy of Rosemary Cramp, whose richly interdisciplinary approach to forms and symbols continues to inform and inspire; we who follow know she has woven well.

54. Kenney, *Sources for the Early History of Ireland*, p. 618.

CONSTRUCTING SALVATION:
THE FIGURAL ICONOGRAPHY OF THE IONA CROSSES

JANE HAWKES

INTRODUCTION

Through her many publications on the subject of Anglo-Saxon sculpture, Rosemary Cramp has helped to establish an approach to the study of the iconography of early Christian sculpture in the Insular world for which text is as important to our understanding of the figural decoration as image.[1] As a result the number of explorations into the iconographic significance of figural carving in the pre-Viking Anglo-Saxon world has increased significantly over the last twenty to thirty years, but by contrast, such approaches to the Early Christian sculptural remains surviving elsewhere in the Insular world are still comparatively rare, and scholarly discussions of the figural decoration of the stone crosses that were erected in and around Iona during the middle of the eighth century provide one example of this neglect.[2] Like some of the contemporary Anglo-Saxon monuments, the Crosses of St. Martin and St. Oran on Iona itself and that at Kildalton on Islay display a considerable amount of figural decoration;

Thanks are due to Gosia D'Aughton, Éamonn Ó Carragáin, and Jennifer O'Reilly for their comments on the points raised in this essay, and to Catherine Karkov for her patience and persistence.

1. For publications that have influenced the recent interest in the iconographic significance of pre-Viking Anglo-Saxon sculpture, see particularly Cramp, *Early Northumbrian Sculpture,* and Cramp, "Evangelist Symbols and Their Parallels." Prior to these publications very few iconographic studies were published that were not concerned with the monuments at Ruthwell and Bewcastle; most notable were Barbara Kurth's on the carvings at Wirksworth (Derbyshire), and Auckland St. Andrews (Co. Durham): "Ecclesia and an Angel," and "Iconography of the Wirksworth Slab." For the more recent tendency to explore sculptures other than the carvings at Ruthwell and Bewcastle, see, for example, Wood, "Anglo-Saxon Otley"; J. Hawkes, "Miracle Scene on the Rothbury Cross-shaft"; J. Hawkes, "Rothbury Cross"; J. Hawkes, "Symbols of the Passion or Power?"; Cassidy, "Dream of St Joseph"; J. Hawkes, "Mary and the Cycle of Resurrection"; Harbison, "Two Panels on the Wirksworth Slab"; J. Hawkes, "Wirksworth Slab"; J. Hawkes, "Question of Judgment"; J. Hawkes, *Sandbach Crosses;* see also the two studies by Bailey: *Meaning of Mercian Sculpture* and "'What Mean These Stones?'"
2. For Pictish sculpture and its relation to sculpture from elsewhere in the Insular world, see G. Henderson and I. Henderson, *Art of the Picts.*

yet unlike their Anglo-Saxon counterparts the iconographic significance of this figural ornament has received relatively little attention.[3]

The nonfigural motifs of the crosses have, of course, been the subject of academic inquiry for many decades. Their relationship to the decoration of manuscripts and sculpture produced elsewhere in the Insular world has been extensively examined, with the distinctive boss ornament and detail of the serpent viewed from above having been compared with similar details in manuscripts such as the Book of Kells (Dublin, Trinity College Library, MS 58) and carvings elsewhere in Scotland.[4] In such discourses the figural carving of the Iona crosses has not been entirely neglected, but consideration of it has focused almost exclusively on style and subject matter as a means of reinforcing the perceived cultural links suggested by the nonfigural motifs. Curle, for instance, discussing the Early Christian sculpture of Scotland in 1939, saw the images of the Virgin and Child as un-Irish "Northumbrian" products, but identified those of Abraham and Isaac and Daniel in the lions' den as "purely Irish"; more recently, Henderson, in her study of David in the art of Early Christian Scotland, has added the depictions of David featured on the Iona monuments to the subjects deemed to betray an Irish connection.[5]

3. Other monuments from the Iona group of carvings, not considered here because of the comparative lack of figural decoration or their extremely fragmentary condition, include the following: on Iona, the Cross of St. John, which displays no figural carving; the fragmentary remains of the Cross of St. Matthew, with the much damaged figures of Adam and Eve; a further fragment that is decorated with the three Hebrews in the fiery furnace; and the Keills Cross in Knapdale: RCAHMS, *Argyll: An Inventory of the Monuments*, 4:197–204, 208–11; Mac Lean, "Keills Cross in Knapdale." The Keills Cross features only a single standing figure set between two (or possibly four) lions in the cross-head (Mac Lean, "Keills Cross in Knapdale," plate 8.1). If this can be identified as Daniel with the lions, its Christological and Eucharistic references are more explicit than is the case with the comparable image on the Cross of St. Martin on Iona (see further below).

4. E.g., I. Henderson, "Book of Kells and the Snake-boss Motif." For the extensive literature on this topic, see further Curle, "Chronology of the Early Christian Monuments"; Radford, "Early Christian Monuments"; Stevenson, "Pictish Art"; Stevenson, "Chronology and Relationships"; Stevenson "Sculpture in Scotland"; F. Henry, *Book of Kells*, pp. 178, 218; Robertson, "St. John's Cross, Iona, Argyll"; Calvert, "Early Development of Irish High Crosses," pp. 160–67, 246–55; I. Henderson, "Pictish Art and the Book of Kells"; I. Henderson, "Review of *Argyll, Vol. 4: Iona*"; RCAHMS, *Argyll: An Inventory of the Monuments*, 4:18–19, 192–209; RCAHMS, *Argyll: An Inventory of the Monuments*, 5:209–10; Mac Lean, "Keills Cross in Knapdale"; Mac Lean, "Snake-bosses and Redemption."

5. Curle, "Chronology of the Early Christian Monuments," p. 96; I. Henderson, "'David Cycle' in Pictish Art"; I. Henderson, *"Primus inter Pares"*; G. Henderson and I. Henderson, *Art of the Picts*, pp. 130–32, 143–45. See also Calvert, "Early Development of Irish High Crosses," pp. 160–66; Mac Lean, "Keills Cross in Knapdale."

ICONOGRAPHIC SELECTIONS

Notwithstanding the claims to regional identity underlying such discussions, these studies have demonstrated the pivotal situation of the
Iona monuments in the Insular world. In these academic constructs, however, the iconographic concerns of the figural carving have been largely
ignored. Henderson's and Mac Lean's work, and a more recent analysis of
the Virgin and Child in Insular sculpture generally, are among the very
few that have even attempted to broach the topic.[6]

In turning to consider this aspect of the decoration, it is worth noting that the extant figural scenes discernible on the Iona monuments are
relatively limited in their selection. They comprise the iconic image of the
Virgin and Child flanked by angels and a series of Old Testament narrative scenes involving Cain and Abel (at Kildalton), Abraham and Isaac (on
the Cross of St. Martin as well as that at Kildalton), Daniel (on St. Martin's
Cross), and David: as Psalmist on the Crosses of St. Martin and St. Oran;
fighting the lion on all three monuments; and overcoming Goliath on St.
Martin's Cross (see figs. 1, 3–5). Nevertheless, limited though this selection
of images is, the scenes do exist (along with the nonfigural motifs) as part
of general iconographic programs that are specific to each monument.

Thus, on the Kildalton Cross (figs. 5–6), the Virgin and Child flanked
by two angels and placed at the point of transition between the shaft and
cross-head on the west face are found in the company of Cain and Abel
and Abraham and Isaac (in panels at the ends of the horizontal cross-arms)
and David Killing the Lion, set in the middle of the upper arm. Above and
below David are (respectively) a pair of angels and two peacocks flanking
a boss. The shaft of the cross, below the Virgin and Child, is filled with an
elaborate series of curvilinear motifs arranged so as to present a prominent central circle contained within a large ovoid lozenge flanked at each
vertical point by circular flourishes. On the other side of the monument
four lions are set around the central medallion of the cross-head, while
another four fill the upper cross-arm. The shaft of the monument is filled
with the nonfigural motifs of serpents and bosses arranged in such a way
as to present the viewer with a series of patterns comprising variations on
cross shapes: a saltire cross in the uppermost panel and a pair of circles
containing "Greek" crosses in the lower panel (figs. 6, 7a).

On the fragmentary remains of the Cross of St. Oran similar methods
of arranging the nonfigural motifs into cross and lozenge patterns seem

6. I. Henderson, "'David Cycle' in Pictish Art"; Mac Lean, "Keills Cross in Knapdale";
J. Hawkes, "Columban Virgins"; see also Ó Carragáin, "Meeting of Saint Paul and Saint
Anthony."

to have been observed (figs. 3, 7b), and a pair of leonine creatures is situated in the upper cross-arm, while the Virgin and Child, flanked by two angels, are set in a comparable position at the point of transition between the cross-head and cross-shaft. This time, however, they are found in the company of David Fighting the Lion and, on the other side, David as Psalmist (figs. 3–4).[7]

On the Cross of St. Martin (figs. 1–2), the nonfigural motifs of bosses and serpents are again organized in such a way that the viewer is presented with a series of cross shapes contained in lozenges and circles (figs. 2, 7c), and leonine creatures are concentrated in the cross-head on both sides of the monument. The Virgin and Child, this time flanked by four angels and situated in the center of the cross-head on the west face, are set over the Old Testament scenes of Daniel in the Lions' Den, Abraham and Isaac, David the Psalmist, and David and Goliath.

In other words, in the immediate context of each individual monument a limited range of figural scenes is repeated in various combinations with the image of the Virgin and Child as a constant. Furthermore, the figural scenes coexist with a select set of nonfigural motifs arranged in ways that are, at the very least, suggestive of the central symbol of Christianity: the cross.[8] It is in this context that the iconographic significance of the figural decoration of these monuments should perhaps be examined.

SALVATION THROUGH CHRIST: THE CROSS OF ST. MARTIN

Turning to the Cross of St. Martin with its Old Testament subjects filling the west face of the shaft (fig. 1), it has been traditional, particularly in the context of the Irish crosses, to regard such images as having been selected to illustrate the theme of the Help of God. Such explanations seem to be conditioned in part by the preservation of Old Irish versions of the ancient prayer for the dying (*Ordo commendationis animae*) in Irish manuscript contexts such as the early ninth-century Stowe Missal (Dublin, Royal Irish Academy, MS D. II. 3) and the so-called "Martyrology of Óengus";[9] in the light of such survivals other potential explanations for

---

7. A figural carving set in the horizontal arm facing the image of David the Psalmist is too damaged to be identified with any certainty (see fig. 4). It seems to have consisted of two figures, one of which is seated and the other standing, but the relationship between them cannot be ascertained, as it can, for instance, with the pair of figures to the right of the David and Goliath panel on St. Martin's Cross (see below). See discussion in I. Henderson, "'David Cycle' in Pictish Art," pp. 94–95.

8. It should be noted that the Keills Cross, although limited in its figural decoration, includes the use of lions in the cross-head (Mac Lean, "Keills Cross in Knapdale," plate 8.1).

9. Warner, *Stowe Missal*, pp. 31–32; Stokes, *Felire Oengussu Celi Dei*.

the selection of Old Testament imagery, although mentioned, tend to be discounted.[10] Yet, while some of the Old Testament scenes on the Cross of St. Martin could be considered as part of an iconographic program signifying God's intervention in the lives of the faithful, not all can be convincingly included. God could be deemed to help Daniel in the lions' den and aid David in his unequal combat with Goliath, but the Abraham and Isaac image is intrinsically open to other interpretations. While the *ordo* (in its Latin and Old Irish versions) does refer to Isaac as being saved from the hand of his father, in patristic literature it is Abraham's willingness to sacrifice his son that is generally deemed praiseworthy.[11] Furthermore, the inclusion of David the Psalmist with these scenes and the depiction of Christ Incarnate in the cross-head suggest other motives may have influenced the selection and arrangement of the scenes comprising the iconographic program of St. Martin's Cross.

DAVID AND GOLIATH (1 SAMUEL 17)

There has been some uncertainty over the identity of the subject matter illustrated by the four figures in the lowermost figural panel on the west face of St. Martin's Cross (figs. 1, 8a),[12] but Henderson's interpretation of the figures as comprising an illustration of the events surrounding David's victory over Goliath, made by comparing the figures with the miniature of the same subject in the tenth-century Cotton Psalter (London, British Library, MS Cotton Vitellius F. xi, fol. 1) and the panel on the so-called Cross of Muirdach at Monasterboice, Co. Louth (fig. 8b) provides the most reasonable explanation.[13]

The four figures in the panel are divided into two pairs: that on the left consists of one crouching figure (on the far left) who, with a hand raised to his head, is half-turned from the second figure who stands facing forward with one hand (possibly holding an unidentifiable object) upraised over the crouching figure's head. The pair on the right consists of one figure

10. See, for example, Françoise Henry's discussion in *Irish Art during the Viking Invasions*, pp. 142–44.

11. See summary in Botterweck and Ringgren, *Theological Dictionary of the Old Testament*, 1:56–57.

12. In RCAHMS, *Argyll: An Inventory of the Monuments*, 4:207, for instance, two of the figures are interpreted as Samuel anointing David and the other two are left unidentified, while in Allen and Anderson, *Early Christian Monuments of Scotland*, p. 382, they are described simply as "a group of four figures."

13. I. Henderson, "'David Cycle' in Pictish Art," p. 95. For the Cotton Psalter (fol. 1), see J. Alexander, *Insular Manuscripts*, nos. 73, 99, plate 349; Roe, "'David Cycle' in Early Irish Art," esp. p. 49; F. Henry, "Remarks on the Decoration," pp. 29–33; Ó Carragáin, "Meeting of Saint Paul and Saint Anthony," p. 20, n. 2.

seated in profile on the right facing a second, standing figure; the two are linked by what appears to be the arm of the standing figure extending down toward the lap of the seated figure. Of these two pairs it is the one on the left that best compares with the Irish manuscript and sculptural images: the crouching figure bears a close resemblance to the pose adopted by the falling Goliath on the Monasterboice Cross who, in both sculpture and manuscript, also has a hand held up to his head, and the standing figure with the upraised arm on the Iona cross corresponds with the figure of David at Monasterboice who has an arm upraised to hold a club. The seated figure on the right of the Iona panel can also be compared with a seated profile figure featured on the Irish cross.

Although such correspondences are clear, both the Psalter and Muirdach images do differ from the Iona group: David is seen in profile and standing to the left of Goliath in both of the Irish versions of the scene, and while the panel on the Monasterboice Cross contains four figures, David and Goliath here form a central pair within the four, flanked on the left by the seated figure and on the right by a standing figure. While such discrepancies are notable, they probably represent no more than different iconographic motifs or traditions underlying the arrangement of the various figural components of a group of four in order to highlight different aspects of the events surrounding David's victory over Goliath. It is thus the relationship of the David and Goliath pair to the other two figures that represents the significant variation between the two panels.[14]

Here it should be noted that although David and Goliath represent a discrete pair flanked by the seated and standing figures on the Cross of Muirdach, David is nevertheless linked to the seated figure (traditionally identified as Saul)[15] by a long flat sword held at an angle behind the shield lying over Saul's lap such that it passes diagonally upward behind David's back; the figure standing to the right of the panel is similarly "linked" to Goliath by means of the giant's sword that is also held at a slight angle behind his shield so that it passes downward over the body of the standing figure beside him. Such details were presumably intended to draw attention to the contrasting relationships and fortunes of Saul the ruler and his faithful servant, David, on the one hand, and Goliath and his follower on the other. On the Cross of St. Martin the manner in which the figures

14. The figures of David and Goliath themselves present the viewer with mirror images of each other on the Muirdach and St. Martin's Crosses, but this is a feature that probably indicates no more than the use of patterns or templates. For discussion of such practices, see Bailey, "Chronology of Viking-Age Sculpture"; Bailey, *England's Earliest Sculptors*, pp. 111–18; Lang, "Continuity and Innovation"; Lang, "Principles of Design"; J. Hawkes, "Anglo-Saxon Sculpture," esp. pp. 206–07.

15. For summary and bibliography, see Harbison, *High Crosses of Ireland*, 1:140–41.

are arranged, insofar as this can be reconstructed, does not appear to be determined by such concerns. While David, being sent out by Saul to combat the Philistine, is still visually linked to him at Monasterboice, on St. Martin's Cross David and Goliath function as a discrete pair, unconnected to the other two figures in the panel.

The worn and indistinct condition of the Cross of St. Martin is such that the identity of these other two cannot be confirmed, but comparison with the Irish carving might suggest that the seated figure is Saul and the figure standing before and connected to him could be identified as David. Having said this, it remains unclear whether the pair (if correctly identified) represents Saul sending David into combat (in which case the order of the narrative, if read from left to right, is reversed) or David returning to Saul having defeated Goliath. Nevertheless, whatever their exact identity this pair of figures can be explained within the context of David's encounter with Goliath, the most likely identification of the left-hand pair of figures.

In patristic literature, David's victory over Goliath was regarded not simply as a moment when God helped his faithful servant, but rather as an incident symbolic of Christ's victory over Satan. As Augustine phrased it in his Commentary on the Psalms: "In figura Christi Dauid, sicut Golias in figura diaboli; et quod Dauid prostrauit Goliam, Christus est qui occidit diabolum" (David is the figure of Christ, just as Goliath is a figure of the devil: and as David overthrew Goliath, so Christ defeated the devil).[16] Here, it is probably relevant to note that when David's victory over Goliath was illustrated in (Insular) Psalters, it was placed between Psalms 50 and 51, not simply to mark the second grouping of the psalms, but because these two were understood to prophecy the coming and destruction of the Antichrist. In the words of Cassiodorus, whose commentary on the psalms was copied in Northumbria in the eighth century: "et per hos geminos psalmos, ne occultus terreat Antichristus, indicatur" (through these twin psalms Antichrist is exposed and prevented from covertly imposing fear).[17]

Explanations such as this were a specific application of more general equations drawn between Christ and David as a result of the struggles endured by the Old Testament figure:

---

16. Augustine, *Enarrationes in Psalmum XXXIII* 4, in *Augustini opera pars X.1*, p. 276; English translation, author's own.

17. Cassiodorus, *Expositio in Psalmum LI, conclusio psalmi*, in *Cassiodori Senatoris opera pars II.1*, p. 477; English translation from *Cassiodorus. Explanation of the Psalms*, 2:7. For Cassiodorus in the Insular world, see Bailey, *Durham Cassiodorus*.

Et quando tale nomen debuit poni nisi com passionis domini-
cae gloriosa certamina referuntur? . . . qui per tolerantiam
suam prostrauit principem tenebrarium, qui mortem moriendo
superauit, qui humanum genus captinum crucifixionis suae
dispensatione liberauit.

(When should such a name [David] be mentioned except when
the glorious struggles of the Lord's passion are recounted? . . .
for by His enduring He laid low the prince of darkness. He
overcame death by dying, He freed the captive human race by
the dispensation of His crucifixion.)[18]

In other words, David's victory over Goliath was well established as an
incident that would have been understood in an Insular context to refer to
Christ's defeat of Death and the devil by becoming human and dying on
the cross of the Crucifixion.

DAVID THE PSALMIST

In the panel above that featuring David and Goliath is the figure of
David the Psalmist, identified by his harp, with an accompanying musi-
cian (fig. 1). It is a pictorial theme that was well established in Insular art in
manuscript and sculptural contexts. As such it is, perhaps, the most commonly discussed of the David images and the extensive academic inquiry
has demonstrated that the scene had a very complex iconographic frame
of reference.[19] At one obvious level it illustrated the understanding that
the psalms were directly inspired by God, but more importantly, it also
illustrated that the words of the psalms, while referring to general historical Old Testament situations, were also the words of Christ and his Church
living under the New Covenant. It thus functioned as a very potent visual
mnemonic recalling Christ. As Augustine explained it in his discussion of
Psalm 54, one of the psalms specifically attributed to David:

Erat quidem Dauid, ut nouimus, propheta sanctus, rex Israel,
filius Iesse; set quia ex eius semine uenit ad salutem nostram
secundum carnem Dominus Iesus Christus, saepe isto nomine
ille figuratur, et Dauid pro Christo in figura ponitur, propter
originem carnis ipsius. Nam secundum aliquid filius est Dauid,

18. Cassiodorus, *Psalmum XXVII* 1, in *Cassiodori Senatoris opera pars II.1*, p. 243; English translation from *Cassiodorus. Explanation of the Psalms*, 1:271.
19. See summary in Bailey, *Durham Cassiodorus*, p. 5. See also summaries and discussions in Roe, "'David Cycle' in Early Irish Art"; I. Henderson, "'David Cycle' in Pictish Art";
D. Wright, *Vespasian Psalter;* J. Hawkes, "Old Testament Heroes."

secundum aliquid Dominus est David; filius Dauid secundum carnem, Dominus Dauid secundum diuinitatem.

(David indeed was, as we know, a holy prophet, king of Israel, son of Jesse; but because out of his seed there came for our salvation after the flesh the Lord Jesus Christ, often under that name He is figured, and David instead of Christ is in a figure set down, because of the origin of the Flesh of the Same. For after some sort He is the Son of David, after some sort He is the Lord of David; Son of David after the flesh, Lord of David after the divinity.)[20]

Thus David, the author of so many of the psalms, was the ancestor of Christ; his anointment by Samuel foreshadowed Christ's baptism by John; his struggles with the lion and Goliath were types of Christ's struggle with the devil; and his kingdom on earth, centered on Jerusalem, foreshadowed the eternal kingdom of Christ, the heavenly Jerusalem. The scene on the Iona cross thus continues, but with a more universal application, the theme of "Christ in David" articulated in the specific incident of David and Goliath below.

SACRIFICE OF ISAAC (GENESIS 22:1–13)

Above this panel is that containing Abraham's sacrifice of Isaac (fig. 1), another Old Testament scene that was commonly reproduced in sculpture throughout the Insular world, and one that was well known as having a Christological significance, being understood as a figure of the Crucifixion.[21] The references are many and varied. For example, in patristic literature, Augustine, explaining Paul's discussion of Christ's Crucifixion in his letter to the Romans,[22] uses the figure of Isaac who, he says: "Propterea et Isaac, sicud Dominus crucem suam, ita sibi ligna ad uictimae locum, quibus fuerat et inponendus, ipse portauit" (carried to the place of sacrifice the wood on which he was to be offered up, just as the Lord himself carried his own cross).[23] In an Insular context, Bede, well versed in such exegetical traditions, describes the image of Abraham and Isaac displayed in the church at Wearmouth as being paired with that of the Crucifixion in order to demonstrate the same concordance between the Old and New

---

20. Augustine, *Ennarationes in Psalmum LIV* 3, in *Augustini opera pars X.2*, p. 656; English translation from *St Augustine: Expositions on the Book of Psalms*, p. 225.

21. Bailey, "Meaning of the Viking-Age Shaft"; Bailey, *Meaning of Mercian Sculpture*, pp. 11–12.

22. Romans 8:32: "he that spared not his own son, but delivered him up for us all."

23. Augustine, *De Civitate Dei* XVI.xxxii, in *Augustini opera pars XIV.2*, p. 537; English translation from *Augustine. City of God*, p. 694.

Testaments.[24] Or, in a more liturgical Insular context, the connection is preserved in the ninth-century Stowe Missal that mentions the sacrifice of Abraham as a type of the sacrifice of the Mass.[25] Thus, the image of Abraham's abortive sacrifice of Isaac presents an event that would have been commonly understood to illustrate, not just an Old Testament incident, but also the actions of Christ, and specifically, the sacrifice of his Crucifixion with its Eucharistic reference points.

DANIEL IN THE LIONS' DEN (DANIEL 6:16–24; BEL AND THE DRAGON 29–42)

The scene at the top of the shaft (fig. 1) illustrating Daniel flanked by two lions presents another instance of an image that refers to more than just the notion of God preserving his own from certain death. Indeed, most patristic commentators understood it to signify Christ's death and Resurrection. The association, however, was not made clearly or commonly in the exegesis; rather, it was made implicitly through the Old Latin text of the Canticle of Habakkuk. As Ó Carragáin has demonstrated, the recitation of verses from this Canticle during the liturgical ceremonies of Good Friday, with its reference to Christ being recognized "in the midst of two animals," was understood by the eighth century to refer to the death and Resurrection of Christ.[26] In a pictorial context knowledge of this text could extend the iconographic reference points of almost any Christian image featuring a central hieratic figure flanked by two others to include an understanding of the liturgy and Christ's sacrifice on the cross. The portrayal of Daniel, therefore, particularly when set between *two* lions (as opposed to the greater numbers found elsewhere as at Moone, Co. Kildare, where seven lions are featured), had the potential to portray both the Old Testament figure and Christ.[27]

As far as the Iona panel is concerned, however, the association of Daniel with Christ through Habakkuk might be further emphasized by reference to the apocryphal episode from the Daniel story: "The History and

24. "imagines . . . de concordia veteris et novi Testamenti": Bede, *Historia abbatum* 9, p. 373.

25. "sacrificium patriarche nostri abrache": Warner, *Stowe Missal*, p. 13; see also comments by Ó Carragáin, "Meeting of Saint Paul and Saint Anthony," p. 15.

26. "in medio duorum animalium innotesceris" (Hab. 3:1). See, for example, Ó Carragáin, "Christ over the Beasts," esp. pp. 385–87; Ó Carragáin, "Liturgical Interpretation," p. 19. For the circulation of this text in "Irish" contexts, see Ó Carragáin, "Meeting of Saint Paul and Saint Anthony," p. 20, n. 2. Of particular interest is the preservation of the Canticle after Psalm 100 in the early tenth-century Cotton Psalter (see above, note 13).

27. For Moone, see Harbison, *High Crosses of Ireland*, vol. 2, fig. 509. See Ó Carragáin, "Meeting of Saint Paul and Saint Anthony," pp. 19–20, for discussion of the liturgical and patristic significance of Daniel in this context.

Destruction of Bel and the Dragon." According to this narrative the Old
Testament prophet Habakkuk, resident in Judea, was interrupted by an
angel while preparing his midday meal (which included broken bread) and
told to take the food to Daniel who was fasting in the lions' den in Baby-
lon. Overcoming his reservations about the logistics of undertaking such
a mission, Habakkuk was instantly transported to Daniel and the food
was duly delivered. It may be that the rather puzzling detail preserved in
the upper right-hand corner of the Iona scene represents the remains of a
pictorial reference to this episode contained in the model from which the
Iona scene is ultimately derived. Habakkuk, when included in images of
Daniel in the lions' den in Early Christian art, was generally set in one of
the upper corners of the scene, as he is, for instance, in the ninth-century
Carolingian copy of an eighth-century Anglo-Saxon version of Sedulius's
Carmen Paschale.[28] Whether this was indeed the case, the image of Daniel
flanked by two lions is one that would have been understood to refer, at
the very least, to Christ, his death and Resurrection.

VIRGIN AND CHILD

The Virgin and Child in the cross-head (fig. 1) functions as confirmation that these scenes together seem to present the viewer with a sustained set of references to Christ and his salvation. Like all such images of
the pair enthroned and flanked by angelic attendants, the scheme refers
explicitly both to the human reality of Christ Incarnate and to the eternal nature of his divinity.[29] The manner in which the Child sits in profile
turned toward his mother (as opposed to confronting the onlooker as he
does on the late seventh-century Northumbrian coffin of St. Cuthbert,
for instance),[30] together with the absence of "divine" attributes, such as
a halo or scroll, and the fact that he does not raise a hand in blessing,
are all iconographic features expressive of his humanity. Complementing
such signifiers are the upright position of the Child's body, the fact that
he does not tip his head up toward his mother (as he does in the Book of
Kells, for example),[31] the hieratic *en face* pose of the Virgin who presents
the Child to the viewer with her right hand, and the presence of the four
attendant angels, their wings spread as a canopy over the seated mother

28. Antwerp, Museum Plantin-Moretus, MS M. 17. 4, fol. 10v: J. Alexander, *Insular
Manuscripts*, nos. 65, 83, plate 289. For discussion of this manuscript and its relationship to
the presumed Anglo-Saxon exemplar, see Levison, *England and the Continent in the Eighth
Century*, pp. 133–34.
   29. J. Hawkes, "Columban Virgins," pp. 123–27.
   30. J. Hawkes, "Columban Virgins," fig. 1.
   31. See Dublin, Trinity College Library, MS 58, fol. 7v (Meehan, *Book of Kells*, plate 7).

and Child. All these are details that accentuate the divinity of Christ. The angels, as the servants of God and attendants on the heavenly throne, traditionally function in Early Christian art as overt symbols of the divine authority of the deity, while the hieratic presentation of Mary not only offsets the potentially close and human relationship with the Child, but also provides an explicit reference to the Virgin as the Mother of God, the instrument of and hence one of the most important elements in the Incarnation. Recognition of this aspect of the Virgin was regarded as particularly apt in the individual Christian's attainment of salvation, and the literature associated with the Columban community during the eighth and ninth centuries demonstrates that such ideas were current at the time the crosses were being constructed.[32]

Together the various iconographic elements of the scheme combine to present the mysteries inherent in the Incarnation. The eternal nature of Christ's divinity is carefully balanced by the human reality of his theophany. Set against the scenes on the shaft below, the group acts as a proof, a summation of all that is implied and foretold in the Old Testament concerning the nature of Christ, his death, Resurrection, and salvation.

NONFIGURAL MOTIFS

It is as further confirmation of these iconographic themes that the nonfigural motifs on the Cross of St. Martin can be understood (figs. 1–2). The lions, for instance, are a recognized symbol of Christ's Resurrection in Christian literature and art (including the Insular), and a number of scholars have explored this significance of these creatures.[33] Literary discussions of lions were common in many texts known to have been circulating in early medieval Britain and Ireland, one of the most popular being those known as the *Physiologus*, a collection of animal lore in which an animal's behavior is described and explained in terms of its Christian signifi-

32. See for instance, the song *Cantemus in Omni Die*, composed by Cú Chuimne of Iona (died ca. 747), which describes Mary as both the Mother of God and Servant of the Lord, the identities that formed the basis of interest in her as heavenly intercessor (Bernard and Atkinson, *Irish Liber Hymnorum*, 1:32–34; 2:124–25; Herbert, *Iona, Kells and Derry*, pp. 9–35, 43–45; Clancy and Márkus, *Iona, the Earliest Poetry*, pp. 177–92; Sieger, "Visual Metaphor as Theology," esp. pp. 84–86; Deshman, "Servants of the Mother of God," esp. pp. 39–40; Leveto, "Marian Theme of the Frescoes," esp. pp. 410–12). For further examination of the Iona Virgin and Child groups in the light of other carvings in Scotland, see Trench-Jellicoe, "Missing Figure on Slab Fragment no 2."

33. Ó Carragáin, "Meeting of Saint Paul and Saint Anthony," pp. 19–20; Hicks, *Animals in Early Medieval Art*, p. 108; Neuman de Vegvar, "Echternach Lion," esp. pp. 172–76; J. Hawkes, "Old Testament Heroes," p. 155; J. Hawkes, "Iconography of Identity"; Gannon, *Iconography of Early Anglo-Saxon Coinage*, pp. 125–36.

cance. In these texts the notion of the lion as symbolic of the Resurrection of Christ is well established and, moreover, encompassed a matrix of ideas involving the duality of Christ's nature, divine power, Resurrection, and rebirth.[34] Thus, as Gregory the Great outlined in his Homily on Ezekiel:

> Ipse enim unigenitus Dei Filius ueraciter factus est homo, ipse in sacrificio nostrae redemptionis dignatus est mori ut uitulus, ipse per uirtutem suae fortitudinis surrexit ut leo. Leo etiam apertis oculis dormire per hibertur, quia in ipsa morte in qua ex humanitate Redemptor noster dormire potuit, ex diuinitate sua immortalis per manendo uigilauit.

> (the only-born Son of God was himself truly made man, and himself considered it worthy to die as a calf for our redemption, and himself rose up as a lion by virtue of his strength. The lion is also said to sleep with its eyes open; thus, in the same death in which through his humanity our Redeemer was able to sleep, he was awake through being infused with his immortal divinity.)[35]

Regarded in this manner the lions in the cross-head of the Cross of St. Martin function iconographically as a fitting apogee, repeating, extending, and emphasizing the ideas surrounding the Incarnation, death, Resurrection, and salvation of Christ expressed in the figural schemes in the center of the cross-head and the shaft below.

Then there are the bosses and serpents that may also, in the case of the serpents, refer the viewer to the Resurrection (the serpent being, by virtue of its tendency to shed its skin, a symbol of rebirth),[36] while the elaborate bosses may refer to the bread of the Eucharist, as has been argued by Ó Carragáin in relation to the Irish high-crosses.[37] The patterns into which these motifs have been arranged, however, are as likely to have been as significant in their frames of reference as any meaning that may attach to the serpents and bosses themselves. As noted, these motifs have

34. The extensive discussion about the dates at which such texts (in the form in which they existed in the eleventh century) may have begun to circulate in Anglo-Saxon England and Early Christian Ireland suggests that the ideas and definitions articulated in the *Physiologus* were in existence in the Insular world in a number of disparate texts from a very early date (see summary in Neuman de Vegvar, "Echternach Lion," pp. 172–73).

35. Gregory, *In Hiezechihelem I: Homilia IV* 1, in *Gregorius Magnus Homiliae in Hezechilhelem Prophetam*, p. 47; trans. in Neumann de Vegvar, "Echternach Lion," pp. 175–76.

36. E.g., Isidore, *Etymologiarum* XII.iv: *De Serpentibus*, in *Isidori Hispalensis Episcopi etymologiarum*, vol. 2; see also I. Henderson's discussion, "Book of Kells and the Snake-boss Motif," p. 65, although Mac Lean, "Snake-bosses and Redemption," does regard the serpents as symbolic of an evil that the cross was meant to overcome.

37. Ó Carragáin, "Meeting of Saint Paul and Saint Anthony," pp. 17–19.

been organized in such a way that they present the viewer with a variety of cross shapes, circles, and lozenges (fig. 7c).

Hiding patterns in the decoration of an artifact is a common tendency in Insular art, and certainly the phenomenon of disguising cross shapes within interlace and curvilinear designs is discernible in the decoration of works of art in most media.[38] It is visible in manuscript decoration in the seventh century in the Book of Durrow (Dublin, Trinity College Library, MS 57); in the seventh- or eighth-century Lindisfarne Gospels (London, British Library, MS Cotton Nero D. iv);[39] in the eighth-century paten from the Derrynaflan hoard (Co. Tipperary); and in sculpture as widely dispersed as the early eighth-century cross at Bewcastle, Cumbria (where the interlace forms a lozenge containing the cross), and those dated to the ninth and tenth centuries at Ahenny and Kilkieran (Co. Tipperary) or Drumcliffe (Co. Sligo).[40]

On the Cross of St. Martin the repetition of the cross shapes, along with the circles and lozenges (which, as O'Reilly has most recently demonstrated, function in Insular contexts as symbols of the cosmological and universal nature of Christ's salvation),[41] suggests that the designs were deliberate: that the monument, the stone high cross, was intended to function as a field of ornament presenting the viewer with elaborate variations on the theme of the cross, *the* symbol of Christianity. However speculative such considerations may seem, it is worth emphasizing that, whatever distinction a modern viewer might make between the "decorative" and "symbolic," the frequency with which such phenomena can be observed in Insular art suggests it would probably (in context) have represented a false distinction to an Insular audience.

SALVATION THROUGH THE CHURCH

The point is that while the nonfigural motifs serve to confirm the Christological themes present in the figural iconography of the monu-

38. Stevenson, "Hunterston Brooch"; Stevenson, "Aspects of Ambiguity"; Stevenson, "Further Notes"; J. Hawkes, "Symbolic Lives."

39. On the date of the Lindisfarne Gospels, see M. Brown, *Lindisfarne Gospels*, pp. 396–408.

40. For the Book of Durrow (e.g., fols. 85v, 124v), see Meehan, *Book of Durrow*, illustrations on pp. 48, 58; for the Lindisfarne Gospels (e.g., fols. 2v, 94v, 138v, 211), see J. Alexander, *Insular Manuscripts*, figs. 34–36, 45; for the Derrynaflan paten, see M. Ryan, *Derrynaflan Hoard*, vol. 1, plate 48; for the Bewcastle Cross, see Bailey and Cramp, *Cumberland, Westmorland and Lancashire-North-of-the-Sands*, illustration 101; for the Ahenny, Kilkieran, and Drumcliffe Crosses, see Harbison, *High Crosses of Ireland*, vol. 2, figs. 9, 213, 393.

41. O'Reilly, "Patristic and Insular Traditions," esp. pp. 77–94; see also Werckmeister, *Irisch-northumbrische Buchmalerei*, pp. 153–67; Kessler, *Illustrated Bibles from Tours*, p. 52.

ment they also highlight (perhaps even clarify) the sacramental Eucharistic references *implicit* in most of the figural scenes, the Eucharist being the sacrament served daily to commemorate the Crucifixion. In the image of Daniel such references lie in the various allusions to Habakkuk and his Canticle. In the portrayal of Abraham and Isaac they lie in the fact that the abortive sacrifice of the son foreshadowed the eventual sacrifice of Christ, the son of God and Man. In the depiction of David the Psalmist they can be understood in that the Psalter was regarded as the foremost of the prophetic books recording the details of the Crucifixion.[42] In the image of David and Goliath they are implicit insofar as that scene recalled Christ's victory over death at the Crucifixion.

This last panel (fig. 8a), however, also includes two other figures, identified as David and Saul, and it is perhaps not immediately obvious how this pair can best be included in a Eucharistic frame of reference. Consideration of the Early Christian, prescholastic understanding of the term *sacramentum*, however, indicates that it may well be possible to regard this pair not only as part of the program but also, perhaps, as essential to understanding the full iconographic significance of the monument.[43]

In biblical, patristic, and therefore Insular contexts the concept of *sacramentum* involved both the sense of the Greek word *mysterion* (mystery), for which it functioned as a synonym, and, in its Latin tradition, a sense of contractual obligation and oath-taking. Thus, in biblical contexts (particularly the Pauline epistles) *sacramentum* was used to refer to God's design to save humanity through the life, death, and Resurrection of Christ.[44] Or, put another way: because Christ embodied God's plan, his will, to save humanity, he was the mystery (*sacramentum*); by extension, the Church, as the body of Christ, was where the believer gained access to that mystery. The manner in which this was to be accomplished was the central concern of the patristic debates on such matters. The answer was: through symbolic participation in Christ's life, death, and salvation; namely, through participation in the mysteries of baptism and the Eucharist, the signs that were regarded as embodying Christ for, as Leo the Great put it, "Quod itaque Redemptionis nostri conspicuum fuit, in sacramenta transiuit" (What was visible in our Redeemer has passed over into the sacraments).[45] That

42. Ó Carragáin, "Meeting of Saint Paul and Saint Anthony," p. 15.

43. A detailed examination of these issues is to be published shortly by Éamonn Ó Carragáin; I am grateful to him for discussions on the subject.

44. For the Pauline Epistles, see, e.g., Romans 6:1–11; 1 Corinthians 2:4; Ephesians 3; for summary, see Ferguson, *Encyclopedia of Early Christianity*, pp. 1011–44.

45. Leo, *Tractatus LXXIV: item alius de Ascensione Domini* 2, in *Sancti Leonis Magni, Romani Pontificis tractatus septem et nonaginta*, p. 457; translation, author's own. See also Augustine, *Tractate VI: in Iohannis Evangelium 1: 32–33* 8, in *Sancti Aurelii Augustini: in Iohannis Evangelium tractatus CXXIV,* p. 57; translated in *St. Augustine: Homilies*, pp. 41–42.

symbolic participation involved not just observing the ritual of the mysteries (as mediated through the Church), but being part of a transaction through which the subject (the believer) and his or her deity bound themselves to each other in a sacred commitment. On one side, God was considered to have made union with humanity in the person of Christ; on the other, each believer was bound in obedience to the divine will, the crucial element in the reception of God's gifts dispensed through the mysteries. Thus, by symbolic participation, each Christian was as much a "figure" in Christ's salvation as those who in the past (in the Old Testament) had foreshadowed those events. As Augustine explains:

> Quia ergo Dauid in figura Christus est, Christus autem . . . et caput et corpus est, nec nos a Christo alienos dicere debemus, cuius membra sumus, nec nos quasi alterum computare; quia "erunt duo in carne una. Sacramentum hoc magnum est," ait apostolus, "ego autem dico in Christo et in ecclesia." Quia ergo totus Christus capus et corpus est, cum audimus: ". . . ipsi Dauid," intellegamus et nos in Dauid.

> (Because then David in a figure is Christ, but Christ . . . is both Head and Body, we ought neither to speak of ourselves as alien from Christ of whom we are members, nor to count ourselves as if we were any other thing, because "the two shall be in one flesh" [Gen. 2:24]. "This is a great mystery" [*sacramentum*], says the Apostle, "but I speak in regard of Christ and the Church" [Eph. 5:32]. Because the whole Christ is "Head and Body," when we hear ". . . David himself," we understand ourselves also in David.)[46]

Thus, in the depiction of David and Saul the Cross of St. Martin presents an Old Testament subject fulfilling his obligation to his king. As such, the image serves to remind the viewer of other oaths made and fulfilled, such as that between God and Abraham who, because of his obedience to the divine will, was promised that his descendents would establish a great nation. It was a covenant that, in biblical and patristic literature, was regarded as being fulfilled in David and the establishment of his kingdom, centered on Jerusalem (2 Sam. 7:27).[47]

Therefore, the figural iconography of the Cross of St. Martin, with its use of Old Testament scenes and the image of Christ Incarnate, provides, in addition to any Christological typologies, a complex commentary on

46. Augustine, *Psalmum LIV* 3, in *Augustini opera pars X.2*, p. 656; English translation taken from *St. Augustine. Exposition on the Book of Psalms*, pp. 209–10.

47. For summary, see Botterweck and Ringgren, *Theological Dictionary of the Old Testament*, 1:56–57; 3:164–69.

the salvation inherent in Christ and available through participation in the mysteries of the Church of the New Covenant of Christ, prefigured in the covenants of the past. Read in this way, the transaction between David and Saul is seen to be completed, the covenants fulfilled between God and Abraham and David are implied, and that between God and his people is figured in the human reality of Christ Incarnate. All that remains is the fulfillment (through participation in the liturgy) of each believer's obligation to Christ and his Church.

SALVATION AND THE IONA GROUP OF CROSSES

In the light of such a reading the figural decoration of St. Martin's Cross would seem to present a coherent series of references, common in biblical and exegetical thought, to Christ, his death, Resurrection, and salvation, which, in the cross-head, culminate in a celebration of the nature of Christ Incarnate. Together with the nonfigural motifs, the decoration may also be understood to offer an extended iconographic program expressing the complexities of Christ's nature and sacrifice, his Church and (crucially) its sacraments, and their relevance to the Christian community on earth—or more specifically, to the Christian community of Iona.

The Cross of St. Martin, however, does not stand alone in this respect. As noted, it is one of a number of crosses displaying similar methods of organizing the decoration and a similar selection of images. Thus the Crosses of St. Oran and Kildalton must also share the iconographic concerns articulated on the Cross of St. Martin in their use of the circle, lozenge, and cross patternings of the nonfigural motifs, the setting of lions in the cross-heads, and the same limited selection of Old Testament subject matter juxtaposed with the image of the Virgin and Child surrounded by angelic attendants.

On both the St. Oran's and Kildalton Crosses (figs. 3, 5) this latter image is varied slightly from the version figured in the cross-head of St. Martin's Cross in that the child is turned to face the spectator, and so presents a more authoritative image than that featured on the Cross of St. Martin where he turns to face his mother. Such comparatively hieratic connotations, however, underlined by the presence of the angels, are balanced by the details expressive of his humanity: the fact that he does not raise his hand in blessing; that he lacks divine attributes, such as the halo, book, or scroll; the way the Virgin bends her head to his; and the manner in which he almost reclines across his mother's lap. Thus, although the details vary, the complexities of Christ's nature, as the Son of God and Man, are fully presented in the images on all three crosses.

On the Cross of St. Oran the Old Testament material accompanying the Virgin and Child scheme around the cross-head is also varied to
include David with the lion (fig. 3)—with David the Psalmist on the other
side (fig. 4). David's struggle with the lion is not an image featured on
St. Martin's Cross, but as with his victory over Goliath, the association of
David with Christ meant his encounter with the lion (1 Sam. 17:34–37) was
a common reference point in patristic discussions on the power of God to
overcome evil. Augustine's commentary on Psalm 7, for instance, refers to
the killing of the lion, symbolic of evil, as a general expression of God's
redeeming power:

> Dicit Apostolus: "Adversarius vester diabolus tanquam leo
> rugiens circuit, uaerens quem devoret." Itaque cum diceret . . .
> "Savu me fac ex omnibus persequentiubus me . . . nequando
> rapiat ut leo animam meam" . . . sciens quis retiterit inimicus,
> et perfectae animae vehementer adversus "dum non est qui rei-
> mat, neque qui salvum faciat" . . . si enim Deus non redimat
> neque salvum faciat, ille rapit.

> (The Apostle says, "Your adversary the devil, as a roaring lion,
> walketh about, seeking whom he may devour." Therefore when
> the Psalmist said . . . "Save me from all them that persecute
> me . . . Lest at any time he tear my soul as a lion" . . . he knew
> what enemy and violent adversary of the perfect soul remained
> "whilst there be none to redeem or save" . . . For if God redeem
> not, nor save, he tears.)[48]

It is an association found throughout the exegetical literature, even
in the Insular world,[49] and the regularity with which such interpretations
were articulated suggests this would have been the intended significance
of the Iona carving. Thus, in conjunction with the patterned crosses and
circles in cross-head and shaft, the lions in the upper arm of the cross-
head, and Christ Incarnate with the Virgin and angels at the top of the
shaft (and the image of David the Psalmist on the other side), the image
of David overcoming the lion on the Cross of St. Oran would have been
part of an iconographic program celebrating Christ's death, Resurrection,
and salvation.[50]

48. Augustine, *Psalmum VII* 2, in *Augustini opera pars X.1*, p. 37; English translation
taken from *St Augustine: Expositions on the Book of Psalms*, p. 21. See also Augustine, *Psalmum IX* 9, in *Augustini opera pars X.1*, p. 63; *Psalmum LVII* 7, in *Augustini opera pars X.2*, pp.
714–15. Other writers include Jerome, Hilary of Poitiers, and Ambrose.
49. E.g., Aldhelm, *De Virginitate*, in *Aldhelm: The Prose Works*, p. 122.
50. If David and Goliath were featured on the cross-arm facing David and the Psalmist
on the Cross of St. Oran, the whole would present a concerted celebration of Christ and his
salvation through the figure of David.

On the Kildalton Cross (fig. 5) the selection of Old Testament images found in conjunction with the Virgin and Child is also varied to include Abel's death at the hand of Cain, along with Abraham and Isaac and David with the Lion, but this event, like that of Abraham's sacrifice of Isaac, was generally celebrated in biblical, patristic, and liturgical contexts as a figure of Christ's sacrifice. Along with Christ's reference to Abel as the first in a long line of prophets martyred for justice (Matt. 23:34–35), Abel is cited in biblical literature by the writers of the Epistles. Paul, for instance, invoking the contractual obligations of participation in the mystery of Christ, offsets the blood of Abel with that of Christ: "Abel, though dead, speaks to God by his merits, to men by his example" (Heb. 12:24).[51] Thus established, Abel's significance was commonly cited in patristic works (Augustine, for example, refers to the "typical" meaning of his sacrifice and death),[52] while in the Gelasian and the oldest of the Gregorian orders, he was celebrated in a hymn sung during the liturgy of Mass on the eighth Sunday after Pentecost.[53] Thus, along with David and the lion and the sacrifice of Isaac, the death of Abel would have been understood to signify the actions of Christ and, specifically, the sacrifice and salvation of his Crucifixion.

The pair of peacocks flanking a boss below David and the lion in the upper arm of the Kildalton Cross, unique to the Iona monuments (as they survive), continues the theme. Although apparently rare among the Iona carvings, the scheme is one that is ubiquitous in Christian art from the fourth century onward where, based on the understanding of the incorruptible nature of the peacock's flesh, it functions as a general symbol of the Eucharist and everlasting life.[54] So fundamental was this understand-

51. See also 1 John 3:12.

52. See Augustine, *De Civitate Dei* XV.xviii, in *Augustini opera pars XIV.2*, pp. 480–81.

53. Cabrol and Leclercq, *Dictionnaire d'archéologie chrétienne et de liturgie*, p. 64.

54. From the fourth century, see, for example, the marble reliefs at San Apollinare Nuovo, Ravenna (Bovini, *Ravenna: Art and History,* plates 39, 43); from the fifth century, the mosaic decoration of La Dauraude, Toulouse (Woodruff, "Iconography and Date of the Mosaics"; Davis-Weyer, *Early Medieval Art,* pp. 59–66); from the sixth century, the throne of Maximianus, Ravenna (Bovini, *La Cattedra eburnean,* plates on pp. 20, 22), holy water vessels from the Merovingian cemetery at Miannay, near Abbeville, and the Saxon grave at Long Wittenham, Berkshire (Allen, *Early Christian Symbolism,* pp. 54–55); from the seventh and eighth centuries, sarcophagi from Italy and Gaul, and Merovingian manuscripts, such as the Gelasian Sacramentary, ca. 750, Vatican City, Biblioteca Apostolica Vaticana, MS Vat. reg. lat. 316, fol. 3v (Schiller, *Ikonographie der christlichen Kunst,* plates 79, 548, 590; Hubert, Porcher, and Volbach, *Europe of the Invasions,* plates 119A, 175). By the ninth century the motif was widespread in Carolingian and Lombardic art (Hubert, Porcher, and Volbach, *Carolingian Renaissance,* plate 203; Schaffran, *Die Kunst der Langobarden,* Taf. 33c), and in Insular contexts is found on the Anglo-Saxon stone column at Masham, Yorkshire (J. Hawkes, "Anglo-Saxon Sculpture," plate 17.5), and the Book of Kells, Trinity College Library 58, fol. 32v (Meehan, *Book of Kells,* plate 63).

Figure 1. Cross of St. Martin, Iona, west face. Photo: RCAHMS.

Figure 2. Cross of St. Martin, Iona, east face. Photo: RCAHMS.

Figure 3. Cross of St. Oran, Iona, front. Photo: RCAHMS.

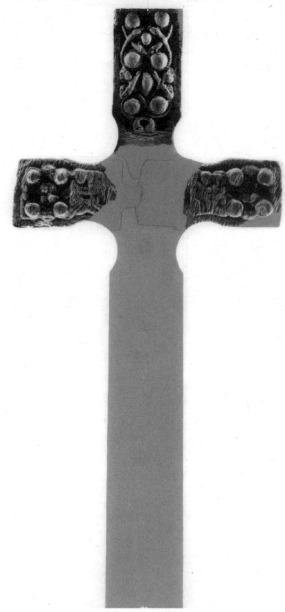

Figure 4. Cross of St. Oran, Iona, back. Photo: RCAHMS.

Figure 5. Kildalton Cross, Islay, west face. Photo: RCAHMS.

Figure 6. Kildalton Cross, Islay, east face. Photo: RCAHMS.

Figure 7. Panels of Cross-patterns: (a) Kildalton Cross, drawing: author; (b) Cross of St. Oran, drawing: author; (c) Cross of St. Martin, drawing: author.

Figure 8a. David and Goliath Panel, Cross of St. Martin. Photo: author.

Figure 8b. David and Goliath Panel, Muirdach's Cross, Monasterboice, Co. Meath. Photo: author.

ing it was not usually deemed worthy of extensive commentary by patristic authors, being generally mentioned only in passing, as for instance, in Augustine's *De Civitate Dei* or Isidore of Seville's *Etymologies*. As such it made its way into the corpus of Insular literature to feature in pieces such as Aldhelm's treatises on Virginity, as well as his riddles.[55] Given the normative understanding, even in the Insular world, of peacocks as being physically incorruptible, and the similarly widespread use of the image in the visual record as a symbol of the immortality afforded all who put their faith in Christ and the sacraments of his Church, it is probable that the carving on the Kildalton Cross would have been understood to signify similar concerns, and as such would have contributed to the overall iconographic presentation of Christ and his mysteries through the use of "figures," both Old Testament and nonfigural.

Thus, although the manner in which the figural decoration is organized over the faces of the Iona crosses is adapted to each monument—on the Cross of St. Martin, filling one side of the cross-shaft and culminating in the cross-head; on the Cross of St. Oran, being concentrated on both sides of the cross-head; and on the Kildalton Cross, filling only one side of the head—the iconographic significances thus constructed provide the onlooker with a series of variations on the theme of Christ and his salvation. This is achieved through the concerted presentation of alternating Old Testament "figures" juxtaposed with the constant of Christ Incarnate, and the setting of the figural alongside the nonfigural. Together these combine to present the intricacies surrounding the death and Resurrection of Christ, the mysteries of his Church, and their relevance to the Christian community of the Iona federation.

55. Augustine, *De Civitate Dei* XXI.iv, in *Augustini opera pars XIV.2*, p. 762; Isidore of Seville, *Etymologiarium* XII.vii, xlviii in *Isidori Hispalensis Episcopi etymologiarum*, vol. 1; Aldhelm, *Riddle XIV*, trans. in *Aldhelm: The Poetic Works*, p. 73; for the poetic *De Virginitate*, see ibid., p. 108; for the prose version, see *Aldhelm: The Prose Works*, p. 66.

Apocalypse Then: Anglo-Saxon Ivory Carving in the Tenth and Eleventh Centuries

Leslie Webster

This essay examines apocalyptic images current in the culture of late Anglo-Saxon England, particularly as expressed in the context of ivory carvings of the perimillennial tenth and early eleventh centuries. The idea that the world might come to an end one thousand years after the time of Christ is based on the passage in the Revelation of St. John (the Apocalypse) where the author describes how, in his vision, he saw an angel binding Satan for a thousand years in the bottomless pit; at the end of this period, Satan would be loosed in the form of Antichrist, accompanied by many and dreadful portents, and would deceive the nations of the earth into false beliefs (Rev. 20:1–10). This period of heresy, omen, and terror is the Last Days. After this would come the overthrow of Satan, followed by the Second Coming, when Christ would return in triumph, to judge the living and the dead, at the end of the world. This period of a thousand years was furthermore sometimes identified in early medieval theology with the end of the sixth and last earthly age.

The prevailing nineteenth-century view, expressed by Michelet and other historians, held that in the course of the tenth century, the whole of Western Europe was consumed by millennial terrors at the prospect of an imminent end to the world in the year 1000.[1] It is true that, by the later tenth century, there was a well-established tradition of commentary on the Apocalypse, most memorably and spectacularly rendered in the many later copies of the eighth-century commentary by the Spanish monk Beatus; and the Michelet interpretation drew heavily on contemporary writers such as Adso of Montier en Der (who wrote a treatise on the Antichrist) and Ralph Glaber, whose influential and lurid *Histories* were a treasure

This essay began as a paper given in 2000 in the sessions in honor of Rosemary Cramp at Kalamazoo; it somehow seemed fitting to choose an apocalyptic subject, not just because of the year 2000, but because of Rosemary's long fascination with, and tremendous understanding of, the workings of the Anglo-Saxon mind in a period of great social and religious change. In focusing on late Saxon ivories in this essay, in which both personal and public aspects of Anglo-Saxon devotion are so visible, I hope this will serve as a small tribute to ways of looking at such things that she has inspired in me and so many of us.

1. Trahern, "Fatalism and the Millennium," pp. 190–205.

trove of millennial terrors and portents.[2] Nowadays, however, the idea of widespread millennial panic and terrors has been rejected by most historians, recognizing that the orthodox theological approach took a more complex view of the end of the world, in which it was seen as near, but not necessarily imminent. In fact, from St. Paul onward, church fathers such as St. Augustine and Bede had cautioned against the popular notion that the world would end a thousand years after Christ's Incarnation (or his death and Resurrection). Their arguments were often complex, and I do not propose to rehearse them here; but essentially they held that there could be no literalistic calculation of the end of the sixth and last earthly age, however tempting it might be to identify that with the year 1000, since the Gospels state that man cannot know the day or the hour of the End, which is known only to God (Matt. 24:36; Mark 13:32). On the other hand, apocalyptic expectation, in the sense of being continually mindful of the Day of Judgment that comes sooner or later, was an ever-present strand in early medieval theological thought; Doomsday was seen as the final consummation of God's redemptive purpose in human time, and with it went a continuing strong emphasis on those elements of the Christian faith that dealt with salvation and man's personal and collective destiny—eschatology, the study of last things. Put thus, orthodox contemporary theological thinking ascribed no special weight to the year 1000; nevertheless, examination of the cultural expression of apocalyptic themes suggests that the particular and critical circumstances of late tenth- and early eleventh-century Anglo-Saxon England may have promoted a heightened perception of the imminence of Doomsday in the decades on either side of the year 1000.

To begin with, it is necessary to set this against a broader cultural perspective. Eschatological ideas from the outset were prominent in the conversion of the Anglo-Saxons, as is clear from the letter sent in 601 by Gregory the Great to King Æthelbert of Kent, and pertinently quoted by Bede. For Gregory, the conversion of the pagan Anglo-Saxons was a matter of urgency, because the end would come when the Gospel had been spread to all the ends of the earth: "we would wish your majesty to know that the end of the world is at hand, as we learn from the words of Almighty God in the holy scriptures; and the kingdom of the saints which knows no end is near."[3]

Bede's own considerable interest in eschatological matters, and the intimately related issue of world chronology, is reflected in many of his

2. Raw, *Trinity and Incarnation*, p. 24; see also, e.g., Wolff, *Awakening of Europe*, pp. 112–18.

3. Bede, *Historia ecclesiastica gentis Anglorum* 1.32, in *Venerabilis Baedae opera historica*, 1:67–70. Trans. in Bede, *Hist. eccles.*

works, including his great work on *De temporum ratione*,[4] and his commentaries on the Apocalypse, as well as an influential poem on Doomsday, *De Die Judicii*.

Nor of course were Anglo-Saxon contemporary ideas about Doomsday expressed in words alone; in sculpture, icons, and manuscript painting, they were powerful images for contemplation, teaching, and study. When Benedict Biscop returned from his fifth visit to Rome in late 679 or early 680, as Bede recounts, he "brought with him pictures of holy images to decorate the church of the blessed St. Peter, which he had built."[5] Among these were painted panels with images from the Revelation of St. John, which decorated the north wall of the church. This famous account has a powerful double resonance; first, because it immediately transports us to the site of St. Peter's monastery at Wearmouth, which Rosemary Cramp has so skillfully brought to life through her passionate and dedicated campaign of excavation; and second, because it so graphically illustrates both the beginnings of an enduring tradition of apocalyptic imagery in Insular art and the accessibility of Early Christian models in England in the later seventh and eighth centuries. Benedict Biscop's installation of apocalypse icons in his own church of St. Peter is clearly a conscious evocation of the church at the heart of the Christian faith. On his visits to Rome, Benedict would certainly have seen not only icons such as these, but also the great mosaic of the apocalyptic Adoration of the Lamb[6] that adorned the facade of Old St. Peter's—literally a central image, and one of the most powerful ones that every pilgrim to the holy city would have remembered; what then more appropriate to adorn this other church of St. Peter, built in stone, as Bede emphasizes, in the Roman manner?[7]

The theme was deeply embedded in other aspects of Insular religious art. From the earliest stage, apocalyptic references appeared in the Gospel books and Bibles that were the essential tools of conversion; these could be overt, as in the Tetramorph figure in the early eighth-century Trier Gospels, a composite of the four creatures of the Apocalypse, deriving from the Old Testament Vision of Ezekiel (Trier Domschatz, MS 61, fol. 5v), and in the image of the Second Coming in the early ninth-century Irish Turin Gospels (Turin, Biblioteca Nazionale, MS O.IV.20, fol. 2a), or they could be more elliptical.[8] As George Henderson and Jennifer O'Reilly have

4. Discussed in this volume by George H. Brown.

5. Bede, *Historia abbatum*, chap. 6, p. 369. My translation.

6. A miniature of this mosaic exists in a late eleventh-century manuscript of Johannes Diaconus, *Life of Pope Gregory*, Eton College Library, MS 124, fol. 122r; illustrated in Stiegemann and Wemhoff, *799 Kunst und Kultur der Karolingerzeit*, cat. no. IX.3, pp. 611–13.

7. Bede, *Historia abbatum*, chap. 5, p. 368.

8. J. Alexander, *Insular Manuscripts*, no. 26, fig. 110; no. 61, fig. 280.

reminded us, the apocalyptic passage preceding the account of the passion in the three synoptic Gospels puts the theme of the coming Judgment
at the very heart of the Gospel narrative.[9] Henderson gives, as example,
the richly resonant image of the Crucifixion at the end of St. Matthew's
Gospel in the late seventh-century Durham Gospels (Durham, Cathedral
Library, MS A.II.17, fol. 38v). It follows a page of script in a cruciform
frame containing the closing verses of Matthew 28, ending with "lo, I am
with you always, to the end of the world." Henderson has argued that this
page of highlighted text encapsulates Christ's Passion and the Judgment
at the Second Coming, and prepares us for the immediately succeeding
miniature of Christ on the cross. This image of a bearded hieratic Christ
stretched on the cross, flanked by Longinus and Stephaton with angels
above, is linked to ideas about the spear wound in the side of Christ as a
source both of the blood of redemption and the water of baptism. It also
bears inscriptions that link it directly with the Book of Revelation (1:8
and 21:6). The letters Alpha and Omega and the words Initium and Finis
on either side of Christ's head further emphasize this image as a densely
symbolic expression of Christian doctrine, in which Christ, as suffering
Redeemer, and Judge and Almighty God, the beginning and the end,
unite in one densely conceived image. Henderson goes on to trace other
layered apocalyptic references in the decoration of some of these early
Gospel books, particularly in the Book of Kells (Dublin, Trinity College
Library, MS 58), which, he argues, draws extensively on apocalyptic tradition in its decoration.[10]

That the expression of ideas about the Last Days is deeply ingrained
in early postconversion Anglo-Saxon art is of course also well exemplified
in other media; for example, Jane Hawkes has demonstrated in the case
of the great late eighth-century mutilated cross from Rothbury that ascension iconography joins with the apocalyptic image of Christ as Judge, above
the damned in hell, very powerfully depicted below.[11] But it is very striking
that by the early ninth century, this tradition had seemingly lost ground
in Anglo-Saxon England. Certainly, none of the surviving Anglo-Saxon
Gospel books of the period display the same kind of overt and multilayered interest in Judgment Day themes that are seen in the earlier Gospel
books and Bibles. Setting aside incomplete codices such as the Barberini
Gospels (Vatican City, Biblioteca Apostolica Vaticana, MS Barberini lat.
570) and the Codex Bigotianus (Paris, Bibliothèque nationale de France,
MS lat. 281, 298), even the major manuscripts of the later eighth and ninth

9. O'Reilly, "Early Medieval Text and Image," esp. pp. 89–91; G. Henderson, *From
Durrow to Kells*, pp. 80–81; see also Raw, *Anglo-Saxon Crucifixion Iconography*, pp. 108–09.
    10. G. Henderson, *From Durrow to Kells*, pp. 131–78, 198.
    11. J. Hawkes, "Rothbury Cross."

centuries exhibit little taste for visual play with apocalyptic subtexts. We search in vain in the St. Petersburg Gospels (St. Petersburg Public Library, MS F.v.1. no. 8), the Stockholm Codex Aureus (Stockholm, Royal Library, MS A.135), or the Book of Cerne (Cambridge, University Library, MS Ll. 1. 10) for the kind of elaborated apocalyptic iconographic elements that can be traced in some of the earlier manuscripts and sculpture. Perhaps the nearest we get to it is in the formidable opening page to St. Luke's Gospel in the early ninth-century Royal Bible (London, British Library, MS Royal 1. E. vi, fol. 43), where the welling clouds that accompany the evangelist symbol may suggest an apocalyptic resonance;[12] but overall, the suspicion grows that the striking paucity of eschatological images in Anglo-Saxon decorated manuscripts of the later eighth and ninth centuries may be due perhaps not just to questions of survival, but also to other less determinable factors, including perhaps deteriorating skills and stagnating knowledge and learning in English monasteries of the day.

The disruption and impoverishment provoked by the long battering of Viking campaigns throughout the main part of the century undoubtedly damaged England spiritually and intellectually as well as physically, as Alfred had cause to lament and strove hard to redress. Nevertheless, a slender thread that suggests the continuing importance of apocalyptic ideas in later Anglo-Saxon religious thought can be traced in a number of ninth- and early tenth-century Anglo-Saxon poems on eschatological themes, for example, in the poems *Christ II, Christ III,* and *Judgment Day II,* usually assigned to the mid-ninth century. It also occurs in the two *Soul and Body* poems; the image of the worm Glutton in *Soul and Body II* is a graphic reminder of the importance of the eternal Soul rather than the eminently corruptible Body, and hence of the Judgment that awaits us all.

Concern with themes related to the Last Days and the Second Coming also continued and developed in the art of the Carolingian courts, and in Carolingian homiletic writing, in the sermons of such as Paulus Diaconus and Haymo of Auxerre, which were to become very influential in England in the tenth century through the monastic Reform movement. Some of the distinctive physical ways in which these ideas were expressed in the tenth and eleventh centuries, and in what contexts, are the subjects of the remaining part of this essay, which will concentrate in particular on the remarkable efflorescence of ivory carving and its role in embodying eschatological concerns in this period.[13] As already noted, early medi-

---

12. J. Alexander, *Insular Manuscripts,* no. 32, fig. 161; Budny, "British Library Manuscript Royal I E.vi," pp. 469–70; Deshman, *Benedictional of St. Æthelwold,* pp. 93, 96–97.

13. Although outside the scope of this essay, it should be noted that a concern with the end of times in the form of the Viking Ragnarok may have influenced Anglo-Scandinavian works such as the tenth-century Gosforth Cross.

eval ideas about Doomsday had an enduring currency quite independent of any perceptions of an approaching millennium in or around the year 1000. Yet, as that date approached, and in the years that immediately followed it, several critical factors seem to have come together in rolling acceleration to produce a very distinctive range of artistic and literary responses to eschatological themes, which seem to reach a climax in the decades on either side of the year 1000.

First among these was the great renewal of religion and learning initiated in the later years of the ninth century by Alfred, who imported Continental and Welsh scholars to spearhead his campaign to reinvigorate and reeducate the failing English church. Alfred's grandson Æthelstan built upon these reforms, nurturing at his court scholars such as Dunstan and Æthelwold, who were to become under Edgar prime movers of the monastic Reform of the Benedictine Order that profoundly transformed church and worship in England in the course of the tenth century. Already, in the style and iconography of the Galba Psalter miniature of Christ enthroned amidst heavenly choirs accompanied by the instruments of the Passion, and of that of the exalted and wounded image of Christ of the Second Coming in the same manuscript (London, British Library, MS Cotton Galba A. xviii, fols. 2v and 21), the influence of Carolingian eschatological iconography is visible; as Deshman has argued, the manuscript has its origins in the reforms of Alfred's reign.[14] The traditions of Carolingian religious scholarship and thought that were already reaching England in Alfred's reign under John the Old Saxon and Grimbald of St. Bertin were amplified and extended under leaders of the Reform, notably, Dunstan, Æthelwold, and Oswald.[15] New texts, such as missals, tropers, pontificals, benedictionals, Continental homiliaries, and so on, introduced new emphases, for instance, on confession and penitence, and with them, different styles and iconographies.[16] The great manuscripts generated from major centers of the Reform movement, such as the 971–84 Benedictional of St. Æthelwold (London, British Library, MS Additional 49598), the Harley Psalter (London, British Library, MS Harley 603), and the Missal of Robert of Jumièges (Rouen, Bibliothèque municipale, MS Y.7), rival in splendor their Carolingian (and Byzantine) exemplars; and they illustrate a revived Anglo-Saxon concern with the iconography of the Apocalypse. Christ strides implacably forward through apocalyptic clouds in the depiction of the Second Coming on folio 9v of the Benedictional

14. Deshman, *Benedictional of St. Æthelwold*, p. 63; O'Reilly, "Early Medieval Text and Image," pp. 84–93; Deshman, "Galba Psalter," p. 135.

15. Keynes, "King Athelstan's Books"; Gretsch, *Intellectual Foundations of the Benedictine Reform*, pp. 248–49, 276–77, and passim.

16. E.g., Gneuss, "Liturgical Books in Anglo-Saxon England."

of St. Æthelwold; his garment is inscribed with the words "King of Kings" (Rev. 19:16).[17] In the same manuscript, Christ as Judge appears as revealed at Doomsday, seated on a rainbow framed against swirling clouds (fol. 70), as described in the vision of Ezekiel and the Apocalypse[18] (Ezek. 1:27–28; Rev. 4:2–3). Some fifty years later, in the Winchester *Liber Vitae* of 1031, we see the image of Cnut and his queen, Emma, presenting a massive gold altar cross to the cathedral; in this draft record of the Book of Life of the saved, the image on the succeeding opening shows the Day of Judgment itself, when the saved and the damned met their final destinies (London, British Library, MS Stowe 944, fols. 6–7).[19]

Second, as the image of the presentation of the great cross in the *Liber Vitae* implies, works of religious art in other media also accompanied the Reform and shared its iconographies. Lavish fitments in precious metalwork—shrines and reliquaries, book covers, altars, crosses, and even large scale gold-sheeted figures of saints and the Virgin—were also made in the new style, as many inventories and other written accounts reveal.[20] Very little of this metalwork has survived the many vicissitudes of time and chance, but fortunately, the survival rate for Anglo-Saxon ivory carving, far less vulnerable to predation of many kinds, is much better. Ivory carving had already assumed a new preeminence in this period, partly due to the influence of Carolingian and, subsequently, Ottonian exemplars, and in part due to regular access to the excellent new medium of walrus ivory, first introduced into England under Alfred's patronage, as we know from the story of the Viking entrepreneur Ottar, as recounted at Alfred's court.[21] With Carolingian ivories to serve as stylistic and iconographic models, this innovative medium too played a notable role in framing an artistic vocabulary for some of the main preoccupations of later tenth- and early eleventh-century religious thought, and in giving compact but revealing form to these eternal, cosmic truths.

The third significant factor here is the striking fact that a great deal of the homiletic literature, and almost all the poetry that addresses apocalyptic themes, was written or collected together in the fifty or so years around the year 1000—sometimes sermons and poetry collected in the same volume, as in the case of the Vercelli Book. Six at least of the longer poems in the Exeter Book are concerned with the Day of Judgment, including *Christ II* and *Christ III*, and *Soul and Body II*; these themes are equally visible in some of the poems in the Vercelli Book (*The Dream of*

---

17. Deshman, *Benedictional of St. Æthelwold*, plate 10.
18. Deshman, *Benedictional of St. Æthelwold*, plate 27.
19. Temple, *Anglo-Saxon Manuscripts*, no. 78, figs. 244, 247–48.
20. Dodwell, *Anglo-Saxon Art*, pp. 202–03, and chap. 7, especially pp. 195–215.
21. Lund and Fell, *Two Voyagers at the Court of King Alfred*, pp. 19–20, 58–62.

the Rood, for example) and are certainly prominent in the homilies in that volume.

The sumptuous manuscripts of the great religious houses and the fabulous wealth of metalwork revealed in the inventories and wills testify to a degree of prosperity and stability in the years approaching the millennium that is to some extent borne out on the political level by the continuities in the tenth-century charter evidence. Though the condition of England was certainly often turbulent and faction-ridden, throughout the reign of most tenth-century kings, up to the death of Edgar in 975, the country enjoyed a degree of security, at least from external forces. All of that came abruptly to an end in the reign of Æthelred II, when England became increasingly the prey of massive Viking attacks by well-organized and ruthless armies from about 980 onward. The tributes by which these successive attacks were temporarily bought off give a graphic picture of the escalating impact on the resources of the country, let alone the graphic accounts of wholesale destruction and slaughter given in the Chronicle. In 991 the sum was £1,000; in 994, £16,000; by 1012, it had reached £48,000; and in 1018 culminated in £72,000 with a further £10,500 paid from London. The attacks culminated in the devastation of much of the country by the army of Thorkell the Tall between 1009 and 1011, by which time the Chronicle bleakly reports that they had "overrun East Anglia, Essex, Middlesex, Oxfordshire, Cambridgeshire, Hertfordshire, Buckinghamshire, Bedfordshire, half Huntingdonshire, much of Northamptonshire; and south of the Thames, all Kent, Sussex, Hastings, Surrey, Berkshire, Hampshire and much of Wiltshire."[22]

It thus seems hardly coincidental that the renewal of Viking raids on England in the late tenth and early eleventh centuries, and the terrors that accompanied them, coincided with a growing intensification of interest in the events and portents of the Last Days, in iconographies associated with these themes, and in how mankind should prepare for the end. This is very clearly seen in the ever-increasing preoccupation with these themes in the homiletic collections, the earliest of which, the Blickling Homilies, has one sermon, Homily XI, preached on Holy Thursday, that is quite explicit about the imminence of Doomsday: "all the signs and portents which our Lord said would come before Doomsday had come to pass, except the Antichrist; and that 971 years, the greater part of the last age, had already passed."[23]

Although this date shortly precedes the main period of Viking raiding, there can be no doubt that here at least the year 1000 was clearly in the writer's mind; and other, less specifically millennial eschatological

22. Whitelock, *English Historical Documents,* p. 244.
23. Morris, *Blickling Homilies,* pp. 115–30, especially pp. 117–19.

topics recur both in this collection and in the slightly later sermons collected in the Vercelli Book. But more significantly, the homilies composed
in the decades on either side of the year 1000 by two of the most influential churchmen of the times, Ælfric and Wulfstan, contain an increasingly
insistent emphasis on eschatological matter, some of it explicitly related
to Viking attacks.[24] To take just a few examples: writing in the early 990s,
Ælfric alludes to the approaching end of the world in the preface to the
First Series of Catholic Homilies,[25] and in a sermon on the sixth Sunday
after Pentecost (Supp. XIV: 126–39), links the Viking incursions with the
tribulations of the Last Days. The theme is returned to often and with rhetorical relish in the sermons of Wulfstan; one of his many eschatological
sermons, III: lines 21–23, specifically identifies the activities of the Viking
armies with the uprising of nations described in the Gospel accounts (e.g.,
Matt. 24:7): "and alien men and foreigners greatly harass us, as Christ in
his Gospel plainly said would come about. He said 'Surget gens contra
gentem.'"[26]

Another of Wulfstan's eschatological homilies, V: lines 44–47, makes
the point that over a thousand years have passed since the Incarnation:
"After 1000 years Satan will be unbound. A thousand years and more is
now passed since Christ was among men in human form, and now are
Satan's fetters completely dissolved and the time of Antichrist is well at
hand."[27]

But it is his best known sermon that, in one version, is prefaced with the
title, "The Sermon of the Wolf to the English, when the Danes persecuted
them most, which was in the year 1014 from the incarnation of our Lord
Jesus Christ."[28] This is an explicit interpretation of the renewed Viking
attacks as divine punishment brought about as a result of the nation's sin-
fulness, as the famous opening lines immediately stress: "This world is in
haste and the end approaches; and therefore in the world things go from
bad to worse, and so it must of necessity deteriorate greatly on account of
the people's sins before the coming of Antichrist, and indeed it will then
be dreadful and terrible far and wide throughout the world."[29] While this
is not explicitly an eschatological homily, the catalogue of evils in the land
that he lists clearly echos the signs and disturbances and civil disasters that
presage the Second Coming. Two other manuscripts of this sermon date it

24. Ælfric, *Homilies of Ælfric: A Supplementary Collection,* nos. XI and XVII; and Wulfstan, *Homilies,* nos. III, IV, and V.
25. Ælfric, *Catholic Homilies, the First Series,* pp. 174–77.
26. Wulfstan, *Homilies,* p. 124. My translation.
27. Wulfstan, *Homilies,* pp. 136–37. My translation.
28. Wulfstan, *Homilies,* no. XX, pp. 267–75.
29. Whitelock, *English Historical Documents,* p. 929.

to the year 1009, possibly referring to an earlier version;[30] this is a date of some significance in terms of Viking activity, to be revisited shortly.

As has often been noted, these later homilies, all written in the two decades around the millennium, lay particular emphasis on confession and penance, while the somewhat earlier Blickling Homilies do not; these acts of contrition enjoined upon a sinful and threatened populace occur elsewhere in texts of this time, and it is also notable that, as has been pointed out by several commentators, the penitential psalms are first adopted into the English rule around 970, shortly before the Viking attacks intensified.

Certain themes, then, are very much in the air in the years around 1000; it is appropriate to examine their iconographic implications, and what this means specifically in the field of ivory carving, the focus of this essay. The late Saxon ivories are of especial interest here: they have been the subject of important discussions in recent years, especially in the wider studies of late Saxon church art and culture by Barbara Raw and Richard Gameson;[31] but their mostly intimate scale suggests they may repay a closer focus, as a devotional phenomenon in their own right. Though none can be precisely dated, their stylistic and iconographic relationship to datable manuscripts of the Winchester school enables us to date the majority of the surviving carvings to the later years of the tenth century and the beginning of the eleventh; and this is particularly true of the significant number that reflect the iconography of Doomsday and related topics, on which I wish to concentrate.

These are all small-scale pieces, of necessity of course, given the narrower diameter of a walrus tusk, compared with that of an elephant. Though ivories were also used in public contexts, as we know from descriptions of lost altar frontals and shrines,[32] many of them imply use in an intimate context, fixed to the cover of a small prayer or Gospel book, or indeed, worn around the neck. These are, for the most part, objects designed for private prayer and meditation, rather than for public display, and their iconography often reflects issues to do with personal salvation. A perfect example of the intimate scale of these ivories is to be seen in a small (10 x 6 cm) carving found at the late Saxon minster site of North Elmham;

30. Wulfstan, *Homilies*, note p. 356.

31. See Beckwith, *Ivory Carving in Early Medieval England*, chap. 2, pp. 27–72, for a fairly comprehensive, if somewhat idiosyncratic, list; Backhouse, Turner, and Webster, *Golden Age of Anglo-Saxon Art;* Raw, *Anglo-Saxon Crucifixion Iconography;* Raw, *Trinity and Incarnation;* Gameson, *Role of Art in the Late Anglo-Saxon Church.*

32. For example, see Dodwell, *Anglo-Saxon Art*, p. 209, citing an Ely inventory describing a silver and jeweled altar frontal with Christ in Majesty in relief, personifications of the Sun and Moon, and representations of four angels in ivory.

it depicts the wounded and exalted Christ enthroned in a mandorla of eternal glory, his garment pulled back to reveal the wound in his side, and his hands upraised to display the nail holes (fig. 1).[33] On the mandorla is an inscription referring to Luke 24:39: "o all of you, regard my hands and feet"—a reference to the wounds of Christ that were inflicted by man. Christ is flanked by Mary and St. Peter with his key (in his role as Heaven's doorkeeper who admits the saved), and below, the cross itself is raised up in the sky by angels—one of the signs of the Second Coming (Matt. 24:30). Below is the community of the faithful awaiting Judgment. This particular iconographic type of Christ displaying his wounds is a regular image of the Second Coming, which, as we have already noted, occurs in the pre-939 Galba Psalter,[34] and has echoes in Reform manuscripts such as the Benedictional of St. Æthelwold and elsewhere, as a Doomsday image. The kind of devotional context in which such an ivory might have been used is illustrated by Gameson who cites a passage in the ecclesiastical section of the laws of Cnut (Cnut I:25), in the drafting of which Wulfstan probably played a part, with its injunction to all men to "have the fear of God constantly in their hearts, and day and night to be in terror of sin, dreading the Day of Judgment, and shuddering at the thought of Hell and ever expecting their last day to be close at hand."[35]

More usual, however, is the image of Christ as Judge enthroned, as for example in the Benedictional of St. Æthelwold (BL Add. 49598, fol. 70), where, as Robert Deshman has argued, the diadem, seething clouds, and the rainbow upon which Christ sits give an apocalyptic resonance to the image.[36] The centrality of this image to the eschatological concerns of the homilists of this period is made manifest in the figure of Christ as the Just Judge that is the frontispiece to a volume of Ælfric's Catholic Homilies (Cambridge, Trinity College, MS B.15.34, fol. 1).[37] Like Christ in the Second Coming depicted in the Benedictional of St. Æthelwold (BL Add. 49598 fol. 9v), his garment bears the apocalyptic text *Rex Regum* (Rev. 19:16), and he holds in his left hand a book inscribed with a further Doomsday reference (*ego sum qui de morte surrexi: ego vivo in eternum, lux mundi: ego venio in dei iudicii*). A similar image in the Boulogne Gospels (Boulogne, Bibliothèque municipale, MS 11, fol. 10) displays a book with the words "Liber Vitae" (Rev. 5:8, 20:12). These figures too wear diadems, emphasizing Christ as the omnipotent royal judge, "coming in the clouds of heaven with much power and majesty" (Matt. 24:30). The

33. O'Reilly, "Early Medieval Text and Image," pp. 73–74, 111.
34. O'Reilly, "Early Medieval Text and Image," p. 92.
35. Gameson, *Role of Art in the Late Anglo-Saxon Church*, p. 252.
36. Deshman, *Benedictional of St. Æthelwold*, pp. 96–97.
37. Temple, *Anglo-Saxon Manuscripts*, no. 74, fig. 241.

five enthroned Christ figures that appear on Anglo-Saxon ivories clearly carry a similar resonance; all have royal diadems and display the Book of Life, and some sit upon rainbows.[38] They comprise a small panel in the Victoria and Albert Museum (fig. 2),[39] the tau cross in Cologne Cathedral treasury,[40] a recently acquired ivory panel in the British Museum (fig. 3),[41] and the central element of a pectoral cross in the Metropolitan Museum, New York (fig. 4).[42] There can certainly be no doubt about the meaning of the awesome depiction of Christ as Judge on this last piece. This is an unequivocally eschatological image, powerfully reinforced by the presence on the back of the apocalyptic Agnus Dei (discussed further below) surrounded by the four evangelist symbols, themselves derived from the beasts of Ezekiel's vision and the Apocalypse (fig. 5).

The same intimate character seen in the pectoral cross is most obviously seen in the numerous small ivory Crucifixion scenes of the period, which, again perhaps significantly, appear for the first time in the later tenth century. In most of these, the hand of God acknowledges Christ, and the cross may be accompanied by the Virgin and St. John and/or angels, in conventional iconography (see, e.g., figs. 6 and 7). Though Christ's sacrifice on the cross is a paramount image of salvation, it also resonates with Doomsday reference in some of these small devotional carvings. The cross may also be flanked by the evangelist symbols, or by the darkened sun and moon (e.g., figs. 7 and 8); these refer to the Gospel accounts of the Crucifixion, of course, but also carry an eschatological meaning, as presages of the Last Days described in the Apocalypse and in the three synoptic Gospels (Rev. 4:7–9; Mark 14:24–26; Matt. 24:29–30; Luke 21:25). In some cases, the Crucifixion is also paired with an image of Christ as

38. I have not counted among these the arguably Anglo-Saxon elephant ivory panel from a book cover, now in the Pierpont Morgan Library, New York, M319A (Backhouse, Turner, and Webster, *Golden Age of Anglo-Saxon Art*, cat. no. 21, pp. 38–39); the image of Christ in Majesty is closely related stylistically to the figure of the wounded and exalted Christ in the Galba Psalter, and the plant scrolls that flank the mandorla closely resemble the decoration of the borders of the dedication page of the *Lives of St. Cuthbert*, presented to the saint's shrine by Æthelstan between late 934 and the latter part of 939 (Cambridge, Corpus Christi College, MS 183; Keynes, "King Æthelstan's Books," pp. 181–84). The figure of a beardless Christ seated on a rainbow, in a mandorla, holding the Book of Life, is surrounded by the evangelist symbols, emphasizing the eschatological significance of the image. Since the origin of this piece remains uncertain, however, it seems best to exclude it from the tally.

39. Backhouse, Turner, and Webster, *Golden Age of Anglo-Saxon Art*, cat. no. 123, p. 121.

40. Beckwith, *Ivory Carvings in Early Medieval England*, no. 30, plates 80–81.

41. See Lasko, *Ars Sacra*, p. 75, plate 109.

42. Backhouse, Turner, and Webster, *Golden Age of Anglo-Saxon Art*, cat. no. 124, pp. 121–22.

Judge, as on the Cologne tau cross or in a lost book cover described in a York inventory, which bore images, apparently in ivory, of the Crucifixion below, with Christ in Majesty and Peter and Paul above.[43] The Crucifixion is of course the central redemptive image of Christianity; but it is striking that in a number of these ivories, as in some related contemporary metalwork, reference to the Last Judgment that is to come coexists with the image of Christ as the redeeming sacrifice—a dual message implicit in another form in the North Elmham ivory referred to above.

The last image I want to examine in detail is intimately connected with both the previous themes. The Agnus Dei is a subject extremely rare in Anglo-Saxon art until the later tenth century when, like many other iconographic subjects, it gained renewed prominence in Anglo-Saxon iconography under the influence of Carolingian exemplars imported in the Reform.[44] The figure of the lamb represents both the Eucharistic, paschal lamb of God, which carries away the sins of the world (John 1:29), and the triumphal apocalyptic lamb, adored by martyrs and elders and the four living creatures, which breaks the seals upon the book (Rev. 5–8). Homily XV, in Ælfric's Second Series of Catholic Homilies,[45] delivered on Easter Day, is a sermon on the significance of the Eucharist, which the homilist compares to the sacrifice of the Passover lamb. The sacrificial lamb that takes away the sins of the world at the heart of the ceremony of the Mass is also bound intimately to the core necessity for confession and repentance. Significantly in this context, however, the image of the resurrected Christ displaying his wounds at the Last Judgment is also invoked by Ælfric toward the close of this sermon. We see a similar combination of the Eucharistic and apocalyptic lamb more explicitly in the eleventh-century Anglo-Saxon portable altar in the Musée de Cluny, where, as Barbara Raw and others have noted, the combination of Christ crucified on the Tree of Life, and the triumphant apocalyptic lamb surrounded by the evangelist symbols express the paradox of Christ's death,[46] in a context of the celebration of the Mass itself (fig. 9). The theme is repeated on a number of crucifixes where Christ on the front is paralleled by the Agnus Dei flanked by evangelist symbols on the back. Two cross-heads from Durham, which may have been made in the early eleventh century, not long

43. Dodwell, *Anglo-Saxon Art*, pp. 202, 312.

44. It should be noted, however, that some depictions of the Lamb of God do survive on the fragments of late eighth- to early ninth-century cross-heads buried at Hart and Hoddom, as well as on the Wirksworth slab. Losses of other such images may have occurred during the iconoclastic destructions of the Reformation.

45. Ælfric, *Catholic Homilies, the Second Series*, pp. 151–52.

46. O'Reilly and Okasha, "Anglo-Saxon Portable Altar"; Raw, *Anglo-Saxon Crucifixion Iconography*, p. 182.

after the arrival of the Community of St. Cuthbert at Durham in 995, show the same idea in stone.[47]

A particularly powerful example may be seen on the early eleventh-century Brussels Cross, made of silver-sheeted wood (fig. 10).[48] Here on the back, we see the familiar configuration of the Lamb surrounded by evangelist symbols; the Crucifixion that once adorned the front is lost, but around the sides are inscriptions that include a reference to a version of the line from *The Dream of the Rood:* "Cross is my name; once trembling and drenched with blood, I bore the mighty king." This is again the living tree, which bore Christ triumphant; but it is also the blood-stained cross described in *Christ III* and in Blickling Homily VII as the red cross shining in the sky at Doomsday (Matt. 24:30). A more sumptuous version of this is seen in the Victoria and Albert Museum's Anglo-Saxon gold and enameled cross set with an ivory figure of Christ crucified;[49] the sacrifice of Christ surrounded by enameled evangelist symbols and delicate filigree plant tendrils on the front is complemented by the gold sheet back, where an Agnus Dei is set at the center of a living vine-scroll cross, its terminals framing the evangelical/apocalyptic beasts.

Another version of the cross as Tree of Life is provided by an ivory pendant reliquary cross from the first half of the eleventh century where, exceptionally, an image of the archer as Word of God adorns the front, with the lamb and symbols on the back (figs. 11, 12).[50] The lamb may also occur in juxtaposition to other apocalyptic images, for example on an early eleventh-century London tau crosier where, in a reference to the vision of Isaiah, a winged seraph in a mandorla appears on one side (Isa. 6:2–7) with the lamb on the other (figs. 13, 14). The tau shape itself may refer to a contemporary perception of the tau expressed in Ælfric's homily on the Eucharist cited above, where he describes how the Israelites, "with the blood of the lamb . . . marked a Tau, that is the sign of the cross, on their door lintels. And we should mark our foreheads and bodies with the sign of Christ's cross, so that we may be saved from destruction, when we are marked both on the forehead and in the heart with the blood of Christ's passion."[51]

---

47. Durham Cathedral Library, nos. xx and xiii; Backhouse, Turner, and Webster, *Golden Age of Anglo-Saxon Art,* cat. no. 139, pp. 132–33.

48. Backhouse, Turner, and Webster, *Golden Age of Anglo-Saxon Art,* cat. no. 75, pp. 90–92, plate xxiii.

49. Inv. no. 7943.1862; Backhouse, Turner, and Webster, *Golden Age of Anglo-Saxon Art,* cat. no. 118, pp. 117–18, plate xxvi.

50. Backhouse, Turner, and Webster, *Golden Age of Anglo-Saxon Art,* cat. no. 125, pp. 122–23; Raw, "The Eagle, the Archer and the Lamb."

51. Ælfric, *Catholic Homilies, the Second Series,* p. 151, lines 52–57.

On the London tau cross, the lamb is supported by two male figures, one in a very short tunic, the other in long garments. I have argued elsewhere that these represent, respectively, St. John the Baptist and St. John the Divine;[52] it is the Baptist who utters the words "Behold the Lamb of God, which comes to take away the sins of the world" (John 1:29), and St. John, author of the Apocalypse, who describes the apocalyptic lamb (Rev. 5:6–12). Thus the two authors of the definitive New Testament utterances on the lamb appear as its supporters and symbolize its twin aspects.

These instances undoubtedly illustrate the popularity of the iconography of the Agnus Dei in the decades around the year 1000. But there is even more telling evidence for a special emphasis, in this perimillennial period, on the Lamb as an image both of salvation and of the Last Days. Michael Dolley some time ago drew our attention to the relationship between a well-dated early eleventh-century brooch bearing the image of the Agnus Dei and the short-lived Agnus Dei coinage of Æthelred II, which can be precisely dated on numismatic grounds to the period between late summer and early Autumn 1009.[53] This was precisely the time (following their arrival at the end of August) at which the raiding army of Thorkell the Tall had launched a massive onslaught throughout southern England, as the Chronicle for that year graphically recounts.[54] And in this same time of great trouble, Æthelred issued an edict (VII Æthelred) headed "This was decreed when the Great Army came to the country."[55] The edict, which is certainly in Wulfstan's style and survives in full only in a manuscript associated with him,[56] urges a general public fasting and penance, confession, and the daily saying of "the Mass against the heathen," and all were to process with the relics and to call on Christ eagerly from their inmost hearts. There can be no doubt that the invocation "agnus dei qui tollit peccata mundi" would have been a focal element in this, with its cry for mercy and peace, chanted by the congregation in the Mass, and possibly also in recital of the Litany accompanying the barefoot procession. In this terrible time of trial, the image of the Agnus Dei both redemptive

52. Backhouse, Turner, and Webster, *Golden Age of Anglo-Saxon Art,* cat. no. 121, pp. 119–20.

53. Dolley, "Nummular Brooch from Sulgrave." Since this paper was presented, a stylistically very similar brooch has been found in Bicester, Oxon., some fifteen miles away. Instead of the Agnus Dei, however, it bears an image of the Dove of the Holy Spirit, more than coincidentally the very motif that appears on the reverse of the Agnus Dei coins.

54. Whitelock, *English Historical Documents,* p. 220. On the connection between Thorkell's invasion, VII Æthelred, Wulfstan, and the Agnus Dei coinage, see Keynes, *Diplomas of Æthelred the Unready;* Keynes, "Vikings in England."

55. Whitelock, *English Historical Documents,* p. 447.

56. Cambridge, Corpus Christi College, MS 20, which also contains the C manuscript of the *Sermo Lupi,* a version that dates that sermon to the same year, 1009 (see below).

Figure 1. Cambridge University Museum of Archaeology and Anthropology, no. Z 15154. Walrus ivory plaque with Day of Judgment.

Figure 2. London, Victoria and Albert Museum, A32-1928. Walrus ivory plaque with Christ in Majesty. Photo: Victoria and Albert Museum.

Figure 3. London, British Museum, PE 1991,4-1,1. Walrus ivory plaque with Christ in Majesty. Photo: Trustees of the British Museum.

Figure 4. New York, Metropolitan Museum of Art, gift of J. Pierpont Morgan 1917 (17.190.217). Walrus ivory plaque with Christ in Majesty. By kind permission of the Metropolitan Museum of Art.

Figure 5. New York, Metropolitan Museum of Art, gift of J. Pierpont Morgan 1917 (17.190.217). Walrus ivory plaque with Agnus Dei and evangelist symbols. By kind permission of the Metropolitan Museum of Art.

Figure 6. London, British Museum, MLA 1887,10-25,14. Walrus ivory
Crucifixion plaque. Photo: Trustees of the British Museum.

Figure 7. London, British Museum, MLA 1980,12-1,1. Walrus ivory Crucifixion plaque. Photo: Trustees of the British Museum.

Figure 8. Private collection; on loan to the British Museum. Walrus ivory Crucifixion plaque. Photo: Trustees of the British Museum.

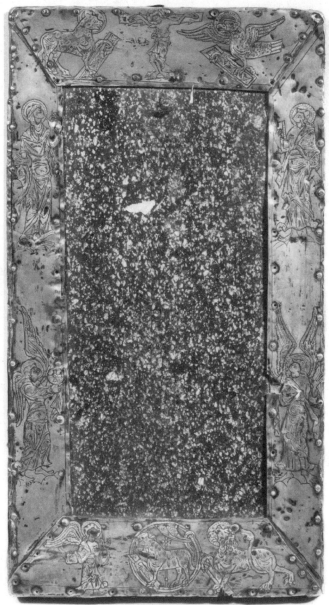

Figure 9. Paris, Musée national du Moyen Age - Thermes et hôtel de Cluny,
CL 11.459. Portable altar in porphyry and silver. Photo: © RMN.

Figure 10. Brusssels, Cathedral of St. Michael and St. Gudula. Silver sheeted cross with Agnus Dei and evangelist symbols. By kind permission of the Cathedral of St. Michael and St. Gudula.

Figure 11. London, Victoria and Albert Museum, A6-1966 (front). Walrus ivory cross with image of the Archer as Word of God. Photo: Victoria and Albert Museum.

Figure 12. London, Victoria and Albert Museum, A6-1966 (back). Walrus ivory cross with Agnus Dei and evangelist symbols. Photo: Victoria and Albert Museum.

Figure 13. London, Victoria and Albert Museum, A.1-1914. Walrus ivory tau cross, with winged seraph in a mandorla. Photo: Victoria and Albert Museum.

Figure 14. London, Victoria and Albert Museum, A.1-1914. Walrus ivory tau cross with Agnus Dei with St. John the Baptist and St. John the Evangelist. Photo: Victoria and Albert Museum.

and triumphant, its foot resting upon the apocalyptic book inscribed with the alpha and omega, carried a powerful resonance; the embattled king's unique coin issue could hardly make the point more starkly. In its other contemporary forms, whether on brooches or on some of the devotional ivories we have seen, it must have symbolized equally serious penitential concerns.

It is perhaps not irrelevant here that the heading of the C manuscript of Wulfstan's *Sermo Lupi* (ascribed in other manuscripts to 1014, a date generally accepted by scholars) and a marginal note in the E manuscript both ascribe the context of its composition to the same year of troubles, 1009—possibly representing the tradition of an early draft of that text.[57] The apocalyptic tone of that sermon, and Wulfstan's likely association with the VII Æthelred edict, reinforce the impression that apocalyptic images of the kinds outlined above and an emphasis on the imminence of the Last Days were indeed an increasingly prominent aspect of Anglo-Saxon thought in the decades around the year 1000. And there are certainly other iconographies that reflect these contemporary concerns, as Barbara Raw has demonstrated: for example, the emphasis on the nature of the Trinity, as an affirmation of orthodox faith in the time of the Antichrist who promotes heretical beliefs, especially about the Trinity, a topic well aired in Ælfric's and other homilies.[58] This and certain other iconographies that appear or are revived in the later tenth and early eleventh centuries carry a deeper freight of meaning than might at first sight appear. The images encapsulated in these small ivories and other personal objects are themselves meditations on the Last Things, on individual salvation and the general fate of mankind, sound bites on eternal matters of life and death.

The fertile literary and artistic traditions of Anglo-Saxon England were well accustomed to absorbing and adapting ideas to new contexts, new conditions, and fresh layers of meaning. What we can trace here, whether in sermons or poems, in the grandest of manuscripts, or on the humblest of ivories or brooches, and even on coins, is a sense of making sense of a disordered world. The references to Doomsday encapsulated in these artifacts, great and small, had a powerful message that both commented on and transcended the troubles of the years around 1000. There can be little doubt that in a real sense they reflect contemporary fears about the end of the world; but in the end, they are also more than that. These were images to be dwelled upon in the heart, visual meditations on individual salvation and the general fate of mankind, the encapsulations of eternal truths about life and death.

57. See Wulfstan, *Homilies*, pp. 261–66, and also the footnote on Millesimo VIIII, p. 356.
58. Raw, *Trinity and Incarnation*, chaps. 1 and 2, and pp. 160–62.

The Glass Beads from St. Ninian's Isle, Shetland

Colleen E. Batey
with contributions from Julian Henderson
and the late Alan Small

St. Ninian's Isle lies to the west of the southern Shetland mainland and is linked to the mainland by a sand bar or tombolo (fig. 1). It is a place of incredible natural beauty and has been a place of burial from the Iron Age to the mid-nineteenth century. The twenty-nine beads discussed in this short essay were originally recovered during the excavations on the island undertaken between 1955 and 1959 under the direction of Professor Andrew C. O'Dell of Aberdeen University (fig. 2). This work was posthumously reported in two magnificent volumes,[1] which concentrated on the record and significance of the unparalleled Pictish silver hoard recovered from a deposit beneath the church in July 1958. The circumstances of recovery of these glass beads are less clear, since there is no account of them in any written record, although the labels attached to the beads (in two separate groups) are in O'Dell's own handwriting and confirm that they were from the St. Ninian's Isle excavations. The reason for the exclu-

My first debt of gratitude must be to Rosemary Cramp, who was my professor at Durham University during my undergraduate years there (1975–78) and postgraduate years (1978–82). Through her skillful tuition, I learned both to be critical of my sources and also to enjoy the thrill of artifact study.

I am grateful for the advice and comments of a number of colleagues in the preparation of this note. Several people have been consulted in my quest for parallels to the beads, and I am grateful to the late Margaret Guido and Trevor Cowie in particular. I wish to thank Professor Charles Thomas for his discussion on the site and material from the original excavations. I am grateful to Professor James Graham-Campbell for making me aware of the beads in the first place and for uncovering and informing me of additional locational information at the last possible moment! Others have provided useful comment on the text, particularly Christopher Morris, Rachel Barrowman, and Hilary Cool, but all remaining inadequacies rest with the author.

A fuller and revised version of this essay is to be published as part of the forthcoming research monograph which provides a reassessment of the past excavations at the site in relation to new investigations there. *The Chapel and Burial Ground on St Ninian's Isle, Shetland. Excavations Past and Present.* R. C. Barrowman with contributions from K. Forsyth et al. Forthcoming Society of Medieval Archaeology Monograph 2008.

1. Small, Thomas, and Wilson, *St. Ninian's Isle and Its Treasure.*

sion of the beads from the main publication is also far from clear, but they subsequently came to light in two tobacco tins in a filing cabinet in University College London.

THE OVERALL ARCHAEOLOGICAL CONTEXT:
DISCOVERY OF THE HOARD AND THE BEADS

The first day on-site for Douglas Coutts, a Shetland schoolboy, in July 1958 was to be momentous, for on overturning a cross-slab in the nave of the medieval church, he uncovered the magnificent Pictish silver treasure, comprising several penannular brooches, chapes, and decorative silver pieces. Conventionally described as a secular hoard, although this is a contested view, it may have been deposited in the face of Viking raids.[2] The precise stratigraphical relationship of this silver hoard is difficult to confirm, although it is clear that it was recovered at some depth below the walls of the surviving church and presumed to be within the bounds of an earlier church. The photographic record of Miss Helen Nisbet shows a stone wall at a considerable depth beneath the later church wall (fig. 3).[3] Whether this was on an alignment similar to the long cists to the south cannot now be known with certainty, but on the published plan there are traces of two fragments of walling that share the alignment of the later church walls, and a tantalizing northwestern fragment that does not obviously share the later alignment (fig. 4).

The immediate archaeological context for the beads is a little obscure, but I am most grateful to Alan Small for the following information. The larger group of beads (Group One) were found in one of the group of long cists situated to the south of the apse of the medieval church. Unfortunately, the lack of a site diary or comprehensive record of small finds has made it impossible to define a more accurate location.[4] These cists lie stratigraphically above a complex Iron Age horizon,[5] and clearly almost one meter below the foundation of the medieval church. Thomas regards these graves as representing the earliest of up to four Christian phases on the island.[6]

The original labeling from the beads suggests that there were two groups recovered. Group One (Nos. 1–21) was labeled "St. Ninian's Isle,

2. Small, Thomas, and Wilson, *St. Ninian's Isle and Its Treasure*, pp. 145–47.
3. In 2000, Miss Nisbet, who had excavated with O'Dell at St. Ninian's Isle, deposited her slide library with the Department of Archaeology, University of Glasgow. This includes several color slides of the excavations and a number of detailed shots of excavation in progress.
4. Small, Thomas, and Wilson, *St. Ninian's Isle and Its Treasure*, p. 5.
5. Small, Thomas, and Wilson, *St. Ninian's Isle and Its Treasure*, fig. 8 B.
6. Small, Thomas, and Wilson, *St. Ninian's Isle and Its Treasure*, p. 12.

Shetland. Beads from grave ca 3' SE of SE nave outer angle." Within the tin that contained this group, Nos. 1–6 were grouped together on a pipe cleaner, as were Nos. 7–15; the rest were loose. Group Two (Nos. 22–29) was simply labeled "St. Ninian's Isle," and all beads were loose in a second tin. Missing information concerning the original context of Group 2 is available in a letter dated 14 July 1967 from Alan Small to Charles Thomas; the beads were found "6" west of side alter [sic] 4' north of wall" with the comment that they "could belong to practically any period from the Iron Age upwards." It is assumed that these beads, which are of a different character to those in Group 1, may have come from a second grave or graves, but it is difficult to prove at this stage (figs. 5–8).

Assuming that O'Dell's measurement is correct, it would place the recovery of Group One in one of the most northerly of the long cists (in the vicinity of the so-called Founder's tomb). Although trial trenches in the area had been opened in 1957–58,[7] it seems most likely that this work was undertaken in 1959, in the last season of excavation at the site. However, recent excavations carried out by Rachel Barrowman have confirmed that in this part of the site there are two levels of cist graves, the lower being on the same level as the earlier church. Either level of cists could be a context for the beads, although the lower level could well be the preferred option.[8] The association of a group of beads with human remains is actually recalled[9] during the later years of the excavation in the area noted in publication as follows: "small area excavation about 12m x 8m was attempted on the south side of the church . . . , which revealed an extensive complex of prehistoric walls, pavements, and graves; all the structures extend [sic] beyond the limits of the excavated area."[10] The artifacts recovered from this area included sherds of pottery (so-called Broch-type)[11] as well as a necklace of bone and antler[12] found underlying the north–south wall shown on figure 3 here, and taken to be from the earliest occupation of the site.[13]

The published plans of the cists to the south of the church show that the northernmost example was in fact cut by modern steps,[14] and it is obvious that several of the side slabs were missing by the time of excavation. Although Small does specifically note that "the early Christian graves in the northeast corner of the excavated area, are separated from the ear-

7. *Illustrated London News*, 23 August 1958: 300.
8. Pers. comm. Rachel Barrowman.
9. Pers. comm. Miss Helen Adamson.
10. Small, Thomas, and Wilson, *St. Ninian's Isle and Its Treasure*, p. 5.
11. Small, Thomas, and Wilson, *St. Ninian's Isle and Its Treasure*, fig. 3 and fig. 4.
12. Small, Thomas, and Wilson, *St. Ninian's Isle and Its Treasure*, fig. 6.
13. Small, Thomas, and Wilson, *St. Ninian's Isle and Its Treasure*, p. 7.
14. Small, Thomas, and Wilson, *St. Ninian's Isle and Its Treasure*, fig. 5.

lier structures by a clear stratigraphical break (i.e. these postdate the cist which produced the bone and antler beads), [they] provide satisfactory confirmation of the deductions from the pottery."[15]

DISCUSSION

Despite the varying bead types and colors in this assemblage (subdivided below), it has proved rather difficult to discover parallels for the types. I am particularly grateful for the assistance in this matter of the late Mrs. Margaret Guido, who confirmed this problem. Examination of other Scottish assemblages, which are generally smaller in scale, with the exception of groups from Viking pagan graves such as Kneep, which produced forty-four beads of predominantly segmented form,[16] has failed to produce any close parallels. There are examples of long cists that have produced groups of beads, such as Dalmeny Park, South Queensferry,[17] and Morham Church, East Lothian,[18] but they are not common. In neither of these assemblages, despite a variety of forms in the Dalmeny group, are there similar examples, although in the Morham group, seven milky opalescent and two oval black beads may be more similar. Ongoing excavations at Scatness broch in southern Shetland include, among an extensive artifact record, two beads that are close parallels; find 2845 from context 2008 is a black glass bead and find 7857 from context 1674 a dark blue one; unfortunately both are from later mixed contexts on the site.[19]

The St. Ninian's Isle beads can be subdivided into a number of groups, and these are considered below:

Bead Type 1: Opaque blue, generally barrel shaped (Nos. 1, 3, 5–10, 12, 17) This is the largest of the groups in this assemblage, with ten examples. Although there are slight differences within the type, for example numbers 1 and 17 are a slightly deeper blue, they form a coherent grouping. Some of the pieces, such as 6, 10, and 12, show more clearly the method of manufacture by winding the glass around a core. At this stage no precise parallels can be found for this bead type, although a "light blue dropshaped bead, quite different from the others" was recorded from Lagore Crannog in Ireland and may be somewhat similar.[20] A single find from the Monarch Islands, North Uist, in the collections of Glasgow Museums, is clearly similar, but sadly an unprovenanced find (GAGM A6116).

15. Small, Thomas, and Wilson, *St. Ninian's Isle and Its Treasure*, p. 7.
16. Welander, Batey, and Cowie, "Viking Burial from Kneep," illustration 9.
17. G. Brown, "Notes on a Necklace of Glass Beads."
18. Pattullo, Donations to the Museum, p. 165.
19. Pers. comm. J. Bond and S. Dockrill.
20. Henchekn, "Lagore Crannog," p. 134, fig. 65 A.

Bead Type 2: Amber colored, generally spherical (Nos. 22–29)
Although yellow beads have been recorded at other sites, the translucent amber color is harder to parallel. Hamilton has also noted several yellow beads of similar form but smaller from Iron Age contexts at Clickhimin Broch, Shetland.[21] These are most commonly a more opaque and bright yellow in contrast to the amber from this group, but these do appear to be glass rather than amber.

Bead Type 6: Dark blue angular (No. 11)
The nearest parallel for this bead has been noted from an unstratified context in Orkney,[22] from the site of Lavacroon, Orphir. Although the color is described rather differently, this is somewhat misleading and there is in fact little difference in either color or form of these beads. Although in the case of the Lavacroon example dating was also problematic, a suggestion of a sixth-century AD date was put forward by comparison with an example from Ipswich.[23] The significance of such a parallel may be disputed, but an additional Northern Isles example is more useful.

Bead Type 7: Translucent amber annular (No. 14)
Examples of this bead type have been recorded from Clickhimin, Shetland, in an Iron Age context,[24] and although those examples are slightly smaller, they are of similar type. Examples here were noted from the period of broch usage and on into the occupation of the wheelhouse at the site.[25] It is difficult to ascribe a particularly close date range to the type, but it would seem likely to be Iron Age.

At this stage no precise parallels can be found for any of the following types of beads.

Bead Type 3: Almost black, flattened sphere (Nos. 13, 16, 19)
Bead Type 4: Opaque off-white, flattened sphere (Nos. 2, 4)
Bead Type 5: Very dark blue, irregular (Nos. 20, 21)
Bead Type 8: Banded decoration, cylindrical (No. 15)
Bead Type 9: Opaque off-white annular (No. 18)

SCIENTIFIC ANALYSIS

Preliminary results of scientific analysis of some of these bead types by Professor Julian Henderson of Nottingham University, using electron-probe microanalysis, are at this stage of little help. Bead types 3 and 4 have been examined so far, and it is intended to examine Bead type 1 to complete the data set. Bead 4 (of type 4), a pale opaque white, and Bead

21. Hamilton, *Excavations at Clickhimin,* p. 90.
22. Batey with Freeman, "Lavacroon, Orphir, Orkney," no. 12 illustration 9.
23. Batey with Freeman, "Lavacroon, Orphir, Orkney," p. 298.
24. Hamilton, *Excavations at Clickhimin,* p. 90, nos. 177–79, fig. 41.
25. Hamilton, *Excavations at Clickhimin,* pp. 133 and 80.

13 (of type 3), which is virtually black, both appear to have unusual compositions. The white one is composed of a potassium-rich mixture of wood ash, silica, and lime with the opaque color being formed by the presence of arsenic. This is highly unusual at such a potentially early date, but the archaeological context is as secure as we can make it at this remove. The black bead, probably to be described as brown since there is apparently no such thing as black glass(!), is of different composition with high aluminia, titania, and iron levels more consistent with an accidentally made glass associated with fuel-ash slag from iron production. Results of the analysis of the largest group of opaque blue glass beads—type 1—is in hand.

Conclusion

It can be assumed that the stratigraphical data available suggests a group of long cists of Early Christian date that were probably associated with a chapel beneath the extant twelfth-century one, and conceivably associated with the original context of the Pictish hoard, dated to the eighth to ninth centuries. The site is very complex, including Iron Age deposits, which have been recently reexamined by Rachel Barrowman. These excavations have confirmed the presence of large amounts of Iron Age pottery as well as an additional three antler cylinders of the type previously identified as beads[26] remaining in situ following the earlier excavations.[27] In addition, the site has been used as a burial ground into the mid-nineteenth century, so it is clear that the memory of this holy place has been long lasting, even after the twelfth-century church disappeared from view in the deep sand that covered the complex so completely.[28]

This group of beads is clearly a significant discovery although a scarcity of contemporary parallels for this type of artifact at this time makes cultural identification somewhat problematic. In order to confirm a Pictish origin for these beads, it will be necessary to compare the glass compositions of some of the beads with datable and culturally diagnostic material, such as a glass eye inset on one of the penannular chapes in the hoard.[29] It is hoped that this work can be undertaken through the National Museums of Scotland, who hold the St. Ninian's Isle hoard. It is, however, certain that these beads, which have eluded publication since their discovery nearly fifty years ago, will provide more information under modern scientific scrutiny.

26. Small, Thomas, and Wilson, *St. Ninian's Isle and Its Treasures*, fig. 6.

27. Rachel Barrowman pers. comm.; excavations undertaken on behalf of Shetland Amenity Trust and Historic Scotland 1999–2000.

28. See Elizabeth O'Brien, this volume, for a discussion of the continued use of traditional burial grounds and sacred sites in the early Middle Ages.

29. Small, Thomas, and Wilson, *St. Ninian's Isle and Its Treasures*, plate xxx, chape number 16.

Figure 1. View of St. Ninian's Isle, Shetland. Photo: Rachel Barrowman.

Figure 2. Excavations at St. Ninian's Isle 1957. Photo: H. Nisbet Collection.

Figure 3. Early wall under E end of Nave, St. Ninian's Isle 1959. Photo: H. Nisbet Collection.

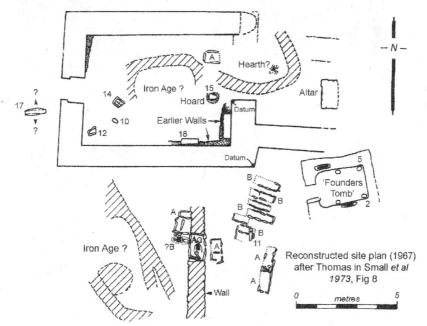

Figure 4. St. Ninian's Isle reconstructed plan (1967). From Small, Thomas, and Wilson, *St. Ninian's Isle and Its Treasure*, fig. 8.

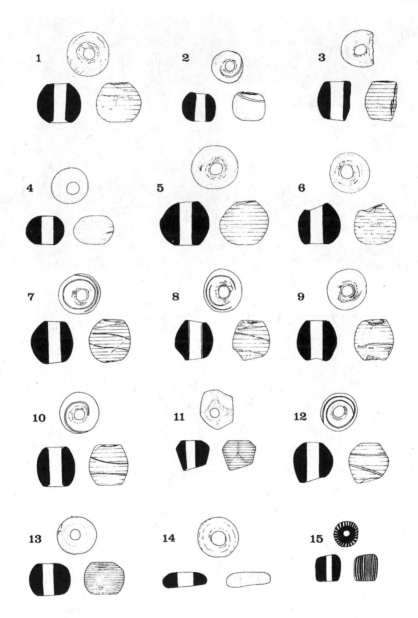

Figure 5. Group One beads, Nos. 1–15. Drawn by N. Emery.

Figure 6. Group One photograph (Beads 1–15).

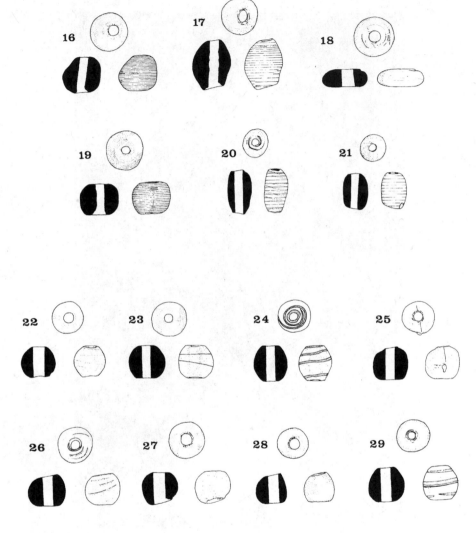

Figure 7. Group One beads, Nos. 16–21, and Group Two, Nos. 22–29. Drawn by N. Emery.

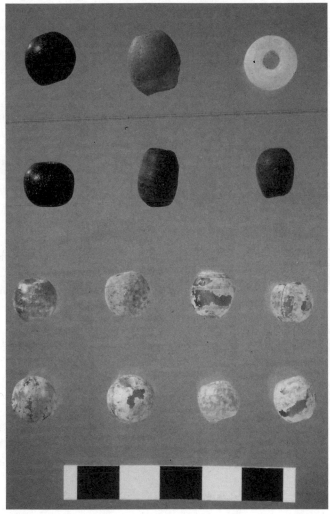

Figure 8. Group One (Beads 16–21) and Group Two (Beads 22–29) photograph.

APPENDIX

CATALOGUE OF THE BEADS

GROUP ONE

1. Opaque blue, flattened sphere is pitted around central perforation. Winding lines slightly visible. Scratched on surface and perforation. Type 1.
   Measurements: 13mm x 12mm. Perforation: 4–5mm in diameter.
2. Opaque off-white, flattened sphere lightly pitted around the central perforation. Surface damaged by pitting and small surface scratches. Winding line partially visible. Type 4.
   Measurements: 10mm x 9mm. Perforation: 3mm in diameter.
3. Opaque blue, cylindrical tapering toward each end. Broken along one side revealing light gray core. Slight surface scratches. Winding lines visible. Type 1.
   Measurements: 9mm x 12mm. Perforation: 4–5mm in diameter.
4. Opaque off-white, flattened sphere. Slightly eccentric perforation, chip at lower edge. Sampled 30.1.91. Type 4.
   Measurements: 11mm x 9mm. Perforation: 4mm in diameter.
5. Opaque blue, flattened sphere. Slightly eccentric perforation. Winding lines visible, some scratching of smooth surface. Type 1.
   Measurements: 14–15mm x 13mm. Perforation: 5mm in diameter.
6. Opaque gray/blue with damage at upper edge, gray core. Central perforation and slight pitting. Winding lines visible. Type 1.
   Measurements: 12mm x 11–12mm. Perforation: 4mm in diameter.
7. Opaque blue, elongated sphere flattened at both ends. Slightly damaged and scratched. Winding lines visible and two particularly distinctive. Slightly eccentric perforation. Type 1.
   Measurements: 11mm x 13mm. Perforation: 4mm in diameter.
8. Variable opaque blue, uneven flattened sphere. Damaged at the central perforation. Winding lines visible and perforation appears to be lined with lighter material. Type 1.
   Measurements: 11mm x 12mm. Perforation: 5mm in diameter.
9. Opaque blue, barrel shaped. Damaged around central perforation revealing lighter material as in No. 8. Type 1.
   Measurements: 12mm x 12mm. Perforation 4mm in diameter.
10. Darker opaque blue, barrel shaped, damaged at perforation. Winding lines visible. Type 1.
    Measurements: 11mm x 12–13mm. Perforation: 4mm in diameter.
11. Dark blue angular bead, unique in group. Faceted slightly eccentric perforation. Slightly scratched. Type 6.
    Measurements: 10–11mm x 10mm. Perforation: 3mm in diameter.
12. Opaque blue, barrel shaped, damaged at both ends around slightly eccentric perforation revealing core. Winding lines clearly highlighted. Type 1.
    Measurements: 11–12mm x 12mm. Perforation: 5mm in diameter.
13. Almost black, flattened sphere. Slightly eccentric perforation, pitted surface. Sampled 30.1.91. Type 3.
    Measurements: 10mm x 12mm. Perforation: 3–4mm in diameter.

14. Translucent amber, annular with slightly eccentric perforation. Scratched surface. Winding lines visible. Type 7.
    Measurements: 12mm x 4mm. Perforation: 4mm in diameter.
15. Very dark blue core with applied smoothed vertical bands of gray/white decoration. Tapering cylinder with central perforation and severe cracking of outer surface. Type 8.
    Measurements: 7–8mm x 8mm. Perforation: 2mm in diameter.
16. Almost black, irregular sphere with central perforation. Slight scratching and patches of wear. Traces of winding lines. Type 3.
    Measurements: 12mm x 11mm. Perforation: 3mm in diameter.
17. Bright opaque blue, barrel shaped with flattened ends. Damage around the oval perforation, indicating gray core and substantial chip removed. Slight winding lines. Type 1.
    Measurements: 12mm x 13–14mm. Perforation: 4mm in diameter.
18. Opaque off-white, annular with a slightly eccentric perforation. Slight scratching and winding lines. Type 9.
    Measurements: 12mm x 5mm. Perforation: 4mm in diameter.
19. Almost black, flattened sphere with central perforation. Slight scratching around perforation and traces of winding lines. Type 3.
    Measurements: 11–12mm x 10mm. Perforation: 2mm in diameter.
20. Very dark blue, cylindrical and tapering toward the slightly eccentric perforation, which is slightly scratched. Winding lines visible. Perforation obstructed. Type 5.
    Measurements: 8mm x 13mm. Perforation: 2mm in diameter.
21. Very dark blue, irregular shape with ends flattened. Striations around bead's body can be seen. Central perforation is blocked (as is No. 20), and has small surface scratches. Type 5.
    Measurements: 8mm x 11mm. Perforation: 2mm in diameter.

Group Two
22. Amber colored, with mottled patina, spherical with ends slightly flattened. Slightly eccentric central perforation. Slightly damaged surface. Type 2.
    Measurements: 10mm x 9mm. Perforation: 3mm in diameter.
23. Amber colored, as No. 22. Type 2.
    Measurements: 11mm x 10mm. Perforation: 3mm in diameter.
24. Amber colored, as No. 22. Winding lines visible. Central perforation, slightly damaged. Type 2.
    Measurements: 10mm x 11mm. Perforation: 3mm in diameter.
25. Amber colored, as No. 22. Cracked in two and slightly scratched. One end slightly raised? Type 2.
    Measurements: 10mm x 9mm. Perforation: 3mm in diameter.
26. Amber colored, as No. 22. Possible winding lines. Chipping and scratches around the perforation. Type 2.
    Measurements: 10–11mm x 9mm. Perforation: 3mm in diameter.
27. Amber colored, as No. 22. Uneven end. Type 2.
    Measurements: 11mm x 9mm. Perforation: 3–4mm in diameter.
28. Amber colored, as No. 22. Eccentric perforation, flattened ends. Slight scratching. Type 2.
    Measurements: 9mm x 8–9mm. Perforation: 3–4mm in diameter.
29. Amber colored, slightly barrel shaped. Flattened around the slightly eccentric perforation, slightly chipped. Winding lines visible. Type 2.
    Measurements: 10mm x 10mm. Perforation: 2–3mm in diameter.

ROMAN TO SAXON IN EAST ANGLIA

CATHERINE HILLS

This essay is an exploration of aspects of the archaeological evidence for the transition from Roman to Saxon in East Anglia. I shall not attempt to provide a new synthesis but, less ambitiously, use aspects of two projects on which I have been engaged as case studies, Spong Hill and Icklingham (fig. 1), to illustrate the extent to which we have still not fully realized the potential of the evidence and ways in which it might further be explored.

There is an even greater contrast in East Anglia than elsewhere in Britain, in terms of quantity, between historical and archaeological sources for the fifth century AD. East Anglia may once have had plentiful early records, but they do not survive, perhaps because they were destroyed in Viking raids. What documentary evidence exists for the pre-Viking period has limited (or no) relevance for the fifth century: the story of Redwald, as recounted by Bede; royal genealogies; references in saints' lives; names of kings on coins; and cryptic words in runic inscriptions.

Archaeological evidence, by contrast, constitutes an already large body of material that increases daily. Yet the texts are more often used to explain the archaeology than the reverse. One reason for this is that it is very difficult to summarize and synthesize our embarrassing wealth of archaeological evidence. There is so much of it that it is not possible either to grasp it all or to present it in neat tidy patterns. It is easier to use the traditional narrative as a framework for explanation, and to select familiar artifacts and sites to support it. Often it is not clear that these selections are in fact no more than the tip of the iceberg, and that they might not be representative or that they might even be misleading. It is also possible to interpret the same evidence in very different ways: what once seemed simple equations between material culture and ethnicity can

My introduction to Anglo-Saxon archaeology took place in the Old Fulling Mill at Durham, where in an overcrowded building overshadowed by the cathedral, and almost in the river, Rosemary Cramp explained manuscripts and monasteries, cruciform brooches and pottery, and also Old English, to a class in which I distinguished myself mostly by arriving late, but that left me committed to the study of Anglo-Saxon England. I think it was clear Rosemary's heart was more in the later, Christian period, and that she had left more to be discovered about the early Saxon period, which may be one reason why I chose that period for research.

no longer be accepted. It used to be relatively easy to take successive slices of time—Iron Age, Roman, Saxon—and look at them in isolation from each other, as separate and distinct episodes in the past. Much explanation of the past has taken, and continues to take, this form, especially in nonspecialist writing and film. It lends itself to explanations of the minimal variety: the Romans came, and then they left; the Saxons came, and then the Normans. Things changed and were different in each separate period because different people arrived. But once you admit that time is a continuum with very few if any complete and sudden breaks, it becomes much more difficult to understand change. The difficulty is compounded if you break the link between material culture and ethnic groups. Perhaps "Anglo-Saxon" burials and pots were used by people whose ancestors thought of themselves as "British." This line of argument has been used to support reinterpretations of the fifth century that involve very little population change. We now have a situation where some scholars argue still for considerable migration, others for very little, usually as much on the basis of their theoretical perspective as from the evidence. I believe that we have still not exploited the potential of the archaeological evidence to cast light on this subject, partly because we have not fully appreciated its extent and complexity.

First it is worth stressing the scale of the evidence overall, as some discussions still appear to suggest that we have a definable, finite set of sites and finds that simply need cataloguing and plotting. This is not the case. In the middle of the last century, aerial photography and field survey began a process that contract ("rescue") archaeology and metal detectorists have recently accelerated. We can see now that the archaeological landscape is not made up of occasional separate, self-contained sites, spots on a distribution map. An archaeological "site" is an arbitrarily defined piece of land, delimited by archaeologists or developers for modern practical reasons. In the past each burial and each house related to other burials and houses. The cemeteries contain the graves of people who lived in the settlements, which consisted not just of houses but of fields, woods, and meadows. Each settlement related to the next and the next in a network across the country. There is seldom a clear edge—even the sea or a river was often less a boundary than a means of communication. Aerial photographs showed us parts of this pattern and field-walking confirmed how widespread and long lived human activity had been in the areas archaeologists thought it worth investigating. What is now happening is that archaeological investigation is largely dictated by modern development.[1]

1. The princely burial at Prittlewell, for example, is located in a known Anglo-Saxon cemetery, but was discovered during excavations undertaken in advance of a proposed road improvement. See Museum of London, *Prittlewell Prince*.

There are many problems attached to this but one advantage is that we are finding evidence in places where it was not expected and so not looked for. West of Cambridge, for example, in areas nearly empty on older maps, every development seems to produce Iron Age to Roman settlements. It was once possible to fill in blank spaces on distribution maps with symbols for forest or marsh and to assume there was nothing there. The blank spaces have now diminished to the point that it could be argued that any left will soon be filled and that the whole of Lowland England should be treated as one continuous site.

Increased reporting of metal detectorists' finds has also revised our ideas of the scale of past activity. Under the Portable Antiquities scheme,[2] thousands of objects are being brought in each year for identification.[3] In East Anglia especially this has not only produced large numbers of artifacts, but also demonstrated the existence of many previously unknown Anglo-Saxon cemeteries: recently in one county alone, Norfolk, several new cemeteries have been recorded each year. Of course, these cemeteries are most often identified by the objects found in the plow soil or excavated in advance of development, so they are discovered and recorded only at the point of destruction.

All of this means that we must revise our ideas of the scale of activity in the past—and also that our distribution maps are not, and never can be, complete. There were many people farming East Anglia in the Roman period, and also many dying and being buried with Germanic-style objects in the following centuries. Exactly how many, and how they related to each other, remains very difficult to define, and this is the core of the problem.

Increase in knowledge comes not only from extensive recording, but also from intensive investigation of excavated material. The Anglo-Saxon cemetery at Spong Hill in Norfolk was excavated in its entirety in the 1970s, producing over two thousand cremations and fifty-seven inhumations of fifth- to sixth-century date.[4] It has been clear since Kemble made the connection in the mid-nineteenth century that the material from Anglo-Saxon cemeteries, especially cremations, can be paralleled in north Germany. Spong Hill and the material from recent excavations of cemeteries in Germany such as Issendorf or Schmalstede confirm and extend the parallels. But it is not clear that the similarity need be explained solely in terms of migration from one place to another. For a start, the English

2. Bland, *Treasure Annual Report 1998–1999.*
3. Some sense of the number and range of the discoveries is provided by Hobbs, *Treasure,* published in conjunction with the exhibition "Buried Treasure: Finding Our Past" (British Museum 21 Nov. 2003–14 Mar. 2004).
4. Hills, "Spong Hill and the Adventus Saxonum."

and German cemeteries continued in use together for generations. There was not an empty desert in the Continent, rather a surviving population in continuing contact with Britain. This contact could have taken various forms and been driven by trade, religious belief, or ideology as much, or more than, population movement. Detailed analysis suggests that all these factors may have been at work.

The parallels between Spong Hill and Germany are strongest in the area to either side of the Elbe—in Lower Saxony and Schleswig Holstein. But these areas do not share all the same traits. Stamped decoration on pottery occurs occasionally in Lower Saxony, not at all in Schleswig Holstein, but is very popular in England. This is partly a developing trend into the sixth century, but it is also possible to argue that the stamp motifs had meaning for those who used them. Two classes of material seem to offer some insight here. The gold bracteates from southern Scandinavia have been extensively studied in recent years. Some have motifs very like those found on pots. At Gudme on Fyn the concentric circles of triangular and semicircular stamps around the central image of one such bracteate are closely comparable to stamps on pots at Spong Hill.[5] If we follow the suggestion of Julian Richards that cremation pots were designed to be viewed from above,[6] as they would be when put into a burial pit in the ground, the similarity becomes even more marked. A religious interpretation seems plausible: in the center of the bracteate are figures interpreted as gods, while in the center of the pot are the cremated remains of the individual, in each case surrounded by patterns that may well have been more than decorative.

Another parallel comes from Fallwerd, near the coast of Lower Saxony.[7] Here there was unusually good preservation of wooden artifacts of Migration-Period date. Among these was a chair- or throne-shaped lid very like the pottery lid in the form of a chair with a seated figure found at Spong Hill.[8] The decoration on the back of the chair includes a complex of interlocking swastikas, very like those on a series of pots from Spong Hill that also have animal stamps. The footstool associated with the chair has an incised linear representation of a hunt scene that is very close to that found on pot no. 2594 from Spong Hill.[9]

5. Thrane, *Guld, guder og godtfolk*, plate 1. Compare with Hills, *Anglo-Saxon Cemetery at Spong Hill, Part I*, plate VIA–D and fig. 57.

6. Richards, "Anglo-Saxon Symbolism."

7. Schon, *Feddersen Wierde, Fallward, Flögeln*.

8. Hills, "Anglo-Saxon Chairperson."

9. Hills, Penn, and Rickett, *Anglo-Saxon Cemetery at Spong Hill, Part IV*, fig. 73; Schon, *Feddersen Wierde, Fallward, Flögeln*, p. 83.

The interesting point about these parallels is that they are not simple transfers of identical artifacts across the North Sea, but images that are being used on different objects, by different craftsmen, in ways that suggest they have common meanings. At a later period we have no difficulty in identifying stone sculpture and illuminated manuscripts as traces of the spread of a religion, Christianity, that had a profound effect on material culture and social and political systems without significant population change.

Examination of grave goods from cremations not only has produced more imported objects, but has also shown that ideas about the patterns of trade and exchange may need revision. Fragmentary artifacts from Spong Hill and other cremation cemeteries have provided information that alters the picture previously created from analysis of more complete skeletons and objects from inhumations. Trade in early Anglo-Saxon England has often been interpreted in terms of Kentish dominance, which seemed to make sense both in terms of geography and in relation to historical accounts. Exotic foreign goods came to England from the Continent through Kent. Either Kent itself, or possibly Frankish rulers controlling or influencing Kentish rulers, limited access for the rest of Anglo-Saxon England to these desirable luxuries. The distribution of imports, such as glass vessels and amethyst beads, in inhumation burials appeared to support this argument. But if account is taken of the large numbers of fragmentary imported objects in cremation burials the picture changes. These fragments of burnt metal, glass, and bone were once disregarded as unidentifiable and tipped away as rubbish. But many can be identified, and while a tiny piece of a glass or bronze vessel may not be as attractive as a complete vessel, it conveys much of the same information. The cemetery that so far has the largest number of recorded glass vessels is Spong Hill.[10] Other cremation cemeteries in eastern England also contained imported objects. The concentration apparent in Kent still applies for some types but no longer exists for others. Direct access to eastern England from the Continent should not be surprising—after all the whole point about the Anglo-Saxon migrations is that the North Sea was crossed, whether by few or many. The importance of Ipswich as a trading center in the Middle Saxon period is unlikely to have emerged from nothing.

One class of imports, elephant ivory bag rings, is found in both cremations and inhumations.[11] These have always had a distribution pattern that does not support transmission via Kent, which led to the suggestion that the rings were made not of elephant ivory but of walrus ivory, a mate-

10. Evison, "Anglo-Saxon Glass from Cremations."
11. Hills, "From Isidore to Isotopes."

rial much used in later periods, an argument that has, however, been refuted.[12] The ivory probably came from Ethiopia, where it was one of the luxuries traded by the kingdom of Aksum, which flourished until the seventh century.[13] In the form of rings or possibly as parts of finished bags, it was distributed as far north as Schleswig Holstein, where it occurs in fourth- and fifth-century cremations. These are precisely the burials with closest parallels to cremations found in eastern England from the mid-fifth century. Initial discussion rested on the relatively small number of inhumations with recognizable rings. In cremations these are often reduced to tiny laminated gray fragments, only found when the contents of cremation urns are meticulously examined. At Spong Hill we found ivory in 205 cremations, and at other recently excavated cremation cemeteries it also occurs in significant numbers, so the weight of the distribution lies clearly in eastern England. In the sixth and seventh centuries ivory rings are found in female inhumations with Germanic-style grave goods from the regions controlled by the Lombards in northern Italy to the Alemanni in southern Germany as well as in England. Such rings are rare in Frankish graves. There may have been more than one route by which ivory arrived in England: up the Rhine and across to eastern England, or into northern Germany and then across the North Sea. A route through Kent does not seem likely. Links between eastern England, Germany, and northern Italy can be seen in other categories of material, including stamped pottery and Style II animal ornament (both of which may have had ideological significance) and in the incidence of horse burials. While the France-Kent connection did exist and Frankish influence may well have been strong in southern England, there were also other independent lines of contact between England and the Continent. It seems to me that the ivory from fifth–seventh-century graves shows the existence already then of the kinds of patterns later detectable especially through imported pottery of middle Saxon date.

Analysis of other aspects of the material has suggested other lines of inquiry, and many more no doubt remain to be explored. The point in this context is that it is necessary to look at the smallest details and then to explore a variety of different explanations for any patterns that emerge. The similarities in material culture observable around the North Sea in the fifth and sixth centuries AD may have part of their origin in population movements, but other mechanisms seem also to have played an important role.

12. Bond, "Explanatory Note."
13. Phillipson, *Ancient Ethiopia*.

Another approach is to turn away from the microexploration of one site to try to see how a whole landscape evolved over time. Changes in styles of jewelry or pottery, or even burial, may not reflect fundamental shifts in the structure of society. But changes in agricultural practice, in settlement patterns, and, of course, in the physical character of the people themselves probably do mean drastic change. Landscape archaeology has become one of the most important focuses for research in Britain and elsewhere, and much recent archaeological fieldwork has pursued this direction, looking at regions rather than sites, plotting long-term patterns of settlement and land-use in the context of changing environments and sociopolitical structures.

In East Anglia the river Lark runs from the claylands in the middle of Suffolk to the eastern fen edge. Between Bury St. Edmunds and Mildenhall the Lark valley is rich in archaeological finds of many periods. There is a linear earthwork, the Black Ditches, that may be of late prehistoric or early historic date. In the first millennium AD the large Romano-British settlement or small town of Icklingham developed near a crossing of the river by the Icknield Way. The Anglo-Saxon settlement at West Stow and the Anglo-Saxon cemetery of Lackford are within two kilometers of Icklingham, and many other Roman and Anglo-Saxon sites are known from stray finds or partial excavation in the area (fig. 1). At present Icklingham and West Stow appear to belong to two separate chapters of history, with no connecting link. According to the traditional account Icklingham, like other Roman towns, fell into ruin, destroyed by invading Anglo-Saxons. The Britons fled or were killed, and the Anglo-Saxons built an entirely new village for themselves at West Stow. An alternative scenario is that there was considerable overlap, with both sites in occupation for a significant part of the early fifth century and the possible survival of the British population beneath an increasing veneer of "Anglo-Saxon" material culture. Recently I have been working on a project designed to reassess the evidence,[14] and to see if any new model can be developed for the transition in this region. This project has so far proceeded only on a limited basis, but some interesting lines of research are emerging.

14. The Lark Valley Research Project has been funded so far by the McDonald Institute and the Salisbury fund, both of Cambridge University. Based in the Department of Archaeology, Cambridge University, it has also received support and advice from relevant specialists within Suffolk Archaeological Services and English Heritage, especially Stanley West and Jude Plouviez. Key staff in the project are Jess Tipper and Katherine Day. John Browning, owner of Weatherhill Farm, inspired the project, and both he and the Rayner-Green family, owners of Mitchell's Farm, have kindly allowed access to their land for excavation.

One reason for choosing this area is that so much is already known and can be built on. West Stow is a well-recorded site, extensively excavated and published by Stanley West.[15] A series of buildings and other features were interpreted as a group of farmsteads, in use from the fifth to the seventh centuries AD. Many artifacts and a large collection of well-preserved animal bones provide an extensive database. West's reconstructions of the buildings, especially the *Grubenhäuser*, have been successfully tested by actual physical reconstructions at what has become an important center for experiment and education about Anglo-Saxon England. Most of the work at West Stow has related to understanding the village as a going concern. A quick reading of the simpler publicity can leave the impression that the Anglo-Saxons arrived from Germany in the fifth century and settled in a largely deserted landscape, creating villages like those they had left on the Continent, and that they had little to do with the preceding Romano-British population. This is partly because that is still the prevailing public perception and also because there are limits to the amount of uncertainty that can be incorporated in a display aimed partly at nine-year-old school children. However, it is of course one of our aims to look very carefully at the evidence for the date and character of the initial settlement and to see how it does in fact relate to what went before. Was there a significant time lapse between the abandonment of Icklingham and settlement at West Stow or could some degree of continuity be argued? Was there a complete break in land use and stock rearing, a new start in an empty landscape; or was there simply a gradual evolution over time, with many elements of continuity, including some of the people?

At Lackford, across the river from Icklingham and West Stow, an Anglo-Saxon cremation cemetery was partially excavated by Lethbridge in 1946.[16] The pottery and grave goods are typical of such sites—like Spong Hill. The bones were unfortunately not kept for study, and the site, part of which now lies under a small plantation of trees, was not completely excavated. In the same field Jude Plouviez excavated small Roman structures in the 1980s. It is also thought to be where the Cavenham crowns, Roman votive objects, were found, and Lethbridge went so far as to claim that this was the true findspot of the Mildenhall treasure. Although this last claim does not seem to be reliably supported, it certainly is interesting that in one field we have traces of both Roman and Anglo-Saxon activity that could be construed as "ritual" on a site close to but across the river from a large Roman settlement. Limited geophysical survey confirms that there are features to be investigated here.

15. West and Cooper, *West Stow*.
16. Lethbridge, *Cemetery at Lackford Suffolk*.

Burials of both Roman and Anglo-Saxon date have been found at various other sites: Roman burials to the south of the main Icklingham site, Anglo-Saxon within the area of the modern village, and also a cemetery associated with West Stow. Stray finds suggest the locations of more Anglo-Saxon burials.[17] One goal of the project would be to compare the people—the human bones—to see if direct evidence could be found of continuity or change in population.

The Roman site at Icklingham was investigated in the nineteenth century by Henry Prigg, who excavated a building with a hypocaust, approximately marked on the Ordnance Survey map as a "villa" and also burials.[18] More recently the Suffolk Archaeological Unit was prompted to commence an investigation after the discovery in 1971 of the third example recorded from Icklingham of a series of lead tanks with Chi-Rho symbols.[19] The small church and baptistery found then, together with the lead tanks, are one of the most substantial pieces of evidence for Christianity in Roman Britain. The site has also suffered attack from treasure hunters, despite the vigilance of its owner, John Browning; a collection of bronze figurines, "the Icklingham bronzes," stolen from the site found their way to an American art gallery, where they remain. Small late Roman coins can be, and still are, picked up from the fields in some numbers. Recorded coin hoards recovered from the site range in date from the third century AD to the early fifth, and the same range has been identified for coins from recent excavations.[20]

The extent of the site was not appreciated until English Heritage carried out a geophysical survey.[21] This showed a complex of roads, enclosures, pits, and structures extending far beyond the two fields that had been designated as a scheduled monument. To the south, toward the river, flood deposits may mask buried features. Extending the survey still further into apparently less densely occupied fields would be a useful way of tracing field or property boundaries and trackways. Some of these features may prove to be post-Roman, but the majority is part of a settlement whose size indicates that it was of some significance at least in the late Roman period, a center for this part of Suffolk. It included some substantial buildings, a church, and inhabitants with wealth to bury. There were also pottery kilns and presumably a range of more ordinary buildings. Armed with

17. West, *Corpus of Anglo-Saxon Material from Suffolk*, pp. 45–51.

18. Moore, Plouviez, and West, *Archaeology of Roman Suffolk*, p. 4, illustration nos. 2, 24.

19. West and Plouviez, "Roman Site at Icklingham."

20. E. Mitchell, "Report on Coins from Icklingham." (With advice from T. Buttrey, Fitzwilliam Museum Cambridge).

21. David and Cole, unpublished magnetometer survey of Icklingham. I am very grateful to Andrew David for access to the results of this survey.

the geophysical plan it is possible to plan limited excavations to define the character, date, and relationships of the features visible there.

From 1997 to 2000 small-scale excavation, carried out as a training dig for Cambridge students, established first the depth and quality of preservation of buried deposits at different locations and then focused on one area where there was good preservation and a complex sequence of archaeological deposits (fig. 2). Over much of the area plowing over many years has eroded occupation layers, leaving major subsoil features, such as boundary ditches and pits, visible in the geophysical survey. In the fill of these ditches pottery, artifacts, and animal bones occur in some quantity, the animal bone usually much better preserved than might be expected in a sandy soil. In this it resembles the nearby West Stow, where a very large collection of animal bones was recovered. One of the aims of the project is to recover a large enough sample for detailed comparison between Icklingham and West Stow. Pam Crabtree's study of the West Stow bones showed the continued use of native species, with some continuity of husbandry practices from the Iron Age and, therefore, also from the Roman period.[22] Comparison with Continental sites, such as Feddersen Wierde, showed differences from West Stow sufficient to argue against the import of Continental animals to replace native ones during the fifth century. A study of a small sample of bones from Icklingham, also by Pam Crabtree,[23] suggested different economic organization: Icklingham was a "consumer" site, West Stow a "producer"; in other words the inhabitants of Icklingham bought meat whereas at West Stow they bred their own animals, the classic urban/rural distinction. This might suggest continued exploitation of existing stock, but within a changed economic structure, or simply that our two sites represent different parts of their contemporary settlement hierarchies. Romano-British village or farm sites might produce animal-bone assemblages closer to that from West Stow. This underlines the need to move away from single-site accounts and to see how each fits into a wider contemporary pattern. Existing site and monument records and aerial photographs already provide much information and show a densely occupied landscape, but this needs to be systematically plotted and also expanded by survey of selected areas, both by field-walking and geophysical means. Programs to do this have not yet been implemented.

We have begun a palaeoenvironmental project[24] because the long-term environmental history of the area should provide evidence for land

22. Crabtree, *West Stow, Suffolk.*

23. Crabtree, "Animal Exploitation in East Anglian Villages."

24. Carried out by Robert Austin-Smith with advice from Peter Murphy (University of East Anglia) and Charley French (Cambridge).

use and the extent to which this changed or remained the same. A recent study of the environment of Britain during the first millennium AD concludes that in the period AD 400–800 there was significant regional variation.[25] In some areas, especially in northern England, there was woodland regeneration, interpreted as the result of the withdrawal of the Roman army. Elsewhere, in the south, there seems to be a trend toward lower-density agriculture, pastoral instead of arable. These conclusions rest on a still-limited series of dated pollen cores, only one of which comes from East Anglia. We have now taken cores from Cavenham Mere and hope to achieve a dated sequence that will clarify the situation within the Lark valley, but also provide key evidence for the wider picture in the region.

We are also remapping the area from existing maps, plots of recorded finds, aerial photographs, and survey, using a GIS system that will eventually allow us to model change through time. Details of the river course are also being investigated through coring across transects of the flood plain. We hope to extend our research into all aspects of the documentary and physical evidence as resources permit.

Excavation was initially directed simply toward establishing the extent and quality of surviving archaeological deposits in different parts of the area covered by the geophysical survey (fig. 2). To the east, in a field on the edge of Weatherhill Farm, toward West Stow, we found a concentration of fourth-century material in the top half of the field, including a roadside ditch. We also found debris from pottery manufacture of first- through second-century date. In the southern part of the field enclosure ditches appeared to be of early or even pre-Roman date, in character similar to those found at West Stow, and predating the Anglo-Saxon village. This is interesting, as it suggests a dispersed pattern of late Iron Age activity. All features in this field have been truncated by plowing.

On the western edge, south of the road, we identified an area of complex features in an unplowed field next to Mitchell's Farm. We established that some of this is due to drainage ditches, including postmedieval and recent channels. However, we also found a sequence of Roman and later features of intrinsic interest, which were a classic example of the frustrating ambiguity some archaeological sequences offer. A road with a hard metaled surface and accompanying ditches was constructed during the Roman period. This appears to be the same road as that encountered by Plouviez in 1974 near the baptistery. It runs to the south of the modern road, which can be seen in its present position in maps from the early nineteenth century. A bank on the edge of this road produced a fifth-century bead: an Anglo-Saxon cemetery is known to have existed in the field on

---

25. P. Dark, *Environment of Britain.*

the other side of Mitchell's Farm, about 250 meters away. A hopeful "Dark Age" scenario for continued use of this trackway into the fifth century was destroyed by the next excavation season, in which it was shown that the road had been reused in the postmedieval period, when a ditch had been cut through the old surface on the southern side; a 1699 coin of William III, found at the bottom of this ditch, suggests that this activity took place in the eighteenth century. The ditch on the north side, however, appears to have been cut and recut on approximately the same line at various dates within the Roman period and possibly also later. There are also pits and other features including two human burials, one with a jet necklace, that are securely dated to the Roman period. The upper fifty centimeters of soil covering these features and extending to the road was very much disturbed by recent and possibly ancient animal, root, and human activity. The moles were visibly active as we excavated, and pottery of all dates to the present was found throughout this level.

In the top of the ditch we found the skeleton of an old woman, who had suffered from arthritis and toothache before meeting her end,[26] lying face down and apparently thrown into a nearly filled ditch in a layer that included charcoal. There was no evidence for the cause of death, which could simply have been old age. Her feet were missing, cut away by a pit that contained the skeleton of a horse. This was a pony, aged three to five years, that had had a savage injury inflicted on its back some weeks before death (fig. 3).[27] Neither burial had associated finds, but the woman was found above layers in the ditch that contained Roman and some later pottery. This, however, could easily have arrived there through one of the disturbances described above—both roots and burrows can move artifacts sideways. There was no sign of cuts for features through the disturbed soil, but this might mean only that the features predated recent reworkings of that layer. A radiocarbon date for bones from the horse date it securely to the Roman period, within the second and third centuries AD.[28]

This means that some alternative interpretations considered earlier can be ruled out. The woman was not an eighteenth-century murder victim, nor was she a victim of marauding Saxons in the fifth century, but she was buried or at least deposited in the ditch at some time during the Roman period. In fact this burial would fit well into a pattern that is now recognized in later Roman sites, although she is rather earlier in date. Although burial in the Roman period would be expected to be in a prop-

26. Dodwell, "Assessment of the Human Bone from Icklingham."
27. Levine, Whitwell, and Jeffcott, "Report on the Horse Burial."
28. A sample of bone from the horse was sent to Beta Analytic, Florida, who provided the following date: Beta-153745: 1 Sigma calibrated result (68% probability) Cal AD 130 to 240 (Cal BP 1820 to 1710).

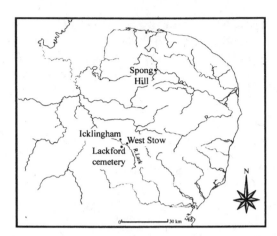

Figure 1. Map of East Anglia showing sites mentioned in text.

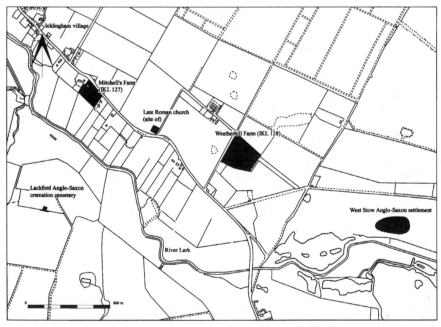

Figure 2. Icklingham, location of survey and excavation. Drawn by Jess Tipper.

Figure 3. Human and horse burials at Mitchell's Farm, Icklingham, July 1999. Photo Jess Tipper.

erly laid out cemetery, there are a number of instances of burials disposed of in apparently less careful ways, including ditches.[29] This might represent a continuation of native burial practices, or might be an indication of the low status of the dead person. There are other interesting features. A large pit next to the horse burial contained many large-animal bones including some of horses, together with a range of Roman pottery. The pit was large, over 2 meters in diameter and at least 1 meter in depth— probably much more but it could not be emptied below the water level. It may have been a simple rubbish pit; but it is perhaps reminiscent of the pit discovered in the 1974 excavations, which predated the church and contained six human skulls.[30] Could our burials relate to pre-Christian Roman ritual practices? There are, however, two other inhumations close by, and an economical explanation would see all three simply as part of an extended series of burials along the southern edge of Icklingham, the other end being marked by the church site.

Had this complex been excavated in the nineteenth century, in the absence of radiocarbon dates it might well have gone into the literature as evidence for the traditional violent end to Roman Britain: the woman murdered by invading Anglo-Saxons who threw her and the ashes of her house into the ditch; the pony also a victim of savage attack, buried later by survivors. So this is partly a cautionary tale, a reminder of the dangers of constructing stories on the basis of what are sometimes shifting sands.

29. Philpott, *Burial Practices in Roman Britain*, p. 232.
30. West and Plouviez, "Roman Site at Icklingham," pp. 68–69, fig. 34.

Literary Insights into the Basis of Some Burial Practices in Ireland and Anglo-Saxon England in the Seventh and Eighth Centuries

Elizabeth O'Brien

It is my pleasure to dedicate this essay to Rosemary Cramp, to whom I am greatly indebted for her many acts of kindness, both personal and professional, to me throughout the years. As her work and that of other archaeologists has demonstrated, those who excavate burials of the early medieval period in Ireland and Britain are often confronted with burial practices that are difficult to explain due to the syncretism of cultural processes in a period of conversion. However, an invaluable insight into the rationale associated with burial practices that prevailed during that period is to be found in references to death, burial, and analogous phenomena that appear in Irish and English hagiography, penitentials, and canons, especially those written in the seventh and eighth centuries. Bearing in mind that texts normally reflect the cultural practices of the world in which they were written rather than the world they purport to describe, these texts do provide references and information that can be of help to the archaeologist and historian alike. This essay will explore three aspects of burial in early medieval Ireland and Britain in order to demonstrate just how much can be learned when the documentary and material records are used to illuminate each other.

The Location of Burials

One of the most basic practices complicating the material record is the reluctance of Christians of the early medieval period to abandon ancestral cemeteries.[1] In the archaeological record this phenomenon is commonly manifested by the presence of apparently Christian burials (that is, extended supine inhumations with heads to the west and without grave goods), either in cemeteries that include burials of earlier eras, in cemeteries that include possible contemporary burials accompanied by a range of grave goods, or in cemeteries with no known ecclesiastical associations. Where burials of this type are dateable, they seldom extend beyond the eighth and ninth centuries.

---

1. See E. O'Brien, *Post-Roman Britain to Anglo-Saxon England*.

The compilers of the early eighth-century *Collectio Canonum Hibernensis*,[2] in an effort to encourage the faithful to abandon their ancestral or familial cemeteries, were on the one hand sympathetic; for example, *Hibernensis* XVIII. *De jure sepulturae* (Law of burial), includes cap. 2. *De eo, quod in paterno sepulcro sepeliendum est* (Concerning the rule that a person should be buried in the paternal grave) that seeks to justify burial among the ancestors by stating that a man or woman may be buried in his or her paternal tomb, and that every man is accursed who is not buried in the tomb of his fathers. The example given is that of Jacob and Joseph requesting that their bones be carried back from Egypt to the land of Canaan in order that they might be buried at the tomb of their ancestors. On the other hand, monks and ecclesiastical tenants, especially those who may have had an affiliation to a particular ecclesiastical establishment, were encouraged to seek burial at that place. *Hibernensis* XVIII. cap. 3 (a). *De eo, quod debet homo sepeliri in ecclesia cui monachus est* (Concerning the fact that a person who is a monk, ought to be buried in the church)[3] quotes rulings from *Sinodus Hibernensis* (a synod of the Irish) that state

> (a) Si quis in ecclesia conjunctus fuerit, in ea sepelietur
> (b) Monachus cum in vita sua libertatem praeter jussionem abbatis non habuerit, quanto magis in morte?

> ([a] if anyone should have been joined to a church, he will be buried there
> [b] a monk who in his life has not freedom without the order of the abbot, how much more so in death?)

Whether or not married women should be buried among their own ancestors or those of their husbands is dealt with in *Hibernensis* XVIII. cap. 4. *De eo, quod mulier post mortem viri libera sit sicut in vita, ita in morte* (Concerning the fact that just as in life a woman may be free after the death of her husband, so also in death):

---

2. Wasserschleben, *Die irische Kanonensammlung* (hereafter *Hibernensis*). This collection of Canons was compiled by Rubin of Dair-Inis (a monastery near Youghal in the south of Ireland) who died AD 725, and Cú Chuimne of Iona, who died AD 747; for full background, see Kenney, *Sources of the Early History of Ireland*, pp. 247–50. A date between 716 and 725 for the compilation is suggested by Charles-Edwards, "Penitential of Theodore," p. 142 n. 5. Translation from the Latin of the relevant *Hibernensis* text was undertaken by the author under the guidance of Professor Thomas Charles-Edwards; I, however, accept full responsibility for the final form of the translation including any errors or omissions.

3. *Monachus* (monk) in this context might also indicate a monastic patron, benefactor, tenant, etc.

(a) Hieronimus: Vir sive mulier honorem dare debet conjugii; sepelietur autem in sepulcro paterno, sive juxta ecclesiam, cui conjuncta est.[4]

(b) Paulus: Mulier alligata est lege viri, quamdiu vivus est vir ejus, post mortem autem viri soluta est lege viri. Quod si licitum est nubere, quanto magis libertatem habebit sepeliendi?

([a] Jerome: A husband or wife ought to give honor to marriage; on the other hand she may be buried in the tomb of the ancestors, or beside the church to which she is joined.

[b] Paul: A woman is bound by the law of her husband during the life of her husband; however, after the death of her husband she has been released from the law of the husband. Because, if she is permitted to marry, how much more freedom will she have for being buried?)

This Irish corollary to 1 Corinthians 7:39 meant that a woman could be buried (a) in her husband's (ancestral?) cemetery (if she predeceased him), (b) in her own ancestral cemetery (if he predeceased her), or (c) in a church cemetery if she became a nun or church tenant. This canon also indicates that in the eighth century it was normal practice to bury men and women in the same cemetery, perhaps even in the same grave.

Ancestral cemeteries were not, however, to be totally abandoned. *Hibernensis* XVIII. cap. 5. *De eo, quod sors mittenda est inter ecclesiam et sepulcrum paternum* (Concerning the rule that lots should be cast to decide between the church and the ancestral tomb) uses a quotation spuriously attributed to Origen to make this point:

Origines ait: Si unusquisque secularis voluerit, dividat sors inter ecclesiam et sepulcrum paternum, sed dona sua plurima ecclesiae suae conferre debet, pauca autem in sepulcro paterno in honorem patrum.

(Origen said: If any secular person has so wished, let lots make the division between the church and the ancestral tomb, but he ought to contribute the greater gift to his church, a few [items] however to the ancestral cemetery in honor of the ancestors.)

This seems to be an indication that while Christians were being encouraged in the eighth century to cease using ancestral burial places, they were nevertheless still being held responsible for the upkeep of these places. This point is further emphasized in *Hibernensis* LI. *De mortuis in somno visis* (Concerning the dead seen in dreams), when in cap. 2. *De causa,*

---

4. This quotation attributed to Jerome is from an Irish exegete, very probably commenting on 1 Cor. 7:39.

qua se ostendunt mortui in somno vivis (Concerning the reason for which the dead show themselves to the living in sleep), it is stated in a quote attributed to Augustine:

> Augustinus ait: Alii putant angelicis operationibus sive ad vivorum qualecumque solatium, ad quos pertinent mortui, sive admonendo humano generi, ut sepulturae prebeatur humanitas, quae licet defunctis non opituletur, tamen culpatur, si in religiositate neglegitur.

> (Augustine said: Some consider it[5] to be by the work of angels whether to give comfort of some kind to the living to whom the dead belong, or to remind mankind that respect should be given to a burial, though it may perhaps not be given to the dead, yet it is a matter for blame if it is neglected by those in the religious state.)

This passage provides a further reminder to those in religion that they were still being held responsible for the upkeep of their ancestors' (probably pagan) graves.

The following canons from *Hibernensis* L. *De reliquiis in deserto humatis* (Concerning remains buried in desert places) make it clear that although Christians were still being buried in ancestral cemeteries (among *mali homines*) in the eighth century, they were earnestly being encouraged to consider burial in "desert" places.[6] *Hibernensis* L. cap. 3. *De eo, quod magis visitantur martyres in deserto humati, quam inter malos homines*[7] (Concerning the fact that martyrs who are buried in desert places are more visited than [those] among evil men) states

> (a) In vitas patrum legimus: Martyres inter malos sepultos ab angelis visitari, sed tamen tristes reversos angelos . . .
> (c) Hieronimus: Post resurrectionem multi audisse voces testantur dicentium angelorum: transeamus ex his sedibus.

> ([a] In the lives of the fathers we read: Martyrs buried among evil persons are visited by angels; however, the angels return sorrowful . . .
> [c] Jerome: After the resurrection many testify that they have heard voices of angels saying: let us depart from these places.)

---

5. "It" being the deed of appearing to the living in dreams.

6. In the seventh century, newly founded Irish monastic centers were often located in areas that would have been perceived as wilderness.

7. *Martyres* are the dead who have witnessed to Christ, as opposed to *mali homines* who are probably pagans (ancestors).

Hibernensis L. cap 1. *De eo, quod multi homines Dei in deserto sepulti sunt, ut ab angelis frequentarentur et a malis vitarentur* (Concerning the fact that many people of God are buried in desert places where they may be visited by angels and avoid evil [men]) reminds the reader that

> (a) Origenes ait: Moyses homo Dei in monte Phasga sepultus est, ut ab angelis semper frequentaretur et a malis vitaretur
> (b) Item: Aaron in monte Or sepultus est
> (c) Item: Paulus heremita in deserto et ceteri in desertis humati sunt.

> ([a] Origen said: Moses was buried on Mount Phasaga so that he might always be visited by angels and be avoided by evil persons
> [b] Aaron is buried in Mount Or
> [c] Paul the hermit, and others, were also buried in desert places.)

If such strong resistance to the abandonment of ancestral cemeteries still existed in eighth-century Ireland after two and a half centuries of Christianity, how much more so must it have been felt in the more recently converted Anglo-Saxon England?

The development of the cult of corporeal relics in the seventh and eighth centuries seems to have provided a strong incentive to substitute burial near the bones of a holy man or monastic founder for burial near the bones of the ancestors. Initially this was especially important in the case of clergy and aristocracy associated with a particular ecclesiastical foundation, but was probably less important for the laity in general. Bede tells us that when Bishop Cedd died and was buried at Lastingham, about thirty of the brothers in his monastery in the kingdom of the East Saxons left that monastery and went to Northumbria, "in order to live near the body of their father or, if the Lord so willed, to die and be buried there."[8] This attitude mirrors that which was current among early Irish missionaries. It is recorded, for example, that when Librán, a monk of Iona, was told by Columba that his resurrection would be in Ireland and not in Britain (i.e., not in Iona) he was extremely upset and had to be comforted by being assured that his part in the Kingdom would be among other Columban monks.[9] Librán eventually died at the Columban monastery at Durrow (Co. Offaly) in Ireland.

The outward appearance of graves, just like their location, could also be ambiguous in the early medieval period. An indication that graves of

---

8. Bede, *Hist. eccles.* 3.23, pp. 288–89.
9. *Adomnán's Life of Columba* 2.39 (92a, b), ed. and trans. Anderson and Anderson (1991), pp. 160–63; *Adomnán. Life of St. Columba*, trans. Sharpe, p. 193.

pagans and Christians could be identical in outward appearance is given in two seventh-century references to similar incidents in writings concerning Patrick. The first reference, given by Muirchú,[10] concerns a grave that was marked by a cross. In reply to questions from Patrick, the dead man in the grave admitted that he was a pagan and that the cross had been placed beside his tomb in error by the mother of another man (a Christian) who was buried nearby; Patrick then transferred the cross to its proper place.[11] The second reference, this time given by Tírechán,[12] concerns a similar incident. Patrick stopped at two new graves, one of which was marked by a cross. Once again, in reply to questions from Patrick, a voice from the grave marked by the cross admitted that the occupant was a pagan and that the cross had been placed beside his grave in error; Patrick pulled the cross from the grave and placed it over the head of the baptized man.[13] Obviously an error like this could not have occurred unless the two graves had been identical in appearance apart from the presence of a cross—a cautionary warning to archaeologists that in seventh-century cemeteries it is not always possible to tell whether a grave is that of a Christian or a pagan from either orientation or outward appearance. The cross in question would appear to have been portable, therefore probably either a wooden cross or a small stone cross or cross-slab.

Writers, and their audience, in the early medieval period were well aware that barrows of all description were ancient burial places. In an Irish context, Tírechán relates a story of Patrick coming through the plains in the territory of Macc Erce in Dichúil (in Co. Mayo?):

> And in Dichuil, Patrick came to a huge grave of astounding breadth and excessive in length, which his people had found, and they were amazed, with great astonishment, that it extended a hundred and twenty feet, and they said: "We do not believe that there could have been such a thing as a man of this length." . . . Patrick opened the grave . . . and a huge man arose whole and said . . . "I am the son of the son of Cass son of Glas; I was the swineherd of Lugar king of Hirota. The warrior band of the sons of Macc Con killed me in the reign of *Coirpre Nie Fer* (a hundred years ago from now)."[14]

10. Muirchú, *Vita Patricii*, in Bieler, *Patrician Texts in the Book of Armagh*, pp. 62–123 (hereafter *Muirchú*). This *Vita* was written between 661 and 700; see ibid., p. 2.

11. *Muirchú* 2.2, pp. 114–15.

12. Tírechán, *Collectanea*, in Bieler, *Patrician Texts in the Book of Armagh*, pp. 123–67 (hereafter *Tírechán*). The *Collectanea* was written ca. 670; see Sharpe, "Palaeographical Considerations," p. 22 n. 64.

13. *Tírechán*, chap. 41, pp. 154–57.

14. *Tírechán*, chap. 40 (1–8), pp. 154–55.

This is an obvious reference to a Neolithic long-barrow.

In another instance, Muirchú describes how Patrick, having landed at Inber Colpdi (Colp) at the mouth of the Boyne, then set off on foot and eventually arrived in the vicinity of Slane (Co. Meath): "in the evening they at last arrived at the burial place of the men of *Fíacc* (*ad ferti virorum Feec*), which as stories tell us, the men (that is, the servants) of *Fíacc* had dug."[15] It is probable that this is a reference to one of the groups of Neolithic passage-grave cemeteries at the bend of the Boyne.

The practice of inserting burials into cemeteries and burial monuments of earlier periods is a phenomenon that is widespread in all eras, and it can readily be identified in the archaeological record up to as late as the seventh or eighth century in both Ireland and Anglo-Saxon England.[16] Literary references to the practice are not so plentiful. The latest recorded incidence of secondary burial in an Irish prehistoric barrow is an entry for 1581 in the *Annals of Loch Cé*, which reads, "Brian Caech O'Coinnegain, an eminent cleric, and keeper of a general house of guests, died; and the place of sepulture which he selected for himself was, i.e. to be buried at the mound of *Baile-an-tobair*.[17] And we think that it was not through want of religion *Brian Caech* made this selection, but because he saw not the service of God practiced in any church near him at that time."[18]

An early eighth-century English reference to the practice concerns Guthlac who lived in a hut that he had built in a chamber in a prehistoric barrow that had previously been opened by grave-robbers.[19] This was the place at which Guthlac was eventually buried; in other words he was buried in a prehistoric burial chamber.

THE TREATMENT OF THE BODY

Bede states that Oswiu buried the head of Oswald at Lindisfarne, but that he buried his hands and arms in the royal city of Bamburgh.[20] The justification for the division of the body or the dispersion of previously dismembered body parts becomes clear when one reads a saying spuriously attributed to Origen in *Hibernensis* XLIX. *De martyribus* (Concerning *mar-*

---

15. *Muirchú* 1.14, pp. 84–85.

16. For a recently excavated Irish example, see E. O'Brien, "Excavation of a Multiperiod Burial Site"; Anglo-Saxon examples abound; see E. O'Brien, *Post-Roman Britain to Anglo-Saxon England*.

17. Probably near Ballintubber Abbey (Co. Mayo).

18. *ALC*, p. 436.

19. Felix, *Life of Saint Guthlac*, chap. 28, pp. 92–95.

20. Bede, *Hist. eccles.* 3.12, pp. 252–53.

tyres [relics]) cap.10. *De resurrectione transmutatorum martyrum* (Concerning
the resurrection of translated relics):

> Alii putant, eos in loco cineris resurrecturos, alii in loco ossium.
> Ubi enim caput fuerit, illic omnia membra congregabuntur. Eze-
> chiel vidit ossa accedisse ad ossa, unumquodque ad juncturam
> suam, et prophetante eo succrescere nervos et carnes et postea
> cutem extensam. Inde spiritum a quatuor ventis in ea flantem.

> (Some believe they will arise in the place of ashes, others in
> the place where the bones are situated. Where for instance the
> head will have been, there all of the members will be assem-
> bled. Ezechiel saw bones approaching bones, each single one to
> its own joint, and he prophesying, their muscles and flesh grew
> up and after that the skin extended. Thence breath from the
> four winds into them may blow.)

In other words Oswald's head was to be buried at his own foundation of
Lindisfarne in the belief that it was there that he would have his resurrection.

Further justification for the movement of corporeal relics, and evidence of the role of such movement in the development of saints' cults, is
found in *Hibernensis* XLIX. cap. 9. *De honore martyrum aliquando migrante,
cum reliquiis alquando remanente* (Concerning the veneration of martyrs,
which sometimes migrates with the remains, sometimes stays behind),
where it is stated,

> Hieronimus: notandum, cum transmutantur alii de martyribus,
> cum his honor conmigrant, aliis vero transmutatis honor in
> locis eorum non cessat.

> (Jerome: It is to be noted that when some of the relics are moved
> to another place, with them veneration moves, but when others
> have been moved the veneration does not cease in their own
> places.)

Such statements help to explain the culting of saints in two or more different locations, as was often the case in both Ireland and Britain.

The removal and movement of body parts, especially the head, have
distinctly negative connotations when they occur in secular burials. Written
sources can throw some light on the practice of postmortem decapitation
where the head is placed in the grave in an incorrect anatomical position.
In the archaeological record for Britain and Ireland the earliest cases of
decapitated burials of this type occur in the late Iron Age cemetery at
Harlyn Bay, Cornwall. This practice, which became fairly widespread in

Romano-British cemeteries especially in the later fourth century, continued to be used sporadically throughout the early Anglo-Saxon period and beyond.[21]

Mutilation of a body after death is an ancient practice. The earliest recorded literary reference is when Aeschylus, writing in the fifth century BC, commenting on the death of Agamemnon, alludes to the custom by which the extremities of the murdered man were cut off and hung about the body, the object of which was to disable the spirit of the dead Agamemnon from taking vengeance on the murderer.[22] That this practice transcends religious beliefs and cannot be regarded as a specifically pagan or Christian act[23] is demonstrated in a passage from chapter 47 of Geoffrey of Burton's *Life and Miracles of St. Modwenna*[24] written in the twelfth century, concerning two villagers of Stapenhill who ran away to the neighboring village called Drakelow, thereby causing dissension between the Abbot of Burton and Count Roger (the Poitevin):

> at the third hour, the two runaway peasants who were the cause of this evil were sitting down to eat, when they were both suddenly struck down dead. Next morning they were placed in wooden coffins and buried in the churchyard at Stapenhill, the village from whence they had fled. What followed was amazing and truly remarkable. That very same day on which they were interred they appeared at evening . . . at Drakelow, carrying on their shoulders the wooden coffins in which they had been buried. The whole following night they walked through the village lanes and fields . . . they spoke to the other peasants, banging on the walls of their houses and shouting, "Move, quickly, move! Get going! Come!" When these astonishing events had taken place every evening and every night for some time, such a disease afflicted the village that all the peasants fell into desperate straits and within a few days all except three perished by sudden death in a remarkable way. . . . Men were living in terror of the phantom dead men . . . and they received permission from the bishop to go to their graves and dig them up. . . . They cut off their heads and placed them in the graves between their legs, tore out the hearts from their corpses and covered the bodies with earth again. . . . Soon after this was done both the disease and the phantoms ceased.

21. E. O'Brien, *Post-Roman Britain to Anglo-Saxon England*, p. 7.

22. *Aeschylus, The Libation-Bearers*, trans. Weir-Smyth, line 439; "Aye, and he was foully mangled" (p. 201).

23. For further information regarding the ambivalent attitude of the church toward this practice, see Bartlett, *England under the Norman and Angevin Kings*, pp. 623–24.

24. Geoffrey became Abbot of Burton in AD 1114. For the *Life*, see *Geoffrey of Burton: Life and Miracles of St. Modwenna*.

In the Icelandic *Saga of Grettir the Strong*, written in the fourteenth century but purporting to relate to deeds that had taken place between 1030 and 1040, when Grettir was attacked by a thrall who was the ghost of Glam "he drew his short sword, cut off Glam's head and laid it between his thighs."[25] And a reference in Ström to an execution on Gotland in the nineteenth century states that "after that we dug a pit near the edge of the wood, dragged the dead man there and shoveled earth over him, after the turnkey had carefully seen to it that the dead man had his head between his legs."[26] The most recently recorded reference relates to an archaeological excavation conducted at an old graveyard in Grimswold, Connecticut, that contained burials of the nineteenth century.[27] One of the burials was that of a male named J. B. whose head and lower limbs had been removed and placed on his chest. Further inquiries disclosed that this man had been the first in his community to die from "the wasting disease" (tuberculosis), and the survivors apparently thought that by disabling his spirit they could stop the disease from spreading to other members of the community. The rationale behind the practice of postmortem decapitation of this type, in whatever era, therefore seems primarily to be prevention of the spirit of the dead from returning to haunt the living, whether because the deceased had been murdered or executed, was considered to be evil, or might bring disease on the living.

PRACTICES ASSOCIATED WITH BURIAL

BURIAL RITES

The burial rite practiced in early medieval Ireland, Iona, and areas of Anglo-Saxon England influenced by Irish missionaries was similar to that recounted by Adomnán when describing the burial in 597 of Columba: "And for three days and three nights the funeral ceremonies were duly carried out in a worthy and honourable manner. When these had ended in the savory praises of God, the venerable body of the holy and blessed patron was wrapped in clean fine cloths (*sindonibus*), and laid in the appointed burial-place."[28] There is no mention of a coffin, so it must be assumed that the body, wrapped in a shroud, was laid into a dug grave and covered with

---

25. Foote and Hight, *Saga of Grettir the Strong*, pp. v and 99.
26. Ström, *On the Sacral Origin*, pp. 164–65, n. 284.
27. Poirer and Bellantoni, *In Remembrance*, p. 146.
28. *Adomnán's Life of Columba* 3.23, ed. and trans. Anderson and Anderson (1991), pp. 230–31.

earth. Alongside this may be placed the details of Guthlac's burial in 715, as described by Felix: "The handmaiden of God (Pega, Guthlac's sister) spent three days in commending the spirit of her brother to heaven with divine praises, and on the third day in accordance with his command she buried his blessed limbs in his oratory, covering them with earth."[29] Guthlac was also wrapped in a linen cloth (*in sindone involvat*) that had been sent to him by Abbess Ecgburg,[30] but a difference between Columba and Guthlac is that Guthlac was placed in a coffin according to the instructions that he gave before his death. The use of the word *sindon* to describe a white linen winding-sheet or shroud is taken from the description of the burial of Christ, as contained for instance in Luke 23:53 in which the body is described as being wrapped in a winding-sheet (*involvit sindone*) before being laid in the tomb. This therefore was regarded as the appropriate mode of burial for Christians in both Ireland and England by the eighth century. Cuthbert, who died 687, had received a gift of a *sindon* from Abbess Verca, and he requested that his body was to be wrapped in this and buried in a stone coffin that he had received from Abbot Cudda.[31] Cuthbert had envisaged a simple burial, but the monks of Lindisfarne decided otherwise and clothed him in rich attire for burial in the Gaulish (Roman) manner. He was clothed in even more sumptuous apparel when in 698 his body was placed in a new coffin on the floor of the sanctuary of the church where it could be seen and venerated by the faithful.[32]

Even seemingly minor articles of dress may have had significance in early medieval burial rites. An unusual item, a single toe-ring, has been noted in occasional male burials in Iron Age cemeteries throughout Britain[33] and in at least one early Anglo-Saxon cemetery, at Burgh Castle, Norfolk (Gaz. 741).[34] While no great importance has been attached to these items in the past, they may actually be of immense significance. My attention was first drawn to this possibility when viewing an exhibition of ancient Near Eastern cylinder seals at the Pierpont Morgan Library in New York in 1998. Two of the seals dating from the Neo-Babylonian period (ca. 1000–539 BC), Numbers 94 and 95, depict a winged hero with one foot unshod, contesting with a lion-demon for a bull; while another seal of the same era, Number 99, depicts an armed hero who also has

29. Felix, *Life of St. Guthlac*, pp. 160–61.
30. See further Kelley Wickham-Crowley, this volume.
31. Colgrave, *Two Lives of Saint Cuthbert*.
32. Bede, *Hist. eccles.* 4.30, pp. 442–45.
33. E. O'Brien, *Post-Roman Britain to Anglo-Saxon England*, chap. 1, p. 21.
34. Johnson, *Burgh Castle, Excavations*, p. 64. "Gaz." refers to the identity number for the site record in the database gazetteer in E. O'Brien, *Post-Roman Britain to Anglo-Saxon England*.

one foot bare, grasping the neck of a kicking ostrich.[35] A subsequent and summary search of the literature has confirmed that the wearing of a single sandal is a motif of great antiquity and is often an indication of sovereignty. The earliest literary reference is in Greek mythology where Jason is described as wearing only one sandal when claiming his father's kingdom from the usurper.[36] In medieval Irish tradition the topos of the single sandal was associated with both kingship and the "otherworld,"[37] and it is probably not without significance that a tenth-century king of Dublin was named Amlaib Cúarán (Norse: Óláfr kváran), which translates as Olaf the Sandal.[38] The presence therefore of the toe-ring of a sandal on one foot of a male burial may be a manifestation in the archaeological record of a social ranking that heretofore has only been recognized in the literary tradition.[39]

BURNING OF GRAIN

There are references in the literature that suggest that pagan practices associated with burial were still being observed by Christians in the early medieval period. The Penitential of Theodore 15.3 states that "He who causes grains to be burned where a man has died, for the health of the living and of the house shall do penance for five years."[40] While this appears to associate the burning of grain with the house in which a person died, evidence that the grain was often put into the grave itself has been found in many Anglo-Saxon cemeteries: for example at Sandy, Bedfordshire[41] (Gaz. 64); Spong Hill, Norfolk[42] (Gaz. 121), where an old find made in 1844 included an urn filled with charred wheat; Balcombe Pit, Glynde, Sussex (Gaz. 244), where a wooden box containing grain was found near the skull of a skeleton in this cemetery of west–east burials, many of which were accompanied only by iron knives; Marston St. Lawrence, Northamptonshire[43] (Gaz. 453); Andover, Hampshire[44] (Gaz. 1110), where burnt

35. Eisenberg, "Glyptic Art of the Ancient Near East," pp. 15–16, figs. 33, 34, 35.
36. Killeen, "Fear an Énais."
37. MacCana, "*Topos* of the Single Sandal."
38. Doherty, "Vikings in Ireland," pp. 296–97.
39. An in-depth examination of the literary evidence of this "Rite of the Single Shoe" is included in Fitzpatrick, *Royal Inauguration in Gaelic Ireland c. 1100 to c. 1600.*
40. McNeill and Gamer, *Medieval Handbooks of Penance*, p. 198.
41. Kennett, "Pottery and Other Finds."
42. Hills, *Anglo-Saxon Cemetery at Spong Hill, Part I;* Hills et al., *Anglo-Saxon Cemetery at Spong Hill, Part II;* Hills et al., *Anglo-Saxon Cemetery at Spong Hill, Part III;* Meaney, *Gazetteer of Early Anglo-Saxon Burial Sites*, p. 175.
43. Meaney, *Gazetteer of Early Anglo-Saxon Burial Sites*, p. 192.
44. A. Cook and Dacre, *Excavations at Portway, Andover.*

grain was found in two female graves of the sixth century; and Burghfield, Berkshire[45] (Gaz. 2180), where carbonized grain was found in a burial that also had two items tied together and placed in a small bag. Several other cemeteries contain burials in which charcoal has been scattered, usually around the upper parts of bodies.[46]

If the burning of grain were associated with some form of purification of the house, then the inclusion in graves of either burnt grain or charcoal might perform the same function. This custom must have been deep-rooted because a repetition of the prohibition is included in the so-called Confessional of Egbert, written about 950–1000, which reads, "Anyone who burns corn in the place where a dead man lay, for the health of living men and of his house, shall fast for five years."[47] There are only a couple of examples of this practice known from Ireland. The first example is at an early medieval cemetery at Kilshane (Co. Dublin)[48] where three of the burials (two adults and a child) had burnt grain deposited around the skulls; and the second example is in the form of a sample of burnt grain listed in the records of the National Museum of Ireland as having been found with a burial at Levitstown (Co. Kildare) in 1943.[49] There is evidence to suggest that the burials at Kilshane have probable Anglo-Saxon connections.[50]

FUNERAL FEASTS

The custom of funeral feasts was condemned in the sixth-century Canons of the Greek Synods, "Non oportet, non liceat Christianis prandia ad defunctorum sepulchra deferre et sacrificari mortuis,"[51] but this did not prevent seventh-century references to the practice. Adomnán, writing at the end of the seventh century, relates a story about an animal thief named Erc, to whom Columba from time to time gave provisions in order to prevent further thieving: "the saint, foreseeing in the spirit the thief's imminent death, sent to Baithéne, then living as prior in the plain of Long, and bade him send to that thief a fat beast and six measures of

45. Butterworth and Lobb, *Excavations in the Burghfield Area*.

46. Individual cemeteries are listed in E. O'Brien, *Post-Roman Britain to Anglo-Saxon England*, p. 55.

47. McNeill and Gamer, *Medieval Handbooks of Penance*, p. 246 and p. 243 for date.

48. E. O'Brien, *Post-Roman Britain to Anglo-Saxon England*, p. 182.

49. Museum record number: NMI 1943.222.

50. E. O'Brien, "Contacts between Ireland and Anglo-Saxon England"; E. O'Brien, *Post-Roman Britain to Anglo-Saxon England*, p. 182.

51. Collection of the Canons of the Greek Synods by Martin, bishop of Braga in Portugal, who died AD 580. See Rolleston, "Researches and Excavations," p. 424.

grain as last gifts. When Baithéne had dispatched these as the saint had asked him to do, the pitiful thief was found overtaken by sudden death on that day; and the gifts that had been sent were used at his funeral."[52] Also, a reference in the early Irish law tract *Dí Dligiud Raith 7 Somaíne*[53] (On the law relating to the fief and profit of a lord) mentions that one of the seven duties that a client must carry out in the event of his lord's death included attendance at a commemorative feast. While these feasts may not have taken place at the actual place of burial, they certainly indicate the continuance of an ancient ritual in a Christian milieu.

BURIAL ENCLOSURES

Tírechán makes an interesting reference to the digging of a circular enclosure around a grave.[54] The episode opens when Patrick, visiting the well of Clébach, on the slopes of Cruachú (Cruachain or Rathcroghan, Co. Roscommon), met with and converted the two daughters of King Loíguire. They then wished to meet the Son (of God), and on receiving the Eucharist,

> they fell asleep in death and their friends placed them on one bed and covered them with their garments and made a lament and great keening. . . . And the days of mourning for the king's daughters came to an end and they buried them beside the well of Clébach, and they made a round ditch (*fossam rotundam*) after the manner of a *ferta* because this is what the heathen Irish used to do, but we call it *relic*,[55] that is, the remains of the maidens. And the *ferta* was made over to Patrick with the bones of the holy virgins, and to his heirs after him for ever, and he made an earthen church in that place.

One could speculate that the ditch must have been penannular in order to provide access to the earthen church. Cruachú is, like Tara, a royal site that is covered with earthen barrows, and Tírechán, who was very familiar with the area, was describing what he considered to be a suitable form of burial for the king's daughters.

52. *Adomnán's Life of Columba* 1.41, ed. and trans. Anderson and Anderson (1991), pp. 74–77.

53. Early Irish law-texts were originally written in the seventh and eighth centuries; F. Kelly, *Guide to Early Irish Law*, p. 30.

54. *Tírechán*, chap. 26 (16–21), pp. 144–45.

55. *Fert:* a burial involving enduring physical signs in the form of a mound or a ditch and rampart, i.e., a permanent change to the landscape by means of the digging of a grave; *relic:* a borrowing from *reliquiae* (the remains of the saints). It would seem that by Tírechán's time the latter had or was beginning to acquire its Irish meaning of *reilig* or cemetery, the meaning that it has retained until the present day.

There is one other reference to the digging of a *fert* in early Irish literature. This occurs in the tract already mentioned above, *Dí Dligiud Raith 7 Somaíne* (On the law relating to the fief and profit of a lord), when another one of the seven duties that a client must carry out in the event of the lord's death was the digging of the lord's *fert* or grave mound.[56] It is important to note that in both of these cases the *fert* is dug and not built, indicating that the major element was the ditch and that such enclosures were, in the seventh century, associated with people of high rank. It might therefore be possible to take the argument one step further and suggest that similar enclosures found occasionally in cemeteries in early medieval Ireland,[57] and more often in seventh-century Anglo-Saxon cemeteries, especially in southeast England, might be substitutes for ostentatious grave goods and wealth displays in the burial of high-ranking individuals.[58]

GRAVE ROBBING

Visible monuments, the display of wealth, or the inclusion of ostentatious grave goods in early medieval burials raises the issue of grave robbing, a practice documented in Anglo-Saxon times by texts such as the *Life of Guthlac* discussed above (p. 293). In general, the evidence for grave robbing in Anglo-Saxon cemeteries is complex, but it does exist and appears mostly to be a phenomenon of the seventh century. At the cemetery at Lord of the Manor, Ozengell, Ramsgate, Kent[59] (Gaz. 1208), for example, up to sixty percent of the graves showed signs of ancient disturbance that appears to demonstrate, among other things, an exact knowledge of the position of graves, what items had been placed in them, and where those items had been placed, thus allowing retrieval with minimum disturbance or labor; this also suggests that the activity may often not have been clandestine.[60] I am of the opinion that the answer lies in the advent of Christianity. It is a central motif in Germanic legend that treasure buried with the dead was cursed,[61] so pagans would be loath to disturb it. If anyone did decide to rob a corpse or a grave the penalties were harsh: in the Frankish Salic Laws compiled in the early sixth century and added to and adapted up to the mid-eighth century, chapter 55 "Concerning the plundering of corpses" states,

56. F. Kelly, *Guide to Early Irish Law*, p. 30.
57. E. O'Brien, *Post-Roman Britain to Anglo-Saxon England*, pp. 182–83.
58. E. O'Brien, *Post-Roman Britain to Anglo-Saxon England*, esp. pp. 132–39.
59. Excavated by Mr. David Perkins, to whom I am grateful for discussing his research on this matter with me.
60. Mr. David Perkins, pers. comm.
61. Dr. Helen Conrad-O'Briain, pers. comm.

(1). If anyone thievishly plunders the body of a slain man before it is buried (known in the *malberg* as *chreomosido*) and it can be proven that he did this, let him be held liable for 2500 denarii, which make sixty-two and one-half solidi. . . . (4). If anyone exhumes and plunders a corpse already buried (known in the *malberg* as *muther*), and it can be proven that he did this, let him become an outlaw until that day when he comes to an agreement with the relatives of the deceased, so that they must ask that he be allowed [again] to go among men . . . let the criminal who is proven to have committed this [deed] or to have exhumed [the corpse] be held liable for 8000 denarii, which make 200 solidi.[62]

In *Beowulf*, lines 3051–57, the poet suggests that any curse on treasure in a burial can be set aside by God:

And this gold of former men was full of power,
the huge inheritance, hedged about with a spell:
no one among men was permitted to touch that golden
store of rings unless God Himself, the true King
of Victories, the Protector of mankind, enabled one
He chose to open the hoard, whichever among men
should seem meet to Him.[63]

In other words, Christians felt that it was in God's power to remove curses, and they would therefore not be afraid to retrieve precious objects that may have been either placed in graves for the benefit of pagan observers of the burial or deposited in the grave of a pagan relative. The (Christian) servants of Guntram Boso certainly did not appear to have been bothered by any curse when they "retrieved" the precious objects that had been buried with a woman in the church near Metz,[64] even though they could still be held accountable for this action under Frankish law. Gregory of Tours obviously thought that the behavior of Guntram Boso, a Christian bishop, was despicable. Bearing all of this in mind, Guthlac's use of a prehistoric burial chamber as a dwelling and burial place may therefore have been his method of demonstrating the dominant power of Christianity over paganism.

---

62. Rivers, *Laws of the Salian and Ripuarian Franks*, pp. 2–7.
63. M. Alexander, *Beowulf*, p. 147. For views on whether or not the writer of *Beowulf* was a Christian, see P. Wormald, "Bede, Beowulf, and the Conversion," esp. p. 65; and Conrad-O'Briain, "*Beowulf* and the Uses of History."
64. *Gregory of Tours. The History of the Franks* 8.21, pp. 453–54.

CONCLUSION

Although archaeologists face the challenge of interpreting correctly both the organization and layout of these eclectic burial sites and the material evidence found in the graves, they are in the same position as the literary historian who attempts to find meaning in the materiality of social customs delineated in literary works. Instances of how written texts can harmonize with the material world of archaeology can be contained in descriptions of early medieval Christian rites. An interdisciplinary approach combining history, literature, and archaeology, undertaken within reasoned parameters, can be of enormous benefit and make a very valuable contribution to our knowledge of the behavior and mind-set of people who lived in Ireland and Britain in the early medieval period.

Buried Truths: Shrouds, Cults, and Female Production in Anglo-Saxon England

Kelley M. Wickham-Crowley

Virginia Woolf wrote not only of a room of one's own, but also of mothers to think back through, those women who come before and challenge us in our intellectual life. Rosemary Cramp's knowledge, authority, generosity, and unflagging energy were constant stimulations in my work at Durham, and still are. I am grateful for the chance to join in offering her our affection and respect, and I hope this essay will pay some tribute to her ability to look where others did not. In her earliest excavations she was famously told not to dig on the south side of Jarrow church, as nothing would be found. How wrong that advice was is only evident because, with typical courage, she ignored it.

In this essay, I have chosen to look for what is hiding in plain sight. While weaving and spinning are usually considered women's work in early Europe, the impact of that production, whether economic, religious, social, or political, remains sparsely examined. Female production of textiles enabled male gift exchange and displays of status at the highest levels, and so enforced social hierarchy and power structures. But even more, I argue here that such textile gifts from the women themselves to honor the holy played a fundamental part in the establishment of many of the major saintly cults for which Anglo-Saxon England is famous. Women's crucial roles in initiating these cults, a formative aspect of the culture, has been a buried truth, obliquely recorded in texts and frequently lost in archaeological contexts, but salvageable. After briefly discussing the issue of whether shrouding was common at all and the attitudes of early Insular Christianity toward the body and soul, I turn to the scanty archaeological record and to specific accounts from Anglo-Saxon England. Identifying the evolution of shrouds into relics, I trace these female productions as they initiate the important saintly cults of the Anglo-Saxons, such as those of Æthelburh, Cuthbert, Æthelthryth, Edmund, and Guthlac. While always visible in these accounts, such female instigation and influence have not been commented on as have, for example, the conversions of husbands and peoples wrought by Christian queens. Yet the thread is there to follow, and here I will track a pervasive context before focusing on Guthlac's life as both the most famous and the fullest depiction of this common and commonly forgotten subject.

Prehistorians have discovered in recent decades a startling fact about past civilizations. On waterlogged sites where organic material survives, instead of what are called hard artifacts (weapons, pottery, metalwork), they found that so-called soft artifacts outnumbered the hard, sometimes by three or four to one. The importance of this new ratio is best seen when we consider who produces the majority of each type of artifact in most cultures. While assumptions about gendered work are always open to revision, the hard artifacts, such as flint or weapons, were objects generally produced by men (based on anthropological cross-cultural surveys such as the Human Relations Area Files [HRAF]), the soft artifacts, such as textiles, woven sandals, mats, baskets, and other perishables, by women. On a site where the conditions do not preserve soft artifacts, the understanding of who produced what, and how much, can radically skew in favor of seeing a culture where males are more productive. When the fuller picture emerges and is adjusted to reflect the fact that many hard artifacts of materials such as metal were rarities, it becomes clear that many if not most artifacts—the things that kept society going and shaped its existence and structure—were made by women.

I would like here to excavate somewhat this buried truth about women as producers. While the standard assumption is that most if not all Anglo-Saxon women were weavers and spinners, the impact of that production, despite its importance both to necessary and to luxury items, dissolves into an accepted background noise. Women's work on cloth must have figured in the economy of any community or family in Anglo-Saxon England. From the harvesting of wool or flax, to its combing or breaking, to its spinning and weaving, women of all classes engaged in the labor of creating cloth to protect the body from the elements and of ornamenting that cloth to reflect beauty. The SFBs or Sunken Featured Buildings (formerly called *Grubenhäuser*) of several sites, such as West Stow, Suffolk, Old Erringham, Sussex, and Upton, Northamptonshire, have provided evidence that weaving sheds existed separate from living quarters. While some have thought these buildings too dark for weaving work (though we know nothing about types of windows or skylights) or too damp, others have seen the additional humidity from a building cut down into the earth as helping keep flax flexible while weaving.[1] The production of such cloth therefore comes with the Anglo-Saxons from the earliest days.

1. In this context, it is interesting to note that the early 1700s Irish farmhouse (originally from the townland of Claraghmore near the village of Drumquin, Co. Tyrone), transported to and reconstructed at the Frontier Culture Museum, Staunton, Virginia, preserves

I focus here on shrouds as a type of case study, and especially on linen as native (not imported) cloth for Anglo-Saxon England, as a means to visualize the roles we have forgotten for these productive women and the impact of their work. I am using shrouds in a broad sense to mean wrappings or garments specially chosen for burial. While limited evidence survives archaeologically, extant saints' lives supplement what we can read of the fragmentary physical evidence left to us. Yet as Clàre Lees and Gillian Overing have commented in their work on Bede's account of Hild of Whitby,[2] women as producers are silenced even in texts otherwise judged to be exemplary. Hild could produce monasteries and the schools in them and educate five eventual bishops in those institutions,[3] but apparently not one of them produced a text about her legacy. Bede's account truncates her life's work in order to serve his larger purpose of writing a Christian history, though to be fair, he often did so to lives of men as well. But think only of what is missing in the account of the Whitby synod when, despite Hild's education of Wilfrid and the synod's being held in Hild's monastery, that account has nothing to say of her influence, learning, or close relationships with those in power; the same is true when her recognition and training of Cædmon's talent is briefly mentioned. The texts used in the present essay to resurrect lost roles have similar gaps, failing to comment on the common contributions of women to what seem to have been common practices. By following what women left behind, we can track back to the women themselves to recoup missing social history. The cloths these women produced testify for them.

In the earlier centuries of Anglo-Saxon disposition of the dead, shrouding may not have been a common practice, or a practice at all. It would be unnecessary if a body were to be placed on a pyre, for example, and the evocative description in *Beowulf* of Hildeburh's mourning of her burning dead suggests that the bodies were visible, if indeed this passage records remembered or actual practice, a debatable point:

---

the original step down for the room built to hold the loom for weaving linen. The reason given by site interpreters for lowering the floor and cutting into soil was that the humidity made weaving linen easier. The site interpreter who spins the flax for this working farmhouse commented also that wetting her fingers regularly made spinning the flax easier (site visited in May 2000). See the museum Web site: http://www.frontiermuseum.org/index .html.

2. Lees and Overing, "Birthing Bishops, Fathering Poets"; Lees and Overing, *Double Agents,* chap. 1.

3. There would have been six, if Tatfrith had lived; the five were Bosa, Ætla, Oftfor, John, and Wilfrid. See Bede, *Hist. eccles.* 4.23, pp. 408–11.

Het ða Hildeburh æt Hnæfes ade
hire selfre sunu sweoloðe befæstan,
banfatu bærnan, ond on bæl don
eame on eaxle. Ides gnornode,
geomrode giddum (1114–18).[4]

(Hildeburh then ordered on Hnæf's pyre her own son to be entrusted to the heat, his bone-vessel to be burned and put in the fire by his uncle's shoulder. The noble woman mourned, lamented with song.)

Beowulf's own funeral records graphic details as well:

alegdon ða tomiddes mærne þeoden
hæleð hiofende, hlaford leofne.
Ongunnon þa on beorge bælfyra mæst
wigend weccan; wud(u)rec astah
sweart ofer swioðole, swogende leg
wope bewunden —windblond gelæg—,
oð þæt he ða banhus gebrocen hæfde,
hat on hreðre (3141–48).[5]

(They then laid amid [the treasure] the famous king, mourning the hero, the beloved lord. Warriors began then on the mound the greatest funeral fire to waken; woodsmoke arose dark over the blaze, the roaring flame wound about with weeping. The windblast subsided when it had broken the bone-house, hot in its heart.)

There is some evidence that a pyre was built over rather than under some cremated bodies,[6] which might suggest why shoulder blades at times do not burn completely. That would shield a full view of the body at least initially, until it had burned to a less recognizable individual. In any case, while shrouding could help bind a body for carrying, the use of fabric would not be necessary either in a cremation or if the body were borne on a bier or platform. It might in fact impede display, if that were a key aspect of the burial. Similarly, bodies kept in chests or coffins might wear elaborate clothing, as in the Continental Köln burials, but would have no real need of shrouding to wrap them. I would argue here that in early Anglo-Saxon times, perhaps even quite late, shrouding was reserved for

4. From Klaeber, *Beowulf and the Fight at Finnsburg*, p. 42. The translation is my own.
5. Klaeber, *Beowulf and the Fight at Finnsburg*, p. 118. The translation is my own.
6. An accessible reconstruction of a tentlike pyre appears in Welch, *Discovering Anglo-Saxon England*, p. 65, fig. 43.

those of high status, especially religious, and was not a universal practice for burial. It may even be that the practice came from Roman influence. It is an example of conspicuous display, of wealth. If we remember that the roots of both "rob" and "robe" are the same, meaning booty or spoil, it reveals that wealth and textiles were often the same thing. (Though the word is from French, the practice is older than the borrowing.)[7]

The early and scanty evidence we have for Anglo-Saxon shrouds, if that is what it is, mainly comes from fabric imprints left in the corrosion on the fronts of metal objects worn on a body. The difficulty with such evidence is that while we can at times distinguish the type and weave of fabric, and evidence for both linen and wool exists, we have no way to prove that such fabric was technically a shroud instead of a cape or shawl wrapped around a body or, indeed, if such garments could themselves function as shrouds. To complicate things, evidence also exists for the wrapping of individual artifacts such as spears, not just bodies.[8] Limbs close together or tight to the body might suggest shrouding, or not, or they might represent some other practice, such as a few bindings to help lower a body into the grave or to bind other cloths tightly about the body. The Bayeux Tapestry, in its depiction of Edward the Confessor's death, shows what may be the shrouding material before it was bound up and a depiction of the procession to Westminster Abbey with canopied bier that suggests body strapping, though with a cloth beneath the bindings that is certainly a shroud. The indentations along the body clearly suggest bindings separate from the shroud itself.[9]

An earlier archaeological example from Darenth Park, Dartford, Kent, demonstrates the difficulty of interpreting evidence. In grave 8 (second half of the sixth century), a woman aged thirty-five to forty-five was buried

7. E. Barber, *Women's Work*, p. 290. See also the relevant entries in the *Oxford English Dictionary*.

8. Elizabeth Coatsworth discusses this practice briefly in her article, this volume, p. 152, and relates it to a type of textile reliquary.

9. Wilson, *Bayeux Tapestry*, plates 29 and 30, captions and translations, p. 172. Plate 29 depicts the procession first (abbreviations expanded): "Hic portatur corpus Eadwardi regis ad ecclesiam sancti Petri Apostoli" (Here the body of King Edward is carried to the Church of St. Peter the Apostle). Plate 30 shows "et hic defunctus est" (and here he is dead). Wilson comments, "The reversal of the death and burial scenes is interpreted by many as emphasizing the hurried nature of the accession" (ibid., p. 183). See also the commentary and bibliography for this scene in Foys, *Bayeux Tapestry: Digital Edition*. Gale Owen-Crocker also discusses these scenes in this volume, in her notes 51 and 52 (p. 118). I do not know the basis for the idea that the head of the dying person is usually depicted to the left, but the two plates from the Hexateuch provided for my article (figs. 1 and 2) show four examples of the head to the right as the body is being shrouded, and a similar orientation occurs for the later illustration of Guthlac's wrapped corpse (fig. 4).

with a rich variety of finds, some of which preserved multiple impressions of textiles, including fine linen, wool, and a tablet-woven braid border. On the left shoulder disc brooch and on the remains of an iron pin in the upper left side of the chest were additional impressions of a coarse tabby weave. In evaluating the evidence, Elisabeth Crowfoot concluded that the woman was buried fully dressed, in a gown of soft, possibly checked wool, a fine linen head veil, and a cloak with patterned border wrapped around her. In addition, "the small coarse fragments (b) caught under the end of the pin and nearby brooch may suggest an extra coarse wrapping or shroud."[10] Because no fragments were found on the right shoulder brooch, however, and because the woman was fully dressed, we might also be dealing simply with a fabric piece used to lower the body, or a small bag that contained the beads and other objects found on the left of the body. Certainly shrouding a fully clothed body would make a bulkier burden; here, it seems unnecessary. But then, signs of status usually are superfluous, which leaves us with an open question.

Texts, on the other hand, often provide incidental confirmation of shrouding, especially in Christian contexts, because of the number of saints' lives recorded. In addition, a change in how the body after death was seen occurs. Before Christian influence, the dead were generally kept separate from the living. Important individuals had graves that were marked, whether by mounds, ditches, or other features, but fears of contamination or of the supernatural also seem to have existed alongside respect. The nuances of belief are lost, since no texts survive. For Christians, however, texts show how a complicated view of the physical body evolved, and it affected that body after death, especially in the case of holy men and women. The desire to keep such people accessible as models and intercessors moved their bodies into contact with the living, and the physical became a sign of and a means to the spiritual power they wielded. Despite a Christian emphasis on the soul over the body, and a gendered, patristic understanding of that hierarchy in which women are seen as more carnal, sensuous, and inferior while men are seen as more spiritual, intellectual, and superior, this dichotomy can be transcended by the idea that the purified body and the soul can be one. So, for example, a dead saint is at once in heaven and also present in any physical remains, and that presence can exercise power through virtue by secondary relics—or those things that have touched or been used by the saint. In this context, the shroud is both a material, carnal veiling for the dead and a signpost that emphasizes the physical as emblem of what is buried beneath and what survives. But even more than a signpost or emblem, the shroud becomes a secondary relic

---

10. E. Crowfoot, "Note on the Textile Remains."

itself, a representation or extension of the saint, endowed with his or her presence as well as God's.[11]

As the interest in relics grew, competition for the most important of them did also, and frequent relocations of relics occurred, what we have interpreted as thefts, as Patrick Geary writes of in *Furta Sacra*. Yet the rationale for such actions often included a clear argument for the saints' endorsements of such relocations; clearly, if they disapproved, it would be impossible to remove them. The presence of the saint must be continuous, not intermittent; therefore, consent was a given if the removal was allowed. As a result, the treatment of the saint's body was as careful as when it lived, or in the case of ascetic saints, often better. An indication of the common presence of women in preparing, shrouding, and mourning the illustrious dead is shown in the Old English Hexateuch (London, British Library, MS Cotton Claudius B. iv), where many of the depictions of Old Testament figures should reflect Anglo-Saxon practice and perceptions, given the originality of the designs.[12] In figure 1, for example, folio 11r depicts the families and deaths of Cainan (top) and Malaleel (Gen. 5:12–17). In the depiction of Cainan, a woman at his feet holds one gathered edge of a large cloth while men at his head hold the other; the image seems to be of his shrouding. The bottom depiction of Malaleel has two men carrying the already swathed body. Folio 12r (fig. 2) has two similar scenes for the burials of Methuselah and Lamech, again with women at the feet of shrouded or swathed figures. The woman near Methuselah's feet has her left hand to her mouth or face, a gesture repeated often in the text in the context of death; it is easy to read it as a gesture of mourning.

In Britain, the tendency was to keep the bodies intact after death, though of course some saints, such as Oswald, died of their dismemberment. Therefore, secondary relics became even more important as the interest in them grew. Without the dispersal of body parts, items associated with saints had to fill the demands of the faithful. There is also an element of native production to this economy. Whereas early on, relics would have to come from the Continent and were often from the apostles or other great saints, as British and English Christians began to produce saints, the process of making someone collectable, as it were, also took root. Because the body was seen as the saint intact in Britain, the process of recognizing and enhancing the visible saintliness of someone would

11. In fact, it strikes me that secondary relics are a different type of the figural mask that Professor Cramp writes of here as connecting to the supernatural, with the lovely pun of such masks being *super*, on top of, the natural, a way to evoke the spiritual power beneath the physical shape (this volume, pp. 8–9).

12. Dodwell and Clemoes, *Old English Illustrated Hexateuch*. "The Basic Originality of the Illustrations" is discussed there, pp. 65–73.

carry great weight and, without implying cynicism, an understanding of
the potential political and spiritual power involved. I would argue that
women had a strong role in this recognition and enhancement through
their production of cloth and embroideries and their care of the dead,
roles now deemphasized yet crucial to creating saints' cults and the cult
of relics and to restoring a more complete understanding of how social
power was constructed.

Anglo-Saxon texts frequently depict details of burial and attitudes
toward the dead and their wrappings. Bede recounts a vision of the nun
Tortgyth that pulls together the points made so far about the absolute
identity of body and soul in sainthood and the inseparability of secondary relics from that reality of absolute identity. Regarding Æthelburh,
the abbess of Barking, Bede relates that the nun Tortgyth left her cell at
dawn:

> Haec ergo quadam nocte incipiente crepusculo, egressa de
> cubiculo quo manebat, uidit manifeste quasi corpus hominis,
> quod esset sole clarius, sindone inuolutum in sublime ferri,
> elatum uidelicet de domo in qua sorores pausare solebant.
> Cumque diligentius intueretur, quo trahente leuaretur sur-
> sum haec quam contemplabatur species corporis gloriosi, uidit
> quasi funibus auro clarioribus in superna tolleretur, donec cae-
> lis patentibus introducta amplius ab illa uideri non potuit. Nec
> dubium remansit cogitanti de uisione, quin aliquis de illa con-
> gregatione citius esset moriturus, cuius anima per bona quae
> fecisset opera quasi per funes aureos leuanda esset ad caelos.

> (One evening, at dusk, as she left the little cell in which she lived,
> she saw distinctly what seemed to be a human body, wrapped
> in a shroud and brighter than the sun, being apparently raised
> up from within the house in which the sisters used to sleep. She
> looked closely to see how this glorious visionary body was raised
> up and saw that it was lifted as it were by cords, brighter than
> gold, until it was drawn up into the open heavens and she could
> see it no longer. As she thought over the vision there remained
> no doubt in her mind that some member of their community
> was about to die whose soul would be drawn up to the skies by
> the good deeds she had done, as though by golden cords.)[13]

The emphasis on Æthelburh's body as being wrapped and dead, and on
her bodily assumption as one with her soul's assumption, shows how literal
the identification of body and soul was. The physicality of wrappings is
included as part of her glorified material and spiritual self, a point worth

13. Bede, *Hist. eccles.* 4.9, pp. 360–61.

stressing in the context of this discussion. Yet the metaphorical accompanies the literal, for the cords are understood to be good deeds.

Other accounts in Bede stress the wholeness of the body, something Rollason and Bynum have commented on in their respective work.[14] Throughout Europe, a body discovered to be incorrupt was understood to be saintly; thus, when the body of Æthelburh, the Anglo-Saxon abbess of Faremoûtier-en-Brie (founded 617), was moved from her unfinished church of the Apostles (itself incidentally another example of women as producers and patrons): "Et aperientes sepulchrum eius, ita intemeratum corpus inuenere, ut a corruptione concupiscentiae carnalis erat inmune; et ita denuo lotum atque aliis uestibus indutum transtulerunt illud in ecclesiam beati Stephani martyris" (On opening her sepulchre they found her body as untouched by decay as it had also been immune from the corruption of fleshly desires. They washed it again, clothed it in other garments, and translated it to the church of St. Stephen the Martyr).[15] Notable as common here is the connection between the identity of spiritual and physical purity after death and the procedure of washing and dressing the body in new clothes. The replaced garments would then have the status of relics. We see this same practice when Cuthbert's body is examined eleven years after death (Cuthbert died on 20 March 687). Bede comments that both body and clothes were incorrupt:

> et aperientes sepulchrum inuenerunt corpus totum, quasi adhuc uiueret, integrum et flexibilibus artuum conpagibus multo dormienti quam mortuo similius; sed et uestimenta omnia, quibus indutum erat, non solum intemerata uerum etiam prisca nouitate et claritudine miranda parebant. . . .
>
> Adtulerunt autem ei et partem indumentorum, quae corpus sanctum ambierant. Quae cum ille et munera gratanter acciperet et miracula libenter audiret (nam et ipsa indumenta quasi patris adhuc corpori cicumdata miro deosculabatur affectu), "Noua" inquit "indumenta corpori pro his quae tulistis circumdate, et sic reponite in arca quam parastis." . . . fecerunt fratres ut iusserat, et inuolutum nouo amictu corpus nouaque in theca reconditum supra pauimentum sanctuarii posuereunt.
>
> (and, opening the grave, they found the body intact and whole as if it were still alive, the joints of the limbs flexible and much more like a sleeping than a dead man. Moreover all his garments in which his limbs had been clothed were not only undefiled but seemed to be perfectly new and wonderfully bright. . . .

---

14. See Rollason, *Saints and Relics*, and two books of Caroline Walker Bynum, *Resurrection of the Body* and *Fragmentation and Redemption*.

15. Bede, *Hist. eccles.* 3.8, pp. 240–41.

So they brought him [the bishop] part of the clothes which had wrapped the holy body. He joyfully received these gifts and gladly listened to the story of the miracle, kissing the garments with great affection as though they were still wrapped round the father's body, and he said, "Put fresh garments around the body instead of those you have brought and replace it thus in the coffin which you have prepared." . . . the brothers did as he commanded; they wrapped the body in a new garment, put it in a new coffin and placed it on the floor of the sanctuary.)[16]

Here, the original garments are removed, and the bishop is described as receiving these as gifts, which he treats as if Cuthbert were present in them. He then causes them to be replaced by a new garment, and a new coffin is added. The garments mentioned first as undefiled could be clothing; the second reference to a single garment may be to a shroud, especially as the bishop says to put fresh garments around the body (*circumdate*). These relics then make available the virtues of the saint. Bede specifically notes, "Sed et indumenta, quibus Deo dicatum corpus Cudbercti uel uiuum antea uel postea defunctum uestierant, etiam ipsa a gratia curandi non uacarunt, sicut in uolumine uitae et uirtutum eius quisque legerit, inueniet" (The garments too, which had covered the dedicated body of Cuthbert while he was alive and after his death, did not lack the grace of healing, as anyone who reads may find in the book of his life and miracles).[17]

In addition, Reginald of Durham's *Libellus de Admirandis Beati Cuthberti Virtutibus* records a now lost embroidered shroud of Cuthbert measuring some sixteen by six feet and in linen. Dodwell comments that it "was unlikely to have been imported since it was of linen, but it does perhaps show how native embroidery could be influenced by fabrics from abroad," by which he means Byzantine or Eastern silks.[18] Reginald's account of the translation of Cuthbert in 1104 details the cloth and the embroidery upon it:

[ch. 42] Quibus superius lodex novem prope cubitorum dimensionem in longitudine tenens, tres autem et semis in sui latitudine protendens, erat circumpositus; cujus operimenti integumento omnis sanctarum reliquiarum cetus decentissimè fuerat obvolutus. Qui villos de filo lineo ad mensuram digiti unius longos ex alterâ regione habuit: nam idem lodex lineus proculdubio fuit. In omni vero lodicis ipsius circumitu

16. Bede, *Hist. eccles.* 4.30, pp. 442–45.
17. Bede, *Hist. eccles.* 4.31, pp. 446–47.
18. Dodwell, *Anglo-Saxon Art*, p. 168.

quadrangulari ipsius textoris prudentiâ artificiali, quibus lim-
bus erat in margine, qui pollicis unius probatur latitudinem
habere. In quâ texturâ videtur quædam de ipsius fili stamine
sculptura subtilissima aliquanto altius prominere; quæ avium
ac bestiarum formas probatur utpote insertas in margine gerere.
Semper tamen in duo avium vel bestiarum paria formabilis
quædam intextura instar cujusdam frondosæ arboris emergit,
quæ hac & illac illarum ymagines disseparando, dirimit & dis-
tinguendo disjungit. Figura etiam arboris sic formabiliter effi-
giatæ ex alterutrû parte videtur suas frondes quamvis minutas
effundere. Sub quibus statim in continenti collaterali scemate
animalium sculptiles texturæ donantur exsurgere; quæ utraque
similiter in panni illius postremis finibus altius visuntur prominere. Pannus iste de sacro corpore tempore translationis suæ
sublatus est, qui ob reliquiarum donaria quæ cotidie fidelibus
præstantur diu integer in ecclesiâ conservatus est. Supra quem
lodicem alius adhuc pannus grossior qui triplicis texturæ fore
dicitur locabatur quo tota lodicis ipsius superficies et omnis reliquiarum inferius locata congeries velabatur. Cui adhuc pannus tertius, totus undique cerâ infusus, preminebat, qui thecam
interiorem sancti corporis una cum omnibus sacris reliquiis
exterius circumdederat. Qui non ad interiora sanctuaria per-
tigisse probabatur, sed potius quasi pro excipiendâ importunâ
foeditate pulveris superadditus fuisse conjicitur. Tres igitur
panni isti a sacri pontificis corpore sublati sunt, pro quibus alii
satis venustiores et multo preciosiores subpositi sunt.

(And above these was wrapped a sheet measuring nearly nine
cubits in length and extending to a width of three cubits and
a half. By this outer covering the whole assemblage of holy relics was properly enwrapped. This sheet had fringes of linen
thread on either side, measuring about one finger's length, for
the sheet was without doubt made of linen. Moreover all round
the rectangle of this same sheet there was a border at the edge
worked by the skillful art of the same weaver, and it is found to
be as broad as a thumb is long. And on this material a very fine
embroidery stands out a little from the strands of thread, which
is found to contain the shapes of birds and beasts, inwoven, that
is, in the border. Always, however, between two pairs of birds or
beasts there appears a woven figure like a tree in full leaf, which
divides and separates their shapes on either side, and so by dis-
joining them makes them distinct. The shapely figure of the
tree also, thus portrayed, is seen to spread out its leaves, tiny as
they may be, on both sides. And immediately beneath them in
similar fashion embroidered forms of animals are presented to
one's view. Both of these features are clearly seen as a raised pattern at the extreme edges of this cloth. This cloth was removed

from the sacred body at the time of its translation, and was long preserved intact in the church as a covering for the gifts of relics which are daily exhibited to the faithful. Above this sheet there was placed another, thicker cloth, which is said to be of three-ply material, and by it the whole expanse of the sheet itself and all the collection of relics placed below was veiled. Visible over this was yet a third cloth, entirely impregnated with wax, which surrounded and enclosed the coffin of the holy body within as well as all the sacred relics. This cloth quite clearly had not touched the holy things within, but is supposed rather to have been a later addition to catch the troublesome defilement of dust. So then, these three cloths were removed from the body of the holy bishop, and instead of them, others, much more beautiful and far more precious were laid over it.)[19]

While it is impossible to prove, the embroidered cloth may be the shroud made for Cuthbert by Abbess Verca and saved by him for his burial. When dying, Cuthbert told Abbot Herefrith:

Est autem ad aquilonalem eiusdem oratorii partem sarcofagum terrae cespite abditum, quod olim mihi Cudda uenerabilis abbas donauit. In hoc corpus meum reponite, inuoluentes in sindone quam inuenietis istic. Nolui quidem ea uiuens indui, sed pro amore dilectae Deo feminae, quae hanc michi misit, Uercae uidelicet abbatissae ad obuoluendum corpus meum reseruare curaui.

(Now there is on the north side of this same oratory a sarcophagus hidden under the turf, which the venerable abbot Cudda once gave me. Place my body in this, wrapping it in the cloth which you will find there. I was unwilling to wear the cloth while alive but, out of affection for the abbess Verca, a woman beloved of God, who sent it to me, I have taken care to keep it to wrap my body in.)[20]

My point in citing this shroud rests in its native production, as linen (*nam idem lodex linens proculdubio fuit*), and its value as the outer, visible

---

19. The translation is that of Edward G. Pace, as printed in Battiscombe, *Relics of Saint Cuthbert*, p. 111. The Latin was transcribed from MS Hunter 101 in the Library of the Dean and Chapter of Durham Cathedral by James Raine; the text here comes from Raine's *Saint Cuthbert*. I am especially grateful to Mr. Douglas A. Anderson for providing a copy of the Latin.

20. Bede, *Life of St Cuthbert*, chap. 37, in Colgrave, *Two Lives of Saint Cuthbert*, pp. 272–73.

shroud of Cuthbert; here, the cloth becomes almost a native silk,[21] imitating that fabric's woven patterns while translating its aesthetic into another medium. Clearly silk was available to be used or copied, but here linen is the valuable cloth. The visible form of the shroud was a native woman's interpretation and production in a form of Anglo-Saxon manufacture, and its gift enhanced the saint's spiritual reputation through its physical beauty.

Such imitations and interpretations could have been numerous. The Casula at Maaseik, which preserves the Anglo-Saxon embroideries there, consists of linen that is this time entirely covered with silk embroidery: the linen *becomes* silk to the eye. Again in support of my thought that the linen embroideries could be valued as silks were, the Maaseik fragment known as the David silk (late eighth or early ninth century) has a pattern that Budny and Tweddle argue is an Anglo-Saxon variation. This half-silk, half-linen fabric, composed of linen, silk, and silver-wrapped linen threads, serves in their opinions "as an extraordinary witness either to the execution of a Western European—probably Anglo-Saxon—design in a Byzantine or Islamic centre, or to the early practice of silk weaving in the West."[22] The embroidery fragments make up a vestment clearly treated now as a relic.

For Anglo-Saxons, even apparently plain, fine linen was often a luxury fabric, enough for Æthelthryth/Etheldreda and Guthlac to forswear wearing it in their lifetimes. Perhaps it is linen that Edgils refers to when he relates in a well-known passage what it was like to live at Coludesbyrig/Coldingham before it was destroyed by a fire which was understood as retribution for sins. He recounted Adomnán's vision to Bede, in which a figure appears to Adomnán and complains that none of the men and women of the monastery are concerned with the health of the soul:

> Nam et domunculae, quae ad orandum uel legendum factae erant, nunc in comesationum, potationum, fabulationum et ceterarum sunt inlecebrarum cubilia conuersae; uirgines quoque Deo dicatae, contemta reuerentia suae professionis, quotiescumque uacant, texendis subtilioribus indumentis operam dant, quibus aut se ipsas ad uicem sponsarum in periculum sui status adornent, aut externorum sibi uirorum amicitiam conparent.
>
> (And the cells that were built for praying and for reading have become haunts of feasting, drinking, gossip, and other delights;

---

21. There is some evidence that linen correlates with wealth and/or status, as silk would, even in early burials (fifth through seventh centuries). See, for example, the report on textiles by P. Walton Rogers in Drinkall, Foreman, and Welch, *Anglo-Saxon Cemetery at Castledyke South*.

22. Budny and Tweddle, "Maaseik Embroideries," pp. 72–73.

even the virgins who are dedicated to God put aside all respect
for their profession and, whenever they have leisure, spend their
time weaving elaborate garments with which to adorn themselves as if they were brides, so imperilling their virginity, or
else to make friends with strange men.)[23]

Here for once the pervasiveness of weaving is acknowledged, though it is
to single out the women as blameworthy for the monastery's destruction.
While the vision's figure blames both sexes for neglect, the pointed specific is directed at women; the text and textiles are filtered through at least
four narrators, an angel and three men (Adomnán, Edgils, Bede). The
women are implicated in drawing attention only to the physical, not the
spiritual. The ornate fabrics call attention to sexuality here (as if they were
brides). Yet even a cursory look at Anglo-Saxon manuscripts impresses
one with the flowing robes both sexes wear, and late Anglo-Saxon wills,
many of them women's, testify to large numbers of textiles available as
behests. Clearly female production, if rightly directed, was valuable.

As a metaphorical and positive reference to ornamentation of fabrics,
Aldhelm comments to the nuns of Barking in "On Virginity" that virginity
should not stand alone, but should be accompanied and adorned by other
virtues to enrich the spiritual harvest. The images of enrichment he uses
are of textiles:

> [15] . . . siquidem curtinarum sive stragularum textura, nisi
> panuculae purpureis, immo diversis colorum varietatibus fuca-
> tae inter densa filorum stamina ultro citroque decurrant et arte
> plumaria omne textrinum opus diversis imaginum thoracibus
> perornent, sed uniformi coloris fuco singillatim confecta fuerit,
> liquet profecto quoniam nec oculorum obtutibus iocunda nec
> ornamentorum pulcherrimae venustati formosa videbitur. Nam
> et curtinae veteris delubri non simplici et singulari tincturae
> genere splenduisse leguntur, sed ex auro, iacintho, purpura,
> bis tincto cocco sive vermiculo cum bisso retorto dispari murice
> fulsisse describuntur.

> (indeed, [in the case of] the weaving of hangings or carpets, if
> threads dyed with purple and indeed with diverse varieties of
> colours do not run here and there among the thick cloth-fibres
> and according to the embroiderer's art ornament the woven
> fabric with the varying outlines of pictures, but it is made uni-
> formly with a monochrome dye, it is immediately obvious that
> it will not appear pleasing to the glances of the eye nor beauti-

---

23. Bede, *Hist. eccles.* 4.25, pp. 424–27.

ful against the most exquisite elegance of ornaments. For the
curtains of the ancient temple are not read to have glowed with
one simple and single kind of dye, but are described as having
blazed with gold, blue, purple, twice-dyed scarlet or vermilion
with twisted cotton of diverse tints.)[24]

For Aldhelm, a single virtue is enhanced by the addition of others: dyed
fabric increases its value when of multicolored threads or embroidered.
He may also be referring to the pseudo-Gospel tales of Mary as spinner
and weaver, where she was chosen to help weave the temple curtain. Ornamentation itself here is akin to additional virtues added to the basic virtue
of the fabric, and it is this point that relates to shrouding as relic. The
ornamentation of fabric becomes a metaphor, grounded in real practice,
amplifying and pointing out the spiritual value of the textile as a text, and
one written by women.

In any case, directing such talents to producing shrouds or reliquary
garments would surely be approved. Though Æthelthryth was of Colding-
ham at first, she became abbess at Ely, perhaps because she gave up such
fine clothes as were singled out for blame. Both Bede and Ælfric record
her life. Believed to have prophesied the plague that would kill her and
many of her sisters, in death she was incorrupt, and also whole again
despite a disfiguring incision that had drained a large tumor on her neck.
When examined by her sister Sexburg (note the presence of a woman) and
the doctor Cynefrith who treated her, her body had entirely healed, and in
parallel, Cynefrith described the linen cloths: "Sed et linteamina omnia,
quibus inuolutum erat corpus, integra apparuerunt et ita noua, ut ipso
die uiderentur castis eius membris esse circumdata" (Besides this, all the
linen clothes in which her body was wrapped appeared as whole and fresh
as on the very day when they had been put around her chaste limbs).[25]
Ælfric, writing in verse on Æthelthryth, said: "Þa wæs seo wund gehæled
. þe se læce worhte ær . / eac swilce þa ge-wæda . þe heo bewunden wæs
mid . / wæron swa ansunde . swylce hi eall niwe wæron" (The wound which
the leech had once made was healed; / likewise the linen clothes in which
she had been wound / were as fresh as if they had been all new).[26] Bede
inserts a comment Æthelthryth made that the tumor was a punishment
for formerly wearing jewelry round her neck, and then proceeds to talk

24. *Aldhelm: The Prose Works*, pp. 71–72. The Latin is found in Aldhelm, *Opera omnia*,
p. 244.

25. Bede, *Hist. eccles.* 4.19, pp. 394–95.

26. Ælfric, "Saint Æthelthryth, Virgin," in *Aelfric's Lives of Saints*, 1:438–39, lines 93–95.
The word Skeat translates as "linen" is *ge-wæde*, meaning "dress" or (archaically) "weeds,"
as in "widow's weeds."

again of the fabrics that had touched her, and of how they were removed and replaced: "Contigit autem tactu indumentorum eorundem et dae-monia ab obsessis effugata corporibus et infirnitates alias aliquoties esse curatas. . . . Lauerunt igitur uirgines corpus, et nouis indutum uestibus intulerunt in ecclesiam" (It happened also that, by the touch of the linen clothes, devils were expelled from the bodies of those who were possessed by them, and other diseases were healed from time to time. . . . So the maidens washed her body, wrapped it in new robes, carried it into the church).[27] Clearly, some robes are kept out and others added. The finery that she eschewed in life was a sign of her power once dead, but in particu-lar, the cloths and clothes she wore at death and was given by her sisters have now become relics themselves and are replaced by yet more textiles from the same women.

The care of Æthelthryth's sisters mirrors the care many women must have taken to honor and enhance the reputations of saints. Stories such as the "Life of Edmund King and Martyr" told by Ælfric record not just the king's deeds and spiritual triumphs, but the effect of his status as martyr after death. Along with miracles recorded, Ælfric tells of how the care of the saint's body is turned over to a woman:

> Sum wudewe wunode oswyn gehaten
> æt þæs halgan byrgene on begedum
> and fæstenum manega gear syððan .
> seo wolde efsian ælce geare þone sanct .
> and his næglas ceorfan syferlice . mid lufe .
> and on scryne healdan to halig-dome on weofode.

> (A certain widow who was called Oswyn dwelt near the saint's burial-place in prayers and fastings for many years after. She would every year cut the hair of the saint, and cut his nails soberly and lovingly, and keep them in a shrine as relics on the altar.)[28]

Women were, of course, often the keepers of reputation and status. While much is made of oral poets who keep history, the hard artifacts of surviving manuscripts have overshadowed the soft artifacts of embroi-dered tapestries and perishable garments offered as gifts. That women kept narratives and enhanced reputations is recorded in such diverse sources as the embroidered Bayeux Tapestry, where Anglo-Saxon women, possibly at Winchester, recorded the victory of the Normans, and literary

27. Bede, *Hist. eccles.* 4.19, pp. 390–97.
28. Ælfric, "St. Edmund, King and Martyr," in *Aelfric's Lives of Saints,* 2:328–29, lines 189–94.

sources such as the *Saga of the Volsungs,* where Brynhild, once a shield maiden, embroiders tapestries of her lover's deeds. The pictures surviving on the Oseberg tapestry could also preserve a similar record, though if so it seems to depict the end of that story, a funeral. If it relates to the woman buried there, and there is much related to weaving in this burial, it is a uniquely recognized survival of a woman's deeds recorded by women, or perhaps even by the woman herself. It is also possible that the many hangings that covered Anglo-Saxon walls, described in wills, were sources of inspiration for more enduring artifacts in sculpture or manuscripts; in this, I concur with Elizabeth Coatsworth's comments in this volume (p. 141). If such a basic point is correct, an entire field of source material and iconography has been lost, to say nothing of the role of women in the history of Anglo-Saxon art. (For example, the Volsung frieze fragment from Winchester, showing the she-wolf and Sigurd,[29] could well be a sculpted translation of a tapestry series.) Women such as Ælfflæd, the wife of Byrhtnoth of Maldon fame, recorded deeds of their husbands; Dodwell comments that the gift of a wall hanging depicting Byrhtnoth's deeds must have predated his final battle, having been made earlier and hung in his home, and so available for his widow to give to Ely. The gift, as Dodwell observes,[30] would make Byrhtnoth a Christian martyr, a new twist on the situation discussed here of giving textiles to honor the saintly dead.

In another example of women honoring the dead, the *Liber Eliensis* records that Æthelthryth was a very talented embroideress who made with her own hands a stole and maniple for Cuthbert with gold and gems. Dodwell casts doubt on this assertion because neither Bede nor the anonymous life of Cuthbert mentions this,[31] but given evidence that Bede has elsewhere reduced coverage of female production, Dodwell's doubt need not erase such a skill. Certainly the fact that she could do so is credible and not unlikely, and the writer clearly expected readers to believe the assertion. In addition, women's textiles were from early on part of the economy of gift exchange between important men. When rulers met or negotiated, gift exchange allowed each to affirm his own status while acknowledging another's, facilitating political life. The silent truth about royal textile exchanges, Continentals wanting good woolen cloaks, or requests for English embroidery for a bishop's vestments is that women made such status perceptible and visible, dressing and reinforcing the church and secular elites. As Elizabeth Wayland Barber puts it, "'Clothes make the man'—but women made the clothes."[32]

29. Illustrated in Backhouse, Turner, and Webster, *Golden Age of Anglo-Saxon Art,* cat. no. 140, p. 134.

30. Dodwell, *Anglo-Saxon Art,* pp. 135–36.

31. Dodwell, *Anglo-Saxon Art,* p. 49.

32. E. Barber, *Women's Work,* p. 127.

The best account of how women and shrouds function as an extension of the female roles of recording reputations and in the economy of gift exchange occurs in the Anglo-Saxon prose *Life* of Guthlac. When Guthlac was twenty-four, he gave up his secular life: "And þa æfter þon þæt he ferde to mynstre, þe ys gecweden Hrypadun, and þær þa gerynelican sceare onfeng sce Petres þæs apostoles under Ælfðryðe abbodyssan" (And after that he went to the monastery which is called Repton and there, under Abbess Ælfthryth, received the mystic tonsure of the Apostle St. Peter).[33] A twelfth-century illustration in London, British Library, MS Harley Roll Y6, the so-called Guthlac Roll, illustrates this scene (fig. 3). The abbess is at least as large as the bishop, and in an interesting reversal, she is mentioned in the *Life*'s account while the male bishop is not. But the role of women in establishing Guthlac's cult as a saint emerges at the end of his life. Having earned a reputation as a holy hermit, Guthlac attracts attention:

> 18. *Be Ecgburhe abbodyssan.* Swylce eac gelamp sume siþe, þæt seo arwyrðe fæmne Ecgburh abbodysse, Aldwulfes dohtor þæs cyninges, sende þam arwurðan were Guðlace leadene þruh and þær scytan to, and hine halsode þurh þone halgan naman þæs upplican kyninges, þæt æfter his forðfore man his lichaman moste ingesettan.
>
> (*Concerning Abbess Ecgburh.* It also happened on one occasion that the venerable virgin, Abbess Ecgburh, the daughter of King Aldwulf [king of the East Anglians 663–713], sent a lead coffin, and a shroud for it, to the venerable Guthlac, and entreated him through the holy name of the Heavenly king, that after his death they should put his body in it.)[34]

Later, when he falls ill just before Easter, he tells brother Beccel that when he is dead, Beccel must find his sister Pega:

> and hi bidde, þæt heo minne lichaman on þa þruh gesette, and mid þære scytan bewinde, þe me Ecgburh onsende. Nolde ic þa hwile, þe ic leofode, mid linenum hrægle gegyred beon, ac nu for lufan þære Cristes fæmnan þa gife, þe heo me sende, ic wylle to þon don, þe ic heold: þonne se lichama and seo sawul

---

33. Gonser, *Das angelsächsische Prosa-Leben*, Kap. 2, lines 78–80, p. 111. Translation from Swanton, *Anglo-Saxon Prose*, p. 43.

34. Gonser, *Das angelsächsische Prosa-Leben*, Kap. 18, lines 1–6, p. 158. Translation from Swanton, *Anglo-Saxon Prose*, p. 57.

hi todæleð, þæt man þone lichaman mid þam hrægle bewinde
and on þa þruh gelecge.

(And bid her set my body in the coffin, and wrap me in the
shroud that Ecgburh sent me. I would not be dressed in linen
clothing while I lived, but now for the love of Christ's virgin I
will put the gift she sent me to the use for which I kept it. When
body and soul part, let them wrap the body in that garment,
and lay it in the coffin.)[35]

Guthlac in life preserves a separation of male and female in his
instructions, even with his blood sister; here the separation is transcended
after death, and the shroud signifies this shift in the status of the physical. The shrouding of his body becomes an entirely spiritual act for him,
representing the change from life to death to rebirth, and he requires this
ritual recognition from his sister. Pega's reaction to his death encompasses
both the expected one of sibling and the recognition of her role as bodily
keeper now that he is dead. She swoons, sighs, prays:

Hi þa þan æfteran dæge æfter þam bebode þæs eadigan weres,
hi becomon to þam eglande, and hi ealle þa stowe and þa hus
þær gemetton mid ambrosie þære wyrte swetnysse gefylde.
Heo þa þone halgan wer on þreora daga fæce mid halgum lof-
sangum gode bebead, and on þam þriddan dæge, swa se godes
wer bebead, hig þone lichaman on cyrcan mid arwurðnysse
bebyrgdon.

(Then on the following day, according to the instruction of the
blessed man, they came to the island and there they found all
that place and the building filled with the fragrance of the herb
ambrosia. Then for a period of three days she commended the
holy man to God with holy hymns, and on the third day, as the
man of God had instructed, they buried the body with honor
in the chapel.)[36]

Worth noting here is the fact that Pega seems to lead the prayers and
hymns in honor of her brother and, as the one chosen by Guthlac, directs
the disposition of the body and its burial in the earth. In the Guthlac
Roll, illustrations show Pega getting into the boat to travel to the island
and, more importantly, holding the shrouded body's head and shoulders

35. Gonser, *Das angelsächsische Prosa-Leben*, Kap. 20, lines 62–68, p. 164. Translation
from Swanton, *Anglo-Saxon Prose*, p. 59.

36. Gonser, *Das angelsächsische Prosa-Leben*, Kap. 20, lines 128–34, pp. 167–68. Translation from Swanton, *Anglo-Saxon Prose*, pp. 60–61.

as Guthlac is placed in his coffin (fig. 4). (Alternatively, this illustration could depict the second burial within the church.) A year later, clearly still in charge, Pega decides to remove, or translate, Guthlac's body to a more honorable place; the text is clear in saying that God gave her the idea, so clearly her status and right to act as she does is sanctioned. Her assessment of how and when to proceed guides the initiation of Guthlac's cult:

> Heo þa þyder togesomnode godes þeowa and mæssepreosta and oþre cyrclice endebyrdnysse, þæt þy ylcan dæge þæs ymbe twelf monað, þe seo forðfore þæs eadigan weres wæs, hi þa þa byrgene untyndon. Þa gemetton hi þone lichaman ealne an-sundne, swa he ær wæs, and þa gyt lifigende wære, and on liþo-bignyssum and on eallum þingum, þæt he wæs slæpendum men gelicra myccle þonne forðferedum, swylce eac þa hrægl þære ylcan niwnysse, þe hig on fruman ymbe þone lichaman gedon wæron. . . . Ða heo þa seo Cristes þeowe Pege þæt geseah, þa wæs heo sona mid gastlicere blisse gefylled, and þa þone hal-gan lichaman mid þære arwurðnysse Cristes lofsangum on oþre scytan bewand, þa Ecgbriht se ancra ær him lifigende to þære ylcan þenunge sende. Swylce eac þa þruh, nalæs þæt hi eft þa on eorðan dydon, ac on gemyndelicre stowe and on arwyrþre hi þa gesetton.

> (Then she gathered together there God's servants and priests and those in ecclesiastical orders, on the same day twelve months after the blessed man had died; and they opened the tomb. Whereupon they found the body as entirely sound as it formerly was, and as though he were still alive; and in the flex-ibility of the joints and in all things it was much more like a sleeping man than a dead one. Moreover the garments were as pristine as when they were first put round the body. . . . Then when Christ's servant Pega saw that, she was immediately filled with spiritual bliss, and then with hymns in honour of Christ wrapped the holy body in another shroud which Ecgberht the hermit had previously sent him, when alive, for the same ser-vice. Moreover, they did not put the coffin back into the earth but they set it in a more memorable and a more honorable place.)[37]

In this extraordinary and detailed account of how a woman directed the disposition of one of England's great saints, Guthlac chooses the Abbess Ecgburh's special gift of a shroud for himself in a fine fabric he gave up

---

37. Gonser, *Das angelsächsische Prosa-Leben*, Kap. 20, lines 142–50, 154–60, pp. 168–69. Translation from Swanton, *Anglo-Saxon Prose*, p. 61.

Figure 1. London, British Library, MS Cotton Claudius B. iv, folio 11r. Top right: a woman and two men shroud Cainan's body. Bottom right: men carry Malaleel's shrouded body. By permission of the British Library.

Figure 2. London, British Library, MS Cotton Claudius B. iv, folio 12r. Top right: a woman and a man sit with Methuselah's shrouded body. Bottom right: women and a man sit mourning by Lamech's shrouded body. By permission of the British Library.

Figure 3. London, British Library, Harley Roll Y6, folio 3, the Guthlac
Roll. At Repton, the bishop tonsures Guthlac as Abbess Ælfthryth looks
on. By permission of the British Library.

Figure 4. London, British Library, Harley Roll Y6, folio 16, the Guthlac Roll. Guthlac's sister Pega supports his shrouded body as Guthlac is placed in his coffin. By permission of the British Library.

during his lifetime, acknowledging both the gift and the judgment of the giver. The shroud may even have been ornamented with embroidery as Cuthbert's was. Pega then is in charge of preparing him for burial, and for initiating an examination of his body a year later, bringing in the male clergy and hierarchy as necessary. Lastly, she reclothes the body in a new shroud, this time the gift of a male hermit (should we see him as a weaver, or as a patron of women?), and presumably the first shroud becomes a relic. At every stage, the judgment and care of women established, confirmed, and enhanced his standing as a saint worthy of veneration.

As stated above, the shroud is both a material veiling for the dead and a signpost that emphasizes the physical as emblem of what is buried beneath. More, it is a surface that allows us to read past it, using the material as a way to the spiritual. But what is also buried and lost is the role women played in conferring and enhancing the status of the dead. Thus the shrouds function as an extension both of the female role of recording male reputations (as seen in "tapestries" of deeds) and of the economy of gift exchange, which frequently traded, literally and figuratively, on women's productions of luxury cloths and embroideries. The gift of a shroud, recorded in *Lives* as the first step in affirming the reputation and status of the dead, establishes women as first patrons of such notables and their legacies; their judgment in making such donations affirms the worth of the dead and lends women a spiritual authority easily missed in the textual accounts. Indeed, such gifts show women to be crucial producers in what may be called the economy of sainthood, in which wrappings become part of the trade in relics and status. The status of the dead, male or female, was confirmed and made visible at the hands of women.

Toward a Definition
of the Irish Monastic Town

John Bradley

It was extremely difficult to keep up any pace over the rocks since they were so unpredictable and so devoid of reason. Their *senselessness* had never so much impressed me. I kept trying to get near the edge of the sea but the rocks kept defeating me, not by malign interest but by sheer muddle, and I kept slipping down slopes into seaweedy pools and confronting black clefts and holes and smooth unclimbable surfaces. I had an intuition of light over the sea and I wanted to be able to look there.

—Iris Murdoch, *The Sea, The Sea*[1]

The term monastic town has achieved a wide currency, replacing "prototown" and "preurban nucleus" in all except theoretical quarters. In large measure this is due to the work of Charles Doherty whose seminal 1985 paper was the first detailed examination of the subject.[2] Several unresolved questions remain, however, notably the issues of what exactly constitutes a monastic town, when did monastic towns begin to emerge, and were they part of a settlement hierarchy that also included "monastic villages." This essay endeavors to address the first two issues and hopes, in the process, to shed some peripheral light on the third.[3]

Christianity came to Ireland from Roman Britain before the fifth century, but it was not until the end of the sixth century that it was accepted throughout the whole island. There were no large nucleated centers in which to establish the initial episcopal sees, and accordingly, the earliest churches were isolated settlements. By the tenth and eleventh centuries, however, some of the larger church sites had acquired urban functions. They were populated centers with a social stratification based upon a literate elite; some were divided into districts and had public buildings, open spaces, and monuments, streets, and marketplaces. These churches

---

1. *The Sea, The Sea* is dedicated to Rosemary Cramp.
2. Doherty, "Monastic Town in Early Medieval Ireland."
3. The claim that "monastic town" is a misleading term "that needs to be excised from our vocabulary" is unconvincing for the reasons pointed out below; see Valante, "Reassessing the Irish 'Monastic Town,'" pp. 17–18.

were closely bound into the local dynastic polity and were the foci for
commerce, education, and administration, in addition to being the main
ceremonial centers, the principal places of refuge, and the major patrons
of art and architecture. Nonetheless, their main aim remained religious,
and the process by which these churches were transformed from hermit-
ages in the sixth century to urban centers in the tenth and eleventh centuries is unclear in many of its details. Some urban functions existed in
the seventh and eighth centuries while others were acquired as a result of
the changing conditions brought on by the arrival of the Vikings in the
ninth and tenth.

Doherty has suggested that the first appearance of these urban functions was connected with social changes in the seventh and eighth centuries.[4] In particular several monasteries found themselves faced with a
dilemma. In origin they had been religious cells set apart from the world
where monks could devote themselves to the contemplative life. From an
early date, however, they also had the function of being refuges and places
of sanctuary. This status not only attracted the sick and the poor, but by
the late seventh century, a mixed population of criminals and offenders
had also begun to settle within or beside the monasteries. The story of
Liabrán of the reed-bed in Adomnán's *Life of Columba*, written ca. 697,
provides one such instance.[5] Liabrán, a member of the Connachta, had
committed murder but had been saved from execution by a wealthy relative in return for pledging lifelong service to his rescuer. Finding, however, that a life of servitude was not to his liking, Liabrán sought refuge at
Iona where he asked to enter the church as a monk. His problem was the
reconciliation of murder and oath-breaking with a life devoted to God.
Columba resolved the problem by imposing a seven-year penance, and
after its completion, he gave Liabrán a highly ornamented sword with
ivory insets to offer his former master as a gift that would release him
from the oath. To its monastic listeners this story was more than simply
an incident in the life of Columba. It was also a parable that provided an
everyday instruction on how to reconcile the sacred with the profane.

The canonical legislation of the early eighth century reflects similar
worries. It speaks disparagingly of monasteries that permitted adulter-
ers, hawkers, jesters, murderers, perjurers, prostitutes, or thieves within
their bounds.[6] In the eyes of the canon lawyers it was improper for abbots

4. Doherty, "Exchange and Trade," p. 71.

5. *Adomnán's Life of Columba*, ed. and trans. Anderson and Anderson (1961), pp. 420–35;
Adomnán, *Life of Columba*, trans. Sharpe, pp. 188–93. On the dating of the *Life*, see ibid., p.
55.

6. Wasserschleben, *Die irische Kanonensammlung*, pp. 176–77: lib. XLIV. cap. 8; Doherty,
"Some Aspects of Hagiography," pp. 301–02; Doherty, "Monastic Town in Early Medieval
Ireland," p. 58.

to allow holy places to be soiled by such persons, and their solution was to restrict access by dividing the site into areas of sanctuary, the *sanctus, sanctior,* and *sanctissimus,* with the most sacred area lying at the core.[7] Others were not so offended by the intrusion of the world into the monastery. Cogitosus, writing ca. 650, shows no sign of moral rectitude in his account of Kildare:

> And who can express in words the exceeding beauty of this church and the countless wonders of that monastic city [*civitas*] we are speaking of, if one may call it a city since it is not encircled by any surrounding wall. And yet, since countless people assemble within it and since a city gets its name from the fact that people congregate there, it is a vast and metropolitan city. In its suburbs [*suburbanis*], which Saint Brigid had marked out by a definite boundary, no human foe or enemy attack is feared; on the contrary, together with all its outlying suburbs [*foris suburbanis*] it is the safest city of refuge in the whole land of the Irish for all fugitives and the treasures of kings are kept there; moreover it is looked upon as the most outstanding on account of its illustrious supremacy. And who can count the different crowds and countless peoples flocking from all the provinces— some for the abundant feasting, others for the healing of their afflictions, others to watch the pageant of the crowds, others with great gifts and offerings—to join in the solemn celebration of the feast of Saint Brigit.[8]

Although what is described here is not a farmstead, it is not a monastic town either. A careful examination of the use of the words *civitas* and *suburbana* has led Cathy Swift to conclude that Cogitosus was describing

> a location in which the church building was surrounded by dwellings of the resident clergy and, at a further remove, by the other, subordinate members of the settlement. These houses were, however, all located within an area of agricultural build-

7. Wasserschleben, *Die irische Kanonensammlung,* p. 175: lib. XLIV. cap. 5 and note e; Doherty, "Monastic Town in Early Medieval Ireland," pp. 58–59.

8. The best text of Cogitosus is generally regarded (see Esposito, "On the Earliest Latin Life of St Brigid," p. 308; Kenney, *Sources for the Early History of Ireland,* p. 359) as the Trèves (now Bibliothèque nationale de France, Paris) text edited by Bolland et al., *Acta Sanctorum,* p. 141, translated by Connolly and Picard, "Cogitosus: Life of Brigit," pp. 26–27. A second text (from St-Amand-les-Eaux, now at Cambrai) was edited by Colgan in his *Triadis Thaumaturgae,* pp. 523–24, and it formed the basis of the fluent translation by de Paor, *St Patrick's World,* pp. 223–24. Although the differences between the texts are slight, they are topographically significant. For the date of Cogitosus's Life, see Connolly, "Cogitosus's Life of Brigit," p. 5.

ings, fields, trees, ponds and pastures and there is no evidence
of a more clustered environment of the type envisaged for the
tenth and eleventh century monastic towns.[9]

The presence of criminals and fugitives almost certainly provided an
impetus to local trade and exchange. The existence of a trading network
in the seventh century into which the ecclesiastical sites were integrated is
evident from the discovery on habitation sites of this period of sherds of
pottery imported from southwestern France.[10] Among the excavations on
which sherds have been recovered are Derrynaflan (Co. Tipperary), Inis-
caltra (Co. Clare), Nendrum (Co. Down), and Reask (Co. Kerry).[11]

From the eighth century the secularization of Irish church sites increased significantly.[12] Hereditary succession to abbacies is found at Lusk
and Slane by the mid-eighth century.[13] Warfare between monasteries is
first evidenced in 760 when Clonmacnoise and Birr fought a pitched battle.[14] Four years later there was a major clash between Clonmacnoise and
Durrow in which two hundred Durrow men died, and by the end of the
eighth century, it was not uncommon for monasteries to engage in secular wars.[15] The worldly quality of saints' lives is increasingly apparent
from the ninth century while the development of vernacular literature is
a feature of monasteries during the Viking Age.[16] The mixture of sanctity
and secularity is clearly seen in the cult of relics, which developed from
around the middle of the seventh century when there are references to
enshrined relics at Armagh and Kildare.[17] Theologically the cult was sus-
pect because it bordered on superstition and idolatry, but church doctrine
justified it on the grounds that it helped and encouraged people to imi-

9. Swift, "Forts and Fields," p. 113. Valante's statement, "Reassessing the Irish 'Monastic Town,'" p. 8, that "*civitas* was used by the Irish to refer to a place with a bishop, whether
that place was urban . . . or not" is incorrect; see Swift, "Forts and Fields," pp. 112–14.

10. Thomas, "Imported Pottery"; Thomas, "Imported Late-Roman Mediterranean
Pottery"; Thomas, *Provisional List of Imported Pottery;* Thomas, "'Gallici nautae de galliarum provinciis'"; K. Dark, *External Contacts and the Economy;* Knight, *End of Antiquity,* pp.
147–65; but see E. Campbell, "E-ware and Aquitaine," pp. 35–38.

11. See the summaries of excavations listed by site name in *MA* 30 (1986), p. 187; *Excavations 1974,* p. 11; Thomas, "Imported Pottery," p. 109; Fanning, "Excavation of an Early
Christian Settlement at Reask," pp. 113–15.

12. Hughes, "Sanctity and Secularity."

13. Hughes, *Church in Early Irish Society,* pp. 161–64; see also Ó Corráin, "Early Irish
Churches," pp. 327–33.

14. Hughes, *Church in Early Irish Society,* pp. 169–70.

15. Hughes, *Church in Early Irish Society,* pp. 170–72.

16. Hughes, "Sanctity and Secularity," pp. 27–28, 32–33; Hughes, *Church in Early Irish
Society,* pp. 230–34; Kenney, *Sources for the Early History of Ireland,* pp. 10–16.

17. Doherty, "Use of Relics in Early Ireland," pp. 92–94.

tate the lives of the saints. To the vast majority of the faithful and, indeed, to many churchmen, it was the miraculous power of relics that made them so important. To the church they were a source of prestige and income as well as spiritual authority. By contrast, secular society held relics in awe: oaths were sworn upon them; they were carried into battle; they were used as insignia of rank; and they lent prestige to abbots on circuit.[18] On such circuits and at the promulgation of saints' laws (*cána*) the display of the enshrined relics was in effect little more than a means of intimidating those who might be reluctant to pay tribute to the church.[19]

FAIRS AND MARKETS

All of these features emphasize the close links that had developed between churches and lay society before the Viking Age. Indeed, they had become so intertwined that the two were virtually indistinguishable. The first reference to a fair at an ecclesiastical site occurs in 800 when the king of South Brega was thrown from his horse and killed at the fair in Lusk on the feast of its patron saint, MacCuilinn.[20] The usual occasion for trade in early Ireland was the *oenach* or fair, generally held at the border of territories, on neutral ground, where peace was assured by the invocation of the saints and the ceremonial gift exchange of kings. It was at once a political assembly, a market fair, and an occasion for races and entertainment. One of the best known of these fairs was the *Oenach Carmain* held near the border of the modern counties of Carlow and Kildare. It had three markets: the market of food, the market of livestock, and the great market of the "Greek foreigners," where gold and fine clothing could be obtained.[21] Fighting, quarreling, theft, and misconduct were prohibited, and peace was guaranteed by the king of Leinster as well as by the invocation of Saints Patrick, Brigid, Kevin, and Colomba.

By the ninth century some monasteries had taken over the function of the *oenach*. The *oenach* of Lynally (Co. Offaly) is mentioned in a text that has been assigned to the end of that century, while the *oenach* of Domh-

---

18. Doherty, "Use of Relics in Early Ireland," pp. 99–100; Lucas, "Social Role of Relics and Reliquaries," pp. 13–27.

19. Hughes, *Church in Early Irish Society*, pp. 167–68; Lucas, "Social Role of Relics and Reliquaries," pp. 14–17.

20. *In circio ferie filii Cuilinn Luscan*, trans. in *AU*, 1:283, as "on the festival of Mac Cuilinn of Lusca," and in Mac Niocaill and Mac Airt, *Annals of Ulster*, p. 255, as "around the feast of MacCuilinn of Lusca." Doherty, "Exchange and Trade," p. 81, pointed out that *circius* (Hiberno-Latin for *circus*) is one of the Latin words used to gloss *oenach*, but see Valante, "Reassessing the Irish 'Monastic Town,'" p. 11, who expresses doubts on this derivation.

21. E. Gwynn, *Metrical Dindshenchas*, 3:2–25; see also Doherty, "Exchange and Trade," pp. 81–84; Byrne, *Irish Kings and High-kings*, pp. 30–31.

nach Sechnaill (Dunshaughlin, Co. Meath) is mentioned in the *vita tripar-tita*, written ca. 830.[22] The same source states that the Oenach Macha at Armagh was marked by a northern and southern cross,[23] and it has been suggested that the crosses outside the monasteries at Armagh, Kells, and Glendalough marked the site of marketplaces.[24] Similar monastic fairs were held at Clonmacnoise, Glendalough, and Roscrea.[25] The word *margad* appears to have been borrowed into Irish in the tenth century from Latin *mercatus* through Old Norse *markaðr,* and the word is used to describe the marketplaces in the Scandinavian towns of Limerick and Dublin.[26] The existence of a similar feature at Kells and Cashel in the early twelfth century is indicated by references to *margad Cenanndsa,* "the market place of Kells," and *margad Caisil,* "the market place of Cashel."[27] The tenth-century cross that stood until recently in the marketplace of Kells may be the same as the "cross of *dorus urdoimh,*" literally "the cross of the entrance door," mentioned in 1156, since it is located at the eastern entrance to the monastery.[28] In this regard it parallels the description of the market cross at Armagh as the "cross of the gate of the rath."[29] The regularity of such fairs and markets, however, is unknown. In early Ireland the *oenach* tended to be an annual event, which, when taken over by the church, was celebrated on the patron's feastday. Markets may have been held more frequently. There are few references to buying and selling at monasteries, but cattle are known to have been sold at the marketplace of Kells, and in the twelfth-century satire known as the *Aislinge meic Conglinne,* the student sells *(recaid)* his possessions for wheaten cakes and ham at Roscommon before embarking on his journey to Cork.[30] In both cases what occurred

22. Doherty, "Exchange and Trade," pp. 81–84, quoting K. Meyer, *Triads of Ireland,* p. 5; see also Plummer, *Bethada Náem nÉrenn,* 1:174, cap. 25; Stokes, *Tripartite Life of Patrick,* 2:394–95.

23. Stokes, *Tripartite Life of Patrick,* 1:238–39; see also *ALC,* sub anno 1021. The town-land name of Enagh, immediately southwest of Armagh, probably derives from *oenach;* see also *ALC,* sub anno 1103.

24. Swan, "Monastic Proto-towns in Early Medieval Ireland," p. 99.

25. Plummer, *Bethada Náem nÉrenn,* 1:178, cap. 30; ibid., 1:144–45; 2:140–41; Todd, *Cogadh Gaedhel re Gallaibh,* pp. 14–15.

26. *AI,* sub anno 1108; *AU,* sub anno 1171; Doherty, "Exchange and Trade," p. 83.

27. Mac Niocaill, *Notitiae as Leabhar Cheanannais,* no. iv (dated 1106x1153); *CS,* sub anno 1130; *A. Tig.,* sub anno 1134.

28. Roe, *High-crosses of Kells,* pp. 26–43; *AFM,* sub anno 1156. Excavations on the site of the cross revealed nothing earlier than the seventeenth century (Heather King, pers. comm.). The cross may have been moved to the other side of the street, however, when it was reerected by Robert Balfe in 1688.

29. *AU,* 2:152 (*crois doruis Ratha*); see also Swan, "Monastic Proto-towns in Early Medi-eval Ireland," p. 99.

30. Mac Niocaill, *Notitiae as Leabhar Cheanannais,* p. 20; K. Meyer, *Vision of Mac Con-glinne,* pp. 8–9; Jackson, *Aislinge meic Con Glinne,* p. 4.

may have been an exchange, but indications of the use of coins at church sites are provided by coin finds of tenth- to twelfth-century date at Ardagh (Co. Longford), Armagh, Clondalkin (Co. Dublin), Clonmacnoise (Co. Offaly), Durrow (Co. Offaly), Glasnevin (Co. Dublin), Glendalough (Co. Wicklow), Kilcullen (Co. Kildare), Kildare, Kilkenny, Monasterboice (Co. Louth), Mungret (Co. Limerick), and Rahan (Co. Offaly).[31]

INTERNAL DIVISIONS

The canonical legislation of the early eighth century divided the monastery into areas of *sanctus, sanctior,* and *sanctissimus:*

> There ought to be two or three termini around a holy place: the first in which we allow no one at all to enter except priests, because laymen do not come near it, nor women unless they are clerics; the second, into its streets the crowds of common people, not much given to wickedness, we allow to enter; the third, in which men who have been guilty of homicide, adulterers and prostitutes, with permission and according to custom, we do not prevent from going within. Whence they are called, the first *sanctissimus,* the second *sanctior,* the third *sanctus,* bearing honour according to their differences.[32]

It is clear from fieldwork that these divisions were more than mere clerical pretension and had a physical reality.[33] At Killabuonia (Co. Kerry) the surviving remains consist of three terraces set into the hillslope.[34] The oratory and a shrine-shaped tomb with an adjacent cross-pillar are on the upper terrace. This was revetted with a carefully built wall of horizontal coursing and upright slabs and was approached from below by a flight of steps. On the middle terrace are two beehive huts and the foundations of two rectangular structures aligned north–south. Below this, the large lower terrace is devoid of remains except for a plain stone cross and a well. The evidence at this site suggests that the most sacred area was the oratory terrace and that the principal dwelling and working area was on

31. Hall, "Check-list of Viking-Age Coin Finds"; Blackburn and Pagan, "Revised Check-list of Coin Hoards."

32. Doherty, "Monastic Town in Early Medieval Ireland," pp. 58–59, quoting the unpublished translation by Sheehy of Wasserschleben, *Die irische Kanonensammlung,* p. 175: lib. XLIV. cap. 5, note e; see also MacDonald, "Aspects of the Monastery and Monastic Life," pp. 295–96.

33. Herity, "Buildings and Layout of Early Irish Monasteries"; Herity, "Layout of Irish Early Christian Monasteries," pp. 105–13.

34. F. Henry, "Early Monasteries, Beehive Huts and Dry-stone Houses," pp. 101–04.

the middle terrace, while the absence of buildings on the lower terrace indicates that it was unlikely to have been used as an area of worship. At Nendrum, the surviving remains are arranged within three concentric enclosures.[35] The church, a round tower, the foundations of a rectangular building, and a large cemetery of lintel-graves were located within the inner enclosure; four beehive huts, one of which was used for metalworking, and a rectangular building (called "the school" by its excavator) lay within the middle enclosure; while the large outer enclosure was devoid of stone structures except for some fragments of cross-walls. Again the impression conveyed by the layout of this site is one of *sanctissimus* (inner enclosure), *sanctior* (middle enclosure), and *sanctus* (outer enclosure). Excavations at Dunmisk (probably the ancient *Domnach Mescáin,* Co. Tyrone) revealed that the site was divided internally into four functional areas. Heavy metalworking was concentrated in the southwest quadrant and fine metalworking, glassworking, and glassmaking in the northeast one. The northwest quadrant was primarily domestic while the southeast was the ecclesiastical and religious zone.[36]

An analysis of twelve of the more important monasteries, including Armagh, Kells, and Kildare, has shown a consistent arrangement of features within the roughly circular or elliptical ecclesiastical boundary.[37] In general, the sites had both an inner and an outer enclosure, the inner of which contained the most important ecclesiastical buildings as well as the burial ground. In those cases where the evidence survived, the entrance was located toward the east and was marked by a special cross that, at Armagh and Kells, was the focus for the marketplace. The positioning of the main structures, in both their orientation and relationship to each other, was found to be an orderly one, and the regularity of the layout suggested that the sites were designed in conformity with an accepted pattern.[38]

Evidence for the existence of internal divisions is also found in the documentary sources. The layout of Derry was reorganized in 1162 when a stone enclosure (*caisil in erláir*) was built *errscardugh na taighi ó thempluibh* (to totally separate the houses from the churches; *AU,* sub anno 1162). In the course of these works, which also involved the rebuilding of the cathedral, eighty houses were demolished (*AU, AFM*). In general these internal divisions are referred to in the annals as *ráth* or *trian. Ráth* implies an enclosure, which appears from the contexts to have contained the princi-

---

35. Lawlor, *Monastery of St Mochaoi.*
36. J. Henderson, "Nature of the Early Christian Glass Industry"; Ivens, "Dunmisk Fort, Carrickmore, Co. Tyrone," pp. 57–61.
37. Swan, "Monastic Proto-towns in Early Medieval Ireland."
38. Swan, "Monastic Proto-towns in Early Medieval Ireland," p. 100; *AU,* sub anno 1166.

pal churches and cemeteries at the core of the monastery. *Trian*, literally "a third," seems to have had much the same meaning as French *quartier*, that is, a precinct. The existence of such a precinct at Cork is indicated by the death in 908 of Ailill mac Eógan, monastic superior (*princeps*) of the *trian* of Cork, at the battle of Belach Mugna (*AU*, sub anno 907; *AFM*). In 1082, the eastern *trian* of Clonmacnoise was burned (*AFM*); in 1111, Downpatrick was burned by lightning "both *ráth* and *trian*" (*AU*), while the destruction in 1020 of *tertia parte Sord Coluim Cille* (Swords, Co. Dublin) may indicate another monastery that was divided into *triana*.[39] The most extensive documentation survives in relation to Armagh where the *triana* are specified by name. The *trian mór* (great precinct) is first mentioned in 1009 (*AU*); the *trian Saxan* (English precinct) and *trian mór* are referred to in 1092 when both were burned (*AU, AFM, ALC*); while the first mention of the *trian massain* (middle precinct) occurs in 1112 when it was burned together with the *ráth* and *trian mór*.[40] The annals frequently use the word *leth*, "half," in relation to ecclesiastical sites without attributing any spatial significance to it, but the word *lár*, "center," may well signify the inner enclosure.[41]

HOUSES AND WORKSHOPS

By the eighth century a range of domestic structures existed within monastic sites. The *magna domus* was a large building used for assembly

39. *AU, ALC*. The burning of a third part (*tertia parte*) of Clonmacnoise in 818 (*AU*, sub anno 817) and again in 835 (*AU*, sub anno 834) may indicate that the *triana* were already in existence by the early years of the ninth century.

40. *AU, AFM, ALC, A. Tig.* Other references to the *triana* of Armagh occur in 1074 (*AU, AFM, ALC*), 1121 (*trian massain* and *trian Saxan: AU*); 1150 (*trian mór: AFM*); 1170 (*trian mór: AU, ALC*); 1173 (*trian mór: AU, AFM, ALC*); and 1189 (*AU, AFM, ALC*). Considering the number of structures that were located within it, it is likely that the *ráth* of Armagh was internally subdivided. The eighth-century *Liber angeli*, for instance, contrasts *in australi bassilica* (the southern basilica) at Armagh with *in aeclessia aquilonalis plagae* (the church of the northern district); see Bieler, *Patrician Texts in the Book of Armagh*, pp. 186–87. See also Hughes, *Church in Early Irish Society*, p. 277, where *plaga* is translated as "quarter." An entry in *AU* and *AFM* for 1091 states that the western half of the *ráth* was burned while the same entry in *ALC* refers to it as the southern half. The possible presence of smaller enclosures is hinted at by the entry of 1195, which states that part of the rath (*ráthaibh*) at Armagh was burned (*ALC*).

41. Kuno Meyer translated *in-descertleth Chorccaige* as "in the southern quarter of Cork" in his edition of *The Vision of Mac Conglinne*, pp. 20–21, but the simpler "on the south side" was preferred by Jackson, *Aislinge meic Con Glinne*, p. 180, glossary under *leth 1*. Other occurrences of *leth* include *Leath Daimhliag Chianáin* (*AFM*: 1149), *Leath Termainn Feichin* (*AFM*: 1149), *Leth iartharach do ráith Arda Macha* (*AU, AFM*: 1091), *Cill-dara dimidia parte cremata est* (*ALC*: 1099).

purposes that also accommodated a number of indoor activities including teaching, reading, and writing.[42] The refectory and kitchen may have
shared a common roof in the earliest monasteries, but they eventually
developed into separate buildings.[43] At Armagh, by 1020, the library was
housed in a structure of its own (*AFM*, sub anno 1020). The sleeping quarters of the seniors (or elders) consisted of individual apartments set apart
from the communal dormitories of the monks,[44] while the guesthouse and
abbot's house were also present.[45] In the course of the tenth and eleventh centuries the abbot's house, which was normally under lay control,
seems to have acquired almost seigneurial attributes. The abbot's house
at Armagh is referred to in 823 as *forad,* a word usually used to describe
an enclosed mound. It is subsequently described as lying within its own
earthen enclosure, and the annalistic reference to its destruction by fire
in 1116 implies that it was a substantial dwelling.[46]

By the tenth century, however, it is clear that, apart from these essentially monastic structures, ordinary dwelling houses were to be found
at monasteries, and Armagh is one of the best-documented sites in this
regard. In 912 the *Annals of Ulster* record the burning of many houses
"in the *ráth* of Armagh through carelessness"; in 996 the round towers,
churches, houses, and the sacred grove (*fidh-neimhedh*) of Armagh were
burned.[47] The entry in the *Annals of Inisfallen* relating to this event provides the additional piece of information that not only were houses burned,
but also that the houses of the elders (*na tech srotha*) within the *ráth* were
destroyed. In 1020, houses in the *ráth* and the *triana* were burned (*AFM, A.
Tig.*), while in 1090 one hundred houses were destroyed around *Na Ferta,*
the eastern suburb of Armagh (*AU*). Other monastic sites referred to during the eleventh century include Kildare where only one house survived a
fire that had started as a result of lightning in 1019 (*AFM*, sub anno 1018;
A. Clon., sub anno 1012). Fires burned both houses and churches at Kells

---

42. MacDonald, "Aspects of the Monastery and Monastic Life," p. 285; MacDonald,
"Notes on Monastic Archaeology," pp. 310–11.

43. MacDonald, "Aspects of the Monastery and Monastic Life," p. 285; MacDonald,
"Notes on Monastic Archaeology," p. 311. An insight into what some of these buildings
may have been like is provided by the excavations at Hamage in northern France, where
seventh-century round houses and an eighth-century communal structure have been discovered on a site almost certainly founded by Irish monks; see Louis, "Aux débuts du monachisme en Gaule du Nord"; Louis, "'Sorores ac fratres in Hamatico degentes,'" esp. p. 32.

44. MacDonald, "Aspects of the Monastery and Monastic Life," p. 287.

45. MacDonald, "Aspects of the Monastery and Monastic Life," p. 287; MacDonald,
"Notes on Monastic Archaeology," pp. 310–11.

46. *AU,* sub annis 822, 1116; MacDonald, "Notes on Monastic Archaeology," p. 310.

47. *AU,* sub anno 911; *AFM,* sub anno 995; *CS,* sub anno 994; *A. Tig.,* sub anno 995.

in 1060 (*AFM*), Glendalough in 1061,[48] Ardpatrick in 1074 (*AI*), and Cork in 1081 (*AFM*). In 1082 houses in the churchyard of the nuns at Clonmacnoise were burnt (*A. Clon.*, sub anno 1080).

These notices increase during the twelfth century when houses are mentioned in passing at Ardagh (*AFM*, sub anno 1137), Ardstraw (*AFM*, sub anno 1179), Armagh (*A. Tig.*, *AFM*, sub anno 1166), Cloyne (*AFM*, sub anno 1137), Derry (*Misc. Irish A.*, sub anno 1135; *AFM*, sub anno 1177), Devenish (*Misc. Irish A.*, sub anno 1157), Emly (*AU, AFM, ALC*, sub anno 1123), Kells,[49] Killaloe (*AFM*, sub anno 1185), Lismore (*Misc. Irish. A.*, sub anno 1157), Louth (*AFM*, sub anno 1164), Ratass (*Misc. Irish A.*, sub anno 1136), Roscommon (*AFM*, sub anno 1135), and Slane (*AU*, sub anno 1161). Attention is also focused for the first time on the numbers of houses. At Armagh, in 1116, the great house of the abbots and twenty houses around it were burned (*AU, AFM, ALC*); seventy or eighty houses were burned at Duleek in 1123 (*AU, AFM, ALC*, sub anno 1123; *CS*, sub anno 1119); eighty houses were destroyed in the remodeling of Derry in 1162 (*AU, AFM*); one hundred and five houses were burned at Clonmacnoise in 1179 (*AFM*); while in 1184 thirty houses were destroyed at Armagh in a plundering raid by the Anglo-Normans of Meath (*AU, AFM, ALC*).

There is little information on the occupants of these houses but a considerable number would have been clerics, lay monks, and students. The king of Fer Mag Ita and Cenél Ennai was killed in the house of a cleric at Derry in 1177 (*AU*), while the thirty houses burned at Armagh in 1184 belonged to "do maithibh muinnterí Arda Macha" (the principal members of the community of Armagh; *AU, ALC*), a description that recalls "na tech srotha" (the houses of the elders) destroyed inside the *ráth* of Armagh in 996 (*AI*). Students also lived in houses as the annalistic reference to the destruction at Armagh in 1020 of "taighibh na mac Léighinn" (the houses of the students) indicates,[50] and it has been suggested that one of the major reasons for the growth of monasteries into urban centers was the influx of large numbers of students.[51]

It is clear, however, that clerics and students were not the only ones to live in these centers. The account of the destruction of the *baile* at Clonmacnoise in 1178 specifically states that the houses belonging to the bishop (presumably the ecclesiastical properties) were excluded from pillage by the Anglo-Normans, implying that the secular properties alone were targeted (*AFM*). Some houses belonged to the lay keepers of shrines. In 1127, for instance, the house of Flann mac Sinach in the *trian Saxan* of

48. *AI.* An earlier reference to a house at Clonmacnoise occurs in 1035: *A. Tig.*
49. *AFM*, sub anno 1156; Mac Niocaill, *Notitiae as Leabhar Cheanannais*, passim.
50. *AFM;* Ó Fiaich, "Church of Armagh under Lay Control," pp. 113–14.
51. F. Henry, *Irish Art during the Viking Invasions*, p. 39.

Armagh was stormed by the Airthir (*AU, ALC*). Flann was a member of the powerful Clann Sinaich family, which provided hereditary lay abbots for Armagh from 965 until 1134, and he himself was the keeper of the *Bachall Íosa*.[52] According to Reeves, the keeper of the Book of Armagh (*Canóin Pádraig*) also had his house in the *trian Saxan*,[53] and further evidence that the custodians of shrines lived in individual houses is indicated by the destruction of the *Bearnán Ailbhe* in 1123 when a house was burned at Emly (*ALC*). Property-owning craftsmen are known to have lived at Kells in the late eleventh and early twelfth centuries. The craftsman MacAedh, whose relative may have made the shrine of the Cathach, sold a "half-house" (*leth lainded*, perhaps a workshop) there sometime between 1117 and ca. 1131.[54] Metalworkers were attached to monasteries from early times, and archaeological evidence for workshops capable of manufacturing fine metalwork has been found at a number of sites including Armagh, Clonmacnoise, Downpatrick, Moville, and Nendrum.[55] A small part (perhaps five percent) of the eastern domestic zone at Clonmacnoise has been excavated, and five buildings dating to the ninth or tenth centuries were uncovered.[56] There were two round houses, one with a diameter of 7 meters, and three D-shaped structures that presumably had ancillary functions, together with associated yards, boundary fences, wells, and refuse pits. The largest D-shaped structure measured 10.5 by 4 meters. There was evidence for a range of craftworking activities including bronzeworking, goldworking, ironworking, jet-bracelet manufacture, comb making, and the remains of an antler workshop.

Documentary evidence for the presence of craftsmen is provided by the eleventh-century account of the death, in 909, of Cerball mac Muirecáin, king of Leinster, at Kildare when he was thrown from his horse opposite a comb-maker's workshop.[57] Antler working, and specifically comb making, were urban crafts in the northern European world of the ninth to twelfth centuries,[58] and such residents were perceived at the time as forming part

52. Ó Fiaich, "Church of Armagh under Lay Control," pp. 82–95; *AFM*, sub anno 1135.

53. Reeves, *Ancient Churches of Armagh*, pp. 19–20.

54. Mac Niocaill, *Notitiae as Leabhar Cheanannais*, no. vi; O'Meadhra, *Early Christian, Viking and Romanesque Art*, 2:164–65.

55. M. Ryan, "Fine Metalworking and Early Irish Monasteries," pp. 40–43.

56. See the summaries of excavations in *Excavations 1990*, p. 49; ibid. *1991*, pp. 40–41; ibid. *1992*, pp. 53–54; ibid. *1993*, pp. 66–67; ibid. *1994*, pp. 74–75; ibid. *1995*, pp. 76–77; ibid. *1996*, pp. 93–94; ibid. *1997*, p. 149; ibid. *1998*, pp. 174–75.

57. Radner, *Fragmentary Annals of Ireland*, p. 167; see also Doherty, "Monastic Town in Early Medieval Ireland," p. 67. Antler tines were discovered near St. Canice's Cathedral, Kilkenny, suggesting the presence of craftsmen there, *Jnl. of the Kilkenny and South-east of Ireland Archaeological Society* 63 (1864–66), 411–12.

58. Nicholson, "The Antler," p. 474.

of a distinctive community. This is hinted at by MacFirbishigh's use of
the word "townsmen" in his seventeenth-century translation of the now
lost *Annals of Clonmacnoise* when describing the killing of one hundred
and seventy of the occupants of Kildare in 1132 (*A. Clon.*, sub anno 1135).
Writing fifty years later, in the 1180s, Giraldus Cambrensis used the word
cives to describe what were almost certainly much the same people.[59] From
the one group of early twelfth-century charters that survives, it is clear
that the community at Kells consisted of clergy and laity, freemen and
strangers.[60]

There was an increasing tendency to locate royal houses at monasteries during the eleventh and twelfth centuries, although it is possible that
this practice may have begun earlier.[61] The Ua Loingsigh lords of Dál
nAraidi had a house in Antrim by 1030 (*AU*); the kings of Mide were living at Duleek in 1123 and had houses at Clonard and Durrow a few years
later;[62] the Mac Carthaig kings of Desmond had a house at Lismore in
1164 (*Misc. Irish A.*); and in the same year, Donnchad Ua Cerbaill, king
of Airghialla, is known to have had a residence at Louth (*AFM*). By 1169,
the Mac Gilla Pátraic kings of Osraige had a house at Kilkenny that they
occupied when in residence, but that was otherwise maintained by a stew-
ard.[63] In 1164, Toirdelbach Ua Conchobair constructed a *caislén ingantach* (wonderful castle) at Tuam (*A. Tig.*). The language used to describe
this structure and Mac Murchada's residence at Ferns indicates that these
were more elaborate buildings than normal royal houses.[64] There are
many notices in the annals of the deaths of kings at church sites, but it is
unknown whether they died at their own houses or not. Nonetheless, the

59. O'Meara, "Giraldus Cambrensis in Topographia Hibernie," p. 151, unaddressed
in the comments on Kildare by Valante, "Reassessing the Irish 'Monastic Town,'" p. 15,
where the citation appears to accept Giraldus as an impartial observer on twelfth-century
Ireland. The implication (ibid.) that Kildare was unchartered is incorrect—see Mills, *Calendar of the Justiciary Rolls of Ireland*, p. 174—as is the statement (Valante, "Reassessing the
Irish 'Monastic Town,'" p. 16) that there were no burgesses at Kildare until the end of the
thirteenth century; see Pembroke Estate, *Calendar of Ancient Deeds and Muniments*, p. 11, for
a burgage at Kildare before 1176. Also incorrect is the statement (Valante, "Reassessing the
Irish 'Monastic Town,'" p. 17, quoting Thomas, *Walled Towns of Ireland*, 2:74) that Drogheda
has "an extant burgage charter [*sic*] dating from 1185"; see Mac Iomhair, "Boundaries of
Fir Rois," p. 171, where the grant of Uriel, together with four burgages in Drogheda, was
redated.

60. Mac Niocaill, *Notitiae as Leabhar Cheanannais*, pp. 29–30.

61. The high king Áed Sláine (d. 604) presumably lived at or near Slane.

62. *AU, AFM, ALC*, sub anno 1123; *CS*, sub anno 1119 (Duleek); *A. Clon.*, sub annis 1136
(Clonard), 1153 (Durrow); see also ibid., sub anno 1162.

63. Orpen, *Song of Dermot and the Earl*, lines 1268–1391, especially 1338–44.

64. *A. Tig.*, sub anno 1166; *AFM*, sub anno 1166; *Misc. Irish A.*, sub anno 1165; see Ó
Corráin, "Aspects of Early Irish History," pp. 69–70.

increasing number of such references in the eleventh and twelfth centuries provides further evidence that the monasteries were functioning as central places within Irish society.[65]

There are hints, too, that some members of the twelfth-century population at such sites had the status of burgesses. Burgesses are documented at Dublin in 1121, and the Anglo-Normans regarded Killaloe as a borough prior to their arrival there.[66] The burgage mentioned at Kilkenny before 1176 was almost certainly at the pre-Anglo-Norman settlement of Irishtown,[67] and the same document also mentions burgages at Kildare and Ferns. Lydon has recently pointed out that Diarmait Mac Murchada's grant to the Augustinian priory at Ferns ca. 1158 of "a certain measure called Sciath, out of every measure called a lagen, or gallon, in the brewing of beer made in the town of Ferns" also implies some form of borough organization.[68] Such organization need not have been particularly complex, and the Scottish model may be relevant here. Twelfth-century Scottish burghs were places that had a trading monopoly over the surrounding countryside, and no one could buy or sell except in the marketplace of the burgh where a toll would have to be paid by those who were not the privileged inhabitants known as burgesses.[69] David I (1124–53) founded the first burghs as part of an endeavor to modernize the Scottish economy along the lines already established in England and elsewhere in Western Europe.[70] He deliberately sought out foreign merchants and tradesmen capable of employing new skills and techniques previously unknown in the kingdom.[71] The first burgesses were attracted by the assurance of individual rights and privileges within the burghs and throughout the king's

65. A few examples will suffice: the assassination of Gilla Pátraic mac Domnaill Mac Gilla Pátraic in 1146 *ar lár Cille Caindigh*, "in the middle of Kilkenny," was almost certainly carried out because he was living there, *AFM*, sub anno 1146. Muircertach Ua Ceallaigh, king of Brega, was killed in a house at Slane in 1161 (*AU*); the king of Fordruim was killed in Moville in 1167 (*AU*). There are instances of kings being killed in buildings other than houses: Murchad mac Flann Ua Máel Sechlainn, for instance, the deposed king of Mide, was killed in the round tower of Kells in 1076 (*AFM*), while Domhnall mac Amhlaoibh Ó Maoil Ruanaidh, king of Fer Manach, was burned to death in the round tower of Devenish in 1176 (*Misc. Irish A.*).

66. Bradley, "Killaloe."

67. Bradley, *Kilkenny*, pp. 1 and 4. Since writing the Kilkenny fascicle it has become clear to me that there is no evidence for Anglo-Norman settlement at Kilkenny prior to ca. 1190 and quite likely not until 1199.

68. Lydon, "Dublin in Transition," p. 140, n. 65.

69. MacQueen and Windram, "Laws and Courts in the Burghs," p. 208.

70. MacQueen and Windram, "Laws and Courts in the Burghs," p. 208; Naismith, *Story of Scotland's Towns*, pp. 18–44.

71. MacQueen and Windram, "Laws and Courts in the Burghs," p. 208.

territory.[72] Given the known presence of Englishmen and Scandinavians at the pre-Norman borough of Killaloe, it is likely that the Ua Briain kings were engaged in similar practices.[73] If something analogous was happening at Kilkenny, under the Mac Gilla Pátraic kings, and at Kildare, under Diarmait Mac Murchada, it would explain the presence of burgages at these sites when the Anglo-Normans arrived.

STREETS

Paved pathways were a standard feature of early monasteries, but it is only during the tenth century and later that roads lined with houses and workshops appear to have developed.[74] The death in 909 of Cerball mac Muirecáin, king of Leinster, is described as having occurred when he rode eastward into Kildare past the workshop of a comb-maker *ar fud sráite in chéime chloichi*, "along the street of the stone step."[75] The stone step may have been a curb or a terrace on which the workshops were built, but it is more likely that it was an edging to the street similar to that found in the excavations at Clonmacnoise.[76] This account of Cerball's death, however, is not a contemporary one although it derives from earlier sources. It was written down in the 1030s and it indicates that by that time the phenomenon of a street with workshops had developed at church sites.

The annals use three words to describe a street: *sreth, sráid,* and *clochán. Sreth* simply means a row, and in the context of Armagh to which its use is largely confined, it seems to mean a row of buildings.[77] The word *sreth* makes its first appearance in 1092 when a street (*sreth*) in the *trian mór* and another in the *trian Saxan* were burned (*AFM*). A range of annalistic references, already cited, indicates that the *triana* were residential areas. Whether these streets had developed at Armagh since the destruction of 1020 or not is unknown, but the use of a new word suggests that a new feature had appeared in the monastery. In 1112, two streets were burned

72. MacQueen and Windram, "Laws and Courts in the Burghs," p. 208.

73. Bradley, "Killaloe."

74. There are indications from the excavations at Clonmacnoise that these developments may have commenced in the ninth century; see below. The word *platea*, which occurs in eighth-century canonical legislation, has been translated as "street," but "open space" is preferable. Compare Doherty, "Monastic Town in Early Medieval Ireland," pp. 58–59, with MacDonald, "Aspects of the Monastery and Monastic Life," pp. 293–97, and Swift, "Forts and Fields," pp. 110–12.

75. Radner, *Fragmentary Annals of Ireland*, pp. 166–67, and see the comments of Doherty, "Monastic Town in Early Medieval Ireland," p. 67.

76. King, "Excavations at Clonmacnoise."

77. *Dictionary of the Irish Language*, S, cols. 370–71; but see *AU*, where it is translated as "stretch," sub annis 1112, 1121.

in *trian massain* and one in *trian mór* (*AU, AFM*), and in 1121, two streets in *trian massain*, described as running from the rath entrance to Brigit's Cross, were also burned (*AU, AFM*). In 1166, the *Annals of Ulster* describe the destruction of Armagh "from the Cross of Colum-cille, the two streets [*sreith*] to the Cross of Bishop Eógan, and from the Cross of Bishop Eógan one of the two streets, up to the Cross of the door of the Close [*ráth*] and all the Close with its churches—except the monastery of [SS] Paul and *Peter* and a few of the houses besides—and a street towards the Close to the west—namely from the Cross of [St] Sechnall to the Crosses of St Brigid."[78] At Clonmacnoise, in 1026, the paved way (*clochán*) from *Garrdha an banab-bad* (the Nun's church, a short distance east of the main enclosure) to *Uluiadh na dtrí gCros* (the mound of the three crosses) was constructed during the abbacy of Breasal Conailleach (*AFM; CS*, sub anno 1024; *A. Clon.*, sub anno 1026). In 1070, Máel Ciarán mac Conn na mBocht built a paved way (*clochán*) from the cross of Bishop Etchen to the sacristy of the church of St. Ciarán, and another road (*clochán*) from the cross of Comgall to the mound of the three crosses, and from there westward to *Bél na sráide*, "the street entrance," presumably the monastery's main thoroughfare (*AFM*). *Clochán* is also the word used to describe a street at Kells ca. 1134–36 that connected the refectory with a granary, and it is described as being six feet (*troigid*) wide and at least forty-two feet long.[79]

The clearest archaeological evidence for the sort of street that the annalists had in mind comes from Clonmacnoise and the Hiberno-Norse settlement at Whithorn in Galloway. At Clonmacnoise, a metaled road, flanked by houses and D-shaped structures of ninth- to tenth-century date, was discovered. It was 3 meters wide and edged with boulders. The surface was exposed over a distance of 18.5 meters, but geophysical work indicates that the road was much longer and extended from the callows beside the river Shannon, through the settlement, and on to the central complex of church buildings. The road was abandoned in the eleventh century, but it had clearly been much used for some time before that because over thirty layers, consisting of lenses of sand, gravel, and peat, had accumulated to a depth of 0.7 meter.[80] This ongoing resurfacing suggests that the stone edging was probably necessary as a revetment to prevent the road from disintegrating, particularly in wet weather. The discovery of an early ninth-century bridge at Clonmacnoise also emphasizes the importance of a good communications infrastructure to the major ecclesiastical sites.[81] It was 120

---

78. Trans. *AU*, ed. Hennessy and Mac Carthy; see also *AFM*, sub anno 1166.
79. Mac Niocaill, *Notitiae as Leabhar Cheanannais*, p. 32.
80. See summary of excavations in *Excavations 1995*, p. 76; ibid. *1997*, p. 149.
81. See summary of excavations in *Excavations 1995*, pp. 75–76; ibid. *1997*, pp. 148–49; ibid. *1998*, p. 174; Boland, O'Sullivan, and Breen, "Early Christian Wooden Bridge."

meters long and 5 meters wide and stood to a height of 10–13 meters, with the walkway placed about 6 meters above the summer water levels.

The close connections of Galloway with Ireland during the tenth and eleventh centuries are clear from its name, which is derived from *Gallgaidil*, as well as from the presence of place-names that have been interpreted as indicating Hiberno-Scandinavian settlement.[82] From 1052 until 1064 it was ruled by Echmarcach mac Ragnaill, former king of Dublin, and he may well have ruled it from Dublin prior to his deposition in 1052.[83] Excavation immediately southwest of the churchyard showed that the monastic town developed in the eleventh century with the construction of buildings of Hiberno-Norse type on either side of a road linking the church with the harbor.[84] A stratified succession of rectangular houses was uncovered, and their alignment remained consistently focused onto the roadway throughout the eleventh and twelfth centuries. Three of these, buildings IV-3, IV-18, and IV-19, are particularly relevant to the Kildare evidence because they produced a range of comb-making debris including tooth-plate blanks, roughly finished side-plates, and antler offcuts and trimmings.[85] Elsewhere, there was evidence for leather- and ironworking as well as for the practice of other crafts. The nearest analogy for the structure and form of these houses occurs at Dublin and Waterford, and the settlement has been interpreted as a trading post that processed raw materials from the hinterland, traded the products, and imported luxuries.[86] The location of this community beside the church, which was the main focus of religious, social, and political life in the region, provides a clear indication that it was also viewed as the natural location for economic activity. Taken in conjunction with the known evidence for a Hiberno-Scandinavian presence at Killaloe, the account in a twelfth-century anecdote of Cell Belaig, beside Rahan, as having "vii sráitte do Gallaibh ann" (seven streets of Galls in it),[87] and the mention in 1098 of the *kaupstad* (market-town) at Iona,[88] Whithorn is a reminder of the important role played by Hiberno-Scandinavians in the economic development of ecclesiastical sites during the eleventh and twelfth centuries.

82. Crawford, *Scandinavian Scotland*, p. 100; Ritchie, *Viking Scotland*, pp. 95–105; Graham-Campbell and Batey, *Vikings in Scotland*, pp. 106–10.

83. Byrne, "Onomastica 2"; Byrne, "Rulers of Man to 1765," p. 466 and n. 2.

84. P. Hill, *Whithorn and St Ninian*, pp. 209–50; see also P. Hill, *Whithorn 2*, pp. 13–21.

85. P. Hill, *Whithorn and St Ninian*, pp. 220, 229–30, 474–95.

86. P. Hill, *Whithorn and St Ninian*, p. 56; P. Hill, *Whithorn 2*, p. 19; P. Hill, *Whithorn 3*, p. 23.

87. Petrie, *Ecclesiastical Architecture of Ireland*, pp. 354–55. I am indebted to Michael Potterton for this reference; see also Ó Cuív, *Catalogue of Irish Language Manuscripts*, 1:78.

88. The Icelandic source *Fagrskinna* (written ca. 1240) records the arrival in 1098 of Magnus Barelegs, king of Norway, at the *kaupstad* of Iona, translated as "market-town" by Anderson, *Early Sources of Scottish History*, 2:109; see Griffiths, "Coastal Trading Ports," p. 65.

DEFENSES

In origin, the boundary of the monastery almost certainly delimited an area of sacred land that constituted sanctuary.[89] It may simply have been marked off with a furrow or a specifically nondefensive ditch such as those that characterize the pre-Christian sacred sites of Ireland.[90] From an early date, however, it is clear that some monasteries were demarcated with a rampart or *vallum,* and in Adomnán's time, if not before, both Iona and Clonmacnoise were so enclosed.[91] Many monasteries restricted their monks to staying within the enclosure. Columbanus, for instance, imposed a penance on anyone who went outside the *vallum* without permission, and the rule of Ailbhe contains a similar stipulation.[92] These regulations seem to have been intended to keep out the distractions of the world as Bede's account of Cuthbert's hermitage on the island of Farne indicates: "The walls on the outside were higher than a man. Out of piety he made the walls higher inside by cutting away the solid rock at the bottom, so that with only the sky to look at, eyes and thoughts might be kept from wandering and inspired to seek for higher things."[93]

The growth of warfare between monasteries during the eighth century, however, and their increasing use in times of attack as places of refuge, both for people and livestock, indicates that enclosures were also needed for security.[94]

In general terms the surviving earthworks at early ecclesiastical sites are comparable with those encompassing secular ringforts, and they show a similar variety in scale and mode of construction. They normally con-

89. Valante's suggestions, "Reassessing the 'Monastic Town,'" p. 14, that I have "argued that any settlement with a wall in the middle ages was a town" and "ignored . . . that the purpose of a monastic *vallum* was to demarcate sanctuary," are uninformed; see Bradley, "Planned Anglo-Norman Towns," pp. 417–20; Bradley, "Monastic Town of Clonmacnoise," p. 47.

90. The Iron Age ritual sites at Tara, Emain Macha, and Dún Ailinne are all characterized by having the bank placed outside the ditch; see Ó Ríordáin, *Tara,* p. 9; Waterman and Lynn, *Excavations at Navan Fort;* Wailes, "Dún Ailinne."

91. *Adomnán's Life of Columba,* ed. and trans. Anderson and Anderson (1961), pp. 214–15, 391–92.

92. Walker, *Sancti Columbani Opera,* pp. 154–55; O'Neill, "Rule of Ailbhe of Emly."

93. Bede, *Vita Cuthberti,* cap. xvii, trans. Webb, *Age of Bede,* p. 66; see also Bede, *Hist. eccles.* 4.28: "surrounded by an embankment so high that he could see nothing but the heavens for which he longed so ardently," trans. in Bede, *History of the English Church and People,* p. 262.

94. Hamlin, "Archaeology of the Irish Churches," p. 281; Lucas, "Plundering and Burning of Churches"; see *Adomnán's Life of Columba,* ed. and trans. Anderson and Anderson (1961), pp. 248–51, for an early instance of neighboring inhabitants taking refuge in a church.

sist of earthen banks with external ditches and, as with secular sites, the available evidence suggests that the more powerful and wealthy the monastery, the stronger and larger was its enclosure. The surviving remains at Seirkieran, said to have been built in 927 by the high-king Donnchadh mac Flann Sinna, are still impressive.[95] They consist of two coterminous banks and ditches that enclose an area of approximately 12 hectares. On the northwest side of the site, the inner bank is 6.8 meters broad and survives to a height of 2 meters, while the inner ditch is 10 meters wide and 3 meters deep. The outer bank is 7 meters wide and 1.8 meters high and has traces of a stone facing on the interior; the external ditch is 4.8 meters wide. These dimensions are necessarily minimal ones because the erosion of the banks and the silting of the ditches have altered both their height and depth. A truer estimate of their original size might be obtained by multiplying these dimensions by a factor of 1.5 to 2. If the inner rampart was topped by a palisade in the manner of secular sites, then Seirkieran would have constituted a formidable site. Durrow is also known to have been bivallate.[96]

Archaeological excavations at Downpatrick have revealed that the monastic site was enclosed by a timber-laced rampart, 6 meters wide, that had an earthen core revetted at the front and back by wooden uprights; outside it was a ditch 3 meters wide and 2 meters deep, beyond which the natural scarp plunges steeply downhill.[97] At Kilpatrick (Co. Westmeath) the ditch was cut into bedrock to a depth of 3 meters and was between 5 and 6 meters wide; traces of a partly leveled internal bank with stone facing or filling were also revealed.[98] There was evidence for ditches of a similar size at Tullylish (Co. Down) where excavation revealed that the site was enclosed by two successive rock-cut ditches each of which averaged 5 meters in width and 3 meters in depth.[99] At Iona, the earliest *vallum*, belonging to the sixth and seventh centuries, was found to have been protected by a water-filled ditch 3 meters deep and 6 meters wide.[100] The height of these ramparts is difficult to gauge but the surviving wall height of 6 meters at Inishmurray (Co. Sligo) provides an idea of the potential height envisaged by monasteries as desirable.

95. Comyn and Dineen, *Foras feasa ar Éirinn*, 3:216–17.
96. See summary of excavation in *MA* 30 (1986), p. 187.
97. Phase V of the rampart excavated in the 1950s and believed then to be of Iron Age construction is now known to be of early medieval date; see Proudfoot, "Excavations at Cathedral Hill," pp. 59, 67–68; and summary of excavation by Brannon in *MA* 30 (1986), 181–82; 31 (1987), 176–77; 32 (1988), 295.
98. Swan, "Excavations at Kilpatrick Churchyard."
99. Ivens, "Early Christian Monastic Enclosure at Tullylish," pp. 58–61.
100. J. Barber, "Excavations on Iona, 1979"; Ritchie, *Iona*, pp. 36–40.

The nearest comparable evidence for these monastic ramparts is to be found at Dublin, where excavations at Fishamble Street revealed four phases in the construction of the defenses between the tenth and twelfth centuries.[101] During the first phase, ca. 925, an earthen bank 1 meter high was built with a shallow ditch outside; about 950 this was replaced with a bank 2 meters high, having an external ditch 2 meters wide and 1.6 meters deep. The flimsy nature of these two phases of the riverside defenses prompted the excavator to view them as little more than breakwaters, perhaps intended to prevent flooding. Around the year 1000, however, a 3-meter-high earthen bank, reinforced with both brushwood and post-and-wattle screens, revetted at the front with boards and post-and-wattle, and topped with a palisade, was constructed. This finds a good parallel in the rampart at Downpatrick and may have been influenced by it or something similar. Indeed the Downpatrick evidence compares favorably with the tenth-century defenses of Hereford, which consisted of a bank 2.5 meters high, revetted by a timber facing and having a breastwork above.[102] The final stage of Dublin's pre-Norman defenses consisted of a stone wall, 1.5 meters thick and an estimated 3.5 meters high, built ca. 1100. Stone defenses are not found on monastic sites, but the entrance gatehouse at Glendalough indicates that the medium was being used on monastic sites during the twelfth century.[103]

In conclusion, it would seem that while the monastic *vallum* was not defensive in origin, it soon became so. By the tenth and eleventh centuries, and perhaps even before, the earthworks enclosing the larger monasteries such as Seirkieran and Downpatrick, instanced above, were comparable in scale to the town defenses of tenth-century Dublin. In view of this it is not surprising to note that in 1103 Armagh resisted a siege (*a forbháisí*) by Muirchertach Ua Briain, which lasted a week (*AFM, AU, ALC*).

Having reviewed a number of general characteristics of the Irish monastic town, the features of seven individual sites will be considered next.

ARMAGH

Founded by St. Patrick, Armagh has been the ecclesiastical capital of Ireland since the seventh century. It was located in Airgialla, a kingdom that began to break up during the eighth century when the Cenél nEó-gain, to the north, became the dominant political power in Ulster. Within Airgialla, two subkingdoms jostled for kingship, the Uí Cremthainn and

101. Wallace, "Dublin's Waterfront at Wood Quay," pp. 110–13; Linzi Simpson, "Forty Years a-Digging," pp. 25–28.
102. Shoesmith, *Hereford City Excavations*, pp. 76–80.
103. Leask, *Glendalough*, pp. 30–32.

Airther. Airther, which included Armagh, pursued a policy of friendship with the Cenél nEógain and triumphed in 827 when the Cenél nEógain defeated the Uí Cremthainn at the battle of Leth Cam.[104] The Airther then began to occupy the principal positions at Armagh, and from the late tenth until the mid-twelfth century, Armagh was run by one of their major families the Clann Sinaich.[105] A lay abbacy was introduced, and under the Clann Sinaich, the role of ecclesiastics became so reduced that Armagh never seems to have had more than one priest at any time.[106] It was during their rule, however, that Armagh developed into Ireland's largest monastic town. The *seniores*, who were responsible for the governing of Armagh and for the administration of its revenues, were all drawn from the Clann Sinaich, while other local families are known to have filled the lesser posts of *secnab*, or administrator of the estate (Uí Bresail Airther), bishop (Cenél nEógain), guestmaster (Mac Gilla Ciaráin), and *cenn bocht*, or master of the poor (Ua hErodáin), while the priest was provided by the Uí Cruinn.[107] The vast majority of the Armagh community consisted of laypeople dedicated to a Christian regimen and bound together by accepted rules and loyalties. In its schools, secular learning seems to have been more highly esteemed than religious knowledge if one is to judge from the obits of its *fir léginn*.[108] The presence of an *oenach*, together with the large number of coin-finds and the evidence for the manufacture of jewelry and fine metalwork, indicates that commercial activities were a part of everyday life. Politically, its pretensions to ecclesiastical primacy gave it a national importance indicated by its use as the principal burial place of the Uí Néill (Cenél nEógain) kings of Ailech, and of a number of high-kings, including Brian Bóruma, who was interred there in 1014.

According to the tradition recorded by Muirchú ca. 680, the first church was on low ground at *Fertae martyrum* (the martyr's burial-ground), and it was some time later that the ecclesiastics were granted the high ground, known as *dorsum salicis* (the ridge of the willow) on which the monastic capital was subsequently built.[109] Normally this should have led

---

104. Ó Fiaich, "Church of Armagh under Lay Control," pp. 81–82; Hughes, "The Church and the World," p. 107.

105. Ó Fiaich, "Church of Armagh under Lay Control."

106. Ó Fiaich, "Church of Armagh under Lay Control," p. 103.

107. Ó Fiaich, "Church of Armagh under Lay Control," pp. 100–05.

108. Ó Fiaich, "Church of Armagh under Lay Control," pp. 111–15. The blend of secular and religious knowledge is reminiscent of the range of intellectual inquiry displayed by Domhnall Ua hÉnna, bishop of Killaloe, in his letter to Lanfranc, archbishop of Canterbury, and the contrast with the doctrinaire reply of the latter; see A. Gwynn and Gleeson, *History of the Diocese of Killaloe*, pp. 105–08; see also Bethell, "English Monks and Irish Reform," pp. 127–28.

109. Bieler, *Patrician Texts in the Book of Armagh*, p. 191.

to a dual origin for the later monastic town, but examination of the topography and the later annalistic sources indicates that the hill summit became the focus for most subsequent development.

The summit is a terrace, about 250 meters across, known in numerous annals of the ninth to twelfth centuries as the *ráth*, a name that suggests it was enclosed by a palisaded earthwork. The gate of this enclosure is mentioned on several occasions, and within it were the principal ecclesiastical buildings. The documentary references cited above indicate that it was a populous center, divided into sectors, having streets and houses in addition to its churches and oratories. The annalistic entry describing the fire of 1020 provides an image of its extent:

> Ard Macha was burned with all the fort (*ráth*), without the saving of any house within it, except the library (*teach screaptra*) only, and many houses were burned in the Trians; and the *Daimhliag-mór* was burned, and the *Cloictheach*, with its bells; and *Daimhliag-na-Toe*, and *Daimhliag an tSabhaill;* and the old preaching chair, and the chariot of the abbots, and their books in the houses of the students, with much gold, silver and other precious things.[110]

Reeves has shown that the churches and round tower mentioned in this entry together with the Célí Dé priory (established before 919), the abbot's house, the kitchen, a sacred grove, and the principal cemetery (including the burial ground of the kings) all lay within the *ráth*. Its former bounds are indicated today on the west, south, and east by the curving street pattern of Callan Street and Castle Street, while to the northeast it is reflected in a curving property boundary.[111] The area outside this enclosure was divided, as we have seen, into three precincts, known as *triana* or trians. The *trian Saxan* (English precinct) was located to the north and northeast, where English Street still preserves its name. The *trian massain* (middle precinct) lay on the southeast, and the *trian mór* (large precinct) on the west.[112] Annalistic references of 1112, 1121, and 1116 indicate that the *triana* contained streets and houses, which were lived in by students,

---

110. *AFM*, see also *AU, A. Tig., CS*, sub anno 1018.

111. Reeves, *Ancient Churches of Armagh*, and *Ulster Jnl. of Archaeology*, 2nd series, 4 (1898), 205–11; F. Henry, *Irish Art during the Viking Invasions*, p. 42; Edwards, *Archaeology of Early Medieval Ireland*, pp. 107–11.

112. The position of the *triana* was established by Reeves, *Ancient Churches of Armagh*, pp. 19–20 and *Ulster Jnl. of Archaeology*, 2nd series, 4 (1898), 212–13. Although apparently following Reeves, F. Henry misplaced the location of the *triana* in *Irish Art during the Viking Invasions*, p. 42 and fig. 2, as did Edwards, *Archaeology of Early Medieval Ireland*, p. 109.

clerics, shrine keepers, and, probably, craftsmen. The *triana* formed part of a large outer enclosure, three sides of which are still delimited by Abbey Street, Thomas Street, and Ogle Street, but its exact western boundary is unclear. It measured approximately 480 by 360 meters and, in the twelfth century, it would have covered an area of roughly 11.5 hectares (29 acres).[113] It is clear, however, from excavations on the east side of Castle Street that parts of this area remained open and were not built upon until the end of the Middle Ages.[114]

Excavations at Cathedral Hill, between Castle Street and the cathedral, revealed that the summit was enclosed in pre-Christian times, and it was almost certainly a place of pagan ritual.[115] It consisted of an enclosure approximately 50 meters across bounded by a ditch with an external bank and roughly coinciding in area with the modern churchyard. The external bank was subsequently pushed into the ditch and the site underwent a change of use, which is probably to be equated with the transition to Christianity. In the seventh, eighth, and ninth centuries the area was used as a workshop by highly skilled metalworkers. *Fertae martyrum* also remained in use, and excavations there revealed a cemetery of narrow graves, in roughly ordered rows, with radiocarbon determinations in the sixth and seventh centuries.[116] One of these (grave A) may be the remains of a shrine, an interpretation that would bear out the statement in the *Liber angeli* that the site was venerated in the seventh century as the shrine of holy men.[117] Stratigraphically later than the cemetery was a workshop with evidence for metal-, glass-, and amber-working, dating probably to the eighth and ninth centuries. Subsequently in the tenth and eleventh centuries, the area was again used by a specialist craftsman who manufactured lignite bracelets.[118] In 1090, the stone church of *Na Ferta* was burned together with one hundred houses around about it.[119] The workshop activity recovered by excavation may well have been associated with some of these houses, which would have constituted an extramural suburb in the eleventh century.

113. Swan, "Monastic Proto-towns in Early Medieval Ireland," p. 84.

114. Lynn, "Recent Archaeological Excavations in Armagh City," p. 278.

115. Gaskell-Brown and Harper, "Excavations on Cathedral Hill."

116. Lynn, "Excavations at 46–48 Scotch Street."

117. Bieler, *Patrician Texts in the Book of Armagh*, p. 191.

118. Lynn, "Excavations at 46–48 Scotch Street," pp. 69–70; *Excavations 1986*, pp. 11–12.

119. *AU*. This is possibly the site of the *vicus* mentioned in Bernard of Clairvaux's *Life of Malachy*, translated as "a hamlet near the city [Armagh]" on p. 8 of Lawlor's translation of the text. Valante confuses the *vicus* with Armagh, while her attribution of Rankean impartiality to Bernard is misplaced when compared with Bernard's agenda in writing the *Life;* see "Reassessing the Irish 'Monastic Town,'" p. 16; for the varying meanings of *vicus*, including that of an urbanized settlement, see Verhulst, *Rise of Cities in North-West Europe*, pp. 47–54.

KELLS

According to the *Annals of Ulster* this monastery was established in 807 on land that appears to have been given by Armagh to the Columban monks of Iona.[120] As at Armagh, traditions survived of the existence of an earlier fort, *Dún Chuile Sibrille*, which was remembered in later lore as the residence of kings.[121] Archaeological evidence for pre-Columban activity on the site is provided by a zoomorphic penannular brooch of sixth-/seventh-century date found in the churchyard[122] and by excavations that were carried out immediately northwest of the stone-roofed oratory known as St. Columba's House. These revealed part of an enclosure that, if complete, would have measured 22 meters in diameter, and dating was obtained from a seventh- or eighth-century bronze brooch with an amber stud found in the fill of the ditch.[123] The importance of Kells increased during the ninth and tenth centuries after the removal to the monastery of St. Columba's relics from Iona. Between the ninth and twelfth centuries, Kells functioned as an administrative center, a place of refuge, and a storehouse for valuables; it was a major patron of art and craftsmanship and an educational center.[124]

The layout of Kells shows that the monastic enclosure measured about 360 meters east–west by 280 meters north–south, an area of roughly 9.5 hectares (22 acres). Its outline is preserved on the north and east by the line of Carrick, Castle, and Cross Streets, on the west by Fair Green, and on the south by the line of the town wall. The boundary is missing in the southeast quadrant where its line would have continued from the surviving piece of town wall toward Cross Street. The lack of definition in this quadrant may be due to an extension of the enclosure along Suffolk Street, a street name derived from Siofóic, an area of Kells mentioned on two occasions in the mid-twelfth century.[125] Simms is almost certainly correct in suggesting that there was an inner enclosure, isolating the principal church as well as the surviving round tower and high crosses in the manner of the *ráth* at Armagh, but topographically it is not as clearly defined.[126]

120. Herbert, *Iona, Kells and Derry*, pp. 68–70.

121. Simms and Simms, *Kells*, p. 1.

122. Graham-Campbell, "Lost Zoomorphic Penannular Brooch."

123. See summary of excavations in *Excavations 1987*, pp. 23–24; ibid. *1988*, pp. 35–36; "Kells," *MA* 33 (1989), 224.

124. Simms, "Frühformen der mittelalterlichen Stadt in Irland." In her comments on Kells, Valante, "Reassessing the Irish 'Monastic Town,'" p. 15, makes no reference to this thoughtful paper nor, indeed, to Mac Niocaill, *Notitiae as Leabhar Cheanannais*.

125. *AFM*, sub anno 1156; Mac Niocaill, *Notitiae as Leabhar Cheanannais*, no. v:21; see also Simington, "Valuation of Kells," pp. 234–35, and O'Connell, "Kells," p. 13.

126. Simms, "Frühformen der mittelalterlichen Stadt in Irland," pp. 32–35; Simms and Simms, *Kells*, pp. 1–3.

Kildare

This monastery is associated with St. Brigit, its traditional sixth-century founder, but Brigit herself is a shadowy figure and is probably a Christianized version of a Celtic goddess.[127] Kildare was associated until at least the twelfth century with a perpetual fire, tended by virgins, a feature that itself suggests a pre-Christian origin for the site.[128] In the seventh century it was described by Cogitosus as "a great metropolitan *civitas*," and its political importance at this time is clear from the fact that any dynasty wishing to dominate Leinster had to control it. From the seventh century until the eleventh it was controlled by the Uí Dúnlainge, one of whom, Muiredach mac Brain, was jointly king of Leinster and abbot of Kildare, but in the late eleventh century, the Uí Dúnlainge were ousted and replaced by the Uí Chennselaig.[129] Kildare's continuing ecclesiastical importance in the twelfth century is shown by its episcopal status at the synods of Ráith Bressail and Kells. An eleventh-century source refers to the workshop of a comb-maker in the "street of the stone step."[130] Additionally described as "eastward running," it is quite likely the same as the modern Claregate Street.

The street pattern of Kildare preserves a number of radial features that are relict remains of pre-Norman enclosures, but despite a number of attempts at analysis no consensus has been arrived at on their exact course.[131] The bulge in Station Road preserves the line of an inner enclosure, while the outer enclosure is reflected in the radial course of Priest's Lane, Academy Street, St. Brigid's Square, and Convent Road. The topography of the northwest and west, which shows higher ground immediately inside the curve of Priest's Lane and Academy Street, suggests that the original *vallum* lay slightly within the road system. For the same reason, its southern boundary is most likely indicated by the long property boundary running east from Bride Street. The eastern boundary of the enclosure is not immediately evident, but it probably followed the line of the later medieval defenses adjoining the Anglo-Norman castle. The

127. Macalister, *Ireland in Pre-Celtic Times*, pp. 340–41; Kildare is the subject of a more detailed treatment by Bradley, "Archaeology, Topography and Building Fabric."

128. O'Meara, *History and Topography of Ireland*, pp. 81–85; Doherty, "Monastic Town in Early Medieval Ireland," p. 61.

129. Doherty, "Monastic Town in Early Medieval Ireland," pp. 62–63.

130. Radner, *Fragmentary Annals of Ireland*, p. 165.

131. Andrews, *Kildare*; Valante's understandable view, "Reassessing the Irish 'Monastic Town,'" p. 8, that Cogitosus "apparently refers to the lack of a monastic vallum at Kildare" overlooks the latter author's statement that the church was surrounded by a *castellum*; see Connolly and Picard, "Cogitosus: Life of Brigid," p. 25, and Bradley, "Archaeology, Topography and Building Fabric," p. 31.

date of the present triangular marketplace is unclear. Swan has proposed a pre-Anglo-Norman origin for it, but as Andrews suggests, it may be of seventeenth-century date.[132]

GLENDALOUGH

Here a progression can be seen from the simple hermitage of St. Kevin on the steep edge of the upper lake to the more spacious terrace on the east, a move dated by Henry to the eighth century.[133] By the middle of the twelfth century, Glendalough was a monastery spread over an area of 2.8 hectares (7 acres), bounded by streams on the north, east, and south and enclosed by a stone-revetted rampart and entered through a stone entrance gate. The chief building was the cathedral and near it was a round tower. The church of St. Mary lay at the other end of the enclosure, and the rest of the *civitas* probably consisted of wooden structures, such as the houses mentioned in 1061, that have now disappeared. Immediately outside the enclosure were the churches of St. Kevin and St. Ciarán. The valley, stretching away from the monastery, was dotted for a length of two kilometers with various establishments dependent on it. It was a center for sculptors, as the high crosses and grave slabs demonstrate, and it had an important scriptorium as the Rosslyn Missal indicates. Its influential school maintained links with Continental centers of learning. It is known, for instance, that the *De abaco* of Gerbert of Aurillac and the *Ars Grammatica* attributed to Clemens Scottus were in use there by 1106, while the lectures of Peter Abelard were transcribed.[134] It was a diocesan center and was a major center of pilgrimage.

The existence of a secular town is suggested by the concentration of bullaun stones, used for grinding food and ores, on the north of the monastic complex.[135] The only excavations have taken place on the flood plain immediately east of the enclosure, which was unsuitable for settlement, and, as expected, these revealed that this area was neither cultivated nor settled in pre-Anglo-Norman times.[136]

TUAM

According to tradition, Tuam was founded by St. Iarlath in the early sixth century, but the first definite evidence for the existence of a monas-

132. Swan, "Monastic Proto-towns in Early Medieval Ireland," p. 86; Andrews, *Kildare*, p. 3.
133. F. Henry, *Irish Art during the Viking Invasions*, p. 45.
134. F. Henry, *Irish Art in the Romanesque Period*, pp. 4, 51.
135. Price, "Rock-basins or 'Bullauns' at Glendalough," p. 162.
136. Manning, "Excavations at Glendalough."

tery occurs in 781 when the *Annals of Ulster* note the death of Nuadu ua Bolcáin, abbot of Tuam. The monastery's rise to prominence, however, was due to its links with the Ua Conchobair family who effectively monopolized the kingship of Connacht from the death of Conchobar mac Tadg in 973. Tuam's position as the preeminent church site of Connacht was reflected in its inclusion as an episcopal see at the Synod of Ráith Bressail and by its elevation to archiepiscopal status at the Synod of Kells in 1152. During the twelfth century it functioned as the Ua Conchobair capital, and a clear indication of its importance is provided in 1164 when Ruairí Ua Conchobair constructed a "caislén ingantach" (wonderful castle) there (*A. Tig.*).

Under the patronage of Toirdealbach Ua Conchobair, king of Connacht, and with the cooperation of Áed Ua hOissín, abbot of Tuam, a new enclosure (*timchill coitchend Tuama dá gualand*) was constructed in 1127 (*A. Tig.*), and this is almost certainly the event commemorated by the two surviving inscribed cross fragments with Urnes style decoration.[137] Tuam was raided by the Anglo-Normans in 1177, but their impact seems to have been slight and Ua Conchobair patronage continued into the second quarter of the thirteenth century.

The town still retains elements of a concentric street pattern, and the outline of two enclosures can be identified.[138] Anglo-Norman documents refer to the abbeys of St. John (Augustinian) and the Holy Trinity (Premonstratensian) as being "in the suburbs," and one presumes that they lay outside the monastic enclosure.[139] Temple Iarlath was the principal church within the enclosure, as is evidenced by both its dedication and its topographical position on the highest ground. It is unusual that St. Mary's Cathedral was not located there in the normal pattern attested at Irish monastic sites, and its situation on low ground and, apparently, at the edge of the monastic enclosure remains puzzling. The marketplace, east of the enclosure, parallels the pattern at Armagh, Kells, and Kildare, and it may well be a twelfth-century feature. The present form of Market Square, however, is clearly a feature of the seventeenth-century town. East of the town, in a similar position to *Na Ferta* at Armagh, was Templenaskreen, which is said to have housed the shrine of St. Iarlath. Its position on the main eastern approach to the enclosure suggests the former presence of a suburb there.

137. F. Henry, *Irish Art in the Romanesque Period*, pp. 141–43; Stalley, "Romanesque Sculpture of Tuam," pp. 182–84.

138. Swan, "Monastic Proto-towns in Early Medieval Ireland," p. 89; Gosling, "Tuam."

139. Sweetman, *Calendar of Documents Relating to Ireland*, 5:226; A. Gwynn and Hadcock, *Medieval Religious Houses: Ireland*, p. 206.

DERRY

The monastery of Derry was situated on an oval-shaped island in a bend of the river Foyle. Although its foundation is traditionally ascribed to Columba, it was in fact established by a relative of his, Fiachrach mac Ciaráin, whose death is recorded in 620.[140] Adomnán indicates that there was a church and burial place here before 700, and communication with Britain and Iona from its harbor (*portus*) was a relatively normal event.[141] It is only during the twelfth century that the monastery seems to have acquired urban functions probably because the Mac Lochlainn kings of Ailech took up residence in Derry ca. 1100.[142] The heyday of the monastery's greatness was in the middle of the twelfth century when it was patronized by Muircertach Mac Lochlainn, king of Ailech (1136–66), and while Flaithbertach Ua Brolcháin was its abbot (1150–75). Together they reorganized the layout of the monastery in 1162, and in the following years its major churches were rebuilt and modified (*AU, AFM*).

By the late twelfth century there were at least three churches in Derry: the *Dubrecles* monastic church, the *Teampall Mór*, and the *Teampall Bec*, while, in addition to many houses, a hermitage (*dísiurt*), a round tower, and a refectory are also documented.[143] In 1173, the settlement is referred to as a *baile*.[144] The precise nature and size of the settlement is unknown, but the demolition of over eighty houses in 1162 implies that many more than that number were left standing or were rebuilt shortly afterwards (*AU, AFM*). Nothing survives of the monastic layout within the modern town plan of Derry, but it has proved possible to pinpoint the major monuments with the aid of early seventeenth-century maps.[145]

CLONMACNOISE

This monastery was founded on what was effectively an island in the Shannon by St. Ciarán, who is said to have died in 549.[146] The site was posi-

---

140. Lacey, "Development of Derry," p. 379; Lacey, "Columba."

141. Lacey, "Development of Derry," pp. 379–83; Lacey, "Columba", p. 39.

142. Lacey, "Development of Derry," pp. 387–88; Lacey, *Siege City*, pp. 33–53; see also Herbert, *Iona, Kells and Derry*, pp. 110–11.

143. Lacey, "Development of Derry," pp. 386–87.

144. *AU, AFM, A. Tig.;* the *baile* is referred to again in 1212: *AU, ALC, AFM.*

145. Lacey, "Development of Derry," p. 381, fig. 2.

146. *AU, AFM, AI,* sub anno 548; *CS,* sub anno 544; but see J. Ryan, *Clonmacnois,* pp. 27–28, where arguments are given for a date of death in 545. These are no more convincing, however, than Macalister's suggestion of 556; see his *Latin and Irish Lives of Ciarán,* p. 159. For a more detailed discussion of this site see Bradley, "Monastic Town of Clonmacnoise."

tioned close to the intersection of two major routeways, the river Shannon and the *Eiscir riada*, a glacial ridge that formed a natural roadway from prehistoric times. Clonmacnoise developed at an early stage into Armagh's main midland rival, and Tírechán, writing ca. 690, accused it of claiming churches in the Sligo area that belonged to Armagh.[147] In return for burial rights, it received major patronage between the tenth and twelfth centuries from the kings of the Southern Uí Néill, of Connacht, and even of one king of Munster. In 909, the high-king Flann Sinna financed Abbot Colmán mac Ailella's building of a *daimhliag mór*, a great stone church, which still survives.[148] The rectangular open space outside the west facade of the *daimhliag mór* seems to have been deliberately conceived as a *platea*, with the cross of the Scriptures placed centrally within it. The inscription on this cross records the names of both Colmán and Flann, whom it styles king of Ireland.[149] At the west end of the *platea* is a round tower, said to have been commenced under the patronage of Fergal ua Ruairc, king of Connacht (956–66), who is also credited with building a causeway across the bog to the monastery.[150] Further patronage is recorded in the twelfth century from Toirdealbach Ua Conchobair. Although it was not included among the episcopal sees at Ráith Bressail, the Synod of Uisneach in 1111 made Clonmacnoise the cathedral church of western Meath (*CS*). The eleventh and twelfth centuries were a period of great prosperity for the monastery and for its scriptorium, which produced the *Annals of Tigernach*, the *Chronicon Scottorum*, the *Annals of Clonmacnoise*, and *Lebor na hUidre*.[151]

The surviving ecclesiastical remains are located within a graveyard wall roughly centrally placed within a large enclosure whose outline survives on the east and south.[152] Internally, the monastery was divided into *triana*, and indications of a dense population are provided by the account of the destruction of one hundred and five houses at Clonmacnoise in 1179, while the burning, in 1082, of houses in the churchyard of the nuns

---

147. Bieler, *Patrician Texts in the Book of Armagh*, p. 142: no. 25, p. 160: no. 4; Doherty, "Monastic Town in Early Medieval Ireland," p. 64.

148. *AFM*, sub anno 904; *A. Tig.*, *CS*, sub anno 908; *A. Clon.*, sub anno 901; Manning, "Clonmacnoise Cathedral."

149. Herity, "Layout of Irish Early Christian Monasteries," pp. 108–09; Ó Murchadha, "Rubbings Taken of the Inscriptions."

150. O'Donovan, "Registry of Clonmacnoise," p. 452.

151. Doherty, "Monastic Town in Early Medieval Ireland," p. 65.

152. Thomas, *Early Christian Archaeology*, p. 29. The eastern stretch of *vallum*, however, which Thomas shows taking a right angle before linking up with the eastern boundary of the New Graveyard, does not exist. Some doubt has been cast on the age of the surviving *vallum*; see C. O'Brien and Seetman, *Archaeological Inventory of County Offaly*, p. 95.

suggests that there was a secular settlement around the nuns' church.[153] Paved ways are known to have existed, and what seems to be the main street is mentioned in the eleventh century.[154] Metalworking evidence has come to light in the course of excavations, and artistic production on a substantial scale has always been assumed at Clonmacnoise because of the attribution to the site of a number of important pieces of metalwork, such as the Clonmacnoise Plaque, the shrine of the Stowe Missal, and the crosier of the abbots of Clonmacnoise.[155]

THE PROBLEM OF DEFINITION

During the tenth century, the fusion of secular and ecclesiastical power, together with a developing economic system based on redistribution, transformed a few of the more important ecclesiastical sites into monastic towns. This was a process that continued during the eleventh century and climaxed in the twelfth century, when monastic towns were large, populated, and politically important centers. Problems remain, nonetheless, due to the patchy and uneven nature of the surviving evidence. In particular, those of definition and character: When is a site a monastery, and when can it be regarded as a monastic town? What was the specifically urban character of a monastic town? And, what did a monastic town actually look like?

Some conclusions can be arrived at from the examination of the seven sites detailed above. Of these, Armagh is the best documented in terms of both written and archaeological sources. It is tempting to interpret all monastic towns as versions of Armagh, but its very preeminence in ecclesiastical affairs must have meant that it was always exceptional. Nonetheless, there are several features that seem to recur at other monastic towns. First, the plan element of an enclosure is characteristic and, while it has been usual to view this as a simple boundary of sanctuary, the substan-

153. *AFM*, sub annis 1179, 1082; *A. Clon.*, sub anno 1080. It is difficult to reconcile the annalistic evidence for 105 houses in 1179 with Valante's statement that "the settlement was anything other than a rural one, and even this did not last [beyond the year 1000]," "Reassessing the Irish 'Monastic Town,'" p. 15. Her comments overlook the facts that late eleventh- and twelfth-century evidence did not survive at the particular point excavated by Heather King in the eastern occupation zone and do not address the issue of settlement elsewhere in the eastern zone, or in the southern or western zones, where geophysical survey and archaeological discoveries reflect the positions of the original *triana*.

154. *AFM*, sub annis 1026, 1070; *CS*, sub anno 1024; *A. Clon.*, sub anno 1026.

155. M. Ryan, "Fine Metalworking and Early Irish Monasteries," p. 42; "Excavation Bulletin 1977–79"; F. Henry, *Irish Art during the Viking Invasions*, p. 123; F. Henry, *Irish Art in the Romanesque Period*, pp. 82, 101–02; Harbison, "Lost Crucifixion Plaque," p. 37; Ó Floinn, "Schools of Metalworking," p. 181; Ó Floinn, "Clonmacnoise: Art and Patronage."

tial earthworks at Downpatrick and the multivallation known from other major sites indicate that some had a defensive function. Second, there was a complex of ecclesiastical structures and features at the core. This is generally typified by a group of churches (including a cathedral in the twelfth century) and a major administrative dwelling, such as the abbot's house and/or a royal residence. Third, there were close links with the local ruling dynasties. Muiredach mac Brain (d. 885), who was jointly king of Leinster and abbot of Kildare, has already been cited. At Kells this situation is typified by Murchad mac Flainn Ua Máel Sechlainn (d. 1076) who was jointly abbot of Kells and Clonard as well as being king of Mide. At Glendalough the closeness of this connection is instanced by Abbot Gilla Comgaill (d. 1127), who was the father of Muirchertach Ua Tuathail, king of Uí Muiredaig between 1141 and 1164. Fourth, there was a social hierarchy in which a branch of the leading political family, such as the Uí Dúnlainge at Kildare, or the Uí Máil, Uí Muiredaig, and Ua Tuathail at Glendalough,[156] formed a ruling elite, while families of lesser political importance supplied nominees to other traditionally held positions. Fifth, there was a dependent population that seems to have been primarily engaged in study, manufacturing, and conducting commercial transactions.

In light of the above, the monastic town may be defined as an enclosed settlement, typified by having a major group of ecclesiastical buildings (including dwellings, monuments, and ceremonial areas) at its core, lived in by a hierarchically organized society with a dependent population (generally consisting of craftsmen, students, traders, and providers) that functioned as a political capital and as a focus for regional trade. Using these criteria, another ten or eleven potential sites may be added to the examples already detailed: Cashel, Downpatrick, Duleek, Emly, Ferns, Kilkenny, Killaloe, Lismore, Louth, Roscommon, and in west Munster, either Ratass or Ardfert. The evidence for their urban status is circumstantial, and the balance of probability suggests that they functioned as monastic towns. There is no evidence from any monastic town for the existence of a burgagelike plot pattern. The Kells charters, however, indicate that property was carefully regulated. Parts of property boundaries were recovered in the excavations at Clonmacnoise, while the presence of a *críochaire* at Armagh, whose job it was to look after boundaries, suggests that such an official may also have been attached to other monastic towns.[157] Nonetheless, the absence of a burgage-plot pattern suggests that

---

156. Mac Shamhráin, "Prosopographica Glindelachensis"; Mac Shamhráin, *Church and Polity in Pre-Norman Ireland*.

157. *AFM*, sub anno 1136; Ó Fiaich, "Church of Armagh under Lay Control," p. 105, and *Dictionary of the Irish Language*, sub *críchaire*.

the social organization of monastic towns was different from their Scandinavian counterparts on the coast.

PARALLELS

Despite presumptions to the contrary the Irish urban experience during the first millennium was not unique, but instead it parallels developments elsewhere in post-Roman Europe. In Britain, the fifth and sixth centuries witnessed the abandonment of towns in favor of rural life, while elsewhere in northern Europe, urban life ceased during the sixth century.[158] Archaeological excavations at Tours have shown that the only continuous link between Roman times and the Middle Ages was one of administration, focused primarily on the monastery of Saint-Martin. "There," comments Galinié, "a society with a minimal hierarchical structure sustained a town without urban life—an administrative town in the 4th and 5th centuries and a holy town . . . thereafter [until the tenth century]."[159] In southern Europe urban life came to a close slightly later—in the late sixth and seventh centuries. Excavations at Brescia, Milan, Naples, Otranto, Pescara, and Verona, among others, have shown that they "were reduced to non-urban proportions" in the course of the seventh century.[160] The documented *civitates* of northern Italy, as Ward-Perkins has said in a memorable phrase, were nothing more than "miserable collections of run-down huts."[161] Seventh-century Rome, once home to one million people, was no longer a city. Rather it consisted of some fifty dispersed ecclesiastical settlements with a population of about five thousand that produced for their own use and for limited exchange.[162] The landscape of Rome consisted of churches with their accompanying farms and agricultural buildings, vineyards, fences, trees, ponds, gardens, fields, and pastures.[163] Even in the Byzantine Empire, with the exception of Constantinople—where the population had dropped from five hundred thousand to perhaps less than twenty-five thousand—there were only four or five

---

158. Clarke and Ambrosiani, *Towns in the Viking Age*, pp. 5–7; Reece, "End of the City"; Dixon, "'Cities Are Not as Populated'"; Verhulst, *Rise of Cities in North-West Europe*, pp. 24–43.

159. Galinié, "Reflections on Early Medieval Tours," p. 61.

160. Hodges, *Towns and Trade*, p. 60; Carver, *Arguments in Stone*, pp. 47–50; see also Liebeschuetz, "End of the Ancient City"; La Rocca, "Public Buildings and Urban Change."

161. Ward-Perkins, "Continuists, Catastrophists, and the Towns," p. 169, quoted in Hodges, *Towns and Trade*, p. 26; see also Ward-Perkins, "Towns of Northern Italy."

162. Krautheimer, *Rome, Profile of a City*, p. 74; Hodges, *Towns and Trade*, p. 56; see also Whitehouse, "Rome and Naples."

163. Krautheimer, *Rome, Profile of a City*, pp. 68–69.

places deserving the name of city by the year 700.[164] As late as the ninth century, Ephesus consisted simply of an administrative center, a church, and a marketplace.[165]

In this essentially nonurban world, churches were one of the few central places, and with the right economic and political conditions, they were ideally placed to nurture urban growth. The synods held at Aachen in 816, 817, and 818–19 initiated a series of reforms that had a wide-ranging impact throughout the Carolingian world.[166] Lay abbots (including Einhard, Charlemagne's biographer) were appointed, metalworking and craftwork were brought within the ecclesiastical enclosure, and the procedures were implemented that enabled monasteries to move away from being purely eremitical sites and to develop into regional capitals.[167] The Plan of St. Gall is generally regarded as a response to these reforms, and it illustrates the problems faced by large Carolingian monasteries.[168] The spiritual task of the ecclesiastical community had to be carried out amid the hustle and bustle generated by schools, servants' quarters, guesthouses, stables, barns, henhouses, cowsheds, pig sheds, a brewery, a bakery, a mill, a hospital, and the workshops of blacksmiths, coopers, fullers, goldsmiths, leatherworkers, shield makers, shoemakers, sword grinders, turners, and wheelwrights. The solution was the division of the monastery into separate sectors, devoted respectively to agriculture, craft production, education, health, hospitality, and spiritual activities. The key development was the creation of an inner sanctuary called the cloister (*claustrum*) into which only monks were to be admitted. This was to be built around a square court on the south side of the church. It included all the buildings that had an exclusive monastic use, such as the monastic portion of the church, the library and scriptorium, as well as the monks' dormitory, refectory, kitchen, privy, laundry, and bathhouse. Communication between the cloister and the outside world was carefully monitored. In his commentary on the Rule of St. Benedict, "a textbook of ninth-century monastic life" written ca. 845, Hildemar of Civate provided detailed instructions on how the duties of the inside as well as the outside world had to be combined as well as separated.[169] Visiting monks, abbots,

164. Mango, *Byzantium*, pp. 50–87; ibid., p. 80 for the population of Constantinople in the seventh and eighth centuries; Hodges, *Towns and Trade*, p. 46.

165. Hodges, *Towns and Trade*, p. 47.

166. Halphen, *Charlemagne et l'Empire Carolingien*, pp. 225–33; McKitterick, *Frankish Kingdoms under the Carolingians*, pp. 112–24; de Jong, "Carolingian Monasticism," pp. 629–51.

167. Horn and Born, *Plan of St. Gall*, 1:349; 2:189.

168. Horn and Born, *Plan of St. Gall*, 1:20–25.

169. Mittermüller, *Vita et Regula SS. P. Benedicti*, quoted in de Jong, "Carolingian Monasticism," pp. 637–38.

bishops, and prominent laity had to have separate guest quarters. After all, he adds, "the laity may stay up till the middle of the night, talking and feasting, while the monks are not allowed to do this; instead they have to be silent and pray."[170] Guarding the *claustrum* was a full-time occupation. Departure and return were surrounded with ritual, and the traveler had to remain silent about what he had seen in the outside world. The abbot was the link between the inside and the outside worlds and supervised all comings and goings in the monastery.[171] The ideal abbot was no longer merely a spiritual father, but rather one who felt as at home within the cloister as he did outside, and who possessed the flexibility to adapt his behavior to different circumstances.[172] He had to be able to handle powerful nobles with care or the community might lose their favor and, perhaps, suffer from their anger.[173]

Monasteries played a major role in the development of marketplaces in the ninth-century Carolingian world.[174] Half of the markets established in northern Italy during the ninth century, for instance, were at monasteries,[175] while production, consumption, and exchange were integrated in monasteries at Brescia, Milan, and Pavia.[176] In northern France and Flanders, monasteries acted as the stimulus for the transformation of the adjoining political centers into trading settlements and afterward into towns.[177] In large measure this was due to the increasing role of Carolingian monasteries as centers of production. Documentary sources indicate that forty craftsmen were needed to manufacture and maintain the material requirements of a monastic settlement consisting of 250 people.[178] Even more were required if the monastic community was producing for the aristocratic elite, as suggested by the presence of arms (swords and shields) manufacturers on the Plan of St. Gall. The concentration of workshops within a sector of the monastery gradually led to the development of a community of craftsmen. At first they worked in the service of the monastic community, but as production increased to satisfy the needs of the immediate (and later of the wider) hinterland, new craftsmen, working for themselves, settled beside the monastery. By 867, in Arras for instance, the *vicus monasterii* had been joined by a *vicus qui vocatur Nova Villa juxta*

---

170. De Jong, "Carolingian Monasticism," pp. 637–38.
171. De Jong, "Carolingian Monasticism," p. 639.
172. De Jong, "Carolingian Monasticism," p. 639.
173. De Jong, "Carolingian Monasticism," p. 638.
174. Hodges, *Towns and Trade*, pp. 84–85.
175. Hodges, *Light in the Dark Ages*, p. 215.
176. Balzaretti, "Cities, Emporia and Monasteries," p. 226.
177. Verhulst, *Rise of Cities in North-West Europe*, p. 43.
178. Horn and Born, *Plan of St. Gall*, 2:195–96.

monasterium.[179] From the phraseology it is clear that the *vicus monasterii* was the older settlement, with its inhabitants working in the monastery and engaging in a range of activities including baking, brewing, smithing, and trading.[180] In contrast, the inhabitants of the newer settlement were working for themselves. As Hodges has pointed out, this development had an enduring impact on European society because the agglomeration of workshops within monasteries set in motion the developments that led to the formation of a new social order—urban craftsmen.[181] The urban settlements of the tenth century and later are characterized by the predominance of craftsmen over merchants, and the emergence of these specialist producers with their own socially interdependent networks eventually broke the ethos of kin-based societies across Europe.[182]

CONCLUSION

The regions of Europe evolved at different rates. During the seventh century there was little functional difference in settlement forms across Europe. It was an urban wasteland, and Cathy Swift's description of the "forts and fields" of the early Irish *civitas* could be applied equally to the *civitas* of Rome itself. In the eighth century, political and economic developments in northern Europe led to the emergence of emporia around the North Sea. It has been suggested that Dalkey Island may have functioned as one such emporium in Ireland, but the evidence is not conclusive.[183] It may well be that the *longphort* established at Dublin in 841 represents the arrival in Ireland and western Britain of the idea of the emporium. The political and economic reorganization of Carolingian Europe in the ninth century led to the abandonment of emporia in favor of manufacturing and trading settlements that were located at monasteries. By the end of the ninth century, however, urban settlements were more commonly located beside elite residences and economically advantageous features such as harbors. However, for a time in the ninth century, the monastic town was the key urban settlement of the Carolingian world. It had emerged in Britain by the end of that century when several of the Alfredian burhs were located at ecclesiastical sites and the "minster-town" was to be a feature of the tenth century.[184] Although Irish monasteries shared

179. Verhulst, *Rise of Cities in North-West Europe*, p. 53.
180. Verhulst, *Rise of Cities in North-West Europe*, p. 53; see also Nicholas, *Growth of the Medieval City*, pp. 32–33, for similar developments at Dijon, Limoges, and Reims.
181. Hodges, *Towns and Trade*, p. 83.
182. Hodges, *Towns and Trade*, p. 83.
183. Hodges, *Dark Age Economics;* I. Doyle, "Early Medieval Activity at Dalkey Island."
184. Blair, "Small Towns," 1:250–58.

many experiences in common with their Continental counterparts, it was only with the reign of the high-king Flann Sinna (879–916) that political conditions favorable to the growth of monastic towns were established in Ireland. Clonmacnoise was reorganized in 909 because it was effectively his capital.[185] From the tenth century onward the documentary, archaeological, and architectural evidence for the monastic town is compelling. At first, like their Continental counterparts, the craftsmen were in the service of the monastery and it is not yet clear at what stage independent craftsmen began to settle at Irish monasteries, but the inscription on the shrine of the Cathach, the charters in the Book of Kells, and the evidence for burgesses at Killaloe all indicate that this development had occurred before the middle of the twelfth century and, if the evidence of the Cathach is accepted, by the end of the eleventh. It may well be that the absence of a burgage-plot pattern at Irish monastic towns reflects the comparatively late development of urban craftsmen as a distinctive social group.

Like its Continental counterparts, the Irish monastic town could not have commenced without elaborating the concept of the monastery as the city of refuge and the city of God. Again like its Continental counterparts, it could not have developed without the emergence of powerful over-kings, strong enough to guarantee the peace and security of the market-place. Finally, it could not have grown without the interaction with the Scandinavian port towns, which provided an important stimulus to craft production and regional trade. Indeed, the relatively late date at which the monastic town began to flower suggests that commercial influence from the Scandinavian towns was much more substantial than hitherto believed.

The names prototown, preurban nucleus, and solar central place have been applied to the monastic town, but none is satisfactory.[186] The Irish monastic town was an entity in its own right, a fully fledged phenomenon with specific settlement characteristics, which was part and parcel of the functioning fabric of society, and far from being unique, it was just one episode in a widespread European experience. Valante's claims that "it was only with Anglo-Norman patronage that towns evolved around a very small number of Irish monasteries . . . [and that] any attempt to view the monastic town, or indeed any urbanism, as an indigenous development in Ireland during the early middle ages cannot be sustained" are without foundation.[187]

185. Bradley, "Monastic Town of Clonmacnoise," p. 49.

186. Swan, "Monastic Proto-towns in Early Medieval Ireland"; Clarke and Simms, "Towards a Comparative History," pp. 678–79; Graham, "Urban Genesis," p. 9; Graham, "Urbanization in Medieval Ireland," p. 181.

187. Valante, "Reassessing the Irish 'Monastic Town,'" pp. 17–18.

BIBLIOGRAPHY

Abbreviations for Latin Sources and Bibliography of Editions. Toronto: Pontifical Institute of Mediaeval Studies, 1995.

Adcock, Gwenda. "A Study of the Types of Interlace on Northumbrian Sculpture." MPhil Thesis, University of Durham, 1974.

Adomnán. *Adomnán's Life of Columba.* Ed. and trans. A. O. Anderson and M. O. Anderson. London: T. Nelson, 1961.

———. *Adomnán's Life of Columba.* Ed. and trans. A. O. Anderson and M. O. Anderson. 2nd ed. Oxford: Oxford University Press, 1991.

———. *Life of St. Columba.* Trans. Richard Sharpe. Harmondsworth: Penguin, 1995.

Ælfric. *Ælfric's Catholic Homilies, the First Series.* Ed. Peter Clemoes. EETS s.s. 17. London: Oxford University Press, 1997.

———. *Ælfric's Catholic Homilies, the Second Series: Text.* Ed. Malcolm Godden. EETS s.s. 5. London: Oxford University Press, 1979.

———. *Homilies of Ælfric: A Supplementary Collection.* Ed. John C. Pope. 2 vols. EETS o.s. 259, 260. London: Oxford University Press, 1967–68.

———. *Aelfric's Lives of Saints: Being a Set of Sermons on Saints' Days formerly observed by the English Church.* Ed. and trans. Walter W. Skeat. EETS o.s. 94, 114. London: N. Trübner, 1890–1900. Reprinted as one vol., London: Oxford University Press, 1966/1967.

Aeschylus. *Aeschylus, The Libation Bearers.* Trans. H. Weir Smyth. Cambridge, Mass.: Harvard University Press, 1926.

Æthelwulf. *De Abbatibus.* Ed. Alistair Campbell. Oxford: Oxford University Press, 1967.

Aldhelm. *Aldhelmi opera omnia.* Ed. Rudolf Ehwald. MGH Auctores Antiquissimi 15. Berlin: Wiedman, 1919. Reprint, 1961.

———. *Aldhelm: The Poetic Works.* Ed. and trans. Michael Lapidge and J. L. Rosier. Cambridge: Cambridge University Press, 1985.

———. *Aldhelm: The Prose Works.* Ed. and trans. Michael Lapidge and Michael Herren. Cambridge: Cambridge University Press; Totowa: Rowman & Littlefield, 1979.

Alexander, J. J. G. "The Illumination." In *The Book of Kells: MS 58, Trinity College Library, Dublin: Commentary,* ed. Peter Fox, pp. 265–89. Lucerne: Faksimile Verlag, 1990.

————, ed. *Insular Manuscripts, 6th to the 9th Century.* London: Harvey Miller, 1978.

————. "The Last Things: Representing the Unrepresentable; The Medieval Tradition." In *The Apocalypse and the Shape of Things to Come,* ed. Frances Carey, pp. 43–63. Toronto: University of Toronto Press, 1999.

————. *Medieval Illuminators and Their Methods of Work.* New Haven: Yale University Press, 1992.

————. "Some Aesthetic Principles in the Use of Colour in Anglo-Saxon Art." *ASE* 4 (1975), 145–54.

Alexander, Michael, trans. *Beowulf: A Verse Translation.* Harmondsworth: Penguin, 1973.

Allen, J. Romilly. *Early Christian Symbolism in Great Britain and Ireland before the Thirteenth Century.* London: Whiting, 1887.

Allen, J. Romilly, and Joseph Anderson. *The Early Christian Monuments of Scotland.* Edinburgh: Society of Antiquaries of Scotland, 1903. Reprinted with an introduction by I. Henderson, 2 vols. Balgavies, Angus: Pinkfoot Press, 1993.

Almgren, Bertil. "Helmets, Crowns and Warriors' Dress—from the Roman Emperors to the Chieftains of Uppland." In Lamm and Nordström, *Vendel Period Studies,* pp. 11–16.

————. "Hjälmar, kronor och stridsrockar—från kejsardömets Rom till Upplands hövdingar." In *Vendeltid,* ed. Ann Sandwall, pp. 158–66. Stockholm: Statens historiska museum, 1980.

Andaloro, Maria. "La datazione della tavola di S. Maria in Trastevere." *Rivista dell'Istituto Nazionale d'Archeologia e Storia dell'Arte,* n.s., 19–20 (1972–73), 139–215.

Anderson, A. O., ed. *Early Sources of Scottish History.* 2 vols. Edinburgh: Oliver and Boyd, 1922.

Andrews, John. *Kildare.* Irish Historic Towns Atlas 1. Dublin: Royal Irish Academy, 1986.

Anon. *JRSAI* 8 (1864–66), 411–12.

Armstrong, Edmund C. R. "Some Irish Antiquities of Unknown Use." *Antiquaries Jnl.* 2 (1922), 6–12.

Arntz, Helmut. *Handbuch der Runenkunde.* Sammlung kurzer Grammatiken germanischer Dialekte, Ergänzungsreihe, 3. 2nd ed. Halle: M. Niemeyer, 1944.

Arnulf, Arwed. *Versus ad Picturas: Studien zur Titulusdichtung als Quellengattung der Kunstgeschichte von der Antike bis zum Hochmittelalter.* Berlin: Deutscher Kunstverlag, 1997.

Arwidsson, Greta. "Valsgärde." In Lamm and Nordström, *Vendel Period Studies,* pp. 71–82.

————. *Valsgärde 7.* Uppsala: Almqvist & Wiksell, 1977.

──────. *Valsgärde 8*. Uppsala: Almqvist & Wiksell, 1954.

Augustine. *Augustine. City of God*. Ed. and trans. David Knowles. Middlesex: Penguin, 1972.

──────. *Augustine: De doctrina Christiana*. Ed. R. P. H. Green. Oxford: Clarendon Press, 1995.

──────. *St. Augustine: Expositions on the Book of Psalms*. Ed. and trans. Philip Schaff. New York: Christian Literature, 1888.

──────. *St. Augustine: Homilies on the Gospel of John; Homilies on the First Epistle of John; Soliloquies*. Ed. and trans. Philip Schaff. Grand Rapids, Mich.: Eerdmans, 1986.

──────. *Sancti Aurelii Augustini: in Iohannis Evangelium tractatus CXXIV*. Ed. R. Willems. CCSL 36. Turnhout: Brepols, 1954.

──────. *Aurelii Augustini opera pars X.1: Ennarationes in Psalmos I–L*. Ed. E. Dekkers and J. Fraipont. CCSL 38. Turnhout: Brepols, 1956.

──────. *Aurelii Augustini opera pars X.2: Ennarationes in Psalmos LI–C*. Ed. E. Dekkers and J. Fraipont. CCSL 39. Turnhout: Brepols, 1956.

──────. *Aurelii Augustini opera pars X.3: Ennarationes in Psalmos CI–CL*. Ed. E. Dekkers and J. Fraipont. CCSL 40. Turnhout: Brepols, 1990.

──────. *Aurelii Augustini opera pars XIV.2: De Civitate Dei, Libri XI–XXII*. Ed. B. Dombarat and A. Kalb. CCSL 48. Turnhout: Brepols, 1955.

Avent, Richard. *Anglo-Saxon Disc and Composite Brooches*. Oxford: British Archaeological Reports, 1975.

Backhouse, Janet A., D. H. Turner, and Leslie Webster, eds. *The Golden Age of Anglo-Saxon Art 966–1066*. London: British Museum Publications, 1984.

Bailey, Richard N. "The Chronology of Viking-Age Sculpture in Northumbria." In Lang, *Anglo-Saxon and Viking Age Sculpture*, pp. 173–203.

──────. *The Durham Cassiodorus*. Jarrow Lecture 1978. Jarrow: St. Paul's Church, 1978. Reprinted in Lapidge, *Bede and His World*, 1:463–90.

──────. *England's Earliest Sculptors*. Toronto: Pontifical Institute for Mediaeval Studies, 1996.

──────. *The Meaning of Mercian Sculpture*. Leicester: Brixworth Lecture, 1990.

──────. "The Meaning of the Viking-Age Shaft at Dacre." *Transactions of the Cumberland and Westmorland Antiquarian and Archaeological Society*, 2nd series, 77 (1977), 61–74.

──────. "Sutton Hoo and Seventh-Century Art." In Farrell and Neuman de Vegvar, *Sutton Hoo Fifty Years After*, pp. 31–41.

──────. "'What Mean These Stones?' Some Aspects of Pre-Norman Sculpture in Cheshire and Lancashire." Toller Memorial Lecture. *Bulletin of the John Rylands University Library of Manchester* 78, no. 1 (1996), 21–46.

Bailey, Richard N., and Rosemary J. Cramp, eds. *Cumberland, Westmorland and Lancashire-North-of-the-Sands.* Vol. 2 of *Corpus of Anglo-Saxon Stone Sculpture.* Oxford: Oxford University Press, 1988.

Bakka, Egil. "Some Decorated Anglo-Saxon and Irish Metalwork Found in Norwegian Viking Graves." In *The Fourth Viking Congress, York, August, 1961,* ed. Alan Small, pp. 32–40. Edinburgh: Published for the University of Aberdeen by Oliver and Boyd, 1965.

Balzaretti, Ross. "Cities, Emporia and Monasteries: Local Economies and the Po Valley, *c.* AD 700–875." In *Towns in Transition, Urban Evolution in Late Antiquity and the Early Middle Ages,* ed. Neil Christie and S. T. Loseby, pp. 213–34. Aldershot: Scolar Press, 1996.

Barber, Elizabeth Wayland. *Women's Work: The First 20,000 Years. Women, Cloth, and Society in Early Times.* New York: W. W. Norton, 1994.

Barber, John. "Excavations on Iona, 1979." *PSAS* 111 (1981), 282–380.

Bartlett, Robert. *England under the Norman and Angevin Kings (1075–1225).* Oxford: Oxford University Press, 1999.

Bateman, Thomas. *Ten Years' Diggings in Celtic and Saxon Grave Hills in the Counties of Derby, Stafford and York from 1848 to 1858.* London: George Allen & Sons, 1861. Reprint, Buxton: Moorland, 1978.

Batey, C. E., with C. Freeman. "Lavacroon, Orphir, Orkney." *PSAS* 116 (1986), 285–300, fiche 5: A3–D9.

Battiscombe, C. F., ed. *The Relics of St. Cuthbert: Studies by Various Authors Collected and Edited with an Historical Introduction.* Oxford: Oxford University Press, 1956.

Beatus Rhenanus. *Castigationes in Libellum de Germania.* Basel: Froben, 1533.

Bebel, Heinrich. *Schardius Redivivus.* 4 vols. Giessen: ex officina Seileriana, 1673.

Beck, Heinrich. "Eber." In *Reallexikon der germanischen Altertumskunde,* 6:328–34. Berlin: De Gruyter, 1986.

———. *Das Ebersignum im Germanischen.* Berlin: De Gruyter, 1965.

Beckwith, John. *Ivory Carvings in Early Medieval England.* London: Harvey Miller & Medcalf, 1972.

Bédat, Isabelle, and Béatrice Girault-Kurtzeman. "The Technical Study of the Bayeux Tapestry." In Bouet, Levy, and Neveux, *Bayeux Tapestry,* pp. 83–109.

Bede. *De templo.* In *Bedae Venerabilis Opera. Pars 2, Opera Exegetica, 2a,* ed. David Hurst, pp. 141–234. CCSL 119A. Turnhout: Brepols, 1969.

———. *De temporum ratione.* Ed. Theodor Mommsen and Charles W. Jones. CCSL 123B. Turnhout: Brepols, 1977.

———. *Bede's Ecclesiastical History of the English People.* Ed. Bertram Colgrave and R. A. B. Mynors. Oxford: Clarendon Press, 1969.

————. *The Ecclesiastical History of the English People, The Greater Chronicle, Bede's Letter to Egbert.* Ed. Judith McClure and Roger Collins. Oxford: Oxford University Press, 1994.

————. *Epistola ad Pleguinam.* Ed. Charles W. Jones. CCSL 123C. Turnhout: Brepols, 1980.

————. "Expositio super Epistolas Catholicas—In Epistolam I Petri." PL 93:66.

————. *Historia abbatum.* In *Venerabilis Baedae opera historica,* ed. Plummer, 1:364–87.

————. *A History of the English Church and People.* Ed. Leo Shirley-Price. Harmondsworth: Penguin, 1968.

————. *Homeliarum Euangelii libri ii.* Ed. David Hurst. CCSL 122. Turnhout: Brepols, 1955.

————. *Bede the Venerable Homilies on the Gospels.* 2 vols. Trans. L. T. Martin and David Hurst. Kalamazoo, Mich.: Cistercian Publications, 1991.

————. *In Cantica Canticorum.* Ed. David Hurst. CCSL 119B. Turnhout: Brepols, 1983.

————. *In primam partem Samuhelis libri iv.* Ed. David Hurst, CCSL 119. Turnhout: Brepols, 1962.

————. *In Regum librum xxx quaestiones.* Ed. David Hurst. CCSL 119. Turnhout: Brepols, 1962.

————. *On the Temple.* Trans. Sean Connolly. Liverpool: Liverpool University Press, 1995.

————. *Venerabilis Baedae opera historica.* Ed. Charles Plummer. 2 vols. Oxford: Clarendon Press, 1896.

————. *Bede: The Reckoning of Time.* Trans. Faith Wallis. Liverpool: Liverpool University Press, 1999.

Beech, George. *Was the Bayeux Tapestry Made in France? The Case for Saint-Florent.* Basingstoke: Palgrave Macmillan, 2005.

Belting, Hans. *Likeness and Presence: A History of the Image before the Era of Art.* Trans. Edmund Jephcott. Chicago: University of Chicago Press, 1994.

Belting-Ihm, Christa. "Das Justinuskreuz in der Schatzkammer der Peterskirche zu Rom." *Jahrbuch des Römisch-germanischen Zentralmuseums, Mainz* 12 (1965), 142–66.

Benediktsson, Jakob. (See Jakob Benediktsson.)

Benjamin, Walter. *Ursprung des deutschen Trauerspiels.* Berlin: E. Rowohlt, 1928. Trans. as *The Origin of German Tragic Drama.* Trans. J. Osborne. London: NLB, 1977.

Beran, Giuseppe. "L'Offertorio 'Domine Iesu Christe' della messe per i defunti." *Ephemerides Liturgicae* 50 (1936), 140–47.

Bernard of Clairvaux. *St. Bernard of Clairvaux's Life of St. Malachy of Armagh.* Trans. H. J. Lawlor. London: SPCK, 1920.

Bérnard, Claude, Jean-Pierre Vernant, et al. *Die Bilderwelt der Griechen.* Mainz: Philipp von Zabern, 1984.

Bernard, J. H., and R. Atkinson, eds. *The Irish Liber Hymnorum.* 2 vols. London: Henry Bradshaw Society, 1898.

Bernstein, David J. *The Mystery of the Bayeux Tapestry.* London: Weidenfeld & Nicolson, 1986.

Bernt, Gunter. *Das lateinische Epigramm in Übergang von der Spätantike zum frühen Mittelalter.* Münchener Beiträge zur Mediävistik und Renaissance-Forschung 2. Munich: Arbeo-Gesellschaft, 1968.

Bertelli, Carlo. *La Madonna di Santa Maria in Trastevere.* Rome, 1961.

Bertrand, Simone. *La Tapisserie de Bayeux et la manière de vivre au onzième siècle.* La Pierre-qui-Vire: Zodiac, 1966.

Bethell, Denis. "English Monks and Irish Reform in the Eleventh and Twelfth Centuries." *Historical Studies* 8 (1971), 111–35.

Biddle, Martin, and Birthe Kjølbye-Biddle. "The Repton Stone." *ASE* 14 (1985), 233–92.

Bieler, Ludwig, ed. and trans. *The Patrician Texts in the Book of Armagh.* Dublin: Dublin Institute for Advanced Studies, 1979.

Bischoff, Bernhard. "Turning Points in the History of Latin Exegesis in the Early Middle Ages." Part 2 of McNamara, *Biblical Studies*, pp. 74–160.

Bjarni Einarsson, ed. *Fagrskinna (Nóregs konunga tal).* Íslenzk fornrit 29. Reykjavík: Hið íslenzka fornritafélag, 1985.

Bjarni Guðnason. *Um Skjöldungasögu.* Reykjavík: Bókaútgáfa Menningarsjóðs, 1963.

———, ed. *Sǫgur Danakonunga.* Íslenzk fornrit 35. Reykjavík: Hið íslenzka fornritafélag, 1982.

Bjork, Robert E., and John D. Niles, eds. *A Beowulf Handbook.* Exeter: Exeter University Press; Lincoln: University of Nebraska Press, 1997.

Blackburn, Mark, and Hugh Pagan. "A Revised Check-list of Coin Hoards from the British Isles, c. 500–1100." In *Anglo-Saxon Monetary History, Essays in Memory of Michael Dolley*, ed. M. A. S. Blackburn, pp. 291–313. Leicester: Leicester University Press, 1986.

Blair, John. "Small Towns 600–1270." In *The Cambridge Urban History of Britain*, ed. D. M. Palliser, Peter Clarke, and Martin Daunton, 3 vols., 1:245–70. Cambridge: Cambridge University Press, 2000.

Blake, E. O., ed. *Liber Eliensis.* Camden Third Series 92. London: Royal Historical Society, 1962.

Bland, Roger, ed., *Treasure Annual Report 1998–1999.* Department for Culture Media and Sport. London: Department for Culture Media and Sport, 2001.

Blindheim, Martin. *Norwegian Romanesque Decorative Sculpture 1090–1210.* New York: Tiranti, 1966.

Boer, R. C. "Studier over Skjoldungedigtningen." *Aarbøger for nordisk Old-kyndighed og Historie,* 3rd series, 12 (1922), 133–266.

Boland, Donal, Aidan O'Sullivan, and Colin Breen. "An Early Christian Wooden Bridge on the River Shannon at Clonmacnoise, Co. Offaly." *Newswarp, the Newsletter of the Wetland Archaeology Research Project* 20 (1996), 23–25.

Bolland, Jean, et al., eds. *Acta Sanctorum.* Februarii, 1. Antwerp: J. van Meurs, 1658.

Bond, J. "Explanatory Note on the Identification of the Ivory Fragments." In Hills, Penn, and Rickett, *Anglo-Saxon Cemetery at Spong Hill, North Elmham Part V,* pp. 35–36.

Boniface. *Briefe des Bonifatius Willibalds Leben des Bonifatius.* Ed. R. Rau. Darmstadt: Wissenschaftliche Buchgesellschaft, 1968.

Bonner, Gerald. *Saint Bede in the Tradition of Western Apocalyptic Commentary.* Jarrow Lecture 1966. Jarrow: St. Paul's Church, 1966. Reprinted in Lapidge, *Bede and His World,* 1:153–83.

Bonner, Gerald, David Rollason, and Clare Stancliffe, eds. *St Cuthbert, His Cult and His Community to AD 1200.* Woodbridge: Boydell, 1989.

Borchardt, Frank L. *German Antiquity in Renaissance Myth.* Baltimore: Johns Hopkins University Press, 1971.

Borchhardt, Jürgen. *Homerische Helme.* Mainz am Rhein: P. von Zabern, 1972.

Borsje, Jacqueline. *From Chaos to Enemy: Encounters with Monsters in Early Irish Texts. An Investigation Related to the Process of Christianization and the Concept of Evil.* Turnhout: Brepols, 1996.

Botterweck, G. Johannes, and Helmer Ringgren, eds. *Theological Dictionary of the Old Testament.* Trans. John T. Willis. 9 vols. Grand Rapids, Mich.: Eerdmans, 1973–.

Bouet, Pierre, Brian Levy, and François Neveux, eds. *The Bayeux Tapestry: Embroidering the Facts of History.* Caen: Presses universitaires de Caen, 2004.

Bourke, Cormac, ed. *From the Isles of the North: Early Medieval Art in Ireland and Britain.* Belfast: HMSO, 1995.

———. *Patrick, the Archaeology of a Saint.* Belfast: HMSO, 1993.

Bovini, Giuseppe. *La Cattedra eburnean del Vescovo Massiamiano di Ravenna.* Ravenna: Longo, 1990.

———. *Ravenna: Art and History.* Ravenna: Longo, 1991.

Bradley, John. "Archaeology, Topography and Building Fabric; the Cathedral and Town of Medieval Kildare." *Kildare Archaeological Society Jnl.* 19, no. 1 (2000–01), 27–47.

————. *Kilkenny.* Irish Historic Towns Atlas 10. Dublin: Royal Irish Academy, 2000.

————. "Killaloe: A Pre-Norman Borough?" *Peritia* 8 (1994), 170–79.

————. "The Monastic Town of Clonmacnoise." In King, *Clonmacnoise Studies,* 1:42–55.

————. "Planned Anglo-Norman Towns in Ireland." In Clarke and Simms, *Comparative History of Urban Origins,* pp. 411–68.

Braga, Gabriella. "*Moralia in Iob*: Epitomi dei Secoli VII–X e loro evoluzione." In Fontaine, Gillet, and Pellistrandi, *Grégoire le Grand,* pp. 561–68.

Branigan, K., and P. J. Fowler, eds. *The Roman West Country: Classical Culture and Celtic Society.* London: David and Charles, 1976.

Brannon, N. F. In "Medieval Britain and Ireland," *MA* 30 (1986), 181–82; 31 (1987), 176–77; 32 (1988), 295.

Brenan, Jane. *Hanging Bowls and Their Contexts.* Oxford: Tempus Reparatum, 1991.

Brøgger, A. W., Hjalmar Falk, Gabriel Adolf Gustavson, and Haakon Schetelig. *Osebergfundet.* 5 vols. Kristiania [Oslo]: Universitets Oldsaksamling, 1917–28.

Brown, David. "Swastika Patterns." In *Angles, Saxons and Jutes,* ed. Vera I. Evison, pp. 227–40. Oxford: Oxford University Press, 1981.

Brown, G. Baldwin. *The Arts in Early England.* Vol. 1, *Saxon Art and Industry in the Pagan Period.* London: John Murray, 1915.

————. *The Arts in Early England.* Vol. 5, *The Ruthwell and Bewcastle Crosses, the Gospels of Lindisfarne and Other Christian Monuments of Northumbria.* London: John Murray, 1921.

————. "Notes on a Necklace of Glass Beads found in a Cist in Dalmeny Park, South Queensferry." *PSAS* 49 (1914–15), 332–38.

Brown, Michelle P. *The Lindisfarne Gospels: Society, Spirituality and the Scribe.* London: British Library, 2003.

Brown, Peter. *The Book of Kells.* London: Thames and Hudson, 1980.

Brown, Shirley Ann. *The Bayeux Tapestry. History and Bibliography.* Woodbridge: Boydell, 1988.

————. "Bibliography of Bayeux Tapestry Studies 1985–1999." In Bouet, Levy, and Neveux, *Bayeux Tapestry,* pp. 411–18.

Bruce-Mitford, Rupert L. S. *Aspects of Anglo-Saxon Archaeology.* London: Gollancz, 1974.

————. "Ireland and the Hanging-bowls—A Review." In M. Ryan, *Ireland and Insular Art,* pp. 30–39.

————. "Late Celtic Hanging-Bowls in Lincolnshire and South Humberside." In *Pre-Viking Lindsey,* ed. Alan Vince, pp. 45–70. Lincoln: City of Lincoln Archaeology Unit, 1983.

————. *The Sutton Hoo Ship Burial.* Vol. 2, *Arms, Armour and Regalia.* London: British Museum Publications, 1978.

———. *The Sutton Hoo Ship Burial.* Vol. 3. London: British Museum Publications, 1983.

Bruce-Mitford, Rupert L. S., and Marilyn R. Luscombe. "The Benty Grange Helmet and Some Other Supposed Anglo-Saxon Helmets." In *Aspects of Anglo-Saxon Archaeology*, ed. R. Bruce-Mitford, pp. 223–52

Bruce-Mitford, R. L. S., with S. Raven. *The Corpus of Late Celtic Hanging Bowls with an Account of the Bowls Found in Scandinavia.* Oxford: Oxford University Press, 2005.

Budny, Mildred O. "British Library Manuscript Royal I E. vi: The Anatomy of an Anglo-Saxon Bible Fragment." PhD diss., University of London, 1984.

Budny, Mildred O., and Dominic Tweddle. "The Early Medieval Textiles at Maaseik, Belgium." *Antiquaries Jnl.* 65 (1985), 353–89.

———. "The Maaseik Embroideries." *ASE* 13 (1984), 65–96.

Butterworth, C. A., and S. J. Lobb. *Excavations in the Burghfield Area, Berkshire.* Wessex Archaeology Report 1. Salisbury: Wessex Archaeology, 1992.

Bynum, Caroline Walker. *Fragmentation and Redemption: Essays on Gender and the Human Body in Medieval Religion.* New York: Zone Books, 1991.

———. *The Resurrection of the Body in Western Christianity, 200–1336.* New York: Columbia University Press, 1995.

Byrhtferth. *Enchiridion.* Ed. Peter S. Baker and Michael Lapidge. EETS s.s. 15. Oxford: Oxford University Press, 1995.

Byrne, F. J. *Irish Kings and High-kings.* London: B. T. Batsford, 1973.

———. "Onomastica 2: Na Renna." *Peritia* 1 (1982), 267.

———. "Rulers of Man to 1765." In *A New History of Ireland*, ed. T. W. Moody, F. X. Martin, and F. J. Byrne, pp. 465–68. Oxford: Oxford University Press, 1984.

Cabrol, Fernand. "L'offertoire de la messe des morts." *Revue Grégorienne* 6 (1921), 165–70 and 205–07.

Cabrol, Fernand, and H. Leclercq, eds. *Dictionnaire d'archéologie chrétienne et de liturgie.* Vol. 1. Paris: Letouzey, 1924.

Calvert, Judith A. "The Early Development of Irish High Crosses and their Relationship to Scottish Sculpture in the Ninth and Tenth Centuries." PhD diss., University of California at Berkeley, 1978.

Cameron, Averil. "The Artistic Patronage of Justin II." In Cameron, *Continuity and Change in Sixth-Century Byzantium*, paper XII. Collected Studies 143. London: Variorum, 1981.

Campbell, Ewan. "E-ware and Aquitaine—a Reconsideration of the Petrological Evidence." *Scottish Archaeological Review* 3 (1984), 35–41.

Campbell, James, et al., eds. *The Anglo-Saxons.* London: Phaidon, 1982.

Capelle, Bernard. "Le rôle théologique de Bède le venerable." *Studia Anselmiana* 6 (1936), 1–40.

Carroll, Judith. "Millefiori in the Development of Early Irish Enamelling." In Bourke, *From the Isles of the North,* pp. 49–57.

Carver, M. O. H., ed. *The Age of Sutton Hoo.* Woodbridge: Boydell, 1992.

———. *Arguments in Stone, Archaeological Research and the European Town in the First Millennium.* Oxford: Oxbow Books, 1993.

Cassidy, Brendan. "The Dream of St Joseph on the Anglo-Saxon Cross from Rothbury." *Gesta* 35, no. 2 (1996), 149–55.

———, ed. *The Ruthwell Cross: Papers from the Colloquium Sponsored by the Index of Christian Art Princeton University 8 December 1989.* Index of Christian Art Occasional Papers 1. Princeton: Princeton Department of Art and Archaeology, 1992.

Cassiodorus. *Cassiodorus. Explanation of the Psalms.* Vol. 1, *Psalms 1–50.* Ed. and trans. P. G. Walsh. New York: Paulist Press, 1990.

———. *Cassiodorus. Explanation of the Psalms.* Vol. 2, *Psalms 51–100.* Ed. and trans. P. G. Walsh. New York: Paulist Press, 1991.

———. *Magni Aurelii Cassiodori Senatoris opera pars II.1: Expositio psalmorum I–LXX.* Ed. M. Adriaen. CCSL 97. Turnhout: Brepols, 1955.

Cather, Sharon, David Park, and Paul Williamson, eds. *Early Medieval Wall Painting and Painted Sculpture in England.* Oxford: British Archaeological Reports, 1990.

Cennini, Cennino. *The Craftsman's Handbook: The Italian "Il Libro dell'Arte" by Cennino d'Andrea Cennini.* Ed. D. V. Thompson. New York: Dover, 1960.

Charles-Edwards, Thomas. "The Penitential of Theodore and the Judicia Theodori." In *Archbishop Theodore,* ed. Michael Lapidge, pp. 141–74. Cambridge: Cambridge University Press, 1995.

Chazelle, Celia M. "Pictures, Books, and the Illiterate: Pope Gregory I's Letters to Serenus of Marseilles." *Word and Image* 6, no. 2 (1990), 138–53.

Childe, V. G. *A Short Introduction to Archaeology.* London: Muller, 1956.

Clancy, Thomas O., and Gilbert Márkus, eds. *Iona, the Earliest Poetry of a Celtic Monastery.* Edinburgh: Edinburgh University Press, 1995.

Clarke, Helen, and Björn Ambrosiani, eds. *Towns in the Viking Age.* Leicester: Leicester University Press, 1991.

Clarke, H. B., and Anngret Simms, eds. *The Comparative History of Urban Origins in Non-Roman Europe.* Oxford: British Archaeological Reports, 1985.

———. "Towards a Comparative History of Urban Origins." In Clarke and Simms, *Comparative History of Urban Origins,* pp. 669–703.

Coates, Simon D. "The Bishop as Pastor and Solitary: Spiritual Authority of the Monk-Bishop." *Jnl. of Ecclesiastical History* 47 (1996), 601–19.

Coatsworth, Elizabeth. "The Embroideries from the Tomb of St. Cuthbert." In *Edward the Elder: 899–924*, ed. N. J. Higham and D. H. Hill, ·pp. 292–306. London: Routledge, 2001.

———. "The Pectoral Cross and Portable Altar from the Tomb of St. Cuthbert." In Bonner, Rollason, and Stancliffe, *St Cuthbert, His Cult and His Community*, pp. 287–301.

———, ed. *Western Yorkshire*. Vol. 8 of *Corpus of Anglo-Saxon Stone Sculpture*. Oxford: Oxford University Press, 2008.

Coatsworth, Elizabeth, Maria Fitzgerald, Kevin Leahy, and Gale Owen-Crocker. "Anglo-Saxon Textiles from Cleatham, Humberside." *Textile History* 27, no. 1 (1996), 5–41.

Coatsworth, Elizabeth, and Gale Owen-Crocker. *Medieval Textiles of the British Isles AD 450–1100: An Annotated Bibliography*. Oxford: Archaeopress, 2007.

Coatsworth, Elizabeth, and Michael Pinder. *The Art of the Anglo-Saxon Goldsmith: Fine Metalwork in Anglo-Saxon England. Its Practice and Practitioners*. Woodbridge: Boydell, 2002.

Colgan, John, ed. *Triadis Thaumaturgae*. Louvain: Coenestenius, 1647. Reprint, Dublin: Edmund Burke, 1997.

Colgrave, Bertram, ed. *The Earliest Life of Gregory the Great by an Anonymous Monk of Whitby*. Lawrence: University of Kansas Press, 1968.

———, ed. and trans. *Two Lives of Saint Cuthbert: A Life by an Anonymous Monk of Lindisfarne, and Bede's Prose Life*. Cambridge: Cambridge University Press, 1940.

Collingwood, W. G. *Northumbrian Crosses of the Pre-Norman Age*. London: Faber & Gwyer, 1927.

Comyn, D., and P. S. Dineen, eds. *Foras feasa ar Éirinn, the History of Ireland by Geoffrey Keating*. 4 vols. London, 1902–14.

Connolly, Seán. "Cogitosus's Life of Brigit, Content and Value." *JRSAI* 117 (1987), 5–10.

Connolly, Seán, and Jean-Michel Picard, eds. "Cogitosus: Life of Brigit." *JRSAI* 117 (1987), 11–27.

Conrad-O'Briain, Helen. "Beowulf and the Uses of History." PhD diss., Trinity College, Dublin, 1990.

Conybeare, John J., ed. *Illustrations of Anglo-Saxon Poetry*. London: Harding and Lepard, 1826.

Cook, A. M., and M. W. Dacre. *Excavations at Portway, Andover, 1973–1975*. Oxford: Oxford University Committee for Archaeology, 1985.

Cook, Jean M. "Bronze-bound Buckets." In *An Anglo-Saxon Cemetery at Great Chesterford, Essex*, ed. Vera I. Evison, pp. 22–24. CBA Res. Rep. 91. London: Council for British Archaeology, 1994.

Crabtree, Pamela. "Animal Exploitation in East Anglian Villages." In *Environment and Economy in Anglo-Saxon England,* ed. D. James Rackham and Martin Carver, pp. 40–54. CBA Res. Rep. 89. York: Council for British Archaeology, 1994.

———. *West Stow, Suffolk, Early Anglo-Saxon Animal Husbandry.* East Anglian Archaeology Report 47. Ipswich: Suffolk County Planning Department, 1989.

Cracco, Giorgio. "Gregorio e l'Oltretomba." In Fontaine, Gillet, and Pellistrandi, *Grégoire le Grand,* pp. 255–66.

Cramp, Rosemary. "The Anglian Sculptured Crosses of Dumfriesshire." *Transactions of the Dumfriesshire and Galloway Natural History and Antiquarian Society,* 3rd series, 38 (1959–60), 9–20.

———. "*Beowulf* and Archaeology." *MA* 1 (1957), 57–77. Reprinted in *The Beowulf Poet: A Collection of Critical Essays,* ed. Donald K. Fry, pp. 114–40. Englewood Cliffs, N.J.: Prentice-Hall, 1968.

———, ed. *Durham and Northumberland.* Vol. 1 of *Corpus of Anglo-Saxon Stone Sculpture.* Oxford: Oxford University Press, 1984.

———. *Early Northumbrian Sculpture.* Jarrow Lecture 1965. Jarrow: St. Paul's Church, 1965. Reprinted in Lapidge, *Bede and His World,* 1:133–52.

———. "The Evangelist Symbols and Their Parallels in Anglo-Saxon Sculpture." In Farrell, *Bede and Anglo-Saxon England,* pp. 118–30.

———. "The Hall in *Beowulf* and Archaeology." In *Heroic Poetry in the Anglo-Saxon Period: Studies in Honor of Jess B. Bessinger,* ed. Helen Damico and John Leyerle, pp. 331–46. Kalamazoo, Mich.: Medieval Institute Publications, 1993.

———. "The Position of the Otley Crosses in English Sculpture of the Eighth to Ninth Centuries." In *Kolloquium über spätantike und frühmittelalterliche Skulptur,* vol. 2, ed. V. Milojcic, pp. 55–63. Mainz: Philipp von Zabern, 1970.

———. "Pre-Conquest Sculptures of Glastonbury Monastery." In *New Offerings, Ancient Treasures: Studies in Medieval Art for George Henderson,* ed. Paul Binski and William Noel, pp. 154–61. Stroud: Sutton, 2001.

———. "A Reconsideration of the Monastic Site of Whitby." In Spearman and Higgitt, *Age of Migrating Ideas,* pp. 64–73.

———. "Schools of Mercian Sculpture." In *Mercian Studies,* ed. Ann Dornier, pp. 192–233. Leicester: Leicester University Press, 1977.

———. *South-West England.* Vol. 7 of *Corpus of Anglo-Saxon Stone Sculpture.* Oxford: Oxford University Press, 2006.

———. *Studies in Anglo-Saxon Sculpture.* London: Pindar Press, 1992.

———. "The Viking Image." In *The Vikings,* ed. Robert T. Farrell, pp. 8–19. London: Phillimore, 1982.

Crawford, Barbara E. *Scandinavian Scotland*. Leicester: Leicester University Press, 1987.

Cronan, Dennis. "Wiglaf's Sword." *Studia Neophilologia* 65 (1993), 129–39.

Crowe, Chris. "Excavations at Ruthwell, Dumfries, 1980 and 1984." *Transactions of the Dumfriesshire and Galloway Natural History and Antiquarian Society*, 3rd series, 62 (1987), 40–47.

Crowfoot, Elisabeth. "Note on the Textile Remains." In D. Batchelor, "Darenth Park Anglo-Saxon Cemetery, Dartford," *Archaeologia Cantiana* 108 (1990), 35–72, at pp. 51–52.

———. "The Textiles." In *The Sutton Hoo Ship Burial*, vol. 3.1, ed. Rupert Bruce-Mitford, pp. 409–79.

Crowfoot, Grace M. "Anglo-Saxon Tablet Weaving." *Antiquaries Jnl.* 32 (1952), 185–91.

Cunliffe, Barry, and Peter Davenport. *The Temple of Sulis Minerva at Bath*. Vol. 1.1. Oxford: Oxford University Committee for Archaeology, 1988.

Curle, C. "The Chronology of the Early Christian Monuments of Scotland." *PSAS* 74 (1939–40), 60–116.

Daremberg, C. V., and M. Edmond Saglio, eds. *Dictionnaire des antiquités grecques et romaines d'après les textes et les monuments*. Paris: Hachette, 1877–1919.

Dark, K. R., ed. *External Contacts and the Economy of Late Roman and Post-Roman Britain*. Woodbridge: Boydell, 1996.

Dark, Petra. *The Environment of Britain in the First Millennium A.D.* London: Duckworth, 2000.

David, Andrew, and Mark Cole. Unpublished magnetometer survey of Icklingham, 1993–97. Ancient Monuments Laboratory, English Heritage.

Davidson, Hilda Ellis. "Archaeology and *Beowulf*." In *Beowulf and Its Analogues*, trans. G. N. Garmonsway and Jacqueline Simpson, pp. 350–60. London: Dent, 1968.

Davis-Weyer, Caecilia, ed. *Early Medieval Art 300–1150*. Toronto: University of Toronto Press, 1986.

de Jong, Mayke. "Carolingian Monasticism: The Power of Prayer." In *The New Cambridge Medieval History*. Vol. 2, *c.700–c.900*, ed. Rosamond McKitterick, pp. 622–53. Cambridge: Cambridge University Press, 1995.

de Lubac, Henri, S.J. *Exégèse médiévale: les quatre sens de l'Écriture*. Paris: Aubier, 1959. Trans. as *Medieval Exegesis: The Four Senses of Scripture*. Trans. Mark Sebanc. Grand Rapids, Mich.: Eerdmans, 1998.

de Margerie, Bertrand. *Introduction à l'histoire de l'exégèse*. Vol. 4, *L'Occident latin*. Paris: Cerf, 1990.

de Paor, Liam. *St. Patrick's World, the Christian Culture of Ireland's Apostolic Age*. Dublin: Four Courts Press, 1993.

"Derrynaflan," *MA* 30 (1986), 187.

Deshman, Robert. *The Benedictional of St. Æthelwold.* Princeton: Princeton University Press, 1995.

———. "The Galba Psalter, Pictures, Texts and Content in an Early Medieval Prayer-book." *ASE* 26 (1997), 109–38.

———. "Servants of the Mother of God in Byzantine and Medieval Art." *Word and Image* 5, no. 1 (1989), 33–70.

DeWald, Ernest Theodore. *The Illustrations of the Utrecht Psalter.* Princeton: Princeton University Press, 1932.

Dickinson, O. T. P. K. "Homer, the Poet of the Dark Age." In *Homer,* ed. Ian McAuslan and Peter Walcot, pp. 19–37. Oxford: Oxford University Press, 1998.

Dictionary of the Irish Language. Dublin: Royal Irish Academy, 1939–.

Dietrich, Franz Eduard Christoph. *De Cruce Ruthwellensi et de auctore versuum in illa inscriptorum qui ad passionem domini pertinent.* Marburg: Typis academicis Elwerti, 1865.

Dixon, Philip. "'The Cities Are Not as Populated as They Once Were.'" In Rich, *City in Late Antiquity,* pp. 145–60.

Dobbie, Elliott Van Kirk, ed. *The Exeter Book.* New York: Columbia University Press, 1936.

Dodwell, C. R. *Anglo-Saxon Art: A New Perspective.* Manchester: Manchester University Press; Ithaca: Cornell University Press, 1982.

———. *Anglo-Saxon Gestures and the Roman Stage.* Prepared for publication by Timothy Graham. Cambridge: Cambridge University Press, 2000.

Dodwell, C. R., and Peter Clemoes, eds. *The Old English Illustrated Hexateuch: British Museum Cotton Claudius B iv.* Copenhagen: Rosenkilde & Bagger, 1974.

Dodwell, Natasha. "Assessment of the Human Bone from Icklingham, Suffolk." Unpublished specialist report, Cambridge, 2000.

DOE: Preface and List of Texts and Index of Editions. Toronto: Pontifical Institute for Mediaeval Studies, 1986.

Doherty, Charles. "Exchange and Trade in Early Medieval Ireland." *JRSAI* 110 (1980), 67–89.

———. "The Monastic Town in Early Medieval Ireland." In Clarke and Simms, *Comparative History of Urban Origins,* pp. 45–75.

———. "Some Aspects of Hagiography as a Source for Irish Economic History." *Peritia* 1 (1982), 300–28.

———. "The Use of Relics in Early Ireland." In Ní Chatháin and Richter, *Irland und Europa / Ireland and Europe,* pp. 89–101.

———. "The Vikings in Ireland: A Review." In *Ireland and Scandinavia in the Early Viking Age,* ed. H. B. Clarke, M. Ní Mhaonaigh, and Raghnall Ó Floinn, pp. 288–330. Dublin: Four Courts Press, 1998.

Dolley, Michael. "The Nummular Brooch from Sulgrave." In *England before the Conquest: Studies in Primary Sources Presented to Dorothy Whitelock*, ed. Peter Clemoes and Kathleen Hughes, pp. 333–50. Cambridge: Cambridge University Press, 1971.

Doyle, Sir Arthur Conan. "The Boscombe Valley Mystery." In *The Adventures and Memoirs of Sherlock Holmes*, intro. Iain Peers, notes by Ed Glinart, pp. 69–93. Harmondsworth: Penguin, 2001.

Doyle, I. W. "The Early Medieval Activity at Dalkey Island, Co. Dublin: A Re-assessment." *Jnl. of Irish Archaeology* 9 (1998), 89–104.

Drinkall, Gail, Martin Foreman, and Martin G. Welch. *The Anglo-Saxon Cemetery at Castledyke South, Barton-on-Humber.* Sheffield Excavation Reports 6. Sheffield: Sheffield Academic Press, 1998.

Duchesne, Louis, ed. *Le Liber Pontificalis.* 2 vols. Paris: E. Thorin, 1886–92. Reprint ed. Cyrille Vogel, 3 vols. Paris: E. De Boccard, 1981.

Duensing, Hugo, ed. "Apocalypse of St. Paul." In *New Testament Apocrypha*, comp. Edgar Hennecke; ed. Wilhelm Schneemelcher et al.; English trans. ed. R. McL. Wilson, pp. 755–98. London: Lutterworth, 1965.

Dumas, A., ed. *Liber Sacramentorum Gellonensis*, 2 vols. CCSL 159 and 159A. Turnhout: Brepols, 1981.

Eddius Stephanus. *The Life of Bishop Wilfrid by Eddius Stephanus.* Ed. Bertram Colgrave. Cambridge: Cambridge University Press, 1927.

Edwards, Nancy. *The Archaeology of Early Medieval Ireland.* London: B. T. Batsford; Philadelphia: University of Pennsylvania Press, 1990.

Einar Ól. Sveinsson and Matthías Þórðarson, eds. *Eyrbyggja saga: Brands páttr orva Eriks saga rauða Groenlendinga saga, Groenlendinga páttr.* Íslenzk fornrit 4. Reykjavik: Hið íslenzka fornritafélag, 1935.

Einarsson, Bjarni. (See Bjarni Einarsson.)

Eisenberg, J. M. "Glyptic Art of the Ancient Near East 'A Seal upon Thine Heart.'" *Minerva* (The International Review of Ancient Art & Archaeology) 2 (July/August 1998), 8–17.

Emery, Pierre-Yves. *The Communion of Saints.* London: Faith, 1966.

Englisch, Brigitte. *Die Artes liberales im frühen Mittelalter (5.–9. Jh.): Das Quadrivium und der Komputus als Indikatorien für Kontinuität und Erneuerung der exacten Wissenschaften zwischen Antike und Mittelalter.* Stuttgart: Steiner, 1994.

———. "Realitätsorientierte Wissenschaft oder praxisferne Traditionswissen? Inhalte und Probleme mittelalterlicher Wissenschaftsvorstellungen am Beispiel vom *De Temporum ratione* des Beda Venerabilis." In *Dilettanten und Wissenschaft: Zur Geschichte und Aktualität eines wechselvollen Verhältnisses*, ed. Elisabeth Strauss, pp. 11–34. Amsterdam: Rodopi, 1996.

Esposito, Mario. "On the Earliest Latin Life of St Brigid of Kildare." *PRIA* 20, C (1912–13), 307–26.

Evans, Angela Care. *The Sutton Hoo Ship Burial.* London: British Museum Publications, 1986; rev. ed. 1994.

Everson, Paul, and David Stocker, eds. *Lincolnshire.* Vol. 5 of *Corpus of Anglo-Saxon Stone Sculpture.* Oxford: Oxford University Press, 1999.

Evison, Vera I. "Anglo-Saxon Glass from Cremations." In Hills, Penn, and Rickett, *Anglo-Saxon Cemetery at Spong Hill, North Elmham Part V,* pp. 23–30.

———. "An Enamelled Disc from Great Saxham." *Proceedings of the Suffolk Institute of Archaeology and History* 34 (1977), 1–13.

———. *The Fifth-Century Invasions South of the Thames.* London: Athlone Press, 1965.

"Excavation Bulletin 1977–79: Summary Account of Archaeological Excavations in Ireland." *Jnl. of Irish Archaeology* 4, no. 63 (1987–88), 77.

Fabre-Vassas, Claudine. *La Bête singulière: Les Juifs, les Chrétiens et le cochon.* Paris: Gallimard, 1994. Trans. as *The Singular Beast: Jews, Christians, and the Pig.* Trans. Carol Volk. New York: Columbia University Press, 1997.

Fadda, Anna Maria Luiselli. "Aspetti e significati della compresnza delle scritture romana e runica nelle iscrizioni anglosassoni." In *Incontri di popoli e culture tra V e IX secolo: atti delle V Giornate di studio sull'età romanobarbarica, Benevento, 9–11 giugno 1997,* ed. Marcello Rotili, pp. 89–101. Bari: Arte tipografica, 1998.

Fadda, Anna Maria Luiselli, and Éamonn Ó Carragáin, eds. *Le Isole Britanniche e Roma in Età Romanobarbarica.* Rome: Herder Editrice e Libreria, 1998.

Falk, Hjalmar. *Altnordische Waffenkunde.* Oslo: Dybwad, 1914.

Fanning, Thomas. "Excavation of an Early Christian Settlement at Reask, Co. Kerry." *PRIA* 81, C (1981), 3–172.

Farrell, Robert T., ed. *Bede and Anglo-Saxon England.* Oxford: British Archaeological Reports, 1978.

Farrell, Robert, and Carol Neuman de Vegvar, eds. *Sutton Hoo Fifty Years After.* Oxford, Ohio: American Early Medieval Studies, 1992.

Fee, Christopher. "*Beag & Beaghroden:* Women, Treasure and the Language of Social Structure in *Beowulf.*" *NM* 97 (1996), 285–94.

Felix. *The Life of St. Guthlac.* Ed. and trans. Bertram Colgrave. Cambridge: Cambridge University Press, 1956.

Ferguson, G., ed. *Encyclopedia of Early Christianity.* New York: Garland, 1990.

Finnur Jónsson, ed. *Lexicon Poeticum Antiquae Linguae Septentrionalis: Ordbog over det norsk-islandske skjaldesprog oprindelig forfattet af Sveinbjörn Egilsson.* 2nd ed. Copenhagen: S. L. Møller, 1931.

———, ed. *Den norsk-islandske skjaldedigtning.* Vols. 1A, 2A, 1B, 2B. Copenhagen: Gyldendal, 1912–15.

Fitzpatrick, Elizabeth. *Royal Inauguration in Gaelic Ireland c. 1100 to c. 1600: A Cultural Landscape Study.* Woodbridge: Boydell, 2004.

Fletcher, Richard. *The Conversion of Europe: From Paganism to Christianity 371–1386 A.D.* London: Harper Collins, 1997.

Fontaine, J., R. Gillet, and S. Pellistrandi, eds. *Grégoire le Grand.* Paris: Editions du Centre de la recherche scientifique, 1986.

Foote, Peter, and G. A. Hight, ed. and trans. *The Saga of Grettir the Strong.* 3rd ed. London: J. M. Dent, 1972.

Foster, Jennifer. "A Boar-Figurine from Guilden Morden, Cambs." *MA* 21 (1977), 166–67.

———. *Bronze Boar Figurines in Iron Age and Roman Britain.* Oxford: British Archaeological Reports, 1977.

Foster, Sally M. *The St Andrews Sarcophagus: A Pictish Masterpiece and Its International Connections.* Dublin: Four Courts Press, 1998.

Fox, Cyril. *The Archaeology of the Cambridge Region.* Cambridge: Cambridge University Press, 1923.

Foys, Martin K. *The Bayeux Tapestry: Digital Edition.* Leicester: Scholarly Digital Editions, 2003.

Frantzen, Allen J. "Prologue: Documents and Monuments: Difference and Interdisciplinarity in the Study of Medieval Culture." In *Speaking Two Languages: Traditional Disciplines and Critical Theory in Medieval Studies,* ed. Allen J. Frantzen, pp. 1–33. Albany: State University of New York Press, 1991.

———. "Writing the Unreadable *Beowulf:* 'writan' and 'forwritan', the Pen and the Sword." *Exemplaria* 3 (1991), 327–58.

Fulk, Robert D. *A History of Old English Meter.* Philadelphia: University of Pennsylvania Press, 1992.

Gale, David. "The Seax." In *Weapons and Warfare in Anglo-Saxon England,* ed. Sonia Chadwick Hawkes, pp. 71–83. Oxford: Oxford Univeristy Committee for Archaeology, 1989.

Galinié, Henri. "Reflections on Early Medieval Tours." In Hodges and Hobley, *Rebirth of Towns in the West,* pp. 57–62.

Galpern, Joyce Ruth. "The Shape of Hell in Anglo-Saxon England." PhD diss., University of California, Berkeley, 1977.

Gameson, Richard. *The Role of Art in the Late Anglo-Saxon Church.* Oxford: Clarendon Press, 1995.

———, ed. *The Study of the Bayeux Tapestry.* Woodbridge: Boydell, 1997.

Gamillscheg, Ernst. *Etymologisches Wörterbuch der französischen Sprache.* 2nd ed. Heidelberg: C. Winter, 1969.

Gannon, Anna. *The Iconography of Early Anglo-Saxon Coinage: Sixth to Eighth Centuries.* Oxford: Oxford University Press, 2003.

Gaskell-Brown, Cynthia, and A. E. T. Harper. "Excavations on Cathedral Hill, Armagh, 1968." *Ulster Jnl. of Archaeology* 47 (1984), 109–61.

Geake, Helen. "When Were Hanging Bowls Deposited in Anglo-Saxon Graves?" *MA* 43 (1999), 1–18.

Geary, Patrick J. *Furta Sacra: Thefts of Relics in the Central Middle Ages.* Princeton: Princeton University Press, 1978.

Geijer, Agnes. *Birka.* Vol. 3, *Die Textilfunde aus den Gräbern.* Uppsala: Almqvist and Wiksell, 1938.

———. "The Textile Finds from Birka: *Birka III Die Textilfunde aus den Gräbern,* revised by the author." *Acta Archaeologica* 50 (1979), 209–22.

Geoffrey of Burton. *Geoffrey of Burton: Life and Miracles of St. Modwenna.* Ed. Robert Bartlett. Oxford: Oxford University Press, 2002.

Glare, P. G. W., ed. *Oxford Latin Dictionary.* Oxford: Clarendon Press, 1982.

Glosecki, Stephen O. *Shamanism and Old English Poetry.* New York: Garland, 1989.

Glover, Julian. *Beowulf, an Adaptation.* Gloucester: Sutton, 1987.

Gneuss, Helmut. "Liturgical Books in Anglo-Saxon England." In Lapidge and Gneuss, *Learning and Literature in Anglo-Saxon England,* pp. 91–141.

Godman, Peter, ed. *Alcuin: The Bishops, Kings, and Saints of York.* Oxford: Clarendon Press, 1982.

Goffart, Walter. *The Narrators of Barbarian History (A.D. 550–800): Jordanes, Gregory of Tours, Bede, and Paul the Deacon.* Princeton: Princeton University Press, 1988.

Goldschmidt, Adolph, with Paul Gustav Hübner and Otto Sigmund Homburger. *Die Elfenbeinskulpturen aus der Zeit der karolingischen und sächsischen Kaiser, VIII.–XI. Jahrhundert.* Berlin: B. Cassirer, 1969–70.

Gollancz, I., ed. *The Cædmon Manuscript of Anglo-Saxon Biblical Poetry, Junius XI in the Bodleian Library.* Oxford: Oxford University Press, 1927.

Gonser, Paul, ed. *Das angelsächsische Prosa-Leben des hl. Guthlac. Mit Einleitung, Anmerkungen und Miniaturen.* Anglistische Forschungen 27. Heidelberg: C. Winter, 1909.

Goscelin. "La Légende de Ste Edith en prose et vers par le moine Goscelin." Ed. A. Wilmart. *Analecta Bollandiana* 56 (1938), 5–101, 265–307.

Gosling, Paul. "Tuam." In *More Irish Country Towns,* ed. Anngret Simms and J. H. Andrews, pp. 119–31. Cork: Mercier Press, 1995.

Gougaud, Louis. "Le témoignage des manuscrits sur l'œuvre littéraire du moine Lathcen." *Revue Celtique* 30 (1909), 37–43.

Graham, B. J. "Urban Genesis in Early Medieval Ireland." *Jnl. of Historical Geography* 13, no. 1 (1987), 3–16.

———. "Urbanization in Medieval Ireland ca. AD 900 to ca. AD 1300." *Jnl. of Urban History* 13 (1987), 169–96.

Graham-Campbell, James. "A Lost Zoomorphic Penannular Brooch from Kells, County Meath." *JRSAI* 116 (1986), 122–23.

————. "The Viking-Age Silver Hoards of Ireland." In *Proceedings of the Seventh Viking Congress, Dublin, 1973,* ed. Bo Almqvist and David Green, pp. 39–74. Dublin: Viking Society for Northern Research, 1976.

Graham-Campbell, James, and C. E. Batey. *Vikings in Scotland, an Archaeological Survey.* Edinburgh: Edinburgh University Press, 1998.

Graham-Campbell, James, and Dafydd Kidd. *The Vikings.* London: British Museum Publications, 1980.

Granger-Taylor, Hero. "The Weft-patterned Silks and Their Braid: The Remains of an Anglo-Saxon Dalmatic of c. 800?" In Bonner, Rollason, and Stancliffe, *St Cuthbert, His Cult and His Community,* pp. 303–27.

Granger-Taylor, Hero, and Frances Pritchard. "A Fine Quality Insular Embroidery from Llangors Crannóg, near Brecon." In Redknap et al., *Pattern and Purpose in Insular Art,* pp. 91–99.

Grape, Wolfgang. *The Bayeux Tapestry: Monument to a Norman Triumph.* Munich: Prestel, 1994.

Green, Miranda Jane. *Celtic Myths.* London: British Museum Press, 1993.

Greenfield, Stanley B. *The Interpretation of Old English Poems.* London: Routledge & Kegan Paul, 1972.

Gregory of Tours. *Gregory of Tours. The History of the Franks.* Trans. L. Thorpe. Harmondsworth: Penguin, 1974.

Gregory the Great. *Gregorius Magnus Homiliae in Hezechilhelem Prophetam.* Ed. M. Adriaen. CCSL 152. Turnhout: Brepols, 1971.

————. *S. Gregorii Magni Moralia in Job.* Ed. Marcus Adriaen, CCSL 143B. Turnhout: Brepols, 1979.

————. *Morals on the Book of Job.* Trans. James Bliss. Oxford: J. H. Parker, 1850.

Gretsch, Mechthild. *The Intellectual Foundations of the Benedictine Reform.* Cambridge: Cambridge University Press, 1999.

Griffiths, David. "The Coastal Trading Ports of the Irish Sea." In *Viking Treasure from the North West, the Cuerdale Hoard in Its Context,* ed. James Graham-Campbell, pp. 63–72. Liverpool: National Museums and Galleries on Mersyside, 1992.

Grimm, Jacob, ed. *Andreas und Elene.* Cassel: T. Fischer, 1840.

————. *Deutsche Mythologie.* Göttingen: Dieterich, 1835; 4th ed. Berlin: F. Dümmler, 1875–78.

Grogan, Brian O'Dwyer. "Eschatological Teaching in the Early Irish Church." In McNamara, *Biblical Studies,* pp. 46–58.

Grosjean, Paul. "Sur quelques exégètes irlandais du VIIe siècle." *Sacris Erudiri* 7 (1955), 67–98.

Guðnason, Bjarni. (See Bjarni Guðnason.)

Gwynn, Aubrey, and D. F. Gleeson. *A History of the Diocese of Killaloe.* Dublin: M. H. Gill, 1962.

Gwynn, Aubrey, and R. N. Hadcock, eds. *Medieval Religious Houses: Ireland.* London: Longmans, 1970.

Gwynn, Edward, ed. *The Metrical Dindshenchas.* 5 vols. Dublin: Royal Irish Academy, 1913.

Hägg, Inga. "Die Tracht." In *Birka,* vol. 2.2, *Systematische Analysen der Gräberfunde,* ed. Greta Arwidsson, pp. 51–72. Stockholm: Almqvist and Wiksell, 1986.

Hald, Margrethe. *Ancient Danish Textiles from Bogs and Burials: A Comparative Study of Costume and Iron Age Textiles.* Copenhagen: National Museum Denmark, 1980.

Hall, Richard. "A Check-list of Viking-Age Coin Finds from Ireland." *Ulster Jnl. of Archaeology* 36–37 (1973–74), 71–86.

Halphen, Louis. *Charlemagne et l'Empire Carolingien.* Paris: A. Michel, 1947.

Hamilton, J. R. C. *Excavations at Clickhimin.* Shetland DoE Archaeological Research Report 6. Edinburgh: HMSO, 1968.

Hamlin, Ann. "The Archaeology of the Early Irish Churches in the Eighth Century." *Peritia* 4 (1985), 279–99.

Harbison, Peter. *The High Crosses of Ireland: An Iconographical and Photographic Survey.* 2 vols. Bonn: Dr. Rudolf Habelt GMBH, 1992.

———. "A Lost Crucifixion Plaque of Clonmacnoise Type found in County Mayo." In *Irish Midland Studies: Essays in Commemoration of N. W. English,* ed. Harman Murtagh, pp. 24–38. Athlone: Old Athlone Society, 1980.

———. "Two Panels on the Wirksworth Slab." *Derbyshire Archaeological Jnl.* 107 (1987), 36–40.

Haseloff, Günther. *Email im frühen Mittelalter: frühchristliche Kunst von der Spätantike zu den Karolingern.* Marburg: Hitzeroth, 1990.

Hatto, A. T. "Snake-swords and Boar-helms in *Beowulf.*" *English Studies* 38 (1957), 145–60 and 257–59.

Hauck, Karl. "Die bildliche Wiedergabe von Götter- und Heldenwaffen im Norden seit der Völkerwanderungszeit (Zur Ikonologie der Goldbrakteaten 18)." In *Wörter und Sachen im Lichte der Bezeichnungsforschung,* ed. Ruth Schmidt-Wiegand, pp. 168–269. Berlin: De Gruyter, 1981.

Hawkes, Jane. "Anglo-Saxon Sculpture: Questions of Context." In Hawkes and Mills, *Northumbria's Golden Age,* pp. 204–15.

———. "Columban Virgins: Iconic Images of the Virgin and Child in Insular Sculpture." In *Studies in the Cult of Saint Columba,* ed. Cormac Bourke, pp. 107–35. Dublin: HMSO, 1997.

———. *The Golden Age of Northumbria.* Morpeth: Sandhill Press, 1996.

———. "An Iconography of Identity: The Cross-head from Mayo Abbey." In *From Ireland Coming: Irish Art from the Early Christian to the Late Gothic Period and Its European Context,* ed. Colum Hourihane, pp. 261–75. Princeton: Princeton University Press, 2001.

————. "Mary and the Cycle of Resurrection: The Iconography of the Hovingham Panel." In Spearman and Higgitt, *Age of Migrating Ideas,* pp. 254–60.

————. "The Miracle Scene on the Rothbury Cross-shaft." *Archaeologia Aeliana,* 5th series, 17 (1989), 207–11.

————. "Old Testament Heroes: Iconographies of Insular Sculpture." In D. Henry, *The Worm, the Germ, and the Thorn,* pp. 149–58.

————. "A Question of Judgment: The Iconic Programme of Sandbach, Cheshire." In Bourke, *From the Isles of the North,* pp. 213–20.

————. "The Rothbury Cross: An Iconographic Bricolage." *Gesta* 35, no. 1 (1996), 77–94.

————. *The Sandbach Crosses: Sign and Significance in Anglo-Saxon Sculpture.* Dublin: Four Courts Press, 2002.

————. "Symbolic Lives: The Visual Evidence." In *The Anglo-Saxons from the Migration Period to the Eighth Century: An Ethnographic Perspective,* ed. John Hines, pp. 311–45. Woodbridge: Boydell, 1997.

————. "Symbols of the Passion or Power? The Iconography of the Rothbury Cross Head." In Karkov, M. Ryan, and Farrell, *Insular Tradition,* pp. 27–44.

————. "The Wirksworth Slab: An Iconography of Humilitas." *Peritia* 9 (1995), 1–32.

Hawkes, Jane, and Susan Mills, eds. *Northumbria's Golden Age.* Stroud: Sutton, 1999.

Hawkes, S. C., and G. C. Dunning. "Soldiers and Settlers in Britain, Fourth to Fifth Century." *MA* 5 (1961), 29–30.

Hawkes, Terence. *Structuralism and Semiotics.* London: Methuen, 1977.

Healey, Antonette diPaolo, et al., eds. *Dictionary of Old English: "E."* Toronto: Pontifical Institute of Mediaeval Studies, 1996.

Hecht, Franciscus X. "De offertorio missae defunctorum." *Ephemerides Liturgicae* 50 (1936), 415–18.

Heller, Steven. *The Swastika: Symbol beyond Redemption?* New York: Allworth Press, 2000.

Hencken, H. "Lagore Crannog: An Irish Royal Residence of the 7th to 10th Centuries." *PRIA* 53, C (1950), 1–247.

Henderson, George. *Bede and the Visual Arts.* Jarrow Lecture 1980. Jarrow: St Paul's Church, 1980.

————. *From Durrow to Kells: The Insular Gospel Books 650–800.* London: Thames and Hudson, 1987.

————. *Vision and Image in Early Christian England.* Cambridge: Cambridge University Press, 1999.

Henderson, George, and Isabel Henderson. *The Art of the Picts: Sculpture and Metalwork in Early Medieval Scotland.* London: Thames and Hudson, 2004.

Henderson, Isabel. "The Book of Kells and the Snake-boss Motif on Pictish Cross-slabs and the Iona Crosses." In M. Ryan, *Ireland and Insular Art*, pp. 56–65.

———. "The 'David Cycle' in Pictish Art." In Higgitt, *Early Medieval Sculpture*, pp. 87–123.

———. "Pictish Art and the Book of Kells." In *Ireland in Early Medieval Europe: Studies in Memory of Kathleen Hughes*, ed. Dorothy Whitelock, Rosamond McKitterick, and David N. Dumville, pp. 79–105. Cambridge: Cambridge University Press, 1982.

———. "*Primus inter Pares:* The St Andrews Sarcophagus and Pictish Sculpture." In *The St Andrews Sarcophagus: A Pictish Masterpiece and Its International Connections*, ed. Sally M. Foster, pp. 97–167. Dublin: Four Courts Press, 1998.

———. Review of RCAHMS, *Argyll*, vol. 4, *Iona*. *MA* 27 (1983), 235–38.

Henderson, Julian. "The Nature of the Early Christian Glass Industry in Ireland: Some Evidence from Dunmisk Fort, County Tyrone." *Ulster Jnl. of Archaeology* 51 (1988), 115–26.

Hennessey, W. M., ed. and trans. *The Annals of Loch Cé*. 2 vols. London: Longman, 1871.

———, ed. and trans. *Chronicum Scotorum*. London: Longmans, Green, Reader and Dyer, 1866.

Hennessy, W. M., and B. MacCarthy, eds. and trans. *Annals of Ulster*. 4 vols. Dublin: HMSO, 1887–1901. Reprint ed. Nollaig Ó Muraíle, Dublin: Edmund Burke, 1998.

Henry, David, ed. *The Worm, the Germ, and the Thorn: Pictish and Related Studies Presented to Isabel Henderson*. Balgavies: Pinkfoot Press, 1997.

Henry, Françoise. *The Book of Kells: Reproductions from the Manuscript in Trinity College Dublin*. New York: Thames and Hudson, 1974.

———. "Deux Objets de bronze irlandais au Musée des Antiquités Nationales." In Henry, *Studies in Early Christian and Medieval Irish Art*, vol. 1, *Enamels and Metalwork*, pp. 195–219. London: Pindar, 1983.

———. "Early Monasteries, Beehive Huts and Dry-stone Houses in the Neighbourhood of Caherciveen and Waterville (Co. Kerry)." *PRIA* 58, C (1956–57), 45–166.

———. *Irish Art during the Viking Invasions (800–1020 A.D.)*. London: Methuen; Ithaca: Cornell University Press, 1967.

———. *Irish Art in the Romanesque Period 1020–1170*. London: Methuen; Ithaca: Cornell University Press, 1970.

———. "Remarks on the Decoration of Three Irish Psalters." *PRIA* 61, C (1960), 23–40.

Herbert, Maire. *Iona, Kells and Derry, the History and Hagiography of the Monastic Familia of Columba*. Oxford: Oxford University Press, 1988. Reprint, Dublin: Four Courts Press, 1996.

Herity, Michael. "The Buildings and Layout of Early Irish Monasteries before the Year 1000." *Monastic Studies* 14 (1983), 247–84.

———. "The Layout of Irish Early Christian Monasteries." In Ní Chatháin and Richter, *Irland und Europa / Ireland and Europe*, pp. 105–16.

Heusler, Andreas, and Wilhelm Ranisch, eds. *Eddica Minora*. Dortmund: Ruhfus, 1903.

Hickey, Helen. *Images of Stone: Figure Sculpture of the Lough Erne Basin*. Belfast: Blackstaff Press, 1976.

Hicks, Carola. *Animals in Early Medieval Art*. Edinburgh: Edinburgh University Press, 1993.

Higgitt, John. "Design and Meaning in Early Medieval Inscriptions in Britain and Ireland." In *The Cross Goes North: Processes of Conversion in Northern Europe AD 300–1300*, ed. Martin Carver, pp. 327–38. Woodbridge: York Medieval Press and Boydell & Brewer, 2003.

———. "Early Medieval Inscriptions in Britain and Ireland and Their Audiences." In D. Henry, *The Worm, the Germ, and the Thorn*, pp. 67–78.

———, ed. *Early Medieval Sculpture in Britain and Ireland*. Oxford: British Archaeological Reports, 1986.

———. "Emphasis and Visual Rhetoric in Anglo-Saxon Inscriptions." Paper delivered at the "Shaping Understanding: Form and Order in the Anglo-Saxon World, 400–1100" conference, London, March 2002. To be published in *Shaping Understanding: Form and Order in the Anglo-Saxon World, 400–1100, a Conference Held at the British Museum, 7–9 March 2002*, ed. Leslie Webster, Helena Hamerow, and Sally Crawford, *ASSAH*. Oxford: Oxford University Press, forthcoming.

———. "Words and Crosses: The Inscribed Stone Cross in Early Medieval Britain." In Higgitt, *Early Medieval Sculpture*, pp. 125–52.

Hill, David. "The Bayeux Tapestry and Its Commentators: The Case of Scene 15." *Medieval Life* 11 (1999), 24–26.

Hill, David, and John McSween. *The Bayeux Tapestry: The Establishment of a Text*. Forthcoming.

Hill, Peter. *Whithorn 2: Excavations 1984–1987, Interim Report*. Whithorn: Whithorn Trust, 1988.

———. *Whithorn 3: Excavations 1988–90*. Whithorn: Whithorn Trust, 1990.

———. *Whithorn and St Ninian: The Excavation of a Monastic Town, 1984–91*. Stroud: Sutton, 1997.

Hills, Catherine M. *The Anglo-Saxon Cemetery at Spong Hill, Part I*. East Anglian Archaeology Report 6. Gressenhall: Norfolk Archaeological Unit, 1977.

———. "Anglo-Saxon Chairperson." *Antiquity* 54 (1980), 52–54.

———. "*Beowulf* and Archaeology." In Bjork and Niles, *Beowulf Handbook*, pp. 291–310.

————. "From Isidore to Isotopes: Ivory Rings in Early Medieval Graves." In *Image and Power in the Archaeology of Early Medieval Britain. Essays in Honour of Rosemary Cramp,* ed. Helena Hamerow and Arthur McGregor, pp. 133–48. Oxford: Oxbow, 2001.

————. "Spong Hill and the Adventus Saxonum." In *Spaces of the Living and the Dead: An Archaeological Dialogue,* ed. Catherine E, Karkov, Kelley M. Wickham-Crowley, and Bailey K. Young, pp. 15–26. Oxford: David Brown, 1999.

Hills, Catherine M., et al. *The Anglo-Saxon Cemetery at Spong Hill, North Elmham Part II.* East Anglian Archaeology Report 11. Gressenhall: Norfolk Archaeological Unit, 1981.

————. *The Anglo-Saxon Cemetery at Spong Hill, North Elmham Part III.* East Anglian Archaeology Report 21. Dereham: Norfolk Archaeological Unit, 1984.

Hills, Catherine M., Kenneth J. Penn, and Robert J. Rickett. *The Anglo-Saxon Cemetery at Spong Hill, North Elmham Part IV.* East Anglian Archaeology Report 34. Gressenhall: Norfolk Archaeological Unit, 1987.

————, eds. *The Anglo-Saxon Cemetery at Spong Hill, North Elmham Part V.* East Anglian Archaeology Report 67. Gressenhall: Norfolk Archaeological Unit, 1994.

Hines, John. "Culture Groups and Ethnic Groups in Northern Germany in and around the Migration Period." *Studien zur Sachsenforschung* 13 (1999), 219–32.

————. *A New Corpus of Anglo-Saxon Square-Headed Brooches.* London: Society of Antiquaries of London, 1997.

————. Review of Owen-Crocker, *The Four Funerals in Beowulf. Notes and Queries* 246 (2001), 319–21.

————. "The Scandinavian Character of Anglian England: An Update." In Carver, *Age of Sutton Hoo,* pp. 315–29.

————. *The Scandinavian Character of Anglian England in the Pre-Viking Period.* Oxford: British Archaeological Reports, 1984.

Hirstein, James. *Tacitus' Germania and Beatus Rhenanus, 1485–1547: A Study of the Editorial and Exegetical Contribution.* Frankfurt am Main: P. Lang, 1995.

Hobbs, Richard. *Treasure: Finding Our Past.* London: British Museum Publications, 2003.

Hodges, Richard. *Dark Age Economics: The Origins of Towns and Trade.* London: Duckworth, 1982.

————. *Light in the Dark Ages, the Rise and Fall of San Vincenzo al Volturno.* Ithaca: Cornell University Press, 1997.

————. *Towns and Trade in the Age of Charlemagne.* London: Duckworth, 2000.

Hodges, Richard, and Brian Hobley, eds. *The Rebirth of Towns in the West AD 700–1050.* CBA Res. Rep. 68. London: Council for British Archaeology, 1988.

Hofmann, Dietrich. *Nordisch-Englische Lehnbeziehungen der Wikingerzeit.* Bibliotheca Arnamagnæana 14. Copenhagen: E. Munksgaard, 1955.

Horn, Walter, and Ernest Born. *The Plan of St. Gall: A Study of the Architecture and Economy of, and Life in, a Paradigmatic Monastery.* 3 vols. Berkeley: University of California Press, 1979.

Hubert, Jean, Jean Porcher, and W. F. Volbach. *The Carolingian Renaissance.* New York: Brazilier, 1970.

———. *Europe in the Dark Ages.* London: Thames and Hudson, 1969.

———. *Europe of the Invasions.* New York: Brazilier, 1969.

Hughes, Kathleen. "The Church and the World in Early Christian Ireland." *Irish Historical Studies* 13 (1962–63), 99–113.

———. *The Church in Early Irish Society.* London: Methuen, 1966.

———. "Sanctity and Secularity in the Early Irish Church." *Studies in Church History* 10 (1973), 21–37.

Ingstad, Anne Stine. "The Functional Textiles from the Oseberg Ship." Trans. C. K. Scott-Moncrief. In *Archäologische Textilfunde: Textilsymposium Neumünster 6–5 to 8–5 1981*, ed. Lise Bender Jørgensen and Klaus Tidow, pp. 85–94. Neumünster: Textilmuseum Neumünster, 1982.

"Inishcealtra," *MA* 30 (1986), 187.

Ireland, Colin. "Aldfrith of Northumbria and the Learning of a *Sapiens*." In *A Celtic Florilegium: Studies in Memory of Brendan O Hehir,* ed. Kathryn A. Klar, Eve E. Sweetser, and Claire Thomas, pp. 63–77. Lawrence, Mass.: Celtic Studies Publications, 1996.

Irving, Edward B., Jr. "Christian and Pagan Elements." In Bjork and Niles, *Beowulf Handbook,* pp. 175–92.

Isidore. *Isidori Hispalensis Episcopi etymologiarum sive originum, libri XX.* Ed. W. M. Lindsay. 2 vols. Oxford: Clarendon Press, 1985.

Ivens, R. J. "Dunmisk Fort, Carrickmore, Co. Tyrone: Excavations 1984–1986. " *Ulster Jnl. of Archaeology* 52 (1989), 17–110.

———. "The Early Christian Monastic Enclosure at Tullylish, Co. Down." *Ulster Jnl. of Archaeology* 50 (1987), 55–121.

Jackson, K. H., ed. *Aislinge meic Con Glinne.* Dublin: School of Celtic Studies, Dublin Institute for Advanced Studies, 1990.

Jakob Benediktsson. "Icelandic Traditions of the Scyldings." *Saga-Book of the Viking Society* 15 (1957–61), 48–66.

Jansson, I. "Wikingerzeitlicher orientalischer Import in Skandinavien." *Berichte der Römisch-Germanischen Kommission* 69 (1988), 564–647.

Jerome. *Commentariorum in Esaiam.* Ed. M. Adriaen. CCSL 73. Turnhout: Brepols, 1963.

Jewell, Richard H. I. "The Anglo-Saxon Friezes at Breedon-on-the-Hill, Leicestershire." *Archaeologia* 108 (1986), 95–115.

Johnson, S. *Burgh Castle, Excavations by Charles Green 1958–61.* East Anglian Archaeology Report 20. Dereham: Norfolk Archaeological Unit, 1983.

Jones, Dan Burne. *The Prints of Rockwell Kent: A Catalogue Raisonné.* Chicago: University of Chicago Press, 1975.

Jónsson, Finnur. (See Finnur Jónsson.)

Jørgensen, Anna Nørgård. *Waffen und Gräber: Typologische und chronologische Studien zu skandinavischen Waffengräbern 520/30 bis 900 n.Chr.* Copenhagen: Det Kongelige Nordiske Oldskriftselskab, 1999.

Kaczynski, Bernice M. "Bede's Commentaries on Luke and Mark and the Formation of the Patristic Canon." In *Anglo-Latin and Its Heritage: Essays in Honour of A. G. Rigg,* ed. Siân Echard and Gernot Wieland, pp. 17–26. Publications of the Journal of Medieval Latin 4. Turnhout: Brepols, 2001.

Karkov, Catherine E. "The Bewcastle Cross: Some Iconographic Problems." In Karkov, M. Ryan, and Farrell, *Insular Tradition,* pp. 9–26.

———. "The Decoration of Early Wooden Architecture in Ireland and Northumbria." In *Studies in Insular Art and Archaeology,* ed. Catherine Karkov and Robert Farrell, pp. 27–48. Oxford, Ohio: American Early Medieval Studies, 1991.

———. "Naming and Renaming: The Inscription of Gender in Anglo-Saxon England." In *Theorizing Anglo-Saxon Stone Sculpture,* ed. Catherine E. Karkov and Fred Orton, pp. 31–64. Morgantown: West Virginia University Press, 2003.

———. *The Ruler Portraits of Anglo-Saxon England.* Woodbridge: Boydell Press, 2004.

Karkov, Catherine E., and George Hardin Brown, eds. *Anglo-Saxon Styles.* Albany: State University of New York Press, 2003.

Karkov, Catherine E., Michael Ryan, and Robert T. Farrell, eds. *The Insular Tradition.* Albany: State University of New York Press, 1997.

Keefer, Sarah Larratt. "Body Language: A Graphic Commentary by the Horses of the Bayeux Tapestry." In Owen-Crocker, *King Harold II and the Bayeux Tapestry,* pp. 93–108.

"Kells," *MA* 33 (1989), 224.

Kelly, Fergus. *A Guide to Early Irish Law.* Dublin: Dublin Institute for Advanced Studies, 1988.

Kelly, Joseph F. "A Catalogue of Early Medieval Hiberno-Latin Commentaries." *Traditio* 44 (1988), 537–71.

———. "The Devil in Hiberno-Latin Exegesis of the Early Middle Ages." In *The Scriptures and Early Medieval Ireland: Proceedings of the 1993 Conference of the Society for Hiberno-Latin Studies on Early Irish Exegesis and Homilectics*, ed. Thomas O'Loughlin, pp. 133–44. Turnhout: Brepols, 1999.

Kemble, John Mitchell, ed. *The Anglo-Saxon Poems of Beowulf: The Traveller's Song and the Battle of Finnesburh*. London: Pickering, 1833–35.

———. "On Anglo-Saxon Runes." *Archaeologia* 28 (1840), 327–72.

———. *A Translation of the Anglo-Saxon Poem Beowulf.* London: Pickering, 1837.

Kendrick, T. D. *Late Saxon and Viking Art.* London: Methuen, 1949.

Kennett, D. H., "Pottery and Other Finds from the Anglo-Saxon Cemetery at Sandy, Bedfordshire." *MA* 14 (1970), 17–33.

Kenney, J. F., ed. *The Sources for the Early History of Ireland: Ecclesiastical. An Introduction and Guide.* New York: Columbia University Press, 1929.

Kerlouégan, François. "Grégoire le Grand et les Pays Celtiques." In Fontaine, Gillet, and Pellistrandi, *Grégoire le Grand*, pp. 589–96.

Kessler, Herbert. *Illustrated Bibles from Tours.* Princeton: Princeton University Press, 1977.

Keynes, Simon. *The Diplomas of Æthelred the Unready 978–1016. A Study in Their Use as Historical Evidence.* Cambridge: Cambridge University Press, 1980.

———. "King Athelstan's Books." In Lapidge and Gneuss, *Learning and Literature in Anglo-Saxon England*, pp. 143–201.

———, ed. *The Liber Vitae of the New Minster and Hyde Abbey, Winchester.* Copenhagen: Rosenkilde & Bagger, 1996.

———. "The Vikings in England, c. 790–1016." In *The Oxford Illustrated History of the Vikings*, ed. Peter Sawyer, pp. 48–82. Oxford: Oxford University Press, 1997.

Keynes, Simon, and Michael Lapidge, eds. *Alfred the Great.* Harmondsworth: Penguin, 1983.

Killeen, J. F. "Fear an Énais." *Celtica* 9 (1971), 202–04.

King, Heather A., ed. *Clonmacnoise Studies.* Vol. 1, *Seminar Papers 1994.* Dublin: Dúchas, 1998.

———. "Excavations at Clonmacnoise." *Archaeology Ireland* 6, no. 3 (1992), 12–14.

Kirby, D. P. "The Genesis of a Cult: Cuthbert of Farne and Ecclesiastical Politics of Northumbria in the Late Seventh Century and Early Eighth Centuries." *Jnl. of Ecclesiastical History* 46 (1995), 318–97.

Kitzinger, Ernst. "The Coffin-Reliquary." In Battiscombe, *Relics of Saint Cuthbert*, pp. 202–304.

Klaeber, F., ed. *Beowulf and the Fight at Finnsburg.* 3rd ed. Boston: D. C. Heath, 1950.

Knight, J. K. *The End of Antiquity, Archaeology, Society and Religion 235–700.* Stroud: Tempus, 1999.

Kock, Ernst A. *Notationes Norroenae.* Lund: H. Ohlsson, 1923–44.

Krautheimer, Richard. *Rome, Profile of a City, 312–1308.* Princeton: Princeton University Press, 1980.

Krautheimer, Richard, et al., eds. *Corpus Basilicarum Christianarum Romae.* 5 vols. Vatican City: Pontificio istituto di archeologia cristiana, 1937–77.

Kurth, Barbara. "Ecclesia and an Angel on the Andrew Auckland Cross." *JWCI* 6 (1943), 213–14.

———. "The Iconography of the Wirksworth Slab." *Burlington Magazine* 86 (1945), 114–21.

Kuypers, A. Benedict, ed. *The Prayerbook of Æduald the Bishop commonly called the Book of Cerne.* Cambridge: Cambridge University Press, 1902.

Lacey, Brian. "Columba, Founder of the Monastery of Derry?—'mihi manet incertus.'" *JRSAI* 128 (1998), 35–47.

———. "The Development of Derry 600–1600." In Mac Niocaill and Wallace, *Keimelia,* pp. 378–96.

———. *Siege City, the Story of Derry and Londonderry.* Belfast: Blackstaff Press, 1990.

Laidcenn. *Egloga, quam scripsit Lathcen filius Baith de Moralibus Iob quas Gregorius fecit.* Ed. M. Adriaen. CCSL 145. Turnhout: Brepols, 1969.

Laing, Lloyd. "The Bradwell Mount and the Use of Millefiori in Post-Roman Britain." *Studia Celtica* 33 (1999), 137–53.

———. "The Mote of Mark and the Origins of Celtic Interlace." *Antiquity* 49 (1975), 98–105.

Laing, Samuel. *Snorri Sturluson Heimskringla, Part Two: Sagas of the Norse Kings.* Rev. Peter Foote. Rev. repr. London: Dent, 1978.

Lamm, Jan Peder, and Hans-Åke Nordström, eds. *Vendel Period Studies: Transactions of the Boat-Grave Symposium in Stockholm, February 2–3, 1981.* Stockholm: Statens historiska museum, 1983.

Landes, Richard. "Lest the Millennium Be Fulfilled: Apocalyptic Expectation and the Pattern of Western Chronography, 100–800 CE." In *The Use and Abuse of Eschatology in the Middle Ages,* ed. Werner Verbeke, Caliel Verhelst, and Andries Welkenhuysen, pp. 137–209. Leuven: Leuven University Press, 1988.

Lane, Alan, and Ewan Campbell. *Dunadd: An Early Dalriadic Capital.* Oxford: Oxbow, 2000.

Lang, James, ed. *Anglo-Saxon and Viking Age Sculpture and Its Context.* Oxford: British Archaeological Reports, 1978.

———. "The Apostles in Anglo-Saxon Sculpture in the Age of Alcuin." *Early Medieval Europe* 8, no. 2 (1999), 271–82.

———. "Continuity and Innovation in Anglo-Scandinavian Sculpture." In Lang, *Anglo-Saxon and Viking Age Sculpture,* pp. 145–72.

————. "The Hogback: A Viking Colonial Monument." In *ASSAH*, vol. 3, ed. Sonia Chadwick Hawkes, James Campbell, and David Brown, pp. 85–176. Oxford: Oxford University Committee for Archaeology, 1984.

————. "Monuments from Yorkshire in the Age of Alcuin." In *Early Deira: Archaeological Studies of the East Riding in the Fourth to Ninth Centuries AD*, ed. Helen Geake and Jonathan Kenny, pp. 109–19. Oxford: Oxbow, 2000.

————, ed. *Northern Yorkshire*. Vol. 6 of *Corpus of Anglo-Saxon Stone Sculpture*. Oxford: Oxford University Press, 2001.

————. "Principles of Design in Free-style Carving in the Irish Sea Province: c 800 to c 950." In Higgitt, *Early Medieval Sculpture*, pp. 153–74.

————. *Viking-Age Decorated Wood: A Study of Its Ornament and Style*. Dublin: Royal Irish Academy, 1988.

————, ed. *York and Eastern Yorkshire*. Vol. 3 of *Corpus of Anglo-Saxon Stone Sculpture*. Oxford: Oxford University Press, 1991.

Lapidge, Michael, ed. *Bede and His World: The Jarrow Lectures*. 2 vols. Aldershot: Variorum, 1994.

————. *Bede the Poet*. Jarrow Lecture 1993. Jarrow: St. Paul's Church, 1993. Reprinted in Lapidge, *Bede and His World*, 2:927–56.

————. "The *Life of Saint Oswald*." In *The Battle of Maldon, AD 991*, ed. Donald Scragg, pp. 51–58. Oxford: B. Blackwell, 1991.

Lapidge, Michael, et al., eds. *The Blackwell Encyclopaedia of Anglo-Saxon England*. Oxford: Blackwell, 1999.

Lapidge, Michael, and Helmut Gneuss, eds. *Learning and Literature in Anglo-Saxon England: Studies Presented to Peter Clemoes*. Cambridge: Cambridge University Press, 1985.

La Rocca, Christina. "Public Buildings and Urban Change in Northern Italy in the Early Medieval Period." In Rich, *City in Late Antiquity*, pp. 161–80.

Larsen, Erling Benner. *Historien om det store sølvfund fra Gundestrup*. Højbjerg: Jysk Arkæologisk Selskab i kommision hos Aarhus Universitetsforlag, 1999.

Lasko, Peter. *Ars Sacra, 800–1200*. 2nd ed. New Haven: Yale University Press, 1994.

————. "The Bayeux Tapestry and the Representation of Space." In Owen-Crocker and Graham, *Medieval Art: Recent Perspectives*, pp. 26–39.

Lawlor, H. C. *The Monastery of Saint Mochaoi of Nendrum*. Belfast: Belfast Natural History and Philosophical Society, 1925.

Leask, H. G. *Glendalough*. Dublin: HMSO, n.d.

Leclercq, Jean. *The Love of Learning and the Desire for God*. New York: Fordham University Press, 1961.

Lees, Clare A., and Gillian R. Overing. "Birthing Bishops, Fathering Poets: Bede, Hild, and the Relations of Cultural Production." *Exemplaria* 6 (1994), 35–65.

———. *Double Agents: Women and Clerical Culture in Anglo-Saxon England.* Philadelphia: University of Pennsylvania Press, 2001.

Le Goff, Jacques. *L'imaginaire médiévale.* Paris: Gallimard, 1985.

———. *Pour un autre Moyen Âge: Temps, Travail et Culture en Occident, 18 Essais.* Paris: Gallimard, 1977.

Leigh, David. "Ambiguity in Anglo-Saxon Style 1 Art." *Antiquaries Jnl.* 64 (1984), 34–42.

Leo the Great. *Sancti Leonis Magni, Romani Pontificis tractatus septem et nonaginta.* Ed. A. Chavasse. CCSL 138A. Turnhout: Brepols, 1973.

Leo, Heinrich. *Bëówulf, dasz älteste deutsche, in angelsächsischer Mundart erhaltene Heldengedicht, nach seinen Inhalte und nach seinen historischen und mythologischen Beziehungen betrachtet: ein Beitrag zur Geschichte alter deutscher Geisteszustände.* Halle: E. Anton, 1839.

Lethbridge, Thomas C. *A Cemetery at Lackford Suffolk.* Cambridge Antiquarian Society Quarto Publications, n.s., 6. Cambridge: Bowes & Bowes for the Cambridge Antiquarian Society, 1951.

Leveto, P. D. "The Marian Theme of the Frescoes in Santa Maria at Castelseprio." *Art Bulletin* 72 (1990), 393–413.

Levine, Marsha A., Katherine E. Whitwell, and Leo B. Jeffcott. "Report on the Horse Burial." Unpublished specialist report, Cambridge, 2000.

Levison, Wilhelm. *England and the Continent in the Eighth Century.* Oxford: Clarendon Press, 1946.

Lewis, Suzanne. *The Rhetoric of Power in the Bayeux Tapestry.* Cambridge: Cambridge University Press, 1999.

Liebermann, F., ed. *Die Gesetze der Angelsachsen.* 3 vols. Halle: Max Niemeyer, 1898–1916.

Liebeschuetz, Wolfgang. "The End of the Ancient City." In Rich, *City in Late Antiquity,* pp. 1–49.

Lightbown, R. W. *Secular Goldsmiths' Work in Medieval France: A History.* London: Thames and Hudson, 1978.

Longfellow, Henry Wadsworth. "Anglo-Saxon Literature." *North American Review* 47 (1838), 90–134.

Longhurst, Margaret. "The Easby Cross." *Archaeologia,* 2nd series, 31 (1931), 43–47.

Longley, David. "The Mote of Mark: The Archaeological Context of the Decorated Metalwork." In Redknap et al., *Pattern and Purpose in Insular Art,* pp. 75–89.

Lorimer, H. L. *Homer and the Monuments.* London: Macmillan, 1950.

Louis, Étienne. "Aux débuts du monachisme en Gaule du Nord: Les fouilles de l'abbaye Mérovingienne et Carolingienne de Hamage (Nord)." In *Clovis, histoire et mémoire*, ed. Michel Rouche, 2:843–68. Paris: Presses de l'Université de Paris-Sorbonne, 1997.

———. "'Sorores ac fratres in Hamatico degentes': naissance, évolution et disparition d'une abbaye au Haut Moyen Âge: Hamage (France, Nord)." *De la Meuse à l'Ardenne* 29 (1999), 17–47.

Lowe, Christopher E. *Angels, Fools and Tyrants: Britons and Anglo-Saxons in Southern Scotland, AD 450–750*. Edinburgh: Canongate Books with Historic Scotland, 1999.

———. "New Light on the Anglian 'Minster' at Hoddom, Recent Excavations at Hallguards Quarry, Hoddom, Annandale and Eskdale District, Dumfries and Galloway Region." *Transactions of the Dumfriesshire and Galloway Natural History and Antiquarian Society*, 3rd series, 77 (1991), 11–35.

Lucas, A. T. "The Plundering and Burning of Churches in Ireland 7th to 16th Century." In *North Munster Studies in Commemoration of Monsignor Michael Moloney*, ed. Étienne Rynne, pp. 172–229. Limerick: Thomond Archaeological Society, 1967.

———. "The Social Role of Relics and Reliquaries in Ancient Ireland." *JRSAI* 116 (1986), 5–37.

Lund, Niels, and Christine E. Fell, eds. *Two Voyagers at the Court of King Alfred: The Ventures of Ohthere and Wulfstan together with the Description of Northern Europe from the Old English Orosius*. York: W. Sessions, 1984.

Lycett, Andrew. *Rudyard Kipling*. London: Weidenfeld & Nicolson, 1999.

Lydon, James. "Dublin in Transition: From Ostman Town to English Borough." In *Medieval Dublin II: Proceedings of the Friends of Medieval Dublin Symposium 2000*, ed. Seán Duffy, pp. 128–41. Dublin: Four Courts Press, 2001.

Lynn, Chris. "Excavations at 46–48 Scotch Street, Armagh, 1979–80." *Ulster Jnl. of Archaeology* 51 (1988), 69–84.

———. "Recent Archaeological Excavations in Armagh City: An Interim Summary." *Seanchas Ard Macha* 8 (1977), 275–80.

Mabillon, Johannes, and Michael Germain. *Museum Italicum seu collectio veterum scriptorum ex bibliothecis italicis*. Paris: E. Martin, J. Boudot, and S. Martin, 1687.

Mac Airt, Seán, ed. and trans. *The Annals of Inisfallen*. Dublin: Dublin Institute for Advanced Studies, 1951.

Macalister, R. A. S. *Ireland in Pre-Celtic Times*. Dublin: Talbot Press, 1919.

———. *The Latin and Irish Lives of Ciarán*. London: SPCK, 1921.

MacCana, P. "The *Topos* of the Single Sandal in Irish Tradition." *Celtica* 10 (1973), 160–66.

MacDonald, A. D. S. "Aspects of the Monastery and Monastic Life in Adomnán's *Life of Columba.*" *Peritia* 3 (1984), 271–302.

———. "Notes on Monastic Archaeology and the Annals of Ulster." In Ó Corráin, *Irish Antiquity,* pp. 304–19.

Mac Iomhair, Diarmuid. "The Boundaries of Fir Rois." *County Louth Archaeological Jnl.* 15, no. 2 (1962), 144–78.

Mac Lean, Douglas. "The Keills Cross in Knapdale, the Iona School and the Book of Kells." In Higgitt, *Early Medieval Sculpture,* pp. 175–97.

———. "Scribe = Artist (but Not Monk): The Canon Tables of Ailerán 'the Wise' and the Book of Kells." Austin: unpublished, diskette.

———. "Snake-bosses and Redemption at Iona and in Pictland." In Spearman and Higgitt, *Age of Migrating Ideas,* pp. 245–53.

Mac Niocaill, Gearóid, ed. *Notitiae as Leabhar Cheanannais 1033–1161.* Dublin: Cló Morainn, 1961.

Mac Niocaill, Gearóid, and Seán Mac Airt, eds. and trans. *The Annals of Ulster (to A.D. 1131).* Dublin: Dublin Institute for Advanced Studies, 1983.

Mac Niocaill, Gearóid, and Patrick F. Wallace, eds. *Keimelia: Studies in Medieval Archaeology and History in Memory of Tom Delaney.* Galway: Galway University Press, 1988.

MacQueen, H. L., and W. J. Windram. "Laws and Courts in the Burghs." In *The Scottish Medieval Town,* ed. Michael Lynch, Michael Spearman, and Geoffrey Stell, pp. 208–27. Edinburgh: J. Donald, 1988.

Mac Shamhráin, A. S. *Church and Polity in Pre-Norman Ireland: The Case of Glendlough.* Maynooth: An Sagart, 1996.

———. "Prosopographica Glindelachensis: The Monastic Church of Glendalough and Its Community, Sixth to Thirteenth Centuries." *JRSAI* 119 (1989), 79–97.

Maertens, Thierry, and Louis Heuschen. *Doctrine et Pastorale de la liturgie de la mort.* Bruges: Abbaye de Saint-André, 1957.

Magnus, Bente. "The Firebed of the Serpent: Myth and Religion in the Migration Period Mirrored through Some Golden Objects." In *The Transformation of the Roman World AD 400–900,* ed. Leslie Webster and Michelle Brown, pp. 194–202. London: British Museum, 1997,

Maguire, Henry. *The Icons of Their Bodies: Saints and Their Images in Byzantium.* Princeton: Princeton University Press, 1996.

Mango, Cyril. *Byzantium, the Empire of New Rome.* London: Weidenfeld and Nicolson, 1980.

Manitius, Max. *Geschichte der lateinischen Literatur des Mittelalters.* Vol. 1, *Von Justinian bis zur Mitte des zehnten Jahrhunderts.* Munich: Beck, 1911.

Manning, Conleth. "Clonmacnoise Cathedral." In King, *Clonmacnoise Studies,* 1:57–86.

———. "Excavations at Glendalough." *Kildare Archaeological Society Jnl.* 16, no. 4 (1983–84), 342–47.

Manselli, Raoul. "L'escatologia di S. Gregorio Magno." *Richerche di Storia Religiosa* 1 (1954), 72–83.

Marcus Manilius. *Astronomica.* Ed. G. P. Goold. Cambridge, Mass.: Harvard University Press, 1977.

Markus, Robert Austin. *The End of Ancient Christianity.* Cambridge: Cambridge University Press, 1990.

Mathew, Gervase. *Byzantine Aesthetics.* London: John Murray, 1963.

McGurk, Patrick, David N. Dumville, Malcolm R. Godden, and Ann Knock, eds. *An Eleventh-Century Anglo-Saxon Illustrated Miscellany.* Copenhagen: Rosenkilde and Bagger, 1983.

McKitterick, Rosamond. *The Frankish Kingdoms under the Carolingians 751–987.* London: Longman, 1983.

McNally, Robert E. "Gregory the Great (590–604) and His Declining World." *Archivum Historiae Pontificiae* 16 (1978), 7–26.

———, ed. *Scriptores Hiberniae minores.* CCSL 108B. Turnhout: Brepols, 1973.

McNamara, Martin, ed. *Biblical Studies: The Medieval Irish Contribution.* Dublin: Dominican Publications, 1976.

McNeill, J. T., and H. M. Gamer. *Medieval Handbooks of Penance: A Translation of the Principal Libri poenitentiales and Selections from Related Documents.* New York: Columbia University Press, 1938. Reprint, 1990.

McNulty, J. Bard. *The Narrative Art of the Bayeux Tapestry Master.* New York: AMS Press, 1989.

Meadows, I. "The Pioneer Helmet: A Dark-Age Princely Burial from Northamptonshire." *Medieval Life* 8 (1997–98), 2–4.

———. "Wollaston: The Pioneer Burial." *Current Archaeology* 13, no. 10 (September 1997), 391–95.

Meaney, Audrey. *A Gazetteer of Early Anglo-Saxon Burial Sites.* London: Allen & Unwin, 1964.

Meehan, Bernard. *The Book of Durrow: A Medieval Masterpiece at Trinity College, Dublin.* Dublin: Town House, 1996.

———. *The Book of Kells: An Illustrated Introduction to the Manuscript in Trinity College Dublin.* Dublin: Town House, 1994.

Megaw, J. V. S. *The Art of the European Iron Age.* Bath: Adams & Dart, 1970.

Mende, Ursula. *Die Türzieher des Mittelalters.* Berlin: Deutscher Verlag für Kunstwissenschaft, 1981.

Menghin, Wilfried. *Das Schwert im frühen Mittelalter.* Stuttgart: Konrad Theiss, 1983.

Mercer, Eric. *Furniture 700–1700.* London: Weidenfeld & Nicolson, 1969.

Meyer, Erich. "Deutschordenskunst im mittelalterlichen England." *Anzeiger des Germanischen Nationalmuseums* 78 (1963), 28–34.

Meyer, Kuno, ed. *The Triads of Ireland*. Dublin: Hodges, Figgis, 1906.

———, ed. *The Vision of Mac Conglinne*. London: D. Nutt, 1894.

Meyvaert, Paul. "An Apocalypse Panel on the Ruthwell Cross." In *Medieval and Renaissance Studies*, vol. 9, *Proceedings of the Southeastern Institute of Medieval and Renaissance Studies Summer, 1978*, ed. Frank Tirro, pp. 3–32. Durham, N.C.: Duke University Press, 1982.

———. "Bede and the Church Paintings at Wearmouth/Jarrow." *ASE* 8 (1979), 63–77.

———. *Bede and Gregory the Great*. Jarrow Lecture 1964. Jarrow: St. Paul's Church, 1964. Reprinted in Lapidge, *Bede and His World*, 1:103–32.

———. "A New Perspective on the Ruthwell Cross: Ecclesia and Vita Monastica." In Cassidy, *Ruthwell Cross*, pp. 95–166.

Milde, Wolfgang. "Paläographische Bemerkungen zu den Breslauer Unzialfragmenten der Dialoge Gregors des Großen." In *Probleme der Bearbeitung mittelalterlicher Handschriften*, ed. Helmar Härtel, Wolfgang Milde, Jan Pirozynski, and Marian Zwiercan, pp. 145–65. Wolfenbütteler Forschungen 30. Wiesbaden: O. Harrassowitz, 1986.

Mills, James, ed. *Calendar of the Justiciary Rolls of Ireland 1295–1303*. Dublin: Court of the Justiciar, 1905.

Mitchell, Bruce, and Fred C. Robinson, eds. *Beowulf: An Edition*. Oxford: Blackwell, 1998.

Mitchell, Elizabeth. "Report on Coins from Icklingham." Practical Project for BA degree. Cambridge, 1998.

Mittermüller, R., ed. *Vita et Regula SS. P. Benedicti, una cum Expositione Regulae a Hildemaro Tradita*. Ratisbonae: Sumptibus, chartis et typis, F. Pustet, 1880.

Mjöberg, Jöran. *Drömmen om sagatiden*. Stockholm: Natur och kultur, 1967–68.

Mohlberg, Leo Cunibert. *Liber Sacramentorum Romanae Aeclesiae Ordinis Anni Circuli (Cod. Vat. Reg. lat. 316 / Paris Bib. Nat. 7193, 41/56) (Sacramentarium Gelasianum)*. 3rd ed., rev. by Ludwig Eisenhofer. Rerum Ecclesiastarum Documenta, Series Maior, Fontes, 4. Rome: Herder, 1981.

Moore, Ivan E., Judith Plouviez, and Stanley E. West. *The Archaeology of Roman Suffolk*. Ipswich: Suffolk County Council, 1988.

Morey, Charles Rufus. *Early Christian Art: An Outline of the Evolution of Style and Iconography in Sculpture and Painting from Antiquity to the Eighth Century*. 2nd ed. Princeton: Princeton University Press, 1953.

Morris, R., ed. *The Blickling Homilies, with a Translation, and Index of Words*. EETS o.s. 58, 63, 73. London: Oxford University Press, 1967.

Much, Rudolf, ed. *Die Germania des Tacitus*. Heidelberg: C. Winter, 1937. 2nd ed., ed. Richard Kienast. Heidelberg: C. Winter, 1959. 3rd ed., rev. by Herbert Jankuhn, ed. Wolfgang Lange. Heidelberg: C. Winter, 1967.

Murphy, Denis, ed. *The Annals of Clonmacnoise*. Trans. Conell Mageeghagen. Dublin: Royal Society of Antiquaries of Ireland, 1896.

Museum of London. *The Prittlewell Prince: The Discovery of a Rich Anglo-Saxon Burial in Essex*. London: Museum of London Archaeology Service, 2004.

Naismith, R. J. *The Story of Scotland's Towns*. Edinburgh: J. Donald, 1989.

"Nendrum," *MA* 30 (1986), 187.

Neuman de Vegvar, Carol. "The Echternach Lion: A Leap of Faith." In Karkov, M. Ryan, and Farrell, *Insular Tradition*, pp. 167–88.

Newton, Sam. *The Origins of Beowulf and the Pre-Viking Kingdom of East Anglia*. Cambridge: D. S. Brewer, 1993.

Ní Chatháin, Proinsias, and Michael Richter, eds. *Irland und Europa: die Kirche im Frühmittelalter / Ireland and Europe: The Early Church*. Stuttgart: Klett-Cotta, 1984.

Nicholas, David. *The Growth of the Medieval City from Late Antiquity to the Early Fourteenth Century*. London: Longman, 1997.

Nicholson, Andrew. "The Antler." In P. Hill, *Whithorn and St Ninian*, pp. 474–85.

Nicolaysen, Nicolay. *Langskibet fra Gokstad ved Sandefjord*. Kristiania [Oslo]: Cammermeyer, 1882.

Nielsen, Karen Høilund. "Style II and the Anglo-Saxon Elite." In *The Making of Kingdoms*, ed. Tania Dickinson and David Griffiths, vol. 10 of *ASSAH*, pp. 185–202. Oxford: Oxford University Committee for Archaeology, 1999.

Niles, John D. "Sign and Psyche in Old English Poetry." *American Jnl. of Semiotics* 9 (1992), 11–25.

Nordal, Sigurður, ed. *Egils saga Skalla-Grímssonar*. Íslenzk fornrit 2. Reykjavík: Hið íslenzka fornritafélag, 1933.

Nordhagen, Per Jonas. "A Carved Marble Pilaster in the Vatican Grottoes: Some Remarks on the Sculptural Techniques of the Early Middle Ages." *Acta ad Archaeologiam et Artium Historium Pertinantia* 4 (1969), 113–19.

———. *The Codex Amiatinus and the Byzantine Element in the Northumbrian Renaissance*. Jarrow Lecture 1977. Jarrow: St. Paul's Church, 1977. Reprinted in Lapidge, *Bede and His World*, 1:435–62.

———. *The Frescoes of John VII (AD 705–707) in S. Maria Antiqua in Rome*. Institutum Romanum Norvegiae: *Acta ad Archaeologiam et Artium Historium Pertinantia* 3. Rome: Panetto & Petrelli, 1968.

————. "An Italo-Byzantine Painter at the Scriptorium of Ceolfrith." In *Studia romana in honorem Petri Krarup septuagenarii*, ed. Karen Ascani et al., pp. 138–45. Odense: Odense University Press, 1976.

————. "John VII's Adoration of the Cross in S. Maria Antiqua." *JWCI* 30 (1967), 388–90.

————. "The Mosaics of John VII (705–707 AD): The Mosaic Fragments and Their Technique." *Acta ad Archaeologiam et Artium Historium Pertinantia* 2 (1965), 121–66.

North, Richard. *Heathen Gods in Old English Literature*. Cambridge: Cambridge University Press, 1997.

Obernhumer, Johannes. "Nochmals: Das Offertorium der Totenmesse." *Theologisch-practische Quartalschrift* 91 (1938), 335–37.

O'Brien, Caimin, and P. D. Sweetman, eds. *Archaeological Inventory of County Offaly*. Dublin: HMSO, 1997.

O'Brien, Elizabeth. "Contacts between Ireland and Anglo-Saxon England in the Seventh Century." In *ASSAH*, vol. 6, ed. William Filmer-Sankey, pp. 93–102. Oxford: Oxford University Committee for Archaeology, 1993.

————. "Excavation of a Multi-period Burial Site at Ballymacaward, Ballyshannon, Co. Donegal." *Donegal Annual* 51 (1999), 56–61.

————. *Post-Roman Britain to Anglo-Saxon England: Burial Practices Reviewed*. Oxford: Archaeopress, 1999.

O'Brien O'Keeffe, Katherine. *Visible Song: Transitional Literacy in Old English Verse*. Cambridge: Cambridge University Press, 1990.

Ó Carragáin, Éamonn. "Christ over the Beasts and the Agnus Dei: Two Multivalent Panels on the Ruthwell and Bewcastle Crosses." In *Sources of Anglo-Saxon Culture*, ed. Paul E. Szarmach with Virgina D. Oggins, pp. 377–403. Kalamazoo, Mich.: Medieval Institute Publications, 1986.

————. *The City of Rome and the World of Bede*. Jarrow Lecture 1994. Jarrow: St Paul's Church, 1994.

————. "A Liturgical Interpretation of the Bewcastle Cross." In *Medieval Literature and Antiquities: Studies in Honour of Basil Cottle*, ed. Myra Stokes and T. L. Burton, pp. 15–42. Cambridge: D. S. Brewer, 1987.

————. "The Meeting of Saint Paul and Saint Anthony: Visual and Literary Uses of a Eucharistic Motif." In Mac Niocaill and Wallace, *Keimelia*, pp. 1–58.

————. "The Necessary Distance: *Imitatio Romae* and the Ruthwell Cross." In Hawkes and Mills, *Northumbria's Golden Age*, pp. 191–203.

————. "The Ruthwell Crucifixion Poem in Its Iconographic and Liturgical Contexts." *Peritia* 6–7 (1987–88), 1–71.

————. "The Term *Porticus* and *Imitatio Romae* in Early Anglo-Saxon England." In *Text and Gloss: Studies in Insular Learning Presented to Joseph Donovan Pheifer*, ed. Helen Conrad-O'Briain et al., pp. 13–34. Dublin: Four Courts Press, 1999.

O'Connell, Philip. "Kells: Early and Medieval." *Ríocht na Midhe* 2, no. 2 (1960), 8–22.

Ó Corráin, Donnchadh. "Aspects of Early Irish History." In *Perspectives in Irish Archaeology*, ed. B. G. Scott, pp. 64–75. Belfast: Association of Young Irish Archaeologists, 1974.

————. "The Early Irish Churches: Some Aspects of Organisation." In Ó Corráin, *Irish Antiquity*, pp. 327–41.

————, ed. *Irish Antiquity: Essays and Studies Presented to Professor M. J. O'Kelly*. Cork: Cork University Press, 1981.

Ó Cróinín, Dáibhí. *Early Medieval Ireland 400–1200*. London: Longman, 1995.

Ó Cuív, Brian, ed. *Catalogue of Irish Language Manuscripts in the Bodleian Library at Oxford*. Dublin: Dublin Institute for Advanced Studies, School of Celtic Studies, 2001.

O'Donovan, John, ed. and trans. *Annals of the Kingdom of Ireland by the Four Masters*. 7 vols. Dublin: Hodges and Smith, 1851.

————. "The Registry of Clonmacnoise with Notes and Introductory Remarks." *JRSAI* 4 (1856–57), 444–60.

Ó Fiaich, Tomás. "The Church of Armagh under Lay Control." *Seanchas Ard Mhacha* 5 (1969–70), 75–127.

Ó Floinn, Raghnall. "Clonmacnoise: Art and Patronage in the Early Medieval Period." In Bourke, *From the Isles of the North*, pp. 251–60. Reprinted in King, *Clonmacnoise Studies*, 1:87–100.

————. "Schools of Metalworking in Twelfth-Century Ireland." In M. Ryan, *Ireland and Insular Art*, pp. 179–87.

Oger, Brigitte. "The Bayeux Tapestry: Results of the Scientific Tests (1982–3)." In Bouet, Levy, and Neveux, *Bayeux Tapestry*, pp. 117–23.

Ó hInnse, Séamus, ed. and trans. *Miscellaneous Irish Annals (A.D. 1114–1437)*. Dublin: Dublin Institute for Advanced Studies, 1947.

Ohlgren, Thomas H., ed. *Anglo-Saxon Textual Illustration: Photographs of Sixteen Manuscripts with Descriptions and Index*. Kalamazoo, Mich.: Medieval Institute Publications, 1992.

————, ed. *Insular and Anglo-Saxon Illuminated Manuscripts: An Iconographic Catalogue c. AD 625 to 1100*. New York: Garland, 1986.

Okasha, Elizabeth. "Literacy in Anglo-Saxon England: The Evidence from Inscriptions." In *Medieval Europe 1992*, pre-printed papers, vol. 7, *Art and Symbolism*, pp. 85–90. York: Medieval Europe, 1992. Reprinted with minor revisions in *ASSAH*, vol. 8, ed. David Griffiths, pp. 69–74. Oxford: Oxford University Committee for Archaeology, 1995.

Okasha, Elizabeth, and Katherine Forsyth. *Early Christian Inscriptions of Munster: A Corpus of the Inscribed Stones*. Cork: Cork University Press, 2001.

Olmsted, Garrett S. *The Gundestrup Cauldron*. Brussels: Latomus revue d'études latines, 1979.

O'Meadhra, Uaininn. *Early Christian, Viking and Romanesque Art: Motif-pieces from Ireland*. 2 vols. Stockholm: Almqvist and Wiksell International; Atlantic Highlands, N.J.: Humanities Press, 1979–87.

O'Meara, J. J., ed. "Giraldus Cambrensis in Topographia Hibernie, Text of the First Recension." *PRIA* 52, C (1948–50), 113–77.

———, ed. *The History and Topography of Ireland by Giraldus Cambrensis*. Portlaoise: Dolmen, 1982.

Ó Murchadha, Domhnall. "Rubbings Taken of the Inscriptions on the Cross of the Scriptures, Clonmacnois." *JRSAI* 90 (1980), 47–51.

O'Neill, Joseph. "The Rule of Ailbhe of Emly." *Ériú* 3 (1907), 104–05.

O'Reilly, Jennifer. "Early Medieval Text and Image: The Wounded and Exalted Christ." *Peritia* 6–7 (1987–88), 89–118.

———. "Patristic and Insular Traditions of the Evangelists: Exegesis and Iconography." In Fadda and Ó Carragáin, *Le Isole Britanniche*, pp. 49–94.

———. "The Rough Hewn Cross in Anglo-Saxon Art." In M. Ryan, *Ireland and Insular Art*, pp. 153–58.

O'Reilly, Jennifer, and Elizabeth Okasha. "An Anglo-Saxon Portable Altar: Inscription and Iconography." *JWCI* 47 (1984), 32–51.

Ó Ríordáin, S. P. *Tara: The Monuments on the Hill*. Dundalk: Dundalgan Press, 1982.

Orpen, G. H., ed. *The Song of Dermot and the Earl*. Oxford: Clarendon Press, 1892.

Owen, Gale R. *Rites and Religions of the Anglo-Saxons*. Newton Abbot: David and Charles, 1981.

Owen-Crocker, Gale R. "The Bayeux 'Tapestry': Invisible Seams and Visible Boundaries." *ASE* 31 (2002), 257–73.

———. "Brothers, Rivals and the Geometry of the Bayeux Tapestry." In Owen-Crocker, *King Harold II and the Bayeux Tapestry*, pp. 109–23.

———. *The Four Funerals in Beowulf*. Manchester: Manchester University Press, 2000.

———. *King Harold II and the Bayeux Tapestry*. Woodbridge: Boydell, 2005.

———. "Reading the Bayeux Tapestry through Canterbury Eyes." In *Anglo-Saxon Studies Presented to Cyril Roy Hart*, ed. Simon Keynes and Alfred P. Smyth, pp. 243–65. Dublin: Four Courts, 2005.

———. "Squawk Talk: Commentary by Birds in the Bayeux Tapestry," *ASE* 34 (2005), 237–54.

————. "Telling a Tale: Narrative Techniques in the Bayeux Tapestry and the Old English Epic *Beowulf*." In Owen-Crocker and Graham, *Medieval Art: Recent Perspectives*, pp. 40–59.

Owen-Crocker, Gale R., and Timothy Graham, eds. *Medieval Art: Recent Perspectives. A Memorial Tribute to C. R. Dodwell.* Manchester: Manchester University Press, 1998.

Page, Ray I. "Anglo-Saxon Runes and Magic." *Jnl. of the British Archaeological Association*, 3rd series, 27 (1964), 14–31. Reprinted in Page, *Runes and Runic Inscriptions*, pp. 118–23.

————. *An Introduction to English Runes.* London: Methuen, 1973. 2nd ed. Woodbridge: Boydell, 1999.

————. "On the Transliteration of English Runes." *MA* 28 (1984), 22–45. Reprinted in Page, *Runes and Runic Inscriptions*, pp. 245–73.

————. *Runes and Runic Inscriptions: Collected Essays on Anglo-Saxon and Viking Runes.* Ed. David Parsons with Carl T. Berkhout. Woodbridge: Boydell, 1995.

Parkes, Malcolm B. "The Contribution of Insular Scribes of the Seventh and Eighth Centuries to the 'Grammar of Legibility.'" In *Grafia e interpunzione del Latino nel medioevo: seminario internazionale Roma, 27–29 Settembre 1984*, ed. Alfonso Maierú, pp. 17–30. Centro del Studio del C.N.R. Lessico intellettuale europeo 41. Rome: Edizioni dell'Alteneo, 1986. Reprinted in Parkes, *Scribes, Scripts and Readers: Studies in the Communication, Presentation and Dissemnination of Medieval Texts*, pp. 1–18. London: Hambledon, 1991.

————. *Pause and Effect: An Introduction to the History of Punctuation in the West.* Aldershot: Scolar Press, 1992.

Parsons, David N. "Anglo-Saxon Runes in Continental Manuscripts." In *Runische Schriftkultur in kontinental-skandinavischer und -angelsächsischer Wechselbeziehung*, ed. Klaus Düwel and Hannelore Neumann, pp. 195–220. Berlin: W. de Gruyter, 1994.

————. *Recasting the Runes: The Reform of the Anglo-Saxon Futhorc.* Uppsala: Institutionen för nordiska språk, Uppsala universitet, 1999.

Pattullo, Rev. James M. Donations to the Museum no. 4, 12 March 1928. *PSAS* 62 (1927–28), 165.

Peers, C. R. "English Ornament in the Seventh and Eighth Centuries." *Proceedings of the British Academy* 12 (1926), 45–54.

Pembroke Estate. *Calendar of Ancient Deeds and Muniments Preserved in the Pembroke Estate Office.* Dublin: Printed for the Earls of Pembroke and Montgomery at the University Press, 1891.

Petersen, Jan. *Viking Antiquities in Great Britain and Ireland, Part V, British Antiquities of the Viking Period found in Norway.* Oslo: H. Aschehoug, 1940.

Peterson, Eric. *The Angels and the Liturgy: The Status and Significance of the Holy Angels in Worship.* Trans. Ronald Walls. London: Herder & Herder, 1964.

Petrie, George. *The Ecclesiastical Architecture of Ireland.* Dublin: Hodges and Smith, 1845.

Phillipson, David W. *Ancient Ethiopia: Its Antecedents and Successors.* London: British Museum Press, 1998.

Philpott, Robert A. *Burial Practices in Roman Britain.* Oxford: Tempus Reparatum, 1991.

Pinder, Michael. "An Aspect of Seventh-Century Anglo-Saxon Goldsmithing." In Redknap et al., *Pattern and Purpose in Insular Art,* pp. 133–39.

Plummer, Charles, ed. *Bethada Náem nÉrenn; Lives of Irish Saints.* 2 vols. Oxford: Clarendon Press, 1922.

Podevijn, Raynerius. "Addendum to Het Offertorium der Doodenmis." *Tijdschrift voor Liturgie* 3 (1921), 249–54.

———. "Het Offertorium der Doodenmis." *Tijdschrift voor Liturgie* 2 (1920), 338–49.

Poirier, D. A., and N. F. Bellantoni, eds. *In Remembrance: Archaeology and Death.* Westport, Conn.: Bergin & Garvey, 1997.

Price, Liam. "Rock-basins or 'Bullauns' at Glendalough and Elsewhere." *JRSAI* 89 (1959), 161–88.

Proudfoot, Bruce. "Excavations at Cathedral Hill, Downpatrick, Co. Down." *Ulster Jnl. of Archaeology* 19 (1956), 57–72.

Prudentius. *Prudentius.* Trans. H. J. Thomson. 2 vols. London: William Heinemann, 1949–53.

Radford, C. A. R. "The Early Christian Monuments of Scotland." *Antiquity* 16 (1942), 1–18.

Radner, J. N., ed. and trans. *Fragmentary Annals of Ireland.* Dublin: Dublin Institute for Advanced Studies, 1978.

Raine, James. *Saint Cuthbert: With an account of the state in which his remains were found upon the opening of his tomb in Durham cathedral, in the year MDCCCXXVII.* Durham: G. Andrews, 1928.

Raw, Barbara C. *Anglo-Saxon Crucifixion Iconography and the Art of the Monastic Revival.* Cambridge: Cambridge University Press, 1990.

———. "The Eagle, the Archer and the Lamb," *JWCI* 30 (1967), 391–94.

———. *Trinity and Incarnation in Anglo-Saxon Art and Thought.* Cambridge: Cambridge University Press, 1997.

Rayburn, Alan. *Naming Canada: Stories about Place Names from Canadian Geographic.* Toronto: University of Toronto Press, 1994.

RCAHMS. *Argyll: An Inventory of the Monuments.* Vol. 4, *Iona.* Edinburgh: HMSO, 1982.

———. *Argyll: An Inventory of the Monuments.* Vol. 5, *Islay, Jura, Colonsay and Oronsay.* Edinburgh: HMSO, 1984.

"Reask," *MA* 30 (1986), 187.

Redknap, Mark, et al., eds. *Pattern and Purpose in Insular Art: Proceedings of the Fourth International Conference on Insular Art*. Oxford: Oxbow, 2001.

Reece, Richard. "The End of the City in Roman Britain." In Rich, *City in Late Antiquity*, pp. 136–44.

Reeves, William. *The Ancient Churches of Armagh: Being the substance of a paper read before the Armagh Natural History and Philosophical Society, on the 14th of March 1860*. Lusk: Privately printed, 1860. Reprinted as "The Churches of Armagh," *Ulster Jnl. of Archaeology*, 2nd series, 2 (1895–96), 194–205; 3 (1896–97), 193–95; 4 (1897–98), 205–28.

Rich, John, ed. *The City in Late Antiquity*. London: Routledge, 1992.

Richards, Julian D. "Anglo-Saxon Symbolism." In Carver, *Age of Sutton Hoo*, pp. 131–47.

Ritchie, Anna. *Iona*. London: B. T. Batsford, Historic Scotland, 1997.

———. *Viking Scotland*. London: B. T. Batsford, Historic Scotland, 1993.

Rivers, T. J., ed. and trans. *Laws of the Salian and Ripuarian Franks*. New York: AMS Press, 1986.

Roberts, Jane. "Some Relationships between 'The Dream of the Rood' and the Cross at Ruthwell." *Studies in Medieval English Language and Literature* 15 (2000), 1–25.

Robertson, W. N. "St. John's Cross, Iona, Argyll." *PSAS* 106 (1974–75), 111–23.

Robinson, F. C. "A Sub-Sense of Old English *Fyrn(-)*." *NM* 100 (1999), 471–75.

Roe, Helen. "The 'David Cycle' in Early Irish Art." *JRSAI* 79 (1949), 39–59.

———. *The High-crosses of Kells*. Kells: Meath Archaeological and Historical Society, 1959.

Roesdahl, Else. *The Vikings*. Trans. Susan M. Margeson and Kirsten Williams. London: Guild Publishing, 1991.

Rollason, David. *Saints and Relics in Anglo-Saxon England*. Oxford: B. Blackwell, 1989.

Rolleston, G. "Researches and Excavations Carried on in an Ancient Cemetery at Frilford, near Abingdon, Berks. in the Years 1867–1868." *Archaeologia* 42 (1869), 417–85.

Ryan, John. *Clonmacnois: A Historical Summary*. Dublin: HMSO, 1973.

Ryan, Michael. "The Book of Kells and Metalwork." In *The Book of Kells: Proceedings of a Conference at Trinity College Dublin 6–9 September 1992*, ed. Felicity O'Mahony, pp. 270–79. Dublin: Scolar Press, 1994.

———. *The Derrynaflan Hoard: A Preliminary Report*. Dublin: National Museum of Ireland, 1983.

———. "The Donore Hoard: Early Medieval Metalwork from Moynalty, near Kells, Ireland." *Antiquity* 61 (1987), 57–63.

————. "Fine Metalworking and Early Irish Monasteries: The Archaeological Evidence." In *Settlement and Society in Medieval Ireland: Studies Presented to F. X. Martin, o.s.a.,* ed. John Bradley, pp. 33–48. Kilkenny: Boethius Press, 1988.

————, ed. *Ireland and Insular Art A.D. 500–1200.* Dublin: Royal Irish Academy, 1987.

Saenger, Paul. *Space between Words: The Origin of Silent Reading.* Stanford: Stanford University Press, 1998.

Salin, E. *Le Haut Moyen Age de Lorraine.* Paris: Paul Geuthner, 1939.

Saxl, Fritz. "The Ruthwell Cross." *JWCI* 6 (1943), 1–19.

Saxl, Fritz, and Rudolf Wittkower. *British Art and the Mediterranean.* London: Oxford University Press, 1948.

Schaffran, E. *Die Kunst der Langobarden in Italien.* Munich: Verlag der Bayerischen Akademie der Wissenschaften, 1941.

Schapiro, Meyer. "The Image of the Disappearing Christ: The Ascension in English Art around the Year 1000." *Gazette des Beaux-Arts,* 6th series, 23 (1943), 135–52.

————. "The Religious Meaning of the Ruthwell Cross." *Art Bulletin* 26 (1944), 232–45. Reprint in Schapiro, *Late Antique, Early Christian and Medieval Art: Selected Papers,* pp. 150–76 and 186–92. London: Chatto & Windus, 1980.

————. *Words and Pictures: On the Literal and Symbolic in the Illustration of a Text.* The Hague: Mouton, 1973.

Schiller, Gertrud. *Iconography of Christian Art.* Trans. Janet Seligman. 2 vols. London: Lund Humphries, 1971–72.

————. *Ikonographie der christlichen Kunst.* Gutersloh: Gütersloher Verlagshaus Gerd Mohn, 1971.

Schliemann, Heinrich. *Mykenae: Bericht über meine Forschungen und Entdeckungen in Mykenae und Tiryns.* Leipzig: F. A. Brockhaus, 1878.

Schmidt, Gary D. *The Iconography of the Mouth of Hell; Eighth-Century Britain to the Fifteenth Century.* Selinsgrove, Pa.: Susquehanna University Press; London: Associated University Presses, 1995.

Schön, Matthias D. *Feddersen Wierde, Fallward, Flögeln: Archäologie im Museum Burg Bederkesa, Landkreis Cuxhaven.* Landkreis Cuxhaven: Der Oberkreisdirektor, 1999.

Schouwink, Wilfried. *Der wilde Eber in Gottes Weinberg: Zur Darstellung des Schweins in Literatur und Kunst des Mittelalters.* Sigmaringen: J. Thorbecke, 1985.

Schrader, Richard J. "The Language of the Giant's Sword Hilt in *Beowulf.*" *NM* 94 (1993), 141–47.

Schwab, Ute. "Eber, aper und porcus in Notkers des Deutschen Rhetorik." In *Annali dell'Istituto Universitario Orientale di Napoli,* sezione linguistica 9, pp. 109–245. Rome: Editione universitarie, 1970.

———. "Das Traumgesicht vom Kreuzesbaum: Ein ikonologischer Interpretationsansatz zu dem ags. 'Dream of the Rood.'" In *Philologische Studien. Gedenkschrift fur Richard Kienast,* ed. Ute Schwab and Elfriede Stutz, pp. 131–92. Germanische Bibliothek. Dritte Reihe: Untersuchungen und Einzeldarstellungen. Heidelberg: Winter, 1978.

Scull, Christopher. "Excavations and Survey at Watchfield, Oxfordshire, 1983–92." *Archaeological Jnl.* 149 (1992), 124–281.

———. "Further Evidence from East Anglia for Enamelling on Early Saxon Metalwork." In *ASSAH,* vol. 4, ed. Sonia Chadwick Hawkes, David Brown, and James Campbell, pp. 117–24. Oxford: Oxford University Committee for Archaeology, 1985.

Serpelli, Bonifacio M. *L'Offertorio della messe dei defunti.* Diss. ad Laurem, Pontificium Athenaeum "Angelicum." Rome: Tipografia Agostiniana, 1946.

Serrailler, Ian. *Beowulf the Warrior.* London: Oxford University Press, 1954.

Sharpe, Richard. "Palaeographical Considerations in the Study of the Patrician Documents in the Book of Armagh." *Scriptorium* 36 (1982), 3–28.

Shoesmith, Ron. *Hereford City Excavations.* Vol. 2, *Excavations on and Close to the Defences.* London: Council for British Archaeology, 1982.

Sicard, Damien. *La Liturgie de la mort dans l'église latine des origines à la réforme carolingienne.* Münster: Aschendorff, 1978.

Sieger, J. D. "Visual Metaphor as Theology: Leo the Great's Sermon on the Incarnation and the Arch Mosaics at S. Maria Maggiore." *Gesta* 26, no. 2 (1987), 83–91.

Siegmund, Frank. *Merowingerzeit am Niederrhein.* Cologne: Rheinland-Verlag GMBH, 1998.

Silvagni, Angelo. "Nuovo ordinamento delle sillogi epigraphiche di Roma anteriori al secolo XI." *Atti della Pontificia accademia romana di archeologia, Dissertazioni* 15 (1921), 181–239.

———. "La silloge epigrafica di Cambridge." *Rivista di Archeologia Cristiana* 20 (1943), 49–112.

Silverstein, Theodore, ed. *Visio Sancti Pauli; The History of the Apocalypse in Latin Together with Nine Texts.* London: Christophers, 1935.

Simington, R. C. "Valuation of Kells, 1663, with Note on Map of Kells, c.1655." *Analecta Hibernica* 22 (1960), 231–68.

Simms, Anngret. "Frühformen der mittelalterlichen Stadt in Irland." In *Genetische Ansätze der Kulturlandschaftsforschung: Festschrift für Helmut Jäger,* ed. W. Pinkwart, pp. 27–39. Würzburg: Im Selbstverlag des Instituts für Geographie der Universität Würzburg, 1983.

Simms, Anngret, and Katherine Simms. *Kells.* Irish Historic Town Atlas 4. Dublin: Royal Irish Academy, 1990.

Simpson, Linzi. "Forty Years a-Digging: A Preliminary Synthesis of Archaeological Excavations in Medieval Dublin." In *Medieval Dublin I: Proceedings of the Friends of Medieval Dublin Symposium 1999*, ed. Seán
Duffy, pp. 11–68. Dublin: Four Courts Press, 2000.

Sjøvold, Thorlief. *The Viking Ships in Oslo*. Oslo: Universitets Oldsaksamling, 1985.

Small, Alan, A. Charles Thomas, and David M. Wilson. *St. Ninian's Isle and
Its Treasure*. London: Oxford University Press, 1973.

Smalley, Beryl. *The Study of the Bible in the Middle Ages*. Notre Dame: University of Notre Dame Press, 1964.

Smith, Charles Roach. *Collectanea antiqua: Etchings and Notices of Ancient
Remains, Illustrative of the Habits, Customs, and History of Past Ages*. London: J. R. Smith, 1852.

Snorri Sturluson. *Edda: Háttatal*. Ed. Anthony Faulkes. Oxford: Clarendon Press, 1991.

———. *Snorri Sturluson, Edda: Skáldskaparmál*. Ed. Anthony Faulkes. London: Viking Society for Northern Research, 1998.

———. *Heimskringla*. Ed. Bjarni Aðalbjarnarson. Íslenzk fornrit 26. Reykjavík: Hið íslenzka fornritafélag, 1941.

———. *Heimskringla*. Ed. Finnur Jónsson. 4 vols. Copenhagen: S. L. Møllers
Bogtrykkeri, 1893–1900.

Soressi, Marino. "L'offertorio della messa dei defunti e l'escatologia orientale." *Ephemerides Liturgicae* 61 (1947), 5–12.

Sozomen. *Ecclesiastica Historia*. Ed. Joseph Bidez. Berlin: Akademie-Verlag,
1960.

Speake, George. *Anglo-Saxon Animal Art and Its Germanic Background*.
Oxford: Clarendon Press, 1980.

———. *A Saxon Bed Burial on Swallowcliffe Down*. Historic Buildings and
Monuments Commission, Archaeological Report 10. London, 1989.

Spearman, R. M., and J. Higgitt, eds. *The Age of Migrating Ideas: Early
Medieval Art in Northern Britain and Ireland*. Edinburgh: National
Museum of Scotland and Alan Sutton, 1993.

Speckenbach, Klaus. "Der Eber in der deutschen Literatur des Mittelalters." In *Verbum et Signum*, ed. Hans Fromm et al., pp. 425–76.
Munich: Wilhelm Fink, 1975.

Stalley, Roger. "The Romanesque Sculpture of Tuam." In *The Vanishing
Past: Studies of Medieval Art, Liturgy and Metrology Presented to Chris-
topher Hohler*, ed. A. Borg and A. Martindale, pp. 179–95. Oxford:
British Archaeological Reports, 1981.

Stancliffe, Clare. "Kings Who Opted Out." In *Ideal and Reality in Frankish
and Anglo-Saxon Society: Studies Presented to J. M. Wallace-Hadrill*, ed.
Patrick Wormald, Donald Bullough, and Roger Collins, pp. 154–76.
Oxford: B. Blackwell, 1983.

Staniland, Kay. *Medieval Craftsmen: Embroiderers*. London: British Museum Press, 1991.

Stanley, Eric G. "The Ruthwell Cross Inscription: Some Linguistic and Literary Implications of Paul Meyvaert's Paper 'An Apocalypse Panel on the Ruthwell Cross.'" In Stanley, *A Collection of Papers with Emphasis on Old English Literature*, pp. 384–99. Toronto: Pontifical Institute of Mediaeval Studies, 1987.

Starensier, Adele La Barre. "An Art Historical Study of the Byzantine Silk Industry." 3 vols. PhD diss., Columbia University, 1982.

Stenton, F., ed. *The Bayeux Tapestry: A Comprehensive Survey*. London: Phaidon, 1965.

Stevens, Helen M. "Maaseik Reconstructed: A Practical Investigation and Interpretation of 8th Century Embroidery Techniques." In *Textiles in Northern Archaeology*, ed. Penelope Walton and John-Peter Wild, pp. 57–60. London: Archetype Publications, 1990.

Stevenson, R. B. K. "Aspects of Ambiguity in Crosses and Interlace." *Ulster Jnl. of Archaeology* 44–45 (1981–82), 1–27.

———. "The Chronology and Relationships of Some Irish and Scottish Crosses." *JRSAI* 86 (1956), 84–96.

———. "Further Notes on the Hunterston and 'Tara' Brooches, Monymusk Reliquary and Blackness Bracelet." *PSAS* 113 (1983), 469–77.

———. "The Hunterston Brooch and Its Significance." *MA* 18 (1974), 16–42.

———. "Pictish Art." In *The Problem of the Picts*, ed. F. T. Wainwright, pp. 96–128. Edinburgh: Melven Press, 1955.

———. "Sculpture in Scotland in the 6th–9th Centuries AD." In *Kolloquium über spätantike und frühmittelalterliche Skulptur, Universität Heidelberg, 1970*, pp. 65–74. Mainz: Philipp von Zabern, 1971.

Stiegemann, Christoph, and Matthias Wemhoff, eds. *799 Kunst und Kultur der Karolingerzeit: Karl der Grosse und Papst Leo III in Paderborn*. Mainz: P. von Zabern, 1999.

Stjerna, Knut. "Hjälmar och svärd i *Beovulf*." In *Studier tillägnade Oscar Montelius*, pp. 99–120. Stockholm: P. A. Norstedt, 1903.

Stokes, Whitley, ed. and trans. "The Annals of Tigernach." *Revue Celtique* 16–18 (1895–97). Reprinted as *The Annals of Tigernach*. 2 vols. Felinfach: Llanerch Publishers, 1993.

———, ed. *Felire Oengussu Celi Dei: The Martyrology of Oengus the Culdee, Critically Edited from Ten Manuscripts*. London: Henry Bradshaw Society, 1905.

———, ed. *The Tripartite Life of Patrick*. 2 vols. London: HMSO, 1887.

Stolpe, Hj., and T. J. Arne. *Graffältet vid Vendel*. Stockholm: K. L. Beckmans Boktryckeri, 1912.

Ström, F. *On the Sacral Origin of the Germanic Death Penalties*. Stockholm: Wahlstrom, 1942.

Strzykowski, Josef. *Origin of Christian Church Art: New Facts and Principles of Research*. Trans. O. M. Dalton and H. J. Braunholtz. Oxford: Clarendon Press, 1923.

Stubbs, William, ed. *Memorials of St. Dunstan*. Rolls Series 65. London: Longman, 1874.

Sveinsson, Einer Ól. (See Einar Ól. Sveinsson.)

Swan, Leo. "Excavations at Kilpatrick Churchyard, Killucan, Co. Westmeath, July/August 1973 and 1975." *Ríocht na Midhe* 6, no. 2 (1976), 89–96.

———. "Monastic Proto-towns in Early Medieval Ireland: The Evidence of Aerial Photography, Plan Analysis and Survey." In Clarke and Simms, *Comparative History of Urban Origins*, pp. 77–102.

Swanton, Michael, trans. *Anglo-Saxon Prose*. London: Dent, 1975. Rev. ed. 1985.

———. "The Manuscript Illustration of a Helmet of Benty Grange Type." *Jnl. of the Arms and Armour Society* 10 (1980), 1–5.

Sweet, H., ed. *The Oldest English Texts*. EETS o.s. 83. London: Oxford University Press, 1885. Reprint, 1938.

Sweetman, H. S., ed. *Calendar of Documents Relating to Ireland 1171–1307*. 5 vols. London: Longman, 1876–85.

Swift, Cathy. "Forts and Fields: A Study of 'Monastic Towns' in Seventh and Eighth Century Ireland." *Jnl. of Irish Archaeology* 9 (1998), 105–25.

Taylor, H. M., and J. Taylor. *Anglo-Saxon Architecture*. 3 vols. Cambridge: Cambridge University Press, 1965–78. (Vol. 3 by H. M. Taylor alone.)

Temple, Elżbieta, ed. *Anglo-Saxon Manuscripts, 900–1066*. London: Harvey Miller, 1976.

Tharaud, Barry, ed. *Beowulf*. Niwot: University Press of Colorado, 1990.

Thomas, Avril. *The Walled Towns of Ireland*. 2 vols. Blackrock: Irish Academic Press, 1992.

Thomas, Charles. *The Early Christian Archaeology of North Britain*. London: Oxford University Press, 1971.

———. "'Gallici nautae de galliarum provinciis': A Sixth/Seventh Century Trade with Gaul, Reconsidered." *MA* 34 (1990), 1–26.

———. "Imported Late-Roman Mediterranean Pottery in Ireland and Western Britain: Chronologies and Implications." *PRIA* 76, C (1976), 245–55.

———. "Imported Pottery in Dark-Age Western Britain." *MA* 3 (1959), 89–111.

———. *A Provisional List of Imported Pottery in Post-Roman Britain and Ireland*. Redruth: Institute of Cornish Studies, 1981.

Thoms, William J. *The Primeval Antiquities of Denmark: Translated and Applied to the Illustration of Similar Remains in England*. London: J. H. Parker, 1849.

Thorkelin, Grímur Jónsson, ed. *De Danorum rebus gestis secul. III & IV. poëma danicum dialecto anglosaxonica*. Copenhagen: Th. E. Rangel, 1815.

Thorn, C., and F. Thorn, eds. *Domesday Book 6. Wiltshire*. Chichester: Phillimore, 1979.

Thrane, Henrik. *Guld, guder og godtfolk*. Odense: National Museum of Denmark, 1993.

Todd, J. H., ed. *Cogadh Gaedhel re Gallaibh: The War of the Gaedhil with the Gaill*. London: Longmans, Green, Reader and Dyer, 1867.

Trahern, Joseph B., Jr. "Fatalism and the Millennium." In *The Cambridge Companion to Old English Literature*, ed. Malcolm Godden and Michael Lapidge, pp. 190–205. Cambridge: Cambridge University Press, 1991.

Trench-Jellicoe, Ross. "A Missing Figure on Slab Fragment no 2 from Monifieth, Angus, the a'Chill Cross, Canna, and Some Implications of the Development of a Variant Form of the Virgin's Hairstyle and Dress in Early Medieval Scotland." *PSAS* 129 (1999), 597–647.

Tristram, Hildegard L. C. *Sex aetates mundi: Die Weltzeitalter bei den Angelsachsen und den Iren*. Heidelberg: Carl Winter, 1985. ·

Tweddle, Dominic. "Silk Reliquary Pouch in Compound Twill." In *Textiles, Cordage and Raw Fibre from 16–22 Coppergate*, ed. Penelope Walton, pp. 378–81. Archaeology of York 17.5. Dorchester: Council for British Archaeology, 1989.

Tweddle, Dominic, Martin Biddle, and Birthe Kjølbye-Biddle, eds. *South-East England*. Vol. 4 of *Corpus of Anglo-Saxon Stone Sculpture*. Oxford: Oxford University Press, 1995.

Valante, Mary A. "Reassessing the Irish 'Monastic Town.'" *Irish Historical Studies* 31 (1998–99), 1–18.

Van der Leeuw, Gerardus. *Sacred and Profane Beauty: The Holy in Art*. New York: Holt, Rinehart & Winston, 1963.

Van Houts, Elisabeth M. C. "The Echo of the Conquest in the Latin Sources: Duchess Mathilda, Her Daughters and the Enigma of the Golden Child." In Bouet, Levy, and Neveux, *Bayeux Tapestry*, pp. 135–53.

———. "The Ship List of William the Conqueror." *Anglo-Norman Studies* 10 (1987), 159–83.

Van Meter, David C. "The Ritualized Presentation of Weapons and the Ideology of Nobility in *Beowulf*." *Jnl. of English & Germanic Philology* 95 (1996), 175–89.

Van Tongeren, Louis. "Vom Kreuzritus zur Kreuzestheologie: Die Entstehungsgeschichte des Festes der Kreuzerhöhung und seine erste Ausbreitung im Westen." *Ephemerides Liturgicae* 112 (1998), 216–45.

Verhulst, Adriaan. *The Rise of Cities in North-West Europe*. Cambridge: Cambridge University Press, 1999.

Vierck, Hayo. "*Imitatio imperii* und *interpretatio Germanica* vor der Wikinger-zeit." In *Les pays du nord et Byzance,* ed. Rudolf Zeitler, pp. 64–116. Acta Universitatis Upsaliensis. Uppsala: Almqvist & Wiksell, 1981.

Vince, Alan. *Pre-Viking Lindsey.* Lincoln: City of Lincoln Archaeology Unit, 1993.

Vogel, Cyrille, ed. *Additions et corrections de Mgr L. Duchesne.* Paris: E. de Boccard, 1981. Vol. 3 of the reprint of Duchesne, *Le Liber Pontificalis.*

———. "Deux conséquences de l'eschatologie Grégorienne: La multipli-cation des messes privées et les moines-prêtres." In Fontaine, Gillet, and Pellistrandi, *Grégoire le Grand,* pp. 267–76.

Volbach, W. F. *Early Decorative Textiles.* Feltham: Hamlyn, 1969.

von den Brincken, Anna-Dorothee. *Studien zur lateinischen Weltchronistik bis in die Zeitalter Ottos von Freising.* Düsseldorf: Michael Triltsch, 1957.

von Wilckens, Leonie. *Die Textile Künste von der Spätantike bis um 1500.* Munich: C. H. Beck, 1991.

Wailes, Bernard. "Dún Ailinne: An Interim Report." In *Hillforts: Later Prehis-toric Earthworks in Britain and Ireland,* ed. D. W. Harding, pp. 319–38. London: Academic Press, 1976.

Walker, G. S. M., ed. *Sancti Columbani Opera.* Dublin: Dublin Institute for Advanced Studies, 1970.

Wallace, Patrick F. "Dublin's Waterfront at Wood Quay: 900–1317." In *Waterfront Archaeology in Britain and Northern Europe,* ed. Gustav Milne and Brian Hobley, pp. 109–18. CBA Res. Rep. 41. London: Council for British Archaeology, 1981.

Walter, Philippe, ed. *Mythologies du porc.* Actes du colloque de Saint-An-toine l'Abbaye (Isère), 4–5 avril 1998. Grenoble: J. Millon, 1999.

Wamers, Egon. "Egg-and-dart Derivatives in Insular Art." In M. Ryan, *Ireland and Insular Art,* pp. 96–104.

———. *Insularer Metallschmuck in wikingerzeitlichen Gräbern Nordeuropas; Untersuchungen zur skandinavischen Westexpansion.* Neumünster: Karl Wachholtz, 1985.

Ward-Perkins, Bryan. "Continuists, Catastrophists, and the Towns of Post-Roman Northern Italy." *Papers of the British School at Rome* 65 (1997), 157–76.

———. "The Towns of Northern Italy: Rebirth or Renewal?" In Hodges and Hobley, *Rebirth of Towns in the West,* pp. 16–27.

Warner, G. F., ed. *The Stowe Missal: MS. D. II. 3 in the Library of the Royal Irish Academy, Dublin.* London: Henry Bradshaw Society, 1906–07. Re-print, Woodbridge: Boydell, 1989.

Wasselynck, René. "Les compilations des 'Moralia in Job' du VIIe au XIIe siècle." *Recherches de Théologie Ancienne et Mediévale* 29 (1962), 5–32.

————. "L'influence de l'exégèse de S. Grégoire le Grand sur les commentaires bibliques médiévaux (VIIe–XIIe s.)." *Recherches de Théologie Ancienne et Mediévale* 32 (1965), 157–204.

————. "Présence de Saint Grégoire le Grand dans les Receuils Canoniques (Xe–XIIe siècles)." *Mélanges de Science Religieuse* 22 (1965), 205–19.

Wasserschleben, H., ed. *Die irische Kanonensammlung.* 2nd ed. Leipzig, 1885. Reprint, Darmstadt: Scientia Verlag Aalen, 1966.

Waterman, D. M., and C. J. Lynn. *Excavations at Navan Fort 1961–71, County Armagh.* Belfast: HMSO, 1997.

Webb, J. F., ed. *The Age of Bede.* Harmondsworth: Penguin, 1988.

Webster, Leslie. "*Ædificia nova:* Treasures of Alfred's Reign." In *Alfred the Great,* ed. Timothy Reuter, pp. 79–103. Aldershot: Ashgate, 2003.

————. "Archaeology and *Beowulf.*" In B. Mitchell and Robinson, *Beowulf,* pp. 183–94.

————. "The Iconographic Programme of the Franks Casket." In Hawkes and Mills, *Northumbria's Golden Age,* pp. 227–46.

Webster, Leslie, and Janet Backhouse, eds. *The Making of England: Anglo-Saxon Art and Culture AD 600–900.* London: British Museum Press, 1991.

Welander, R., C. E. Batey, and T. Cowie. "A Viking Burial from Kneep, Uig, Isle of Lewis." *PSAS* 117 (1987), 163–65.

Welch, Martin G. *Discovering Anglo-Saxon England.* University Park: Pennsylvania State University Press, 1993.

Werckmeister, Otto K. *Irisch-northumbrische Buchmalerei des 8. Jahrhunderts und monastiche Spiritualität.* Berlin: De Gruyter, 1967.

Werner, Joachim. "Die Eberzier von Monceau-le-Neuf (Dép. Aisne): Ein Beitrag zur Entstehung der völkerwanderungszeitlichen Eberhelme." *Acta Archaeologica* 20 (1949), 248–57.

West, Stanley E. *A Corpus of Anglo-Saxon Material from Suffolk.* East Anglian Archaeology Report 84. Ipswich: Suffolk County Council, 1998.

West, Stanley E., and Valerie Cooper. *West Stow: The Anglo-Saxon Village.* East Anglian Archaeology Report 24. Ipswich: Suffolk County Planning Department, 1985.

West, Stanley E., and Judith Plouviez. "The Roman Site at Icklingham." In *Suffolk,* ed. John Wymer, pp. 63–134. East Anglian Archaeology Report 3. Ipswich: Suffolk County Planning Department, 1976.

Whitehouse, David. "Rome and Naples: Survival and Revival in Central and Southern Italy." In Hodges and Hobley, *Rebirth of Towns in the West,* pp. 28–31.

Whitelock, Dorothy, ed. *English Historical Documents.* Vol. 1, *c. 500–1042.* 2nd ed. London: E Methuen, 1979.

Wickham-Crowley, Kelley M. "The Birds on the Sutton Hoo Instrument." In Farrell and Neuman de Vegvar, *Sutton Hoo Fifty Years After,* pp. 43–62.

Wilde, William R., ed. *A Descriptive Catalogue of the Antiquities of Stone, Earthen and Vegetable Materials in the Museum of the Royal Irish Academy.* Dublin: Royal Irish Academy, 1857.

William of Malmesbury. *Willelmi Malmesbiriensis Monachi De Gestis Regum Anglorum Libri Quinque.* Ed. William Stubbs. 2 vols. Rolls Series. London: Eyre & Spottiswoode, 1887.

Wilson, David. *Anglo-Saxon Paganism.* London: Routledge, 1992.

Wilson, David M. *Anglo-Saxon Art from the Seventh Century to the Norman Conquest.* London: Thames and Hudson, 1984.

———. *The Bayeux Tapestry.* London: Thames and Hudson; New York: Alfred A. Knopf, 1985.

———. *The Vikings and Their Origins: Scandinavia in the First Millennium.* London: Thames and Hudson, 1970.

Wilson, David M., and Ole Klindt-Jensen, *Viking Art,* 2nd ed. London: Allen & Unwin, 1980.

Wolff, P. *The Awakening of Europe.* Vol. 1, *The Pelican History of European Thought.* Harmondsworth: Penguin, 1968.

Wood, Ian. "Anglo-Saxon Otley: An Archiepiscopal Estate and Its Crosses in a Northumbrian Context." *Northern History* 23 (1987), 20–38.

Woodruff, H. "The Iconography and Date of the Mosaics of La Dauraude." *Art Bulletin* 13 (1931), 80–104.

Wormald, Francis. "Style and Design." In Stenton, *Bayeux Tapestry,* pp. 25–36.

Wormald, Patrick. "Bede, Beowulf, and the Conversion of the Anglo-Saxon Aristocracy." In Farrell, *Bede and Anglo-Saxon England,* pp. 32–95.

———. "The Uses of Literacy in Anglo-Saxon England and Its Neighbours." *Transactions of the Royal Historical Society,* 5th series, 27 (1977), 95–114.

Wright, Charles D. *The Irish Tradition in Old English Literature.* Cambridge: Cambridge University Press, 1993.

Wright, David. "The Byzantine Model of a Provincial Carolingian Ivory." In *Eleventh Annual Byzantine Studies Conference; Abstracts of Papers,* pp. 10–12. Toronto: Pontifical Institute of Mediaeval Studies and Centre for Medieval Studies, University of Toronto, 1985.

———, ed. *The Vespasian Psalter: B. M. Cotton Vespasian A.i.* Copenhagen: Rosenkilde & Bagger, 1967.

Wulfstan. *The Homilies of Wulfstan.* Ed. and trans. Dorothy Bethurum. Oxford: Clarendon Press, 1957.

Youngs, Susan. "Medium and Motif: Enamelling and Early Manuscript Decoration in Insular Art." In Bourke, *From the Isles of the North*, pp. 37–47.

———. "Recent Finds of Insular Enameled Buckles." In Karkov, M. Ryan, and Farrell, *Insular Tradition*, pp. 189–209.

———, ed. *'The Work of Angels': Masterpieces of Celtic Metalwork, 6th–9th Centuries AD*. London: British Museum Publications, 1989.

CONTRIBUTORS

COLLEEN F. BATEY is a half-time lecturer in the Department of Archaeology at the University of Glasgow. She is an expert on Scandinavian and North Atlantic archaeology and has directed excavations at sites from Tintagel in Cornwall to the Shetland and Orkney Islands.

JOHN BRADLEY is senior lecturer in the Department of History at the National University of Ireland, Maynooth. He specializes in the archaeology of Ireland, especially urban archaeology. He has also published on crannogs, death and burial, and the medieval Irish town.

GEORGE H. BROWN is professor emeritus of English at Stanford University. He is currently editing Bede's historical works for the Corpus Christianorum Series Latina.

ELIZABETH COATSWORTH is senior lecturer in the Manchester Institute for In-novation in Art and Design, Manchester Metropolitan University. She is co-director of the Manchester Medieval Textiles Project and editor of the West Riding of Yorkshire volume of the *Corpus of Anglo-Saxon Stone Sculpture*.

ROSEMARY CRAMP is professor emeritus in the Department of Archaeology, University of Durham. She is general editor of the *Corpus of Anglo-Saxon Stone Sculpture* and an acknowledged expert in all aspects of Anglo-Saxon art and archaeology.

HELEN DAMICO is professor of English, founder of the Institute for Medieval Studies, and presidential teaching fellow at the University of New Mexico. She is currently completing a book on *Beowulf*.

ROBERTA FRANK is Douglas Tracy Smith Professor of English at Yale University. She has published widely on both Old English and Old Norse poetry and culture and is a past president of the Medieval Academy of America.

JANE HAWKES is lecturer in the Department of Art History at the University of York. She is currently working on the historiography of Insular sculpture and its context in nineteenth- and twentieth-century medievalism.

CATHERINE HILLS is senior lecturer in the Department of Archaeology at Cambridge University. Her research focuses on the early medieval period in Europe, especially the region around the North Sea. She directed the excavation of the Anglo-Saxon cemetery at Spong Hill, Norfolk.

JOHN HINES is Professor of Archaeology at the University of Cardiff. He is interested in the integrated study of archaeology, language, and literature and is currently researching the chronological basis for Anglo-Saxon England c. 580–720.

CATHERINE E. KARKOV is Chair of Art History at the University of Leeds. She is currently completing books on Anglo-Saxon art and Anglo-Saxon drawing and is co-director of the Visionary Cross project.

CAROL NEUMAN DE VEGVAR is Professor of Art History at Ohio Wesleyan University. She has published widely on all aspects of Anglo-Saxon art and is currently working on a book on early medieval Rome.

ELIZABETH O'BRIEN is an archaeologist and independent scholar based in Dublin.

ÉAMONN Ó CARRAGÁIN is professor emeritus in the English Department at University College Cork. He has published on many aspects of Anglo-Saxon and medieval art and literature, but is perhaps best known for his many publications on the Ruthwell and Bewcastle crosses.

GALE R. OWEN-CROCKER is a professor in the Department of English at the University of Manchester. She is an acknowledged expert on the Bayeux Tapestry and is currently directing a research project entitled *The Lexis of Cloth and Clothing in Britain c. 700–1450*.

LESLIE WEBSTER is former curator in the Department of Prehistory and Europe at the British Museum. She is co-editor of a number of exhibition catalogues, including *The Golden Age of Anglo-Saxon Art*, *The Making of England*, and *The Transformation of the Roman World*.

KELLEY M. WICKHAM-CROWLEY is Associate Professor of English at Georgetown University. She is currently working on a book on the intersection of the physical and intellectual cultures of the Anglo-Saxons and a second book on women and weaving in Anglo-Saxon texts and archaeology.

SUSAN YOUNGS is a former curator in the Department of Prehistory and Europe at the British Museum. She is an expert on Insular metalwork and editor of *The Work of Angels*.

INDEX OF MANUSCRIPTS

417

PUBLICATIONS OF THE RICHARD RAWLINSON CENTER

The Old English Hexateuch: Aspects and Approaches
  Edited by Rebecca Barnhouse and Benjamin C. Withers

The Recovery of Old English: Anglo-Saxon Studies in the Sixteenth and
Seventeenth Centuries
  Edited by Timothy Graham

Typeset in 10/12 New Baskerville
Designed by Linda K. Judy
Composed by Tom Krol
Manufactured by Thomson-Shore, Inc.

Medieval Institute Publications
College of Arts and Sciences
Western Michigan University
1903 W. Michigan Avenue
Kalamazoo, MI 49008-5432
http://www.wmich.edu/medieval/mip

 WESTERN MICHIGAN UNIVERSITY